ENERGY AND THE FEDERAL GOVERNMENT

ENERGY and the FEDERAL GOVERNMENT

Fossil Fuel Policies, 1900–1946

John G. Clark

UNIVERSITY OF ILLINOIS PRESS

Urbana and Chicago

Library of Congress Cataloging-in-Publication Data

Clark, John Garretson, 1932–
    Energy and the federal government.

    Includes index.
    1. Energy policy—United States—History—20th
century. 2. Fuel trade—Government policy—United
States—History—20th century. 3. Fossil fuels—
Government policy—United States—History—20th century.
I. Title.
HD9502.U52C57 1987   333.8'2'0973   85-20505
ISBN 0-252-01295-X

To the grandchildren:
Stevie,
Ann Elizabeth,
and John Brandon

ACKNOWLEDGMENTS

MANY PEOPLE and several institutions provided me with aid and encouragement while I researched and wrote this book. Most of the archival research was completed during 1976–78 while I served as a visiting scholar at the United States Department of Energy; the unflagging support of Richard G. Hewlitt, chief historian (retired), and Jack M. Holl, assistant chief historian (now chief historian), DOE, was essential to the completion of this study. Laine Moore and Jerry Hess, archivists at the National Archives, went beyond the call of duty in making records available to me. The first draft of the manuscript was completed while I was a Fellow at the National Humanities Center, Research Triangle Park, North Carolina; to all the Fellows of 1981–82 and to the center's wonderful staff, in particular Ineke Hutchison, Madeline Moyer, and Jan Paxton Cuddy, I express my profound appreciation for their help and patience. The University of Kansas provided summer research support through the General Research Fund. Librarians at the University of Kansas, the Library of Congress, and several other depositories served me well. A number of colleagues gave generously of their time in my behalf; among those who must be singled out are Alfred Chandler, Jr., Arthur Donovan, August Giebelhaus, William Hambleton, Linda Lear, Thomas McCraw, Martin Melosi, Bonnie Morrison, Mark Rose, and Theodore Wilson. My family did not complain excessively about the time I devoted to this project. To all of the above, my sincere thanks.

CONTENTS

14

Wartime Administration of Solid Fuels, 348

15

TABLES

FIGURES

CHARTS

MAPS

ABBREVIATIONS APPEARING IN
THE TEXT AND NOTES

ACWA   American Coal Wholesalers Association
API   American Petroleum Institute
ARA   American Railroad Association
BCD   Bituminous Coal Division (DI)
BCon   Bureau of Conservation
BCorp   Bureau of Corporations
BFDC   Bureau of Foreign and Domestic Commerce
BM   Bureau of Mines
CCC   Central Coal Committee (USRA)
CIC   Capital Issues Committee
CMA   Coal Mines Administration
CND   Council of National Defense
DC   Department of Commerce
DI   Department of the Interior
DOE   Department of Energy
DPC   Defense Plants Corporation
DSC   Defense Supplies Corporation
EHFA   Electric Home and Farm Authority
ERC   Energy Resources Committee
FEA   Foreign Economic Administration
FFD   Federal Fuel Distributor
FOCB   Federal Oil Conservation Board
FPC   Federal Power Commission
FTB   Federal Tender Board
FTC   Federal Trade Commission

GPO	Government Printing Office
ICC	Interstate Commerce Commission
IOC	Interstate Oil Compact
IPAA	Independent Petroleum Association of America
KNG	Kansas Natural Gas Company
NAM	National Association of Manufacturers
NARUC	National Association of Railroad and Utility Commissions
NBCC	National Bituminous Coal Commission
NBCIB	National Bituminous Coal Industry Board
NCA	National Coal Association
NCBA	National Coal Board of Arbitration
NELA	National Electric Light Association
NICB	National Industrial Conference Board, Inc.
NIRA	National Industrial Recovery Act
NRA	National Recovery Administration
NRB	National Resources Board
NRC	National Resources Committee
NRCMA	National Retail Coal Merchants' Association
NRPB	National Resources Planning Board
OCC	Oklahoma Corporation Commission
OD	Oil Division (USFA)
ODT	Office of Defense Transportation
OPA	Office of Price Administration
OPM	Office of Production Management
OSAC	Oil States Advisory Committee
OWM	Office of War Mobilization
PAB	Petroleum Administrative Board
PAW	Petroleum Administration for War
PCC	Planning and Coordination Committee
PCND	Petroleum Committee for National Defense
PCW	Petroleum Coordinator for War
PFDC	President's Fuel Distribution Committee
PIWC	Petroleum Industry War Council
PRC	Petroleum Reserves Corporation
PWA	Public Works Administration
PWSC	Petroleum War Service Committee
REA	Rural Electrification Administration
SFAW	Solid Fuels Administration for War
SFCND	Solid Fuels Coordinator for National Defense
TNEC	Temporary National Economic Committee
TRC	Texas Railroad Commission

TVA	Tennessee Valley Authority
UMWA	United Mine Workers of America
USBM	United States Bureau of Mines
USCC	United States Coal Commission
USFA	United States Fuel Administration
USGS	United States Geological Survey
USHR	United States House of Representatives
USRA	United States Railroad Administration
USS	United States Senate
WFC	War Finance Corporation
WIB	War Industries Board
WLB	War Labor Board
WMC	War Manpower Commission
WPB	War Production Board
WSB	War Shipping Board

INTRODUCTION

The Promises of 1904

IN THE CENTER of an enormous building, the Palace of Machinery, whose ceiling vaulted several hundred feet above ten acres of densely packed space, stood a great engine and electric generator. Crafted by the Allis-Chalmers Company, it was the newest model, 40 feet in height, weighing 720 tons, and capable of generating 6,500 horse-power or 5,000 kilowatts. Nearby stood four massive Westinghouse Electric and Manufacturing Company generators, each with a 2,000 kw capacity. Surrounding these engineering wonders were dozens of other giant machines—steam turbines, gas engines, hot air pumping engines, diesel engines, hydraulic presses—manufactured by a dozen different firms, American and European. Not far from this palace, with its seven lofty towers, stood the Palace of Electricity, surrounded by lagoons, covering four acres of exhibition space and jammed with the fruits of modern electrical technology: telephone and telegraph systems, working models of incandescent light systems, dynamos, electric motors, storage batteries, the newest Westinghouse electric railway equipment, large scale models of electrical equipment manu-facturing factories. These were but two of 1,586 new buildings, spread over 300 acres and housing 55,000 individual displays, all designed for the edification of the 19 million visitors who poured into the Louisiana Purchase Exposition of 1904—the St. Louis World's Fair.[1]

At night, the Allis-Chalmers and Westinghouse generators lit up the entire park in a brilliant display of electric lighting visible for miles. With the present filled with such wonders as gasoline- and electric-powered vehicles and a myriad of new mechanical contrivances for home, farm, and factory, visitors envisioned a bright future.

In bigger and bigger boilers, coal made steam which passed under pressure to ever larger turbines and generators. New chemical processes turned oil and coal into dozens of valuable products. Pipelines carried natural gas over longer distances to more and more homes and factories. All this, and more, the real and the potential, was on display in St. Louis. Only four years into the new century and the air was laden with the heavy scent of sweeping change.

There are few static societies in the real world. Certainly there were no static nations in the Western world in 1900. At the turn of the century, America moved more smartly than most other countries, and most Americans approved of the general direction and the pace. Among the diverse goals sought, economic prosperity and security beckoned to many as the most important, and in 1900, they seemed within reach. Most Americans agreed that democracy had been achieved and required only constant defense. The economy, however, had always been volatile, and Americans in 1900 were especially sensitive to its unpredictability, having just emerged from a severe depression. But the new technology, the power that moved it, and the organizations that managed it held forth the promise of new jobs, larger incomes, an improved quality of life, and an acceptable level of personal security. The new forms of energy, raw and manufactured, that swept into the ken of Americans during the late nineteenth and early twentieth centuries were keys to the transformation of dreams into reality.

Seemingly inexhaustible supplies of cheap energy had already contributed to the triggering of momentous change in American society. Between 1870 and World War I, the nation became urban and industrial. Towns became cities and cities became metropolises, crisscrossed above by tracks and wires and below by pipes and conduits. Towering buildings, vast rambling factories, and densely packed residential neighborhoods sprang up across the land. Farmers mechanized or went out of business and joined the flood of people moving to the cities.

Millions of foreigners made their way to America, seeking freedom, economic opportunity, and a better life. The capacity of the nation to absorb the newcomers rested to a significant degree upon new forms and new uses of energy. Each fresh application of energy to productive processes created new jobs and new demands. The jobs may have been dreary and dangerous and the wages low, too low for an adequate standard of living, but for many these were better than most jobs available in the old country—and there was hope for future generations.

American industrial production spurted ahead at a rapid pace in the 1880s, the decade in which coal became the preeminent source of energy. Despite the severe depression of the mid-1890s, commonly used economic indicators attest to remarkable gains in manufacturing between 1880 and 1900: Value added by manufacturing and the capital invested in manufacturing both increased by two and one-half to three times. During the same interval, total national energy consumption almost doubled, rising from 5,000 trillion Btu to 9,600 trillion. By 1920, total energy consumption had doubled again, reaching 22,000 trillion Btu. During these years of remarkable growth and development, the per capita consumption of energy also doubled, as did the nation's population.[2]

Between 1880 and 1920, the sources and forms of energy that Americans consumed changed dramatically. As late as 1880, wood served as the most widely used fuel. But by the mid-1880s, coal was providing over half of the nation's energy requirements and continued to do so until World War II. Coal's input to energy consumption peaked in the first two decades of the twentieth century when it provided over 70 percent of energy needs. The production of coal quadrupled between 1880 and 1900 and doubled again during the next two decades, reaching a maximum output of 678 million tons in 1918, a tonnage not again surpassed until 1947 (see Table 4, p. 9). The absolute predominance of coal, although lasting until 1940, was challenged in the early twentieth century by discoveries of large supplies of other mineral fuels and the concurrent emergence of a technology to utilize them. Petroleum and natural gas, while providing no more than 25 percent of energy needs in 1925, competed seriously with coal for the business of large and small energy consumers. The production of crude oil and natural and manufactured gas is summarized in Table 4. Water power (hydropower), too, provided a small portion of energy needs—never exceeding 5 percent—during the early decades of the twentieth century.[3] In some markets, the Denver area as an example, hydropower competed directly with the mineral fuels.

The St. Louis World's Fair officially opened when President Theodore Roosevelt, at the White House, pushed a button that started hundreds of motors whirring in St. Louis. It was the dawn of a revolutionary era in the production and use of energy. Fuel generated electricity, that "subtle fluid," still in its infancy in application and organization but on the verge of spreading its uses throughout society, affecting routines of life in the home and in the store and in the factory. The kilowatt-hour (kwh) production of central stations, at 6 million in 1902, was new enough to still excite awe and wonder and some fear among beholders, yet it reached relatively few Americans. By 1920, most urbanites and innumerable commercial, industrial, and transportation firms used some of the 56 million kwh generated by the electric utility companies and isolated generating plants that served a particular plant or building.[4] The birth of the electric utility industry provided an expanding market for the mineral fuels. In this study, treatment of the electric utilities is confined to their role as consumers of the basic mineral fuels and, therefore, as an occasionally influential participant in the formulation of fuel policies.

As of 1904, the oil needs of the nation had yet to feel the impact of the motor vehicle. Most of the petroleum requirements of the more populous eastern half of the nation were met from the Appalachian and Lima (Ohio)-Indiana fields. Spindletop, the first great flush pool in Texas, had exploded on the oil scene in 1901, and for a few years production in Texas hovered at 18 to 21 percent of national production. But the initial foray in the Gulf area soon petered out; production in Texas as a share of U.S. output reached only 10 percent in 1917, compared with 30 percent in 1930. Even during the few years of Spindletop's peak productivity, 1902–5, the real center of U.S. crude production shifted to the Mid-Continent field of Kansas and Oklahoma with the discoveries of the Glenn (1905), Cushing (1912), and Healdton (1913) fields (see Table 7, p. 94). California was the largest producer from 1905 through 1914, but its output had little impact on the states east of the Sierra Nevada. By 1918, the Mid-Continent field contributed over one-half of domestic crude oil production.[5]

All these production increases—in coal, liquid fuels, electricity—accompanied and precipitated significant changes in the fuel consumption patterns of the nation and in the internal organization of the fuel industries. In turn, technological and administrative innovations, the magnitude of energy available, its relative cheapness, and the possibility of choosing among a variety of energy sources combined to transform, sometimes rapidly and at times more gradually, the social, economic, and political routines of American society.

Chapter 1 treats the basic organizational structures of the coal, oil, and natural gas industries and the developing competition among the basic fuels. Natural gas receives less attention than coal or petroleum, because during this period natural gas served essentially local or, at best, regional markets. Chapter 2 summarizes the general impact of all this on the urban-industrial complex while emphasizing the pre-World War I involvement of governments with fuel industries. Chapters 3 and 4 deal with government policies toward the fuel industries during World War I.

The armistice of 1917 ushered in a period of peace for the United States lasting two decades. But peace did not come to the coal fields. Strike after strike periodically closed large numbers of mines, causing shortages and escalating prices. Simultaneously, fears of diminishing oil reserves engendered discussion and controversy within the industry and interested federal agencies. As a result, a federal role persisted in both the coal and oil industries during the 1920s, a time of significant energy transition throughout the nation. These are the central concerns of Chapters 5, 6, and 7.

Depression struck swiftly in 1929 and 1930 and lingered for what seemed to Americans an eternity. Chapters 8, 9, and 10 treat the various federal policies adopted to bring a modicum of stability to the fossil fuel industries. Chapter 11 offers an evaluation of interwar federal fuel policies that centers around the proposals of the National Resources Committee's subcommittee on energy resources. In 1939, another war in Europe and spreading violence in Asia captured the attention of Americans and stimulated the economy sufficiently to end the depression. A complicated superstructure was gradually erected by the federal government to manage first defense production and then a wartime economy. Chapters 12, 13, and 14 describe and analyze federal wartime policies toward the fossil fuels and the wartime agencies that emerged to administer those policies. Finally, the courageous reader who has persevered will reach Chapter 15, which tenders a brief evaluation of the meager results achieved by federal fuel policies between 1900 and 1946.

ENERGY AND THE FEDERAL GOVERNMENT

ONE

The Fuel Industries
in the Early Twentieth Century

THE ORGANIZATIONAL STRUCTURES created by the fuel industries prior to World War I differed as a result of the location of the
resource, the difficulty of extraction, processing requirements, available transportation or distribution options, marketing considerations,
and related factors. While organizational patterns varied, a dominant
mode emerged relatively early in the history of each industry and was
further refined (or unrefined) with the passage of time, the introduction of new technologies, economic or political crises, shifting consumer demands, and other variables.

The Coal Industry

Bituminous coal was mined commercially in about thirty states,
and anthracite coal was found only in Pennsylvania. Most of the
bituminous originated from mines east of the Mississippi River; in
the peak year, 1918, eastern mines produced 88 percent of the national
total. Pennsylvania alone mined 30 percent of the country's bituminous, and if anthracite is included, 41 percent of all coal produced. As
Table 1 indicates, West Virginia, Illinois, Ohio, and Kentucky were
also major coal suppliers. But as displayed in Map 1, a dozen or more
other states also competed with the leading bituminous producers for
local and regional markets.

The corporate structure of the anthracite industry differed considerably from that of bituminous, just as the uses of anthracite differed
from soft coal. By far the larger part of anthracite was used in the East

TABLE 1. *Primary Bituminous Producing States, by Percentage of Total Production, 1900–1919 (million tons)*

	Pennsylvania	West Virginia	Ohio	Illinois	Kentucky
1900	38	11	9	12	3
1904	35	11	9	13	3
1909	36	14	7	13	3
1914	35	17	8	14	5
1919	31	16	8	14	6

Source: "Coal produced in the United States, by states, 1900–1919," Coal Investigation, COR5 NAT85, FTC, RG 122.

for home heating purposes, although from time to time price and supply factors made it economical to use anthracite for steam raising. Normally, however, bituminous and anthracite were noncompetitive. Bituminous coals varied far more in quality than anthracite and, as bituminous was the major industrial fuel, the different qualities or kinds of bituminous were used for different purposes such as blacksmithing, coke, gas making, and steam raising. Each consumer group demanded a different performance from coal, and the bituminous mines geared their production and preparation to suit the needs of their customers. Thus, there were dozens of sizes and qualities (measured in Btu generation per pound) of coal. Most mines produced several sizes of single quality, normally suitable for several different purposes.

Bituminous mines varied widely in productive capacity. Between 1905 and 1916, the number of commercial mines operating in any single year fluctuated between a low of 5,060 in 1905 to 5,887 in 1911. World War I stimulated the opening of large numbers of new mines, the total reaching 6,939 in 1917, 8,994 in 1919, and an industry high of 9,331 in 1923. Unlike anthracite, a small number of coal producers did not dominate the industry. In 1920, 6,277 producers operated 8,921 mines. At the small end, 2,322 operators, or 37 percent, produced under 10,000 tons annually and contributed but 1.5 percent of total soft coal production. Another 2,121 operators, or 34 percent of the total, producing between 10,000 and 50,000 tons annually, mined 9 percent of total production. Thus, 71 percent of the operators produced just above 10 percent of total output. At the large end of the scale, 70 operators produced 34 percent of bituminous, each mining

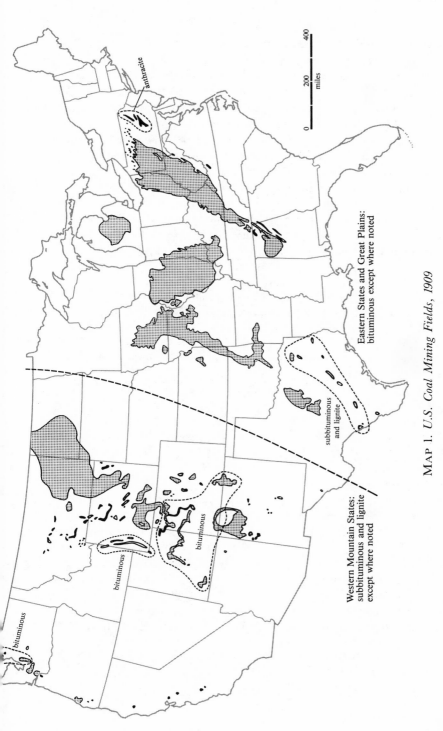

MAP 1. *U.S. Coal Mining Fields, 1909*

Source: U.S. Bureau of the Census, *Statistical Atlas of the United States* (Washington, D.C.: GPO, 1914), Plate No. 452.

Eastern States and Great Plains: bituminous except where noted

Western Mountain States: subbituminous and lignite except where noted

anthracite

subbituminous and lignite

bituminous

bituminous

bituminous

over one million tons annually. In the middle rank, 1,727 producers, each mining 50,000 to one million tons annually, contributed 55 percent of soft coal output. In each of the major coal fields, a small number of companies emerged that produced the bulk of the field's coal. Thus, in the Kansas-Missouri-Oklahoma-Arkansas field, seven or eight firms produced 80 to 85 percent of total production. These large firms established the Southwestern Coal Operators Association, but they exercised no particular dominance over the amount of coal produced or its marketing. Such associations functioned primarily as the management bargaining agent with the miners' union.

In the anthracite industry, 13 of 254 companies engaged in business in 1916 produced 79 percent of total production; 11 of these were railroad companies that engaged directly in mining or owned mining companies. The Reading Railroad, for instance, part of the Morgan system, in 1900 produced 20 percent of all anthracite. These so-called captive mines aroused intense suspicion and resentment in both private and public circles.[1] A comparison of the degree of concentration in bituminous and anthracite, based upon the value of product, is offered in Table 2.

TABLE 2. *Concentration in the Coal Industry, by Value of Product, 1919*

Annual $ value of product per enterprise	Number of enterprises	% value of total product
Anthracite		
under $100,000	118	<1
$100,000–$1,000,000	71	10
$1,000,000–$5,000,000	48	23
$5,000,000 and over	17	67
Bituminous		
under $100,000	4,442	11
$100,000–$1,000,000	2,028	56
$1,000,000–$5,000,000	156	25
$5,000,000 and over	10	8

Source: U.S. Bureau of the Census, *Fourteenth Census of the United States, 1920*, vol. 11, Mines and Quarries, 1919 (Washington, D.C.: GPO, 1922), 267.

In the bituminous industry, railroads and steel companies were the major owners of captive mines. For a number of reasons, dealt with in subsequent pages, the major coal-carrying railroads, some of which owned and leased coal lands or held controlling interests in coal companies, attracted the most public scrutiny. In 1915, the United States Geological Survey (USGS) identified almost a hundred railroads that carried coal, some earning a substantial portion of their income in this traffic. Eight lines carried 186 million tons, or 42 percent of total production; the Pennsylvania system alone transported 64 million tons, followed by the Baltimore & Ohio, the Norfolk and Western, and the Chesapeake & Ohio. These four carried 33 percent of total production. Each of these lines and many of the others, particularly in the West, owned or controlled a large tonnage. Between 1920 and 1924, tonnage classified as captive represented about 20 percent of national production. In 1924, the mines of steel plants alone produced about one-half of all captive production and 12 percent of total production, while the railroads produced 24 percent of captive and 6 percent of total production. Other industries, especially the by-product coke plants and public utilities, mined another 6 percent of the nation's soft coal.[2]

The owners of captive mines were among the dominant consumers of soft coal. Virtually all coal moved to final markets at least partly by rail, although by World War I motor trucks were becoming more important in local distribution and marketing. Since railroads were the single largest consumers of coal, the relationship between the coal industry and the railroads was especially significant, threatening conflicts of interest during periods of coal or transportation scarcity.

The domestic market for coal escalated in the last quarter of the nineteenth century in direct response to the growth of the iron and steel industry and the completion of the railroad network. Not only did the railroads convert from wood- to coal-burning locomotives, but the expansion of track mileage from 35,000 in 1865 to 74,000 in 1875 and over 200,000 by 1890 provided an enormous stimulus to the steel industry. Railroads, then, not only required great quantities of coal as fuel, but in their frenetic haste to expand their trackage, contributed to the rising coal requirements of the steel industry. The major categories of soft coal consumers and the tonnage used by them from 1915 through the 1920s are summarized in Table 3.

Table 4 attests to a steady rise in coal production and use through World War I. Thereafter, the industry failed to benefit from the prodigious increase in energy consumed domestically. Technological advances in industry, transportation, electric generation, and home

TABLE 3. *Consumption of Coal, by Consuming Groups, 1915–1929*

	1915		1917		1920		1929	
	% pro-duction	million tons	% pro-duction	million tons	% pro-duction	million tons	% pro-duction	million tons
Railroads	28[1]	124	24	133	27	154	24	131
Steel Plants					6	36	5	26
Coke, Bee-hive, and By-product	14	62	15	84	15	84	17	89
Other Industrials					24	139	23	124[2]
Electric Utilities			6	34	6	36	8	43
Bunker	2	10	1	8	2	10	1	7
Mine Fuel	2	9	1	12	2	12	<1	5
Exports	4	18	5	26				
Domestic Consumers (incl. commercial heating)	16	71	10	57	10	57	23	122[3]
All Industrials (incl. steel and utilities)	33	146	32	176				
All Other			9	48	3	14		

[1] May include only Class I railroads.

[2] Includes stone, clay, glass, machinery, transportation equipment, paper and other forest products, food and related products, petroleum refineries, noncoal mines, and quarries.

[3] Includes all commercial and small industries.

Sources: "Users of Coal, 1915," Box 364, Coal, 21A-A4, Technology or Commodity File, WIB, RG 61; Sidney A. Hale, "The Marketing of Bituminous Coal," Box 1, Entry 4, USCC, RG 68; W. C. Trapnell and Ralph Ilsley, *The Bituminous Coal Industry with a Survey of Competing Fuels* (Washington, D.C.: Federal Emergency Relief Administration, 1935), 154.

TABLE 4. *Annual Supply of Energy from Mineral Fuels, 1880–1925*

	Bituminous coal (million tons)	Anthracite coal (million tons)	Crude oil (million barrels)	Natural gas (billion (cubic feet)	Manufactured gas (billion (cubic feet)
1880	51	29	26		
1890	111	46	46		
1900	212	57	64	128	
1901	226	67	69	180	102
1902	260	41	89	206	
1903	283	75	100	239	
1904	279	73	117	257	113
1905	315	78	135	320	112
1906	343	71	126	389	
1907	395	86	166	407	
1908	333	83	179	402	
1909	380	81	183	481	151
1910	417	84	210	509	
1911	406	90	220	513	
1912	450	84	223	562	
1913	478	92	248	582	
1914	423	91	266	592	204
1915	443	89	281	629	
1916	503	87	301	753	231
1917	552	99	335	795	264
1918	579	99	356	721	272
1919	466	88	378	746	306
1920	569	90	443	812	320
1921	416	90	472	674	
1922	422	55	556	776	
1923	565	93	732	1,025	386
1924	484	88	714	1,162	
1925	520	62	764	1,210	

Sources: U.S. Bureau of the Census, *Historical Statistics of the United States, Colonial Times to 1957* (Washington, D.C.: GPO, 1960), 356–57, 359–61. For natural gas, in any given year, probably 10 percent more was wasted. For manufactured gas, Herbert B. Doran, ed., *Materials for the Study of Public Utility Economics* (New York: Macmillan, 1930), 11.

heating equipment all combined to produce a relatively stagnant demand for coal during the 1920s and thereafter, a condition apparent even prior to World War I but somewhat masked by actual coal production increases. For example, the U.S. merchant marine and U.S. Navy had hardly converted to coal from sail when they initiated a major conversion to fuel oil.[3] More is said in the last section about the competition between fuels.

The major industrial, utility, and home-use markets for coal were located in the heavily populated urban and metropolitan areas of New England, the Middle Atlantic states, and the East North Central states. Since coal was mined at a distance from these markets, it all had to be moved by rail or water carriers or both. Because mines did not store coal but produced only as much as could be carried away, the daily output of most mines—western as well as eastern—depended entirely upon the number of coal cars made available by the railroads that served them. Determining the carrying capacity of a railroad were such factors as the number and capacity of cars suitable for coal transportation and their state of repair, the proportion of coal cars used to carry other goods, the number of locomotives on line at any given time, the coal-handling capacity of yards and terminals, and the manner in which coal cars were distributed among coal mines. Unless the roads ordered new cars, any increase in the number of mines would diminish the number of cars available per mine.

By World War I, the coal-carrying railroads had developed a system of mine rating to determine the share of cars a mine received. New mines automatically received a share, regardless of their efficiency or marketing potential, that share determined by a formula measuring the mine's daily capacity. Unfortunately, the roads did not order sufficient new equipment or invest enough in repair to keep up with the demand for coal cars. The shortage of cars figured heavily in the coal scarcity caused by World War I and the coal strikes of the postwar years. During such periods, coal operators frequently accused the mine-owning railroads of favoring their own mines in the assignment of cars.[4]

Two separate distribution and marketing systems functioned in the coal industry. One, the least complicated but involving the most coal, supplied the dominant consumers: railroads, utilities, and by-product and steel plants that consumed some 40 percent of all bituminous produced. The other system managed to get soft and hard coal into the hands of millions of small domestic and commercial consumers. Each category of consumer—and consumers within each category—

required different types and sizes of coal, the sizing generally being done at the mine. Some mines offered as many as fifteen different sizes. Domestic consumers, for instance, used block coal (capable of passing over a six-inch opening), lump (between three and six inches), or nut (between two and three inches). Steam-raising plants frequently used slack coal or screenings as did the by-product plants. Railroads also had their size preferences.

The larger consumers normally purchased on contracts of six months or more; in a few cases contracts ran for as many as five years. An estimated 70 percent of bituminous tonnage was sold on contract in 1920, with railroads taking the largest share. The Jackson, Walker Coal & Mining Company of Kansas City, Missouri, produced and shipped in 1920 and 1921 1.5 million tons of coal, 95 percent of which filled contracts. The Santa Fe railroad took 75 percent of total production. To reach the smaller consumers, mines shipped to thousands of retailers located in thousands of American communities, some of whom purchased through wholesalers and some of whom sold to wagon peddlers who sold coal by the bushel basket or the sack. In 1916, local coal dealers were just beginning to shift from horse-drawn coal wagons to trucks, some of which were electric.

Some coal companies, particularly in anthracite, operated, as did the Delaware, Lackawanna & Western Coal Company, their own retail outlets. Others shipped to an exclusive list of wholesalers, in some cases to only one that was an affiliate of the coal company. Few anthracite producers sold directly to unaffiliated retailers. In bituminous, prior to World War I, some eastern mines operated through joint sales agencies that handled the marketing of their entire production. This effort to regularize and stabilize the marketing of coal tiptoed uneasily along the edge of violation of antitrust statutes.

The largest market area along the northeastern seaboard, from Washington, D.C., north to Boston, was supplied by the Pennsylvania anthracite mines and the Appalachian bituminous fields. The Chesapeake & Ohio, Norfolk and Western, and other roads moved their bituminous tonnage to tidewater, to Norfolk for instance, where the coal was loaded in barges for shipment to New York, Boston, and other coastal distribution points. In 1908, New England imported by barges 5 million tons of anthracite and 11 million tons of bituminous, one-third of which arrived at Boston and the remainder at New Haven, Providence, and Portland. The coal discharged at Boston originated at Baltimore (33 percent), Philadelphia (17 percent), Norfolk (16 percent), and Newport News (25 percent). Another 15 million tons arrived in New England by railroad, but at Boston all but one percent arrived by barge. Both Boston and New York maintained large bunker stocks.

Each city, then, had its own coal distribution patterns, depending upon its location relative to the coal fields, its proximity to water, and the railroad serving it. Interior cities such as Buffalo, Pittsburgh, or Indianapolis were on all-rail routes and drew from mines on both sides of the Ohio River. Cincinnati and Louisville operated a part-river trade and purchased in many fields. The so-called lake trade—rail from fields to Lake Erie ports, barge to Duluth and Superior, rail to Minneapolis-St. Paul and North and South Dakota markets—serviced consumers in the upper Great Plains. In that trade, as elsewhere, coal fields competed with one another for the market. At St. Paul, the all-rail coal from Illinois and Indiana clashed with the eastern dock coal arriving at Duluth or Superior. Six producing fields shipped at least 10 percent of their total production to lake ports.

Distance from field to market was not the determining factor since differential freight rates and relative costs of production largely determined what coals could enter what markets. Mid-Continent coal operators, for instance, complained loudly in 1916 that the Interstate Commerce Commission (ICC) freight rates allowed Illinois and Indiana coal to invade trans-Missouri markets. Illinois and Indiana coal companies, in their turn, opposed freight rates conferring benefits on southern mines that already enjoyed a competitive advantage as a result of low wages paid to nonunion miners. Southern coal competed vigorously in markets north of the Ohio. While anthracite and bituminous normally did not compete, since the former filled home heating purposes more effectively than soft coal, a rise in the price of bituminous could open up the steam-raising market for anthracite. Such a situation occurred in 1917. Anthracite producers accepted large-quantity contracts from industry, causing a serious shortage of home-use coal. The coal industry was intensely competitive, both internally and with other fuels. When business was going poorly, or when an aroused public attacked the coal producers, the latter hastened to blame the selfish attitudes of railroads, utilities, and other large coal users for all the difficulties.[5]

The Petroleum Industry

The oil industry rose to prominence in response to the discovery of new uses for the refined product and the bringing in of new pools to supply the enhanced demands of a burgeoning, urbanizing, and mobile population. Table 4 documents a thirtyfold increase in crude oil production between 1880 and 1925. The annual consumption of oil per household unit, at 1.9 barrels in 1880 and 4 barrels in 1900, zoomed to 34 barrels in 1929. The 26 million motor vehicles racing along the nation's rutted and potholed highways in 1929 explain much of this swollen demand. The value of crude oil produced rose from $25 million in 1880 to $1.2 billion in 1925, or 25 percent of the total value of all mineral products and 41 percent of the value of mineral fuels. During those years, the value of refinery output soared from $44 million to $2.3 billion. The book value capital invested in petroleum refining rose from $95 million in 1899, or 1 percent of the capital invested in all manufacturing, to $5.7 billion in 1929, or 10 percent of manufacturing capital. By 1925, oil provided over 18 percent of the nation's energy needs, compared to under 1 percent during the 1880s. In the meantime, total energy use increased by over four times.[6]

Studies of late nineteenth and early twentieth century developments in the oil industry naturally focus on the emergence of Standard Oil as the initially unchallenged giant in the industry. Standard and a few serious competitors pioneered in exploration and recovery, the invention of superior refining techniques and new products, the construction of pipelines, and the creation of national and world-wide marketing organizations. To be sure, thousands of obscure wildcatters and others—to say nothing of Henry Ford—contributed to the fashioning of the industry, but overwhelming attention has centered on the practicality of vertical integration, the economies of scale, and the inexorable advance of giantism in oil as in other industry groups. While the antitrust dissolution of Standard in 1911 (occurring even as Standard's hold on the industry perhaps weakened) did open up the industry to a certain degree of competition, the monopoly of Standard was replaced by the oligopoly of the majors, among whose numbers were several original affiliates of the old Standard combination. All of this seemed to prove the inevitability of bigness and the necessity of vertical integration from production through marketing.[7]

As the center of crude oil production shifted rapidly from pools east of the Mississippi to pools west of the river, thousands of new wells towered over the corn fields and prairie grasses of the Mid-Continent field (see Table 7, p. 94). By 1919, the Kansas-Oklahoma field contained one-quarter of 258,000 wells that produced over one-half of the domestic supply. Thousands of oil companies operated in the Mid-Continent, the Gulf, and the older oil fields, some owning a few wells on a few leased acres, and a few others like Standard, which moved into the Mid-Continent before 1900, leasing several hundred thousand acres. In the Gulf field before World War I, four companies, of hundreds operating in the area, emerged as major integrated firms: Gulf Oil, the Texas Company, Sun Oil, and the Security Oil Company (a subsidiary of Standard of New Jersey). Production rapidly became concentrated in relatively few firms. In 1919, fifteen fully integrated firms produced 35 percent of the nation's crude and thirty-two companies produced 60 percent.

The prolific Mid-Continent and Gulf fields attracted an enormous investment in refining capacity and pipeline construction. A complex of refineries sprang up in Kansas and Oklahoma and along the Gulf Coast in Texas. The number of refineries, under 100 through 1900, rose to 147 in 1909 and 320 by 1919. Standard constructed its first Mid-Continent refinery at Neodesha, Kansas, in 1897 and in 1904 completed a larger refinery at Sugar Creek, near Kansas City, Missouri (see Map 2, p. 17). At this time Standard's refineries produced about 85 percent of all refined products. But the successful penetration of the industry by Gulf, the Texas Company, Sun Oil, Royal Dutch Shell, Sinclair, and Cities Service, in addition to the dissolution of Standard, greatly reduced Standard's share of production, refining, and marketing by World War I. In 1917, Cities Service was the largest producer of Mid-Continent oil, followed by Magnolia Petroleum Company and Prairie Oil and Gas Company, both former Standard subsidiaries.[8]

Refining capacity, after an initial locational concentration in the Great Lakes and Middle Atlantic states, diffused widely throughout the country as new fields opened in the nation's midsection and in southern California. By the end of the 1920s, eastern refineries, virtually all owned by major integrated firms, refined some 21 percent of all crude (Table 5), while refineries in California yielded another 25 percent for use along the West Coast. The remaining plants were scattered about the interior oil fields, with large refineries located in and near Houston and Port Arthur, and others in Oklahoma, Kansas, and Illinois.

In 1911, Standard refineries produced 64 percent of the nation's output, a marked reduction from the 90 percent they produced at the turn of the century. A number of integrated firms then filled the vacuum. In 1920, the thirty largest firms, including former members of the Standard combine, controlled 72 percent of refining capacity. In 1929, seventeen firms accounted for 70 percent. To jump further into the future for purposes of perspective, by 1938 ten majors refined 59 percent of the crude and twenty majors refined 77 percent. So,

TABLE 5. *Regional Distribution of Refining Production, by Percentage of Total Crude Refined, 1925–1926 and 1928–1929*

Refining Regions	1925	1926	1928	1929
Total crude refined (million bbls)	740	779	913	988
East Coast and Appalachian	21%	20%	22%	21%
Indiana-Illinois	9	9	11[1]	11[1]
Oklahoma-Kansas	13	12	12	12
Texas	19	20	20	21
(Texas Gulf)	(15)	(15)	(15)	(15)
Louisiana and Arkansas	9	9	8	8
(Louisiana Gulf)	(7)	(7)	(6)	(5)
Rockies	4	4	3	3
California	25	25	23	25

[1] Includes Kentucky.

Sources: USBM, *Petroleum Refining Statistics 1926*, Bulletin 289 (Washington, D.C.: GPO, 1927), 22; ibid., Bulletin 339 (1929), 34.

whether it be Standard alone or the former Standard group and a dozen others, concentration remained the predominant feature of the industry.[9]

Arthur Johnson's two definitive volumes on the oil pipelines explain how Standard and other major companies utilized the pipelines as a competitive weapon, first against the railroads, then against one another, and finally against the smaller so-called independent oil firms.[10] Standard's rise to dominance in the late nineteenth century depended as much upon its rebate and rate-fixing agreements with the railroads as upon its technological or organizational efficiency or its size. Transport cost advantages permitted Standard to engage in predatory pricing in order to force competitors to merge or go out of business. Once Standard entered the pipeline business, partly in response to the construction of lines by competing firms, the railroads quickly lost out in this traffic for the pipelines moved oil to tidewater much more efficiently and cheaply than could the railroads. By the early twentieth century, pipelines were the key element in the expansion of the industry. In 1910, 20,000 miles of trunk line and 24,000 miles of gathering line were operating; by 1920, 70,000 miles of all pipeline were in place (Map 2).

In the Mid-Continent field, Standard in 1901 formed the Prairie Oil and Gas Company, which became the largest pipeline company in the region. Prairie's lines pumped oil to the Standard refineries at Neodesha, Sugar Creek, and Whiting, Indiana. For a few years, it was virtually the only pipeline available and, therefore, the only purchaser of crude in the Kansas-Oklahoma fields. While the proportion of total Mid-Continent crude sold to Prairie diminished from 97 percent in 1906 to 58 percent in 1912, by World War I it still owned 38 percent of total trunk line mileage and 70 percent of storage capacity in the field.

Needless to say, Prairie's dominant position made it a determining force in the price Mid-Continent producers received for their crude. In the Gulf field, lines moved the crude to tidewater and oil tankers then shipped crude and refined oil to eastern refiners and distributors. Before World War I, Gulf field companies moved into the Oklahoma producing region, particularly the Glenn pool. Perhaps as much as 25 percent of Kansas-Oklahoma production traveled south to the Gulf by World War I. This left about 25 percent of the production in the hands of the independents.[11]

In 1915, at least fifty-five independent refineries operated in Kansas and Oklahoma. Only one of these, the Cosden Company plant at Tulsa, had a daily capacity comparable to Standard's Neodesha refinery, about 12,000 barrels. Over half had a capacity of under 1,000 barrels. Fewer than one-half owned any pipeline, and those that did connected only with their producing wells. Virtually all depended entirely on the railroads for the shipment of the refined product. While the major firms, with their own trunk lines, transported their crude to refineries within central metropolitan regions far distant from the producing fields, the Mid-Continent producers and refiners, lacking competitive transportation to the East Coast, were confined to midwestern markets. They faced the competition of the majors in those markets also.

In 1915, R. L. Welch of the Western Oil Jobbers Association, E. E. Giant of the Independent Oil Men's Association, and H. G. James of the Western Petroleum Refiners Association all complained about the effects of rapidly rising eastern gasoline prices. The jobbers maintained that they were forced to pay higher eastern prices while selling at lower western prices since the more active eastern markets attracted additional supplies of crude. James accused Prairie of adding a high premium to the posted price that independent refiners paid for crude

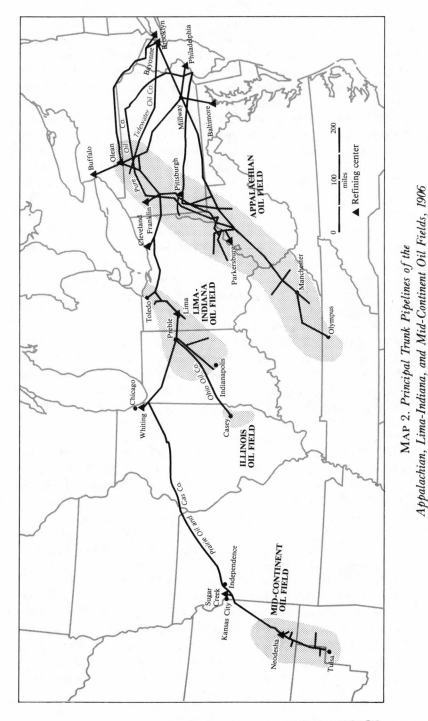

MAP 2. *Principal Trunk Pipelines of the*
Appalachian, Lima-Indiana, and Mid-Continent Oil Fields, 1906

Source: Arthur M. Johnson, *The Development of American Pipelines: A Study in Private Enterprise*
and Public Policy, 1862–1906 (Ithaca: Cornell University Press, 1956), facing page 208.

oil. Producers, refiners, and jobbers alike operated in an inflexible system because they lacked access either to transportation to the East, to crude oil, or to markets beyond the reach of the price-setting powers of the majors. All these grievances represented core elements in the case of the independents versus the majors that enlivened oil politics into and beyond World War II.[12]

The rise of the independents and the expansion of the majors was fostered by revolutionary changes in the uses of oil. As *The American Petroleum Industry* points out, the refining industry of 1900 was capable of producing lubricants and kerosene. Then, coincident with the great Mid-Continent and Gulf discoveries, came the explosive demand for gasoline and the escalating use of fuel oil for steam raising, process heat, and domestic purposes. Refiners scrambled to devise techniques to extract from the crude enormous quantities of gasoline. An increase in the volume of gasoline refined from Mid-Continent and Gulf crude, neither possessing good lubricant-making characteristics, automatically increased the quantity of fuel oil produced. Marketing the fuel oil became a matter of high priority for the industry.

Over a period of twenty years, new refining processes appeared, culminating with thermal cracking in the 1920s and causing a major shift in the products of crude refining. Between 1899 and 1923, gasoline production jumped from 6.6 million barrels, or 13 percent of the crude run to stills, to 180 million barrels, or 31 percent of the crude run to stills. Kerosene production increased, too, but its share of crude usage declined from over 50 percent to 9 percent. The increase in fuel oil production, from 7 million barrels in 1899 to 89 million in 1914, or 39 percent of the crude refined, reflected the flow of oil from Mid-Continent fields. After 1917, about one-half of all crude was turned into fuel oil and, much to the dismay of the coal industry, the production of fuel oil kept rising, reaching 182 million barrels in 1919 and 287 million in 1923.[13]

The domestic industry evolved its modern forms within the context of this product revolution. The majors perfected their integrated mode by developing new marketing structures and tactics, both for overseas and domestic sales. While the proportion of exports to domestic supply for all refinery products declined from 41 percent to 16 percent between 1899 and 1919, the volume of oil exported rose almost threefold. Simultaneously, some major firms became interested in the potential of overseas crude production, particularly in Mexico and South America.[14] Mexican fuel oil supplied a substantial portion of the fuel oil burned along the East Coast. Independent refiners participated but little in the international market but were sensitive to its

18

real or imagined impact on their own fortunes. Their major concern, however, was keeping afloat in the domestic market.

The products of the refineries moved to market by rail, water, wagon, and truck. During the pregasoline years when kerosene composed the essential refined product, Standard and the few other large firms had developed a nationwide distribution system. Each of Standard's subsidiaries, such as the Waters-Pierce Oil Company in Oklahoma and Kansas, or the United Oil Company of Denver, operated in a strictly defined marketing area and supplied hundreds of retailers, most purchasing exclusively from Standard, scattered about in the villages and towns of the marketing region. Standard's refining subsidiaries, at Neodesha, Kansas City, and Denver (The Continental Oil Co.), shipped their products to wholesaling subsidiaries. As other large firms successfully entered the oil industry and Standard's share of refining output declined, the newcomers established distribution systems and independent distributors emerged along with independent refiners. Standard's marketing share, at some 85 percent in the pre-World War I decade, declined by 1920 to under 50 percent nationally.

Standard, Sinclair, the other majors, and the independents distributed their commodities through tank wagon or bulk stations, normally located on railroad sidings in the preautomotive days, but then diffused throughout cities once truck delivery became common. The advent of independent refiners stimulated the establishment of independent jobbers or wholesalers who constructed bulk stations, at first to sell kerosene to retailers or directly to such dispersed consumers as farmers or small industrials. As fuel oil became more important, the kerosene stations were easily accommodated to the new product. Gasoline distribution in its early years was similarly handled, but before long a new marketing system based on roadside gasoline and automotive service stations emerged as the dominant method of marketing motor fuel, motor lubricants, and a host of other products.

Of the more than fifty independent refiners in Kansas and Oklahoma, about ten owned their own bulk stations, virtually all within their own state. In 1915, some 60 percent of the distributing stations in those states was owned by Standard. Even fewer independent refiners owned gasoline retail stations, selling instead to independent operators in the wholesaling and retailing end of the business. *Oildom* in 1917 remarked on the many filling stations appearing in the Mid-Continent, a phenomenon replicated in even greater magnitude in other more populous regions. By 1916, over 18,000 garages and other outlets dispensed gasoline, most curbside. Drive-in stations quickly replaced the curbside variety, and just as quickly specialized businesses concentrating on gasoline sales, lubrication, and retail sale of auto accessories replaced the nonspecialist as the chief purveyor of motor fuel. By 1919, filling stations and garages handled 85 percent of the value of gasoline sales. Garages soon relinquished the retail trade to the corner filling station.

While Standard's share of the market for petroleum products declined markedly between 1900 and 1920, the beneficiaries of this were a small number of new major firms. After the dissolution of Standard, such former Standard firms as Jersey Standard and Indiana Standard integrated their own operations by acquiring production and pipelines (which severely weakened Prairie Oil and Gas Co.). These former Standard companies, in addition to the new majors, dominated the industry just as completely as had the old Standard Company.[15]

Such small refiners as the Kanotex Refining Company of Caney, Kansas, complained bitterly in 1907 of frequent Standard reductions of tank wagon prices even as the price of crude advanced and demand for refined products seemed active. To Kanotex officials, Standard was "carrying out a policy of oppression . . . that, if allowed to continue, means the extermination of the independent refineries." In later years, such Mid-Continent refiners as the Chanute Refining Company and the Kansas Oil Refining Company of Coffeyville, as well as independent jobbers, all agreed that Standard and "other" companies manipulated oil prices to suit their own purposes. "All they would have to do now," said a Chanute official, "to put the Independent Refineries out of business is to raise the price of crude oil a little more and keep reducing the prices on refined oil and gasoline." As the independents perceived their situation, one master had been replaced by several.[16]

The internal structure of the oil industry was established in its modern form by 1920 or so. Full integration ruled among the major firms and was even achieved by a number of independents. Technological improvements in exploration, drilling, and refining were introduced during the interwar years, in some instances the technique being fully controlled by a major firm. But company structure and approaches to marketing in 1939 remained quite similar to those maturing in 1920.

However, perceptions of this industry varied radically, depending upon the beholder's angle of vision. The image articulated by the president of Standard of Kansas, for instance, accentuated a market ruled by supply and demand, vulnerable to the intrusion of aggressive competitors, and dependent upon a raw material difficult to find and rapidly depleted. Independents beheld a market in which the availability of crude, access to transportation and markets, and prices were subject to the manipulation and control of the majors and the railroads.[17] These contrasting and conflicting portraits provided the information base, impressionistic as it was, for the evolution of public attitudes toward the industry. Chaos, cutthroat competition, and labor violence emerged as central elements in the public picture of coal. Giantism, power, amorality, all muted by a subtle appreciation of efficiency, formed the dominant lines of the public image of oil.

The Natural Gas Industry

During the early years of the twentieth century, natural gas appeared as a relatively new source of primary energy. In certain sections of the nation, particularly in the Mid-Continent where the largest natural gas discoveries occurred, natural gas began to replace manufactured or artificial gas (produced from coal or oil). Prior to the commercial introduction of electricity in the 1880s and 1890s, the artificial gas produced by almost 1,000 companies was used chiefly for street lighting. Thereafter, the artificial gas industry focused upon interior illumination and home cooking; it was too expensive for industrial use or for home heating. In areas with access to natural gas, that fuel quickly penetrated domestic and industrial markets. Both manufactured and natural gas gradually lost the interior illumination market in urban areas to electricity. Table 4 indicates that the use of both types of gas rose steadily into the 1920s, with about 75 percent of all artificial gas consumed in households and 75 percent of natural gas consumed by industry. In such places as Kansas City, Tulsa, and Oklahoma City, the gas companies converted from manufactured to natural gas as soon as pipelines could be constructed from the gas fields. By the 1920s, perhaps 7 million natural-gas-burning appliances heated space and water and cooked beans in American homes.

The distributors of natural gas to consumers early became defined as public utilities, subject to some degree of regulation first by municipal authorities, then by state agencies, and finally, in the late 1930s, by the federal government. The initial impact of the natural gas industry was greatest in cities and larger towns proximate to the gas fields, there being no long-distance pipeline system until the late 1930s. In the urban areas of the Mid-Continent, the rate-setting policies of the natural gas distributors precipitated frequent and noisy political controversy. The intrusion of natural gas into these areas also engendered intense competition with coal, oil, and electricity.

A tendency toward consolidation typified the evolution of the natural gas industry (and the electric utilities as well). By World War I, most gas utilities composed a part of one or another holding company. Advocates of this organizational structure maintained that the parent company could more effectively market the securities of the operating companies, thereby providing the capital for expansion. Other economies resulted through the mass purchasing of equipment and the standardization of rate making, billing, and other administrative routines. Detractors were not absent. They pointed to real and potential abuses of the holding company form of organization, especially in matters of equitable rate making and quality of service. The critics offered municipal ownership or rigid public regulation as alternatives.

Great contention swirled around the natural gas industry because of the real threat of depleted gas fields, interrupted service, and chilled householders. In Kansas City, Missouri, consumers and civic leaders frequently attacked the rates charged by the Kansas Natural Gas Company (KNG) to the local gas distribution company. Both KNG and the local distributor were subsidiaries of the United Improvement Company, a Philadelphia holding company. Regulatory bodies in Missouri exercised no authority over KNG, which operated only in Kansas and turned over the gas at the state line. Utilities, unlike coal and petroleum, developed their politics in a municipal setting.[18]

The Search for Markets

In 1908, a report of the Bituminous Coal Trade Association predicted a happy future for the coal industry and projected a domestic production of one billion tons by 1935. This report assumed that coal would continue to provide its current share of the nation's energy requirements. It completely overlooked numerous signs of market encroachment by other forms of energy. In the pre-World War I years, industries throughout the Mid-Continent conducted many experiments involving the substitution of fuel oil for coal. J. P. Cudahy of the Cudahy Packing Company, Kansas City, Missouri, reported favorably on the efficiency and lesser cost of fuel oil relative to coal. Other firms—Swift & Company, the St. Louis & San Francisco Railroad, Peet Brothers Manufacturing Company, the Kansas City electric utility—organized similar tests. Firms in Wichita and Oklahoma City replicated these experiments, as did industries in other parts of the country.

Fuel oil became an increasingly damaging competitor of coal, particularly in the railroad fuel market. Railroad use of coal peaked during the early 1920s (see Table 3) and then declined by 1930 to roughly 60 percent of the 1920 tonnage. In the meantime, fuel oil burning in locomotives had grown from 20 million barrels in 1909 to around 70 million barrels in 1930.[19] Coal also suffered displacement among other groups of consumers. While manufacturing remained the largest single category among coal consumers, coal use by industry failed to keep pace with the post-World War I expansion of manufacturing output and rose only fractionally in actual tonnage consumed through 1930. Coal gave way to fuel oil and natural gas almost entirely in the industries of the Mid-Continent. Little coal was used along the West Coast. In New England and the Middle Atlantic states, fuel oil competed vigorously and successfully for industrial customers.

Coal lost out everywhere as the primary source of domestic and commercial heat. Advances in household oil-burner technology far surpassed those in coal-burner fabrication. The domestic anthracite market proved extremely vulnerable to cleaner, cheaper, and less troublesome types of fuels. The petroleum refining industry, faced with the need to dispose of an enormous volume of fuel oil as a result of the vigorous demand for gasoline, energetically sought and captured an impressive share of the domestic and industrial space heating and steam-raising markets. In November 1906, the Uncle Sam Oil Company of Kansas, ran advertisements for three consecutive days in every Kansas newspaper promoting oil heaters and cook stoves. In eastern and central Pennsylvania, gas ranges replaced coal ranges. Anthracite dealers reported in 1916 that Philadelphia had almost completely converted from coal to gas. In Harrisburg, 15,000 of 16,000 homes used gas ranges.

The market for coal in the electric power[20] industry experienced gradual growth during the first three decades of the twentieth century. But the volume involved—34 million tons in 1917 and 43 million tons in 1929 (see Table 3)—hardly compensated for losses in other consumer markets. The coal-burning apparatus used by the utilities improved with each passing year. As steam-generated kilowatt-hour generation reached 80 billion in 1929, compared with 10 billion in 1907, the kwh generated per ton of bituminous improved from 475 to about 2,000. Fuel oil and natural gas cut into the utility market for coal in the Mid-Continent.[21]

While coal faced stiff competition from other fuels, the competition between natural and manufactured gas and fuel oil and between gas and electricity also intensified. While it became more and more common for electricity and gas to be distributed by the same company, in markets where the two energy sources were sold by separate companies, intense competition occurred involving fuel oil as well. Electric industry spokespersons emphasized the inherent safety of electricity in the home while broadcasting warnings about the unhealthiness of coal, oil, and gas and the explosive qualities of the latter two fuels. Both the electric and gas companies quickly organized departments for the direct retail sales of appliances to consumers and hired a squad of women to spread the word about the quality of their wares. Gas and electric utilities promoted the use of central heating systems to replace coal and oil stoves, which also served as space heaters. By 1921, homes, hotels, clubs, restaurants, and institutions were switching from coal to gas and oil and electricity.

In some regions at some times, natural gas also dominated the industrial process-heat market. Nationally, industry burned 65 to 80 percent of all natural gas distributed; in the Mid-Continent, industry normally used above 75 percent of the metered gas consumed. Industries that owned their own gas supplies also consumed enormous quantities of unmetered gas. Such was the case in the southeastern quadrant of Kansas, where the availability of free gas stimulated the rise of a major industrial complex, including zinc and lead refineries, glass factories, and cement and clay products plants. While gas was plentiful, some of the plants supplied contract gas to neighboring communities at cheap rates. But in the 1910–20 period, the depletion of the gas fields caused serious shortages in the Kansas-Oklahoma area. Almost overnight, the industries of southeastern Kansas closed down or moved elsewhere. Many towns were then forced onto the KNG system, at higher rates and with poor service. Gas companies serving metropolitan areas found it necessary to greatly extend their pipelines in order to supply domestic consumers with regularity. A politics of gas emerged, distinct from oil but similar to electricity in that rate and service became all-consuming issues.[22]

At one point or another each source of energy contested for markets with some other source. Oil, natural gas, and electric power entered a vigorous state of growth, partly at the expense of coal, which proved most susceptible to product substitution. Howard Mitchell, secretary to the Coal Credit and Correct Weight Bureau of Kansas City, Missouri, in explaining a discrete problem faced by Kansas City retailers, also evoked aspects of the general vulnerability of coal:

> The coal retailing business in this city has undergone a considerable change in recent years. There used to be a heavy trade in steam coal . . . in coal . . . used [for heating in] large office buildings and the apartment houses. But . . . a large part has gone out of the hands of the retailers [and] many of the large office buildings in the uptown district are now heated from a central heating plant.[23]

Mitchell went on to complain of the serious price competition of small, fly-by-night mines—variously called "snowbird mines" or "wagon mines"—that sold directly to consumers, thus bypassing "legitimate" retailers. All in all, he opined, the coal industry in Kansas and Missouri was quite demoralized.[24]

The few options available to the coal industry could do little more than postpone its decline. Individual mining companies could achieve modest economies by modernizing or joining a sales agency. Remedies aplenty were proffered and some were even adopted. But the primary cost-saving strategy pursued was the slashing of miners' wages, which precipitated long and vicious strikes and coal shortages. While some railroads commandeered coal during periods of scarcity, most industries were unable to guarantee their fuel supply even when under contract. The uncertainties of coal supply during the early 1920s accelerated the substitution of other fuels for coal, among domestic as well as industrial consumers.

Few of the remedies propounded by advocates of modernizaton possessed much relevance. After all, coal is a filthy fuel. Coal mining was costly in lives and, as people well knew, its production and use damaged the environment. What sane householder who had the financial wherewithal would continue to use coal when cleaner fuels and new fuel-burning equipment appeared on the market? As fuel cost differentials and other factors came to favor the newer fuels, industrial engineers and the American householder rapidly abandoned coal.

Federal policies toward coal, even when intervention was forced by strikes and attendant coal shortages, were predicated upon the erroneous belief that the industry could be revitalized. If only freight rate differentials between the fuels could be equalized; if only fewer mining companies competed in the marketplace; if only other fuels would use fair competitive methods; if only. . . . The evolving fuel-use patterns and preferences of Americans belied such notions.

Conclusion

The energy industries, founded on seemingly inexhaustible supplies of coal, petroleum, and natural gas, experienced striking growth between 1880 and 1920. The coal industry dominated the energy scene while the petroleum, natural gas, and electric industries assumed their modern structures. Among them, the fuel industries and the technologies that supported and supplemented them thrust Americans into an era of major energy transition. Chapter 2 discusses the transformation of America from a low-energy to a high-energy society.

Signs of weakness within the coal industry were visible well before World War I; and soon enough the coal industry proved less capable of exploiting the great opportunities that a mass consumption society offered than did the oil, natural gas, and electric industries.

The fuel industries also injected new considerations into political arenas. The federal government, as Chapter 2 demonstrates, intervened gradually and hesitantly in the affairs of the fuel industries, and both government intervention and industry performance became the subjects of intense public scrutiny. Many Americans recognized that these industries were of more than ordinary importance to the general welfare and, thus (or perhaps), warranted more-than-ordinary monitoring by public authority. The fuel industries rejected this notion. How this controversy was resolved describes the central theme of the remainder of this book.

TWO

Emergent Government Fuel Policies
before World War I

As AMERICAN COMMUNITIES confronted and coped with the outpouring of new technologies—itself a gradual process—transformations
occurred in the size, form, and organization of these communities.
Compared with the experiences of the past, the technological transition
seemed rapid, but in fact it did not transpire overnight, or in a year,
but over the course of a generation or more. The industrial city, powered
by inanimate energy sources, spread across the land to Pittsburgh,
Dayton, East St. Louis, Kansas City, and beyond; but it was, after all,
a type of city that had appeared in New England even before the 1830s.

Still, as Sam Bass Warner, Jr., points out, the industrial metropolis
became the archetypical city of the period 1870–1920. Within those
years, new and exciting and foreboding things swept into the vision
and the lives of most Americans. If the technological transition was
gradual, so too was the energy transition, itself but a part of the
former. Relatively few Americans possessed an automobile before
1920; fewer still cooked on an electric range or enjoyed the convenience of central heating. William Cottrell views this period as a key in
the long transition from a low-energy to a high-energy society that
commenced early in the nineteenth century with the introduction of
steam power to replace water, wind, and animal power. Steamboats
and steam locomotives and stationary steam engines spurred the
evolution of a national network of cities and a national market. But
prior to the Civil War, after six decades of steam development, industrialization and urbanization had, as Allan Pred argues, still to
converge, to reach a point where industrial growth rather than com-

27

mercial growth provided the chief impetus to urban development. The new technologies of the late nineteenth and early twentieth centuries brought these initial advances to maturation.[1]

This chapter first outlines the extent of the energy transition and then attempts to identify the points at which the federal government, and occasionally other jurisdictions, intervened in fuel and utility industry affairs. At no time during the years covered in this study did the federal government evolve a comprehensive energy policy; instead, policies emerged that dealt with each fuel individually. Although there were efforts to transcend a fuel-by-fuel approach, they bore no fruit.

An Energy Transition

Energy transitions, like technological transitions, are overlapping and are experienced slowly. During the first decades of the twentieth century, American communities experienced the introduction of new kinds of energy and new systems to distribute the energy to consumers. An energy transition began, building upon yet superseding an earlier transition decades in the making during which coal rose to dominance as a source of energy. One mark of the new era was a decreased use in the home of raw power—wood, coal, kerosene burning in stoves for cooking and space or water heating—and the increased use of energy purchased through a central distributor such as an electric company. Proceeding slowly in the city, this trend penetrated the countryside at an even more leisurely pace.

Over time, this transition altered the physical appearance of the city. Hundreds of horse-drawn wagons hauling coal from yards to consumers gradually disappeared from the streets of the central city, replaced by motor trucks, some of which were electric, and by the tunnels of central steam-producing plants. One or two energy utility companies and a few fuel oil tank wagon stations slowly replaced many small coal yards. Gas street lights gave way to incandescent lighting, and tens of thousands of central city offices substituted interior electric lighting for gas fixtures. Hundreds of miles of highly visible wires strung from countless poles entered factories, stores, and residences in the city and its suburbs and powered the ubiquitous city trolley car.

With the demise of the city horse—a demise not complete even in the 1930s—urban smells, and the daily work of the street sanitation crews, became somewhat less obnoxious. But if the scent of the city improved, surely the look of the city did not, until most of the crisscrossing overhead wires went underground to join the steam tunnels and water and gas mains. The incessant digging up of city streets as utility systems laid new kinds of pipe or extended their systems to hook up with more consumers produced great irritation for motorists and nearby residents—but did provide momentary playgrounds for the street children who clambered over the piles of earth.

But all this proceeded at a slow pace, the more so in rural America. The age of coal, despite such aggregate indicators as Btu contribution to American energy needs, was a long time dying (and, of course, has never died) while the advent of the age of oil or electricity occurred steadily but not abruptly. Perhaps it makes little sense to speak in terms of the "age" of this or that form of energy. Americans could make new choices among fuels or sources of energy, but all are being used even now, including wood and kerosene. Still, over the period 1890–1920, the artifacts of change and accommodation were highly visible. Americans believed in the world of science, and while society exercised little direct control over the rate of technological introduction or over its impact on the social order, physical evidence of scientific discovery surrounded Americans and intrigued them and confused them.

Metropolitan areas responded quicker to new and cheaper forms of energy, as attested to by the shifting spatial arrangements within metropolises. The stationary electric motor not only decreased the cost of energy per unit of output, permitting enhanced flexibility in the actual organization of production within a plant, but it encouraged factories to move from the interior of cities, close to rivers or coal depots, to less expensive lands on the city's periphery. Imposing, and somewhat frightening, new centers of industry sprang up in such places as Gary, Indiana, the home of U.S. Steel, Akron, Ohio, the headquarters of Goodyear, and East St. Louis, Illinois, the site of large steel plants. (Proximity to coal fields prompted the development of East St. Louis.) Trolley cars, autos and trucks, and electric power lines all contributed to weaken the older imperatives of central city location and gradually decentralize industry within metropolitan regions. Within the cities themselves, the trolley lines extended the feasible distance for journeying to work and opened up large amounts of land to residential and business development. In the central city, buildings soared skyward as did urban land values. Overcrowding and daily congestion became the hallmarks of central business districts.[2]

This energy transition produced countless innovations in the physical structure and social organization of cities. While cities may be perceived by urbanologists as systems both in their internal and external relations, urban folk experienced their cities partially and subjectively, encountering innovation in a random and piecemeal fashion. For the ordinary city dweller, encounters with new uses of energy and other technologies occurred in the office or factory, on the street and in the park, in the kitchen and living room.

Promoters of the new energy technologies promised manifold blessings from public acceptance of their commodities. Flexibility in industrial organization contributed to rising productivity per labor hour, particularly in such basically new industries as steel and chemicals. As the economy benefited, or so it was alleged, so would the environment and the quality of life. "Spring days make you yearn for a home" and "health demands freedom from coal smoke and dust," J. C. Nichols, home builder of Kansas City, advertised in 1906; thus, "deed your wife a nice new 5 or 6-room cottage, [with] flowers, grass, trees, city water, [and] electric light."[3] In many cities, especially in the East, the electrification of railroads eliminated the soot, cinders, and black smoke of locomotives. Even as these gains—marginally effective, at best—were being made, however, the introduction of the auto introduced a new, though less visible, pollutant into the air while the spread of industry into suburbs dispersed toxic substances as well as jobs more evenly throughout metropolitan regions.[4]

As population growth and new technologies combined to advance the demand for energy, the fuel and utility industries labored to meet demand and competed aggressively to win new customers. The electric and gas utilities initiated vigorous sales campaigns, emphasizing economy, reliability, and service by experts, and aimed at coal users and operators of isolated generating plants. Convenience, cleanliness, and status were also touted in sales pitches aimed at the residential market. In 1905, Henry L. Doherty, owner of Denver Gas and Electric Company, and founder of Cities Service Corporation, employed forty salesmen to scour the city and environs for new business. The Denver Gas and Electric Company, and other utilities, offered cooking instruction and lectures on domestic science. In 1912, the municipally owned electric firm of Kansas City, Kansas, cooperating with seventeen local businesses, demonstrated irons, washing machines, vacuum cleaners, and other appliances to some 10,000 visitors to City Hall over a four-day period. On the Pacific Coast, in 1916, the electric companies sponsored an "Electric Week" and devised demonstrations and displays of their new electrical equipment in Reno, San Francisco, Seattle, Ogden, and Salt Lake City. The electric companies in Denver, Kansas City, and elsewhere pushed electric signs for retail and wholesale firms and advocated outdoor lighting of buildings, plazas, billboards, streets, and so on. These were new markets and created demand dur-

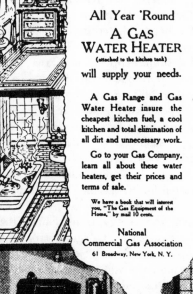

FIG. 1. *Advertisement Used by the National Commercial Gas Association in 1911 in a national campaign to promote gas use.*

Source: Louis Stotz and Alexander Jamison, *History of the Gas Industry* (New York: Press of Stettiner Brothers, 1938), 276.

ing nonpeak hours. "White ways"—brilliantly illuminated streets—became a mark of distinction in many cities.

Fuel oil and coal dealers did not rest idle in the face of the skillfully articulated sales campaigns of the utilities. Factory owners could still be convinced by an appeal to cost statistics that gas or fuel oil was cheaper and more efficient than electricity for such special purposes as process heat, steam raising, and space heating. But fuel and coal oil dealers were of smaller size and less well organized than the utilities. The utilities in Kansas City (both Missouri and Kansas), for example, worked diligently in cooperation with industrialists, the chambers of commerce, and realtors to attract new industries or commercial establishments to the area.

Domestic or household consumers, less susceptible to economic arguments, required a sales pitch that emphasized convenience, comfort, status, and similar enticements. Price, of course, was not an insignificant consideration, but within the income groups that could afford to select from the full range of domestic energy choices—families, for example, who purchased homes in J. C. Nichols's Country Club District—non-cost-related benefits proved most appealing. Gas and electric companies pioneered in developing sales techniques and service organizations that beguiled middle-class and upper-class consumers. Fuel oil wholesalers and retailers also targeted these groups for special sales attention, while the coal industry fought a defensive battle to retain its share of the domestic market.[5]

As indicated, the energy transition in the household proceeded gradually in urbanized areas, slower still in rural America, and had not been completed as far as coal use was concerned even in the late 1940s. Table 3 indicates widespread domestic coal use during the late 1920s. Such complex and interwoven factors as the size of living quarters, the number and distribution of single-family residences and multi-family dwellings within regions and among income groups, family size, individual preferences, the availability of particular sources of energy for household use, and the sales tactics of and prevailing credit arrangements offered by the distributors of the new household technology all must be sorted out to comprehend the pace of the transition. Suffice it to say that in promoting their wares, the utilities and the oil industry promised Americans a pure and synthetic environment and in addition asserted that all these gadgets would release the overburdened housewife from household drudgery. The energy industries did, indeed, succeed in packing American homes and apartments with modern appliances.[6]

FIG. 2. *Natural gas and fuel oil distributors also promoted a version of the hot-air furnace pictured. Electric blowers were soon introduced to circulate the hot air throughout the house.*

Source: E. S. Keene, *Mechanics of the Household, A Supplementary Course of Physics Dealing with Household Appliances* (n.p., 1911), 46.

Government and the Energy Industries[7]

The energy transition of the late nineteenth and early twentieth centuries did not escape the notice of government. During these years, governments at the municipal, state, and federal levels evolved roles that had a lasting impact on the production, distribution, and pricing of energy as well as upon the organizational structure of the energy industries. As with the energy transition itself, governments only gradually defined their areas of responsibility. Changing conditions— rapid national growth, war, strikes, product shortages—compelled frequent alterations in the position of governments toward the energy industries. In the long run, the role of the federal government was expansionist, but in the short run, federal intervention was marked by a crooked course, graphically portrayed by a slowly ascending but meandering curve. Not all energy industries simultaneously felt the weight of federal intervention or regulation. The coal and petroleum industries fell within the federal purview at an earlier date than did natural gas or power.

Each of the energy industries, all of which touched national life at numerous points, developed a somewhat distinct style of politics in their governmental relations. Coal, oil, natural gas, and power were viewed as separate industries, each with its own problems and each with its own impact upon society. Policy makers during the first half of the twentieth century did not treat the industries as a unit, as energy industries.[8] Although the individuals involved in each of these industries were cognizant of the web of interrelationships that bound them together as they impinged on the economy and on society, governmental authorities treated them discretely, thinking not of national energy needs but of national needs for coal, for oil, or for natural gas. This pattern persisted throughout the period encompassed in this study—and beyond into the 1980s.

The U.S. Congress, the president, the regulatory and investigatory agencies they created, and the federal courts frequently appealed to "the public interest" as a justification for action (or inaction) taken with regard to the energy needs of the nation and the performance of the energy industries in filling them. While the term "public interest" may be an exceedingly "vague construct," I do not believe it to be either "indefinable" or "analytically counterproductive."[9] Others agree the term is indispensable, however difficult to manage. Richard Flathman asserts its usefulness as a normative concept necessary for the evaluation of governmental policies. Without it, how can one determine justifiable government policy?[10] Without it, how can one formulate government policy at all?

While this is not the place to initiate an extended discussion of the meaning of the term "public interest," it may not be inappropriate to present my own notion of its essential components. In doing this, in giving subjectivity its head, other equally vague phrases or terms that cry out for definition will be cavalierly passed over. My purpose here is solely to inform the reader of my own philosophical point of departure.

A policy cannot be in the public interest if it condones, directly or indirectly, immoral or unethical behavior. What precisely such behavior consists of is for society to decide, and it is not to be expected that society will agree on all or even on most points. The supreme test of policy is the degree to which it achieves equity (sharing), justice (fairness à la John Rawls), and liberty all in the spirit of the principles enunciated in the Declaration of Independence.[11] Policies that promote the fair sharing of burdens and benefits throughout all segments of society and that carry the nation a step closer to a realization of the Declaration's principles are in the public interest. It is simple enough to so state such a meaning of the public interest; more difficulty may be encountered in evaluating fuel or energy policies against such amorphous criteria. It might also be legitimately asked whether historians should engage in such assessments. I have no doubts as to the propriety of evaluation if it is done openly and with due regard to the facts.

During the two or three decades prior to the outbreak of World War I, considerable and frequently heated attention was directed toward the question of the public interest inherent in the specific energy industries. The remainder of this chapter briefly treats the early involvement of government with the energy utilities, particularly natural gas, and then proceeds to the halting development of federal investigative and regulatory authority over the fuel industries prior to World War I.

Between the 1880s and World War I, local governments and, more gradually, state governments explicitly recognized the public interest in power and natural gas distribution and extended regulatory authority over those industries. These developments did not carry over to either coal or oil. Municipalities such as Kansas City and St. Louis received authority from the Missouri legislature in 1908 to establish public utility commissions with the power to fix electric and natural gas rates and to oversee the supply and service performance of the utilities. A handful of cities owned the local utility companies, but this never became the prevailing mode of control. The private utilities in New York and Wisconsin were brought under state regulatory control in 1907. During the next several years many other states created new bodies—Oklahoma Corporation Commission (1907), Kansas Public Utilities Commission (1911), Missouri Public Service Commission (1913)—or endowed older regulatory commissions with authority expanded to include the utilities. The state commissions, of course, supervised only intrastate commerce.[12]

It soon became clear, however, that neither municipal nor state regulation could adequately regulate utilities that provided service throughout a state and, increasingly, across state lines. Regulation of the natural gas industry posed difficult problems to municipal and state bodies because of the intrastate and interstate nature of the business. Municipal authority ended at the city line, and state authority terminated at the state line. The gas supplies for Kansas City, Missouri, and for Omaha, Nebraska, were located, for instance, in Kansas and Oklahoma.

In the electric industry, the operating company both generated and distributed its power. In natural gas, at least two firms were normally involved, one producing and pumping the gas and selling at wholesale to another firm that distributed it to consumers and operated under a municipal franchise. The threat of gas field depletion, a reality in the Kansas gas fields around World War I, and attendant gas shortages, inadequate pressure, interrupted service, and chilly consumers added to the complexity of gas regulation.

The history of Kansas City between 1900 and 1920 is punctuated by recurrent battles, bitterly fought, between the local gas company and municipal and state authorities. But the interstate nature of the business thwarted the assertion of effective public control over rates, supply, or service. Missouri police power simply did not touch the Kansas Natural Gas Company, which sold its gas to the local distributing company at the state line. Consumer prices were determined by the wholesale prices charged by KNG. Neither could the Missouri Commission compel KNG to build new lines, drill new wells, or favor domestic consumers over industrial consumers during periods of gas scarcity. Municipal efforts to reduce gas prices by franchising competing local distribution companies came a cropper, both in Denver and Kansas City, in the face of holding company price cutting. In Kansas City, the United Gas Improvement Company responded to one such threat by slashing prices and destroying its competitor.

Opponents of regulation and those interested in the KNG blamed state authorities, Kansas as well as Missouri, for so weakening KNG that it declared bankruptcy. In fact, KNG was not insolvent but was the object of a takeover fight waged by various gas interests. Once in receivership administered by a federal court, KNG was beyond the reach of state police power.[13] The Missouri Commission, then, did fail to establish its regulatory authority over the gas industry, but not because it was "captured" and not because it ignored the public interest.[14] By placing beyond the reach of the regulators the producing companies that established prices, the legal system obstructed the commission from performing its duties.[15]

To a limited degree, the petroleum industry displayed characteristics similar to those of natural gas. The interstate character of crude oil distribution protected oil companies from state regulatory efforts. Unlike the case of natural gas, however, the federal government prior to World War I did assume certain responsibilities over the distribution system and did apply antitrust laws in an effort to assure a competitive market. The emergence of a federal stance toward oil and coal claims the attention of the remainder of this chapter.

Federal intervention in the affairs of both the oil and coal industries derived from the same ideological commitment to a free market economy that motivated municipal and state authorities to create a regulatory system to control the energy utilities. The latter, quickly defined as natural monopolies within definable market areas, required strict regulation in the public interest. From time to time, various public bodies attempted to apply the concept of the public interest to the oil and coal industries. Some voices in society even called for the nationalization of all or some phases of those industries. However, both state and federal governments generally confined themselves to the application of antitrust laws to those industries in the same way and prompted by the same standards or criteria that justified intervention in the affairs of any other industry. The degree to which public officials perceived trends in oil and coal as threatening to the free marketplace determined the character of government intervention. Similar criteria explained intervention in the match, beef, oilcloth, and other industries.

Federal responsibility for the management of grass, timber, water, and mineral resources on the public domain did establish a specific federal role in the exploitation of energy resources. Laws passed in the 1870s and thereafter controlled access to the public lands for purposes of drilling for oil and mining for coal. Federal responsibility for the disposition and use of Indian lands also affected production, particularly of oil, in places such as the Indian Territory (later Oklahoma). Beginning in the early 1900s, successive federal administrations commenced the withdrawal of public lands containing oil and other mineral deposits from private exploitation and, in 1912 and 1915, established the naval oil reserves.

The debate over withdrawal and leasing policies, through and including the final passage of the General Leasing Act of 1920, hinged on two interrelated questions, the rights of private capital to drill for a marketable resource and the requirements of national security for accessible proven reserves to meet possible emergencies. By and large, adherents of the national security position emerged victorious. But, in fact, the national interest was only minimally involved if adequate supply is the fundamental consideration. The public lands contributed but a small proportion of the nation's crude. Far more productive pools were located on private lands, and it was on those lands that the dominant oil companies built their empires and that the wildcatters and independents sought to carve out a niche of their own. The fight between supporters of withdrawal and of exploitation, while waged passionately and while producing much political furor, especially when the Teapot Dome scandals surfaced after World War I, contributed little to the fashioning of a federal stance toward the petroleum industry.[16]

Beginning with the Interstate Commerce Act of 1887 and the Sherman Antitrust Act of 1890 and continuing through the passage of the Clayton Act and the establishment of the Federal Trade Commission in 1914, the attention of the federal government increasingly focused on the transportation and industrial sectors of the economy. During those years, and particularly after 1900, a complex of new federal investigatory and regulatory agencies emerged while Congress strengthened the authority of the ICC.[17] The U.S. Industrial Commission's hearing in 1899 on the trust problem precipitated a rancorous debate over the position of the Standard Oil combine. Thereafter, the fuel industries became a central target of antitrust action in the early twentieth century and the subject of much legislation dealing with transportation and the responsibilities of the ICC. The protection of the free market economy from the evils of monopoly defined the objectives of much of this activity.

Federal scrutiny of the oil industry originated in the concern engendered by the dominant position won by the Standard Oil Trust during the 1890s and early twentieth century. Virtually all the investigations launched by Congress and the Bureau of Corporations, prior to the dissolution of Standard in 1911, emphasized Standard's monopolistic position and the function of transportation in consolidating its superiority. Public suspicion of and antagonism toward Standard resulted in numerous attacks on the firm in the media and in various books that portrayed Standard "as the very embodiment of monopoly."[18]

Pervasive antagonism toward the trust characterized the attitudes of hundreds of operators within the oil industry. Action against the combination by the federal government, then, responded to imperatives originating along a broad social spectrum. The crusade encompassed people of such opposing ideological commitments as Henry George and Richard T. Ely, Henry Demarest Lloyd and Ida M. Tarbell, James R. Garfield, Commissioner of the Bureau of Corporations (and Secretary of the Interior, 1907–9), and Scott Ferris, an Oklahoma oilman elected as a Democrat in 1907 to the U.S. House of Representatives. It was not a campaign drummed up by sensation-seeking muckrakers.[19]

The documentary evidence gathered by the federal government

fully substantiated the monopolistic position achieved by the Standard combination in the 1880s and the 1890s and the great power Standard exercised over the industry even as some competitors entered the field and gained a share of production, refining capacity, and markets. The justification offered by its supporters for the consolidation of Standard, that is, achieving vertical integration in order to rationalize operations and achieve economic stability within the industry, received short shrift from the critics of the trust.

Two reports of the Bureau of Corporations released in 1906 and 1907 and a report submitted in 1907 by the U.S. House Committee on Interstate and Foreign Commerce proved the case to the satisfaction of Standard's opponents. Commissioner of Corporations Garfield, in transmitting findings to President Roosevelt in 1906, wrote that the "control of the Standard Oil Company over the entire oil industry is so great as to require a special study of its relations to transportation companies." Garfield emphasized Standard's employment of pipelines to assert control over crude oil production in the Mid-Continent field, the discriminatory rates and minimum tender requirements imposed by Standard's pipeline subsidiaries, the illegal secret rates and rebates offered Standard by the railroads, and the effective price control thereby attained by Standard. The bureau's two reports and the House documents sketched a picture of overwhelming power, used consciously to rid the industry of competitors; thus, the critiques concluded that Standard was a threat to the free market economy and inimical to the public interest.[20]

In the minds of Justice Department officials, Congressional and Bureau of Corporation investigations of Standard generated sufficient evidence to warrant the institution in 1906 of a suit to dissolve Standard (resolved in the government's favor in 1911). Other strategies were also employed in an effort to weaken Standard's hold on the industry. In Congress, the transportation of oil claimed serious attention. In two states in particular, Kansas and Texas, local crude oil producers and refineries succeeded in bringing state power to bear on monopoly in oil, but with indifferent results.

In 1906, Congress passed the Hepburn Act, which enhanced ICC rate-making powers, prohibited railroads from carrying commodities they had produced or mined except those necessary for their own use (commodities clause), and defined pipelines as common carriers, thus subjecting them to regulation by the ICC. The impetus for attaching the pipeline provision to the bill benefited directly from Bureau of Corporations evidence documenting Standard's use of pipelines to achieve its awesome power. Passage of this bill did not resolve the problem of concentration in the oil industry any more than did the dissolution of Standard in 1911.

Prior to World War I, the ICC chose not to intervene actively in pipeline affairs. The commission not only lacked the expertise and reeled under the burden of railroad rate cases but did not consider common carrier status an efficient device to stimulate increased competition in the oil industry. Also, the common carrier clause quickly became tied up in the courts (the clause was declared constitutional in 1914) when the ICC ordered the major pipelines to file tariffs. To complicate matters, the Mann-Elkins Act of 1910, in creating the U.S. Commerce Court, compromised ICC jurisdiction. Not much had changed by 1916, compared with 1906, when the Federal Trade Commission (FTC) published a report on the petroleum pipelines. Although Standard had been dissolved, the dominant firms, including several from the old Standard Trust, firmly controlled the trunk pipelines of the nation and refused to operate them as common carriers.

All the grievances of the non-Standard firms of 1906 pertained in 1916, only in 1916 the place of the Standard combination was filled by a dozen major corporations.[21] Independent producers still sold their oil to major firms that controlled their own pipelines. In the Mid-Continent, Prairie Oil and Gas Company, reorganized in 1915, still gathered almost 50 percent of the crude. Sales of crude that bypassed the major pipelines suffered from the high freight rates charged by the railroads. Independent refineries located near the producing wells could not economically market their products in distant territories. Within the producing territories, Standard continued to exercise price leadership. In 1913, Walter T. Munn, general manager of Kanotex Refining Company, in Caney, Kansas, expressed virtually the same grievances against Standard of Indiana leveled against the Standard combination in 1907 by an officer of the same firm.

Federal antitrust action did not produce more favorable competitive conditions for the independents. Neither did state intervention. Both Kansas and Texas passed legislation designed to eliminate or mitigate the absolute power of Standard. Mass meetings of Kansas oil producers at Chanute and Independence in 1904 passed resolutions demanding state action against the Standard Trust, particularly its subsidiary Prairie Oil and Gas. The Kansas legislature responded with laws to prevent discrimination in selling oil, to fix maximum freight rates for oil shipment, to make pipeline common carriers, and to establish a state oil refinery to sell oil at cost; the latter measure was speedily declared unconstitutional by the state supreme court.

For a brief and exciting moment, Kansas oil interests believed they had tamed the tiger. E. L. Gros, owner of thirty-one oil wells and investor in a refinery, thought these laws among the greatest ever enacted by a state, a sentiment echoed by members of the Kansas Oil Producer's Association and the Mid-Continent Oil Refiners Association, interest groups organized to combat Standard. State-fixed oil rates did reduce the cost of crude and did lower shipping costs of refined products, but only within the state of Kansas. Standard initiated a boycott of Kansas crude while the railroads manipulated their intrastate freight rates to the disadvantage of Kansas oil. Common carrier status for intrastate pipelines failed to change much since a vastly greater volume of oil was produced than the state could consume. Kansas, for unaccountable reasons, failed to initiate an antitrust suit against Standard even though the state had a potentially strong case.

Though filled with much sound and fury, efforts in Texas to prevent eastern interests and integrated oil companies from dominating the state's oil industry proved equally feeble. Texas did manage to throw out several Standard affiliates, but other integrated firms—the Texas Company, Gulf, Magnolia—managed to operate in the state. Nor did passage of a pipeline common carrier law and the regulation of pipelines by the Texas Railroad Commission have much impact on the structure of the state's oil industry.[22]

What had public policy toward oil accomplished prior to World War I? Standard Oil had been dissolved into its constituent parts. But application of the Sherman Act, as Alfred D. Chandler, Jr. asserts, simply "increased the number of competitors in . . . already oligopolistic industries." Antitrust action did not "prevent the rise of the giant integrated firm when markets and technology made administrative coordination profitable."[23] At hearings on gasoline prices held by the House in 1916, witnesses attested to the continued price leadership of the Standard group. The City Council of Minneapolis accused the Standard group of creating artificial domestic shortages so as to raise prices. Similar accusations came from a Georgia congressman, gasoline retailers, and spokespersons for various oil jobber associations. Independent refiners in the Mid-Continent complained that in order to purchase crude, large premiums were demanded by Prairie pipeline, raising costs from fifteen to seventy cents per barrel above the price paid by the Standard group. Some sentiment supported an embargo on crude petroleum exports. While it was true that Standard's overall share of the petroleum industry had been reduced and that the various Standard firms met stiff competition from rising giants such as the Texas Company, Standard firms, in 1917, still consumed 30 percent of all crude production and controlled between 35 and 50 percent of the domestic market.

The Standard Oil group and the other majors owned and operated the oil pipelines. Access to the lines was denied the nonowners by the imposition of large minimum quotas for shipment. As it became apparent to the independents that the common carrier laws brought no improvement in access, the antimajor interests called for divorcement, a strategy endorsed by the FTC in 1917, 1922, and 1925 and a central factor in oil politics through the 1930s. The FTC recognized the persistent domination of the oligopolistic oil industry by the Standard companies, attributing wide price variations on products of similar quality to Standard manipulation and the absence of price competition between Standard companies. Both before and after its dissolution, the independents perceived Standard as a capricious and willful monopoly that threatened their existence.[24]

The independents formulated a strong case demonstrating that their interests suffered from the policies employed by Standard and then the majors. Bureau of Corporations and FTC officials made these arguments their own, integrating them into the several reports issued on the oil industry. By 1917, it was conceded that dissolution of Standard had failed to diminish the power of the Standard units within their marketing territories. That the common carrier principle had affected no change was also conceded, thus the demand for divorcement. The linchpin of federal policy, antitrust, proved incapable of coping with the rise of the modern oil industry—or, for that matter, industry in general.

The grievances of the independents were real, but it did not follow that a resolution of their difficulties would benefit the consuming public. The supply of crude oil would not have changed; at no time did the independent producers claim that the power of the majors discouraged exploration and discovery. Nor did the independents advance the proposition that the supply or quality of refined products would improve with the advent of a competitive structure more to their liking. The independents claimed, on the one hand, that the price they received for their products was too low, and, on the other hand, that the implementation of their remedies would result in lower consumer prices. While the former contention may have been true insofar as they actually did operate on a narrow margin, the latter assertion went unsubstantiated.[25]

The independents could demonstrate the illegality of the majors' pipeline practices. They could, perhaps, make a case that so closely linked Standard's price policies in a market area with prevailing prices in that area that only those willingly deceived could interpret the relationship as coincidental. To the extent that these accusations demanded and did not receive corrective attention by the federal government, to that extent the public interest was ill served. But at a more general level the independents failed to prove that the public would benefit from their continued existence; they failed to demonstrate the convergence of their particular interests with the public interest.

The majors argued that their accrued advantages stemmed from their size and integrated operations. While Americans feared monopoly, they accepted the notion that in modern business, efficiency improved with size. But great size, unopposed, was unacceptable. Dissolving Standard, or American Tobacco, relieved certain anxieties. Whether, in fact, operational efficiency, innovativeness, product quality, and other industrial desiderata actually depended upon great size and could not be readily achieved at some smaller size remained unproven. The federal government contributed little, beyond dissolving Standard, to the resolution of these questions or others regarding the preferred structure of the oil industry.[26]

The Coal Industry

As early as 1844, the federal government turned its attention to coal when the Department of the Navy supported experiments on the burning properties of coal. Occasional experiments of a similar sort were authorized in later years. Beginning in 1890, the U.S. Commission of Labor commenced the publication of annual reviews of coal production. Three years later federal interest in the structure of the industry surfaced. In 1893, a House committee held hearings concerning an alleged combination between the Philadelphia and Reading Company and other rail lines and producers of coal. These hearings derived naturally from the statutory authority of the Sherman Act; that thrust, less publicized and less dramatic than in oil, since there was no equivalent of Standard in the coal industry, persisted into the twentieth century.[27]

Labor-management strife in the coal fields exerted pressure on the federal government to assume a more active role in coal. The anthracite strike of 1902 precipitated the first major federal intrusion when Roosevelt established the Anthracite Coal Commission to settle the controversy. Subsequent strikes in bituminous—1904, 1906 (particularly serious), 1908, 1912, 1914—gave rise to no direct federal intervention but served to confirm prevailing public opinion as to the essentially chaotic nature of the industry. Labor disputes after World War I, especially those of 1919 and 1922, prompted direct federal intervention and intense federal scrutiny of the industry. In this study, the specific nature and the history of the labor-management disputes receive only incidental attention; instead, the focal point is the evaluation of federal policies affecting production, distribution, allocation, and price.[28]

Although dissension among producers in the coal industry was not absent, its political impact remained muted before World War I, at least when compared to the internal bickering of the petroleum industry. Coal operators competed intensely within local and even regional markets; and, as noted in Chapter 1, confronted threatening competition from other fuels. Excepting labor, transportation was the major cost incurred in coal operations. Naturally, then, coal operators evinced marked concern about railroad freight rates, an area that somewhat dovetailed with federal expressions of interest in the role of coal-carrying railroads and railroads that owned coal mines or coal land.

Between 1907 and 1917, the House published at least three reports on the coal industry that emphasized rail transportation, and the FTC published a major analysis of general conditions in the soft and hard coal industries. The House report of 1907, actually an ICC report of investigations carried out in response to a congressional joint resolution of 1906, concentrated on discrimination in coal by eastern bituminous coal-carrying railroads, many of which owned mines. Among the provisions of the Hepburn Act of 1906 was one prohibiting railroads from carrying commodities they had produced or mined, except those necessary for their own use. As interpreted by the Supreme Court, however, the Hepburn Act did not prevent railroads from mining, selling, and hauling their own coal.

The pre-World War I investigations solidly documented the unfair trade practices of mine-owning bituminous railroads, and the FTC report of 1917 confirmed prior knowledge about the extent of railroad control prevalent in the anthracite industry. The hearings in both 1913 and 1914 devoted much attention to the need for the divorcement of railroads from owning and operating coal mines, a policy recommended by the ICC in 1907 and again in 1909. In oil, support for divorcement originated largely among the small refineries and producers of the Mid-Continent that owned no trunk pipelines, while larger independents frequently opposed it. The issue of pipeline divorcement aroused little interest outside oil circles, an indication, perhaps, that consumers perceived no connection between it and their own interests. Divorcement in coal appealed to a broader range of interests, including nonrailroad mine operators in the bituminous fields and various individuals speaking for eastern consumer groups.

At the coal hearings, numerous New Englanders testified in favor of the divorcement of anthracite mines from railroad ownership. New Englanders knew that a dozen mine-owning railroads controlled a large percentage of anthracite production (see Chapter 1, p. 6). Supply and price inequities were attributed to this concentration of power. Anthracite railroads, according to witnesses from New England and New York, compensated for losses incurred in mining coal by charging excessive freight rates for carrying their own coal. These freight rates, charged against distributors (some owned by the railroads), were then passed through to domestic consumers.

Coal shortages in 1911 and 1912, in Boston, Providence, New Haven, and elsewhere in New England, reflected no drastic lack of coal but stemmed from market manipulation by the anthracite roads (see Table 4). Prices soared skyward, as U.S. Representative William F. Murray, a Boston Democrat, explained it, partly because the anthracite roads compelled independent distributors to pay premiums for coal. The hearings of 1913 confirmed the findings of earlier ICC investigations of the major bituminous-carrying railroads. Favoritism and discrimination in car supply that favored captive mines, oddly structured freight rates that benefited the railroads' mines, the offering of stock in coal mines to railroad employers, the discouragement of new mine openings by the denial of sidings, and other abuses were uncovered by ICC investigators. Similar practices described the activities of western mine-owning roads, according to witnesses at the hearings of 1914. In that year, Colorado independents accused the Denver and Rio Grande Western Railroad and its subsidiary fuel companies with unfair competition in coal markets and the denial of coal cars to competitors.

In hearings that spanned a decade, coal operators and consumers from widely separated regions responded to congressional interrogators with a documented litany of complaints against the railroads and with demand for divestiture. The charges and supporting evidence went uncontested by the railroads or their fuel company affiliates. The federal government, however, felt no disposition to press for divorcement. The FTC opted for enforcement of the commodities clause of the Hepburn Act, even though the courts had rendered it impotent. Many congressmen believed that such blatantly unfair practices as did exist should be remedied through the courts, although small coal operators denied their ability to finance such suits against major railroads with their army of lawyers. Nor was any effort made, by either coal or oil operators, to coalesce and campaign for a general divorcement bill applicable to all common carriers. Not to say that such an alliance would have, in fact, strengthened their position, but only that it would have reflected a recognition of the broad implications of the issue.[29]

These hearings and investigations about the coal roads and about railroad freight rates, coupled with the reports of the Anthracite Coal Commission in 1902, the U.S. Commission of Labor in 1912, and the FTC coal investigation in 1916 (authorized by a congressional resolution), produced a comprehensive body of data on the nation's coal industry. By the time of America's entrance into World War I, the federal government recognized several serious problems. Many coal-producing units, dependent upon rail transport and burdened by high freight rates, competed madly for local and regional markets while trying to shave costs by keeping wages down. The bituminous industry had a developed capacity and labor force far in excess of demand. Year in, year out, the mines were idle seventy to ninety working days annually. Irregular operation, aggravated by periodic coal car shortages, upset the distribution of coal, causing unpredictable fluctuations in price. Accumulated evidence pointed to the intrusion of other fuels into traditional markets. Some federal officials, as James P. Johnson points out, sympathized with coal industry experiments with joint selling agencies, price agreements, and other marketing tactics; some, particularly in the Justice Department, held these practices illegal.[30] All this, as many realized, directly and adversely affected the interests of the public.

As Johnson suggests, traditional commitments to protecting and encouraging competition by means of antitrust legislation may have obstructed industry stabilization efforts.[31] Too, the industry itself recognized no leaders or spokespersons and followed no dominant firm as oil firms followed the leadership of Standard. The competitive structure of the industry virtually precluded effective intraindustry cooperation. Mid-Continent coal operators railed at ICC rates that permitted Illinois and Indiana coal to compete west of the Mississippi and that then threw Kansas coals into markets served by Colorado mines. Appalachian bituminous operators north of the Ohio fought with southern operators who invaded Great Lakes markets and with the anthracite producers who occasionally penetrated the steam-raising markets of bituminous. Even assuming the absence of such barriers as antitrust statutes, what, precisely, other than divorcement, could have been done by public authorities to rationalize a historically competitive, contentious, and violent industry? FTC Commissioner Edward N. Hurley's panacea, uniform cost accounting, or F. G. Tryon's emphasis, seized upon by engineers during the 1920s, on improved coal storage to smooth out seasonal production irregularities were almost laughable given the industry's chronic difficulties.[32]

Conclusion

Two knowledgeable students of the petroleum industry, Gerald D. Nash and August W. Giebelhaus, perceive trends in oil policy formulation prior to World War I that are not apparent to me. Nash refers to the emergence of an oil policy between 1890 and 1917 as a direct result of the actions of private entrepreneurs who "sought governmental sanctions and restraints to cope with problems of their rapidly changing industry."[33] For his part, Giebelhuas also senses new attitudes evolving after 1911 regarding industry-government cooperation. He writes: "The government moved to protect the public's interest in a valuable national resource, while business executives realized the economic gains possible through legislation to effect stabilization of the industry."[34]

On several counts a demurral should be provided, which applies in part to the coal industry as well. Intraindustry strife best captures the flavor of oil industry politics, and coal as well. In oil, those most actively seeking government intervention did so with very narrow objectives in mind and harbored no desire for other than a negative, prohibitory role for the government. The majors, insofar as they actually advocated cooperation with government, defined that cooperation as a relationship in which a permissive federal government eschewed efforts to tamper with free market forces or interfere with the benefits of economies of scale. While the independents demanded a more active federal government, they narrowly defined intervention to include only enforcement of the antitrust laws and use of the amended Interstate Commerce Act to eliminate certain practices of the majors that damaged their own interests. Essentially, the independents confined their demands to pipeline divorcement and the reduction of railroad freight rates for crude oil.

Neither the independents nor the majors trusted the FTC, nor did they demand, in the name of the public interest, broad FTC action against unfair trade practices. Some independents viewed the FTC as an information gathering and disseminating agency which, in publishing cost figures for all branches of the petroleum industry, would equalize access to information. Others complained loudly when the FTC attempted to gather confidential data. In short, the majors believed that an inactive government would best serve their interests; the independents wished federal intervention at certain well-defined points. The coal industry, really without an expressed collective position, wanted little from government aside from freight-rate adjustments—that is, again intervention at a specific point.

The federal government—Congress, the executive, the courts—had no notion of the public interest which went beyond routine and rhetorical assertions that a free market must be preserved. Perhaps the dissolution of Standard was compatible with the public interest. But that action was not initiated in an effort to protect a nonrenewable natural resource. The unenthusiastic federal response to coal industry problems reflected even less concern with the public interest. The ICC, the Bureau of Corporations, and the FTC failed to develop ideas about oil and coal that distinguished them from nonfuel industries.[35] Prior to World War I, then, neither an oil nor a coal policy emerged, while the term "public interest" served as a blind behind which lurked particular interests.

THREE

Wartime Coal Policies

AMERICAN BELLIGERENCY in April 1917 compelled the federal government to assume unprecedented responsibility for the mobilization of goods, services, and manpower necessary to wage a war on fronts thousands of miles from home. With little experience to guide it, the federal government reacted slowly and spasmodically to emerging necessity, applying short-run remedies to long-term problems and inadequately anticipating problems of all kinds. Lacking expertise in many fields, the federal establishment depended upon the knowledge and competence of the private sector, temporarily recruiting hundreds of individuals from private enterprise and the professions to staff the offices and agencies created to manage the massive war effort. Serious disagreement concerning the degree of centralization demanded to conduct the war hampered the efforts of the war managers, in part reflecting the carry-over into the war years of controversies and uncertainties about the proper roles of the public and private sectors in the American economy.

Prewar progressivism represented an ideological current characterized by widespread disbelief that giant corporations served the public interest. Some voices called for strict regulation; others demanded the nationalization of key industries, particularly the railroads. Antitrust suits against several large industrial combinations, passage of the Hepburn Act, and the establishment of state railroad and utility commissions and such federal regulatory commissions as ICC and FTC at once demonstrated the political potency of these gnawing concerns and the essential moderation of political responses. Conserva-

49

tives fought against an expanding federal role, arguing forcefully for a hands-off policy that would permit free market forces to spur economic development. For business, the war in Europe opened up great opportunities for profit through an expanding foreign trade. As many businessmen viewed it, American entrance into the conflict provided no compelling reasons for a swollen federal economic role.[1]

In 1917 and 1918, the federal government hesitantly developed an organizational framework to manage the nation's fuel supplies. The United States Fuel Administration (USFA) coordinated this enormous effort by developing a sprawling network of subordinate units located in thousands of localities and staffed by public officials and by persons drawn from all walks of life. USFA never developed into a superagency, nor did its only administrator, Harry A. Garfield, emerge as a fuel czar. Garfield preferred decentralized authority as an operational mode even though USFA possessed considerable statutory power.[2]

Mobilizing fuel supplies for war compelled the U.S. government to confront problems of price, production, and transportation and to choose from among various uses of fuel those most necessary to the war effort while simultaneously making judgments about how much fuel should be allocated to certain classes of users. Houses, offices, and factories had to be kept warm, electricity had to be generated to light homes and run machinery, locomotives consumed enormous quantities of coal, and process heat was required by the industrial sector. The USFA and peer agencies whose duties also impinged upon fuel supply assumed the task of defining the public interest and devising policies to achieve goals in consonance with it. To most Americans, winning the war quickly was obviously in the public interest. Not so easily answered, however, was the extent to which victory would demand restructuring the home front.

The Fuel Crisis of 1916

When the United States declared war in April 1917, it was already in the throes of a fuel emergency that boded ill for a future characterized by vastly increased demands upon all resources and distribution systems. Prior to 1915, public perceptions of rising fuel prices, uncertain supplies, and fear of monopoly had, as recounted in Chapter 2, prompted Congress to authorize various investigations of the petroleum and coal industries. Stable price levels ruled prior to 1915, but inexplicably coal prices started to rise in late 1915 (Table 6), and within a matter of months, coal shortages became severe. Since production was not falling (see Table 4), all this confused and embittered

TABLE 6. *Average Spot Prices per Ton of Bituminous Coal FOB Mines, 1915–1922*

	1915	1916	1917	1918	1919	1920	1921	1922
January	$1.13	$1.53	$4.15	$2.48	$2.57	$2.57	$3.26	$2.26
February	1.12	1.40	4.18	2.53	2.49	2.58	2.77	2.20
March	1.09	1.27	3.89	2.58	2.47	2.58	2.63	2.12
April	1.08	1.24	3.21	2.64	2.43	3.85	2.62	2.23
May	1.07	1.21	4.14	2.67	2.38	4.59	2.68	3.09
June	1.07	1.26	4.00	2.57	2.40	7.18	2.52	3.32
July	1.05	1.22	3.17	2.58	2.47	8.24	2.40	4.38
August	1.07	1.30	3.24	2.58	2.76	9.51	2.42	6.10
September	1.10	1.57	2.02	2.58	2.91	8.52	2.37	5.06
October	1.12	2.26	2.02	2.58	3.09	7.78	2.33	4.37
November	1.17	3.87	2.48	2.58	2.57	5.87	2.35	4.10
December	1.33	4.01	2.48	2.58	2.58	4.38	2.26	4.07

Source: Box 4, Entry 8, USCC, RG 68.

consumers. Crude oil prices at the well also rose, although less steeply than either bituminous or anthracite prices.[3]

In December 1916 and January 1917, the Cincinnati Traction Company and utilities in Louisville, Oklahoma City, and elsewhere frequently came within a few hours of total exhaustion of fuel supplies. Although these companies purchased all but a small portion on contract, suppliers failed to deliver, forcing the firms to enter the coal spot market and pay inflated prices. The utilities and other large consumers blamed the railroads for aggravating supply conditions. In 1916, the United Gas Improvement Company, one of the country's largest utility holding companies, investigated the railroad car shortage and concluded that the railroads assured their own supply by seizing and reconsigning loaded coal cars without regard to contracts. The Louisville & Nashville Railroad, for instance, admitted to the confiscation of 1,782 coal cars from November 1916 through April 1917.[4]

As early as January 1916, *The Retail Coalman* had warned its readers to anticipate brisk demand and pressures on car service, partly as a result of British and French armaments orders, and partly because of uncertainty about the mine workers' contract due to expire on 1 April. But few were prepared for the severity of the problem or its duration. Railroad officials blamed coal producers and distributors for the shortages, accusing producers of inefficient loading and dealers of inefficient unloading. Coal people blamed the railroads and one another. Irate consumers, casting their net most widely, impugned the motives of all involved, including the federal government for its apparent powerlessness.

After sifting through the charges and counterchanges, the FTC concluded that car supply shortages were at the root of bituminous supply difficulty. These shortages, appearing early in 1916, not only reduced coal production but induced major consumers to place extraordinarily large coal orders. Panicky consumers stimulated producers and distributors to advance prices and to renege on contracts worth much less than sales on the spot market. This forced more large consumers to place orders and reduced the quantity of domestic (household) coal available. During 1916, bituminous prices in Kansas City, Oklahoma City, and New York rose by 50 to 70 percent, reaching $6.50 to $7.00 per ton. Rising soft coal prices induced eastern steam coal users to switch to anthracite which, in turn, seriously diminished the stock available to householders. The public's fear of anthracite shortages permitted anthracite dealers to charge what the market would bear. The FTC discovered that numerous dealers held their coal in the cars, awaiting the most favorable moment to auction off the coal to the highest bidder. The poor, or those purchasing by the bushel basket or sack, suffered most, for while average retail prices per ton rose by over 50 percent in many communities, prices per hundred pound sack rose 100 percent—and these customers were the last to receive any coal. Culpability, then, could be evenly ascribed to individuals and firms in all sectors of coal production, transportation, and distribution.

Inflationary pressure and inadequate coal supply persisted into the early months of 1917. Open-market bituminous prices reached $7.50 per ton in Memphis and Newark. Steadily rising fuel oil and gasoline prices in eastern markets exacerbated the inflationary pinch and produced some dislocation within the Mid-Continent oil industry. Independents attributed this to the pricing policies of Standard and the majors. A good part of the Mid-Continent's problem, however, derived from a marked production decline in the Cushing field that forced up the price independents paid for crude oil from $1.20 barrel in late 1915 to $2.10 in 1916; frequently a premium of $.50 was demanded on top of the posted price. With a brisk eastern market, larger than normal quantities of crude flowed eastward, precipitating feedstock shortages among smaller western refiners and thus significantly higher gasoline prices.[5]

FIG. 3. *In 1916, the coal industry believed it was unfairly singled out for criticism about price hikes.*

Source: *The Retail Coalman*, 28 (October 1916), 38.

Energy and the Federal Government

The wholesale price of all goods rose steeply beginning in 1915. Wholesale coal prices moved upward at about the same rate as other commodities, thus supplying some credence to the cartoon that appeared in *The Retail Coalman*. However, retail coal prices increased much more sharply than wholesale prices. Furthermore, other commodities, excepting food, were less essential than fuel. Purchase of less essential items could be postponed, and shopping around might unveil an acceptable product at a lower price. Not so with heating fuels where scarcity could cause sickness and even death.[6]

Organizing for War

The inflationary spiral of 1915–16 and its unequal impact on people throughout the land coincided with a growing apprehension within the Wilson administration that American participation in the European war was likely. Preparedness—an obscene term to many patriotic Americans—surfaced as a political issue in November 1915 when President Woodrow Wilson proposed a moderate expansion of the nation's military forces. From that time until the final declaration of war, the issue of America's involvement never disappeared, and, indeed, Wilson narrowly won another term in 1916 only by emphasizing that he kept us out of the war. In January 1917, only two months after Wilson's victory, Germany announced the resumption of unrestricted submarine warfare and commenced sinking American vessels. By late winter, the president was convinced of the necessity of American participation and simply waited for events to dramatize that tragic need to the people. Even before the election of 1916, the federal government had taken the first halting steps to prepare society for the threatening eventuality of war mobilization.

In 1916, Congress created the Council of National Defense (CND), delegating to it the responsibility for coordinating efforts to prepare the economy for war, but neglecting to clothe it with substantial power.[7] Early in its career, CND focused its attention on winning over major industrial sectors, which had been neutral toward its inception; by encouraging the organization of a number of industry-based advisory committees, the CND hoped to engender industry cooperation with the government in preparing for war. Even in its first faltering steps to stake out its responsibilities for war mobilization, CND reflected the Wilson administration's dependence upon the private sector for expertise and its commitment to develop "national policy through the public institutional recognition of private individuals and private interest groups."[8]

As CND launched its initial preparedness efforts, the state of the nation's fuel supplies steadily deteriorated. The shortages of 1916 persisted into 1917, as did car shortages at the mines and railroad congestion at major terminals. With the declaration of war in April, federal procurement of a vast array of goods rested on the shoulders of the cooperative committees of CND. Lacking power, the CND committees employed moral suasion and appeals to patriotic feelings to transform the economy from a peacetime to wartime posture.

In April and May 1917, CND organized many committees to place the various industrial sectors on a war footing. The Cooperative Committee on Railroad Transportation, staffed by railroad personnel, functioned until 26 December 1917, when the railroads were nationalized. A special committee on national defense, formed by the American Railway Association (ARA) in April, established subcommittees on car service and military traffic. The ARA subcommittees and the CND committee suggested a general preference system for coal supply and moved cars and engines to places of need. Even before the war, in March, the CND rail committee intervened to prevent a railroad strike. But the entire system depended upon the voluntary compliance of the separate rail companies. The president did have statutory authority to take possession of any transportation system, a power granted in the Army Appropriation Act of 1916. In May 1917, Congress expanded the power of the ICC to establish car service rules. In August 1917, Congress passed the Priority Act, empowering the president to order carriers to give preference to transportation essential to national defense. But throughout the remainder of 1917, these powers were rarely and but lightly used. The CND transport committee, cooperating with the ARA, remained the primary authority in rail (and fuel) transport, a fact that severely limited the effectiveness of the U.S. Fuel Administration.[9]

On 21 April, the CND appointed a coal committee, chaired by Chicago coal executive Francis Peabody, and charged it to increase coal output and, in cooperation with the transportation committee, to move the coal to necessary locations. The Peabody committee recruited ten of its fourteen members from the ranks of coal industry management, a mistaken tactic that immediately drew the fire of John P. White, president of the United Mine Workers of America (UMWA).[10] White declared that such appointments "place all the great coal areas of the nation at the dictation of the avowed enemies of union labor [and] would disrupt all standards, all decency, all glowingly patriotic ideals."[11]

Although distrusted by labor and some officials in government, including the FTC and Secretary of War N. D. Baker, and dependent upon the cooperation of operators, carriers, and large coal users, the Peabody committee threw itself into its war work. It launched a survey of coal resources, studied the impact of conscription and competing lines of industrial work on mine labor, probed the nation's rail and distribution facilities, and acknowledged that chronic car shortages would sabotage efforts to increase production. The coal committee attempted to speed up mine loading, discourage miners from moving from mine to mine, guarantee the navy a continuous flow of coal, and encourage shipments by the most direct route. It also tried to convince the railroads not to use coal cars for other purposes, to employ box cars in coal transport, and to meet the specific coal demands of various users such as the utilities or steel and consuming regions such as the upper Great Lakes states. Pooling arrangements were worked out to handle coal at tidewater rail and water depots for the lake trade, the success of which depended upon the availability of transportation.

Peabody committee appeals to patriotism and a spirit of sacrifice were not entirely ineffective. In its first two months, the committee, without any coercive power, did keep coal moving to such strategic points as eastern tidewater ports and Lake Erie and Lake Michigan ports by means of pooling. Some cross-hauling of coal was eliminated, and the confiscatory practices of railroads were much abated. Numerous coal operators ceased shipping coal to traditional and distant markets and searched out markets closer to their mines. Many argued, however, that such ad hoc arrangements could not possibly succeed in the long run, that more centralized and more authoritative control must be quickly applied. Consumers feared that industry voluntarism and patriotism could not hold prices in line. Abnormal demands on transportation and rising fixed transportation costs, as the Baltimore & Ohio president, Samuel Willard, admitted, would necessarily cause the railroads to protect their own interests at the expense of operators and consumers. Moreover, as critics asserted, the committee had ignored that part of the distribution system which put coal in the bins of homeowners or other small consumers.

In May 1917, as average off-season mine prices uncharacteristically rose (see Table 6), angry consumers accused dealers of charging exorbitant retail prices. Associations of citizens and property owners in New York City addressed letters to their congressmen and to the FTC complaining bitterly about the inflated price and short supply of coal and warning of epidemics, riots, and general misery should the scarcity persist. Far to the west, in Kansas City, Missouri, Miss M. E.

Cavanaugh echoed the frustration of the New Yorkers about coal prices that cost her $2 more per ton than in 1916. *"What are we to do,"* she implored, "if we are to be held up in this manner?" Another Kansas Citian called local coal dealers "the most cold blooded and heartless bunch of speculative sharks that ever went unhung." Concurrently, oil refineries in Kansas and Oklahoma shut down for lack of crude oil or because crude prices were too high to warrant processing. Jobs and comfort were at stake. Aggrieved Kansas Citians and New Yorkers contributed to the fashioning of a case for federal control over fuels.[12]

The Peabody committee, aided by Secretary of Interior F. K. Lane, attempted to deflect criticism from the coal industry by calling a meeting of producers and hammering out a maximum mine-mouth price for coal, fixed on June 28 at $3 per ton. The friction precipitated by this figure (I will return to this matter later in a section on price-fixing procedures) led directly to the passage of the coal provisions of the Food and Fuel Control Act of August 1917 (Lever Act). The Wilson administration disavowed the operators' price and substituted lower prices in August. Wilson also made the decision to endow a new agency with authority to administer the Lever Act rather than granting that power to the Federal Trade Commission which had actively campaigned for that role.

Congressional hearings in the summer of 1917 on the regulation of the coal industry, particularly the imposition of maximum prices, revealed that many within coal accepted the need for some centralized control, but not by the FTC which was viewed as hostile to the industry. J. G. Puterbaugh, president of the McAlister Fuel Company, Oklahoma's largest distributing company, argued in July 1917, that price and supply conditions demanded the imposition of tight federal regulations to prevent price gouging and inequitable allocation by producers and railroads. John L. Lewis of the UMWA considered the FTC incompetent in coal and preferred a new agency composed of people familiar with the industry and representatives of consumers. Others, especially within FTC, viewed the entire debate as irrelevant to the central problem: the continuing ability of the railroads to divide and allot the nation's traffic according to their own self-interest. Nonetheless, the Lever Act, which itself aroused little adverse notice, permitted presidential discretion in establishing the appropriate administrative mechanisms. The act authorized the president to regulate the price, production, sale, shipment, and allocation of coal and coke.[13]

Wilson's decision to form a new agency, the U.S. Fuel Administration, confirms analyses offered by Cuff and Kennedy which suggest that the Wilson administration, while reluctant to create new agencies, believed firmly in the dispersion of power.[14] Wilson's awareness of industrial hostility toward the FTC furnished an equally important reason. All advice reaching Wilson from various sources, while disagreeing on many particulars, counseled against lodging the new powers within FTC.[15]

Organizing the USFA

The fuel provisions of the Lever Act were without precedent. They empowered the president to regulate totally the coal industry. Although the preamble of the act included gas and oil in its definition of fuel, the law omitted specific authority to set prices for gas or oil. Those fuels were subject to fewer restrictions than coal. Vocal support from a variety of organizations and interests accompanied passage of the legislation. But the disturbing reality of federal control precipitated the organization of at least two national coal industry associations, The National Retail Coal Merchants' Association (NRCMA) and The National Coal Association (NCA), a producers' group. Both associations anticipated key roles in the operation of the USFA and patriotically pledged their support to the administration. Nonetheless they defined their essential task as defending their members against unnecessary and foolish federal intervention.[16]

USFA administrator Harry A. Garfield was a humane and intelligent man but knew little about coal. He came to Washington armed with rather well-formed ideas about the proper role of government in the social and economic life of the nation and in September 1917, applied those ideas to the molding of USFA. Garfield, Wilson, and others were apprehensive about concentrating more power in federal hands, but were no less disturbed about the economic power and political influence of giant private corporations. Believing in a cooperative approach to industrial mobilization, Garfield imposed a decentralized organizational structure on USFA, trusting that the call to arms would foster a spirit of sacrifice and harmony. From the beginning, Garfield struggled in vain against the imperatives of war. In refusing to make concessions to centralization early on, when he possessed some flexibility, he was forced later on, as pressure intensified, to exercise power swiftly—and, it therefore appeared, arbitrarily and ruthlessly. By December 1917, Garfield's faith in the cooperative order had dimmed. If the war continues for a long time, he sadly confided to a Senate subcommittee, the government would exercise more and more control.[17]

USFA's permanent internal organization unfolded at a rather leisurely pace between September 1917 and the reorganization embarked upon in late December 1917. The administration's most persistent operational difficulties flowed directly from Garfields first administrative act, the organization of separate state fuel administrators gathered loosely together into a bureau of state organizations. State administrators received considerable authority over prices, distribution, allocation, and conservation. Decentralized management worked well enough when applied to such matters as national fuel conservation campaigns. But the critical issues—price, dealer margins, allocation of fuels to users, transportation priorities—were national in scope and required centralized coordination. So frequently did state administrators act as advocates of the interests of their own states that headquarters officials gradually assumed responsibility for decisions of local as well as national import. By mid-1918, state administrators were confined to orchestrating conservation crusades, lecturing Washington about state and local conditions, and pleading for exceptions to rules perceived as detrimental to state interests. Nor did all of the special constituencies affected by USFA trust state and local officials who numbered in the thousands.[18] At its first annual meeting in 1918, NRCMA adopted a resolution calling on Garfield to exercise detailed oversight of the activities of state officials. The imperatives of federalism and Garfield's proclivity for cooperation, voluntarism, and decentralization assured that hoary traditions of local autonomy would retreat slowly in the face of pressing national needs.

A related problem of equal significance, emphasized in Cuff's study, stemmed from the absence of a sufficient cadre of federal employees expert in fuel and transportation problems. As did the War Industries Board (WIB) and the defense council before it, USFA recruited most of its chief employees from the ranks of the coal industry. The various coal field and coal distribution center committees were staffed entirely by coal industry personnel. J. D. A. Morrow, general secretary of the National Coal Association, became director of the bureau of distribution; all of his assistants held management positions with coal railroads or coal companies. Alfred M. Ogle, director of the state distribution bureau, had managed mines and mining companies in Indiana since 1911, and just prior to the war had organized the Ogle Coal Company, a sales organization headquartered in Indianapolis. After the war, Ogle served as vice-president of NCA from 1919 to 1922 and as president in 1922. Samuel B. Crowell, Garfield's chief advisor on retail coal, was most recently resident vice-president of the NRCMA.

While this relationship, particularly in the oil division, fomented discontent in progressive circles and provided ammunition for those accusing USFA of being a captive of the coal and oil industries, in fact, Garfield's options were limited. A pool of trained and neutral individuals did not exist outside the fuel industries, save for a few persons coopted from various federal agencies. Nor did Congress appropriate funds for the development of a staff with no industry ties. Time was pressing, and Garfield seized upon available expertise, using industry trade associations and industry personnel as best he could. While the state fuel administrators were frequently unassociated with the fuel industries, the chairpersons of the 3,800 local and county committees frequently came from fuel firms.[19]

Garfield's reluctance to bureaucratize his agency derived partly from his belief that once mine-mouth coal prices were fixed, existing agencies and voluntary compliance would get fuel to proper destinations. This conviction, naive given the absence of transportation coordination, postponed the creation of a USFA division of distribution until January 1918. And the preeminent concern with coal retarded the organization of an oil division until the same month. Problems concerning electric power slid by default to the conservation division, but the real center of control in electricity rested with the Army Corps of Engineers and the War Industry Board's power division. Until early 1918, USFA operated more or less through ad hoc committees.

USFA's internal weaknesses were exacerbated by the failure of Congress and of Wilson to recognize that business-as-usual attitudes coupled with a piecemeal approach to reorganization severely hampered war mobilization. While USFA authority reached into all sectors of the coal industry and penetrated deeply into petroleum, the agency did not operate with superagency powers. Possessing primacy in all matters relating to fuel supply, USAF's wide sphere of interest necessitated cooperation with several other federal agencies.[20] These agencies were not created simultaneously, according to some master plan, but as necessity—even *after* necessity—demanded. Cuff skillfully details the painstaking evolution of WIB from CND and the latter's General Munitions Board. WIB itself was a composite of several agencies, and in accomplishing its primary duty, the assignment of priorities for resource use among competing users, acted more as a broker than as a dictator. Even this role fully emerged only in the spring of 1918.[21]

Until the organization of the United States Railroad Administration in December 1917, ad hoc committees of CND, all filled from the ranks of railroad management, attempted to coordinate railroad transportation. These committees and the Interstate Commerce Commission interfered minimally with the independent operations of the railroads. Power existed but was not exercised. ICC commissioners disagreed as to their actual power to regulate car supply under the Esch Act of May 1917. Car shortages paralyzed coal mines in the Mid-Continent and elsewhere, obstructed beef shipments from Texas and Oklahoma and feed shipments into cattle states, and caused fruit to rot unpicked on the trees. Numerous individuals and groups, including the ICC, urged unification of the roads under federal aegis. But into late fall of 1917, evidence of threatened disaster failed to galvanize the Wilson war managers into action on the railroad front. Many of USFA's difficulties, particularly in December and January, can be attributed directly to such inaction. Unilaterally, USFA could not remedy a 40 percent shortfall in the provision of cars to the coal mines. As with priorities, so with transportation; the USFA could request but not command. These weaknesses ultimately shattered Garfield's reliance upon voluntarism.[22]

Price Fixing

USFA's mission encompassed three basic responsibilities: fixing mine-mouth coal prices, readjusting the geographic distribution of coal, reordering distribution among consumers. Of the three, the fixing of prices was attempted first and generated great controversy, but may have been the least important.[23]

Severe inflationary pressures vexed the nation in the months following the declaration of war. CND acknowledged the need for a more centralized approach to prices by forming a committee to search for a stabilizing policy. Some advocated across-the-board government price fixing; others claimed the federal government and business leaders could jointly and cooperatively formulate guidelines for the establishment of fair prices. Miss Cavanaugh and thousands of other householders were understandably upset over inflated coal prices, because it was well known that the bituminous mines had a production capacity far in excess of even the swollen demands of late 1916 and 1917. Harry N. Taylor of the Peabody committee denied the prevalence of price abuse in the Mid-Continent. Evidence submitted by the Kansas Buff Brick and Manufacturing Company and the attorney general of Missouri flatly contradicted Taylor's assertions, and both parties called for government possession of the mines. The Fuel Engineering Company of New York, a fuel consulting firm representing about a hundred manufacturers with 250 plants, which consumed 3 million tons annually, advocated federal control over prices and contracts as the only means of preventing extortionary prices. In Denver, the *Denver Post* declared war against Colorado's "coal barons" and soon added the Colorado fuel administrator to their hit list.

Public antipathy toward the coal industry prompted the Peabody committee to call a meeting of coal operators to discuss price. After listening to Secretary of the Interior Lane exhort them not to coin the blood of soldiers into dollars, the operators tentatively agreed upon a maximum price of $3 per ton for bituminous. This price elicited an extremely favorable response from the press. The *Richmond Times-Dispatch* called it a "sweeping reduction" while the *Youngstown Telegram* claimed it would save consumers $180 million annually. The *Atlanta Journal*, the *Boston Journal*, and newspapers in other cities responded with equal enthusiasm. But Newton D. Baker and others in the Wilson administration considered $3 unconscionably high. Baker denounced the price as exorbitant and oppressive and charged that the Council of National Defense lacked the authority to fix prices. Congressman William A. Cullop of Indiana labeled CND a "Council of Oppression."[24]

The Peabody price, according to James P. Johnson, convinced Wilson and his cabinet of the necessity of formal federal control over the coal industry. To be sure, the $3 price, whether it was actually too high or not, contributed to Wilson's decision to support the Lever Act. But the generally poor performance of the Peabody committee, at least as most Americans perceived it, in distributing and allocating coal provided the larger reason for a perceptible shift toward centralized control of the fuel industries. Whatever price the coal operators had suggested, compelling reasons for federal regulation would have remained. Peabody defended the $3 price, but he also recognized the need for government regulation. In agreeing upon a maximum price, the operators may indeed have been attempting to short-circuit the move toward federal regulation. If so, their strategy backfired, though the price itself hardly merited such expressions of administration and congressional outrage. Moreover, the Lever Act alone could not stabilize the industry or assure the efficient movement of fuels. As events demonstrated, without equivalent attention to the railroads, the Lever Act could produce at best minimal improvements in coal production and delivery.[25]

On 21 August 1917, two days before the appointment of Garfield, Wilson issued an executive order that fixed average maximum mine prices of coal for the several coal districts at about $2.40 per ton. This first large-scale attempt by the federal government to establish prices for industry provoked a torrent of protest from mine operators and coal distributors who claimed the low prices would discourage production and damage the war effort. However, the executive order figures were based upon hasty and incomplete FTC production cost studies covering only 20 percent of total production, and it was understood that these prices would be amended by USFA. The fuel administration immediately launched a more encompassing study of coal production costs in each producing district, but much confusion attended each aspect of the price-fixing procedure.

To determine if the Wilson prices should be adhered to, FTC accountants examined the cost sheets submitted by the operators. USFA also utilized data gathered by state fuel administrators, but this was much more impressionistic than the FTC information. Some state administrators received help from reassigned employees of FTC's coal section while others ignored this source of expertise; overall, the FTC data warranted smaller increases of the Wilson prices than did data compiled by USFA personnel. Also, while state administrators collected data on prices, sometimes provided by local fuel committees, and forwarded them to the price bureau for analysis, individual operators and district operator associations often submitted their own statistics to the price office. Furthermore, some state officials identified more closely with operators than with consumers, a charge repeatedly leveled at the Colorado fuel administrator by the truculent Denver newspapers. In addition to loyalties or prejudices that may have skewed price figures submitted to USFA, few state fuel administrators possessed sufficient economic expertise to offer informed analyses of the costs of coal production.

It was out of this confusion that USFA compiled its data, but nonetheless, amend Wilson's figures they did. On 1 October 1917, six weeks after the president's executive order, Garfield issued the first revised prices; maximum prices for each district were, on the average, raised thirty to fifty cents per ton above those fixed by Wilson. Prices were revised constantly during the remainder of the war. But not until January 1918 did Garfield finally organize a committee of professional coal engineers to analyze the operator cost sheets. By then the major requirement in pricing was to make adjustments that compensated for inflationary pressures but did not markedly increase operator profits. FTC economists criticized the USFA engineers for recommending unnecessarily high mine-mouth prices, pointing out that the industry-wide rate of profit reached 29 percent in 1917, compared with 8 percent in 1916; coal producer profits in 1918 did decline to 18 percent, but were still high by any standard.[26]

In mid-October 1917, Emerson Carey, fuel administrator for Kansas, had informed headquarters of widespread retail coal price increases. Dealers hurried to protect their profits from the further federal price setting announced in Garfield's 1 October order establishing retail gross margins and other regulations governing retail dealers. The 1 October order recognized that maximum prices at the mines did not fully control retail price levels, which were subject to distributor and dealer manipulation before consumers put coal in their basements. Arthur Capper, governor of Kansas, confirmed such manipulation in his state and accused retail dealers of collusion "in advancing prices to unreasonable figures, apparently with a determination to ignore federal action."[27]

Even more confusion attended the establishment of retail margins than in fixing mine prices. Responsibility for the latter rested in Washington; the state administrators determined retail margins.[28] In September, to prepare for the 1 October order, Garfield had authorized state administrators to instruct local committees to study local retail costs. But few retailers knew, or would reveal, their costs; and fewer still employed standardized accounting procedures. Costs varied from dealer to dealer and from area to area within a state. The local committees, pressed for time and sensitive to the criticism of their neighbors, were more often than not composed of individuals who knew nothing of the coal business—a situation much complained of by retail coal dealers. As the winter progressed and coal became more difficult to obtain, retailers blamed scarcities on inadequate margins and lobbied to raise their prices. Investigations by local fuel administrators of dealer arguments in Detroit and Kansas City denied any linkage between margins and supply, but pressure mounted to recalculate margins so as to allow higher retail prices. The policing of prices became more and more random. Counterpressure from consumers mounted, but it was a seller's market.

Garfield's agency claimed that mine-mouth price policies, fixed margins, the licensing system for jobbers, wholesalers, and retailers inaugurated in April 1918, and regulations to prevent engrossment by distributors had stabilized prices by early 1918 at fair levels. Producers, distributors, and consumers frequently disagreed. What was reasonable to a retailer seemed outrageous to a consumer. Mine-mouth prices remained stable from fall 1917 through 1919, except for a brief upward flurry in fall 1919 (see Table 6). But the differential between low and high prices in fall 1919 was only $.71. Retail prices proved less tractable. Retail anthracite prices per ton rose dramatically from July 1916 through January 1919: in Baltimore by $2.60, in

Boston and Philadelphia by $2.25, in New York by $1.87.

As early as August 1917, Treasury Secretary W. G. McAdoo had argued for price controls to buffer consumers against the extortionary prices of the anthracite trust. In May and June 1918, Detroit coal dealers and state local fuel officials in Michigan traded accusations about the level of retail prices, the adequacy of profit margins, and the relation of price to supply. In Denver, both the municipal government and the *Denver Post* operated public coal yards that sold coal at prices below those charged by local retailers. The *Post* and the *Denver Express* published scathing attacks on USFA, the Colorado fuel administrator, William J. Galligan, and the coal barons; the retail dealers labeled their opponents socialists, and Galligan linked the *Post* with pro-German interests.[29]

Producers and distributors viewed the prices differently and bombarded state administrators with demands for upward adjustments of prices or margins. According to FTC field personnel, state officials too often acceded to coal industry arguments. In December 1917, Garfield had established a procedure allowing an appeal to Washington against retail prices set by state administrators, but it proved a mechanism better serving suppliers than consumers. So little was really known about costs as to preclude any certain judgment about the justice of individual pleas, either by coal people or by consumers; or, for that matter, about the justice of actual decisions of the fuel officials. Everyone felt oppressed. This assured that most decisions precipitated immediate criticism from one interest or another.

The price policies of USFA and its state arms exposed the agency to incessant criticism, predominantly from individual and unorganized consumers. When citizens could obtain the support of congressmen, USFA responded by reviewing and occasionally reversing the decisions of state officials; but without political support, individual protests were unproductive. However, the cumulative impact of consumer complaints about widespread and flagrant price abuse did produce USFA action. In late 1917, numerous reports of coal hoarding by distributors prompted the agency to authorize state administrators to seize and distribute hoarded coal. Hoarding and other forms of engrossment also convinced USFA to apply a licensing system for retailers and jobbers and otherwise control delivery to domestic consumers, a decision that provoked controversy with the coal retailers' association, NRCMA, and the National Coal Jobbers Association.[30]

Once USFA promulgated a general policy, it resisted pressures to intervene at the state level to ensure implementation. Even in early 1918, as Garfield recognized the urgency of reorganizing his agency, adding distribution and oil divisions and an engineers committee and concentrating decision-making authority in Washington, the state branches retained significant roles in application and enforcement. Complaints addressed to headquarters were referred to the state administrators who were, more often than not, the subject of the complaints. USFA shrewdly manipulated the policy of decentralization to shelter itself from criticism. In this scheme of things, the buck never stopped.

Production

The Lever Act authorized President Wilson to implement coal production controls. Many consumers, large and small, who had suffered from inadequate coal supplies during the winter of 1916–17 and who anticipated even more severe shortages now that the nation was at war, demanded nationalization of the mines. This was never seriously considered by Wilson or his close advisors during the months prior to the establishment of USFA, nor by USFA officials after its organization. A few FTC commissioners lobbied for federal control of all coal as it left the mines—a giant national pool as it were—but no one in FTC proposed federal takeover of the mines. The pressing need was for increased production and rapid distribution. Few knowledgeable people believed that federal operation of the mines offered a greater assurance of more coal than continued private ownership.

During the course of the war, USFA officials consistently projected a wartime demand for coal that surpassed current or anticipated production by anywhere from 20 to 30 percent. Optimistic assessments of expected production increments normally fell at between 10 and 15 percent, close to the actual gain of 16 percent from 1916 to 1918 (see Table 4). Garfield viewed price as the key to production and set prices, above those fixed by Wilson in August 1917, at a level sufficient to induce greater production in existing mines and to encourage the opening of new mines. Whatever the fairness of the prices set for each district, production rose and new mines opened. Between 1917 and 1918, the number of mines rose from 6,939 to 8,319, representing an increase in capacity not matched by a proportionate rise in production. Still, the prices fixed by USFA discouraged neither production nor the opening of new mines. Other factors, inadequate car supply and transportation bottlenecks, prevented actual production from reaching a larger proportion of real capacity than the 83 percent achieved in July 1918. Even at the height of the war, not all mines or miners were working during each work day.

Later United States Coal Commission studies indicated that the average days of work lost per year during the war fell far below pre-war (or postwar) norms for soft coal and anthracite. While anthracite interests excused a stationary production for 1917 and 1918 by inveighing against the excessive number of holidays taken by miners, USFA officials as well as eastern consumers blamed production and distribution inefficiencies on the anthracite mine-owning railroads. In bituminous, few operators pointed at labor as inhibiting production, and price levels were scored less frequently than car supply. Car supply, most argued, was the single most persistent difficulty, one beyond the direct influence of the USFA. Anthracite shortages were particularly excruciating because so many people in the east warmed their homes with hard coal, and when it was in short supply were forced to enter an inflated soft coal market already hard pressed by the abnormal demands of war industries, utilities, and railroads.[31]

The USFA encouraged the opening of new mines. As a general practice, USFA accepted the service railroad's evaluation of a new mine and once satisfied on that score endorsed requests for equipment which the defense council's various priorities committees then acted upon. Equipment requests for operating mines followed a similar channel, with the state fuel administrator making the initial recommendation. Only in 1918 did USFA undertake the direct investigation of requests for the opening of new mines; and only in 1918, with the establishment of the U.S. Railroad Administration, did a somewhat independent agency attempt to evaluate transport needs for new mines—sidings, car availability, and so on. By spring 1918, very few new mine applications received approval, and only if a new mine could function without taking labor from operating mines and if cars were available. If new mines required capital investment, USFA utilized state fuel administrators for initial assessments which, if favorable, were forwarded to the local committee of the Capital Issues Committee (see note 20). If these evaluations were positive, that is, if a new mine project was considered financially sound, the CIC-state fuel administrator recommendation went to USFA, which then made a decision about throwing the application into the priorities hopper. Hundreds of new mines escaped all of this because of their small size and their ability to make use of wagons or even trucks to carry the coal out. Some of this production traveled directly to final consumers and aroused the ire of established jobbers, wholesalers, and retailers.

The lure of high prices enticed many new operators into the fields, especially south of the Ohio River where nonunion labor prevailed. Each new mine, large or small, efficient or not, rightfully demanded of the service railroad its fair quota of cars. Even during the war, as USFA officials were well aware, the production of a new mine may not have increased total field production if its establishment resulted in the assignment of fewer cars to existing producing mines. FTC field men frequently pointed this out to state fuel administrators who as frequently ignored the warning. To a nonexpert in coal it seemed reasonable that a new mine meant additional production. Unfortunately, reason possessed limited value in understanding the operation of the coal industry. The policies of the fuel administration and other federal agencies encouraged the building up of excessive productive capacity and contributed to the severe postwar economic travail that weakened the coal industry. To prevent such an outcome demanded more comprehensive federal controls over coal and transportation than Wilson's fuel managers could acquiesce to.[32]

Distribution

Rapidly advancing coal prices and public demands for action compelled Wilson and Congress to experiment with coal price fixing and the regulation of allowable dealer margins to moderate inflationary pressures. Mine-mouth prices did level out after the fall of 1917, and while less success attended USFA measures to control wholesale and retail prices, the fuel agency did intensify its efforts in 1918 to prevent price gouging. Inflationary pressure roiled the entire economy as a result of the war. Federal policies to finance the war by means of borrowing rather than taxation contributed heavily to the rising costs of goods and services. Wilson's refusal even to consider comprehensive wage and price controls diluted the effects of USFA coal price policies. Steel, petroleum, and other industries, in the meantime freely negotiated prices with the War Industry Board or the military. While federal cajoling and the fear of public scrutiny might moderate the price demands of a particular industry at a particular time, the net result was inflation and great industrial profits. In price and finance, as in other sectors of the wartime economy, emergency measures were adopted that "would do the least possible violence to the monetary and business arrangements that had proved so profitable in the neutrality period."[33] From this perspective, federal fuel management policies seemed quite radical.

The government demonstrated little alacrity in formulating comprehensive distribution policies. Railroads were the key carriers as well as the largest consumers of coal, and their inability to provide expanded and rapid service endangered the entire mobilization program. As the nation entered the war, many of the major lines evinced serious operational weaknesses. According to some, the inability of the railroads to meet the nation's pressing needs stemmed directly from a financial structure weakened by years of ICC regulations and Justice Department hostility toward pooling agreements. Railroad spokesmen instructed the ICC, Justice, and the CND (a form of self-instruction) about the facts of railroad credit and operating costs, the urgent need for larger revenues, and, therefore, the need for higher rates.[34] Others, less impressed with railroad performance, emphasized the consequences of a decade of financial manipulation and misman-agement that deprived the roads of development capital and forced several lines into bankruptcy while leaving other lines enervated. To extract maximum performance from the roads demanded policies that subordinated the particular interests of the roads to the national in-terest; such policies failed to emerge during the first nine months of the war.[35]

Notwithstanding irrefutable evidence that linked the fuel shortages of 1916 and early 1917 with the failure of the rail transportation sys-tem, the federal government relied upon voluntarism to move goods and soldiers. From April through December 1917, chief responsibility resided in the CND Committee on Transportation and a special American Railroad Association (ARA) committee on national de-fense. Although the ICC possessed authority to promulgate car ser-vice rules, the commission even as late as November 1917 seemed unwilling to recognize the imminence of a transportation crisis or that specific commodities required special treatment. As a result, policy decisions regarding the movement of fuels and other essential com-modities were formulated hesitantly by ad hoc committees that lacked statutory authority to issue orders or otherwise impose their will on the railroads or other inland carriers. ARA rules to compel eastern carriers to return empty western box cars swiftly were simply ignored by roads such as the New York Central, an expression of self-in-terested indifference that exacerbated the coal shortage of 1916–17. Similarly, joint USFA-ARA regulations, which established fuel ship-ment preferences, were honored by the lines only when it suited them.

CND's committees did piece together the skeleton of a fuel trans-portation policy, giving coal first priority in car assignment and move-ment and then determining delivery priorities. Coal for the U.S. government ranked first, followed by fuel for railroads and fuel for other purposes. Within the latter category, utility use ranked higher than domestic. This preference system warranted further explication, but it was not forthcoming; and, indeed, the roads abided by it only casually. A Kentucky producer charged that the railroads virtually sold their cars to producers submitting the lowest bid on railroad fuel contracts and denied cars to other mines. The railways, moreover, accepted all freight, confined loaded coal cars to sidings in order to move more profitable cargoes, and filled coal cars with other commodities.

The car service subcommittee of ARA undertook the regional distribution of cars and locomotives, a responsibility delegated by Congress to ICC but unused. Producers and consumers (industries to retailers) applied to the car service committee for coal cars until the organization of USFA's distribution division in early 1918. CND claimed that cars "circulated as freely as bank notes." However, Oklahoma coalman J. G. Puterbaugh asserted in June 1917 (and Emerson Carey, Kansas fuel administrator, in October 1917) that Mid-Continent car shortages reduced coal production by 40 percent and that the railroads used coal cars for lumber traffic, an observation corroborated in November by an FTC investigator.[36]

In conjunction with the Peabody committee, ARA initiated in May 1917 the pooling of coal shipments at Great Lakes and Atlantic Coast ports, a tactic approved by USFA, thus facilitating the more general policy of moving coal eastward toward the strategic industrial shipping cities. Coincident with this was the effort to organize more efficiently the port of New York (and other shipping centers as well) through the creation of the New York Port War Board. But the serious shortage of lake and coastal shipping, including barges and tugs, partially negated the effectiveness of such plans. Shortfalls in the delivery of coal to Lake Michigan and Lake Superior ports, as Garfield warned Wilson in September 1917, threatened a severe crisis, unrectifiable once the ports were closed by ice.[37]

CND's committees possessed enormous responsibility but inadequate power, and the transportation systems slid toward paralysis during the last quarter of 1917. Traffic backed up at key terminals and along major trunk lines throughout the country. New York harbor shuddered under the impact of barge, shipping, and rail congestion. Ohio municipalities, down to a few lumps of coal, seized fully laden coal cars passing through; the governor confiscated 4,000 cars. In December, Emerson Carey warned Garfield of the imminent closing of several meat packing plants in Kansas City, Kansas, because of lack of coal. So scarce were railroad cars that by mid-December, bituminous mines operated at only 60 percent of capacity. By then, many cities had been without coal deliveries for days, and in the Mid-Continent a long stretch of zero-degree weather caused illness and suffering. Severe weather in many sections of the country hampered traffic. The assignment of cars to essential shippers, the key device adopted by the ARA committee on national defense, failed to assure cars to anyone, and those with cars found them backed up, unmoving, or with coal frozen solid in the gondolas. After the war, McAdoo wrote that in the fall of 1917 "the inefficiency of the American railroads was the greatest ally of the Imperial German Government."[38] The traffic was simply more than the railroads could bear; a new system was urgently required.

By early December, Secretary McAdoo was exerting unceasing pressure on Wilson to nationalize the railroads. Garfield, allied with McAdoo in this campaign, offered substantive evidence to the president to refute the case made by ARA against nationalization. In Senate hearings on coal and transportation held in late December, Sen. James Vardaman of Mississippi excoriated the railroads for their self-serving refusal to fully cooperate in the war effort.

Wilson established the United States Railroad Administration (USRA) on 26 December 1917, under Director-General McAdoo, and placed all railroads under its jurisdiction. Now, presumably, USFA and USRA could clear up the congestion that clogged the nation's tracks and terminals—145,000 loaded cars idled in yards west of Chicago and St. Louis, for instance.[39] How to accomplish this consumed the attention of Garfield and McAdoo in late December 1917 and early January 1918. No swift and effective measures could be painless. Following rounds of conferences, including one with President Wilson on 16 January to gain his approval of the action agreed upon, USRA, under USFA authority, issued the Closing Order of 17 January 1918. Designed to close down most businesses and industries throughout the country, the Closing Order prohibited all manufacturing plants save the most essential from burning fuel or using power from 18 January through 22 January and on each Monday beginning 28 January and continuing through 25 March 1918. Monday closings also applied to most office buildings, stores, recreational establishments, and businesses selling intoxicating liquors.

Rarely had so many Americans been so directly affected by a single act of the federal government. Within the next few days, chambers of commerce, manufacturers, labor unions, and citizens from all sections of the land deluged USFA with letters of bitter protest. *Insanity* it was called, a cure worse than the disease. Millions were compelled to forego paychecks for a week. Tens of millions of dollars of profits were lost. Given the utter failure of prior transportation policies, the demonstrated inability of the railroads to move and discharge goods, the

Wilsonian commitment to voluntarism (to which Garfield sub-scribed), and the general American preference for business and plea-sure as usual, only purgative action could cleanse the system. Madness it was not. The Liberty Loan agents in New York City who proposed to promote bond sales by digging thirty acres of trenches in Central Park were the unhinged ones. Nor was the order universally condemned; the Merchant's Association of New York, for example, admitted that the order was preferable to the continuation of coal shortages and railroad congestion. Republicans lambasted the Wilson administration and considered the order proof of administrative in-competence, particularly Garfield's incompetence, a point pounded into his Senate colleagues by Henry Cabot Lodge—and recently re-vived by David Kennedy. As Secretary Lane remarked to an acquain-tance, "We do not take kindly to orders when they are not explained." Still, the temporary dislocation caused by the order would be worth it, Lane believed, since coal and other goods would now move more freely. No longer would soldier boys freeze in American camps.[40] Those who condemned the Closing Order were missing the point. The American system of waging war had proven wanting.

The Closing Order had little to do with coal production and much to do with railroad congestion. While it obviously reduced coal use by several million tons of coal, the significance of this was minimal. The order did quicken car movement to and unloading at the central rail and water terminals. The order's effect on householders is unclear. Coal was moving; presumably some of it reached retailers and, thence, homes. In keeping people from work, however, the order must have caused severe hardship to many families who even in the best of times lived in actual poverty—or on the edge.

Hectic USFA activity accompanied the Closing Order. Garfield cen-tralized his agency by organizing a distribution division and an oil division, also responsible for natural gas. The distribution division, USRA, and the priorities division of WIB formulated a national plan for coal distribution and allocation (see note 21). The new plan estab-lished a zone system that prescribed coal and coke shipping patterns and impinged heavily on the Mid-Continent region, an anthracite dis-tribution scheme that drastically reduced or prohibited the movement of hard coal to the West and South, and a priority-based quota system for the receipt of coal. Cumulatively, these policies diverted rolling stock and coal eastward toward the Atlantic.[41]

Zoning took effect at the commencement of the coal year, 1 April 1918. The system was designed to eliminate unnecessary long hauls and cross hauls, thus inducing users to purchase coal from the nearest possible producer. The nation was divided into thirteen bituminous zones, some of which were further subdivided and each of which could ship bituminous only to designated points. Coal Zone A, as an example, consisted of the producing districts of Iowa, Missouri, Arkansas, Kansas, and Oklahoma; coal from that zone could move freely within the zone and to Nebraska and the western portions of Louisiana and Texas. Coal zones located east of the Mississippi River were prohibited from exporting coal west of the river. Chicago, normally the destination for millions of tons of Kentucky and West Virginia coal, now depended upon the production of southern Illinois mines. Virtually all of the coal produced from southern Indiana eastward was earmarked for Atlantic Coast use. In effect, the zone system defined the East Coast as an importing region, the regions from central Pennsylvania to the Mississippi as essentially self-sufficient but capable of exporting a surplus, and the vast expanse stretching from St. Louis to Denver as an entirely self-sufficient region without significant export capability.

The zone system produced the desired results. Coal and rolling stock moved eastward in successive waves. Domestic consumers and nonwar industries in the East continued to suffer from coal shortages, but they were caused more by production shortfalls and allocation policies than by inadequate transportation. The coal stocks of iron and steel plants, mostly located east of the Mississippi, rose from 800,000 tons in March 1918 to 1.9 million tons in mid-August while New England's industrial plants stored nine weeks' supply on 1 April 1918 and twenty-six weeks' supply on 9 November.[42]

Across the Mississippi, however, depleted rolling stock and the embargo imposed on coal by the zone system caused persistent coal and oil shortages. USFA assumptions about the fuel self-sufficiency of the western states were inaccurate even had the region's mines operated at full capacity, which they did not. Lt. Gov. Wallace Crossley, Missouri's fuel boss, predicted calamitous shocks from zoning. St. Louis and Kansas City were doomed to suffer, Crossley warned, if contracts already made for Illinois coal were abrogated. The contracts were voided, and cities and towns from St. Louis to Witchita experienced nagging and frequently severe fuel shortages during the late winter of 1918 and again in the fall.[43] Mid-Continent industrial and domestic fuel requirements were, then, subordinated to the needs of other regions judged by USFA as contributing more to the war effort and/or less self-sufficient in fuels.

Zoning produced major consequences; some are treated in Chapter 4. The distribution pattern achieved by zoning represented a more serious invasion of the private enterprise system than did price controls; zoning erected impassable barriers between groups of states. The prohibition of anthracite shipments to the Plains states and to the South forced thousands of homeowners to convert to other fuels, and anthracite lost markets never fully recovered after the war. The bituminous industry gained little even when soft coal was readily available, for other fuels offered significant advantages. Coal production declined throughout the grain belt. This transition to new fuels occurred in the East as well, but at a slower pace in areas relatively close to the anthracite fields.

Allocation

The zone system was not a miraculous cure for the nation's fuel distribution ills. USFA officials recognized that bituminous demand outstripped supply and that anthracite scarcities forced homeowners to utilize bituminous, thereby diminishing the stock normally consumed by large steam raisers. Nonetheless, zoning assured eastern residents a monopoly of available anthracite and siphoned transportation, bituminous, oil, and trains from the Mississippi region to eastern industrial areas. Thus, Michigan fuel officials complained to their congressional delegation about the diversion of 2 million tons of coal from Michigan to eastern states.

Allocation policies, once established, functioned in tandem with zoning, favoring the East over the West, industrial over domestic users, and some industries over others. But specific priorities regarding the allocation of fuel to scores of industries were slow in appearing. At first, the Council of National Defense assigned priorities to broadly defined categories such as transportation and manufacturing. When this proved useless, CND (during the summer of 1917) tried to identify specific nonessential industries and then limit their access to transportation and fuel. But many obstacles vitiated this effort. For one, railroads frequently ignored CND's priority orders and accepted freight from all sources, and CND lacked the power to enforce its orders. Too, as USFA decided in late 1917, CND's labeling of certain industries as nonessential carried heavy political liabilities. For instance, in November 1917, a CND effort to so define the auto industry and thus release steel for locomotive and railroad car construction enraged car manufacturers, compelling the council to back down. And corset, casket, and hosiery manufacturers and laundry owners offered heated objections to being categorized as nonessential.

USFA, sensitive to the uproar over CND's use of the term "nonessential," employed a semantic tactic designed to cover up the continued use of the nonessential category. In *Nation's Business* (February 1918), Pierrepont B. Noyes, director of conservation at USFA, shrewdly if not cogently argued that there were no nonessential industries. USFA then adopted the practice of identifying "preferred" industries.[44]

None of these subtle maneuvers resolved the central problem: No single agency possessed the authority to assign or enforce priorities of any kind. In spite of the proclamations and moral fulminations of USFA and CND, industries essentially competed in the open market for materials, fuels, and transportation. Only with the establishment of USRA in December 1917 did an agency possess the power to set priorities, and that for only a single service: transportation. Finally, in March 1918, President Wilson lodged responsibility for priorities with the newly created War Industries Board. Even this lacked comprehensiveness; McAdoo, for instance, insisted that transportation priorities remain with USRA. Too, as Cuff points out, WIB relied upon industry-staffed committees for decisions about the specific orders to fill. Still, however tardily, a giant step forward had been taken.

The provocative problem of actually determining priorities remained. WIB accepted USFA's semantic strategem of identifying "preferred" industries. In April 1918, WIB's priorities board issued Preference List No. 1, a preliminary list governing coal and coke deliveries. By June, the priorities system, constantly in process of refinement, was being implemented at the state level.

Preference List No. 1 circumvented the need to identify any single class of industry as nonessential by developing four classes of coal users. Class I coal users were of such exceptional importance to the war effort that their fuel needs must be fully satisfied at all times. Industries in Classes II through IV, in descending importance, were to be serviced before industries that failed to make the list. (Laundries, for instance, did make the list, but only into Category IV.) Actually, in the thinking of WIB and USFA officials, any industry below Class II was nonessential; its fuel supply was substantially reduced.

USFA determined the specific industries that fit the specific classes; the state fuel administrations provided the basic data and the initial recommendations. Through questionnaires and on-site inspections, engineers from the Bureau of Conservation studied the fuel efficiency of over 115,000 plants; efficiency ratings then played a role in actually allocating fuel to a given plant. To speed the process, Garfield appointed district representatives, all coal mine executives, for each of the coal zones. Upon the request of a state fuel administrator, the district representative attempted to match a priority order for fuel with a coal producer. Only as a last resort were problems referred to Washington.

Official allocation criteria left little discretionary power to state officials. District representatives actually possessed more authority in these matters than the state administrators, a situation quickly recognized by the Missouri and Kansas administrators, for example. Although headquarters flatly denied any intention to limit the jurisdiction of state officials, the district representatives did further centralize authority and did circumvent state fuel offices, all of which fit the pattern of USFA evolution in 1918. Emerson Carey of Kansas vigorously opposed the appointment of prominent coal executive Harry N. Taylor as district representative. Taylor had been critical of USFA, Carey argued in February 1918, and would manage allocation in the interests of the Southwestern Interstate Coal Operators Association. But such criticism fell on deaf ears. USFA appointed as district representatives only men acceptable to district coal producers.

District representatives operated in territories coequal to a coal zone or a subdivision. Thus their authority frequently covered several states. They appointed other coal executives as their assistants— Taylor appointed J. G. Puterbaugh as his Oklahoma assistant—and reported directly to the distribution division. In servicing the emergency requests of retailers and industries, district representatives chose from among area producers and grades of coal. In the Mid-Continent field, Taylor attempted to force retailers to accept mine run coal (slack or screenings), normally used for steam raising, at much higher prices than usual. Operators benefited because slack was the cheapest to produce and the most difficult to market. Mid-Continent fuel administrators opposed Taylor but received no support from Washington. The appearance of the district representatives and the evolving USFA policy of limiting the fuel consumption of particular industries rapidly drove state fuel administrators into an adversarial relationship with USFA headquarters.[45]

During the remainder of the war, WIB, the Capital Issues Committee, and other agencies also intervened to reduce the flow of raw materials, finished products, fuel, transport, and capital to industries and activities only tangentially related to the war effort. State fuel officials and state CND officials routinely provided CIC with initial evaluations concerning new stock issues by oil companies and public utilities and performed the same function when municipalities or private parties applied to WIB for construction permits. Fuel supply represented but one criterion, but it was applied at the local level; other factors such as the availability of construction materials were evaluated by WIB. Construction proposals received thorough scrutiny because the building materials industry consumed some 32 million tons of coal annually and furnished some 100 million tons of freight to railroads. WIB discouraged nonessential public and private construction. Although construction industry complaints aroused congressional interest in this policy and forced WIB to justify it to the Senate, by and large the policy prevailed.[46]

USFA focused its attention on the fuel use of such specific industrial groups as window glass, cement, brick and tile, and quarrying, all highly fuel-intensive. Using fuel consumption data gathered by FTC field personnel, USFA issued orders reducing the allowable delivery of fuel to those industrial groups by 25 to 50 percent. Not unexpectedly, these orders precipitated an outpouring of criticism from the affected industries and from state fuel administrators in states that housed significant concentrations of the curtailed industries: Pennsylvania (cement), Colorado (cement), Indiana (glass), Oklahoma (glass and brick and tile), and Kansas (glass, brick and tile, and cement). USFA assumed that some of these industries could switch from coal to gas, a mistaken premise discussed in Chapter 4. State administrators, under pressure from particular firms, inundated Washington with requests for exceptions. In Kansas alone, at least fifteen glass companies and a dozen cement companies each wrote at least one scathing letter to the besieged Emerson Carey and innumerable letters to Garfield and other USFA officials (all referred back to the state office) and to congressmen. But USFA proved virtually immovable—rigid and inflexible as perceived by midwesterners. More than that, the curtailment orders, followed by the zone system, convinced many in the Mid-Continent, and the South as well, that the entire war machine discriminated against their region in favor of the East.[47]

Mid-Continent fuel officials, aware of regional shortages of natural gas, suggested that curtailed industries be permitted to use unlimited quantities of slack coal, a grade produced far in excess of demand (see note 45). In a lengthy correspondence with USFA, William J. Galligan, Colorado's chief fuel official, promoted this tactic. As he explained it, Colorado's mines faced a limited steam coal market and experienced difficulty disposing of their slack. In Colorado, Kansas, and Oklahoma, cement and clay products plants consumed sizable quantities of slack. Reductions in the size of that market by curtailment orders would so reduce the volume of prepared sizes that a domestic coal shortage would ensue. Galligan proposed that cement and clay products plants be permitted to consume as much slack as full production warranted, thereby guaranteeing an adequate supply of domestic sizes. His persistence, vocal support from fuel administrators in neighboring states, and repercussions from the closing of plants in at least three states combined to achieve a limited success for the Galligan proposal. On 9 August 1918, a USFA order permitted cement and clay products plants west of the Mississippi to purchase unlimited quantities of slack for a thirty-day period; the original restrictions were then reimposed. Galligan's further efforts were rebuffed by USFA with lectures that the general good required Colorado to suffer.[48]

Western fuel administrators understood quickly that the basic thrust of the distribution and allocation system awarded western needs the lowest priority both for domestic and industrial fuel use. Demography and the eastern locations of the bulk of war industry almost predestined the consequences westerners denounced. Federal intervention in oil as well as coal, particularly the imposition of regulations ill-suited to western needs, threatened established competitive relationships. Prior to the war, cement and clay products from southeastern Kansas had penetrated markets throughout the Missouri and Mississippi river valleys, from Idaho to Louisiana, and even as far west as the Pacific Coast. Colorado and Nebraska cement plants also competed in those markets. These gains were all but eliminated by the fuel curtailments.[49]

Even after the establishment of USRA and the implementation of zoning, domestic consumers and others purchasing in the retail market experienced local and subregional shortages, most seriously along the northeastern seaboard. Consumers suffered from the profiteering and discriminatory practices of retailers and some wholesalers and the general inability of the fuel managers to match available supply with pressing need on some reasonable basis. The task was monumental and the personnel available hardly adequate. Regular policing of retailer practices never developed. WIB even questioned the ability of USFA to correctly identify localities with severe fuel shortages. As the summer of 1918 passed, USFA evinced an increasingly pessimistic attitude concerning the coming winter's domestic fuel supply. After attending a meeting with USFA in July 1918, one WIB official confessed sadly that "the more you get into it the more hopeless the situation becomes. Simply shifting the present output of coal from one point to another is mighty unsatisfactory business."[50]

Cities were warned to expect the worst and advised to prepare some form of rationing—Philadelphia's plan was suggested as a model. All local fuel officials were exhorted to increase their efforts to encourage early summer ordering and early delivery, as Galligan was doing in Denver. The Kansas City, Missouri, fuel committee with state approval ordered all dealers to have in their yards by 1 September 1918 a certain percentage of their annual tonnage. Upper Great Lakes and New England communities viewed the approach of winter with dread, and USFA could offer little encouragement to assuage their fears. J. F. McGee, Minnesota fuel administrator, demanded a national order forcing owners of palatial residences to reduce the number of rooms heated. In Detroit as well as Kansas City, citizens sorely abused local fuel officials for rising prices and short supply. In September 1918, Kansas City Alderman Harry Sandler castigated the local fuel committee as servants of the city's coal dealers and characterized the recent $.30 per ton price hike as "rotten injustice to the poor people of the city."[51]

In May 1918, USFA informed its state officers and the district representatives that "sufficient coal will not be transported to all parts of the country to satisfy the needs of all consumers." State officers were warned to expect a deluge of requests from consumers unable to obtain coal through their usual sources. By October, it was apparent that the allocation policies were coming apart. Under the pressure of inadequate supply and rising prices, the controlling regulations collapsed. The licensing system initiated in April, regularizing the distribution of coal through middlemen, only worked if there was coal to distribute and if that coal arrived through normal channels. So in October, jobbers and wholesalers were scrambling frantically to find a source of supply with adequate transportation. But the capacity of the transportation system had not increased in proportion to the demands made upon it. Wholesalers, jobbers, and retailers could not reasonably expect to receive as much coal as they had in 1917. Under such extreme conditions, the rules established for domestic distribution in March became obsolete. In New York City, where bituminous reached $11.75 per ton in October, a resident of Inwood, in uptown Manhattan, reported that landlords refused to turn the heat on until 1 November, claiming that USFA had issued an order to that effect; New York's Consolidated Edison and the city's retailers took up the refrain. USFA, of course, had not; but it did not matter, given the small volume of coal available and the unlikelihood of larger supplies reaching the city.[52]

Mercifully—for many reasons—the war ended in November. While severe problems remained and aftershock struck, the inordinate pressure on transportation and fuel supply eased. Increased domestic fuel supplies appeared none too soon, for the influenza pandemic, already in evidence prior to the armistice, claimed tens of thousands of American lives as it swept across the nation. Had the war continued into another winter, the halfway measures adopted by the war managers could have failed entirely. Coal (and perhaps food as well) shortages would have been fearsome, and weakened people would have succumbed in even greater numbers to the deadly virus. As it was, the halfway measures were visibly inadequate to wage a fulltime war that consumed soldiers and materials so voraciously. Americans had cause to rejoice in the armistice.

FOUR

Wartime Power, Natural Gas, and Oil Policies

UNDER THE LEVER ACT, USFA authority to formulate distribution and allocation policies, to generate use restrictions, to intervene in the production process, and to mount conservation campaigns extended to all fuels. Price-fixing authority, however, applied only to coal. Notwithstanding this broad authority, the fuel agency concentrated largely on coal, the source of most of the power and heat in America. As a result of this single-minded attention to coal during the harsh winter of 1917, an oil division was not even established until January 1918. Thereafter, and even though oil branches were organized in state fuel offices, the oil division operated in a segregated sphere, its functions never properly integrated into the overall mission of USFA.

Electric power, an essential component of the eastern war industry complex, received even less attention than oil and natural gas. Several federal agencies and dozens of state utility commissions dabbled in power, with none possessing final authority to make decisions regarding plant expansion, distribution policies, or other matters. Only in December 1917 did the War Industries Board organize a power section that attempted to coordinate the activities of such other agencies as USFA. By then, the Department of War had emerged as the most active federal unit engaged in power management. Simply put, a power policy capable of meeting swollen demands failed to emerge during the war. As a result of this and of the scattered authority that did exist, power policies frequently clashed with policies applied to the fossil fuels.

The fuel administration and the railroad administration assumed responsibility for providing fuel to the utilities. Less susceptible to quick resolution were problems involving the capital needs of the electric industry; the relationships among rates, fixed costs, and debt financing; and the expansion of generating capacity. By early 1918, several of the most critical war production regions experienced severe electric energy scarcity. Federal authority, minimal as it was, achieved little in resolving these difficulties. Initiatives by WIB, USFA, and other interested agencies to secure federal authority to subsidize and coordinate electric industry expansion died in Congress.

While the Wilson administration marshaled its arguments in favor of utility expansion, USFA, WIB, and other agencies promoted a variety of plans to reduce energy consumption. Many of these schemes, frequently orchestrated by USFA's conservation bureau with the fervor of crusaders, involved electricity as well as fuels; these campaigns are discussed in the following section. Later, the section on natural gas treats USFA efforts to promote the substitution of natural gas for other fuels in the Mid-Continent.

Conservation Campaigns

In January 1918, USFA statisticians projected an annual increase in coal use of 15 percent, while supply would rise only 7 percent.[1] A serious conservation effort, it was believed, could narrow the difference between consumption and production. Restrictions on the fuel consumption of florists and cement plants, the denial of transportation to corset manufactures, and the prohibition of long hauls of coal were the sort of practices adopted. Other devices depended upon the good will and patriotic commitment of the community at large. USFA's conservation bureau spread its campaign along a broad front but focused most intently on the domestic and commercial sectors. Their projects were basically two types: 1) the elimination of fuel waste in both production and consumption and the improvement of technologies and delivery systems; and 2) limitations on use either by regulation or by appeals to patriotism and economy.

The conservation bureau attacked waste wherever it was discovered, frequently cooperating with the Bureau of Mines, the U.S. Geological Survey, USRA, and WIB. Programs were launched to reduce the consumption of coal by railroads and interurbans, protect consumers from poor quality coal, rate the fuel efficiency of industrial plants, consolidate ice plants, eliminate isolated electric power plants, electrify mines and oil well drilling, and standardize the manufacturing of furnaces.

The bureau of conservation, the bureau of production, and the oil division of USFA and WIB's conservation division assigned a high priority to the electrification of mine and oil production in the Mid-Continent and the promotion of industrial purchasing of central station electricity by plants with their own generating equipment. USFA officials believed that electrification would both reduce coal and oil consumption used in on-site operations and increase production. But these plans achieved little success, partly because of electric company reluctance to extend lines into remote regions of marginal profit potential and partly because of electrical equipment shortages. Similar constraints prevented the achievement of significant results in eliminating isolated generating plants even though many manufacturers and commercial establishments sought the lower costs coincident with central station connections. USFA and WIB officials also promoted the pooling of electricity and the interconnection of contiguous systems, a thrust persisting into the 1920s. But utility reluctance to enter the capital market or invest current income to expand or interconnect systems and the failure to obtain federal monies to finance these schemes precluded notable success.

The conservation bureau of USFA estimated coal savings in 1918 at 27 million tons. How this was calculated is unclear. The gap between supply and demand undoubtedly accounted for greater "savings" than the conservation campaigns, although it was also true that consumers sought faithfully to use fuels more efficiently. Programs to upgrade or substitute technologies were long-term propositions and confronted serious obstacles when attempted in the short-term. For instance, some isolated stations did disappear, and continued to do so after the war; but available data from Denver, Oklahoma City, Kansas City, Dallas, and Richmond indicate that almost as many isolated plants existed at the end of the war as at the beginning. Electrification of coal and oil fields in the Mid-Continent produced minimal savings; many mines and wells used natural gas rather than coal. Had the war continued for several years, these efforts might have proven more fruitful.[2]

Programs to upgrade or substitute technologies relied exclusively upon engineering expertise. The war years facilitated the first marshaling of fuel technologists under one banner. The American Institute of Mining Engineers aided the USFA engineers committee in studying the costs of coal production. The war service committee of the Illuminating Engineers Society prepared a report for the conservation bureau on the lighting of public buildings, drawing upon data gathered by the U.S. Bureau of Standards.[3] Electrical engineers participated in USFA, WIB, and War Department investigations of electric power while petroleum engineers and geologists associated closely with USFA's oil division. Dependence upon engineering solutions to resource problems became habitual during the war years and thereafter, as revealed in the published reports of the U.S. Coal Commission, the American Engineering Council, and the National Industrial Conference Board. The proclivity to seek technological solutions to energy resource problems ignored the fact that such problems frequently demanded more attention to considerations of equity than to the application of mechanics.

Conservation policies adopted by USFA and implemented by state fuel administrators affected daily routines of life. In July 1918, as entrenched American troops in the Rheims sector came under attack by waves of German infantry during the second battle of the Marne, home-front warriors complained about the more stringent street and outdoor lighting restrictions just announced by USFA. Beginning in November 1917, USFA issued a series of orders that restricted the use of street lights, advertising and display signs, and ornamental lights. These orders, labeled as useless by a Mid-Continent electric holding company, were revoked in April 1918. Reimposed in July, they prohibited such lighting four nights weekly along the Atlantic seaboard and two nights weekly in the rest of the country, thus precipitating anguished cries of discrimination from easterners. These orders, and others prohibiting fuel consumption by yacht owners and country clubs, were all abolished in November 1918, unless expressly continued by written order of state fuel chiefs.

State administrators and their local committees enforced compliance with the lighting regulations. Wallace Crossley of Missouri enthusiastically approved the November 1917 orders and reported general cooperation. But by July 1918, Crossley had changed his mind, offering USFA detailed criticism and objecting to the reimposition of the order; William Galligan in Colorado agreed. Both asserted that while less electricity was used, little coal was saved; the utilities agreed. As they explained it, a diminished use by industrial and commercial consumers, many of whom burned steady amounts over sixteen or even twenty-four hours, would not greatly alter the generation required to handle peak-load demand. Little coal would be saved, the amount of fuel per kilowatt-hour would rise, and plant efficiency would suffer. Operating revenues would inevitably decline at a time of rising fuel costs. State utility commissions, reluctant to contribute to inflation or antagonize the public, resisted rate increase petitions. These arguments were pressed most vigorously by utilities in Kansas, Colorado, and Pennsylvania, which served curtailed industries such as cement, glass, and brick.[4]

Federal fuel managers viewed fuel usage in American homes as a source of great potential savings, particularly in coal. The zone system confined anthracite consumption to eastern householders and forced midwestern homeowners to rely on regional production. From time to time during the winter of 1917–18, state administrators rationed fuel deliveries to residences. In Philadelphia, Greenwich, Connecticut, and other places, the type of house—row, duplex, freestanding—and the number of rooms determined fuel allotments. On 16 January 1918, Crossley ordered Missouri's local committees to limit residential fuel deliveries to a maximum of one ton per week until 15 March 1918. Two days later, he issued delivery priorities that placed residences and hospitals before all other structures. Closing orders were also imposed on restaurants, saloons, recreational establishments, office buildings, and nonfood or drug retail stores. On 1 February 1918, Emerson Carey announced a universal closing order for Kansas; it turned off all advertising and display lights and set opening and closing hours for all types of businesses. As Carey reported to Garfield, at least seventy-five Kansas towns faced ten-degree weather without coal.

For the most part, state fuel bosses reported good-to-excellent response to the emergency orders and the permanent regulations. Apparently, most Americans believed that a fuel crisis existed—those without coal in Kansas had little choice—and willingly accepted the minor inconveniences and discomforts attending such regulations as early store closings. Edward Bok, editor of the popular magazine, *The Ladies' Home Journal*, took Garfield and P. B. Noyes to task for resorting to such watered-down restrictions. Domestic consumers were constantly importuned to save coal, while advertising and other signs and lights blazed away, Bok observed; he advised USFA to turn them *all* off, since few would object save the owners. Noyes, in June 1918, assured Bok that a more stringent curtailment order would take effect in July. On 18 July, USFA released its order prohibiting certain kinds of outdoor lighting.

Early closing hours for commercial establishments engendered debate within the conservation bureau; some argued for uniform nationwide closing hours, while others insisted that final decisions remain with local officials. Merchants, too, debated the issue, some opting for one set of hours and some for another. Department stores generally preferred shorter hours during the week, while small stores supported longer hours. In late 1917, USFA decided to issue general guidelines within which state officials would make the final determination; in February 1918, the agency published a list of maximum conservation regulations. The allowable was hardly onerous. Few stores were compelled to close before 10:00 P.M. State fuel officials called for more severe limitations, but they were unsuccessful. And by fall 1918, USFA had stripped state officials of all flexibility even while fuel famine threatened many locales. Therefore, state fuel managers such as Crossley and Carey lacked the authority to impose restrictions; but they did so nonetheless, hoping that pressures on supply would be relieved before Washington could order the abrogation of the state orders. In fall 1918, as supplies dwindled, USFA forbid state officials to order any closings or other restraints.

As Carey reported in September 1918, merchants in Kansas were prepared to abide by USFA restrictions. And the National War Service Committee of Retail Dry Goods and Department Stores, for example, promised to support winter restrictions. Nonetheless, in the fall of 1918, USFA decided to scrap the lightless night and store-closing programs—though agency records fail to reveal the reasons behind the decision. USFA apparently believed that the liabilities of such campaigns, which saved very little coal, exceeded the benefits. USFA admitted to possible psychological problems of such programs. For instance, shivering householders contemplating their last shovelful of coal might well feel oppressed as they passed gaily lit theaters, saloons, and food halls strung out along fully illuminated main streets; for not all merchants acquiesced, and not a few complained to their congressmen. USFA officials had little inclination to antagonize countless local chambers of commerce. The utilities thought the entire program a farce, useless as a coal saving measure and damaging to their financial structure.[5]

In mid-March 1918, it occurred to the power and light section of USFA's conservation bureau that the power required to start a trolley far exceeded the power required to keep it rolling. USFA proposed that trolley lines reduce the number of scheduled stops by about one-third and thereby save an estimated 1.5 million tons of coal. Through fall 1918, conservation officials and state fuel personnel invested considerable time getting the "skip-stop" system adopted in the nation's cities. By late April, skip-stop systems functioned in Washington, D.C., Brooklyn, Evansville, Oakland, and other communities; but in many, state, local, and street railway authorities moved less swiftly, if at all. With so many jurisdictions involved, state fuel administrators settled for less rapid progress than headquarters desired, and in some places no progress at all. The conservation bureau estimated that as of July some 25 percent of the trolley lines had adopted the program, so perhaps 30 or 35 percent compliance was obtained by November.

USFA officials agonized over local inertia and exhorted local fuel administrators to hurry adoption of skip-stop. Local and state officials generally ignored these pleas, sensitive as they were to jurisdictional complexities and to the unknown economic impact of the program on street railways. Street railway companies in a number of cities complained that reducing the number of stops stimulated competition from jitney buses. Moreover, many street railways teetered on the edge of economic collapse anyway. The Kansas City Railway Company, for example, generated its own power and sold surplus energy to commercial users, but in 1917 verged on bankruptcy as a result of soaring fuel costs, a sacrosanct five cent fare, a limited ridership, and the loss of power customers to the Kansas City Power & Light Company. Its generating plant, built in 1900, required extensive and costly repairs. Reductions in power demand by the adoption of skip-stop combined with market losses to decrease total generation without reducing operating expenses. Quite probably, the adoption of skip-stop hastened the bankruptcy of the company; it passed into receivership in 1920.[6]

The skip-stop scheme, like electrification of fuel extraction, the elimination of isolated generating plants, and gasless Sundays (treated later in the section on petroleum) flowed from the fertile minds of headquarters officials, depended for success upon the cooperation of local, state, and regional personnel, often rested upon erroneous perceptions of local or regional conditions, aroused varying degrees of hostility among those whose cooperation was sought, and fell far short of achieving the savings projected in Washington offices. Given the abbreviated time within which USFA and other wartime agencies operated, the confusion attending an only partially centralized administration, and the reluctance of individuals like Garfield to ride roughshod over local jurisdictions and interests, modest success, or less, is not surprising. As suggested earlier, had the war continued through another winter of severe fuel scarcity, perhaps a less tender regard toward local and interest-group autonomy would have been forced upon federal fuel managers.

The conservation bureau managed a host of other fuel conserving crusades. "National Tag Your Shovel Day," scheduled for 30 January 1918, dramatized the need for coal conservation. Tags by the millions were distributed through local school districts, except in Kansas where state education officials refused to permit such blatant federal interference with the educational system. In Kansas City, Missouri, where coal shortages forced the closing of eighty grade schools and twenty-eight parochial schools for ten days beginning 13 January, the schools opened for the ceremony and shut down again. "Save a shovel of coal a day" became the rallying cry in January and culminated in the tagging of the president's own shovel by two Washington school children. Whether or not such moral suasion succeeded in reducing coal consumption, programs such as this did involve people, and for those with a shovelful left dramatized the urgency of the fuel shortages. Conservation officials knew that the intelligent use of fuel in the home and elsewhere could effect great savings.[7]

Natural Gas

In 1923, over one trillion cubic feet of natural gas was marketed, reflecting an increase since 1900 of almost eight times (see Table 4). By 1923, the Mid-Continent field produced about 40 percent of the total and the Appalachian field under 50 percent. In 1920, natural gas contributed just under 4 percent of the nation's aggregate energy requirements. The national significance of natural gas paled before dependence upon coal and the rising demand for oil; between 1910 and 1920, the contribution of oil to national energy needs increased from 6 to 12 percent.[8]

However, gas provided an important energy source in regions such as the Mid-Continent. There, industries, utilities, and towns utilized apparently endless supplies for process heat and for residential and business purposes. By World War I, Mid-Continent consumers sadly recognized the finite nature of once bountiful natural gas fields (see Chapter 1). This was generally recognized shortly after the war when George Otis Smith of USGS stated: "Natural gas is a mine that is largely worked out; it has seen its best days and future dividends to the nation cannot equal those of the past."[9] Smith, of course, was wrong; but the recent history of the industry provided solid reasons for such an assertion. The USFA's oil division, responsible for federal natural gas policies, somehow failed to obtain or absorb the correct facts about Mid-Continent gas supplies and founded its approaches on the mistaken assumption that a virtually unlimited volume of gas was available.

Within the oil division of USFA, responsibility for the production, transportation, and distribution of natural gas resided in the bureau of natural gas. At this time, natural gas markets were regional in nature, more like coal than petroleum and, in the intrastate transportation and distribution phase of the business, subject to state and local regulation. In both the Appalachian and Mid-Continent regions, USFA policies focused on the diversion of natural gas from nonessential to essential industries. (The oil division exhibited much less reluctance than other USFA units to employ these hard categories.) In the Mid-Continent distribution area, USFA also emphasized the substitution of natural gas for fuel oil and coal in both war and nonwar industries. In its efforts to control end-use, USFA seemed to recognize a supply problem, but in its fuel substitution efforts, belief in an abundant supply dominated thinking. Recognition of a supply problem also prompted the oil division, late in the war, to assign the highest priority to domestic consumers, but the war ended before these priorities were applied. Although natural gas companies persistently articulated the need for vigorous drilling programs if need were to be met (and therefore, as did the electric utilities, demanded higher gas rates to supply the capital for drilling), USFA expended less effort on stimulating production than on the diversion or substitution of fuels.

Recent events attested to the uncertainty of gas supply in the Mid-Continent. By 1917, depleted Kansas pools, inefficient delivery systems, pipeline companies weakened by stock manipulations and disorganized by a sequence of corporate takeovers had caused serious economic dislocation in parts of northeastern Oklahoma, southwestern Missouri, and southeastern Kansas. Industries closed down, and consumers in municipalities as far north as Kansas City, St. Joseph, and even Omaha suffered from erratic supply, frequent interruptions of service during the coldest peak-use months, and permanent low pressure in pipelines. Kansas Citians had experienced all of these hardships during most winters from 1909 through 1917, blaming their difficulties on the corporate maneuvers of the Doherty interests, which owned the Kansas Natural Gas Company (KNG) as well as the local distributing companies. Oklahomans, in the center of the nation's newest and largest gas pool, suffered no less than more northern consumers. Shortages and discontinued service plagued consumers during the exceptionally harsh winter of 1917–18.[10]

In spite of this evidence, which failed to pierce the awareness of oil division officials, USFA in spring 1918 decided without prior investigation to initiate a vast fuel substitution program in the Mid-Continent. Natural gas was to be diverted from nonessential industries such as brick and tile and cement to more essential industries that used fuel oil or coal, particularly oil refineries and various manufacturing firms engaged in filling military contracts. The oil division assumed that the fuel saved from industrial curtailment, some of which was natural gas, could be diverted to noncurtailed industries and thus free up a large volume of petroleum for shipment to the East. All this could be accomplished, so the oil division insisted, without diminishing service to domestic consumers.

As described in Chapter 3, beginning in February 1918, regulations imposing curtailments of up to 50 percent were applied to several industrial groups. However, many of the brick and cement companies no longer burned natural gas, precisely because they had converted to coal or fuel oil in response to inadequate gas supplies. And in Tulsa, for instance, virtually all industries producing or refining oil had switched to fuel oil by 1918. Therefore, USFA instructions to natural gas pipelines and local distributors to provide gas to industries using fuel oil and instructions to industries using fuel oil to convert to natural gas could *not* be complied with unless a massive exploration and discovery effort were launched simultaneously and attended by instant success. Of course, nothing resembling this transpired. Natural gas companies echoed the electric utilities in complaining about reduced cash flow caused by stable gas rates and rising fixed expenses. Industries willing to convert and gas distribution companies willing to extend service faced extended delays in obtaining pipe and other necessary equipment.

Contrary facts in no way deterred the oil division from plunging ahead by assiduously identifying all oil- or coal-burning firms in the Mid-Continent and sending out scores of letters and telegrams importuning them to switch to natural gas. Responses from the gas companies and from the industrial sector flowing back to Washington were discouraging. KNG informed USFA in August 1918 that as a result of a court order to divert gas from industrial to domestic consumers, it was unable to supply manufacturers. One month earlier, the Kansas Gas and Electric Company of Wichita reported adamant industrial refusal to convert from oil to gas because of short supply. Both the *Wichita Beacon* and the *Wichita Eagle* warned readers to prepare for a serious gas shortage by laying in coal stocks. Admitting to a shortage of gas, the Oklahoma Natural Gas Company confided to the natural gas bureau that during the gas shortage of the previous winter, "we were compelled to eliminate practically all of the industrial gas in order to protect our domestic consumers as much as possible."[11]

Municipal officials, veterans of the natural gas wars and cognizant of the insecurity of supply, fumed over the potential effects of the USFA program on residential supply. The agency's natural gas bureau blamed Kansas City's problems on leaky gas mains and waste in general, a conclusion based on the findings of a local investigation conducted in August 1917. Spokespersons for the city were quick to point out that the volume wasted comprised but a fraction of the total shortfall.

State fuel administrators, at first merely skeptical about the program, swiftly adopted a hostile attitude. Wallace Crossley informed headquarters that substitution of gas for oil or coal would be ruinous. Two letters from the Kansas City Gas Company confirmed Crossley's views. Very little cold weather would be required, wrote the company in September 1918, to cause serious shortages. KNG avowed its ability to meet the domestic needs of Kansas City, but the firm exaggerated its supply position; it experienced a decrease of flow from productive wells averaging 15 percent per month from January through May 1918. Information from the distributing companies of other communities indicated that the fuel substitution occurring was precisely the opposite of USFA intentions.[12]

In other parts of the country, particularly the upper Ohio River valley, USFA policies toward natural gas developed in conjunction with oil policies and adhered to similar imperatives. USFA sought to control gas use by assigning priorities to various groups of users. Domestic consumers received the highest priority, followed by utilities, preferred war industries, and less essential industries. In Pennsylvania, Ohio, and West Virginia, cement plants suffered curtailments similar to those of their Mid-Continent counterparts. By late summer 1918, however, Appalachian gas companies complied less willingly with USFA industrial-use priorities and seemed prepared to cut gas service to municipalities. Alliance, Ohio, Louisville, Kentucky, and communities in western New York feared interruption of service during the approaching winter.

To counter natural gas producer and distributor circumvention of or utter noncompliance with USFA programs, the oil division prepared a licensing regulation for natural gas and most of the oil industry; Wilson promulgated this order on 25 September 1918. Thereafter, no natural gas company was permitted to deliver gas without a license, which was obtained only by proof of compliance with priority regulations.

In October 1918, at the request of municipal authorities in Louisville and several Pennsylvania and New York communities, USFA imposed natural gas rationing in those communities. In Louisville, studies uncovered gross inequity in natural gas use, with 8 percent of the consumers using 50 percent of all gas delivered. The USFA order permitted a maximum consumption of 1,000 cubic feet per day unless permits for additional amounts were authorized by the Kentucky fuel administrator. On 21 January 1919, the Jefferson County Circuit Court at Louisville upheld that order, but by then the war was over and most USFA regulations had been revoked. A prolonged war would have compelled further use of this rationing authority, perhaps in gasoline and fuel oil as well as natural gas.[13]

Oil division policies regarding natural gas emerged belatedly, just as the oil division itself did, partly because of the intense preoccupation with oil and partly because of the regional rather than national importance of the fuel. In formulating policies, the oil division favored the producer over the distributor, the gas industry over consumers, and, until fall 1918, the industrial consumer over the domestic consumer. Efforts to induce industrial conversion to natural gas ignored regional resource history while controverting the opinion of most fuel experts that domestic users should receive first priority in gas supply. Industrial users could switch from one fuel to another, if necessary and if possible, and pass costs on to their customers. Domestic consumers, many of whom lived in multifamily dwellings, could hardly move furnaces and duct work or steam pipes in and out of their homes in response to temporary policies. USFA managers, faced with a steadily deteriorating fuel picture, paid ever less attention to local and regional opinion and in their haste to meet last week's problems made ineffective use of locally derived data. For instance, rationing at Louisville was typical of belated sensitivity to local conditions and to questions of equity in allocation.

Requa's Oil Division

Domestic production of crude oil rose by 35 percent during the five years 1909–13 and by another 35 percent during the next five, 1913–17. Exports to Europe between 1914 and 1917 rose from 45 million barrels to 61 million barrels, or 35 percent. American entry into the war did generate additional demand-side pressures, but these were not extraordinary if compared with prewar and postwar demand.[14] Still, the likelihood that demand would exceed supply during a long war disturbed many oil industry experts.

Concern about the nation's oil supplies antedated the declaration of war and the establishment of USFA. In 1916, crude production in Oklahoma's great Cushing field fell off so suddenly and drastically that refiners throughout the Mid-Continent found themselves without crude to refine. Mid-Continent crude prices, averaging $.78 per barrel in 1914 and $.58 in 1915, jumped to $1.26 in 1916 and had reached

$1.60 when the nation entered the war. Crude prices in other fields also moved steadily higher. By spring 1917, demand-side as well as supply-side pressure produced an upward movement in price that seemed in line with general inflationary trends. In spite of the drop in Cushing's flow (see Oklahoma, Table 7), crude production rose steadily with Mid-Continent (and Texas) crudes contributing 55 percent of production in 1916, 59 percent in 1917, and 62 percent in 1918.

Cushing, however, called attention to the finiteness of even the largest oil reserves. Simultaneously, Americans learned that the nation actually produced less oil than it consumed. According to one report, crude production for the first seven months of 1917 exceeded production for the same period in 1916 by 21 million barrels, but consumption rose by 31.5 million barrels. Wartime requirements pushed demand still further above supply, thus requiring the use of oil in storage almost continuously from 1915 through 1918. Many oil experts agreed that the United States would soon be dependent upon foreign crude.[15]

The daily needs of a giant war machine postponed until the early 1920s further investigation of the implications (or accuracy) of such assessments (see Chapter 6). In 1917, the United States took its oil as it could; and although need intensified, the federal government procrastinated in imposing its full power over oil, and when it did the system was applied less rigorously than on coal. Without doubt coal was the more critical fuel both in industry and domestic use. But federal hesitancy to move as swiftly in oil might also be explained by the great concentration of economic power and attendant political influence that characterized the organization of the oil industry. Competitiveness within coal, its regional rather than national marketing structure, the relatively small size of even its largest producing units, and its labor-intensiveness offered a more vulnerable target for the federal government than did the giant integrated firms that dominated the oil industry. These considerations more satisfactorily explain the evolving system in oil than does an emphasis on such amorphous concepts as the ideology of cooperation and industrial self-government.

Prior to the organization of USFA, the Peabody coal committee of the Council of National Defense had its equivalent in oil, the petroleum advisory committee, chaired by A. C. Bedford, chairman of the board of Standard Oil of New Jersey, and dominated by the major integrated firms. The oil committee, without statutory authority, assumed the task of providing oil supplies to the military and to America's allies and distributing oil to the various sectors of the infant wartime economy. The leading elements within oil welcomed the or-

TABLE 7. *Domestic Crude Production, by Major Fields, 1900–1920 (million barrels)*

	Applachian field[1]	Pennsylvania	West Virginia	Lima-Indiana field[2]	Illinois field[3]
1900	36	14		22	
1901	34	13	14	22	
1902	32	13	14	23	
1903	32	12	13	24	
1904	31	12	13	25	
1905	29	12	12	22	
1906	28	12	10	18	4
1907	25	11	9	13	24
1908	25	11	10	10	34
1909	27	10	11	8	31
1910	27	10	12	7	33
1911	24	9	10	6	31
1912	26	9	12	5	29
1913	26	9	12	5	24
1914	24	9	10	5	22
1915	23	9	9	4	19
1916	23	8	9	4	18
1917	25	9	8	4	16
1918	25	8	8	3	13
1919	32	9	9	3	13
1920		8	8		

[1] Encompasses New York, Pennsylvania, Kentucky, West Virginia, and eastern Ohio. Pennsylvania's production includes a small amount from New York.

[2] Includes east central Indiana and northwest Ohio.

[3] Includes a portion of southwest Indiana.

[4] Normally includes Kansas, Oklahoma, and Texas; sometimes Arkansas and northern Louisiana. For 1904–6, the Kansas figure includes Oklahoma production.

[5] Includes southern Louisiana and southern Texas. After 1912, some Texas production is included in the Mid-Continent field totals.

[6] Includes Colorado, New Mexico, Montana, and Wyoming.

Mid-Continent field[4]	Kansas	Oklahoma	Gulf field[5]	Texas	Rocky Mountain field[6]	California field
						4
			4	4		9
			18	18		14
2			18	18		24
6	5		25	22		30
13	12		37	28		33
23	22		21	13		33
47	2	44	16	12		30
49	2	46	16	11		45
51	1	48	11	10		56
60	1	52	10	9		73
67	1	56	11	10		81
66	2	51	9	12	2	87
85	2	64	9	15	3	98
98	3	74	13	20	4	100
123	3	98	21	25	4	87
137	9	107	22	28	7	91
164	37	108	24	32	9	94
180	46	103	24	39	13	98
	35	81	23	85	13	101
	39	106		96	18	106

Sources: Joseph E. Pogue, *The Economics of Petroleum* (New York: John Wiley & Sons, 1921), 54; Harold F. Williamson et al., *The American Petroleum Industry: The Age of Energy, 1899–1959*, vol. 2 (Evanston: Northwestern University Press, 1963), 16; FTC, *Advance in the Price of Petroleum Products* (1920), 66th Cong., 2d sess., 1920, H. Doc. 801, 8.

ganization of this committee as a defense against further intrusions of federal authority—a threat perceived by oilmen as stemming from a hostile FTC. The majors viewed the Bedford committee as a mechanism to achieve production and price stability through pooling, refinery quotas, and other cooperative arrangements frowned upon (if not prohibited as illegal) by the FTC and the Justice Department during peacetime. The committee seized the opportunity that war presented to promote American penetration of Middle Eastern and Indonesian producing areas, hitherto tightly monopolized by European oil interests.[16]

Oil interest pressures on federal policy emanated from this oil committee that essentially represented the most powerful companies; but other sources of pressure within oil also existed, and these quickly became more vociferous in expressing their displeasure over the major's influence on oil policy. The oil committee enjoyed something less than the complete confidence of the oil industry. Burt Lyon, a Mid-Continent oil producer, wrote Bernard Baruch in July 1917 about a letter from Bedford to Kansas and Oklahoma oil producers urging them to increase production. "I fail to observe," Lyon said, "any intimation of a willingness on his part to have the dividends of the Standard Oil Company . . . in any way reduced in the interest of the national government." Lyon expressed "serious doubts as to the unselfish motives of . . . A. C. Bedford" and others at the head of various subcommittees.[17]

In what amounted to an exercise in self-policing, the oil committee established functional divisions and subcommittees responsible for the various phases of oil mobilization. As with the organization of coal, the confused system of priorities and the absence of federal control over the railroads hampered the oil committee's work. Bedford and his subcommittee chairmen could only request and plead that individual firms adhere to programs adopted by the committee. With the tacit approval of the ICC and FTC, the committee pooled and distributed large volumes of oil, but the jerrybuilt structure performed less and less efficiently as military and domestic demands expanded. The committee system lacked coherence and the coercive power to enforce its will.

Strangely enough, the passage of the Lever Act and the organization of USFA brought little improvement. Except for price fixing, the Lever Act delegated to the president the same powers over oil as over coal; but Garfield, preoccupied with the complexity of setting coal prices and moving coal along the railroads, essentially ignored oil, allowing the oil committee to continue its work without much central supervision.[18] But by mid-November 1917, it was painfully obvious to Garfield that this ad hoc arrangement required reorganization no less than the railroads. Oil prices were rising. Refiners blithely ignored the distribution decisions of the oil committee. Refiners in the Mid-Continent suffered from the exaction of exorbitant premiums. Production lagged behind demand, and exploratory efforts were obstructed by inadequate supplies of drilling equipment. Centralized direction seemed the only solution. Garfield proposed to Wilson the organization of a separate oil division within USFA and under the direction of Mark L. Requa. Wilson reluctantly agreed, confiding:

> I am a little shy about creating a separate oil control. There are enough separate things now and the greatest need in every direction is coordination and unification of administration. But I dare say it is true that we need an extension of powers over the fuel oil situation.[19]

Requa was with the Food Administration but had impressive credentials in western oil ventures. In his acceptance, Requa expressed some rather broad-ranging opinions about his new job and about the oil industry. He believed that the petroleum office should be an independent department, deriving authority directly from the president, instead of existing as a subdivision of USFA. Requa obviously recognized the pitfalls of assuming responsibility without adequate power. Furthermore, Requa understood his duties as encompassing all phases of the oil industry, of which fuel oil was but one small part. The central problem hinged on adequate reserve supplies and the most efficient use of "nature's bountiful endowment." He accused the industry of outrageously wasting oil and of timidity in increasing production. In itemizing the critical difficulties—conservation, production, materials allocation, pooling and shipping, and possibly zoning—Requa treated price as a minor factor. He also distrusted Great Britain, ascribing to that nation a drive to control the world's oil supply. Since Requa was among those who foresaw increasing dependence upon foreign crude, American penetration of overseas oil fields bulked large in this thinking both during and after the war.[20]

Requa's division housed a full complement of bureaus responsible for natural gas, production, domestic supply, traffic, transportation, conservation, and other duties, some of which dispatched personnel to the state fuel offices. In the producing states, offices invariably contained oil conservation and transportation officials. State fuel administrators received orders to do nothing about oil without first contacting headquarters.[21]

Requa also reorganized the industry arm, now called the National Petroleum War Service Committee (PWSC). Garfield agreed with his oil chief that this committee should serve as the primary contact with the industry, and at Requa's suggestion the PWSC enlarged its membership to include jobbers, oil well supply representatives, and additional independents. By March 1918, a new subcommittee system had been developed, centered around geographically based units for production, refining, and marketing. Other subcommittees advised on natural gas, pipelines, tank cars, oil tankers, and oil well supplies. One important unit from the old committee, now the PWSC Committee on Conciliation and Cooperation, retained its original duties. Chaired by J. F. Darby, vice-president and manager of the Mid-Continent Oil and Gas Association and a large independent operator, that committee allocated crude to refineries and mediated intraindustry disputes over prices and contracts. Garfield and Requa soothed the industry's fears that the new division represented a harbinger of further federal regulation by assuring PWSC that the industry would continue to govern itself whenever possible.[22]

Requa and others recognized that a long war would seriously strain American productive capacity, deplete oil stocks, and lower proven reserves. Evidence compiled by the Bureau of Mines from sources in the various producing fields attested to slumping or stable production in virtually all fields save the Mid-Continent (see Table 7). In 1917 and again in 1918, Van H. Manning, director of the Bureau of Mines, warned the U.S. Senate to anticipate severe petroleum shortages, particularly gasoline, as wartime needs intensified. In March 1918, Requa predicted an oil shortage for the year of 74 million barrels, of which 30 million would be imported from Mexico. It was absolutely necessary, he told Garfield, that domestic production increase, otherwise stocks in storage would quickly disappear.[23]

Requa, then, launched a vigorous effort to stimulate domestic production, curtail nonessential consumption—thus promoting the substitution of natural gas for fuel oil—and further advance American oil interests in foreign lands. Requa focused on encouraging new exploration and discovery, particularly by wildcatters, and the more efficient withdrawal of oil from proven but declining fields. He also insisted, along with California and western oil interests, that such naval reserves as Teapot Dome be opened to exploitation, a demand strongly opposed by CND, the Department of the Navy under Josephus Daniels, the FTC, and USGS. Ray Lyman Wilbur, president of Stanford University and later secretary of the Interior, accused Secretary of the Interior Franklin Lane of contributing to the oil shortage by supporting the navy's view. This particular debate by no means monopolized Requa's attention, and only the notorious Teapot Dome scandal of later years infected it with apparent significance relative to the oil division's role in production. In fact, Requa emphasized the drilling of new wells on private lands in the Mid-Continent and Gulf Coast fields.

The oil division developed an intimate working relationship with the Capital Issues Committee and the priorities board of WIB. Requa's essential contribution was the education of personnel in both agencies as to the critical relationship between wildcat drilling and the development of new fields. Both CIC and WIB, the former ruling on permissible capital investment and the latter controlling the manufacture and allocation of oil drilling equipment and supplies, manifested justifiable suspicion that a large but unknown proportion of the $550 million invested in the oil industry in 1917 (an amount equal to the total investment of the three previous years) represented stock jobbing, fraudulent promotions, and unneeded speculative ventures, all stimulated by rising oil prices. To separate the essential from the spurious, both agencies relied upon the judgment of the oil division and the Bureau of Mines and USGS.

Requa and his field subordinates who advised regional CIC committees contended that although 90 percent of each dollar invested in wildcatting produced no oil, without it oil production would decline at an alarming rate. CIC then adopted the policy that drilling ventures approved by their expert advisors must be encouraged in order to assure the additional capital investment that would transform a find into a producing well. Once convinced by USFA that a wildcatter's application was bona fide, CIC further scrutinized the corporate structure for signs of fat, unnecessarily high overhead costs, or other evidence of inefficiency or even camouflaged fraud. Commonly, a negative USFA evaluation produced CIC disapproval.[24]

At least two smaller producers, Liberty Oil & Refining in Kansas City and Apex Refining & Drilling in Denver, believed that the CIC scruntiny of projected securities issues discriminated against small operators. Large operators, Liberty pointed out, could bypass CIC by employing current revenue to develop fields; by denying small operators access to capital markets, CIC strengthened the dominance of the integrated firms. The validity of this argument is difficult to evaluate. And such large firms as Cities Service and Sinclair did submit numerous development applications. The following example illustrates that there was at least a tear in any blanket charge of favoritism. In early 1918, Cities Service sought approval for a $15 million issue to finance exploratory drilling by its subsidiary, Empire Gas & Fuel Company. Requa approved this request without comment. But both the local CIC subcommittee and its regional superior in Kansas City believed that Cities Service could finance a major portion of the request out of earnings and recommended approval of only $3 million unless the firm could provide additional justification. The application was still pending at the time of the armistice.[25]

Once cleared by CIC, the future of a particular exploratory or drilling venture depended upon the favorable attitude of WIB's priorities committee and then upon the availability of oil well equipment. Again USFA recommendations, now coupled with CIC recommendations, assumed central importance. The calculus employed in reaching a decision was extraordinarily complex: How much steel should be allocated to produce destroyers or tanks vis-a-vis oil pipe, casings, or drill bits? Until spring 1918, when the priority system became more regularized, oil well equipment manufacturers (and manufacturers of other oil industry equipment) competed in an essentially open market for raw and semifabricated materials, perhaps armed with USFA approval but by no means assured that this would suffice to obtain supplies. In fall 1917, Mid-Continent producers complained of serious shortages of equipment and of equipment suppliers passing on higher costs for steel and fuel by adding a premium to list prices.

The equipment industry also looked to USFA for high fuel priority ratings, which in the days before USRA could not be counted on to assure actual deliveries. When the zone system took effect, Mid-Continent manufacturers operated in an attenuated fuel market with eastern coals no longer available. Oil division efforts to induce the substitution of natural gas for oil and coal also aggravated the fuel situation of equipment producers in Oklahoma, Wichita, and Kansas City (both Missouri and Kansas), most of which used fuel oil and special-purpose coke. The Kansas City Bolt & Nut Company, manufacturer of mining and agricultural equipment, and the Kaw Boiler Works, makers of refinery stills, were but two of dozens of firms that sought priority certificates from USFA for various items: a nut burring machine, steel plate, 100,000 barrels of fuel oil, and twelve carloads of coke. Gradually, the oil division counterparts in WIB regularized the procedure for granting priorities. But demand for all kinds of strategic goods exceeded supply; and the priority system, essentially resting on the assessment of individual applications, verged on collapse in fall 1918. By October, Requa and E. B. Parker, priorities chief at WIB, agreed to the necessity of strict rationing of oil industry equipment. As Requa informed CIC, the question of financing new companies would resolve itself, because no new supplies would be allocated to them.[26]

Crude production increased by some 55 million barrels between 1916 and 1918, with Mid-Continent fields accounting for 78 percent of the increase, a result at least partly attributable to Requa's decision to favor Mid-Continent equipment applications above those of the eastern fields. The oil division, in association with CIC and WIB, successfully protected the production branch of petroleum from some of the dislocations and repercussions of wartime mobilization. In October and November 1918, the oil division was poised to advance another step toward a centralized command.

After the war ended, individuals within the oil industry such as Darby and W. S. Farish (Humble-Standard Oil) and industry groups such as the Mid-Continent Oil and Gas Association and the American Petroleum Institute (the direct descendent of the PWSC) applauded the industry's record in raising production and maintaining prices at levels high enough to stimulate production but reasonable relative to prices of other commodities. As major units within the industry recalled the flow of events, the industry, by avoiding price fixing that would discourage production, had proven beyond a shadow of doubt that self-regulation and cooperation with government worked more efficiently than wholesale federal intervention. Bedford, chairman of CND's oil committee, in a speech in 1917, had promised these results if the government had the foresight to leave the industry alone.[27]

The actual course of events in pricing and in the distribution and allocation of crude and refined products followed a somewhat rougher path, involving the threat of federal price fixing, the imposition of a licensing system in oil, and the likelihood in fall 1918 of rationing. Not all these intrusions or potential actions can be attributed to oil industry obduracy; neither can they be attributed solely to short supply. Rather, the amorphous and disaggregated nature of the system itself, the uncertain realms of responsibility in which oil division and industry units performed, persistent transportation snarls in 1917 and early 1918, and the incompatible definitions of self-interest that divided various segments of the industry all combined to force the government to intervene or consider intervention in 1918.

Under the Lever Act, USFA lacked authority to establish prices for oil. The maintenance of price stability rested entirely upon the self-restraint of the industry. The incline in the posted price of Mid-Continent crude oil was steeper from 1915 through 1918 than for all commodities. Regional disparities existed, which in some instances moderated and in other instances exaggerated general price trends.

Fuel oil prices through 1917 rose more rapidly nationally than in the Mid-Continent and more acutely still in New England. Gasoline prices in New York City for 1916 exceeded those in Kansas City by an average of $.055 per gallon, but only a $.02 spread prevailed in 1918.

Most significantly, the posted price of crude oil—the normal oil industry standard and that used in USFA assessments of price—did not reflect the actual prices paid for crude by many refiners. The posted price for Mid-Continent crude was $.58 per barrel in 1915, $1.26 in 1916, $1.79 in 1917, and $2.20 in 1918. To this must be added the premiums charged by producers and such carriers as Prairie Oil and Gas Company. While the posted price of Mid-Continent crude in 1916 averaged $1.26 per barrel, the Kansas City Refining Company paid between $1.50 and $1.90 per barrel *plus* a premium of $.15 to $.60 per barrel. On the average in 1916, the difference between the posted price and the actual price paid for crude by small, independent refiners in the Mid-Continent stood at $.38 per barrel, in 1917 at $.68, and in 1918, as a result of USFA jawboning, at $.35. Independent refiners in the Mid-Continent paid much higher prices for crude than did the majors while they marketed refined products in regions where the price of those products failed to advance commensurately. The high fuel oil prices in New England did not benefit Mid-Continent refiners because they were excluded from that market by high transportation charges.[28]

When the producers and transporters of crude oil defended the legitimacy of crude price hikes during 1917 and 1918, they pointed to the moderate rise in posted prices. In fact, these were the prices paid by the major integrated firms. USFA's oil division viewed as unwarranted the same price increases, including one of $.25 per barrel achieved by Texas and Mid-Continent producers in February and March 1918. Independent refiners without their own production regarded this hike plus the required premiums as potentially destructive. In fact, the Great Western Oil Refining Company responded to rising crude prices in February 1918 by closing its Erie, Kansas, refinery. North American Refining Company of Oklahoma City closed down two refineries while working three others at only 12 percent capacity. Throughout 1918, other reports of closings and of refineries operating at under 25 percent capacity reached the oil division and the FTC.

Some refiners refused to pay the premiums; others, willing to pay any price for crude, could not secure even medium-term contracts from producers. Prairie Oil and Gas and Cities Service affiliates in the Mid-Continent field forwarded all the crude obtainable to East Coast markets. Independent producers, even those holding contracts with independent refineries, found it more convenient to dispose of their crude through the major pipeline operators than to sell it within the field. The existence of the Mid-Continent refining industry seemed threatened by the combination of rising crude prices and diminishing crude supplies. Independent refiners attributed much of their difficulty to the predominant influence of the majors on USFA.[29]

Requa, philosophically sympathetic to the weeding out of small refiners who utilized crude less efficiently than larger refiners, did consider crude price increases in spring 1918 as unwarranted, largely because of higher prices paid by the government for refined products. Garfield, more sensitive to the plight of small refiners and reluctant at all times to disturb existing competitive relations within an industry, also criticized additional price increases. Neither Requa nor Garfield believed that a runaway market existed, but both agreed that further price advances were unnecessary. In the absence of price-setting authority, Requa resorted to jawboning. In an open letter of 17 May 1918, he informed the oil industry that the government would not accept further price increases. Faced with the implied threat of federal intervention and smarting from recent FTC charges of profiteering, the Petroleum War Service Committee succumbed. At a meeting in Tulsa on 22 July 1918, attended by both Bedford and Requa, the industry agreed to freeze prices as of July and implement the agreement in August.

Thereafter, prices for crude remained reasonably stable, but gasoline and fuel oil prices continued to rise in numerous markets. In September 1918, distributors of gasoline in Chicago and Kansas City paid two cents more per gallon than they had in April; and fuel oil in Boston had advanced by 35 percent over spring prices. USFA responded to these trends with an order, dated 14 August 1918, that established an oil products price scale for all government contracts. In September, USFA responded to criticism regarding persistent price advances by announcing its intention to fix gasoline prices at the pump at a figure lower than the current inflated market price.[30]

Preliminary USFA planning to initiate gasoline rationing and fixed prices coincided with Wilson's proclamation of 19 August requesting Americans to cease driving on Sundays—known as "Gasless Sundays." USFA promoted this effort at voluntary conservation at a time when eastern gasoline stocks were very low. Some considered it entirely unnecessary. *Oildom* denied that a shortage existed. A number of U.S. senators attributed the scheme to the machination of the majors who sought to create the impression of a shortage so as to justify higher prices. But the shortage was real. Although gasless Sundays ended in October, USFA was prepared to implement a voluntary rationing program to reduce consumption by 20 percent; if that failed, mandatory controls would be implemented, despite the opposition of PWSC's committee on distribution.[31]

Wilson's proclamation of 25 September 1918 extended the partial licensing system instituted in February 1918 to oil companies that produced or distributed over 100,000 barrels annually and to retailers with gross sales above $100,000 annually. Licensing derived as much from USFA's determination to hold prices firm as from a demonstrated need to further regularize distribution. Requa, pressing Garfield in August to speed up the announcement, revealed his intention to use the licensing power to control gasoline prices and to compel compliance with existing priorities on the allocation of fuel oil and gasoline. While Requa did not overtly dispute PWSC's argument for a continuation of voluntary gasoline rationing, he harbored serious doubts as to the adequacy of gasoline and fuel oil stocks and recognized that the voluntary price agreement did not prevent excessive wholesale or retail prices. Garfield's licensing regulations established the necessary preconditions for a rationing system, the details of which USFA and WIB's priorities committee were discussing in September and October.[32]

By mid-1918, then, Requa had decided that further bidding up the price of oil would not produce a single additional barrel. He also recognized the political costs of overseeing the demise of the Mid-Continent oil refining industry and the accrued liabilities of policy decisions that many interpreted as favoring the major integrated firms. Garfield seems to have restrained Requa in the pursuit of efficiency that promised to strengthen further the majors at the expense of the independents. The crude allocation policies adopted by the CND oil committee and retained by the oil division and PWSC worked counter to the interests of independent refiners and excited their vigorous opposition. The Western Petroleum Refiners Association viewed allocation programs in 1917 and 1918 as a continuation of practices (first surfacing in 1916) damaging to small refiners.

The oil division relied upon PWCS's regional field committees to supervise pooling arrangements, distribute tank cars, mediate contract disputes, and allocate crude to refineries. The Mid-Continent committee on conciliation and cooperation and the committee on refining and marketing shared responsibility for dividing crude among refiners. J. S. Cosden, president of Cosden & Company, refiners of 1.4 percent of the nation's crude, chaired the refining and marketing committee. Independent refiners voiced considerable displeasure over the allocation policies of Cosden's committee. In August 1918, the Oklahoma-Kansas Refining Company of Tulsa telegraphed USFA that the crude allocation practices of Cosden's committee so reduced crude supplies as to compel the closing of its Tulsa refinery. The firm asserted that the arbitrary diversion of crude from normal channels, while greatly benefiting the larger firms, made it difficult for small refiners to remain open. The oil division replied that it was not involved in the allocation of crude and that the case should be submitted to Cosden's committee, the body that had authorized the diversion in the first place.[33]

Smaller refiners had always operated at a competitive disadvantage because of the greater efficiency of the larger and integrated units; their ability to protect themselves was not enhanced under the wrenching wartime repercussions. The majors fully utilized their crude pipelines and avoided the railroad congestion that obstructed oil as well as coal shipments. Between January 1917 and March 1918, *Oildom* chronicled the alleged inefficiency, if not perfidy, of the railroads that had the temerity to press the ICC for increased freight rates by using contrived delays of freight to buttress their arguments. USFA, USRA, and the ICC all grappled with the tank car shortage and sought a system of equitable distribution, but success eluded them. As late as August 1918, PWSC's Kansas City tank car committee reported severe congestion at regional terminals with empty tank cars resting idle on sidings. When the war was over, the inland traffic office of the oil division produced impressive statistics of expedited car movements, longer trains, shorter hauls, priorities granted oil shipments, and so on, little of which squared with the perceptions of refiners or of *Oildom*.

The disadvantage faced by the independent refiners under normal conditions stemmed from discriminating practices as well as the efficiency of integrated firms. Prairie Oil and Gas Company, the largest purchaser of Mid-Continent crudes, not only charged refiners a premium but refused the shipments of small producers. The Hepburn Act remained unenforced by ICC. Refiners lacking pipelines from producing fields were denied tank cars to carry the crude while the cars were redeployed to carry the refined products of the larger refiners. Mid-Continent refiners continued, then, to pay an overt premium for their finished products. Neither USFA nor ICC intervened since railroads fell under the control of USRA, which permitted customary practices to continue. PWSC, managed by executives from the largest companies, found no reason to tamper with the system.[34] These inequities persisted into the 1920s and beyond. Combined with the dynamics of a growing industry dependent upon its ability to locate and exploit a finite resource and the ever-growing size and power of the major integrated firms, they produced a politics of oil characterized by divisiveness and, increasingly, by appeals to government authority to rectify alleged inequities or disadvantages.

Conclusion

In early November 1918, rumors and false reports of an armistice unleased premature celebrations across the land. Wallace Crossley, for example, revoked lightless night restrictions in Missouri on 8 November; three days later hostilities ceased. USFA, WIB, CIC, and other emergency agencies began to liquidate their affairs. During the remainder of the year, restrictions on fuel use were rapidly rescinded. WIB cancelled all restrictions and orders in late November and was all but dissolved by the end of the year. On 1 February 1919, USFA suspended all regulations on prices and eliminated the zone system. Between December 1918 and May 1919, USFA revoked all oil and natural gas regulations.

Within the coal industry, where opposition to any and all federal intervention had seemed most intense, some elements questioned the wisdom of abrupt federal disengagement. In late November, a coal producer in Helena, Montana, warned Sen. Thomas J. Walsh that the ravages of influenza had already reduced production and that the lifting of price controls would play directly into the hands of speculators who, in holding back supplies for higher prices, would cause coal shortages in the state. The executive committee of the National Retail Coal Merchants Association resolved that USFA price restrictions and the zone system be maintained at least until 1 April 1919, the beginning of a new coal year. NRCMA reminded Garfield that USFA had urged dealers to stock up on coal during late summer and early fall. To do this dealers had accepted inferior coal on contract at maximum prices; now, retailers were caught with those high-priced coals in a declining market and were vulnerable to the competition of cheaper and better coal shipped in from other zones. Throughout the spring and summer of 1919, complaints from western dealers confirmed NRCMA's reasoning. But USFA believed, as did Crossley of Missouri, that the public chafed under the restraint of wartime controls; therefore, this outweighed other considerations.[35]

When America went to war in April 1917, the government moved cautiously to shape an economy capable of waging total war. The timid approach of Wilson and his war managers toward full-scale and unambivalent wartime controls, convincingly documented by Cuff and Kennedy, cannot be denied.[36] Garfield's predilection for a decentralized USFA, his failure to organize a distribution office or an oil division until 1918, and his reliance upon the state offices all attest to his unwillingness to thoroughly regiment the fuel industries to the wartime situation. In fact, by attempting to dilute the centralizing impact of USFA, Garfield conducted an experiment in the sharing of authority. Thus, the state and local branches of USFA (and CND, also) afforded tens of thousands of citizens the chance to participate directly in the war effort. Sensitivity to local autonomy probably moderated the resentment of individuals to fuel restrictions. Garfield moved to gain greater mastery over the fuel industries only at the eleventh hour when, in late 1917, it seemed that the nation's distribution system was on the verge of collapse.

In 1918, the management of the fuel industries underwent a perceptible, if not radical, transformation. State branches of USFA lost power as Garfield gathered authority in the central office. An oil division was created, the railroads were nationalized, a zoning system went into effect, a system of priorities emerged, and the licensing of fuel dealers tightened control over distribution and allocation. Controlling wholesale and retail coal prices, however, proved an elusive quest, even though both USFA and the Federal Trade Commission gathered conclusive evidence of widespread price gouging by coal dealers. Coal profits for 1917–18, according to FTC studies, averaged 29 percent.[37] While the cost of fuel, rent, and food soared, wages rose but moderately. Clearly the war cost some people more than others.

As federal agencies assumed larger responsibilities, they abridged the permissible fields of action allowed the industry fuel committees. However, to a degree disturbing to many, the evolving regulatory mechanisms masked a system in which implementation of fuel control rested in the hands of individuals with a direct and pecuniary interest in the fuel industries. Nonetheless, the system, strengthened in 1918, achieved its primary goal: moving goods and men swiftly to overseas destinations. Even more comprehensive federal controls, including gasoline rationing, were being developed as a hedge against the possibility that the war would continue into 1919.

Zoning and the complex rules that determined who would get coal and oil fostered regional and intraindustry inequities. The Mid-Continent cement industry lost markets as a consequence of fuel restrictions imposed by USFA. The competitive strength of independent refiners in the Mid-Continent was weakened by the inability of USFA to control crude prices and by allocation procedures that favored the major integrated firms. Zoning permitted low-cost and nonunion coal from the South to penetrate markets previously dominated by unionized coal mines in the North. The war induced a great expansion of productive capacity in coal, a condition that weakened the industry and inflamed labor-management relations during the 1920s. The coal operators, even though influential within USFA, still bridled over the unprecedented degree of federal control imposed upon the industry. The National Coal Association and other industry groups quickly adopted the policy of adamant opposition to federal involvement in the coal industry that persisted during the postwar decade and even beyond. But coal's severe difficulties, visible before the war and reaching a destructive state during the 1920s, can by no means be blamed on the war or federal controls. Coal was the victim of endemic illness.

Through late summer or fall 1918, USFA more often than not honored its promise to allow the oil industry maximum freedom to manage the mobilization of oil for war. Thus, Nash and Williamson and other later accounts of the wartime experience emphasize industrial self-governance and the cooperative efforts that provided gasoline for the lorries, ambulances, and airplanes stationed in western France. According to Nash, the war nurtured the cooperative partnership between oil and government that first emerged prior to the war. Describing the prewar industry as "rent asunder by bitter competition," Nash suggests that the exigencies of war fostered a general spirit of "cooperation in many spheres to achieve stabilization." "Public policy," he asserts, "recognized the change by encouraging voluntary self-regulation among oilmen under the aegis of federal supervision."[38]

Such conclusions overlook at least two contradictory trends: 1) the chronic and corrosive distrust of the independents toward the major integrated firms and 2) centralizing pressures that surfaced in early 1918. Disharmony plagued the oil industry for decades after Standard's dissolution. During World War I, Mid-Continent oil interests, particularly the independent refiners, accused USFA of favoring the major firms by allocating proportionately more crude to the larger refiners and fewer tank cars to the smaller refiners. Centralization gained momentum as the oil industry's voluntary committees proved incapable of coping with fuel shortages or preventing price increases that USFA deemed unwarranted. The oil industry's war committee acquiesced in the price agreement of July 1918 not because of its desirability and not because of a genuine wish to cooperate, but to avoid further coercion. While oil industry personnel held administrative positions in USFA and WIB and filled the PWSC committees, federal regulations steadily reduced their ability to take independent action. The comprehensive licensing system of September 1918 encompassed all but the industry's smallest units and laid the groundwork for price fixing and rationing that a longer war would have necessitated.

Overly sensitive to the criticisms and demands of powerful economic interests, many with representatives in the inner sanctums of official Washington, USFA imposed its restrictions gently upon industry and domestic consumers. USFA officials constantly worried that the limits of public acceptance had been reached. While the war and the government's unending appeals to patriotism caused Americans to accept the regimen imposed by the government, the *fact* of fuel scarcity more satisfactorily explains widespread acquiescence to specific restrictions on fuel use. The formation of USFA encountered general public approbation; so, too, did price fixing. People expected USFA to bring relief. Citizens criticized USFA for displaying a lack, not an excess, of vigor. Given the actual suffering in communities large and small, it would appear that conditions warranted more stringent regulations (some on the drawing boards in November 1918) than the federal government saw fit to impose. To assure fair prices and equitable allocation, more people than the government reckoned would have stomached more government.

In the immediate postwar years, the skeleton of wartime fuel policies would reappear during the fuel crises of 1919 and 1922, which caused even greater shortages than those experienced during the war. Concern over the nation's oil resources, apparent during the war, would stimulate the establishment of a federal board authorized to investigate ways and means of protecting the national interest by assuring an adequate oil supply. However, as subsequent chapters demonstrate, the many useful lessons to be learned from USFA's history were generally ignored by later federal fuel mangers.

FIVE

The Coal Crises of the 1920s

By LATE WINTER 1919, coal was again an essentially unregulated industry. Rapid federal disengagement, however, did not attest to a naive belief on the part of government personnel that the war in any way had worked a miraculous cure of chronic industry problems. During the next several years, a series of violent strikes so disrupted the coal supply of the nation that the federal government and many states reinstituted some of the wartime controls. Simultaneously, Congress and other units of the government launched studies and investigations of the apparently irresoluble difficulties that plagued the volatile industry. Knowledgeable individuals desperately sought permanent solutions to coal's disabilities, but such cures eluded them, and the cumulative efforts of a decade appeared as little more than ventures in crisis management. By the end of the decade of the 1920s, before the Great Depression struck and gloom descended upon a startled people, the coal industry and its travail had struck a historic nadir.

Federal Awareness of Coal Problems

Even as Garfield busied himself with the details necessary for an orderly end to federal regulation of the coal industry, he cast about for an acceptable plan of industry stabilization, finally deciding to sponsor a conference in February 1919, to which he invited officials from the National Coal Association (NCA) and the United Mine Workers of America (UMWA). Garfield's initiative derived from his wartime experience, his belief that the root causes of the coal crisis of

1916 remained unresolved, and his vision of a postwar world that offered meager prosperity to most mine operators and little security for the 615,000 men employed in mining. Perhaps, too, he persuaded himself that careful nurturing could strengthen and bring to maturity the cooperative spirit evoked by the war. As Garfield pursued this line of thought, he concluded that industry stabilization required the creation of a permanent independent unit of government responsible for the coal industry. Under his guidance, a committee of nine, divided equally among the NCA, the UMWA, and the government, drafted a rather remarkable stabilization scheme to present to President Wilson.

Wilson's rejection of Garfield's proposal stemmed not from any intrinsic weaknesses in the plan itself, but from his disbelief in the willingness of Congress to accept such a comprehensive regulatory program. Too, Wilson's preoccupation with his ambitious plans for a just peace with the Central Powers left little time to devote to domestic difficulties, even though Garfield's proposal had the approval of cabinet members F. K. Lane, J. Daniels, and N. D. Baker, and of Walker D. Hines, director-general of USRA. In brief, the Garfield scheme called for the appointment of a regulatory commission that would license all coal operators engaged in interstate commerce; establish rules governing the production, distribution, allocation, storage, and sale of coal; formulate fair trade practices and forbid unfair practices; review and mediate labor disputes; establish regulations regarding employee welfare; and exempt licensed operators from the provisions of the Sherman Anti-Trust Act of 1890.[1]

Garfield's idea was the most far-reaching solution to coal's problems that emerged during the interwar years, excepting only later proposals for the nationalization of the entire mining phase of the industry. Dismissed by Wilson as politically infeasible, the plan escaped public airing—and the inevitable cacophony of objections it would have precipitated. Never clothed with the fabric of detailed procedure, the Garfield proposal advanced the premise that the industry faced a declining market for coal while simultaneously supporting excess capacity and that these realities, if unchecked, could only result in uncontrolled competition for markets, operator demands for reduced wage scales, and strikes. Thus, such concrete elements in the plan as licensing and exemption from antitrust action were intended to limit the number of new mine openings while permitting groups of mine owners to market their coal cooperatively through joint-sales agencies. Presumably, the unspecified regulations affecting production, distribution, and allocation would mitigate transportation difficulties and stabilize prices.

Garfield's plan and other far more superficial proposals which followed all rested on a full body of information detailing the history of the industry. Experience taught that because of inadequate coal car supply, inefficiencies in coal routing, and a four-tiered system of distribution, coal shortages occurred even when peace prevailed between miners and owners. The convergence of these factors, aggravated by wartime demands, had resulted in coal scarcity from 1915 through 1918. Congressional and other investigations in the immediate postwar years simply confirmed what was already known and what the Garfield scheme presumed to address. In September 1919, two months before the first of several damaging postwar coal strikes, the *Bulletin* of the American Coal Wholesalers Association accused the Senate of conducting hysterical and uninformed hearings on coal, which by their intemperate warnings about impending coal shortages impugned the integrity of the entire coal industry.[2] A coming coal famine may have been problematical at that time, but that facts about the coal industry were lacking was entirely erroneous. Mountains of information, accessible to Congress, had been accumulated by the FTC, the USFA, and other public and private organizations.

Hardly had Garfield's plan been obscurely interred than a familiar cycle of coal ills made itself felt. Stimulated by wartime demand and high prices, the number of operating mines (and capacity) rose rapidly from 6,939 in 1917 to 8,319 in 1918 and 8,994 in 1919, far outstripping the rate of increase in production. The cessation of wartime demand and the apparent end of the fuel emergency caused a reduction in new coal orders, particularly by such major consumers as utilities and industries. During the first four months of 1919, bituminous production fell to 78 percent of production for the same months in 1918. With consumers relying upon stocks on hand, operators closed mines, reduced hours, and eliminated jobs. By midsummer 1919, stocks were dangerously low, and the miners were threatening a coal strike in response to operator insistence on large wage reductions.

Even before the likelihood of a strike penetrated public awareness, a noticeable rise in coal prices prompted hearings in Congress, which rehearsed a familiar litany of coal industry woes but generated little new information. Neither did these prestrike hearings suggest remedies that compared with the Garfield proposals in comprehensiveness. Instead, familiar charges of operator monopoly, especially in anthracite, emanated from some consuming states, while coal operators defended themselves by blaming consumers for their diminished orders and the railroads for distribution foul-ups. These hearings in the Senate and the House made it clear, however, that all coal industry associations opposed any federal intervention in the industry, including mild suggestions about the Bureau of Mines or the USGS gathering information concerning coal mine operations. The cooperative spirit of early 1919 between NCA and the government had evaporated by the summer of 1919.

Well before the miners struck on 1 November, then, reports from operators and large consumers attested to serious car shortages and the depletion of coal stocks: about six weeks' supply in December 1918, under three weeks' supply by August 1919. But the railroad administration took no steps to relieve the car shortage problem. Indeed, USRA's Director-General Hines accused the coal industry of rumormongering in order to justify price hikes. Hines testified that "in the first six months of [1919], there were virtually no transportation difficulties."[3] Information submitted prior to October 1919 by the coal industry, the railroads, and a wide assortment of consumers attested to inadequate coal transportation and warned of impending coal famine whether the miners struck or not—flat contradictions of Hines's assertions.

As of summer 1919, reliable information existed about the cost of coal production, price trends, costs of distribution (including freight rates), dealer margins, and other aspects of coal industry operation as well as about current supply and demand conditions. The brutal competitive situation in coal, particularly between nonunion southern mines and unionized northern mines, was well known. The procedures by which railroads assigned coal cars to mines, the inefficiencies of the cross-haul, the speculative purposes of reconsigning loaded coal cars, the peculiar requirements of lake dock operators, all these facets of the industry were by 1919 public knowledge, part of the lore of coal. The formulation of federal coal policies did not suffer from want of data, nor did the postwar crises strike without ample warning.[4]

More hearings and investigations inevitably followed the coal crisis of 1919–20, and still more were generated by the coal strike of 1922, including the report of the United States Coal Commission (USCC), which more or less summarized all the findings of prior studies. The results of this outpouring of data graced the pages of coal and other trade publications and provided grist for several popular books on the subject. Almost without exception, this body of material emphasized the chaotic condition of the industry, perceiving over-capacity as the crucial factor. Everyone involved in the industry, from the operators to small consumers, were castigated for ignorance, irresponsibility, and greed. Investigators and authors singled out the oligopolistic anthracite industry for special abuse since its product fed the hearths of so many millions of American homes; some critics tarred the bituminous industry with the same brush. The railroads were damned because of their seizure of coal during periods of scarcity and their inability to guarantee the efficient movement of coal. Virtually all these studies agreed that those involved in the coal business trampled upon the public interest. But as to appropriate remedies, no consensus emerged, even after disastrous strikes.[5]

Sen. William E. Borah, Father John A. Ryan, George W. Perkins, and other old-line Progressives agreed that government ownership of the mines afforded the best solution. Leaders of the coal industry viewed even an investigation as threatening and, of course, denied the need for more regulatory authority than ICC already commanded. Most interested parties fell between these two camps, but the character of the solutions ranged widely from further fact finding to rather intensive regulation. Two of the bills introduced, one in 1919 by Rep. George Huddleston, Democrat of Alabama, and one in late 1921 by Sen. John S. Frelinghuysen, Republican of New Jersey, created mechanisms to control production, transportation, prices, and coal sales. Both these bills resembled the Garfield proposals in recognizing the competitive weakness of the coal industry relative to other fuel industries.

Another futile legislative gambit, led by Sen. William S. Kenyon, Republican of Iowa, proposed that Congress declare coal a public utility and establish a coal industry code to regularize labor relations and abridge the right to strike. But most bills and less formal suggestions, recognizing only the tip of the iceberg, emphasized such palliatives as seasonal coal rates, discounts for early ordering, and greater coal storage by consumers, especially the railroads and utilities. At most hearings, the various interest groups persistently engaged in shooting at adversaries, in constructing elaborate justifications for their practices and performance, and in deflecting blame elsewhere. Harry N. Taylor, president of NCA, portrayed a virtuous coal industry sincerely committed to serving the public interest but beseiged and unjustly impugned by such hostile and self-serving interests as organized labor, the railroads, and everyone else.

Most discussions of the coal industry casually disregarded mounting evidence of consumer inclination to substitute other fuels for coal whenever possible. With many miners on strike and mines closed in July 1922, *Oildom* gloated at the opportunity presented to fuel oil distributors to penetrate and seize markets heretofore dominated by coal. While the coal retailers' organ, *The Coal Merchant*, blasted communities for establishing municipal coal yards during the strike of 1919, the oil industry unleashed regiments of salesmen who scurried from factory to factory preaching the cheapness, cleanliness, efficiency, and constant supply of fuel oil. While *The Coal Merchant* pressed "buy early" campaigns and the American Engineering Council, at the behest of USCC, produced a lengthy report on the economies of coal storage, many consumers longed for the day when they would see their last lump of coal.[6]

The Coal Crisis of 1919–1920

The American economy of the immediate postwar years moved sluggishly into a recession in 1919 as rapid demobilization reduced industrial demand and as 4 million discharged soldiers sought jobs. Unemployment and underemployment rose, but a recession was prevented from becoming a depression by the essential strength of the economy, by continued federal expenditures for completed or almost completed war contracts, as in ship building, and by a still vibrant export sector, particularly in agricultural commodities. Indeed, by 1920, a short-lived boomlet was in progress, serving as a prelude to the serious but abbreviated economic collapse of 1921. During these unsettled years, the federal government played a passive role, refusing to venture into the realm of depression prevention or resolution.[7]

One of the striking characteristics of federal investigations of the coal crisis of 1919–20 and of 1922–23 was the almost total absence of analyses that related coal's many maladies to the fluctuating economy or to the general economic structure of the nation. The coal strike that commenced on 1 November and involved over 600,000 bituminous and anthracite miners was dramatically prefaced in September by a great and violent steel strike. In 1919 alone, some 4 million workers engaged in over 3,600 strikes. Coal miners, then, were not alone in their militancy or in their willingness to defend such hard-won and all-too-tenuous economic security as had been achieved.

By midsummer 1919, the large coal stockpiles of late 1918 had disappeared. In July, the American Mining Congress, NCA, and the National Electric Light Association, among other groups, instructed their members to prepare for a coal shortage. Demand for coal and transportation, declining throughout the winter, would inevitably rise in the fall as orders for new coal arrived at the mines at just the moment when the demand for cars to move crops would peak. As indicated earlier, while USRA's Hines expressed confidence in the ability of the railroads to handle this traffic, few in the know believed him; NCA witnesses at Senate hearings on coal prices directly refuted Hines. In

August, Sen. Atlee Pomerene, Democrat of Ohio, pointing to car shortages in West Virginia, demanded that USRA take immediate steps to relieve the operators.[8] In many ways the situation resembled that of 1916. A coal crisis of some magnitude was developing even before the UMWA threatened to strike.

The coal strike commenced on 1 November 1919, lasted until mid-December, and closed down over 60 percent of bituminous production and 100 percent of anthracite. Later USCC and NCA tabulations suggested that the strike reduced normal production by some 43 million tons of coal. The loss of only one month's production, then, can be attributed to the strike.[9] But this followed a period of reduced ordering and diminished production and occurred during a period of heavy demand in railroad transportation. The strike alone did not cause the crisis. Indeed, the most severe shortages of coal struck in the months following the resumption of coal production, particularly in the East where anthracite warmed millions of homes. Buyers already low on coal in early fall frantically entered the market in an effort to bring their stocks up to normal, but their orders were larger than normal as a result of their failure to purchase during the previous spring and summer.

Well before the strike, consumer and producer groups exerted pressure on the Wilson administration and on USRA and ICC to forestall a coal shortage whether or not the miners struck. But the fuel and railroad agencies were engaged in liquidating their affairs, and the ICC was assiduously avoiding entanglement with the coal industry. Only the actual issuance of a strike order by UMWA catalyzed the administration into action.

One week before the coal strike, Wilson resurrected the USFA, authorizing it to reimpose maximum mine-mouth prices, maximum jobbers' commissions, and maximum wholesale and retail profit margins; and to manage distribution and allocation. However, appropriations for USFA had terminated the previous June, and although Garfield returned to his old job, his agency lacked both money and personnel. Garfield, then, issued an order on 31 October delegating all authority over shipment, distribution, allocation, and storage to the director-general of USRA, which still possessed a full staff and a functioning network of regional and local committees. Presumably, the attorney general was to enforce the price controls. USRA, responsible for car supply, immediately issued a list of priority consumers which simply reiterated the wartime priority list.[10]

In assuming responsibility without power, Garfield committed the deadliest of bureaucratic blunders. What induced him to assume the burden? Loyalty to Wilson, his old friend and patron, and, perhaps, Garfield's belief that he more than any other individual possessed the confidence of both miners and owners and could therefore settle the dispute swiftly and equitably. His calculations, however, proved faulty. His proposed 14 percent wage increase rested on the belief that the cost of the settlement should not be passed through to consumers in the form of higher coal prices; Garfield argued that operator profits could well bear that wage increase. The operators accepted the wage proposal, but the UMWA rejected it, and no promise of stable prices was forthcoming. Secretary of Labor William Wilson, however, advocated both a larger wage increase—averaging 31.6 percent—and higher coal prices. The cabinet, although preferring Wilson's approach, if not his precise recommendation, referred the entire matter to a commission of three, called the U.S. Bituminous Coal Commission. Garfield, convinced of his rightness but now denied a role in the settlement, resigned on 11 December. The miners agreed to accept commission arbitration and returned to work in mid-December; the commission eventually offered wage increases of from 20 to 27 percent. With Garfield's resignation and that of his assistant administrator, USFA consisted only of the general counsel, and he soon went home to Chicago.[11]

Prior to the recall of Garfield and the strike, retail coal prices moved sharply upward, this despite an actual decline in mine-mouth prices (see Table 6) and a relatively inactive market, an anomaly that prompted Senate hearings on the price of coal. In the Kansas City, Missouri, market, retail prices advanced from $6.50 per ton in January 1918 to $9.56 per ton in December 1919. Before the crisis had ended, late in 1920, small consumers in Kansas City paid $11.00 and more per ton for soft coal, when they could find it. Prices in Philadelphia, Memphis, and elsewhere ascended similarly, and in some cases, Boston for example, spot market coal sold at $20.00.

The wartime price controls reimposed in November succeeded in stabilizing mine-mouth prices but failed to control wholesale or retail prices. Some part of the increase, about 10 percent in Kansas City, for instance, reflected freight rate increases allowed by the ICC in August 1920. But the largest share of the advance resulted from the higher margins exacted by wholesalers and retailers. Even the most credulous of Kansas City buyers found it difficult to accept the wholesalers' plea of defenselessness against the exorbitant demands of mine owners. With USFA functioning without the enforcement mechanisms available during the war, dealers, unafraid of punishment for noncompliance, charged what the market would bear. Truly defenseless were the small customers, generally poor and working class, who lived in cramped quarters heated by a single anthracite coal stove and who paid $1.25 to $1.50 per fifty-pound sack of coal, or some $60.00 per ton. Scavenging for coal along railroad tracks and around coal yards became a daily routine for many families.[12]

Falling production during late winter and the spring months of 1919 and minimal consumer ordering generated a nervous market in late summer and fall as large users entered the market to build up depleted stocks and prepare for a possible coal strike, thereby stretching to the limit the capacity of railroads to deliver. The strike transformed a nervous market into a panicked market with large contracts outstanding, severe weather ahead, and 70 percent of productive capacity shut down. The railroad administration seized all the coal on wheels, established a Central Coal Committee (CCC) to coordinate distribution, and reimposed the old wartime system of fuel priorities. Both Garfield and Hines believed that a quick settlement of the strike and the reopening of the mines would terminate the emergency. They were wrong.

Federal efforts to cope with the coal crisis divide naturally into three periods. In the first period, November and December 1919, USRA assumed the commanding role. The second period, commencing in January and lasting until May 1920, followed the demise of USFA and witnessed the lifting of USRA's emergency orders and the abrogation of federal authority over coal distribution and allocation. The worsening crisis ushered in the third period, spring–fall 1920, dominated by the Interstate Commerce Commission, which, armed with new power, acted unilaterally to meet serious transportation deficiencies and to ameliorate pronounced inequities in distribution and allocation. One prevailing characteristic of all three periods was the absence of an overall plan that measured total national need against total coal supply and then moved coal from areas of surplus to areas of want by the shortest and most efficient routes. A second common thread was the failure to control prices, not only from November to April 1920, when the maximum price regulations were in force, but especially thereafter when no price limitations were in effect.

The distribution and allocation mechanisms imposed by USRA in November and December 1919 lacked the comprehensiveness of the World War I strategies while retaining all the discriminatory features. Instead of reinstituting the zone system, USRA seized all coal in transit and relied upon the CCC and its regional and district committees to move coal to the places of greatest need. However, CCC, even if capable of identifying need, was constrained by USRA's coincident order of 31 October to deliver coal according to an earlier wartime preference list.[13] Much confusion followed as CCC committees adhered to either the "greatest need" criterion or the wartime preference list, or neither. Eventually, the order of 31 October prevailed. But that order did not assure the movement of coal to the points of most urgent need. A disproportionately large supply reached the public utilities and industries designated as preferred on the basis of their contribution to the war effort, a criterion hardly germane in 1919–20.

The regional coal committees functioned in isolation from one another so that a surplus in one region was of little use to a region of scarcity. Thus, great difficulty attended the coordination of distribution from operating coal mines that traditionally shipped into two or more market areas. Railroads consumed one-third of the coal produced in Illinois. The remainder supplied the Chicago metropolitan area, Michigan, Wisconsin, Minnesota, Iowa, Nebraska, Missouri, and Indiana, competing in many of those markets with coal from Indiana, Ohio, Kentucky, West Virginia, and Pennsylvania. Under the zone system of World War I, Illinois coal was restricted to specified market areas, as was the coal of competitors. Users in Kansas City knew for certain that Illinois coal was unavailable. Under the USRA regime, little was known for certain. District and local coal committees wheeled and dealed in seeking coal to meet this or that discrete emergency. Areas normally served by several fields could not be certain that even one of those fields could or would ship in coal. The indefiniteness of it all especially plagued the consuming markets served by lake and tidewater docks.[14]

Rail and rail-water routes supplied the northeastern quarter of the nation as well as funneling coal into the upper Great Lakes states. By the time USRA intervened, the winter freeze had virtually shut down lake traffic, but according to general preference lists, traffic was to be diverted to lake ports from other destinations. Some time elapsed before coal was rerouted from the frozen lake ports, especially on Lake Erie, to other points. USRA also assumed that the East Coast required more attention than interior regions. In fact, the entire midsection of the nation experienced equally severe shortages that persisted into mid-1920. In December, Chicago inaugurated lightless nights and reduced work days in an effort to conserve coal. In far-off Montana, the Montana Cattlemen's Association protested against the inadequate amounts of coal being delivered to meat packers.

USRA functioned without an overall distribution and allocation formula which it could apply to regional needs. Users who first convinced USRA's coal committees of their desperate fuel situation re-

TABLE 8. *Days' Supply of Bituminous Coal on the First Day of the Month, 1919–1923*

	Jan. 1919	April 1919	March 1920	June 1920	April 1921
By-product coke plants	32	23	15	8	28
Steel plants	42	35	<11	11	38
Other industrials	65	47	27	24	47
Coal gas plants	81	58	31	22	66
Electric utilities	49	48	21	22	48
Bituminous coal dealers	39	25	13	10	26
Railroads	32	N/A	21	10	24

Sources: Bituminous Operators' Special Committee on Transportation, "Statement on Coal Transportation, 1923," Box 4, Entry 8, USCC, RG 68;

ceived priority attention; those who failed to catch the ear of USRA quickly enough went without. Steps were not taken, for instance, to prevent the diversion of short anthracite stocks from domestic to industrial use, and even railroad use. Without strict enforcement of mine-mouth prices and distributor margins, operators and dealers sold to the highest bidders. Railroads and utilities bid against each other in an effort to obtain coal, forcing prices up and in effect denying coal to the domestic market. Without zoning, without regional allocation policies founded on peacetime consumption patterns, and without price enforcement the policy of robbing Peter to pay Paul eventually robbed Paul also.[15]

Hardly had the USFA/USRA regulations taken effect than Garfield resigned, USFA withered and died, and the miners, accepting the appointment of the United States Bituminous Coal Commission on 19 December 1919, agreed to resume work. For some inexplicable reason, in January USRA proceeded to revoke its emergency orders and in February federal control of the railroads terminated under the terms of the Transportation Act (Esch-Cummins Act) of 1920. But the most severe repercussions of the strike and of the developing transportation shortage that preceded the walkout lay in the future. Purchasers rushed into the market to restore stocks already low prior to the strike and further depleted in November and December 1919. Industrial stockpiles of coal dwindled rapidly during the first half of 1920, falling dangerously below the margin of one month's supply that railroads,

March 1922	Sept. 1922	Oct. 1922	Nov. 1922	Jan. 1923	Feb. 1923	March 1923	June 1923
39	11	14	18	19	20	19	23
48	12	17	21	27	26	26	29
56	32	33	39	40	36	34	39
82	34	38	55	60	62	58	75
54	26	30	32	33	35	34	45
23	11	18	21	16	15	11	27
42	13	15	13	16	18	16	21

for March 1920, F. G. Tryon, "Consumers' Stocks of Bituminous Coal, March 1 and June 1, 1920," Box 9, Entry 20, USCC, RG 68.

steel plants, and by-product plants preferred to have on hand; and even further below the two to three months' supply that utilities normally stored (Table 8). During this period, however, the federal government exercised no authority over the deteriorating coal situation. While coal production rose during the first three months of 1920. surpassing production in the first quarter of 1919 by 28 percent and even exceeding the 1918 volume by a small fraction, the inability of the railroads to haul the new production caused coal shortages surpassing in severity those experienced during the war.[16]

The Transportation Act of 1920 delegated extensive new authority to the ICC. It now had the power to declare a fuel emergency and then regulate car service and assign priorities in the movement of fuel. This authority could have been applied directly and immediately to moderating the coal crisis, but ICC eschewed the application of its new powers until the latter part of May 1920. In his testimony at Senate hearings in 1921 on coal and transportation, James J. Storrow, New England fuel administrator during World War I and the Massachusetts fuel administrator in 1920 and 1921, soundly criticized the ICC for failing to assume its new obligations in March and April 1920. According to Storrow, prompt action during a time of slackening coal demand and prior to the onset of seasonal calls on transportation by the agricultural sector would have relieved immediate congestion and facilitated both coal and crop movements in late summer and fall of 1920. As it was, ICC stepped in only when directly faced with disabling congestion along trunk lines and in terminals and when petitioned in May by the principal carriers to intervene. Thus, ICC bestirred itself only when forced to by a crisis within a crisis.

In May, the principal carriers announced their inability to manage the flow of food and fuel, and ICC declared an emergency. But ICC's powers, although sufficient for the control of rail transportation, did not encompass price and contracts or distribution and allocation to wholesalers and retailers or final consumers. ICC's authority ranged less broadly and penetrated less deeply than did the pastiche of federal powers existing in 1918. The later fulminations of the coal merchants' association that the ICC misused its authority so as practically to control prices and the entire distribution of coal reflected the paranoia of a group who imagined a regulator lurking behind every coal pile. It also attested to a degree of self-awareness, that the retail branch of the industry could not bear searching public scrutiny.[17]

The ICC launched its venture in coal management at an unpropitious moment. Prices had risen, and a wildcat strike of the nation's railroad yard switchmen in late spring gravely exacerbated the developing coal car shortage while prices advanced still further: by 50 percent in Illinois and 100 percent in central Pennsylvania. From all parts of the country reports flowed in of a decrease in coal loadings, reflected in April and May production which fell to but 80 percent of the production of the three prior months. The USGS reported that, as a result of the car shortage, running time at the mines averaged fewer than twenty-four hours a week. By 1 June 1920, commercial stocks of bituminous were 25 percent lower than normal (see Table 8) and lower than the stocks of winter 1917–18, a time when coal shortages caused the widespread closing down of industry. In 1921, an official of the Brooklyn Union Gas Company, for instance, recalled that inadequate coal deliveries in 1920 almost compelled the plant to shut down.[18]

Between May and October 1920, ICC issued twenty-one Service Orders. To administer these orders, the commission organized thirty terminal committees at key railroad and traffic centers. Charged with maintaining a regular flow of coal through these gateways, the committees reported on local conditions, advised ICC concerning specific Service Order (SO) requirements, cooperated with local or regional units of NCA and the American Railway Association to assure that coal producers received a fair share of rolling stock, and dealt with emergencies as they could. ICC decided against identifying coal as a priority commodity, but treated it as a special case requiring special measures to guarantee movement to certain sections by the most efficient routes.[19]

ICC made no effort to improve upon the USRA system and in replicating it reproduced all of its weaknesses. The Service Orders reestablished many of the coal traffic regulations first implemented by USFA and USRA during the war and again in late 1919. A majority of the orders sought greater efficiency in the movement and handling of open-top equipment. Seven of the orders aimed at speeding coal cars eastward, required the railroads to give preference to coal mine requests for cars, and penalized consignees for failure to unload cars within a twenty-four-hour period (unless it was the carrier's fault). The highway and building material industries, the iron and steel and glass industries, and the American Coal Wholesalers Association all protested the discriminatory effects of these orders. Wholesalers felt oppressed because SO No. 7 prevented reconsignment of loaded coal cars while prohibiting delays in unloading, both of which obstructed wholesalers from keeping coal off the market in anticipation of higher spot market prices. James Storrow, Massachusetts fuel administrator, viewed SO No. 7 as of little use to his region since the railroads were already pulling a maximum number of cars to New England. The ICC, however, maintained that New England benefited from the order because more coal moved to tidewater and then to New England by water.[20]

Complementary to the above Special Orders were others that awarded preferential treatment to public utilities and to industries that had appeared on World War I priority lists. The ICC justified its decision to authorize a preferential supply of cars to meet the needs of utilities on the basis of dangerously low stocks in the hands of the utilities, pointing to less than a twelve-day supply in New York and Chicago and the closing of some utilities in Michigan, Wisconsin, and elsewhere. But, of course, there were critics. For instance, J. D. A. Morrow of the NCA accused the utilities of exploiting the orders to build up unjustifiably large stocks at the expense of domestic consumers.

Still other orders targeted regions of extraordinary scarcity, including the Great Lakes ports and New England, for preferential treatment. Every effort was made, for example, to move coal to the Great Lakes before winter freezing closed down the ports. John F. McGee, fuel administrator in Minnesota, claimed that in late summer 1920 his region possessed 6 million fewer tons of coal than at the same time in 1919, while only 35 percent of the region's normal car supply was available. Thus, great reliance was placed on lake transportation, which would close down in the winter. SO No. 5 (9 June 1920) failed to move sufficient coal toward Lake Erie and was superseded by SO

No. 10, which stipulated that a given volume of coal should move to the lakes from a specific district, totaling in the aggregate 4,000 cars per day, or 1.2 million tons. SO No. 5 reestablished a lake cargo pool, gave coal assigned to the pool preference over other lake coal, and embargoed the movement of coal to Erie ports for water transport unless accompanied by a permit issued by the pool management. These restrictions were designed to prohibit the speculative practices of brokers who withheld contract deliveries in order to enter the spot market. Service Orders No. 6 and No. 11 established a similar pool system for shipments to New England after the closing of the lake ports and assigned preference to coal destined for New England by water from tidewater ports.[21]

The regionally oriented SOs whipped up as much disagreement as the car supply and public utilities orders. Consumer groups, including municipalities in such nonpreferred regions as central New York, documented equally urgent needs and argued that the SOs aggravated already serious coal shortages by withdrawing cars. Testimony from mine operators in fields compelled to supply the Great Lakes or New England corroborated these criticisms. Mines in Ohio were ordered to move 35 percent of daily production to the lakes before shipping a single lump to other destinations; but a reduced car supply provided only enough transportation to meet the lake requirements. Other customers went begging, even if they held supply contracts with the producers. Operators with a car supply over and above that assigned to the lakes frequently ignored their contracts and entered the spot market, while the railroads often favored the mines that offered them the lowest price. The result, as the chambers of commerce of Akron and Cleveland complained, was to deny contract coal to the larger consumers, including retailers, and force all consumers to pay the exorbitant prices of the spot market.

To avoid the appearance of arbitrariness in the issuance of SOs and to win the support of affected groups, ICC conducted hearings on many of the orders. But too many interests clamored for satisfaction, and in the hearings the influence of producers and carriers clearly predominated. Reconciling the demands of the two latter interests, both essentially opposed to ICC intervention at any level, meant that the needs of unorganized domestic and small consumers went unheeded. Without effective enforcement procedures, much noncompliance went undetected. The ICC, unfamiliar with the vagaries of the coal trade or with pricing mechanisms and relying principally on advice from producers and carriers, refused to take chances, construed its power narrowly, and ignored advice that clashed with the position assumed by its principal counselors. ICC's politics were arbitrary by definition, since the SOs singled out certain regions or consumer groups for special attention while ignoring other regions and consumer groups. If the wartime system was unfair to some areas and consumers, it did function systematically and predictably throughout the entire nation.

Fuel administrators operated in only a few states and rarely enjoyed the cooperation of carrier organizations or the NCA and its state branches. In Indiana, NCA and its state affiliates succeeded in preventing federal efforts to determine how much coal was being produced within the state and almost succeeded in blocking a state law regulating the industry during the emergency. The National Coal Association obtained a court injunction that prohibited FTC from gathering information about coal production in Indiana, arguing that this was purely a state matter. Then, NCA went to court against the Indiana coal control law which permitted the fixing of mine-mouth prices and the licensing of dealers and required coal producers to ship coal to dealers identified by the Indiana coal administration. NCA, in this instance unsuccessfully, contended that the law interferred with interstate commerce and the prior contract obligations of producers. NCA, then, came close to stonewalling all public measures to ameliorate the severity of the coal famine.

State fuel administrations, few in number, could not provide ICC with the grassroots support available to USFA during the war. The governors of Wisconsin, North Dakota, South Dakota, and Minnesota telegraphed President Wilson requesting the immediate appointment of a federal fuel distributor. Under the Lever Act, Wilson possessed this authority and, as the Justice Department advised the president, without a federal fuel distributor the power of the Lever Act could not be brought to bear on the crisis. However, Wilson, weak in body and drained of spirit by the Senate's rejection of his treaty, chose not to act.[22]

In a 10 July 1920 telegram to the president, Calvin Coolidge, governor of Massachusetts, and his peers in Vermont, Connecticut, New Hampshire, and Rhode Island, urged the immediate reduction of coal exports.[23] As the governors and others in New England and adjoining states insisted, rising coal exports during the first half of 1920—averaging 807,500 tons in January and February and 1.7 million tons during each of the subsequent four months, not including exports to Canada—reduced supplies to New England by almost 50 percent. At least two ICC commissioners agreed to the necessity of an embargo of coal exports but, reluctant to press for unilateral ICC action, sought some expression of the president's position. While few denied ICC's claim that it could not prohibit exports as USRA/USFA had done during December 1919–February 1920, Wilson and the New Englanders apparently believed the ICC's authority over car supply enabled the commission to restrict transportation to shippers supplying domestic wants. In fact, ICC in early June did establish a partial embargo on exports by authorizing the Tidewater Coal Exchange (the operating pool at Virginia's ports) to deliver cars only to domestic shippers and by permitting the carriers to embargo all export shipments. Not only did this arouse the opposition of NCA and the U.S. Shipping Board and maritime interests, but its effectiveness was minimized by the operational latitude enjoyed by the producers and railroads. As a result of ICC's conservative and legalistic interpretation of its authority, something over 10 percent of the coal arriving at tidewater moved to foreign destinations while the utilities in New York City had only a six-day supply.[24]

By November or December 1920, the coal emergency was over. Production during the final quarter of the year averaged 52.3 million tons monthly, 30 percent greater than the output of the final quarter of 1919 and 12 percent greater than the last quarter of 1918. Simultaneously, coal stocks increased (see Table 8). By November, ICC had revoked all its orders except those assigning cars to the utilities, a decision requested by the utilities and considered unnecessary by Daniel Wentz, NCA's president.

The crisis of 1919–20 disappeared less because of ICC policies than because production and transportation eventually achieved an equilibrium. ICC, an agency without expertise in fuel management, promulgated Service Orders that fell far short of establishing a national fuel distribution policy. Indeed, the cumulative impact of the SOs forced prices up and reduced the supply of coal available to domestic, commercial, and nonpreferred industrial consumers. ICC's maladroit tactics left a residue of ill will and mutual suspicion that tarnished the postcrisis relationships of the central protagonists. Harry N. Taylor told the coal retailers in 1920 that "Uncle Sam must be pried out of the coal business . . . and all other business which has been invaded."[25] In December 1920, Sen. William M. Calder's committee declared coal profiteering to be a national disgrace and suggested legislation to prevent irregularity of delivery, inferior quality of coal, profiteering, and the monopoly of transportation facilities. This Senate report met with little congressional enthusiasm. While hearings were held on a coal regulation bill prepared by Senator Calder, Republican of New York, only a bill diluted of all authority save requiring regular reports from the coal industry emerged from committee in February 1921; it died in the Senate shortly thereafter. At an NCA meeting in May, J. D. A. Morrow congratulated the membership for defeating the Calder bill, a maleficent intrusion of federal power into private enterprise. Very little time elapsed between the death of the Calder bill and warnings of impending coal shortages for winter 1921–22.[26]

The Coal Crisis of 1922–1923

In February 1922, the bituminous operators of the Pittsburgh district, southern Ohio, and Indiana announced wage reductions of 30 to 40 percent effective 1 April, making a coal strike on 1 April all but inevitable. Desultory negotiations between the United Mine Workers of America and the operators in March produced no settlement. The bituminous miners ceased work on 1 April and were followed in May by the anthracite miners. The coal operators, of course, scored the miners for their unreasonable demands and blamed the federal government for the high wage scale established by the U.S. Bituminous Coal Commission in 1919. As Morrow explained the operators' position, the lower wage scales of the nonunionized mines south of the Ohio River permitted those mines to invade and capture the traditional markets of the unionized mines. Instead of demanding a higher wage for southern miners, Morrow asserted the necessity of reduced wages for northern miners. For their part, the miners rejected any reduction in wages, demanded the continuation of the present wage scale, and refused to submit the dispute to arbitration.[27]

During the prestrike months of 1922, uncertainty prevailed concerning the sufficiency of coal stocks. In January and February, *Coal Review* reported production declines during the last quarter of 1921. The American Engineering Council singled out inadequate coal storage in early 1922 as a major factor in the shortages that followed the strike.[28] While Table 8 indicates higher stocks on 1 March 1922 than in prior months, Table 9 identifies many states in which the stocks of retailers and utilities fell substantially below the national average. A USGS report in March warned that a strike of any length would cause steep price increases, severe winter coal shortages, and the closing of many factories. Mitigation of these consequences depended upon efficient distribution of available supplies. But, the USGS reminded its constituents, in 1919 distribution was facilitated by the government's wartime powers to control coal and transportation. Without similar authority, the situation could deteriorate seriously even after the mines reopened. USGS also counseled against a reliance upon increas-

TABLE 9. *Days' Supply of Bituminous Coal in the Hands of Retailers and Utilities, in Selected States, 1 March 1922*

	Retail Dealers			Public Utilities		
	April 1919	*April 1921*	*March 1922*	*April 1919*	*April 1921*	*March 1922*
National average:	25	26	23	48	48	54
	States with fewer than 20 days' supply			*States with fewer than 40 days' supply*		
Rhode Island	11					
Pennsylvania	18					
Maryland	14					
Delaware	19			33		
District of Columbia	10			30		
Minnesota	14			33		
North Dakota	7					
South Dakota	7					
Nebraska	18					
Missouri	14					
Oklahoma	18			23		
Arkansas	18					
Colorado	15			18		
New Mexico	16			16		
Arizona	9					
Wyoming	3			13		
Montana	15			18		
Idaho	18					
Washington	14					
Wisconsin				26		
Virginia				30		
Kentucky				34		
Tennessee				33		
Mississippi				37		
Texas				21		

Source: *Coal Review* 4 (29 April 1922), 11.

ing production of nonunion coal to compensate for losses of union coal: "To haul this coal into the Middle West, which is solidly union, is a very difficult traffic problem."[29]

Few hearkened to the advice offered in this excellent analysis. The data in Tables 4, 9, and 10 substantiate the USGS conclusions. Coal production in 1921 barely exceeded the volume mined in 1911, while in 1922 coal production dipped below the output of 1911. Production during the last quarter of 1921 fell far below that produced during the final quarter of 1920. For the three prestrike months (January–March) of 1922, output was higher than the January–March period of 1921 and October–December 1921, but not enough to compensate for the production losses suffered during April–August 1922 when only 113.9 million tons were mined, or some 60 to 65 percent of normal bituminous production for that period. Production in Illinois, Indiana, and Ohio all but ceased, while production in Pennsylvania was reduced by 50 percent in bituminous and 100 percent in anthracite (Table 10). In the Mid-Continent, mining in Kansas, Missouri, and Colorado declined precipitously. West Virginia's output also dropped significantly. Alabama's output fell only marginally, and production in Kentucky rose, but their total output hardly made up the losses experienced in the major producing states (Table 10).

Public apathy greeted the work stoppages of April and May, but this quickly changed as coal prices shot up later in May and as consumers began to realize, in July and August, that they held only a small portion of winter's coal requirements. Early in June, the USGS warned of the possibility of a runaway coal market as buyers, finally recognizing the shortage, rushed into the market eager to purchase at any price. In July, public anxiety about winter replaced earlier complacency. As of August, less than half of Chicago's residences had even a partial winter supply, and some retailers were rationing coal to regular customers (and hoarding some coal in anticipation of higher prices.)

In September 1922, with consumer stocks far smaller than during March (Table 8), industrial consumers bid against one another, sending prices to $9 and more per ton in the Chicago, Cincinnati, and St. Paul markets. Boston, too, experienced severe coal shortages in August. While deliveries to New England for the first three months of 1922 exceeded by 1.2 million tons those for the same period in 1921, deliveries from 1 April through 15 August fell 1.7 tons under the receipts of 1921. Shrinking deliveries, caused in part by the July wildcat strike of railroad shop workers (which reduced production in the

TABLE 10. *Bituminous Production of Selected States during the Coal Strike,
April–August 1922*

	March (thousand tons)	Average Monthly Production April–August as percentage of March Production
Alabama	1,372	96
Colorado	988	65
Illinois	9,503	1
Indiana	3,039	1
Kansas	459	18
Kentucky	3,425	121
Missouri	461	6
Ohio	3,451	11
Pennsylvania	13,347	32
West Virginia	8,317	77
Total above	44,362	38 (16,852 avg.)
Total U.S.	49,976	38

Source: Federal Fuel Distributor, *Final Report of the Federal Fuel Distributor to the President of the United Sates, September 21, 1923* (Washington, D.C.: GPO), 25.

nonunion mines), propelled prices upward. The regional railroads and utilities received such a large proportion of the incoming coal that spot market coal was virtually unavailable at any price in Boston.[30]

The strike stimulated but a lethargic federal response. The Harding administration, although forewarned of the strike and its potential repercussions, prepared no plans to alleviate its effect on the public. President Harding adopted a hands-off stance, insisting that he possessed no authority to intervene beyond appealing to both parties to reconcile the dispute in a rational way. Secretary of Commerce Herbert Hoover did gain the president's approval in late May to intervene in an effort to prevent further coal price increases. A firm adherent of cooperation between business and government, Hoover called a conference of nonunion operators and won their voluntary agreement to hold prices at the levels established in 1917 by Garfield. In reaching this agreement, Hoover, perhaps unintentionally, laid the major responsibility for preventing exorbitant prices at the door of the distributors. An editorial in *The Coal Merchant* severely criticized

Hoover for displaying such complete ignorance of the common practices of the retail coal trade and questioned his competence to manage price stabilization. Only when convinced that Hoover would no longer wildly blame retailers for price increases, did the National Retail Coal Merchants' Association lower its guns. Furthermore, recognition that Hoover's plan just might prevent even more drastic federal intervention convinced both retailers and wholesalers to publicly avow their compliance with the price arrangements.

For the brief moment in June, prices were stable, prompting Senators William Borah of Idaho and David I. Walsh of Massachusetts to postpone an immediate probe into the matter of coal profiteering. National coal prices on the spot market, above $4.00 in early May, averaged about $3.50 throughout June and into July. Nonunion coal did find its way to market, but not in sufficient quantities to make up for the loss of both bituminous and anthracite. Anthracite users entered the bituminous market, while large bituminous consumers such as the railroads, steel, and the utilities began to bid against one another and other purchasers. Then on 1 July, the wildcat strike by railroad yard shopmen cast a flimsy system into utter disarray. Nonunion bituminous production of some 8.1 million tons weekly in June plunged to 4 million tons weekly in July, an amount unequal to the demand of railroads, utilities, and food producers alone. In late July, Alabama's operators renounced the price agreement. By 7 August, average spot prices approached $6.20 per ton, and in early September, a Wichita, Kansas, consumer sent Hoover a retailer's circular that listed bituminous prices from $8.25 to $14.25. Voluntarism proved wanting in defending the public against the virus of quick and high profits.[31]

As the fuel supply situation worsened throughout the country (and particularly in the North Atlantic and Great Lakes states), President Harding stepped up his efforts to cajole the hostile parties to reach a solution. Congress busied itself with hearings and debates on a variety of coal bills ranging from almost total federal control to the creation of yet another investigative body; the latter was vigorously supported by Senator Borah and Secretary Hoover. By mid-July, Harding had decided on two approaches: First, convince the miners to return to work at prestrike rates and promise the establishment of a coal commission to investigate the entire industry; second, organize an executive fuel distribution committee to cooperate with the ICC and state fuel organizations (Hoover, on 26 July, requested the states to appoint fuel administrators) in moving coal to points of need. In late July, Hoover convened an organizational meeting of the President's Fuel

Distribution Committee (PFDC), consisting of Attorney General H. M. Daugherty, Clyde B. Atchinson of the ICC, and Henry B. Spencer, appointed permanent chairman of PFDC at this initial meeting. While PFDC organized itself, the ICC issued SOs No. 22 and No. 23, giving priority in coal transportation to public institutions, railroads, public utilities, and vital industries and ordering the railroads to ship by the most efficient route. By early August, PFDC had established eight district committees in the nonunion fields to process emergency orders for fuel and to assign transportation priorities. Possessing no statutory authority, PFDC's effectiveness rested upon the coercive powers vested in ICC.

During July and August, PFDC and ICC directed particular attention to the needs of the East Coast and on moving coal to Lake Erie for shipment to ports along the upper Great Lakes. As in 1920, and with equally mixed results, nonunion districts in southern Ohio, Kentucky, Tennessee, and Alabama were ordered to load specified quantities for Lake Erie before filling other orders. PFDC also strove to prevent the railroads from entering the spot market and bidding up the price of coal far above the now lapsed voluntary prices, but the railroads invariably ignored these directives. PFDC recommended punitive action, but the ICC declined, preferring at all times to avoid coercion and to rely on moral suasion. The railroads paid no attention to such appeals and continued to grab coal and cars when and how they could. In Colorado, for example, the Union Pacific, Chicago, Burlington & Quincy, and Rock Island lines used open cars belonging to the Denver and Salt Lake and the Denver and Rio Grande Western lines for nonfuel freight, refusing to return them to the owners and greatly reducing coal shipments from Colorado to western Kansas, Nebraska, and South Dakota. From 1 August through 11 September, PFDC succeeded in moving some 3 million tons of coal, roughly 8 percent of the total mined during the period or the equivalent of a two-month supply for New England.[32]

With the settlement of the strike in mid-August, PFDC and ICC terminated their oversight of distribution, and ICC suspended SO No. 23, leaving in effect only the orders pertaining to the Great Lakes. Fuel Distributor Spencer informed the states that since the emergency had ended, fuel distribution was now entirely the responsibility of the states. But unlike 1919–20, few agreed with Spencer that the resumption of coal mining meant the disappearance of the emergency. As the strike ended, Harding requested emergency powers over coal, and for the next month Congress conducted hearings on special coal legislation. Even Hoover, the champion of voluntarism, seemed prepared to accept legislation to control prices and prevent rail congestion that would inevitably accompany the return to normal coal production. Hoover admitted the necessity of a federal body to coordinate coal movement with the assistance of equivalent state agencies. The coal industry, on its part, opposed any coercive measures. *Cushing's Survey* reflected the extreme individualist and antigovernment position among coal trade journals, denying, in the midst of the worst coal crisis, any coal operator responsibility for shortages and, indeed, doubting the existence of scarcity.

While some, like Senators Thomas J. Walsh of Montana and Borah of Idaho and the governors of North and South Dakota and Wisconsin, urged the nationalization of the coal mines and the railroads, Congress never seriously considered such proposals. On 22 September 1922, Congress passed and the president signed two bills: one declaring a national emergency to exist in the production, transportation, and distribution of coal and other fuel; the other creating the U.S. Coal Commission. Accumulating evidence pointing to dangerous coal car shortages and a wildcat strike by railroad switchmen in early August, reducing to a trickle the shipment of coal from producing mines, hastened the passage of this legislation.[33]

The emergency coal act enlarged the powers of the ICC by authorizing the commission to issue priority orders for coal delivery, to impose embargoes against shippers or carriers, to assure equitable distribution, and "to prevent . . . the purchase or sale of coal or other fuel at prices unjustly or unreasonably high." The act also created the office of Federal Fuel Distributor (FFD) to assist and advise the ICC in administering its new responsibilities. Conrad E. Spens, vice-president of the Chicago, Burlington & Quincy, was appointed fuel distributor.

In a separate act, Congress authorized the president to establish the U.S. Coal Commission to investigate the entire coal industry and report its findings to Congress. Support for an independent investigative agency had first surfaced in April when Rep. Oscar E. Bland, Republican of Indiana, offered such a bill with Harding's support. Although the Bland bill was effectively killed by the Republican leadership, interest was maintained; and in July, Senator Borah introduced a new bill for a fact-finding commission. Harding convinced Borah to postpone the matter until the strike was resolved, at which time the president and Hoover came out in favor of Borah's bill. Borah and his allies campaigned vigorously for this legislation, which sought a commission composed equally of representatives of the operators, labor, and the public. As ultimately passed, no restrictions were placed on the president's choice of commissioners except that members of Congress were ineligible. Of the commissioners appointed, only two, the director of USGS and a former commissioner of labor, possessed any special knowledge of the coal industry. The act specified that the new commission was to conduct separate investigations of anthracite and bituminous.[34]

Congress had created a study group and an administrative arm for ICC. In granting ICC virtual blanket power of embargo, Congress obviously intended that ICC deny transportation to parties who charged unreasonable prices. The act also clearly granted to ICC the authority to set mine-mouth, wholesale, or retail prices. The emergency legislation permitted the establishment of a fuel control system even more comprehensive than that allowed by the Lever Act, because power was centralized in one agency, the ICC, rather than distributed among several, as had been the case during World War I. Moreover, the price-fixing powers in the 1922 legislation applied to all fuels, whereas those clauses in the Lever Act specifically excepted oil. However, neither FFD nor ICC considered the invocation of embargo or price powers. While prices were set by some states, the federal agencies relied upon the importuning of coalmen to act reasonably, a method quite acceptable to coal operators and dealers—but barren of results.

During this acute crisis, ICC took few actions that improved upon its performance in 1919–20. Virtually the same Service Orders were issued, and they produced virtually the same results. For a brief moment in October and November, the coal crisis appeared to be waning. Prematurely (as during December 1919–January 1920), ICC withdrew its orders and FFD prepared to liquidate its operations. But by mid-December, all the transportation difficulties experienced in 1919 and 1920—car shortages; congestion; inefficient car assignment procedures; the hoarding of coal by industries, railroads and utilities; the siphoning off of the coal cars of western lines by eastern roads— had reappeared, and they persisted into early summer 1923.

Panicky accounts of dangerous coal shortages inundated FFD. The Denver Gas & Electric Company in October possessed coal sufficient for seven days of operation, and its supplier received only one-third the cars required. In Oklahoma, the Missouri Pacific Railroad complained of thousands of cars lost to the Wabash and other eastern lines, and the Denver and Rio Grande Western road accused the Missouri Pacific of hoarding cars. While reports indicated that coal car loadings for the last quarter of 1922 fell some one million cars lower than in the same period of 1921, FFD and ICC merely lectured the car service division of the American Railway Association (ARA) about the need for equitable car distribution. ARA promised to investigate the situation and to improve its performance in 1923.

Far to the north, the state fuel administrators of Minnesota, Wisconsin, and the two Dakotas agonized over a coal supply that was but 25 percent of normal. To the east, the Rhode Island fuel administrator, describing terrible anthracite shortages and wildly escalating prices, warned of the danger of epidemic unless fuel arrived quickly. In Newark, New Jersey, long queues of men, women, and children with pails and bags waited for hours in the bitter cold to purchase a bushel of coal for which they paid at a rate exceeding $20 per ton. In New York City, the public health commissioner documented a deadly increase in influenza and pneumonia cases during December 1922–February 1923 and declared the public health imperiled.[35]

All of these problems were interrelated and impervious to resolution by reshuffling coal cars or by SOs that applied to specific carriers and to specific demands, as did all the SOs issued between November 1922 and February 1923. The FFD and ICC, however, operating in a vacuum, incapable of matching regional productive capacity with regional coal consumption, and loath to coerce producers, carriers, or distributors treated each problem discretely. The fuel needs of New England were ignored while the Great Lakes remained open. But the withdrawal in December of orders compelling shipments to Lake Erie, the lack of railroad equipment along north-south lines, the congestion resulting from the steady diversion of rolling stock eastward, the refusal of upper Ohio River valley operators voluntarily to reroute shipments northward, and the opposition of lake coal distributors to all-rail shipments from Indiana and Illinois into the upper lakes combined to leave the upper Great Lakes states dangerously undersupplied. In early December, with lake navigation terminated for the season, the upper lake states had received only 25 percent of the anthracite allocated to them. The fuel administrators of Minnesota, Wisconsin, and the Dakotas appealed to FFD for an ICC order directing the anthracite carriers to send them 250 cars daily; ICC, however, turned the whole problem over to the Pennsylvania Fuel Commission, which advised the stricken states to burn bituminous.[36]

When the ports along Lake Erie closed for the winter, attention shifted to New England. FFD advised ICC to apply emergency measures to the northeastern quadrant, but ICC elected to meet the emergency through voluntary cooperation with the ARA and its carrier members rather than through the issuance of Service Orders.[37] Although the ICC possessed adequate statutory authority to compel shipments from Pennsylvania to New England and other eastern states, the commission clung to the belief that the anthracite mine-owning railroads would act in the public interest. Abundant evidence to the contrary proved no catalyst of federal action.

In fact, the state of Pennsylvania wielded more power over anthracite than the federal agencies.[38] Pennsylvania's fuel commission established national anthracite quotas (embargoing shipments west of the Missouri and south of the Ohio) and fixed anthracite prices at the mine. But even with those extensive powers, the Pennsylvania commission could not enforce its directives upon those anthracite-carrying railroads that engaged in interstate commerce. Only the ICC could compel the adherence of the anthracite lines to shipment priorities assigned by the Pennsylvania commission, and ICC consistently refused to do so. ICC shrewdly acted as if the Pennsylvania commission could act unilaterally and deflected criticism and demands toward the state unit. But the railroads protected their own self interests, shipping coal to markets where the highest prices prevailed, regardless of quotas.

In February, snow and subfreezing temperatures in New York, Pennsylvania, and New England led to the seizure of coal in transit by local officials who then distributed it among local residents. Boston appropriated $250,000 to purchase coal for distribution among its neediest citizens. New England's fuel administrators accumulated convincing evidence that anthracite exports to foreign countries, particularly Canada, exacerbated the supply problems of the entire region. However, the ICC, in February, denied the need for an export embargo and thereby won the applause of the NCA and the General Policies Committee of the Anthracite Operators. The latter group congratulated itself for achieving an unsurpassed record of self-restraint and moderation in meeting the fuel emergency.[39]

Only the merry breezes of spring brought relief to a thoroughly chilled nation, but no assurances that similar shocks would be avoided in the future. A thankful FFD and ICC withdrew from the coal management business, having successfully ignored the lessons of earlier crises, abstained from virtually all coercive acts, and naively relied upon the willingness of operators, carriers, and distributors to treat fairly one another and the general consuming public, thereby nullifying the intent of the emergency fuel act. Meanwhile, the U.S. Coal Commission amassed evidence that the coal industry impinged mightily upon the public interest, a fact hardly needing emphasis to those who suffered through the winter of 1922–23 short of coal. But a public consciousness more explicit and more systematic about the matter was emerging. For instance, the editors of *Electrical World*, characterizing the coal industry as a public menace, joined President John W. Lieb of New York's Consolidated Edison Company in demanding the regulation of coal.[40]

Results of the U.S. Coal Commission Probe

The coal commission completed a penetrating investigation of all phases of the coal industry within its appointed time. The work of the commission has been judged a failure by Ellis Hawley and a fiasco by James Johnson.[41] Hardly a fiasco, the total effort cannot, however, be construed as a success. It should not be rejected as a total failure simply because it affected no immediate change in the coal industry. The commission's conclusions and recommendations, frequently contradictory, irritatingly ambiguous, and overcautious to a fault, rested on a solid factual foundation that was readily accessible to Congress and that provided ample substantive support for the reformation of the industry. The coal commission should not be held responsible for congressional inaction or the absence of executive leadership.

As the commission's staff accumulated and analyzed its data, preliminary reports were submitted to Congress.[42] For the next decade and more, congressional and executive studies of the industry utilized the commission report as the basic reference. In terms of factual presentation, the separate reports and the final report cannot be faulted. Whatever one wished to know about coal had received exhaustive treatment. But the commission's recommendations were incongruous with their facts and the general conclusions derived from the data. The commission declared that public health and safety depended upon an unfailing supply of coal, thus attributing to the industry a significance equal to the railroads and utilities. Since the industrial might of the nation rested on bituminous, as did the health, comfort, and convenience of innumerable citizens, the coal industry ought to be subject to public control. The experience of the current coal crisis as well as earlier periods of scarcity, high prices, and failed distribution systems provided ample justification for these conclusions.

But these portentous words prefaced recommendations so timerous and innocuous that they almost failed to provoke a caustic comment from organs of the coal industry. While the commission hinted that coal ought to be regulated like the railroads, utilities, and interstate pipelines, in concrete terms it recommended a vague form of licensing of producers shipping in interstate commerce and the lodging of fact-finding authority with the ICC, which presumably would subject the industry to the glare of publicity. After expending hundreds of pages to portray the individualistic coal industry as an anachronism in modern America, the commission in essence placed its ultimate hopes for improvement in voluntary reform and internal policing by the industry itself.

How had the commission arrived at such a useless position? It denied the competence of the federal government to regulate the coal industry. Having adopted that premise, albeit in blatant disregard of their own description of the energetic and successful management of fuels by the federal government during World War I, only one recommendation could logically emerge: do nothing and hope for the best, a nostrum dear to Herbert Hoover, coal industry associations, and other business interests.[43]

Although Congress delayed publication of the coal commission's final report until 1925, its findings attracted some media attention when they were made public in 1923, and they were widely referred to as serious coal strikes erupted between 1924 and 1927.[44] The United Mine Workers suffered shattering defeats between 1924 and 1927, by which time the union wage scale and the union itself had disappeared from many previously organized producing districts. This unremitting chaos in the coal industry repeatedly caused hardship in many regions of the country, particularly in 1925–26, when the anthracite miners walked out.[45]

Despite the insistence of the coal industry that it suffered from no problems and was unaffected with a public interest, and therefore required no federal attention, legislators introduced dozens of bills into Congress. In 1925–26, Congress registered at least fifty bills that focused on the coal industry, some calling for full nationalization of the mines and many empowering the president to seize and operate the mines in the event of an emergency (an authority sought by both Harding and Coolidge). Other bills sought to extend the regulatory power of ICC or FTC, or to create a new agency. Still other bills isolated the anthracite industry for regulatory attention.

None of these bills survived the legislative grinder. Not even the lengthy strike of 1927 forced Congress to act. While many of the bills enjoyed the strong support of various consumer interests (mostly localized in the northeastern states) and their representatives (both Republicans and Democrats), the hearings of 1926, as a typical example, were dominated by the antiregulatory forces of coal and its allies, particularly the railroads. The coal industry, in addition to painting a rosy picture of its present condition and prospects for the future, a depiction utterly at odds with the findings of the coal commission or with the facts of 1925–27, asserted that ICC already possessed sufficient authority to deal with temporary periods of emergency. Many congressmen agreed with this view of ICC authority, perhaps forgetful or ignorant of ICC's inept employment of its powers in 1922–23. Only a handful of congressmen expressed an interest in full-scale reform of the industry.[46]

The League for Industrial Democracy, Norman Thomas, and others campaigned for nationalization of the industry, the creation of a cabinet-level department of mines, and the linking of coal with giant power, that is, stabilizing coal production through the construction of an interregional power system that would "electrify" America; the latter was a favorite panacea of Gifford Pinchot, Senator Borah, Herbert Croly, and others.

On the other hand, one bill that would have merely created an anthracite division within ICC was denounced by the New York Chamber of Commerce as socialistic, the most dangerous bill ever introduced in Congress. For those between the extremes, a common ground for action failed to evolve. Herbert Hoover's faith in associationism, emphasizing the cooperation of the federal government with the disciplined and self-restrained individuals and corporate units comprising the coal industry, best captures the attitudes of most congressmen.[47]

Hoover and individual congressmen recognized the severe problems afflicting the coal industry, foremost among them overcapacity, the inexorable effect of competitive fuels, and the consequences of this on wage rates and labor-management relations. However, while sensitive to the dangers of piecemeal reforms that could aggravate rather than remedy ills, they were unwilling to consider comprehensive changes affecting the entire industry. From this perspective, one shared by the U.S. Coal Commission, trust in the willingness and ability of the coal industry to reform itself seemed the wisest course. Not even the frightening dislocation of national depression sufficed to overcome this inertial drift.

Conclusion

Several reasons can be suggested to explain the ambivalent, inconsistent, and partial responses of the federal government to the severe coal crises of 1919–20 and 1922–23. For some, ideological beliefs precluded the application of World War I strategies to peacetime problems. Still, Congress did grant ICC broad powers over price and distribution; but in both crises, ICC interpreted its mandate as narrowly as possible, confining its efforts to the Parcheesi-like movement of rolling stock and coal from one point to another. Apparently, the commission never considered seriously the use of its control over car distribution or the authority it possessed under the emergency coal act of 1922 to apply embargoes against shippers or carriers, to deter further price increases, or to prevent shippers or carriers from discriminating against certain classes of users. ICC erroneously believed that the railroads could manage coal distribution if only shown the proper path by the government, and naively assumed that coal dealers would voluntarily exercise restraint in advancing prices. ICC and the office of Federal Fuel Distributor also relied too heavily on the action of individual states to stem the upward price trend.

The threat of federal intervention aroused the immediate hostility of the organized coal industry. Although the coal industry suffered from debilitating internal divisions, a condition exacerbated by coal's deteriorating competitive position relative to other fuels, the industry managed to ward off repeated efforts to impose on it a regulatory regimen. The coal commission's warning against tampering with the coal industry aided coal in its defense. Somewhat ironic was an article in *Cushing's Survey* in 1923 that responded to a flurry of coal regulation bills by counseling the industry to rest its case on the recommendations of the U.S. Coal Commission.[48]

For its part, Congress proved incapable of generating a consensus on solutions to coal's malaise, unaided as it was by executive leadership. While the NCA and other coal associations invariably opposed coal legislation as destructive to the free market economy, congressional inaction might best be attributed to the chronic inability of Congress to produce policy in the absence of presidential direction and to the relatively short-lived nature of particular crises, none of which was caused by the lack of resources in the ground.

SIX

Federal Responses to the Energy
Transition of the 1920s

WRITING IN THE JULY 1921 issue of *The Central Station*, Chester A.
Gauss suggested a variety of sales tactics to convince people to purchase electric appliances they did not want. One sure-fire approach
depicted a salesman, electric vacuum in hand, cornering the man of
the house and asking, "Do you love your wife? If you really do, help
her by eliminating the drudgery of old fashioned ways of doing house-
work." All the while, the sales specialist casually sprinkled his cigar
ashes over the new carpet, ground them into the nap with his heels,
and then magically sucked the dirt into the vacuum. The enterprising
salesperson might also carry a jar of fine coal dust to use along with
the cigar ashes, and could perhaps sell an electric range as well—all
on the installment plan.[1] Countless reenactments of this readily im-
aginable scene, featuring perhaps an oil stove salesperson or an engineer demonstrating a new gas-burning process-heat furnace, hurried
along the energy transition that reshaped American life during the
interwar years.

The Energy Transition of the Interwar Years

This energy transition did not occur in a moment, any more than
had the earlier gradual and never complete substitution of coal and
steam power for wood, animal power, and water power. This later
transition originated even before the turn of the century, as attested
to by the commercialization of electricity and the advent of the internal combustion engine; it continued into the post–World War II years.

THE JOBBER'S NIGHTMARE

FIG. 4. *Unfortunately for future generations, the jobber's nightmare never came true.*

Source: *National Petroleum News*, 19 (6 April 1927), 73.

The so-called "age" of electricity and "age" of petroleum, which seemed to characterize the 1920s and the 1930s despite the lingering depression, emerged from an accommodating culture long accustomed to and desirous of rather rapid change. Neither the quotidian lifestyles and values of Americans nor the institutional networks of the growing nation proved obstructive to the advance of technological innovation or to the social and economic changes accompanying the new mechanics.

By the 1920s, two innovations in particular reflected the dynamic quality of American inventiveness and wrought exciting and lasting changes in American society. The automobile assumed a permanent place in the landscape (and cityscape) during the 1920s, while as many Americans as could hooked up to electricity. In purchasing cars, trucks, and tractors, adding convenience outlets, and placing electric motors in shops and factories, Americans rearranged the shape of metropolitan America, hastened the decentralization of the industry and residential areas, created such new industries as electric appliances and equipment, rubber tires, and gasoline service stations, and greatly increased agricultural productivity.[2] These transformations impelled significant alterations in the use of energy and in the fuel-mix that produced the energy.

Energy consumption in the United States increased two-and-one-half times between 1900 and 1930, and then rose minimally during the depression. Coal contributed 75 percent of all energy in 1905–10, its historic peak, declined to under 60 percent in 1930, and fell to under 50 percent by 1940.[3] Tables 4 and 11 show an essentially stable bituminous and declining anthracite production (excepting during the strike years) for the 1920s. Crude oil production pushed above the billion barrel mark just prior to the depression while natural gas output more than doubled during the 1920s, and except for 1931–33 rose steadily even during the hard times.

Coal's central problem, however identified with overcapacity, anarchical labor-management relations, inadequate transportation, and so on, boiled down to a shrinking proportion of the market as consumers displayed their preference for cleaner, more efficient, more dependable, and more convenient fuels. While the coal operators of the North and South engaged in brutal competition, the drummers of other sources of energy penetrated the traditional domains of coal with remarkable success. Even those sectors that continued to rely heavily on coal, such as the electric utilities, dramatically improved the energy output of a ton of coal. In 1920, 3 pounds of coal produced one kilowatt-hour; in 1930, only 1.5 pounds were required. In the railroad industry, electrification further reduced coal requirements; and in still other industries, including the utilities, improved furnaces permitted the substitution of fuel oil for coal. As a result, while kilowatt-hour generation in the nation doubled between 1920 and 1930, coal consumption by utilities increased by only 19 percent (see Table 3).

Bad news for coalmen poured in concerning industrial markets for coal. The rapid electrification of manufacturing, particularly chemicals and steel, reduced coal consumption significantly. By 1926, every steel foundry in the Chicago area was equipped with one or more electric furnaces. Commonwealth Edison of Chicago also announced the connection to company lines of many hotels, office buildings, bakeries, industrial kitchens, and other commercial establishments,

143

TABLE 11. *Annual Production of Fuels 1926–1950*

	Bituminous coal (million tons)	Anthracite coal (million tons)	Crude oil (million barrels)	Natural gas (billion cubic feet)
1926	573	84	771	1,336
1927	518	80	901	1,471
1928	501	75	901	1,596
1929	535	74	1,007	1,952
1930	468	69	898	1,979
1931	382	60	851	1,722
1932	310	50	785	1,594
1933	334	50	906	1,597
1934	359	57	908	1,816
1935	372	52	997	1,969
1936	439	55	1,100	2,225
1937	446	52	1,279	2,473
1938	349	46	1,214	2,358
1939	395	51	1,265	2,538
1940	461	51	1,353	2,734
1941	514	56	1,402	2,894
1942	583	60	1,387	3,146
1943	590	61	1,506	3,516
1944	620	64	1,678	3,815
1945	578	55	1,714	4,042
1946	534	61	1,744	4,153
1947	631	57	1,857	4,582
1948	600	57	2,020	5,148
1949	438	43	1,842	5,420
1950	516	44	1,974	6,282

Source: U.S. Bureau of the Census, *Historical Statistics of the United States, Colonial Times to 1957* (Washington, D.C.: GPO, 1960), 356, 359–61.

many of which previously burned coal. The coal industry took some comfort in the knowledge that heating an eight-room house electrically cost twice as much as heating with a good coal furnace, but this did little to soften the bad news on the industrial and commercial fronts.

The industry was also very concerned about residential uses of natural gas and fuel oil, and quite sensitive to claims for their superiority in American homes. Coal dealers in Kansas City and Chicago, for example, organized booths at business fairs to demonstrate the efficiency of coal-burning furnaces and stoves. And *The Retail Coalman* even responded vituperatively to the "propaganda" of competitiors by reporting deaths attributed to exploding gas and oil equipment. But gas and fuel oil inroads in the domestic market could not be stayed. Between 1924 and 1930, those fuels combined to replace, for home use, an estimated 17 million tons of coal per year.

Transportation of natural gas was limited by the pipeline technology of the late 1920s to distances of 300 miles or so; therefore, dramatically expanded domestic, commercial, and industrial use had to await the technological improvements of the 1930s. In the meantime, however, in certain areas of the nation, the regional availability of natural gas allowed the utilities to substitute that fuel for coal. As a result, utility consumption of natural gas rose from 22 billion cubic feet in 1920, or 2.7 percent of total natural gas use, to 120 billion cubic feet in 1930, or 6 percent of the total.[4]

The sensational growth of the auto industry contributed to coal's problems. As the number of registered motor vehicles rose from 10.4 million in 1921 to 26.7 million in 1930, vast quantities of gasoline were required. Gasoline consumption rose more than fourfold between 1919 and 1929, triggering the rise in crude oil production displayed in Tables 4 and 11. As new refining processes quickly increased the quantity of gasoline removed from each barrel of crude oil, there remained a great and steadily augmenting volume of fuel oil to dispose of. The 250 million barrels of fuel oil produced in 1919 doubled by 1929, prompting a concerted campaign by oil refineries to sell fuel oil to domestic and industrial consumers.

On the domestic front, trends in housing construction favored the promoters of fuel-oil use. In 1921, 75 percent of all dwellings constructed were one- or two-family buildings; by 1929, multifamily residences composed 49 percent of all new construction. Many of these were located in cities and employed fuel-oil furnaces rather than coal-burning equipment. In 1923, a report of the Massachusetts Fuel Commission noted the inroads of fuel oil into the markets of New England and attributed the trend to the uncertainties of coal supply, the cheapness of Mexican oil, and the many conveniences of fuel oil.[5]

The exigencies of intraindustry competition and recurrent strikes blinded coal operators to the long-term implications of fuel substitution. Many coal experts in government recognized the danger signs much earlier than leaders in the industry but could not transform their knowledge into effective policy. Some, in both government and industry, saw the electric power industry as the ultimate savior of coal, perceiving central station generation, especially at mine-mouth, as the most efficient way to use coal.[6] But the federal government, essentially ignorant of the striking changes in the electric power industry during the 1920s, assumed only a minor role in this energy transition. Only toward the end of the decade did the federal government cast its glance at the power industry and the position it had established in the national economy.

The energy utilities avoided federal regulation during the 1920s and circumvented the regulatory efforts of many state utility commissions. The coal industry, although ever in the public eye, escaped reform and regulation because of the depth and complexity of its problems and because of its consistent and well-orchestrated opposition to even minimal federal intervention. Of the major producers of energy, only the petroleum industry was forced to cope with concrete expressions of federal concern in its affairs, arising from apprehension about the sufficiency of the nation's oil reserves and the persistent opposition of antitrusters to the alleged monopolistic position of the major firms. While the industry managed to deflect the thrusts of the antitrusters, it did come under the scrutiny of the Federal Oil Conservation Board, created by President Coolidge in 1924; this was the chief reflection of federal concern about oil supply.

The Oil Paradox: Too Little and Too Much

At a conference held in 1927 between officials of the Federal Trade Commission and the American Petroleum Institute (API), R. L. Welch, general secretary and counsel of API, asserted that the internal combustion engine "produced a new oil industry." With the exception of the business organization of the oil industry, Welch claimed, "everything that lies behind the advent of the automobile is relatively as unimportant in the oil situation as would be a consideration of the harness industry prior to the advent of the automobile."[7] Welch exaggerated but slightly. American crude oil production doubled between 1914 and 1922, with 47 percent of the increase occurring during the three years 1920–22. Then, during the succeeding seven years, crude production rose by another 81 percent (see Tables 4 and 11), while gasoline output expanded by almost 200 percent. However, beginning as early as 1915, domestic crude consumption exceeded domestic crude production by a steadily widening margin, amounting to 9 million barrels in 1915, 57 million in 1918, and peaking at 78 million barrels in 1920. During the four years 1921–24, the supply-consumption gap averaged 29 million barrels annually. While the importation of Mexican crude closed the gap, the failure of domestic production to meet internal demand aroused intense concern among many involved in the industry.[8]

In January 1917, one oil magazine writer detected dark clouds in the future of oil as demand advanced faster than production. Six months later a U.S. Geological Survey memorandum estimated proven recoverable reserves at 6 billion barrels. During the next few years, the best assessments of probable and proven reserves ranged between 6 and 9 billion barrels (Table 12). Van H. Manning, director of the Bureau of Mines (BM), warned the Council of National Defense in early 1919 that the undersupply of oil would require drastic measures, including perhaps direct governmental intervention to assure increased production and equitable allocation. One year later, J. C. Lewis, chief petroleum technologist at BM, informed the Independent Oil Men's Association that "we cannot rely upon our own Crude Production to meet the Ever Increasing Demand for Petroleum Products." With consumption approaching 600 million barrels in 1920–21, Lewis calculated reserves for fewer than twenty years. Another BM official, F. G. Cottrell, asked in 1920, "Where is the fuel supply of increasing numbers of motor vehicles to come from?" Not from new discoveries, answered Joseph E. Pogue, noted petroleum economist, pointing out that for ten years new discoveries had not replaced withdrawals. In 1922, J. E. O'Neal, president of Prairie Oil and Gas Company, foresaw shortages within ten years unless abundant new sources were discovered.[9]

Federal officials and a few individuals from the oil industry feared both short-run scarcities and long-term depletion of reserves. They viewed the decline in production of Oklahoma's Cushing and Healdton fields as the harbinger of a future in which America lost its self-sufficiency in oil. Cushing, for instance, produced 49 million barrels in 1915, only two years after its discovery; by 1920, its production had fallen to 11.6 million barrels, a decline hastened by wasteful and negligent production methods which, if persisted in, threatened all fields during their flush stages. Pogue, Cottrell, and others concerned about the longevity of domestic reserves recognized that the steady depletion of reserves did not preclude periodic gluts of oil, as production at any given time could exceed domestic consumption. Short-term oversupply could occur as a result of improved recovery techniques, because of new refining technologies, and, most disturbingly, by the continued application of the rule of capture to both old and new fields.[10] Since the driller with the most operating wells re-

TABLE 12. *U.S. Petroleum Reserves and Estimated Duration, 1918–1938*

	API reserve estimate (million bbls.)	Duration of reserve at current annual rate of production (years)
1918	6,200	17
1919	6,700	17
1920	7,200	16
1921	7,800	16
1922	7,600	13
1923	7,600	10
1924	7,500	10
1925	8,500	11
1926	8,800	11
1927	10,500	11
1928	11,000	12
1929	13,200	13
1930	13,600	15
1934	13,250	14
1938	15,800	12

Sources: Henrietta M. Larson and Kenneth W. Porter, *History of Humble Oil and Refining Company: A Study in Industrial Growth* (New York: Harper & Bros., 1959), 695, for API estimates, 1918–30; for 1934, Stanley Gill, *A Report on the Petroleum Industry of the United States, Prepared for Presentation to the Sub-Committee on Petroleum Investigation of the Committee on Interstate and Foreign Commerce, House of Representatives, 73rd Congress* (n.p., 1934), 43; National Resources Committee, *Energy Resources and National Policy* (Washington, D.C.: GPO, 1939), 291–92.

covered the most oil, it behooved all drillers to pump as much and as swiftly as possible, disdainful of demand and without regard to maintaining sufficient gas pressure in the field to permit the recovery of a maximum amount of oil. The presumed diminution of domestic reserves and wasteful recovery practices coupled with attendant periods of glut, fluctuating prices, and questionable end-uses of refined products constituted the most critical issues within the oil industry during the first half of the 1920s.

Federal officials in the Wilson, Harding, and Coolidge administrations accepted the shortage thesis and discussed, designed, and advocated programs and policies to protect the national security by means of conservation and to assure access to both domestic and foreign crude. But the shortage thesis provoked vigorous rebuttal from the oil industry. Thomas A. O'Donnell, a former USFA official and president of API in 1922, castigated as dangerous and misinformed those presumed experts who harped on the near-future exhaustion of oil. Walter C. Teagle, president of Standard Oil of New Jersey, Frank Haskell, Tidal Oil Company president, the Pews of Sun Oil, and others who agreed with O'Donnell pointed to the new drilling and new finds of the early 1920s, particularly in California, as proof that abundant crude was immediately available and readily discoverable. API's position was best reflected in its famous report of 1925, which sought to allay all fears of threatened oil scarcity by denying that great waste attended oil production and by asserting that the nation possessed one billion acres of potential oil-bearing land, sufficient to last for decades. Dozens of state geologists quickly challenged API's happy picture, labeling the estimates reckless. Individuals within and without the industry attributed API's conclusions to the fear of federal regulation. If API could demonstrate the falsity of the shortage thesis and the nonexistence of waste, then, as Earl Oliver, Oklahoma oilman and API member, reasoned, the danger of federal intervention would dissipate and the wisdom of a laissez-faire philosophy emerge triumphant.

Critics of the position officially adopted by the API in 1925 argued that present rates of production created a false image of great abundance when in fact oil was of limited supply and irreplaceable. They further accused API and earlier proponents of the unlimited-supply thesis of narrowly measuring waste against short-run business profits. If profits were the standard of measurement, then indeed waste seemed quite negligible; but the apparent profitability of the oil industry masked appalling long-run social waste both in rule of capture production tactics and in the profligate and inefficient end-use of petroleum. Pogue, for one, feared near-future gasoline shortages as a result of technological inadequacies in gasoline production, the remarkable popularity of the automobile, and the indifference of automobile manufacturers to the development of efficient (high mileage per gallon) engines. Others worried that future eastern demand for fuel oil would exceed the supply of domestic fuel oil plus Mexican imports.[11]

What to do engendered even more divisiveness than defining the problem. One strategy that evolved directly from awareness of the essentiality of oil during World War I encouraged the active participation of American oil companies in the exploitation of foreign fields.

Mark Requa, Pogue, and others considered the exploitation of overseas oil fields by Americans a partial solution to the supply problem and consistent with a view of national security that counseled the use of cheap and accessible foreign oil while conserving the domestic reserve. The problem was accessibility. While American oil firms gained strong footholds in Mexico, Columbia, and Venezuela, less success attended federal efforts to apply a version of the old Open Door policy to such areas as the Middle East and the Dutch East Indies, regions within the spheres of influence of western European nations. Americans believed, and rightly so, that while this nation allowed foreign oil interests such as Royal Dutch Shell to operate in the United States, Great Britain and the Netherlands conspired to deny or retard American exploitation of oil fields in the Near East and in the Pacific. The departments of the Interior and Navy accused Britain of seeking to control the world's petroleum industry (this at a time, 1921–23, when America produced 83 percent of the world production) and of employing unfair methods in denying to American nationals the same concessions in British producing fields that British nationals enjoyed in American producing fields.

Requa and the Wilson administration assumed that government-industry cooperation, in the form of a public-private U.S. Oil Corporation, could gain American entry to overseas fields. The industry unanimously rejected such a partnership as destructive of private initiative and portending comprehensive federal control and regulation. The major companies preferred the use of American diplomatic muscle to force an opening, and this indeed was the strategy pursued, although with indifferent results. During the 1920s, the U.S. failed to gain any influence in either Middle Eastern or East Indian oil fields through the use of formal diplomacy. Through sheer persistence, a group of ten U.S. firms, led by Standard of New Jersey, did win some concessions from the powerful Anglo-Persian Oil Company.[12] Complicating the issue was the emergence of strong opposition from independent domestic producers to expanded crude oil imports. The independents' demand for an oil import tariff, opposed by both Harding and Coolidge as incompatible with the interests of national security, persisted into the depression years and beyond. Overshadowing the issue of American overseas oil production were the dual issues of waste in oil recovery and the regulation of domestic oil production, both of which darkly promised an enhanced government role in the oil industry.

Most Americans during the 1920s were either ignorant of or indifferent to the unbelievably large waste of energy resources in the field, in processing, and in end-use. The API report of 1925 to the contrary notwithstanding, studies of engineers, scientists, and government officials offered to those interested abundant and accumulating evidence of waste. Indeed, as Erich Zimmerman notes, the incidence of waste in oil and natural gas production captured the attention of professionals much sooner than it did individuals in the oil industry (or coal and electric power). Factory boilers wasted about one-half the heat value of the fuel used to raise steam while another one-half of the energy used to propel a coal-burning locomotive went up the stack in smoke. A session on fuels at the American Society of Mechanical Engineers in 1920 catalogued the causes of notorious waste in fuel use and called for a policy of conservation. Experts in natural gas estimated a waste of over 80 percent of the caloric value of pumped natural gas because of production, transmission, and use inefficiencies. Investigations in the Texas, Oklahoma, and Kansas oil fields at various times documented a ruthless waste of natural gas, amounting to the flaring and other dissipation of hundreds of billions of cubic feet during the recovery of oil. As the engineers knew, the presence of natural gas pressure in the pool determined the rate of recovery. Too rapid a rate of oil withdrawal or the uncontrolled escape of the natural gas from the well meant that much oil remained in the ground, unrecoverable by existing technologies.[13] Again, the question was: How can efficiency be improved and waste eliminated?

While many oilmen publicly denied that great waste attended oil production, the general consensus admitted wastefulness and attributed it to competitive conditions, which retarded the application of new production methods and technologies. In the 1920s, the states were responsible for the controls that did exist. Several states, even prior to World War I, passed laws to regulate drilling and other natural gas and oil production operations. Oklahoma functioned under the most comprehensive oil conservation regulations. In 1907, the state delegated authority to the Oklahoma Corporation Commission (OCC) to eliminate waste and stabilize production. In 1913 and 1915, OCC applied prorationing to the Healdton and Cushing fields and even established minimum prices in a futile effort to control the great production of those flush fields. (Prorationing is the sharing of total allowable daily flow in a field among the wells of the field.) Enormous waste accompanied the Healdton and Cushing finds as many producers without storage facilities and unconnected to storage facilities by pipelines simply allowed their excess production to flow away on the ground.[14] A Common Purchases Act passed in 1909 and requiring each pipeline to take a fair share (a ratable taking) of the oil produced in its immediate vicinity proved to be impotent in the face of such unmarketable surpluses of oil.

These events led to the passage in 1915 of a new conservation statute in Oklahoma, which served as a model for other states and which embodied three crucial definitions. First, included in the definition of waste the OCC was authorized to eliminate or control were physical waste resulting from production exceeding storage capacity or transportation facilities, subsurface waste that depleted reservoir pressure, and economic waste resulting when production surpassed market demand. The failure of other states, Texas as an example, to authorize regulatory commissions to control economic waste severely obstructed efforts to regulate production during the late 1920s and the 1930s. Second, production limitations could be applied if full (maximum) production in any given field caused waste. Thus, pumping the maximum volume daily could be curbed if it so reduced reservoir pressure as to result in unrecoverable oil. Third, the statute defined prorationing as the volume of oil OCC permitted to be withdrawn from a pool. That volume was expressed as a percentage of the pool's maximum production; the specified percentage determined the allowable production for each of the pool's wells.

Texas in the 1920s and Kansas in 1931, passed state-wide oil and gas conservation measures. But neither Oklahoma nor Texas seriously enforced their laws until after 1926, when a series of enormously productive oil fields were discovered. Political opposition, especially by the smaller producers, and the decisions of federal courts during the 1930s stymied conservation efforts in Texas. In short, the regulatory efforts of these states failed to modify the rule of capture or to compel the application of the best technology and scientific knowledge to the exploitation of particular pools.[15]

Calls for federal action were prompted by the commingling of incontrovertible evidence of waste in oil and gas production with gloomy forecasts of shrinking national oil reserves and with price instability accompanying sudden deficiencies of crude and refined oil or sudden short-term surpluses. (Short-term surpluses, measured in months, did not signal a plethora of oil reserves but rather that production and demand were out of sync.) These calls for federal action in turn quickly triggered adamant denials from industry spokespersons: There was no need for and the Constitution prohibited *any* federal intervention. As the shortage thesis gained currency in 1920 and as the FTC pursued an investigation (ordered by the House of Representatives) into the sudden rise in the prices of refined products, Walter C. Teagle, president of Jersey Standard, asked rhetorically, "Is there any justification . . . for believing that there is in Government operation any of those qualities necessary for the development of great business with boldness, initiative, and efficiency?" To Teagle and many within the API and other industry groups, conditions failed to justify federal attention, particularly by the FTC; according to R. L. Welch, API's general secretary, the FTC, by directing its efforts "toward 'getting' somebody . . . has harassed and not helped business." Welch vividly recalled the Randall Resolution (H.R. 175) of 1916, which, if it had passed, would have ordered the secretary of the Interior to study the expediency of government ownership and operation of oil-bearing properties and refineries.[16]

The Randall thrust, reflecting a deep and long-lived suspicion of the major firms, periodically resurfaced in Congress following World War I, fed by both ancient antagonisms and such contemporary excitements as the Teapot Dome scandal. Congress focused its attention, then, on monopoly in the petroleum industry: the organization, financing, and concentration of power in the hands of the majors; and the presumably deleterious affects of such power on the public. As critics of these probes pointed out, such investigations reflected the continuation of concern with monopoly that had led to the antitrust suit against the Standard Oil combine and its ultimate dissolution. Now, the critics asserted, too much rather than too little competition plagued the industry. George Stocking described the congressional predilection with monopoly as demonstrative of "ignorance of the real problems involved" and productive of much more harm than good. Stocking and others wished the target shifted to the increasing instability of the industry and the actual extent of domestic reserves, and to such remedies as conservation and production controls.[17]

Congress, however, persisted in its scrutiny of the internal workings of the oil industry, the methods by which prices were established, the influence of the Standard Oil group, and the performance of the pipelines as common carriers. Congressional hearings and FTC inquiries spawned an enormous quantity of detail on the petroleum industry as it had evolved since the dissolution of Standard Oil in 1912; but neither Congress nor the executive was prepared to sponsor comprehensive regulation, even though some of the inquiries reflected hostility toward the industry and apprehension over the concentration of economic power lodged in the hands of the major companies. Some of these conclusions are treated in the following chapter, which analyzes the politics of the fuel industries. For now, the point to be made is that for the most part Congress concerned itself with problems that many within and without the industry considered irrelevant to the needs of the modern industry and of the nation. Of course, within the industry itself, the dominant mood deplored all federal attention, but it could not be wholly evaded.[18]

Congress and the executive did bestow favors upon the oil industry in the form of an oil depletion allowance and the opening of the public domain to exploratory ventures under certain conditions. In 1913, Congress passed the "notorious" (as Davis terms it) depletion allowance as part of the federal income tax law. Although the allowance engendered bitter debate in the 1950s and 1960s, this incentive aroused no controversy in 1913. Later amendments in 1916, 1918, 1921, 1924, and 1926, which changed the method of calculation from a deduction from income tax to a percentage depletion allowance, raised few eyebrows among the industry's antagonists. Its purpose was to stimulate exploration, and the tax break recognized that the financial losses incurred in dry holes must be compensated for in the successful wells.[19]

Fears of oil shortage permitted the continuation of the depletion allowance after the war and hastened passage of the Mineral Leasing Act of 1920, which opened to exploitation and development a vast acreage on the public domain which had earlier been withdrawn from private use. (Unsuccessful efforts in 1911, 1914, and 1918 to amend the Land Withdrawal Act of 1910 preceded passage of the act of 1920.) More controversial than the depletion act, the opening up of oil-bearing public lands to private ventures failed to arouse much interest outside the oil industry. The real furor broke out with the revelation of corruption, involving congressmen and cabinet members, in the awarding of leases in the naval oil reserves, which, prior to the Coolidge administration, were closed to private capital.

When Coolidge called for bids on naval reserve leases, he raised two significant issues: private versus public development to meet naval needs, and rapid development versus controlled development of the public domain. But the Teapot Dome scandal smothered serious discussion of those questions. Independent producers had opposed the leasing of the public oil lands all along, recognizing that only the large companies possessed the investment capital necessary to develop leases. But the independents could offer no arguments against a law that offered hope for increasing the nation's oil reserves. Van H. Manning, BM director, viewed their objections as entirely self-serving. Neither could conservationists muster a solid defensive line against the development wedge led by federal officials and actively supported by the large producing firms. So the new leasing act passed and, aside from the furor aroused by Teapot Dome, slumbered in relative obscurity until the great oil glut of the late 1920s and early 1930s induced President Hoover to politicize the issue of oil development on the public domain. But despite Hoover's renewed interest in it, few considered this aspect of production a central issue.[20]

While independents objected to the new leasing act as more beneficial to the majors and larger producers than to themselves, they assigned far more significance to current transportation inequities and pressed the ICC to enforce the common carrier provisions of national law. Pipeline expansion proceeded rapidly during the 1920s with the mileage of trunk and gathering lines expanding from 43,000 in 1917 to 116,000 in 1931, most of which carried crude to the Gulf Coast or to refineries as far east as Ohio and Buffalo. During the early 1920s, competition within the industry forced oil companies searching for economies in all phases of their operation to expand or build pipelines. Then, following the great oil finds of the late 1920s, increasing volumes of crude compelled the integrated firms to once again increase their carrying capacity. None of this benefited the independents. Some owned gathering lines that linked them directly to a refinery. Most producers, however, owning no lines, sold their crude to such major transporters as Prairie Oil and Gas at whatever price Prairie chose to offer, or they transported their crude by rail to refineries. Mid-Continent refiners, far removed from the large eastern markets, were priced out of those markets as a result of rail freight charges.

All this was soundly documented in testimony before the La Follette committee in 1923 and substantiated by ICC and FTC investigations. Still, the ICC refused to proceed against the minimum tender requirements imposed by the pipelines that made a mockery of the common carrier provisions. The La Follette committee found remarkable the "complete failure to make the pipeline facilities of the country available to the independents engaged in the oil business," a failure corroborated in the FTC report of 1928. In lieu of enforcement of the common carrier principle, independents demanded a reduction of railroad freight rates on petroleum products; and Congress, in 1925, ordered ICC to investigate the entire rail freight rate structure. ICC, however, determined that revisions were unnecessary. This conclusion stemmed less from a consideration of intraindustry competition in various markets and the enormous advantages enjoyed by the pipeline-owning integrated firms than from a hesitancy to initiate rate reforms that required consideration of interindustry competition. Railroads derived some 25 to 30 percent of their freight revenue from coal and 10 to 13 percent from petroleum products. Tinkering with rates would seriously affect railroad operating revenues and intensify and politicize the widening struggle between oil and coal for market superiority. ICC defended the status quo. As a consequence of ICC inertia, the independents and others distrustful of the major integrated firms escalated their campaign for the divorcement of pipelines from the integrated firms. In this particular case, congressional attention to competitive relationships, deemed irrelevant by some, dovetailed smoothly with the contemporary structure of the industry and its historical antecedents.[21]

FOCB: First Stage

The federal government pursued two lines of inquiry relative to the oil industry, one concentrating on internal organization and competitive relationships, the other manifesting concern over the size of the nation's reserves. Only rarely did these paths converge, and even less frequently did these distinct emphases widen to encompass other fuel and energy industries. Congress and the FTC devoted their attention almost exclusively to competitive structures. The Harding and Coolidge administrations, convinced of the essential accuracy of the shortage thesis, sought the means to protect national security by assuring adequate reserves (of an irreplaceable resource) and the achievement of this without impinging upon the private property rights of the industry or disturbing its organizational framework.

Short of defining oil as within the public interest (much as the definition was applied to electric power by the states), which would have infuriated the oil industry, the federal government could either ignore the problem and await the course of events or devise some framework for federal-state-industry cooperation. Despite fond memories of quasi-mythical government-industry cooperation during the Great War, industry for the most part employed the cooperation refrain as a barricade against real government intrusion into their private affairs. Any initiative would have to originate with the federal government and would have to allay industry's fears of federal regulation by confirming industry's right to manage its own household.

When Jersey Standard's Walter Teagle used the word cooperation, he meant intraindustry cooperation and the elimination of such federally imposed obstacles to industry growth as the antitrust laws. W. H. Gray, the independent leader, supported cooperation that would eliminate the unnatural competitive advantages of the major integrated firms. Mark Requa, not wholly trusted by the dominant elements within the API, perceived cooperation as the application of federal production guidelines by the industry to conserve oil and stabilize the industry—all enforced jointly by the industry and the oil-producing states. At the outer edge, and anathema to Teagle and to the Pews of Sun Oil, stood the influential Henry L. Doherty, head of a sizable electric power holding company and of Cities Service, one of the largest integrated firms. Doherty's commitment to conservation by means of production controls—unit management of oil fields and pro-rationing of production—admitted to the possibility of direct federal control if state-industry cooperation failed to materialize, a heretical stance to majors and independents alike and disturbing to most federal officials as well.[22]

President Coolidge accepted the opinions of his closest advisors, including Doherty, that the nation might confront a shortage of domestic oil within a generation. Approving of the principle of federal-industry cooperation, convinced that great waste attended the production of oil, and, perhaps, wishing to prevent further political damage from Teapot Dome, Coolidge, in 1924, established the Federal Oil Conservation Board (FOCB), consisting of the secretaries of Interior (serving as chair), War, Navy, and Commerce. Coolidge instructed the board to formulate methods of safeguarding national security through the conservation of oil. FOCB clearly reflected the president's belief that oil was of national concern and just as clearly reflected Coolidge's distaste for precipitate action or for an enlarged federal role. FOCB was designed as a purely deliberative body that would carefully study the condition of the nation's oil reserve and recommend techniques to prolong its life.[23]

During the next several years, FOCB existed at the center of the debate over conservation policy and the role of the federal government. Its history has been misunderstood. Its career can be divided into two periods: The first, 1924–27, corresponded to the peaking and gradual waning of fears of oil shortage; and the second corresponded with the discovery of new oil fields, a flood of crude into markets, and the onset of national depression. The board's emphases and proposals displayed a precise congruence with the flow of events, but its history has been told as if its first stage never existed.[24]

FOCB recognized two interconnected problems. One stemmed from the gloomy predictions of future oil shortages and rapidly diminishing reserves. What if these speculations were correct? The second confronted the recurrence of periods of short-term overproduction that hastened the process of field depletion. As indicated, overproduction did not imply a great surfeit of oil reserves but indicated that current production practices were unsynchronized with demand. In its early years, FOCB was keenly aware of the constancy of rapid growth in the demand for petroleum products and aware that national requirements must strike a balance between the rising demand and future reserves. To FOCB, overproduction represented a temporary problem, a phase of the larger problem. Industry, on the other hand, allowed its myopic, if understandable, scramble for short-term profits to blind it to the long-term repercussions of uninhibited production. To cope with shortage and the stretching-out of reserves, FOCB turned to a study of end-use. In adopting this strategy, the board confronted what is clearly the critical question in energy policy: What form of energy should be used to achieve a given work task?

As mentioned, historians of oil and of FOCB have ignored this first stage of FOCB development. Instead, they have evaluated the board on the basis of ideas and proposals fully developed only during its last stage and reflecting the severe oil glut caused by the coming in of the Seminole, Oklahoma City, and East Texas oil fields. By that time, since its first strategy had been dismissed as unachievable, FOCB's options had attenuated and increasing divisiveness characterized the industry. The remainder of this chapter deals largely with FOCB's reasoned but unsuccessful efforts to achieve consensus on efficient end-uses for oil and other fuels. Of course, production controls and price stabilization came within FOCB's purview even during its early career, but they assumed paramountcy in response to events only in the second stage. Chapter 8 covers the second stage.

Though polite and superficially positive, industry response to the formation of FOCB masked grave suspicions of coming danger. API pledged its cooperation, appointed a committee to represent it before the board, and, in 1925, agreed to conduct a nationwide survey of future supply and demand. But API's unanimity had already been fractured by the radical production-control proposals of Doherty, an officer of API but considered by many in the industry a renegade. Neither API nor the independents evinced much interest in conservation. Both camps viewed FOCB as a potential threat, the opening wedge of federal intervention, coming as it did hard on the heels of the La Follette hearings. API strategy, then, was to agree to cooperate with the board and perhaps win some benefits such as modification of the antitrust laws, while simultaneously preparing a case to demmonstrate the nonexistence of problems within the industry. Perhaps FOCB would then go away. For their part, many independents perceived the board as the instrument of the majors and viewed with hostility the imposition of production controls whether by voluntary means or under law.[25]

The president's mandate to FOCB prescribed conservation as the essential mechanism to assure adequate oil supplies. FOCB's program of investigation, conducted through studies by specialists, industry-wide questionnaires, and public hearings rested on three basic propositions: the exhaustibility of crude reserves, the possibility that production controls would be necessary, the wisdom of first attempting to achieve conservation by improving end-use efficiency. While the industry busied itself preparing a case that essentially denied the first proposition and constructing a Maginot Line against the second, the board pursued the third line of inquiry.

Data derived from an impressive number of experts in fuel use, users as well as engineers, convinced the board of the interrelationship of fuels in the production of energy and of the misuse of oil. The relatively low price of oil and its apparent abundance stimulated a variety of uses and keen competition with coal and natural gas. As E. R. Rochester, secretary of FOCB, analyzed the problem: "Oil is being used in homes, by the railroads, in industries, on the high seas, and in a hundred other different ways, whereas coal which we have in inexhaustible abundance might well as satisfactorily be utilized. It is this non-essential use of our national oil supply that represents ... overproduction."[26] FOCB's report of 1926 maintained that oil's current cheapness stimulated waste in the fields and waste through inefficient use. The proper solution to the problem, therefore, was to define efficient uses, a task requiring the formulation of a strategy encompassing all fuels and energy sources, and to promote the substitution of other sources of energy for oil in the performance of certain types of work. In short, FOCB sought to divert the energy transition from its current path to a course deemed more efficient.

FOCB identified the burning of oil as a domestic, industrial, and electrical generating fuel as the least efficient use and the use most susceptible to the substitution of other fuels. The board defined the transformation of oil into gasoline, lubricants, and other petrochemicals as the most efficient use. Somehow, society must be convinced of the economic waste implicit in refining crude into fuel oil that boilers consumed to produce process heat or domestic heat or electricity. But the contemporary availability and use of fuels had evolved, in the main, from choices made in a relatively free market place. FOCB, an agency of two national administrations thoroughly attached to laissez-faire doctrines, suggested that the free market place could not always be trusted to make choices consonant with the public interest. FOCB's theoretical formulation of the problem of resource use manifested a modern and sophisticated understanding of the complexities involved, and invoked considerations with marked affinity to those forced upon the attention of the United States during the 1970s.

Wasteful production and inefficient end-use nurtured one another. The presumed need to withdraw oil at the maximum daily rate and without regard to reservoir pressure or ultimate recovery produced oil so low in price that only inferior uses provided sufficient markets for such vast quantities. The oil companies alone, in 1925, burned 57 million barrels of crude as fuel, that is, without any refining at all—or 7 percent of total crude production. In response to low prices, the market for fuel oil expanded rapidly, more than doubling between 1918 and 1929, thus inducing continued rapid withdrawals from the oil pools and persistent oversupply and low prices. FOCB proposed to break this cycle by intervening on the end-use side, arguing that producers would then recognize the merits of adopting more efficient production methods and would benefit as prices rose and the volume of oil recovered from longer-lived pools increased. In effect, FOCB would stimulate the rise of oil prices from artificially low levels to real market prices. This would not only encourage exploration but conservation as well. For the higher price of crude would be passed through to fuel oil users who would then seek a cheaper fuel. Gasoline prices would also rise, but since demand for gasoline was inelastic, current trends in use would not be radically disturbed by the upward movement of price. Policy makers in the 1970s sought to implement this strategy relative to both oil and natural gas but without the end-use controls necessary to reduce inefficient use by consumers willing to pay higher prices.

FOCB's reconstruction of the nation's fuel mix assumed a constant advance in technological capabilities over an extended period of time. In identifying gasoline as the superior use of crude oil, FOCB and others anticipated that continuous improvement of refining processes would substantially increase the proportion of gasoline produced from a barrel of crude. And so it came to pass; yields per barrel rose from 25 percent to almost 40 percent during the 1920s, allowing a fivefold increase in gasoline production while crude production advanced only half as much. Such improvements prevented from materializing the long-term gasoline shortages predicted by Pogue and the Bureau of Mines at the beginning of the decade. FOCB also devoted considerable attention to the potential of producing oil from shale and coal, the technologies for which were well advanced by the mid-1920s, although not at commercially competitive prices. FOCB advised continued experimentation, anticipating a time when shale would be considered a proven reserve.

In its emphasis on the application of new production and processing methods, the board demonstrated considerable restraint and common sense. FOCB never indulged in predictions that this or that technology would soon resolve all future fuel problems, as API's report of 1925 did. Recall that API's report concluded that the nation's one-billion-acre oil reserve assured a sufficient supply—"beyond the time when science will limit the demand by developing more efficient use of, or substitute for, oil, or will displace its use as a source of power by harnessing a natural energy."[27]

Instead, FOCB's reports and statements, while assuming constant technological advance, offered no assurances that the practical application of new knowledge would provide sufficient new resources to compensate for the profligacy with which Americans consumed energy. Requa best expressed the caution of the oil board in remarks made at the hearings of 1926: "I am not unmindful of what science may develop in the future . . . I wish to repeat that we can not today found any national policy upon the assumption that scientific discoveries will supply our future demand for minerals from sources now undiscovered."[28] In the abstract, then, FOCB's reports of 1926 and 1928 projected an idea of energy resource use, including the exploitation of foreign oil, that derived from the board's vision of the rational individual capable of postponing immediate gratification in anticipation of long-term social benefits.[29]

Whether or not FOCB actually believed that this approach could win the acquiescence of the practical men who directed the oil industry cannot be determined from the records. Contemporary students of the industry recognized the validity of the board's analysis. Even the API called for the engineering of more efficient automobile engines, and, as noted earlier, engineers applauded an end-use approach. According to the historians of Humble Oil Company, the FOCB's first report gained friendly acceptance in the industry because it allayed fears of further federal intervention. But could this be translated into acceptance of the direction FOCB wished to move the industry? At the hearings of 1926, L. V. Nicholas, president of the National Petroleum Marketers Association, vigorously advocated restrictions on the use of fuel oil, asserting that "oversupply has forced the industry to find new outlets through inferior uses." In contrast, Doherty termed such restrictions illegal and un-American. The Texas Company's Amos L. Beaty, then president of API, opposed any restrictions, arguing that economic demand would determine use, a position diametrically opposed to the FOCB position.

In fact, with the exception of a few odd souls in the industry,

FOCB's plan met with prompt rejection, whether it was to be implemented voluntarily or otherwise. Standard of New Jersey's Walter C. Teagle, like Beaty, would leave all to price and natural market forces, and he reiterated in his testimony of 1926 all the arguments advanced in API's report of 1925. Too many interests were involved in one or another end-use to allow the defining of any single use as superior. In his testimony, Leon D. Becker, official of the American Oil Burner Association, categorically denied that the burning of fuel oil was an unessential, uneconomic, or inferior use of crude; the steadily rising number of fuel oil burners in use attested to its efficiency in the home. Others questioned the social benefits of substituting coal for oil, given the polluting effects of the former. In truth, FOCB had not given much thought to the environmental consequences of its fuel-substitution proposals. FOCB's general outline envisioned no wholesale substitution, but rather sketched a program that might differ in its details from region to region according to the availability of one or another or several sources of energy. Both Hoover and Secretary of Interior Hubert Work, for instance, were sympathetic to the idea of superpower and the private development of hydroelectric capacity.[30]

The hearings conducted by FOCB demonstrated a number of truths. The industry was sorely divided on the proper definition of the oil problem, with some, Doherty as an example, warning of the day when the United States became an oil-poor nation. Others nodded affirmatively after reading an article in the *National Petroleum News* entitled "Those Who Would Regulate Coal Industry May Drag In Oil Also." To nip that frightening possibility in the bud, API hired the respected jurist, Charles Evans Hughes, to represent it at the hearings. Hughes, ignorant of all phases of the oil industry, presented a strict constructionist critique of federal regulation of the industry, a presentation vigorously disputed by Doherty. Indeed, Doherty was so incensed at the API for presenting Hughes's uninformed views as those of the oil industry that he ran a full-page advertisement in several newspapers in support of federal regulation. While Hughes's foray into the morass of oil politics may have been unfortunate, his total rejection of federal intervention did correspond with majority opinion in the API and among independent groups. The hearings, in quick order, convinced FOCB of the futility of pursuing further the application of end-use restrictions. The hearings also obstructed FOCB's efforts to discover an acceptable compromise regarding the control of production. Neither strictly voluntary nor government-enforced controls seemed to have many adherents.

Oil industry distrust of FOCB was also reflected in the desultory and uninformative response of the industry to a series of questionnaires prepared by the board and distributed among scores of individuals involved in the industry. Responses to the questionnaire on "Waste in Production" were, according to USGS director G. O. Smith, who summarized the returns, "frankly defensive, as such a proposal, in their opinion, would seem to imply that remedial action can come only through Governmental intervention. . . . In most of the replies, physical waste of oil is termed negligible or practically nil." Answers to other questionnaires on efficiency in production, waste in refining, waste in utilization, and the economics of fuel oil, among others, revealed little of substance, couched as they were in very general, nonempirical terms and frequently consisting of little more than a lecture on the value of laissez faire. "Endorsement of the principle of cooperation," Smith concluded in an understatement, "is not unanimous." One oil executive suggested that the FOCB would render a great service to the country and to the industry by reassuring the public "that there is no danger."[31]

During its first two or three years, FOCB operated on the assumption that America risked oil shortages within a generation unless conservation was applied to both production and end-use. Neither strategy appealed to the oil industry, nor did FOCB ever threaten to push for coercive authority to implement conservation. The board's end-use proposals failed to generate enthusiasm but succeeded in raising serious opposition within the industry. Production controls, of secondary interest to the board, stimulated visceral responses from oilmen apprehensive about federal intentions. A cooperative program could advance only a short way if, as the API insisted, there were no problems to resolve. As of 1926, few reasons could be cited to justify the board's continuing existence. Dramatic events in the fields, however, pumped new, life-giving fluids through the atrophying agency.

The discovery of vast new oil fields transformed a threat of scarcity into a serious overabundance. Between 1925 and 1931, flush production from the Greater Seminole and West Texas fields, from the Oklahoma City field, the Hobbs pool in New Mexico, and, finally in 1931, from the magnificent East Texas field overwhelmed oil markets. These developments followed earlier discoveries in the Los Angeles basin and the sizable exports of California oil to the East Coast in 1923 and 1924. The new finds forced a revision upward of estimated proven reserves to volumes that ranged between 10 and 12 billion barrels, twice the USGS estimate of 1918. Even though consumption in 1929 surpassed one billion barrels, leaving a reserve of thirteen years, or *less* than the estimates for 1918–21 (see Table 12), attention shifted quickly to the immediate impact of overproduction. As Chapter 8 shows, the rhetoric of conservation assumed a new guise as its purpose was transformed from that of nursing diminishing reserves to controlling production in order to achieve price stability by bringing demand and supply into equilibrium.

Doherty's proposals, as they emerged through the filter of FOCB, suddenly appeared quite acceptable to the leaders of API. Chapter 8 further considers unitization and prorationing, the nuclear mechanisms proposed by FOCB, with the sanction of API, to protect the oil industry from the consequences of its discoveries. While the techniques themselves gained the ready acquiescence of the majors, the independents persisted in their opposition during the Hoover and Roosevelt administrations. Nonetheless, FOCB vigorously promoted the unit operation of oil pools, the strengthening of state conservation laws (particularly prorationing requirements), the passage of federal and state legislation permitting producer cooperation to restrict production, and the negotiation of controlled production agreements by the producing states. These objectives confronted effective opposition from various elements within the industry.

In 1927, E. W. Clark, president of API, challenged his peers to accept the "ideals of coordination, of cooperation, of understanding, of confidence rather than suspicion" proffered by the FOCB, which he characterized as an exemplar of "moderation and reasonableness."[32] Mutual suspicions had apparently evaporated. FOCB stood ready to cooperate, even to the extent of sanctioning the revision of the antitrust laws as an incentive to producer cooperation. The threat of federal regulation seemed less intimidating as FOCB emphasized the preeminent role of the states, a position midway between Doherty and those refusing to compromise their laissez-faire values.[33]

Poised to enter the most important era of its life, FOCB in its three years had achieved little of a concrete and measurable quality. Its countenance of production controls had engendered antagonism from the independents, although the breach had been healed with the majors. Unorganized consumers failed to grasp the benefits implicit in higher oil prices or restrictions on the use of fuel oil. The board's abortive endeavor to achieve a consensus on end-use, however, should not be dismissed as a complete failure. Although sterile of actual results and having little discernible influence on future thinking about energy, it was, in my opinion, the most appropriate and the most correct method to pursue.

Conclusion

What of the evolution of federal fuel policies during the predepression years of the 1920s? Successive crises in coal after World War I generated successively weaker federal responses, none of which transcended simple crisis management, and that with indifferent results. Crises of a different nature, rooted more in perception and speculation than in empirical proofs, disturbed the tranquility of the oil industry and caused some to demand federal regulation. But, excepting for the purely consultative FOCB, this was beaten back. Both the oil industry, particularly the major firms, and the energy utilities pursued a path of structural development uninhibited by governmental restraints. FOCB displayed no concern about the majors' steadily increasing control of all phases of the oil industry, while FTC and congressional inquiries into the realities of economic power failed to elicit a formal statutory response.

While some applauded this era of benign neglect and hoped it would last forever, others, far fewer in number, questioned its wisdom and its implications for the future. Doherty wished to protect the economic value of his firm's oil reserves against the plunging prices that accompanied unrestrained production. His call for federal regulation incurred for him the disfavor of his peers, not that he cared one iota about the opinion of others. Nonetheless, he opened a Pandora's box for the oil industry. Adopting a somewhat larger view, Sen. William E. Borah, in a Denver speech of 1927, argued that government must carve out an active role in the oil, coal, and power spheres. Great economic empires exploited those sources of energy. Known waste accompanied production. Aggrandized corporate units made unilateral decisions that seriously affected the lives of millions. Many of those decisions were economically unsound and thus "morally wrong." "What," he asked, "is the public welfare?"[34]

SEVEN

The Politics of Energy during the Prosperity Decade

Policy-Making Agendas

In what ways did politics, broadly defined, affect the ongoing energy transition of the 1920s? In searching for the answer, I assume that the political process enveloped all discussions by public and private bodies of current problems for which policy solutions were offered or which were ignored, as well as the formulation and implementation of actual policy by executive agencies, courts, and legislators. Local, state, and national governments constituted the policy-formulating arenas. Much of the material presented in this chapter is familiar to the reader but is approached from a different perspective and, insofar as possible, couched in a comparative framework. Many issues, some of particular significance at the local and state level, fall beyond the range of this chapter. Coal-trade efforts to soften restrictions imposed by local smoke abatement ordinances, community-utility clashes over rates and service, and other relevant issues are ignored. Attention is directed to the national arena and national fuels policy, or the lack thereof.

Were policy objectives enunciated during the 1920s; can they be identified? President Coolidge invoked the concept of national security as a justification for the creation of FOCB. To achieve this noncontroversial goal implied the discovery of new fields, perhaps overseas as well as at home, the conservation of known domestic reserves, and the more efficient uses of energy resources. Selecting from among these practical options and determining the extent to which their accomplishment required public action triggered vigorous argument among contending interests. Furthermore, the controversies swirling around these options rarely included consideration of other energy sources, although the oil board's brief fling with end-use control posited the interrelationships of all sources of energy. Recurrent coal crises evoked frequent calls for order but only infrequently took cognizance of developments in the other energy industries. Electric power developed its own mystic. A few individuals, mostly in government service, sought to integrate policy debates around the inclusive term "energy" but were doomed to disappointment. A fuel-by-fuel format dominated agendas and must be replicated in analysis if the energy policies of the era are to be understood. Historians must embark from and conclude their journeys at the same terminals as their subjects.

The mind set of this generation imposes further constraints on analysis. Typically, policy discussion pursued a path that reflected the functional organization of the industry. The U.S. Fuel Administration, for example, created divisions responsible for production, processing (in oil, refining), transportation, and distribution (and allocation) or marketing, a structure resurrected in less comprehensive form in 1919 and 1922 by the U.S. Rail Administration, the ICC, and the Federal Fuel Distributor. The organization of the industry—its financial structure, its integration, the degree to which single units controlled resources—imposed still another dimension upon policy discussions, often without reference to the efficiency with which a firm drew resources from the ground, processed them, and moved them to ultimate consumers. The scheme of this chapter reflects the organizational imperatives accepted by contemporaries.

This chapter, then, discusses the political issues arising from production, processing, transportation, marketing, and organizational structure. Fundamental differences in production distinguished coal from oil, and this determined that the politics of production would also differ. The comparative perspective adopted will, I hope, return integrative benefits. Past policies had a continuing impact. Freight rate decisions for coal produced positive and negative consequences for coal and other energy marketers.

Did participants approach these complex problems from some set of common assumptions? The central issue, of course, revolved around the responsibilities of the federal government. Analysis would be much facilitated if, for instance, all representatives of industry consistently and adamantly opposed all federal intervention on philosophical and pragmatic grounds. But an unyielding commitment to laissez faire clouded the minds of theoreticians, not industrialists. Fuel industry leaders were, if anything, hard-nosed realists who sought advantages where they could and strove to deflect threats to their security from whatever the source.

Henry L. Doherty believed in free enterprise and blasted as unconstitutional, indeed un-American, the feeble effort of FOCB to devise end-use controls. But Doherty also championed the constitutionality of federally imposed production controls. As A. W. Giebelhaus tells us, J. N. Pew of Sun Oil supported the antitrust suit against Standard Oil and applauded the dissolution of the monopoly. Years later, faced with an oil glut of frightening dimensions, Pew's successors advocated the weakening of antitrust laws to allow industry cooperation in restricting production.[1]

Neither did representatives of the federal government subscribe to some common formula that, if applied to energy, would define the public interest. Sen. William E. Borah believed that the public welfare required the exercise of federal authority to compel oil conservation. Secretary of Commerce Herbert Hoover felt uncomfortable with federal controls even during the coal crises of the 1920s and concocted a vague notion of associationalism to justify some role for the federal government. As secretary of commerce, Hoover advocated oil industry cooperation to control production. As president, Hoover attacked an oil industry plan to limit production as a device to fix prices. The U.S. Coal Commission proclaimed the public interest in coal but, unable to devise methods of protecting the public interest short of comprehensive federal intervention, withdrew into the safety of vacuous recommendations for greater publicity of industry conditions.

Problem-solving (or even problem-defining) formulas did not emerge during the 1920s. A profusion of discordant and confused views epitomized thinking about energy difficulties. As an uncontrollable malignancy seemed to seize the body of the coal industry, George Cushing, editor of *Cushing's Survey,* informed Senator Borah in 1925 that government persecution had pushed the industry to the edge of bankruptcy. A year later, Walter Barnum, president of the National Coal Association, dismissed all criticism of coal as irresponsible and professed difficulty in accounting for any agitation for federal regulation—given such creditable performance of the industry.[2] Coal achieved relative unity in opposing federal controls over any phase of the trade. Less unity characterized oil. Mavericks such as Doherty or Mark Requa espoused radical views of federal responsibilities. The independents, too, sought to exploit federal power on their behalf against the dominance of the majors.

Ideological stances rarely explain satisfactorily the political course pursued by these protagonists. Ideological rhetoric served to guard against the entrance of various interests into the political arena in search of concrete advantages or to counter specific threats. Awesome complexity characterized the seamless web of America's ongoing energy transition. New technologies, improved performance of established technologies, demographic changes (particularly in metropolitan areas), consumer preferences shaped in part by increasingly subtle advertising and whetted by inviting new financing programs, proximity to a power line or a pipeline, all of these variables and more explain the nation's fuel mix. Among the variables, it may be that policy or its absence contributed one iota to a decision to use a particular fuel or energy source.

In 1924, the Southeastern Millers Association informed Hoover of the conversion of numerous mills from coal—costly, inconvenient, and of uncertain supply—to oil and hydroelectric. Government inability to assure supply during recent crises had convinced the millers of the wisdom of substitution. To reverse this trend, coal dealers in Texas and New England in 1924–25 developed sales campaigns that trumpeted federal estimates of diminishing oil reserves. Coal, they claimed, was coming back. "It is our firm belief," the New Englanders wrote, "that oil as a house heating fuel will not be permanent. . . . Anthracite is really the only Fool Proof Fuel For The Home."[3] Thus a connection between policy and use can be traced. The intent of a policy decision might be construed narrowly, while its results, probably unanticipated, ripped through the entire society.

For the most part, decisions to implement policy proved less consequential than decisions to abstain from devising policy, since the latter supported the status quo. Those engaged in the process invariably predicted dire results from action or inaction. Most of the sound and fury emanated directly from those employed by the energy industries or those, like Sen. Robert M. La Follette, who consistently attacked them. Momentary interest among the general public might be stirred up, as over the Teapot Dome scandals, warranting front-page coverage in the newspapers. Price advances in late 1924 and early 1925 produced the *New York World* headline: "Oil Industry, Ill, Is Quickly Cured by Price Advance of $100,000,000."[4] The popular press devoted somewhat less space to reservoir pressure, railroad coal car assignment practices, or the other arcane matters that confronted policy makers.

The policy-making wars of the 1920s, particularly those involving the ICC and the FOCB, turned on the axis of such details. By construing narrowly the implications of such factors, both ICC and FOCB succeeded in avoiding such explosive issues as monopoly or oligopoly. Not all participants subscribed to such a limited view. Oil independents attributed their weaknesses to the unnatural strength of the majors. Were they right or wrong? Other Americans justifiably questioned the implications for political democracy and for the free enterprise system of the fact that fifteen firms in 1926 controlled some 63 percent of the proven domestic oil acreage, and twenty-one firms in 1929 produced almost 60 percent of domestic oil production. What was to be done about this? Why should this be a concern if the large firms operated efficiently and charged reasonable prices to consumers? Independents supplied answers to those questions and proposed, for instance, the divorcement of pipelines from the integrated companies. Assuredly, this was in their interest, or so they believed, but they failed to convince many people that it was also in the public interest. Those who believed that the Standard group and the other majors possessed an unacceptable degree of power proposed few remedies that promised a certain cure. While the La Follette committee of 1923 advanced specific recommendations as remedies for specific grievances, it offered no clear vision of a system that would serve the public interest more effectively than the present system.

Many imponderables hindered the elucidation of a clear view of the "total picture" of oil or coal, let alone of energy. It seemed more practical to focus on production or transportation. Freight rates from Kentucky coal fields to the lake ports were definable. The amount of oil produced in the Cushing or Hobbs field could be measured against estimated demand. The web of energy was intricate, its separate filaments numerous and interlaced; best to proceed strand by strand.

Production as a Factor in Energy Politics

The physical nature and geographic location of the fuels determined basic marketing patterns; so, too, did those qualities imprint upon the fuels distinguishable political characteristics. The physical properties of coal, oil, or natural gas circumscribed their use and commanded or encouraged the use of separate transportation or transmission facilities. Use-technologies and consumer preferences contributed to the political calculus. Since each resource could be used, directly or indirectly, to boil water in a pot or a boiler full of water, a theoretical point of convergence existed, but this commonality seemed less susceptible to political response than the unique conditions of production.

The location of each resourse shaped its political configuration. The production and transportation of natural gas for regional markets remained unhindered by regulation, except insofar as affected by state oil conservation laws. At the point of distribution from a carrier to users in a municipality, local and state regulations impinged upon the industry, as it did in electric distribution. But local and state regulation was limited in effectiveness by the interstate nature of the industry. In the absence of competition, a strong consensus emerged within national electric and gas industry associations about the acceptable degree of regulation and in opposition to public ownership. Oil and coal politics diverged radically from this pattern.

Coal was located in two dozen states, and only the Pacific states lacked access to adequate coal supplies (Map 3). The lion's share of production lay east of the Mississippi River. The northern Appalachian fields plus Illinois and Indiana supplied 84 percent of the bituminous output in 1920 and 86 percent in 1929, and all anthracite came from Pennsylvania. Each producing district, the essential supplier of its own regional needs, also sought markets in contiguous regions, with the largest volume of coal moving from the Appalachian states east to the Atlantic Coast, north to the coal ports of Lake Erie, and west to the High Plains states.[5]

To compete successfully against other operators and against other fuels, each operator sought to reduce fixed costs, primarily wages and transportation charges. Wages bulked large in the labor-intensive coal industry, and during the entire twentieth century, bitter and frequently violent biennial wage negotiations in the highly unionized northern and western fields dominated and shaped the internal politics of coal. Recurrent strikes disrupted the nation's coal supply after World War I and compelled federal and state intervention, with the results described in Chapter 5. Government intervention neither prevented subsequent strikes against wage reductions nor resulted in the adoption of a coal policy.

Although Congress considered many regulatory bills before 1928, none dealt with production per se, that is, with excessive productive capacity. In 1929, bills were submitted that would establish coal-field production quotas, but New Deal legislation—the coal codes and the two Guffey acts—rejected production controls and adopted minimum price controls as the key stabilization strategy.[6] In oil, just the opposite occurred. Neither did a single national forum develop for coal politics; in oil, FOCB performed this function. Instead, a diffused pattern of coal politics evolved, based on several key producing districts, each competitive with one another in one or more market areas. Since adverse freight rates could close markets to particular producing districts, coal operators were forced before the ICC where they contested high rates imposed by the railroads and sought advantageous rates relative to competing producing districts. A subsequent section describes the transportation politics of the fuels; the competitive situation in coal is outlined here.

Increasingly, anthracite dealers faced competition from bituminous in domestic markets, a development attributed by some to strikes and the competition of other fuels and by others to the collusion of the major mine-owning railroads which purposefully underproduced in order to keep prices high. Operators in the southern bituminous fields, encouraged by the opportunities presented during recurrent work stoppages in the union fields, moved coal across the Ohio River into the traditional market areas of northern operators. Operators in Ohio, Pennsylvania, and West Virginia who served the coal ports of Lake Erie and the Lake Erie dock operators confronted stiff competition in the markets of the upper Great Lakes states and the High Plains from Indiana and Illinois producers who moved coal by rail to those North Central markets. Coal freight rates played a crucial role in this interregional struggle.[7]

All the while, traditional coal markets throughout the country experienced penetration by other fuels and by electricity. While the nation grew, coal production did not (see Tables 4 and 11). The number of operating mines, peaking at 9,331 in 1923, fell to just over 6,000 by 1929, a number only insignificantly larger than prior to World War I; and mine employment plunged from 705,000 in 1923 to 503,000 in 1929, fewer by 100,000 than in 1916. Two-thirds of the mine closings occurred among marginal mines (producing under 200,000 tons annually) that had opened during World War I and again in 1919 and 1922. In that production category, the number of mines declined from 6,636 to 4,476 between 1920 and 1929, while their percentage of total production fell from 33 percent to 20 percent. The number of mines operated by firms producing over 500,000 tons annually also diminished by several hundred, but their contribution to total production rose from 47 percent in 1920 to 60 percent in 1929, reflecting the adoption of mechanized mining equipment and a concomitant reduction of the work force. Mechanization proceeded less rapidly in southern mines where wage levels were below those north of the Ohio. Northern operators argued that southern competition compelled both wage reductions and mechanization, but this was a spurious argument as it applied to the larger companies. Productivity per miner rose steadily during the 1920s, yet operators continued to slash wages.[8]

The turmoil and human suffering accompanying these readjustments reposed somewhere on the edge of the nation's political vision. Experts discussed excess capacity, transportation inadequacies, the need for early coal storage, mine mechanization, the growing significance of strip mining, and the desirability of improving the technology of coal utilization through the development of superpower, the use of pulverized coal, coal gasification, and even the transportation of coal by pipelines. Except during strikes, the plight of the miners aroused negligible, and not entirely sympathetic, public attention. Coal was, after all, available in great abundance. Few feared its ultimate depletion. Unlike oil, risk of discovery was not an important factor. Coal's competitive problems with other fuels, one could say, attested to technological advance. Although the Garfield reform scheme and the Huddleston and Frelinghuysen bills (see Chapter 5, p. 114) indicated that the trauma of coal elicited some concern, few congressmen or public officials were inclined to tackle the industry's problems. Coal industry organizations were unalterably opposed to any such efforts. The politics of coal, then, reflected the atomized, individualistic structure of the industry itself.

So, too, did the politics of oil echo its organization. Significant petroleum pools existed in relatively few states; in 1929, the Mid-Continent—Oklahoma, Kansas, Texas, Arkansas, and part of Louisiana—and California produced 89 percent of the domestic supply.[9] Shifts in the relative importance of production in each state occurred during the period, with Texas emerging at the end of the decade as the leading oil producing state and a major refining center as well.[10] In the politics of oil, Oklahoma and Texas carved out predominant roles during the 1920s, although the independent producers and refiners in Kansas participated actively and effectively. The independents of those three states orchestrated the strongest dissent to the oil policies, in embryonic form in the 1920s, that the federal government adopted during the depression.

The inescapable risks involved in discovery, the migratory nature of the oil locked far beneath the earth's surface, the customary methods of recovery, the judicial concept of law of capture, leasing and royalty practices, the processing required, the wide variety of products that refining produced, the great distance separating the producing and central consuming areas—these describe the substantive components of oil politics. The vagaries of location and the imperatives of national and international marketing gradually resulted in the formation of two potentially hostile groups within the universe of oil, the oil-producing states and the oil-consuming states, a distinction that never quite took hold in the rhetoric or practice of coal politics. Thus, such issues as tariffs and import quotas or policies designed to limit production (thereby inflating prices), all of great moment to the oil industry, remained essentially irrelevant to the coal industry. FOCB's early emphasis on end-use not only ran afoul of the spirited opposition of refiners and the oil equipment trade but of eastern fuel oil consumers as well.

Producing states demanded cheap access to national markets and remunerative prices for petroleum products. Consuming states, also interested in cheap transportation, expected a continuous and adequate supply at low prices. At no time during the 1920s did anything resembling a consuming-state bloc materialize, and only sporadically did residents of those states express a vague concordance of views regarding the oil industry, complaining perhaps of a sudden rise in gasoline prices or responding negatively to independent efforts to impose a tariff on Mexican crude. In the 1930s, however, spokespersons from the consuming states were more likely to articulate a shared opposition to the demands of independents for oil tariffs or import quotas and to respond suspiciously to the inflationary thrust of national oil policy and the mechanisms adopted to achieve price stabilization (see Chapter 8, pp. 197–201). In that decade, some of the oil-producing states united in a federally sanctioned Interstate Compact to Conserve Oil and Gas, designed to control production and achieve price stability.[11] But in the early debates over these strategies which enlivened FOCB's deliberations, the opinions of consuming states carried little weight. The fight remained in-house.

In the politics of production, internal divisions received further expression in the long-lasting antagonism between the independent oil companies and the majors. The coal industry, without an equivalent of Standard Oil, did not replicate a similar internal division. The independent producers and refiners, largely unintegrated and located overwhelmingly in the producing states, coalesced with the majors during the early 1920s to squash the production-control proposals of Doherty and others and to water down conservation and control legislation considered by the producing states. But with the great outpouring of oil during the late 1920s, this alliance broke down as independents consistently opposed the control policies advocated by the majors. These small producers, powerful in the state capitols of the producing states, acted in concert to obstruct or moderate demands for production controls originating with the federal government and the majors. Wildcatters and independent producers with small capital and without storage or transportation facilities could not afford to keep their oil in the ground.

In coal, except for the anthracite mine-owning railroads of the East Coast, separate firms handled mining, wholesaling, and retailing. Coal underwent little processing beyond sizing and cleaning before passing into the hands of the consumer. Virtually all oil was refined. The location of refineries relative to oil fields and markets, coupled with the large number of small producers operating in most Mid-Continent fields, created the essential dimension of oil industry politics and induced some cooperation between independent producers and independent refiners, both of whom felt oppressed by the majors. Independents accused the majors of violating the letter and the spirit of antitrust laws. As noted in Chapter 2, both Kansas and Texas passed laws aimed at weakening Standard Oil. Independents frequently generalized their hostility toward the majors, primarily in testimony before committees of Congress, but the most serious confrontations occurred over discrete issues. Tariffs, as an example, assumed increasing significance during the Hoover and Roosevelt years. But the most enduring issue involved pipeline transportation of crude to refineries and rail transportation of refined products to end-users. Critical elements included the location of independent refineries close to producing fields, control of pipelines by the major integrated firms, and the level of rail freight rates on refined products between western and eastern points. Discussion now shifts to transportation, a most salient factor in coal politics as well as in oil.

The Politics of Fuel Transportation

This section focuses on the transportation of energy rather than on the use of energy in the movement of people and goods. Absent from the discussion is a consideration of the gradual extension of interstate natural gas transmission systems, which fell beyond the regulatory authority of local and state governments (see Chapter 10, pp. 280–81; Chapter 11, note 31).The dominant ingredients are oil and coal, pipelines and railroads, and the ICC.

Transportation constituted a key fixed expense for both coal and oil. Virtually all coal moved to market by railroad at least part of the way, and each producing field watched closely the freight rates paid by competition to reach common markets. The daily availability of rail transportation, as earlier chapters made clear, determined the daily production of each mine. Thus, the adequacy of transportation at producing points affected delivery at consuming points, so that the interests of electric utilities and the steel industry intersected with that of the coal industry. Small and large coal producers, wholesalers, and retailers depended upon the railroad system and, as we have seen, were frequently harmed by its inefficiency.

In oil, the transportation system assumed added complexity because the larger firms owned production, transportation, refining, and marketing facilities, an integration that gave them substantial competitive advantages over the small and nonintegrated producers or refiners and even over the somewhat larger independent firms who owned both production and refining facilities. In the coal trade, then, producing districts scattered about the eastern two-thirds of the nation acted as political units in seeking favorable freight rate differentials vis-a-vis one another in traditional markets. In oil, small producers and refiners in the Mid-Continent producing region sought to reduce the great advantages enjoyed by the integrated majors. The independents supported a sustained campaign against the pipeline policies of the majors and against discriminatory railroad rates that combined to deny the independents access to eastern markets.

A sizable complex of independent refineries emerged in Oklahoma and Kansas during and after World War I. Another huge concentration developed in Texas where the larger units were owned by the majors and located on or near the Gulf. The number of refineries in the United States rose from 176 in 1914 to a high of 547 in 1924 and then declined to 341 by 1929. In 1921, Oklahoma and Kansas possessed 125 refineries (an increase of 37 percent since 1917), or 30 percent of the national total, with 19 percent of total refining capacity; Texas housed 82 refineries (almost four times as many as in 1918), or 20 percent of the national total, with 19 percent of total refining capacity.

The economies available through the use of tanker transportation of crude and refined products to the Atlantic Coast spurred growth in Texas just as proximity to enormous markets for fuel oil and gasoline encouraged a Middle Atlantic or Chicago area location for the largest refineries. During the 1920s, Mid-Continent refining declined in relative importance as refineries in Oklahoma, Kansas, and the non-Gulf portion of Texas closed down or operated at considerably less than full capacity.[12] By 1929, fifty-seven refineries operated in Kansas and Oklahoma. Refining capacity in those states plus the non-Gulf portion of Texas fell from 33 percent in 1920 to 22 percent in 1930.[13] Table 13 indicates only marginal absolute growth in Mid-Continent refining

TABLE 13. *Refining in the Mid-Continent, 1925–1929*

	1925	1926	1928	1929
Total crude refined (million bbls.)	740	779	913	988
Total refined in Mid-Continent[1] (% of total)	134 (18)	133 (17)	159 (17)	174 (17)
Total gasoline produced (million bbls.)	260	300	377	435
Total produced in Mid-Continent (% of total)	61 (24)	65 (22)	79 (21)	85 (19)

[1] Includes Kansas, Oklahoma, and the non-Gulf portion of Texas.

Sources: USBM, *Petroleum Refinery Statistics, 1926*, Bulletin 289 (Washington, D.C.: GPO, 1927), 22, 26; ibid., *1927*, Bulletin 339 (1929), 28–29, 36.

output and the complete absence of relative growth. Mid-Continent refiners did not benefit from the enormous market for gasoline that developed during the 1920s. Mid-Continent independents entered the political arena—as they had before World War I when Standard Oil was the enemy—to redress disadvantages perceived as stemming from the unfair and illegal competitive tactics of the majors.

The ongoing efforts of Mid-Continent refiners to gain access to eastern markets by political means won the support of independent producers as well. Unless the independent refiners expanded their markets, the producers would remain the captive suppliers of the major-controlled trunk pipelines of the region, compelled to accept whatever price the pipelines offered for crude. The refiners aimed their political weaponry first at the pipelines. But the statutory definition of the pipelines as common carriers failed to rectify conditions, because the pipeline companies ignored it, common carrier legislation by the states was ineffective, and the ICC chose not to enforce the law. Both the La Follette committee of 1923 and the FTC oil investigation of the mid-1920s sternly criticized the ICC for its indifference, but to no avail. While not abandoning the campaign to compel ICC enforcement of the Hepburn Act, the independents, acting through the National Association of Independent Oil Producers and other independent trade associations, shifted their immediate objectives to reducing rail freight rates for refined products (also requiring ICC action), curtailing foreign crude imports (these crudes provided fuel oil for the Atlantic seaboard), and divorcing the pipelines from the integrated firms. Both the La Follette committee and FTC endorsed divorcement.[14]

The majors contested each independent demand, arguing that managerial skill, product quality, efficiency, and size explained their market supremacy. The independents gained no relief from the ICC or Congress. Still, the independents persevered, organizing in 1929 the Independent Petroleum Association of America as a means to aim their intensifying animus at the majors and their federal tools, the Federal Oil Conservation Board and the Interstate Oil Compact— and later the New Deal's Petroleum Administrative Board. The unity of the independents much reduced the probability that oil policies would ever spring from an internal consensus and thwarted the effectiveness of the policies adopted.

Transportation charges accounted for over half the price consumers paid for coal. In the competition among producing fields for markets, freight rate differentials carried a significance exceeding wage differentials, despite producer claims to the contrary. The miners absorbed the social costs of reduced wages as well as the social costs resulting from injury, death, and vocational disease. Additions to gross industry income gained by lowering wage costs were not distributed equally among all the operators in unionized fields, but redounded primarily to the advantage of the larger operators who mechanized production and abandoned marginally productive mines. As noted earlier, bituminous mine attrition occurred primarily among those producing less than 200,000 tons annually; those producing above 500,000 tons annually improved their market position. During each round of wage negotiations between the United Mine Workers of America and northern operators, the latter blamed the threatening competition of southern mines on the favorable wage differentials enjoyed by southern operators. But these wage advantages merely supplemented basic freight rate advantages that permitted southern penetration of northern markets. Once the wage rate issues were settled, the operators refocused their attention on the central issue, freight rates.[15]

Three producing regions, northern Appalachia, the upper South, and the North Central states, engaged in intense competition for two great northern trades, the tidewater route to Atlantic Coast markets and the rail-lake route to distribution centers on Lake Michigan and Lake Superior. Chart 1 depicts production trends in these three regions. While production in northern Appalachia dropped sharply

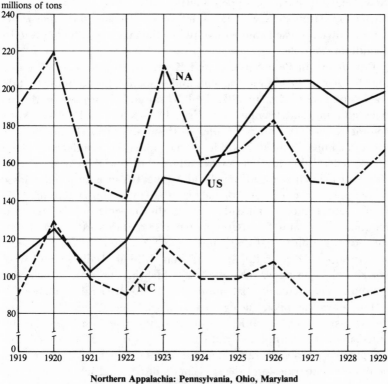

millions of tons

Northern Appalachia: Pennsylvania, Ohio, Maryland
Upper South: Virginia, West Virginia, eastern Kentucky
North Central: Illinois, Indiana, western Kentucky

CHART 1. *Coal Production of Three Producing Regions, 1919–1929*

Source: National Industrial Conference Board, *The Competitive Position of Coal in the United States* (New York: NICB, 1931), 151.

during each of the post-World War I strikes, output increased in the upper South. Production in the North Central states, while falling, demonstrated more stability. For the three years 1927–29, northern Appalachia supplied 30 percent of all soft coal, compared with 40 percent in 1919 and 1920; and the upper South accounted for 38 percent of production, compared with 23 percent in 1919 and 1920. Northern Appalachia lost out in the lake trade to coal moving from the upper South to lake ports and to all-rail coal from the North Central states to the upper lake states. But some North Central coal was also displaced in the Chicago-Milwaukee area by southern coal. Northern Appalachian coal also lost out in the Middle Atlantic and

New England states to upper South coal moving to tidewater and thence by barge to New York and Boston. Because the same issues were involved at each competitive point, the lake cargo trade provides a suitable example.

Production in West Virginia and Kentucky expanded rapidly during the war as new mines opened and gained entry to both the tidewater and lake trades. In 1917, the ICC raised freight rates on the rail lines entering and leaving Lake Erie docks and failed to raise rates commensurately on all-rail routes to the upper lakes. In an effort to move as much coal as possible to the upper lake and High Plains states, federal distribution policies adopted during the emergencies of 1919 and 1922 encouraged the all-rail traffic, because the strikes closed more mines in northern Appalachia than in western Kentucky, Indiana, and Illinois. Railroads serving the upper South offered promotional coal rates for southern exports to the North, and the resulting rate differentials remained intact into the 1920s. This rate structure favored all-rail shipments from Illinois, Indiana, and western Kentucky to upper lake markets, which had been the province of Ohio and Pennsylvania coal shipped in a rail-water-rail sequence.

The all-rail shippers, using such roads as the Illinois Central and the Louisville & Nashville, emphasized their proximity to the disputed markets; the rail-lake-rail shippers and the coal dock operators complained of higher rail rates per mile than charged their competitors. Unfair rates and the exegencies of national fuel emergencies, rather than a natural advantage, fostered the encroachment of Illinois and Indiana coal. Similar historical circumstances produced lower rates to Lake Erie from the upper South than from mines north of the Ohio River, despite the shorter distance of the latter haul. Northern operators charged that low southern rates acted as a subsidy to southern mines, encouraging the opening of new mines and adding further excess capacity. Large rate increases permitted by ICC in 1920 weighed more heavily on eastern and northern shippers than on southern, since the lower wage scales of southern mines buffered the operators from the full impact of the rate advances allowed southern railroads. The rate increases of 1917 and 1920 also aroused the ire of petroleum independents. The Independent Oil Men's Association and the Western Petroleum Refiner's Association accused ICC of furthering the advantage of those eastern refiners receiving most of their oil by pipeline.

Between 1922 and 1927, northern operators and the lake dock interests initiated repeated attempts to obtain reduced rates from ICC, but secured only minor reductions in 1927. The ICC in 1922 and again in 1927 denied the validity of the northern operator's essential contention: that unfair rates that blatantly disregarded distance encouraged the unfair competition of southern mines, thereby threatening the existence of the northern mines. During the entire decade, the ICC virtually ignored general rate structures—for petroleum products as well—and avoided consideration of distance of haul. According to the commission, northern wage scales satisfactorily accounted for successful southern competition. The commission consistently opted against disturbing existing competitive relationships (as if it had no hand in their creation) and opted for the status quo in the marketing of coal and oil. As a result, southern operators secured transportation and hence market advantages over northern operators, the competitive strength of coal deteriorated, and the major oil companies further consolidated their control over Mid-Continent producers and over eastern markets.[16]

The theme of ICC passivity was encountered in Chapter 2 but particularly in Chapter 5 where the agency emerges as one endowed with broad powers but hesitant to apply them. In abstaining from correcting rate inequities favoring southern mines, the commission actually nurtured less efficient producing fields, fields whose average costs of production, even with lower wages, were higher than production costs in the northern fields.

The commission also avoided the issue of mine ownership by the anthracite lines. The anthracite roads charged excessively high rates, garnering their profits more from carrying than from mining the coal, and thus compelled high retail prices, a situation resembling the use of pipelines by the major oil companies. The ICC eschewed use of its authority to establish a more efficient coal car distribution system. Traditional distribution policies had aggravated shortages during World War I and during the strikes of the 1920s, as had railroad favoritism toward mines holding railroad supply contracts. Consumers, many producers, Congress, and the U.S. Coal Commission all criticized these policies. Yet, ICC rejected all recommendations for reform, including a specific USCC mine-rating scheme, and continued its practice of guaranteeing cars to all mines however inefficient and however much the practice contributed to overdevelopment.[17]

In summary, coal and oil shippers failed to obtain reduced freight rates from the ICC, the dominant policy-making body in fuel transportation. How, then, is ICC's utter lack of responsiveness to the urgent demands of fuel shippers and its indifference to the common carrier clause of the Hepburn Act to be explained? Eugene Rostow labels the commission inept and ignorant of energy economics. Joseph

Lambie, agreeing with the ICC, views the differential rate structure of the 1920s as of dubious value in explaining either the so-called redundant capacity of the coal industry—a capacity of great value in 1941—or the competitive situation that favored southern roads and mine operators. Harold Williamson implies that ICC tampering could not improve the competitive position of independents vis-a-vis the natural superiority of the major integrated firms. Arthur Johnson links the inaction of ICC to the general indisposition of the federal government to introduce changes in federal oil policy, but this does not correlate smoothly with the formation of FOCB and the unleashing of acrimonious debate about the federal role.[18]

Another reason can be suggested. For the four-year period 1928–31, coal and oil provided the railroads with some 38 percent of total freight revenues, with coal (the single largest revenue source) contributing 20 percent in 1929. ICC protected the railroads against the impact of rate reductions on key commodities. Lowering pipeline rates or compelling the pipelines to reduce minimum-tender quotas would deprive the roads of freight—51 percent of refined products moved by rail—at a time when the roads were already suffering to some degree from truck and water competition. This may have been shortsighted. High petroleum rates stimulated, in part, the development of product pipelines and the expanded use of intermediate-distance tank trucks. While coal had few transport alternatives aside from well-developed water routes, high rates weakened its competitiveness with other fuels and narrowed its role in the nation's energy mix. An over-protective commission, unschooled in energy economics and lacking authority over competing water and motor transport, sustained rates that aggravated the vulnerable position of the railroads and hastened along the energy transition.[19]

Industry Structure and Politics

The properties of energy resources, their geographic locations, the processing required to change them into marketable commodities, the transportation employed to haul them to consumers, user preferences for a particular quality of energy to perform a specific task—all these were *interrelated* facets of a national energy system but evoked *fragmented* political responses, which seemed incapable of comprehending the essentially holistic character of the system. In 1923, M. W. Potter, ICC commissioner, described the coal freight rate structure as inimical to the public interest. USCC declared a public interest in the entire coal industry, a position enthusiastically seconded by the electric utility industry. President Coolidge's mandate to FOCB linked the performance of the oil industry with the "safety of the whole people."[20] Public utility regulation was familiar to all and frequently alluded to in discussions that clothed oil or coal (or both) with a public interest. But to proceed from the assertion of the public interest to the application of that undefined concept to coal or oil, let alone to synthesize all elements into a coherent whole, proved impossible. As FOCB learned, discrete interests thwarted coalescence around a consensus that transcended particularism.

The conflicting interests within and among the fuel industries, the marshaling of free-market defenses against government intrusion, and an apparent abundance of energy precluded the formation of more than random, crisis-oriented, superficial policies. But one available strategy—use of the antitrust laws—was deeply rooted in a commitment to free enterprise and in opposition to monopoly. Furthermore, an antitrust approach presumed studious attention to the structure of industry—to the production, processing, transportation, and marketing and pricing phases. The antitrust laws afforded Congress and the FTC a firm statutory foundation, as some believed, for the resolution of energy industry problems. The extent to which politics could resolve economic difficulties was, of course, problematic; but at the least the antitrust laws constituted a paradigmatic guidepost, acknowledged by most participants, if unenthusiastically, as the law of the land.

At the La Follette hearings of 1923 on the oil industry, again in House hearings on coal legislation in 1926, and yet again in FTC's petroleum investigation of 1926–28, attention focused on the lack of conformity between industrial organization and an ideal of the free market economy. The obvious relationship between fuel competition in markets and the structure of the industry served as a conceptual surrogate for an unarticulated and more inclusive view of national energy policy. Other forums—state legislatures, annual meetings of NCA or API, city councils, the public press—served a political purpose as well, extending their reach to include natural gas and electric power, energy sources still beyond the ken of the federal government. The structure of the energy industries provided the broadest energy agenda item, facilitating an integrated and comprehensive approach, whereas a focus on transportation frequently narrowed attention to, say, rail rates between the Pocahontas coal field and Chicago.

The organizational structure of each energy industry, well-known to contemporaries, derived from a body of knowledge accumulated over several decades. Oil independents were not mystified by the organizational structure of the Standard combination or by the restructuring that occurred after Standard's dissolution. The independents and a small but interested public were well aware—it was certainly no secret—of the proportion of production, refinery capacity, and pipeline mileage controlled by the majors. That the old Standard subsidiaries, acting as independent units, competed with one another as well as with newer majors held little consolation to independents or others concerned with the concentration of resources and power in few hands.

If the degree of control over production, refining, and transportation owned by the former components of the Standard combination diminished, as it did in refining from 80 percent in 1906 to 45 percent in 1926, did this demonstrate the success of dissolution? Was it more germane that the former Standard subsidiaries still controlled close to 80 percent of refining capacity in the eastern district during the 1920s and that Standard Oil of New Jersey alone controlled a share rising from 10 percent in 1920 to 14 percent in 1930? During the 1920s, the proportion of total crude produced by twenty-one majors increased from 53 to 60 percent.[21] The ten largest firms owned a share of refining capacity that rose from 46 percent in 1919 to 60 percent in 1929. The largest fourteen firms controlled above 70 percent of pipeline mileage during the entire decade.[22] What were the appropriate questions suggested by these facts?

The structural form of the natural gas and electric power industries could be similarly depicted, although the implications of the holding company device was not fully appreciated until the publication of the results of two FTC investigations between 1928 and 1936. Still, in 1929, eight holding companies in natural gas, including Cities Service as the largest and Standard Oil (New Jersey) as the fourth largest, supplied 85 percent of all gas consumed, with 60 percent supplied by the top four. In the electric power industry, twenty-two firms possessed 61 percent of national generating capacity.[23] At the least, then, current information irrefutably documented the substantial control of three key energy industries by relatively few firms.

It made little sense to consider the organizational structure of the coal industry as a unit, since clear differences distinguished anthracite from bituminous. Our discussion that accompanied Table 2 touched upon essential structural differences as of 1920, and these persisted during the 1920s. In bituminous, the largest 17 companies produced 20 percent of total tonnage, and the next 201 firms produced 40 percent, a degree of concentration far less marked than in the oil or the energy utilities. Moreover, few bituminous companies owned any part of the transportation upon which they depended or any part of the firms that wholesaled or retailed coal. Except for the captive bituminous mines, integration had not occurred in soft coal.

In anthracite, the eight leading mine-owning railroad companies contributed almost 70 percent of total tonnage and owned an equivalent share of the reserves. Captive mines were not absent from the bituminous industry. Steel plants, railroads, and utilities in 1924 owned 23 percent of the total soft coal output; in 1929, the production of captive mines contributed 27 percent of bituminous production. And, of course, a handful of large railroads earned a high proportion of freight revenue from carrying coal. Railroad ownership of anthracite mines, coupled with the total concentration of production in Pennsylvania and the consumption of three-quarters of all the anthracite in the northeastern seaboard states (a portion of which was marketed through wholesale houses also owned by the railroad mining companies), precipitated demands for the divorcement of mines from railroads. A similar rationale motivated those seeking the separation of the pipelines from the integrated oil companies.[24]

While the bituminous industry reeled from the blows of strikes and market dislocation, the wisdom of the 1920s excluded monopoly from among the primary causative factors.[25] Indeed, bituminous operators frequently bewailed the application of monopolistic power against them, be it the UMWA, the coal-carrying railroads, or other dominant purchasers such as the utilities and steel, and berated the large consumers for using market leverage to beat down prices. The ICC proved insensitive to coal operator complaints about rates while other difficulties appeared insusceptible to correction through the application of the antitrust laws. More than enough soft coal existed for a shrinking market, hardly a condition replete with monopolistic potential.

The anthracite producers, it was charged, conspired to keep production stable and prices artifically high. In fact, production fell steadily after 1923 (see Tables 4 and 11). The anthracite-burning public turned increasingly to bituminous and other fuels as anthracite prices failed to reflect a declining demand. During the anthracite strike of September 1925–February 1926, an estimated 17 million tons of bituminous replaced anthracite. Anthracite use in New England dropped by 15 percent. Strangely enough, lost markets stimulated little change in the tactics of the mine-owning railroads. Coal freight earnings contributed a larger portion of railroad profits than coal mining. The anthracite roads, then, maintained high freight rates on their own and on independent coal, the costs of which were eventually passed on to consumers. Many of those consumers wisely sought cheaper fuels.[26]

Control of transportation permitted a relatively few firms in both anthracite and oil to dominate the production phase and capture the lion's share of the national (regional for anthracite) market. Critics of these industries correctly emphasized the crucial role of price leadership exercised by the key firms—in oil, singling out the former Standard Oil companies as the price setters. In anthracite, the case appeared indisputable; freight rates determined wholesale or retail prices. In oil, the evidence indicated that the Standard firm in each marketing area fixed a price for crude or gasoline that other firms followed. Divorcement of the pipelines from the oil companies and of the mines from the railroads would reduce, it was insisted, the swollen power of the largest firms and foster competitive marketing.

The merit of the cases made against the anthracite railroads and the pipeline companies weighed but lightly in the political arena of the 1920s. Narrow Supreme Court interpretations of the commodity clause of the Hepburn Act diluted its usefulness, and the ICC made no effort to clarify its precise meaning, thus relegating that clause to the same political limbo that nullified the intent of the common carrier clause. ICC indifference forced the aggrieved to seek legislative relief. Nor did the Justice Department evince any interest in applying the antitrust laws to the anthracite or petroleum combinations.

Those laws, in any event, were seriously weakened in 1920 by the Supreme Court in the U.S. Steel Case. The Court rejected the government's contention that U.S. Steel used its power to eliminate competition and should therefore be dissolved into its constituent parts. In effect, the Court sanctioned informal industry cooperation to stabilize prices. Shortly thereafter, the Court almost destroyed FTC's authority to investigate and proceed against unfair methods of competition, a development that terminated FTC scrutiny of major oil company domination of gasoline service stations and of the gasoline price-fixing tactics of the former Standard companies. The power of FTC to investigate investment in and profits of the bituminous industry was similarly vetoed by the courts. In the Maynard Coal Company case (1920), an action initiated by the National Coal Association, the decision stated that FTC possessed no authority to demand information regarding the intrastate coal trade and that Congress could not delegate such power.[27]

With the ICC and FTC virtually eliminated as sources of relief, the opponents of big anthracite and big oil turned to the Congress. In

Pennsylvania, for instance, Gov. Gifford Pinchot, in 1923 and 1924, fought rising anthracite prices, attempted to mobilize the anthracite-consuming states against the anthracite roads, and promoted regulatory legislation in Congress, but all unsuccessfully. A malleable anti-anthracite constituency existed in neither Pennsylvania nor the other eastern states. The independent anthracite operators closed ranks with the mine railroads when confronted with the threat of regulation. The independents, after all, could pass on high freight rates to consumers.

Not even the severe hardship suffered by easterners during the winter anthracite strike of 1925–26 gave birth to a constituency. As anthracite prices soared to $40 per ton in New York City, Boston, and Manchester, New Hampshire, many turned to bituminous as a substitute. Many unfortunates in New York suffered injury and even death because of the incompatibility of their anthracite furnaces with soft coal use. Numerous bills were introduced in Congress calling for the granting of emergency powers to the president, but Coolidge withheld support and insisted that Pennsylvania handle the emergency. USCC's final report adopted the view that "a limited natural monopoly like anthracite, held by a relatively small number of individuals, estates, and companies and supplying a necessity of life for millions of our people, can not continue to be treated as if it were not affected by a public interest." The industry, the report maintained, must be regulated like railroads and telephones.[28]

Some of the legislation considered in the strike-induced hearings of 1926 proposed regulatory schemes. Few witnesses unconnected with the anthracite industry denied the basic assumption of the USCC report. While ARA, NCA, and the anthracite organization proclaimed the success of voluntary efforts in moving coal and opposed further federal intervention, others like Governor Pinchot, Senator Borah, Mayor James W. Curley of Boston, and various eastern newspapers pressed for regulatory action. But as Eugene McAuliffe detected, "the American people and their legislators forget quickly. . . . They are rapidly forgetting the anthracite strike of September 1, 1925, lasting 165 days . . . which cost the country millions of dollars."[29]

Certainly this shrewd observation captured a truth that applied in 1920 and 1923 as well as in 1926. But an even more telling criticism of regulatory legislation, particularly if calling for divorcement, emphasized the adequacy of the powers already possessed by the ICC. This position also contained a truth, as did the assertion that the aggrieved could seek judicial remedies. But, of course, the ICC and the courts formed a key part of the *problem*, the former refusing to enforce the law and the latter tightly circumscribing the effectiveness of the law. Trapped in a cocoon of circular reasoning, Congress gave desultory attention to a fact-finding commission and, feeling no pressure from a vocal public, terminated the debate.[30] Legislative proposals that followed in 1928 and 1930 (see Chapter 10) influenced both the NRA coal code and the Guffey acts.

Many individuals and groups expressed outrage over the performance of the coal industry, but this failed to produce a sense of urgency in Congress. Inertial forces similarly precluded congressional action relative to oil, despite the endeavors of some legislators to restructure the industry. A number of hearings occurred before 1924, the most important of which was the La Follette investigation. The organization of FOCB in 1924 reduced the pressure on Congress to deal with oil. As the debate shifted from the floors of Congress to the FOCB, the emphasis shifted as well, heralding a redefinition of the central issues and the prescription of new remedies. FOCB abandoned the ground staked out by the La Follette committee, and it was not returned to until the mid-1930s.

Concluding that the oil industry "is clothed with a great public interest," the La Follette committee's recommendations pursued a strict antitrust strategy and were linked to two basic assumptions: that the dissolution of Standard had not stimulated competition and that the overwhelming power of Standard, if not checked, would eliminate competition. "The dominating fact in the oil industry today," the final report asserted, "is its complete control by the Standard Companies." Through its control of the pipelines, Standard Oil "fixes the price which the producers of crude oil receives at the well, the price which the refiner receives for his gasoline and kerosene, as well as the retail price paid by the consumer." The committee recognized the rise of major firms competitive with Standard, but from time to time in its report subsumed those new giants into an amorphous, allegorical being called "The Standard." A strict segregation of the Standard companies from the rest of the pack would only marginally influence the conclusions. After all, in 1920, five former Standard firms controlled 29 percent of national refining capacity. Consolidation and the concentration of enormous market power in a few firms characterized the industry.[31]

If a competitive market were to survive, the committee believed, such power demanded immediate dilution. Industry defenders argued that the integrated firms were in the process of achieving an optimum size that guaranteed efficiency, quality, and low prices. According to some, the nonintegrated oil firms, many small and inefficient, obstructed reform by opposing the conservation proposals of FOCB.[32] In demanding the enforcement of the antitrust laws and the common carrier clause, the independents deflected attention from the critical problems of the industry. The La Follette committee's recommendations coincided with the political demands of the independents, drew support from that source, and defined the problem of oil in terms of the absence of competition. FOCB essentially ignored the competitive struggle for markets and emphasized the waste inherent in current production practices. The antitrust strategy of the La Follette committee gained adherents from among the nonintegrated firms; FOCB's proposals, until 1927 or so, encountered unyielding opposition from both independents and majors. Neither the antitrust nor the conservation strategies stimulated much interest outside of oil.

The key recommendations of the Senate committee included enforcement of the common carrier clause, divorcement, the reduction of freight rates on petroleum products moving eastward from the Mid-Continent, the initiation of antitrust suits against the price-fixing power of the Standard companies, and an investigation of the legality of gasoline cracking patents owned by, for example, Jersey Standard, Indiana Standard, and the Texas Company.[33] The committee's proposals furnished part of the impulse behind the FTC investigation of petroleum initiated in 1926, which, as published in 1928, exonerated the oil industry from charges of price fixing. FTC's earlier reports and studies, while skeptical of the social benefits derived from the overall control exercised by the majors and aware of the price leadership of the Standard companies in many market areas, had not uncovered solid evidence of collusive price fixing. FTC's findings, however, did support the La Follette committee's conclusion as to the close relationship between transportation and market accessibility.[34]

These deliberations yielded no tangible returns in policy formulation during the 1920s. The postulates undergirding an antitrust strategy in oil as well as coal encountered hostile courts, indifferent regulatory agencies, national administrations promoting cooperation rather than coercion, and an apathetic public. Indeed, FOCB's definition of the issues and its faith in industry-government cooperation fathered an American Petroleum Institute proposal to trade industry cooperation for immunity from antitrust prosecution, a result achieved during the early New Deal despite the loud opposition of the independents.

The La Follette committee believed that the oil industry had attained a degree of concentration that ceased to produce socially desirable results, a supposition difficult to prove. The relationship between an oligopolistic industry—anthracite as well as oil—and the social whole remained unclear to the general public. A few did take note of the division of the oil industry into two hostile camps and frequently acknowledged the legitimacy of independent assertions attributing their problem to the majors.[35] According to the independents, further consolidation would drive them from the industry. The independents were undoubtedly correct in accusing the pipeline companies of noncompliance with the common carrier clause. What proved impossible of unequivocal demonstration was the conjunction between the public interest and the survival of the independents. The absence of such an understanding precluded enlisting a supportive public into the camp of the independents. During the 1930s, while the independents inveighed against the power of the majors and reiterated all their old demands, the major companies successfully pursued a politics of price stabilization and production controls.

An Inventory for the 1920s

The scope of federal regulatory involvement in the energy industries did not diverge radically in the 1920s from that carved out earlier. Industry leaders and government officials frequently employed the rhetoric of cooperation, or associationalism, but the industries sought a form of cooperation that minimized the federal role, while the government failed to crystallize its thinking regarding appropriate responsibilities. If the proper duties of the federal government included the guarantee of an adequate supply of energy at reasonable prices and the prevention of serious interruptions in energy supply, the government would receive low marks in coal. In the other energy industries, the government played an insubstantial role. Congress pursued an antitrust tack without results and, along with FTC, wielded a weapon effectively spiked by the courts. The Harding and Coolidge administrations hoped that intraindustry cooperation would resolve the problems of coal and oil. Ideas were in the air—and remained there.

The La Follette committee and the production-control propositions of Henry L. Doherty and FOCB instilled some fear in API and at the headquarters of major companies. Neither challenge attracted a constituency sufficiently large to achieve the desired ends. The key developments in the oil industry, particularly in gasoline refining and marketing, occurred because of decisions made within the industry. The process of concentration in pipeline and refinery ownership proceeded without inhibition. The fight for markets between the integrated and nonintegrated firms further defined the mutuality of interests within each contending group, and some of these interests were translated into political demands. The interests of independents—producers, refiners, wholesalers and jobbers, and retailers—suffered as a result of federal inaction and the ever accumulating advantages of the majors. The depression further threatened the economic viability of the independents and incited them to frenzied political action.[36]

Coal, certainly vulnerable if measured against a reasonable standard of performance and an apparently waning industry compared with oil or electric power, successfully evaded permanent federal controls, despite a series of strikes causing public hardship and productive of much antagonism toward the industry. The operators deflected much of the blame to the railroads and the UMWA and refused to cooperate with the federal government. As in the case of petroleum, neither the executive nor the legislature could agree upon a preferred industrial structure for coal. Nationalization was the fanciful panacea of a few; giant power captured the imagination of others. But a politically feasible solution failed to evolve from among the suggested remedies. The idea of coal as an ordinary commodity, like corks or oil cloth, persisted. USCC clothed the industry in the public interest; the La Follette committee clothed the oil industry in the public interest. In both instances, the garments resembled the emperor's new clothes.

Of all the fuel industries, natural gas received least attention from the federal government or from the state commissions that regulated the public utilities. Gas conservation emerged as an issue in several states, but only as a result of its intersection with the techniques of oil recovery. While a component of the energy mix in certain regions, the industry had yet to assume a level of national importance comparable with oil, coal, or electric power. When, in 1927, the American Gas Association (AGA) received a plea from NCA for support against federal intervention in the coal industry, AGA's officials chose not to respond.[37] Only in the 1930s, as FTC probed deeply into the structure of the electric and gas holding companies, did AGA hurriedly construct political defenses.

As the decade passed midpoint, the oil industry felt the first buffeting from crude pouring out of newly discovered fields, and coal careened into another round of strikes. The major oil companies, faced with severe price deflation, looked more favorably upon such remedies as production controls. The decade ended in disaster. Millions lost their jobs, markets disappeared, and prices tumbled. The nation joined the coal miners and farmers in depression. The jerry-built edifices of the holding companies trembled, as did their investors. Hard times compelled new and more searching inquiries into the relationship between the energy industries and the common good. Although the Hoover years introduced no changes that seriously affected the energy industries, the ideas of the 1920s began to germinate and, finally, to yield some fruit during the New Deal. Whether an expanded role for the federal government and a concomitant narrowing of market-place power would better serve the public interest than the arrangements evolved during earlier years is explored in subsequent chapters.

EIGHT

Oil Politics
during the Early Depression Years

APPREHENSION about the nation's future oil supply launched the
Federal Oil Conservation Board on its career in 1924 and explained
its conservationist impulses. Within a few years, however, the exigencies of flush field production compelled the board and its intractable
clientele to alter course and attend to the flood of oil entering the
market and depressing prices. The strategies of field unitization and
prorationing initially suggested by Henry L. Doherty and a few others
and soundly rejected by most elements within the organized oil industry, now seemed, in the context of the discoveries of 1926 and 1927,
more appealing to the larger firms that dominated API. Could not
the same strategies be utilized to achieve supply and demand equilibrium? Could not the rhetoric of conservation be employed in the cause
of industry price stabilization? As a decade of prosperity came to an
abrupt end in 1929 and as depression strangled the economy, FOCB
thought so, and so too did an increasing number of oilmen.

Implementation of unitization and prorationing advanced but little
during the Hoover years. Even in principle the oil industry could not
reach consensus about unitization and prorationing. Neither could
proponents agree as to whether they should be voluntary or compulsory and, if the latter, who should enforce them—states or the federal
government. Blocking FOCB's endeavors to formulate an acceptable
policy were independents who resisted all controls, other independents
and majors who sought some sort of voluntary program, and still
others (including both independents and majors) who disagreed about
the location of authority. FOCB and API failed to convince many inde-

pendents that their persistent and depression-intensified harping on such traditional issues as oil imports, freight rates, pipelines, and monopoly obstructed the implementation of a program that treated the truly germane problems. A few oil producing states did achieve a tenuous production-control agreement, but it collapsed when the East Texas fields came in. The situation became so desperate that the governors of Oklahoma and Texas, in August 1931, declared martial law in the oil fields and dispatched armed guardsmen to stop production.

During the Hoover administration, the political cleavages within the oil industry occurred within an atmosphere of profound despair and hopelessness and mounting distrust of the business community. The Hoover administration responded to the depression with homilies to individual effort, with a few billion dollars plugged into banks and railroads in the hope that some would trickle down, by denigrating efforts to institute public works programs, and by lecturing municipalities on their responsibilities for unemployed breadwinners upon whose exiguous resources some 40 million Americans depended for food, clothing, and shelter. The crisis of oil composed but a part of this larger disaster, and its leaderless and purposeless politics bogged down in a morass of particularism. The New Deal brought purpose and leadership to strategies available to Hoover and compatible with his political philosophy but beyond his political abilities to realize. This chapter deals with drift, the next with purpose and program. It should not be assumed that the latter were synonymous with correctness or wisdom. New Deal oil policies, expeditiously enacted as part of a grand recovery strategy, were neither imaginative nor free from the defects of political opportunism.

Reserves and Future Supply

The oil discoveries of the late 1920s and early 1930s and the resulting crisis of oversupply somewhat muted expressions of concern over future oil scarcity. Still, during the 1930s, a few federal officials addressed the problem of long-term supply. Even though discoveries exceeded domestic production between 1926 and 1938, Interior officials believed that shortages could be expected within a couple of decades (see Table 12). In 1934, assessing the nation's petroleum future, an Interior committee on mineral policies emphasized a number of salient, if speculative, points. Liquid fuels from shale or coal were not to be relied upon because of cost and the time required to commercialize such processes. The rate of future national consumption would advance more rapidly than replacement from new discoveries. The cost of new oil would increase as greater attention was devoted to secondary recovery. The largest reserves were likely to be found in foreign countries, especially the Middle East and South America, and American reserves would be exhausted sooner than the deposits of other nations. "The position of the United States with respect to the future supply of petroleum," the committee concluded, "is much weaker than that of the outside world."[1] Given this reasoning, a conservation campaign seemed eminently sensible. Should, the committee asked, the U.S. begin importing large volumes in order to conserve its own reserves against some future threat to national security?

To desperate oilmen and members of Congress, such projections seemed more hallucinatory than even the American Petroleum Institute's one-billion-acre reserve. So much oil was produced in 1930 and 1931 that prices for Mid-Continent crudes plunged to ten cents per barrel, while markets for refined products contracted sharply under the impact of falling consumer spending. While a few oil executives such as Frank Phillips, president of Phillips Petroleum Company, accepted the credibility of the shortage thesis, most agreed with W. S. Farrish, president and chairman of the board of Standard Oil of New Jersey, in totally rejecting such pessimistic prognostication. Rep. Charles A. Wolverton, Republican of New Jersey, defended the interests of his consuming constituency in opposing all production-control schemes. Wolverton's stance represented the common position assumed by the eastern consuming states.[2] While consumer objections ultimately succumbed to New Deal and major oil insistence upon production controls as a price-inflation mechanism, consuming interests did exercise leverage against independent producer demands for a prohibitive oil tariff or import quotas. The consuming states prevented the imposition of effective import restrictions, designed to subsidize domestic production, until 1957. In the evolution of depression energy policies, arguments for conservation derived from national security considerations carried little weight compared with the burdensome realities of oversupply and price deflation.

In 1925, FOCB embraced Doherty's proposals for unitization and prorationing as part of a larger scheme to promote conservation and to prolong the life of America's reserves. But from the beginning, production controls were the target of an enveloping fusillade discharged from the rival independent and major camps. The impact of new discoveries so distressed the industry that by 1927 the majors and API had moved into the camp of their former adversary and were actively promoting some form of production control. This left only the independents, numerous but armed with less political firepower, to train their puny weaponry against government controls. Independents, while admitting the theoretical need to produce more efficiently, viewed compulsory unitization of an entire field and the setting of well-production quotas as threatening to their livelihood. They suspected that such controls would severely disadvantage them in competing with or selling to the majors.

Independent unity broke down somewhat in the face of the surpluses of 1929 and 1930. Some independents were willing to support production controls administered by the separate states. By that time, both FOCB and API had opted for state rather than federal controls and launched a campaign to achieve uniformity in the conservation legislation of the producing states. Doherty, Mark Requa, and Sen. William E. Borah argued for direct federal controls, but this was not politically feasible during either the Hoover or the Roosevelt administration. As the states tentatively applied prorationing to limited areas before 1929, FOCB had, to all intents and purposes, ceased worrying about reserves and about conservation.

Early prorationing laws in such states as Texas and Oklahoma defined waste in terms of efficiency of extraction—damage to productive strata, the escape of gas or oil above ground, reservoir pressure—not in terms of economic waste—production in excess of market demands. Indeed, the Texas law was amended in 1929 to exclude economic waste, a troublesome change when East Texas exploded on the scene in 1930 and 1931. Initial prorationing efforts, as in the Yates field of Texas, and court approval in 1928 and 1929 of state-wide prorationing in Oklahoma and Texas, encouraged the proponents of state controls. But in 1928 and 1930–31, the unimaginable bounty of the Oklahoma City and the East Texas fields completely undid this progress. The initial impact of both fields occurred during the depression, and the magnitude of oil produced far exceeded that of older fields, threatening to totally inundate a skidding market.

Thereafter, FOCB and its allies single-mindedly pressed for the application of production controls to raise prices and, in the face of the East Texas glut, embraced a broader federal role. Within the producing states, agreement could not be reached on the issue of federal supervision or federally imposed quotas. Independent producers were powerful in most fields and obstructed the application of prorationing and contested the imposition of federal restraints. If controlled production meant the reduction of cash flow, then producers would oppose its implementation, hold fast to older production techniques, and, perhaps, disregard laws applied to their fields and wells. Small producers never admitted that their methods were at variance with the public interest. They believed that the practices of the majors severely damaged the public welfare.[3]

The Reemergence of Ancient Issues

The issue of national reserves was filed away in some remote corner of the U.S. Geological Survey, not to be retrieved until the establishment of the various mineral and fuel policy planning committees that skulked forlornly in the darker wings of the New Deal. A sufficiency of other issues—or nonissues as FOCB would have it—remained. The often convulsive perturbations of oil industry politics during the Hoover and Roosevelt administrations involved far more than the rejection or acceptance in some form of FOCB production-control proposals. The board's schemes ignored most of the issues that agitated oil independents and a variety of lay people. Independents clung tenaciously to hallowed remedies through good times and bad, but rarely so fervently as during the depression. The issues have been encountered in previous pages: tariffs or quotas on imports, discriminating freight rates and pipeline practices, marketing competition, the alleged monopoly of the major integrated firms.

FOCB and API considered these issues as irrelevant to the problem of overproduction and price deflation. Nonetheless, the independents succeeded again and again in interjecting them into the politics of oil in 1929 and thereafter because they struck a chord to which antitrusters could positively respond. Even President Hoover scotched FOCB efforts to weaken the Sherman Anti-Trust Act. From FOCB's perspective, the concerns of independents were viewed as of small moment, or worse, as obstructing a united attack on the most pressing problems of the oil industry. As the grand strategies designed by the early New Deal to end the depression lost their glittering appeal, the focus of the independents upon monopoly intermeshed more tightly with the antitrust emphasis of the later New Deal, but before anything could be resolved, World War II intervened.

During the 1920s, a number of American oil companies developed foreign oil fields, particularly in Mexico, Peru, Columbia, and Venezuela, and imported foreign crude for refining and sale along the East Coast. In 1929, American firms owned 30 percent of all foreign crude oil produciton, amounting to 329 million barrels or double the quantity owned by Americans in 1922. By 1931, Jersey Standard's foreign production surpassed its domestic, and in 1932 the firm acquired a large refinery on the island of Aruba, off the coast of Venezuela. As early as 1921, independent producers had sought an oil import tariff to stem the flow of Mexican crude to the Atlantic seaboard where it was used as fuel oil, but President Harding and the majors opposed the tariff. The issue lay dormant until resurrected by the market collapse in 1929 and 1930. Congress, in 1931, considered a joint resolution imposing a tariff on petroleum imports and companion bills in both houses, sponsored by Sen. Arthur Capper, Republican of Kansas, and Rep. Milton C. Garber, Republican of Oklahoma, placing import quotas on crude and prohibiting the importation of refined products for three years.[4]

During the course of congressional hearings, all the interest groups affected by the bills offered testimony. The producing states of Texas, Oklahoma, Kansas, California, Colorado, and several others lined up in support of the measures and paraded innumerable witnesses before both committees. The essence of all the oral and written testimony was summarized by Senator Capper. The Standard Oil group, Royal Dutch Shell, and Gulf Oil imported oil amounting to about 10 percent of annual consumption. This cheaper oil fixed the price of crude and fuel oil throughout the country. Independent refiners, Capper explained, dared not purchase large quantities of crude in advance for fear that imported crude would be thrown on the market at very low prices. Foreign imports of crude depressed domestic prices (reduced in the Mid-Continent to thirty cents per barrel by Standard of Indiana in June 1931) and replaced American crude in refineries supplying eastern fuel oil requirements. Coupled with the pipeline monopoly of the majors, the flood of imports would, Capper and Sen. John W. E. Thomas, Democrat of Oklahoma, insisted, ruin most independents within a few years, leaving the producing fields and refining entirely to the majors. Dozens of independent Mid-Continent refiners, such independent organizations as the Independent Petroleum Association of America (IPAA), the recently organized Governor's Oil Relief Conference, and communities in the oil producing states provided Capper ample corroborative data.

A host of seaboard consuming interests, transport companies, and coastal refiners (owned by the majors) opposed any form of import limitation. Representatives from consuming states argued straightforwardly that imports provided cheap fuel oil. The Associated Industries of Massachusetts reflected the opinions of many eastern consuming groups when it told the Senate committee that passage of either the Capper or the Garber bill would do the inland refiners no good at all. Railroad rates on fuel oil from the Mid-Continent to New England were simply too steep, and if either bill passed New England would switch back to coal, a point that partially explains the favorable attitude of the National Coal Association toward these bills. Sen. Millard E. Tydings, Democrat of Maryland, bluntly told Capper that he would not harm the Maryland shipping or asphalt industries or residential fuel oil users for the sake of Mid-Continent interests. The Pan American Petroleum & Transport Company argued that passage of the bills would rapidly deplete domestic oil reserves and damage national security, but such an argument, coming as it did from a subsidiary of Indiana Standard, a major importer, fooled no one. Still, Wirt Franklin, president of IPAA, was wrong, and he knew it, when he charged that only a few major importing firms opposed this legislation.[5]

Such influential opponents of import restrictions as Mark Requa, Henry L. Doherty, and Secretary of Interior Ray Lyman Wilbur, chairman of FOCB, denied any influence on price or marketability of such a marginal volume of imports. But in 1931, FOCB, still opposed to mandatory quotas or a tariff, recommended that the major importers agree to voluntary reductions. In an effort to win independent support for prorationing, Secretary of Commerce Robert P. Lamont appealed to the importing companies to render a national service by reducing imports, a concession elicited by political rather than economic considerations.[6]

In fact, even as the hearings commenced, events in the Mid-Continent in late 1930 and early 1931 substantiated independent claims that imports caused a disastrous fall in prices and a shrinking market for oil. In 1930, Humble Oil (a Texas-based subsidiary of Standard New Jersey) announced a drastic cut in prices offered for North Texas crude and soon stopped purchases altogether. In December 1931, Prairie Oil and Gas Company, the largest purchaser and carrier of Mid-Continent crude, ceased purchasing Oklahoma and Kansas crude, leaving thousands of small producers without a market. Shrinking markets forced this action upon Humble and Prairie. In Humble's case, Standard of New Jersey substituted Columbian crude for domestic. Between 1929 and 1933, Humble's crude sales declined by 14.2 million barrels, with 77 percent of the decline attributable to reduced Standard purchases. In Prairie's case, not only did a number of its normal customers construct pipelines and develop their own domestic sources of crude during the 1920s, but its three largest customers, Gulf, Standard of Indiana, and Standard of New Jersey, all imported large volumes of South American crude. In 1930, according to Prairie, those imports replaced 143,000 barrels of crude daily formerly obtained from small Mid-Continent stripper wells. As Prairie informed an API committee established to find an outlet for this "distressed" oil, the major refineries "have assured us that they can no longer furnish us a market for any of this oil." With so much surplus crude on the market, Standard of Indiana, in June 1931, reduced the price offered for Mid-Continent crude by an average of thirty-three cents per barrel.[7]

This crisis energized the drive for a tariff which had bogged down in both houses. In 1932, FOCB succeeded in negotiating an informal agreement with the importing firms to reduce imports during the last half of the year by 25 percent, which, in modified form, became part of the National Recovery Administration Petroleum Code of 1933. Protariff forces, somewhat strengthened by the support of API and several nonimporting major firms, won an amendment to the Revenue Act of 1932 that placed an excise tax of twenty-one cents per barrel on imported crude and fuel oil and higher taxes on gasoline and lubricants. Hearings conducted on the revenue bill of 1932, at which the testimony of 1931 was repeated, indicated that substantial opposition to a tariff remained. The shift from a tariff of forty-two cents per barrel to an excise tax and the abandonment of the Capper embargo dulled the opposition of such as Senator Tydings, representative of both free trade Democrats and eastern consumers, and sapped the strength of industrial users who rejected any surcharges on oil. But the measure was received cooly by adherents of a tariff. Independent producers and refiners doubted that the compromise figure was high enough to open up any new markets for their products. Senator Tydings believed that it would benefit only the nonimporting majors. The historians of Humble, however, maintain that the tax brought relief to Humble as its customers looked increasingly for domestic supplies. Indiana Standard, for example, sold its foreign properties to Jersey Standard. But Humble's sales declined from 37.7 million barrels in 1931 to 27.4 million barrels in 1934, while sales to Jersey Standard plunged from 29.6 million to 19.4 million. Mid-Continent producers had hardly recovered from the Prairie affair of 1931, when East Texas oil inundated markets and shattered prices. All in all, the placebo-like effect of the excise tax on the marketing position of Mid-Continent producers assured the persistence of agitation for a real tariff during the remainder of the 1930s.[8]

In the tariff debates of 1931–32, rather clear-cut oil zones of interest responded to immediate economic considerations. The producing states of the Mid-Continent, in addition to California, stood together against the Atlantic consuming states. Within the industry, the various branches divided along lines consistent with their location. Mid-Continent producers and refiners presented a solid protariff front.

Eastern refiners divided into two camps as most nonimporting firms aligned themselves with the Mid-Continent, while the importers and their transportation allies united in opposing restrictions. Among marketers, opposition to or support of import restrictions depended upon their access to Mid-Continent supplies. Arguments derived from considerations of conservation or national security were neutralized since both could be employed to sustain any position.

To Requa, all this proved that the industry, by itself, could not put its house in order and that some sort of federal commission was urgently required to monitor the use of the nation's resources.[9] FOCB, without any coercive powers, did essay this difficult brokerage and did convince the importers to curtail their imports. But FOCB's basic opposition to tariffs, quotas, or embargoes earned only the further enmity of the independents, already alienated by the board's commitment to production controls. FOCB's reputation with the independents suffered further damage when the issue of divorcement resurfaced as a direct result of Prairie's decision to cease purchasing Mid-Continent crude.

Prairie's announcement in December 1930 exposed the transporter to the burning hostility of Mid-Continent oil interests, which attributed their weak market position to the baneful policies of the pipeline companies and to the unwillingness of ICC to enforce the common carrier clause of the Hepburn Act. During the 1920s, trunk pipeline mileage increased from 24,000 to 44,000 miles. During the three years 1927–29, when the Greater Seminole, Oklahoma City, West Texas, and Texas Panhandle discoveries came in, over 9,000 miles were constructed. Particularly disturbing to Prairie's dominant competitive position in the Mid-Continent were lines constructed by firms such as Pure Oil and Jersey Standard, formerly customers of Prairie but now integrating backward to their own production. By the late 1920s, as Prairie's vulnerability became more evident, its managers looked to the possibilities of integration forward into refining or merger with an integrated firm. Prairie's market weakness in 1930 and 1931, reflected in revenues that fell from $38 million in 1929 to under $10 million in 1931, precipitated its purchasing decision.[10]

Thousands of small producers lost their only market while Prairie continued to transport the production of its own leases. FOCB and API scrambled frantically, and with reasonable success, to find alternative purchasers for the 15,000 to 20,000 barrels of distressed oil produced daily. At this very moment, the Kansas legislature was debating a new conservation law, which, as enacted in March 1931, defined waste to include economic waste and authorized the Kansas Corporation Commission to prevent waste by imposing prorationing in the fields and ratable taking from competing fields. Gov. Clyde Reed of Kansas was preparing to participate in a governors' conference in March which created The Oil States Advisory Committee. FOCB and API moved with alacrity to neutralize the substantial political power of the aggrieved oil interests, fearful that Prairie's decision might deflect Kansans from participating in a compact of producing states to limit production to current market needs and incite the state to pursue counterproductive antitrust policies.[11]

The Mid-Continent refused to be pacified by emergency relief measures and responded as if no changes had occurred within the oil industry since the La Follette hearings. The fact that Prairie, an ancient antagonist, could be battered by even larger enemies offered no solace to the independents. Prairie's deteriorating position proved that imports denied markets to domestic production and depressed prices; Prairie's decision proved that the policies of uncontrolled pipeline companies could ruin thousands of small producers. FOCB and API lectured Governor Reed and Senators Capper and Thomas as to the real culprit: the flush production of unregulated fields from which Prairie and other pipeline companies could gather great volumes of crude at much less expense than from the thousands of stripper wells yielding but three to ten barrels of oil daily. Independents, however, identified the power of the majors as the true culprit.

Homer Hoch, Republican congressman from Kansas, introduced a bill in 1931 that applied the commodities clause of the Hepburn Act of 1906 to the pipeline companies, thereby compelling divorcement.[12] In the House hearings of 1931 on the Hoch bill, all the old arguments against ICC and Prairie—the symbol for all the pipelines—tumbled from Fibber McGee's closet. Independents asserted that divorcement would loosen prices for crude and thus stimulate competition. A. S. Ritchie, Derby Oil Company, Wichita, Kansas, told the committee that control of the pipelines permitted the integrated firms to post low prices for independent crude. Independent producers were forced to sell to the pipelines. The pipelines then charged artificially low carrying rates on the crude passed through to eastern refineries. There, Charles E. Bowles, IPAA official, reminded the committee, the refined product was sold much more cheaply than independent refiners could sell their products, encumbered as they were by rail freight rates much higher than pipeline rates.

Hoch argued that divorcement would open the pipelines to independent producers, raise prices for independent crude, weaken the competitive advantages of the majors over independent refiners in central market areas by narrowing freight rate differentials, and, in fostering the expansion of independent refiners, provide an additional outlet for independent producers. Alfred M. Landon, independent oilman from Kansas, warned that without divorcement, tariff restrictions, and lower rail rates on petroleum products, hundreds of small firms would succumb to the power of the majors. To the direct House testimony favoring divorcement could be added scores of communications directed to President Hoover, FOCB, and Mid-Continent congressmen by railroads, producers, refiners, oil royalty owners, and community organizations in Tulsa, Kansas City, and numerous smaller places such as Coffeyville, Chanute, and Iola, Kansas.[13]

The Hoch bill worried API sufficiently to induce it to organize a committee to contest divorcement. API, as well as most other expert opinion, completely rejected the need for divorcement or its practicality. API denied the existence of monopoly in the oil industry, a position supported by the so-called Splawn report of 1932, which argued that pipelines should be considered an integral piece of the petroleum industry rather than an industry in itself.[14] Viewing the pipelines as an extension of the refinery—its limbs—back to the fields or forward to refined storage facilities jeopardized even the common carrier principle. Others, while less willing to ignore the economic power of the integrated firms, thought divorcement an ineffective remedy and advocated the enforcement of the common carrier clause. Although the Hoch bill went no further than committee, a new administration would assume power in 1933. Among its central figures, Harold L. Ickes, secretary of Interior, endorsed divorcement. Ickes's advocacy, in addition to a number of bills introduced into Congress, kept the issue alive and led to the inclusion of a divorcement clause in the NRA oil code.

FOCB assumed no official position on the divorcement bill but could hardly have viewed it as desirable. Cutthroat competition among producers in the Oklahoma City and East Texas fields threatened to drown the industry in a torrent of oil. FOCB's entire program was designed to reduce, not induce, competitiveness. For this reason, the oil board, in 1928–29, looked on sympathetically as API and FTC cooperated in the development of a code of fair practices for the marketing branch of the industry.

In 1922, *Oildom* introduced a new section devoted to the filling station. As millions of Americans took to the road in their new cars, tens of thousands of retail outlets for gasoline opened up along the streets and highways of the nation. In the early days of the auto, many garages, buggy shops, stables, and stores of various kinds hawked gasoline, often by the pailful. But by 1929–30, 317,000 gasoline service stations (roughly three times the number in 1920) dispensed 90 percent of the fuel purchased by motorists while also selling all the accessories and minor repairs and service required by autos.

Intense competition characterized this industry from the very beginning. The major firms quickly entered the field, at first by leasing equipment to already established retailers and then, by the mid-1920s, by building their own stations and leasing them to other parties (lease and agency agreements). In 1921, Indiana Standard operated 4,875 service stations in eleven states, and in 1926, 19,400 stations. In greater Kansas City, this firm operated 30 percent of all filling stations. By the late 1920s, the major integrated firms owned probably one-half of all the service stations and sold 70 to 80 percent of all the gasoline, including a sizable volume of unbranded gasoline distributed to and sold by independents. In the marketing territory of Jersey Standard, for example, that firm accounted for 43 percent of all gasoline sales in 1926, six other majors for 46 percent, and the independents for 11 percent.[15]

In the Mid-Continent, with numerous independent refiners in close proximity, a large number of independent stations sought their share of business. Indiana Standard marketed its product in twenty-five midwestern states and sold 36 percent of all the gasoline, while other majors sold 28 percent and smaller firms sold 37 percent. Since few of the small refiners possessed marketing organizations, most independent stations purchased their gasoline through independent jobbers or wholesalers, a group with greater political power in the Mid-Continent than elsewhere. A few of the larger independent refiners such as Derby and Champlin opened their own service stations within a marketing territory delimited by the cost of rail transportation. In order to compete with the highly advertised regular brands of the majors, the independents sought to maintain a price one or two pennies below the retail price of the major brands.[16] Maintaining this margin, complicated by the introduction by the larger marketers of a lower-than-regular or cut-rate grade, was essential to the independents and stimulated furious competition in service and accessories as well as in price.

The competitiveness of the industry commanded FTC attention immediately after World War I when independent retailers, particularly those in the Mid-Continent, accused the major firms of utilizing franchising or lease and agency agreements to drive independents from the streets. In the lease and agency contract, the refining company negotiated a lease with the proprietor of an established filling station, designating the proprietor as the company's operating agent, or the refiner constructed a station and then leased it to another party. Under this exclusive contract, the operator retailed company products at a designated price and leased pumps, storage tanks, and other equipment from the company.

Independent gasoline refiners and manufacturers of so-called Pennsylvania grade lubricants—Pennzoil or Quaker State—opposed the lease and agency system as an unfair limitation on the distribution of their products. During the early 1920s, FTC instituted actions against such arrangements on the grounds that they violated the Clayton Act, but the courts held against the commission. The problem intensified as the number of service stations proliferated to a point far beyond economic necessity, fostering gasoline price wars throughout the nation.

It was generally acknowledged that the separate Standard companies fixed the daily pump price in their marketing territories and that independents set their prices accordingly. Price cutting by any station normally precipitated equal or greater cuts by neighboring stations. Independent and major companies then traded accusations about which party initiated hostilities. Independents needed to maintain a steady gallonage and retain a price margin between their gasoline and the branded product of the majors. According to the independents, the majors frequently cut prices, forcing independents to sell at or below cost, and built stations rapidly in an effort to increase the gallonage dispensed, even though new stations were unneeded and served only to diminish the gallonage sold by nearby independents and majors alike. In Kansas City, for example, each new intersection begat new stations, irrespective of real demand. In most places, if land was available a filling station could be placed on it—and frequently was. Such draconic competition spawned a host of promotional techniques to attract new customers. The major companies vigorously promoted their brands in newspapers and on the radio. Unable to afford such advertising, the independents countered as best they could with on-site advertising, gifts or premiums such as glassware, free auto washing, and so forth. By the early 1930s, major firms had introduced the credit card as a competitive weapon.

Inelastic demand for gasoline within local market areas guaranteed motorists the benefits of frequent price wars. The attendant chaos and high rate of failure that plagued the industry prompted API to formulate a code of marketing ethics in 1928, which received the sanction of FTC in 1929. Sponsored by FTC's Trade Practices System, the code was adopted by a large majority of oil marketing and refining companies in all states except Texas and California. The code, administered by regional committees of API, sought the discontinuation of those practices that caused cutthroat competition. The depression, coupled with the price-deflating pressure of enormous quantities of Oklahoma City and East Texas oil, so aggravated conditions that the code quickly lost its effectiveness. The average price of gasoline at the pump (excluding taxes) in fifty American cities declined from eighteen cents in 1929 to thirteen cents in 1931, while the price paid by the retailer declined by only four cents. In spite of the dismal prospects for business, the number of service stations (primary outlets, not including 195,719 secondary outlets such as garages and general stores) rose from 121,513 in 1929 to 170,404 in 1933. Inevitably, price slashing once again became common.

All the marketing issues of the early depression, and new ones such as antichain-store laws passed by states to retard the monopolistic tendencies of A&P as well as Indiana Standard, became the inheritance of New Dealers. Despite the opposition of the National Association of Gasoline Retailers, which played no role in developing the oil code, the API code formed the nucleus of the marketing code of the NRA oil code. Gasoline price wars persisted throughout the 1930s, preventing the stabilization of the retail branch of the industry. The number of all gasoline retailers continued to grow, rising from 317,000 in 1929 to 450,000 in 1939, or from one outlet per eighty-four vehicles to one per sixty-nine vehicles. The lease and agency arrangements similarly troubled the code's administrators. To some, price fixing seemed the answer. Some advocated antichain-store and other antitrust strategies. Still others believed that limiting production to market demand offered the best solution. The inability of oil code authorities to bring a modicum of order to retailing alienated independent marketers and their trade organizations who perceived the Petroleum Administrative Board (see Chapter 9, p. 226), as did independent producers and refiners, as the instrument of the integrated firms. However, even had New Deal policies successfully controlled production in the flush fields, the surfeit of service stations and the inelasticity of demand assured the persistence of marketing instability.[17]

FOCB and Production Controls

As various sectors of the oil industry gathered their forces to achieve or combat import restrictions, divorcement, or marketing rationalization, FOCB pursued almost single-mindedly its own objectives: the

conservation of an irreplaceable natural resource for future generations of Americans and the stabilization of the industry by means of
the application of unitization and prorationing. Contemporary critics
labeled the board a tool of the majors. As the Independent Oil Men
of America contended, the monopolistic intentions of big oil, hidden
behind the smokescreen of conservation and legitimated by an alliance with FOCB, guaranteed that independent producers would be
the losers. Such New Deal critics as the National Resources Committee echoed those views, faulting the board for soft-pedaling conservation in order to achieve short-run price stability that induced the
further concentration of power in the hands of the integrated firms.
FOCB, however, viewed conservation and stabilization as compatible
and vigorously denied the imputation that conservation was designed
to conserve business profits.[18]

As noted earlier, the launching of Doherty's proposals and their
adoption by FOCB met instant rejection by the oil industry on two
grounds: that America possessed an abundance of petroleum and that
government intervention was as unnecessary as it was undesirable.
Industry objections to unitization, a concept possible of scientific vali-
dation, were less strenuous than opposition to prorationing, at least
among the major firms and within API. By the mid-1920s, sufficient
engineering evidence existed to demonstrate that gross inefficiency
and waste, of natural gas as well as petroleum, attended the rule of
capture procedures applied in the oil fields. Engineers, geologists, and
federal officials, joined by a few from within the oil industry, agreed
that uninhibited flush production in fields jammed full of oil rigs, each
pumping oil as rapidly as possible, quickly reduced reservoir pressure,
vented billions of cubic feet of natural gas into the air or wasted it by
flaring, and left much oil in the ground, irrecoverable with current
technology or at current prices. Corrective procedures for efficient
drilling and pumping were available and included the measurement
of oil pool gas pressure, the determination of the most efficient flow
per well, and the proper spacing of wells on a particular tract. The
unit management of pools would, FOCB claimed, eliminate waste
and, combined with prorationing, reduce unnecessary production, defined as production in excess of market demand, and shave production costs by eliminating uneconomic drilling.

The theory of unitization clashed with vested interests in the oil
fields. Independents, working on leased land, constituted a significant
portion of operators within each of the major fields—and were numerically dominant in the Oklahoma City and East Texas fields. Both
lessor and lessee, but especially the former, earned income according

to the amount produced. The pecuniary interests of both parties encouraged maximum daily production. Small producers, weak in capital resources and without storage facilities or direct access to refineries, depended upon daily sales. Submitting to unitization and allowable withdrawals calculated for the entire field rather than by the individual well benefited the large firms which could afford to tie up capital, owned storage tanks, and, frequently, owned transportation and refineries. Independent producers, royalty owners, and refiners resisted unitization regardless of its sponsor. Yet, even when faced with defeat, the independents wielded sufficient power in state politics to shape a system that minimized their losses.

Adherents of prorationing viewed it as the application of scientifically derived estimates of total national oil demand to the daily production of each field. Unitization offered no assurances of supply-demand equilibrium. Even if each well, suitably spaced, withdrew oil at its optimum rate, production could still surpass demand. Prorationing, then, was the economic prerequisite for achieving orderly production and, as FOCB exclaimed, as much a conservation as an economic stabilization strategy. But, as FOCB recognized, the objective need for conservation alone could not—did not—motivate the oil industry or the states to reform the system. Erupting after 1929, demands for economic stabilization, rather than appeals to conservation, provided the incentive to change the system.[19]

As part of its strategy to reach agreement on production control, FOCB first emphasized the desirability of voluntary agreements among the producers of each field to allocate production among the wells. An effort in 1927 to achieve voluntary limitation in the Yates field in Texas aroused the opposition of many independent producers. The latter obtained a court injunction preventing those who wished to limit production voluntarily from participating in the scheme. Although producer groups such as the Mid-Continent Gas and Oil Association preferred a voluntary system, antitrust laws as well as the opposition of small producers and royalty holders assured the failure of voluntarism. FOCB then shifted to a two-pronged campaign. The board sought an amendment to the Sherman Act that permitted the cooperation of producers in limiting production. The second tactic coupled uniform state regulation to control production and prevent waste with the adoption of an interstate agreement to apportion allowable production among its members. In 1927, FOCB sponsored the formation of the Committee of Nine, composed of three former presidents of API, three representatives of the American Bar Association, and three federal appointees, to which was delegated the task of formulating a production control scheme based on industry-state-federal cooperation and on recommending federal legislation that would promote conservation by loosening the antitrust laws.

Both the API and individual oilmen, largely from the integrated firms, favored the dilution of the antitrust laws. As the general counsel of the Continental Oil Company explained to Secretary of Interior Hubert Work in 1926, the antitrust laws blocked all possibility of cooperative oil conservation, as in the Yates field, and should be amended to permit combination for purposes of conservation.[20] Doherty publicly denounced the Committee of Nine, characterizing its API members as the most reactionary in the business and appointed because of their known opposition to federal regulation. Doherty's views, however much they enlivened the discussion, elicited little sympathy from the industry or FOCB. The Committee of Nine recommended two basic legislative requirements: 1) granting FOCB the authority to declare a state of emergency in times of oil overproduction and to stop production, 2) a law declaring that producer agreements to control production in the fields were not in violation of the antitrust laws and delegating supervisory powers over such agreements to FOCB. Similar legislation, said the committee, should be passed by the oil-producing states, which would then shoulder the responsibility for enforcement. For the most part these recommendations were consonant with resolutions adopted by the API's board of directors in late 1927.

The committee's recommendations to change the antitrust laws ran into immediate opposition from independents, and, in 1929, President Hoover came out flatly against it as a form of price fixing. In a moment of frankness, Hoover confided to the secretary of the Interior his suspicion that oil industry and government meetings derived from the desire of oil men "to have legalized some control which is illegal, otherwise they would do it themselves."[21] API proposals in early 1929 to restrict production to the 1928 level, as FOCB informed R. C. Holmes, API member and president of the Texas Company, constituted a violation of the Sherman Act. Of the Committee of Nine's proposals, then, there remained the possibility of convincing the states to use their police powers to regulate production and to assure common action by the formation of an interstate compact that confined federal responsibility to the recommendation of production quotas to each member state. This was the strategy pursued by FOCB during the Hoover administration and ultimately adopted, with the addition of a "hot oil" prohibition, by the Roosevelt administration. Much, then, depended upon the advocates of production controls in the producing states and their ability to persuade influential independent interests to accept some form of curtailment.[22]

Before 1929 or 1930, few individuals outside of FOCB manifested a sense of urgency concerning surplus production; nor could the oil board be accused of moving with undue haste. In 1926, discovery of the Seminole field in Oklahoma caused the state's production to explode from 179 million barrels in 1926 to 278 million barrels in 1927, or 30 percent of the national total. Seminole, producing 490,000 barrels daily at its peak in July 1927, contributed 50 percent of the state total.

As prices plummeted, twenty of the field's largest producers attempted in 1926 and 1927 to impose a voluntary curtailment plan. Those producers, including Indiana and Jersey Standard, Gulf Oil, Cities Service, several other majors, and a few independents, gained the support of FOCB to help pressure the Oklahoma Corporation Commission (OCC) to sanction the agreement and order the compliance of all producers. A large number of smaller producers, particularly the Okmulgee District Oil and Gas Association, rejected all controls, contested the commission's jurisdiction, and demanded divorcement, reduced rail rates, and the cessation of imports. Although the commission issued its orders, compliance was negligible, as it was again in 1928 when OCC issued a statewide conservation order. The Okmulgee association passed a series of resolutions in May 1927 which were forwarded to FOCB. The resolutions identified the major firms as the primary cause of overproduction and as the sponsors of production restrictions. State-imposed quotas would force smaller producers to relinquish their leases, which the majors could then grab up. This analysis, consistent with the normal portrait of the majors offered by independents, was no more extreme than that offered by dozens of other independents in the Seminole field and elsewhere. The likelihood of success for FOCB's program looked gloomy as 1928 ended.[23]

Four years later, the balance of forces within the oil industry remained unchanged in its essentials. Meanwhile, a deepening depression tore at the vitals of the economy, weakening all industries, eliminating millions of jobs, and eroding purchasing power. As confidence in the natural recuperative powers of the economy dissipated, two enormously prolific oil fields were brought in. Oklahoma City in 1929 and East Texas in 1930–31, threw tens of millions of barrels of flush production onto a shrinking market. In 1931, East Texas recovered 106 million barrels and in 1933, 172 million barrels. Even as prices of Mid-Continent oil plunged to absurd levels—fifty cents per barrel, thirty-five cents, ten cents—the pace of drilling activity accelerated. By 1933, East Texas contained 9,300 producing wells, two-and-one-half times the number of 1931. Most parties in oil recognized the existence of a crisis of monumental proportions, but despite the dogged efforts of FOCB to win a consensus for its solutions, the industry remained fractional and fractious.

API and most of the major integrated firms accepted the necessity of production controls and, with FOCB, had resolved the issue of the locus of authority by opting for state control. President Hoover's refusal to sanction any tampering with the antitrust laws compelled this choice, since neither the majors nor FOCB upheld the constitutionality of federally mandated state production quotas. To assure coordination among the states, FOCB, the majors, and influential individuals within the producing states proposed an interstate compact. All of this was presented formally at a meeting of the oil industry, billed as national and all-inclusive, that was arranged by FOCB and held at Colorado Springs in June 1929. Mark Requa, selected by Hoover to chair the conference, and Secretary of Interior Ray L. Wilbur vigorously promoted the solution developed by FOCB.[24]

From FOCB's perspective, the conference proceeded unsatisfactorily. Requa undoubtedly antagonized some with thinly veiled threats of direct federal intervention in lieu of state action. E. B. Reeser, president of API, countered Requa's thrusts by flatly denying the authority of either the federal government or an interstate compact to regulate production within a state. At least the Requa-Reeser exchange was to the point, as defined by FOCB, but most of the debate at the conference dwelt upon issues considered peripheral by the board. Even less acceptable to the sponsors was the hostility directed at President Hoover's decision of March 1929 to close the public domain to further oil leasing and to cancel permits that had not complied with the provisions of the lease.

According to Interior figures, holders of 15,000 of the 34,000 drilling permits on public lands were in noncompliance with the requirements of the mineral leasing law of 1920. As Hoover asserted, conservation and stabilization demanded the cessation of further withdrawals from the public domain. Delegates at Colorado Springs from Wyoming, Colorado, Montana, and New Mexico deplored the withdrawal order as patently unfair to the public-land states and useless as a measure to remedy overproduction, since total production on the public domain for the five years 1926–30 amounted to less than 5 percent of the national total. Prohibiting the development of western oil resources might, western delegates warned, result in the rejection of an interstate compact by their state legislatures.[25] The public-land states also injected the tariff into the discussion, a tactic enthusiastically seized upon by independents from the Mid-Continent. Wirt Franklin, president of the Independent Petroleum Association of America (organized during the conference), delivered a long speech on behalf of a crude and a refined tariff as an integral part of any conservation program that expected the support of independents.

A separate session of delegates, selected by the governors of the producing states to discuss the principle of an interstate compact, revealed serious differences of opinion. The delegates from Texas, Oklahoma, and California, representing states with 85 percent of national production, rang the alarm over the possibility of relinquishing State rights to some superior agency. Requa's impolitic utterances had stirred up a hornet's nest. The Kansans, Gov. Clyde M. Reed and Alfred M. Landon, emphasized the necessity of joint action by state and federal authority, admitting that circumstances argued for the acceptance of a degree of federal control. For Reed, an interstate compact seemed the most suitable instrument. In the end, the delegates agreed to disagree, committed themselves to further study of the issue, and promised to meet again . . . sometime.[26]

The meeting in Colorado Springs exposed the disunity of the industry. The independent wholesalers and jobbers, unrepresented at the conference, questioned its legitimacy and the motives of FOCB. The tariff issue, independent harangues against the pipelines, western grumbling over withdrawals, the intransigence of State righters, all accentuated the rifts that plagued the industry. Colorado Springs attested to the inability of the oil industry to resolve its own problems. The inexorable downward slide of the economy demanded, more than ever before, consistent and forceful leadership from President Hoover. Without that, intraindustry differences could not be negotiated and an acceptable industrywide program could not be hammered out. That leadership was not forthcoming.[27]

The Colorado Springs conference occurred before Oklahoma City and East Texas worked their full impacts on the industry. Those fields produced as much panic as surplus oil. At this point FOCB became irrelevant. The price skid precipitated by flush production forced the states to take action, both unilaterally and cooperatively. The cooperative endeavor did move the states one step closer to the achievement of FOCB's goals but had no influence at all on the oil glut which threatened the viability of hundreds of firms. In neither joint nor individual state action were issues confronted and resolved. Fear prompted action, and little time was devoted to reasoned discussion. Besides, everything had already been discussed. The issues were familiar to all interested parties, and attitudes were fixed. The ingredient lacking was honest brokerage, a talent not possessed by President Hoover. While he personally favored an interstate compact, he did not intervene to speed up its formation. For its part, FOCB had done all it could. In 1931 and 1932, FOCB's enemies simply ignored it, as did even its allies, sunshine soldiers for the most part.

Chaos and distress in the Oklahoma and Texas oil fields and the effects of flush production on Kansas, New Mexico, and other producing states prompted an immediate and positive response, in early 1931, to an urgent call issued by Gov. William H. Murray of Oklahoma for a meeting of the governors of the oil-producing states. In Oklahoma City, in February 1931, governors or their representatives from Oklahoma, Texas, Kansas, and New Mexico established the Oil States Advisory Committee (OSAC) to bring the production of the member states into alignment with market demand. Northcutt Ely, a friend of Wilbur's and an FOCB staff expert on oil conservation, acting as Wilbur's liaison with OSAC, informed Wilbur that OSAC was financed by New York oil money with E. B. Reeser, still president of API, passing the money along to the committee. By April, OSAC included Louisiana, Colorado, Wyoming, California, Arkansas, and Ohio. The committee agreed to focus on four objectives: the adoption of an interstate compact; the passage of state laws promoting unit operations, thereby reducing economic waste and conserving gas energy; voluntary import restrictions; production quotas for the major producing states (determined by the Voluntary Committee on Petroleum Economics which FOCB had organized, or by a new oil board).[28]

The organization of OSAC encouraged Ely and Wilbur to press in each member state for coordinate legislation that assured interstate cooperation. Ely drafted a model bill, with help from the staff of the Texas Company, but the states reacted indifferently to it. Wilbur and FOCB then offered their enthusiastic support to the Thomas-McKeon bill (drafted by OSAC), which created an interstate compact and a federal oil board authorized to recommend quotas and approve private unitization agreements. An early version of this bill provided for a uniformity of conservation laws among the major producing states and sufficient authority to enforce the compact in the courts, both of which were deleted before the bill reached committee and neither of which turned up in the compact finally formed during the New Deal. According to Gerald Nash, the Thomas-McKeon bill, approved by API, was withdrawn from consideration in order to smooth the passage of the tax on imported oil; why this was necessary is not explained. The bill then languished while a new administration took office; the bill finally disappeared into the enveloping maw of the National Industrial Recovery Act.[29] It is clear that the strongest support for production controls through some form of compact between the producing states came from API and the majors.

Had these initiatives surfaced during a more or less stable period, they would be described as encouraging, progressive, or statesmanlike, but such encomiums are perhaps less warranted given the circumstances impelling the governors to action. From 1929 through 1933, state conservation laws, the only available weapons to stanch the demoralizing flow of Oklahoma City and East Texas oil, proved useless, while hope for voluntary agreements among producers survived only in the hearts of believers in magic. By 1930, before East Texas, a one-billion-barrel production had led to the accumulation of huge stocks of stored oil; yet drilling increased. In imposing statewide prorationing in 1929, the Oklahoma Corporation Commission confronted the bitter opposition of thousands of independents, widespread noncompliance in the fields, and obstructive court challenges, an experience replicated in Texas in 1931 and 1932. The plans of some nine major operators to organize unit pools in the Oklahoma City field engendered vitriolic attacks from independent producers and such independent refiners as Champlin Refining Company.

By midsummer 1931, oil prices in the Oklahoma City field had descended to twenty-two to thirty-seven cents per barrel. A survey of Oklahoma and Kansas producers indicated that fully 75 percent were producing at a loss. Thirty thousand wells in northeastern Oklahoma and southeastern Kansas, the very wells that had been affected by the Prairie decision, faced shutdown. Conditions in West Texas and New Mexico were no better. Most observers agreed with FOCB that "there would be no situation in Oklahoma if Texas would cooperate with other states in control of her new oil pools."[30] East Texas production, at 100,000 barrels per month in January 1931, reached 12 million barrels monthly by August 1931, or 16 percent of national production. The Texas Railroad Commission order of 1 May for the prorationing of the East Texas field was unenforceable and finally voided by a federal district court on the grounds that state conservation law did not provide for restrictions on the basis of market demand. With East Texas largely controlled by antiprorationing, antimarket-demand producers, no possibility existed that producers would restrain themselves or allow a market-demand law to move through the state legislature without a bitter fight. Although such a law did win enactment in 1932, the politics of oil in Texas stymied railroad commission stabilization efforts until 1935. "The selfish and irresponsible interests operating the East Texas pool have," FOCB intoned, "demonstrated their ability to prevent control by the State and are apparently determined upon wholesale ruin."[31]

In July, with prices in the Mid-Continent dipping below $.22 per barrel, 350 Oklahoma City producers voluntarily closed their wells; but without the cooperation of East Texans, prices sank to $.10 in August, and large quantities moved at $.05. Frustrated producers in Oklahoma City, particularly the smaller firms, began pumping again. Frank Phillips of Phillips Petroleum foresaw quick economic annihilation. Sinclair, Champlin, and Shell oil companies appealed to the governor. One producer favored calling out the militia. Exciting days followed in Oklahoma City, for this was precisely the step taken in August 1931 by Gov. William Murray of Oklahoma and Gov. Ross Sterling of Texas.

Governor Murray, on 4 August, declared martial law in twenty-nine flush Oklahoma fields and called out the Oklahoma National Guard to enforce shutdown orders. The governor's sycophantic cousin, Cicero I. Murray, chairman of OSAC, sporting the rank of lieutenant colonel and attended by a full retinue of militia officers and grubby enlisted men, marched around the Oklahoma City field, striking fear and awe in the hearts of operators.

On 17 August, Governor Sterling mobilized a cavalry brigade of the Texas National Guard to enforce martial law and well-closing in the East Texas field. One thousand troops bivouacked amid the rigs. Both governors swore to keep the wells shut down until oil reached $1.00. By the end of August, prices had advanced to $.70 or $.75 cents, and production was resumed on a limited basis, but still policed by militiamen. Thereafter, in East Texas, only periodic shutdowns proved successful in controlling production.

Governor Murray, popularly called Alfalfa Bill, discovered the single effective method of production control that emerged during the Hoover administration. Although this novel strategy was quickly voided by the courts, troops remained in East Texas in defiance of court injunctions and continued to enforce prorationing. Few bothered to probe the anomalies and ironies implicit in the declaration of martial law. Had democratic processes been abandoned completely? Could the executive through force achieve what legislatures had explicitly denied? Was the use of force a fair competitive practice? What of the sight of soldiers enforcing noncompetition in the world's leading free enterprise economy? What provisions were made for 3,000 to 4,000 employees in the Oklahoma City fields suddenly thrown out of work?

Unquestionably, independent opposition to prorationing had frustrated production restrictions in Oklahoma and Texas and would continue to do so. A. L. Derby, H. H. Champlin, and other independents, large and small, continued to denounce prorationing and interstate compacts as harmful to their interests. Other independents, notably Wirt Franklin and his IPAA, favored prorationing only if coupled with strict import limitations and divorcement. Although Franklin incurred the wrath of many independents, he, no less than his critics, viewed the majors with hostility. At the least, one must assume that experienced oilmen such as Derby and Champlin recognized their own interests. Still, nickel oil was patently absurd and the resort to martial law explicable on that ground alone. The major firms in the Oklahoma City and East Texas fields did not protest the use of force.[32] In a speech to the United States Chamber of Commerce in 1932, C. B. Ames, head of the Texas Company and president of API, expressed the views of the majors:

> Adequate control, therefore, depends upon and requires cooperation of the principal oil-producing States. . . . A great many of the enlightened units in the oil industry are anxious to see the compact created and coordination of control by agreement between the principal oil-producing States made effective.[33]

Here the matter rested until a new administration assumed command.

Unresolved Problems: Past and Future

If anything should have been clear, it was that the oil industry could not reform itself. Independents and majors alike decried wasteful overproduction, but each blamed it on the other. Not even five-cent oil induced cooperation. Equally clear was the consistent inability of state authorities to reduce production through the enforcement of state conservation laws. OSAC possessed no power, exercised no influence over California or Texas, and relied solely upon the ineffective state public service commissions. Oklahoma independents abhorred OSAC, as much because of its chairman, Cicero I. Murray, considered morally delinquent and of little talent by many, as because of its objectives. The quotas recommended by the FOCB's forecasting committee and accepted by OSAC were consistently disregarded.

While the Texas Railroad Commission did receive authority in 1932 to prorate according to market demand, a majority of its members denounced the idea of a state compact with authority to do more than suggest quotas. Conceivably, prorationing could be applied in East Texas but yield no results in terms of market stabilization. As the Humble Oil historians explain it, small producers and refiners enjoyed numerical preponderance in East Texas; small producers "preferred . . . to produce 10,000 barrels daily over a few months even at 25 cents a barrel rather than 300 daily at $1.00 over several years."[34] In this, producers received the unqualified support of royalty owners. Without the cooperation of Texas, as subsequent events demonstrated, the entire exercise in control was futile. To achieve a supply-demand balance required a superior power to impose a structure and enforce a set of rules that acted on both individuals and states.

To discover the public interest in this maze of individual, state, and national interests is no easy task. It was at least in the public interest to protect the nation's oil supply by preventing the wasteful practices that so rapidly depleted the pools. Petroleum engineers stood ready to conserve reservoir pressure and increase ultimate recovery through well-spacing and advanced drilling techniques. Most producing states did have laws that attempted to reduce waste incident to recovery methods. But what if current market forces and profit considerations encouraged rates of production that diverged from the optimum flow science assigned to each well? The waste resulting from production in excess of market demand remained the major unresolved issue in 1932. Some denied the validity of this concept of waste, arguing that in a free market producers must determine rates of production. In the independent's scenario (in a truly free market), a normally advancing national demand freed from monopoly prices and costs would efficiently use the volume produced. Thus the independent solution, in depressed times as in normal times, called for import restrictions, pipeline divorcement, and the prosecution of firms that conspired to fix market prices.

To FOCB and its successors, the independent's case seemed, if not suicidal, then dangerously tilted and out of touch with reality. Surely nickel oil could lead only to the demise of the independents who lacked the physical and financial resources of their larger competitors. Ten-cent gasoline, a temporary boon to consumers, would soon destroy most independent marketers. Moreover, even had the independents realized all their political objectives and even had the depression necessitated no special action, the question of ultimate supply remained. Independents acted as if the nation's oil reserves were inexhaustible. The majors, more accepting of production controls as a stabilization device, rejected no less forcefully the entire notion of future depletion. To design an oil policy in conformity with the public interest required the acceptance of some estimate of recoverable oil reserves. If a pessimistic estimate was adopted, conservation appeared as an urgent requirement, and the use of foreign oil made sense. If optimism prevailed, conservation by whatever methods seemed less urgent than short-term stabilization.

During the 1920s and into the depression, the federal government adopted a broader view of public needs, derived from a more pessimistic assessment of the country's reserves, than did the oil industry. But FOCB proved unsuccessful in translating these ideas into a functioning political structure. In adding the necessary bureaucratic framework, the Roosevelt administration deviated but marginally from the FOCB formula. The New Deal prescription inevitably subordinated the peculiar needs of oil—and energy in general—to the ultimate objective: recovery from the depression. Thus, in emphasizing the raising of prices by controlling production rather than the stimulation of demand, New Deal economic policies conformed smoothly with conservationist aims.

The cooperation of oil producers, the enactment and enforcement of state conservation laws, and the coordination of production controls by the separate states joined together in an interstate compact was not the only option available to the new administration. As early as 1924 or so, Henry L. Doherty and Mark Requa had advocated the direct federal control of production, grounding their claims of constitutionality in the general welfare and national defense clauses of the Constitution. Harold L. Ickes, as the new secretary of Interior the dominant figure in energy politics from 1933 to the conclusion of World War II, emerged as the most powerful spokesperson for this position. Ickes subordinated the particular problems of producers, processors, and marketers to the overarching demands of the general welfare, particularly national security. In adopting the goals earlier formulated by FOCB, he sought to bypass the states and to minimize the need for industry cooperation by applying federal authority to each well.

In 1932, a memo drafted by FOCB Chairman Wilbur noted that the discovery of new pools instilled in many the belief that the nation had more than enough oil. This opinion, Wilbur warned, has "fostered a spirit of wastefulness and general lack of concern about the future which more or less jeopardizes efforts to achieve proper conservation."[35] But whereas Wilbur would impose general responsibility upon a compact of producing states, Ickes would centralize power in the federal government. As Chapter 9 makes clear, Ickes's view of the public interest and the structure required to protect it confronted powerful antagonists and suffered an inevitable dilution in the political arena.

NINE

Regulating the Oil Industry
during the New Deal

As the Roosevelt administration mobilized to battle hard times and widespread despair, the newly empowered depression warriors confronted not only a seriously divided oil industry but internal disagreements about the strategies to be employed to stay and ultimately reverse the economic downswing. During the distressing spring of 1933, banks, businesses, and industries teetered on the edge of irremediable collapse. And soup lines lengthened. Could a comprehensive strategy be devised that would stabilize all industries, prevent further unemployment, and strengthen consumer purchasing power? Was it possible to invent a legislative program that could effectively and equitably deal with the disparate problems of oil, textiles, coal, or steel without sacrificing the interests of owners, workers, or the consuming public? What measure of federal authority would be required to protect the weak from the exactions of the strong, guarantee participation of weakened but still powerful economic interests, and pump new vigor into the free enterprise system?

The New Deal answer, of course, was multifaceted, rooted in American traditions, and designed to ease the suffering of millions, to stimulate recovery, and to effect the reform of obvious weaknesses in the economic system. Roosevelt, the Congress, and thousands of enthusiastic New Dealers who invaded the capital in 1933 launched simultaneous campaigns to strengthen the banking system, save the farmers, provide unemployment relief and spread employment opportunities through public works programs, legitimize organized labor, and induce increased production in the nation's factories and mills.

To achieve many of these heroic objectives, the New Deal sponsored and secured the passage in June 1933 of the National Industrial Recovery Act (NIRA), a bill encompassing all the fuel industries and establishing the essential mechanisms applied to fuels through 1935. Even though NIRA was declared unconstitutional in 1935, the central objectives of the system evolved under NIRA were written into new legislation that determined federal fuel policies into and beyond World War II.

The broad-gauged NIRA was administered by the National Recovery Administration (NRA) under the leadership of an old Progressive and War Industries Board official, Gen. Hugh Johnson. In addition to spawning the Public Works Administration, NIRA sought to eliminate child labor, establish minimum wages and maximum working hours, strengthen labor unions by recognizing the right of labor to organize and bargain collectively, and reform industry and business by eliminating cutthroat competition and wasteful production. To reorganize industry, NRA assumed the monumental task of devising codes of fair competition for hundreds of discrete industries or lines of business, each code to include blanket protections for labor, including the mandated collective bargaining provision of Section 7(a) of NIRA. Each code was to be formulated by industry representatives working under the general supervision of Johnson's staff, and, as anticipated by the proponents of industry-government cooperation, each code would foster effective industry self-policing by means of an industrywide code authority.

According to Ellis Hawley's cogent description, the initial debates over NIRA and the process of code formation precipitated serious disagreements. In contention were those who sought intraindustry cooperation with a minimum of federal control; those preferring a centralized planning structure to supervise the cooperative efforts of business leaders, labor representatives, and consumers; and those who, fearful of a resurgence of monopoly, deplored the anticompetitive aspects of NIRA and responded skeptically to visions of industry self-regulation.[1] Within the oil industry, champions of those positions struggled for paramountcy, first in the debates over NIRA and then in the struggle to formulate an oil code.

Oil Interests and the Oil Code

Recent events in the Oklahoma City and East Texas oil fields quickly convinced Secretary of Interior Harold L. Ickes of the urgency of imposing comprehensive federal production controls on the oil industry. For Ickes, concern for the national security transcended all other objectives in the evaluation of oil policy. Petroleum was essential and irreplaceable, and the nation could ill afford to permit producers to kill themselves off in cutthroat competition while wantonly squandering "the very life blood of the nation."[2]

Ickes harbored no deeply embedded belief in the capacity of the states or the industry, acting unilaterally or jointly, to bring production under control by means of state prorationing laws. To be sure, martial law in Oklahoma and Texas had staunched the flow of oil temporarily, but such a draconic approach held out little hope for the future and, to Ickes's mind, demonstrated conclusively the inability of the states to limit production to market demand. Nonetheless, Ickes and his staff inherited a decade's worth of FOCB policy proposals that emphasized the role of the producing states and looked askance at direct federal regulation. Secretary Ickes, in his first official act relative to oil, felt constrained to convene a conference of governors of the oil-producing states; this conference, held in March 1933, was attended by some 200 industry leaders.

Studies by Linda Lear and Gerald Nash, among others, have convincingly demonstrated the significance of this conference in the development of Ickes's ideas about oil policy. Ickes, if he ever believed a policy consensus could be reached, was quickly disabused of that possibility. As in the past, groups of independents argued among themselves and with the majors, some condemning production controls out of hand and others willing to accept controls if enforced by the states and if accompanied by tariffs and divorcement. Some majors demanded direct federal control over production while some preferred state control. Texas adamantly refused to consider federal controls of any kind, while Oklahoma and Kansas expressed their readiness to formally replace the Oil States Advisory Committee with an interstate compact. Minority and majority reports were filed, the latter opting for state production controls and federal legislation prohibiting shipment in interstate commerce of oil produced in violation of state law (so-called hot oil). While resolutions were adopted to impose import quotas and protective tariffs, the gist of the majority report, approved by all attending associations save the Independent Petroleum Association of Texas, recommended federal participation "but not government control of oil production."[3]

Face-to-face contact with a sorely divided, mutually antagonistic oil industry hardened the resolve of Ickes to insist that the Roosevelt administration adopt direct federal controls over production, even at the risk of an adverse decision in an unsympathetic federal court. But the very divisiveness of the industry, permeating each subsequent stage leading to the adoption of the oil code, thwarted him at every turn. The ambiguity of the president's own position proved a key (if not the key) element in the fuzzy formula ultimately adopted. By early summer 1933, while Roosevelt could admit that overproduction appeared to have ruinous consequences relative to price as well as to waste, he was reluctant to commit the administration to a strategy that divorced the oil industry from proposals in the legislative mill to produce a single, all-encompassing solution to the nation's industrial ills. For that reason, Ickes failed to win Roosevelt's active endorsement of the Marland-Capper bill, which, following the recommendation of the governors' conference, prohibited the transit of hot oil across state lines. But just as Texas lifted virtually all production controls in the East Texas field and the price of oil plunged to ten cents or less, Roosevelt opted to include the oil industry in the recovery legislation being considered in House and Senate committees. Ickes then sought, as a last resort, to force the inclusion of separate oil regulations in the recovery bill. By this time, Roosevelt's preference for a weak rather than a strong federal presence in oil was clear. Without the support of his boss, Ickes could not hope to obtain legislation that broke new ground or that deviated substantially from the proposals of FOCB or the governors' oil conference. After the invalidation of NRA, Roosevelt would again undercut Ickes's efforts to impose production controls upon the oil industry.

The demoralizing impact of the East Texas and Oklahoma City fields had, in fact, worked somewhat to Ickes's advantage. A large group of independents, termed the "majority independents" by René de V. Williamson and best represented by the Independent Petroleum Association of America (IPAA), actively supported Ickes's campaign for direct federal controls. Wirt Franklin, IPAA's chief spokesperson, campaigned vigorously against the concept of industry self-government reflected in the recovery bill. To IPAA, industry self-government was likely to produce a system controlled by the majors while state controls had demonstrated a singular inability to reduce production. Ickes, less obsessed than IPAA with the crimes of the majors, recognized nonetheless that efficient resource conservation, the desideratum, could only be assured through federal action. For different reasons, then, IPAA and Ickes could agree on certain proposals. But this alliance proved too weak to overcome the opposition of the majors and the minority independents, especially Texans, to direct controls. The latter angrily denounced Ickes and the IPAA and demanded the dissolution of the integrated companies. IPAA and Ickes, less naive than Roosevelt concerning industry self-government, sought a broader federal role than the majors or the other independents but could not penetrate the defenses of producing states jealous of their sovereignty, suspicious of one another's intentions, and strongly influenced by numerous small producers and refiners.[4]

The NIRA contained special provisions relating directly to the oil industry. The experience of recent years, confirmed at the Marland-Capper bill hearings, proved indisputably that the states could not prevent the movement of hot oil across state lines. Ickes proposed and Sen. Tom Connally of Texas introduced an amendment incorporating the intent of the Marland-Capper bill into the oil section (Title I, Section 9) of NIRA. Section 9(c) authorized the president to "prohibit the transportation in interstate and foreign commerce of petroleum and the products thereof produced or withdrawn from storage in excess of the amount permitted to be produced or withdrawn from storage by any state law." Sections 9(a) and (b) dealt with pipelines, a tactical bow to the independents; the first authorized the president to initiate proceedings before the ICC to regulate the operations of oil pipelines and to establish reasonable rates, and the second authorized the president to institute divorcement proceedings when a pipeline through unfair practices or unreasonable rates tended to create a monopoly. Section 3(e) gave the president regulatory power over imports, and Section 4(a) provided for presidential approval of agreements between companies. In addition, NIRA permitted the president to establish an administration separate from NRA to oversee the operation of the oil code.

NIRA, then, awarded the federal government only fringe powers. The essential prerequisite for either stabilization or conservation, setting production quotas for states and fields, remained in the hands of the producing states. If, as was the case with California and later with Illinois, a state had no prorationing law, the federal government possessed no authority to interfere with its interstate commerce in oil. The federal government could interdict interstate shipments of oil produced above state quotas but could not compel the states to set quotas that cumulatively matched estimated national market demand.[5]

Haggling over the specific provisions of the oil code consumed the summer months of 1933, forcing both Ickes and Johnson into the role of brokers between contending oil factions which sought a code protective of their specific interests. Simultaneously, Ickes and Johnson competed for authority to administer the code. The operating theory underlying the code, as Petroleum Administrative Board Vice-Chairman (later Chairman) Charles Fahy understood it, would foster sound public policy by coordinating state law and national policy to achieve balanced and efficient recovery, production, and marketing programs. But, in fact, the separate branches and interests composing the oil industry were less concerned with sound public policy than with advancing their own fortunes. Oil code negotiations with NRA demonstrated the chronic inability of the industry to reach a consensus on virtually every issue that arose. The disunity evidenced in oil replicated that of many other American industries which were divided by size and degree of integration, geographical location, and production, distribution, and marketing practices. These differences, circumvented but not resolved in code formulation, presaged extraordinary difficulties in enforcing code compliance. In oil, disaffected independent producing and refining interests, especially in Oklahoma and Texas, proved particularly intractable, and they violated code provisions whenever possible.

API initiated code formulation proceedings by organizing a meeting in Chicago in June 1933 to devise a code for submission to NRA. Although independents from Texas and California boycotted the meeting, a preliminary code emerged that included provisions for production quotas, federal permits for new drilling and the licensing of producers, and minimum price fixing but which ignored the labor requirements stipulated by NIRA. The "Chicago Code" aroused much caterwauling from some independents and certain majors who opposed quotas and/or minimum prices. As René de V. Williamson suggests, this version can be viewed as representing a preliminary victory for IPAA and for Ickes who, at this stage, sought minimum price-fixing authority. Subsequent revisions, demanded by Johnson and lobbied for by various dissidents, while lessening the attractiveness of the code for IPAA did assure at least the tacit approval of most majors. But the amendments failed to moderate the rigid opposition of many independents.

General Johnson forced the NIRA labor provisions into the code and, after much debate, succeeded in removing the price-fixing and licensing provisions. At this stage, late June and July 1933, members of IPAA began referring to the code as a creature of Standard Oil, while other independents, agreeing with that description, further confused the process by demanding oil tariffs, import quotas, the divorcement of pipelines, and the abolition of lease and agency agreements. Independent marketers perceived the code as an instrument of the major integrated firms, designed to "put the Independent Concerns out of business."[6] Johnson and Ickes both coveted administrative responsibility for the code, a contest won by Ickes to the applause of IPAA. But the code, as approved by Roosevelt in August 1933, failed to provide firm price-fixing authority and denied the federal government authority to do more than recommend production quotas.[7]

Withdrawing the oil code from NRA jurisdiction—the only code so treated—and awarding its administration to Ickes represented, according to Nash, a triumph for the secretary.[8] But if so, it was a victory only in the narrowest and most bureaucratic sense, for the code failed to include powers considered essential by Ickes, and it did not assuage the antagonism of many independents. For all its complexity and detail, the oil code was a gloss on NIRA. It represented no improvement over the proposals of FOCB and, except for the vague pricing authority, was therefore quite acceptable to the major integrated firms. The delegation of administrative authority to Ickes rather than to Johnson resolved a fight over turf rather than over principle or program. Still, it was probably the best decision considering that Johnson was essentially ignorant of oil industry problems. Whether one accepts oil industry stabilization or resource conservation or some amalgamation of the two as the primary objectives of the oil section of NIRA and the oil code, Ickes, backed by the resources of Interior, stood a better chance of realizing them than General Johnson.

Two executive orders in July and August established the Department of Interior as the locus of authority in petroleum.[9] Ickes created the Petroleum Administrative Board (PAB) in September as an advisory body to himself as oil code administrator and a Planning and Coordination Committee (PCC) to make recommendations on all matters relevant to the oil code.[10] Ickes appointed three NRA officials to PCC along with twelve industry representatives, four from major firms and eight from independents associated with IPAA. Wirt Franklin, president of IPAA, was designated PCC chairman. These initial appointments have been characterized as favorable to the pro-price-fixing elements of the industry, the IPAA in particular, and, in completely ignoring the antiprice-setting, antiprorationing, and antigovernment intervention wing of the independents, as hostile to that group and by implication to State rights. Ickes also neglected to appoint to PCC representatives of nonproducing and nonrefining sectors of the industry. Predictably, the composition of the committee stirred up considerable furor among the unrepresented groups and from those, particularly the majors, who opposed industrywide price fixing. Ickes, later on, did enlarge PCC by eleven members, mostly from among the unrepresented independents and the marketing branch of the industry.[11]

Both PAB and PCC reported directly to Ickes, the code administrator. PCC was not organized as a constituent part of PAB and sought to exploit this independence by transforming itself into the central policy-making arm of the oil code, thereby undercutting PAB. With a majority of PCC members supporting price fixing, that issue became the crucial test of PCC power. But before plunging into the maze of issues and controversies that characterized code administration, it will be useful to scrutinize the content of the oil code.

The Operation of the Oil Code

The oil code and PCC and PAB were patterned after the division of the industry into production, transportation, refining, and marketing sectors. The oil code contained separate articles dealing with each of those divisions and provided the legal authority for the district committees established by PCC.[12] General powers were conferred upon the president to modify or eliminate code provisions not required by NIRA and to consent to all agreements between competitors devised to promote the objectives of the code.[13]

Article III dealt with production. Section 1 codified Section 3(e) of NIRA and "requested" the president to limit oil imports, while Section 2 required the approval of PCC for withdrawal of crude oil from storage (NIRA, Section 9(c)). Section 3 authorized the president or his designated agent to "estimate" the production required to meet consumer demand and "recommend" an equitable allocation among the producing states. If states did not allocate production among their producing wells, the president (as Sections 4 and 5 stipulated) could appoint a state agency to determine the allocation and regulate the interstate commerce of the resulting production (NIRA, Section 9(c)). Section 6 defined as an unfair trade practice the pricing of crude below the cost of production, arrived at by a complex formula manipulating specific gravity, octane rating, and average tank car prices for regular gasoline. Section 6(a) allowed the president to set base prices for gasoline for no longer than ninety days. Section 7 declared illegal the shipment in interstate commerce of oil produced from new pools (discovered after 19 August 1933) that did not obtain presidential approval of field or pool development plans.

Article IV focused on the refining of gasoline, seeking to prohibit the production of gasoline in excess of market demand as established by PAB, while also guaranteeing the equitable access of refiners to allowable crude supplies. PCC was authorized to appoint subcommittees for each refining district which would recommend production quotas for each district. Complaints regarding the availability of crude were first heard at the district level, and if unresolved the complaint was referred to the Adjustment Committee of PCC for arbitration. Excessive gasoline in storage, a volume determined by PCC, was defined as an unfair trade practice.

Marketing was the subject of Article V and comprised thirty-one rules, far too many for detailed summary. The article was intended to prevent price wars and to curb the unfair trade practices that precipitated them. Theoretically, the production and refining controls of Articles III and IV would so limit supplies as to preclude further general price deflation, but it was recognized that price wars could flare up as a result of particular competitive conditions in various locales. The temporary price-fixing authority (Article III, Section 6(a)) would suffice, presumably, to prevent long, debilitating price wars. The code applied to all distributors of petroleum products but was particularly aimed at retail filling and service stations, all of which were bound by the code. Prices for all petroleum products were to be posted on the pumps at retail outlets. All distributors were prohibited from using false advertising, selling below cost, giving discounts (permitted to wholesalers under certain conditions), and employing premiums, trading stamps, other free goods, or games of chance in connection with the sale of petroleum products or accessories.

Rules 7 through 22 attempted to regulate the relationship between refiners and retail outlets. For example, Rule 19 defined any new lease and agency agreement as an unfair trade practice; Rules 7, 8, and 9 forbade oil companies to sell, loan, or repair the service station equipment supplied by the companies to retailers. Rule 22 prohibited the granting of free service to oil burner owners by those selling fuel oil. Many of these rules replicated earlier FTC decisions and recommendations concerning the lease and agency arrangement. Their collective purpose was to promote free and fair competition among establishments of various sizes and facing diverse competitive conditions. To police these rules would have required an army.

Article VI dealt very briefly with transportation. PCC's subcommittee on transportation was required to investigate transportation practices and rates and recommend appropriate action to the president. NIRA, it will be recalled, delegated power to the president to take certain steps regarding freight rates and the divorcement of pipelines. In fact, neither PAB, PCC, Ickes, nor Roosevelt assigned much importance to those powers or to Article VI even though many independents pressed for their implementation.[14]

The experience of the industry under the short-lived code can be described most effectively by commencing with the efforts to control production and proceeding through refining and marketing, the latter including price policies; in other words, by conforming to the actual operational organization of the industry. However, I deviate somewhat from this plan in order to deal immediately with the ambition of PCC to assert its dominance over PAB by imposing price fixing upon the entire industry.

A majority of PCC members, among them Chairman Franklin and Amos L. Beatty of Phillips Petroleum, favored the imposition of minimum crude and product prices, a position adopted by IPAA during the debates over NIRA and strongly objected to by most major integrated firms and a host of other independents. Walter Teagle and W. S. Farish of Jersey Standard, the Pews of Sun Oil, C. B. Ames of the Texas Company, all opponents of price setting, had suffered a setback when Roosevelt awarded Ickes, considered by some to be a proponent of price fixing, administration of the code instead of Johnson, an opponent of fixed prices. PCC, in September, devised a price schedule for crude and refined products which Ickes accepted. But uncertainty as to the expediency or the practicality of this step convinced Ickes to postpone the effective date until 1 December.

Few on Ickes's staff knew much about oil pricing; moreover, they readily admitted to this ignorance. PAB's chairman, Nathan Margold (solicitor of Interior), in a memorandum to his chief argued that price schedules were economically unjustifiable, impossible to enforce, and probably unconstitutional. PAB and Bureau of Mines experts cautioned Ickes about the inadequacy of production cost data, a shortcoming which would foment inequities and disturb, perhaps severely, existing competitive relationships. Continued allusion to price fixing emanating from those involved in oil administration may have been designed to win a readier compliance with production quotas. (Linda Lear, Ickes's biographer, leans in this direction.) In any event, this internally generated advice carried more weight with Ickes than did a flood of letters supporting or condemning the schedules but containing little new information. The opponents of fixed prices counterattacked by circumventing PCC and appealing directly to Ickes or PAB. Moreover, they devised an alternative plan. In the meantime, Ickes, sensitive to criticism concerning the composition of PCC, had determined to expand it to include more majors, non-IPAA independents, and marketers. This undermined the superiority of the pro-price fixers and hastened the adoption of the alternative plan to control refinery production and gasoline purchasing by agreements among refiners and marketers.[15]

Ickes's seeming shift in position over pricing has been characterized as "chamelonlike," but this seems unfair.[16] Ickes was new to his job and relatively uninformed about the intricacies of oil pricing, but he recognized this. If he appeared inconsistent it was because he was never unalterably committed to fixed prices. Instead, he viewed effective production controls as the key prerequisite for waste prevention and the conservation of petroleum for future generations.[17] A shrewd politician and a rapid learner, Ickes recognized the PCC gambit as a strike for power and deflected it by increasing its membership. The inclusion of more majors, including Teagle, Ames, and E. G. Seubert, president of Indiana Standard, and some marketers did recast the committee into a form more representative of the entire industry, but the reconstituted group also better mirrored the divisions which rent the industry. No longer could any single faction dominate the committee. PCC became a body advisory to Ickes and tacitly subordinated to PAB, rather than, as René de V. Williamson suggests, a cohesive group capable of a sustained contest with PAB.[18]

Ickes, no ideologue of price fixing but instead seeking expanded federal control over production, was more than willing to escape a situation fraught with political peril, especially since a plan emerged that might accomplish similar results. That the new marketing scheme outraged many independent marketers, hurled antitrusters into the fray, and never took effect were problems for the future. In late 1933, Ickes was quite happy to avoid in oil the terrible complexity of price fixing that threatened NRA efforts to stabilize the coal industry.[19]

Throughout the final months of 1933, monopolized by the price issue, it remained clear to Ickes and PAB that the short-term stabilization of the industry and the dampening of deflation demanded the immediate imposition of production controls. During the first months of 1933, weekly oil production rose, prices plunged to under ten cents per barrel, and the Texas Railroad Commission (TRC) announced an allowable for East Texas of 800,000 barrels per day, double estimated market demand. In May 1933, East Texas production approached one million barrels daily, some 200,000 above an already excessive allowable and one-half of total national demand. The states, it appeared, either could not or would not enforce their prorationing laws, establish reasonable allowables, or prevent hot oil from pouring across state lines into the holding tanks of refiners. Over a ten-month period in late 1932 and 1933, some 75 million barrels of hot oil were produced.

As authorized by the code, PAB immediately calculated national consumption demand and then allotted shares to the producing states. In September 1933, as an example, total daily national consumption was estimated at 2,413,700 barrels. Texas received a production share of 975,000 barrels (40 percent), Oklahoma, 540,000 (22 percent), California, 480,000 (20 percent), and Kansas, 111,000 (5 percent). Thereafter, quotas differed insubstantially from September's figures, with the highest national allotment at 2,530,000 barrels in July 1934 and the lowest at 2,183,000 in January 1934, both explicable by seasonal demand.

The states allocated the total state allowable among their pools and fields. Success in controlling production rested with Texas and Oklahoma, together producing some 80 percent of national output. California's importance was less substantial as its production did not greatly affect the markets of the eastern two-thirds of the country. The Corporation Commission of Oklahoma and the Texas Railroad Commission allocated quotas and enforced the prorationing laws. While both agencies complained regularly about the unfairness of federal allocations, both normally conformed. The critical problem faced by the states, and addressed by the hot oil provision in NIRA, was enforcement of production quotas through the interdiction of interstate commerce in hot oil or the products of refiners using hot oil. According to federal investigators, the Oklahoma City field consistently produced illegal oil that made its way to local refiners and then out of state. One agent estimated in summer 1934 a prevailing 10 percent overage in Oklahoma City. The Corporation Commission loudly denied all charges and in their turn pointed to East Texas as the source of the industry's problems. And they were right, in a manner of speaking and ignoring questions of equity, for the excess production from Oklahoma hardly influenced price as sharply as the bootleg oil from East Texas.[20]

Oklahoma and Kansas complained bitterly to PAB and Ickes about the flood of hot oil from East Texas in late 1933 and 1934. PAB considered such bootlegging as a threat to the entire crude and refining structure of the code and identified the culprits as largely independent producers in Texas and independent refiners in Texas and neighboring states. Texas accounted for some 70 percent of the hot oil entering the market. Homer Hoch of the Kansas Corporation Commission informed Ickes in several telegrams that East Texas oil caused disastrous market conditions for Kansas producers and for Kansas refiners who used prorated oil. Rep. Wilburn Cartwright, Democrat of Oklahoma, attributed severely depressed Oklahoma crude prices to hot oil from Texas. These men, and many others as well, asked why their states should abide by the code rules and federal allocations when East Texas blithely ignored them and went unpunished.

Ickes admitted the justness of these grievances but possessed insufficient authority to remedy them without the cooperation of TRC. Throughout the life of the code, Ickes and TRC traded accusations. Ickes blamed TRC for not enforcing the laws and implied that TRC did not want to stop hot oil production; according to PAB, TRC could have indicted refiners using hot oil for intrastate purposes. East Texas, more than any other factor, induced Ickes energetically to seek the enlargement of federal control over production in 1934 and especially in 1935 when the courts first invalidated the hot oil section of NIRA and then demolished the entire code edifice. Simultaneously, TRC led a successful campaign against delegation to the federal government of authority to establish mandatory quotas in the producing states.

In fairness to TRC, it must be pointed out that the Texas Market Demand Act of 1932 was not sustained in federal courts until 1934.[21] In the interim, Texas independents swarmed into the courts seeking and easily obtaining countless injunctions against the imposition of allowables by TRC. A thoroughly politicized TRC succumbed to the independents by setting grossly excessive allowables and ignoring production above the permissible level. In November 1934, however, TRC reduced the East Texas allowable from 800,000 to 400,000 barrels daily.

Once reasonable allowables had been established by the states, the problem narrowed to the prevention of production above the allowables and of hot oil from moving in interstate commerce. While prices improved, reaching $.75 per barrel in early 1934 and $1.00 by midyear, the flow of hot oil continued. According to Humble Oil's *Weekly Digest*, hot oil production ranged from 100,000 to 145,000 barrels daily in late 1934. TRC could not possibly police each of the 15,000 wells in East Texas, let alone 51,000 state wells. Moreover, once the crude left the field it was considered interstate commerce and beyond the jurisdiction of TRC. To plug up the substantial leakage from East Texas, PAB created the Federal Tender Board (FTB) in October with personnel stationed in Oklahoma City and East Texas. All shipments of oil and gasoline required a permit from FTB, and any railroad accepting oil products without a permit became liable to prosecution. Refiners could only receive oil under the crude allocation system by proving they used no hot oil. Now, tardily according to TRC, FTB watched the outlets—trucks, railroads, pipelines, and refineries. As much as 30,000 barrels daily of hot oil continued to slip through federal defenses in early 1935, but FTB did greatly improve the effectiveness of state prorationing laws. And prices remained fairly stable during the remainder of the code's life.[22]

The regulation of refinery output, particularly gasoline, formed an integral part of the conservation and price stabilization program. Hot oil would be produced at any price as long as refiners purchased it and could sell their products. The continued overproduction of oil, then, directly affected gasoline production, and excess gasoline supplies fostered price-cutting wars in retail markets. Under Article IV of the code, PCC established production quotas by refining districts, but performance under that article was entirely unsatisfactory during the final quarter of 1933 and almost all of 1934. An initial effort spearheaded by PCC to win the compliance of refiners by fixing well-head and refined prices met defeat as a result of the opposition of major integrated firms and many independents and the lukewarm attitude of Ickes and PAB toward fixed prices. Other efforts to impose order on the refining branch followed but in the absence of effective controls over production yielded inconsequential results.

One scheme, proposed by the major firms in late 1933 as a substitute for price fixing, was designed to prevent independent refiners from obtaining cheap oil to produce gasoline then sold below desired market prices. The majors suggested that the oil administrator fix the total quantity of permissible gasoline production. That quota would be shared among refining districts and among refiners within a district. The majors further agreed to purchase surplus—distressed —gasoline from the independents and to accept a modest reduction of their own gasoline quota.[23] With a guaranteed outlet for their gasoline, the independents, or so it was believed, would cease purchasing hot oil; now denied an outlet, hot oil would pose no further problem.

A PAB report of early 1934 counseled Ickes to support this program as likely to achieve a better balance of gasoline supply and consumption and afford some relief to hard-pressed small refiners. Ickes accepted this recommendation, conforming as it did with his obligation to preserve the existence of small refiners, and attempted to implement it in 1934. The plan—referred to as a pooling and marketing arrangement—recognized that insofar as prorationing reduced the access of independent refiners to cheap oil and, therefore, eliminated part of their market, a guaranteed market at a higher price must be found for gasoline produced from more costly crude. By September 1934, a subcommittee of PCC was actively negotiating purchasing agreements between major refiners and distributors and nonintegrated or semi-integrated refiners to dispose of distress gasoline, particularly in East Texas and Oklahoma. Although in theory the scheme appeared airtight, its effectiveness depended upon the drying up of sources of hot oil.

Independent refiners made money by breaking the law, and they manifested great suspicion, if not outright hostility, to the new proposal which they perceived as more beneficial to the major firms than to themselves. The opposition of independent refiners, however, was less strident than that emanating from independent wholesalers and retailers. In late 1933 and early 1934, the latter interests took Ickes and PAB and PCC to task for imposing upon them an organization called the National Petroleum Agency. This agency, composed of the major oil companies, intended to formalize the pooling and marketing agreements by establishing fixed margins between crude and refinery gasoline on the one side and refinery gasoline and retail gasoline on the other side. Mid-Continent refiners protested the narrow price differentials between crude and gasoline, asserting that only the majors could operate within such margins because of their control over pipelines, their storage facilities, and their large marketing organizations. Independent marketers also concentrated their ire on the proposed margins, arguing for greater price differentials between nonbranded and branded gasoline (expressed in octane ratings) so as to assure the competitiveness of retailers at the pump. Danciger Refineries of Tulsa interpreted the pooling and marketing agreement as accomplishing through subterfuge the objectives of the discarded price-fixing schedule. Danciger and numerous marketers predicted that the manipulation of the gasoline pool by the majors would result in the extermination of independents.

Consumer interests and assorted antitrusters such as Sen. Borah also launched assaults on these agreements. The Consumer's Advisory Board of NRA foresaw industry control over supply and price as leading to the gouging of consumers by the major companies. In the state of Washington, the Independent Progressive Clubs published a pamphlet *Citizens of Washington, You Are Being Robbed*, which recounted the methods used by the majors to take over several independent concerns and warned Washingtonians to "remember, the big oil companies are fighting you."[24]

Despite this opposition, Ickes and PAB persevered in their efforts to implement these agreements. Pooling agreements for distress gasoline did materialize in California, the Mid-Continent, and East Texas, but the marketing provisions lacked the support necessary for implementation. As PAB's Margold assured Borah, Secretary Ickes could modify or withdraw approval if it appeared that the agreements damaged the interests of independent refiners. In fact, PAB's Margold and Fahy both believed that refining overcapacity developed during the 1920s contributed greatly to the overall problem. Many small refiners, even during prosperous years, experienced competitive difficulties as a result of their inadequate technology, small scale of operation and relatively high unit cost of production, and marketing disadvantages. Now, PAB was expected to nurse these weak units through a time of depression and do so while denying them the one advantage they possessed: access to very cheap crude. As PAB-FTB and state control over crude production tightened in late 1934, the strength of independent refiners deteriorated, squeezed as they were between rising crude prices and the inability of the code authority to raise gasoline prices significantly and eliminate price wars.[25]

Control or chaos—those were the choices confronting the oil industry in 1934, according to Phillips Petroleum's Amos L. Beatty, successor to Franklin as chairman of PCC.[26] For many, within and outside the oil business, the control or order desired by Beatty seemed no more than order imposed by the major integrated oil companies, while the chaos Beatty fought described a competitive system liberated from the dominance of the majors. Beatty, Margold, and Fahy might well emphasize the disadvantages faced by independents in marketing their products. Independents perceived those disadvantages not as derived from economic inefficiencies but rather from the unnatural structural advantages evolved—or seized—by big oil over the years. Here, of course, the independents alluded to pipeline control, discriminatory rail freight rates, foreign crude imports, and such retail marketing arrangements as lease and agency.[27]

In no sector of the oil industry was competition more severe than in retailing, where the number of gasoline stations increased from 317,000 in 1929 to some 450,000 in 1939, about one-half owned by independents and the remainder owned or under contract to the majors. The code prohibited new lease and agency agreements and placed restrictions on renewals, but the status of the lease and agency agreement remained confused during the NRA period. In fact, a number of the majors cancelled existing contracts, substituting a new and more binding contract that tied operators ever more tightly to the integrated company.[28]

Article V of the code spelled out in some detail the restrictions placed upon the sale of petroleum products, particularly gasoline. Working in tandem with production controls and refinery regulation, the prohibition of specified unfair trade practices would, it was anticipated, bring stability at higher prices to the retail market. As we have seen, however, retailers leveled pointed objections against the marketing and pooling arrangements of the aborted National Petroleum Agency, which, they charged, placed them in total dependence upon the majors for gasoline supplies. The marketers also rejected as too small the margins allowed between their unbranded and the major's branded gasoline. Independent marketers in the Mid-Continent received virtually all their gasoline from independent refiners. Prorationing threatened to limit refinery output; reduced supplies implied higher wholesale prices. Independent retailers could survive only by maintaining a significant margin between their pump price and the pump price of the majors. With so much at stake, independent retailers habitually circumvented the code, purchasing gasoline regardless of its legality, offering whatever incentives they could dream up to attract customers, and, if necessary, cutting prices to protect the required margin.

In 1933 and 1934, the steady availability of East Texas hot oil kept the retail sector in constant disarray, according to the perceptions of those advocating an imposed stability. PAB saw it this way: "When the code went into effect, the marketing branch of the industry was suffering from chaotic conditions and prices were at a beggar's level. Thousands of dealers faced extinction. Their stations have been kept open by the code."[29]

Others, including independent marketers, interpreted events somewhat differently, blaming the majors for establishing an excessive number of service stations during the 1920s and even during the depression as part of a callous strategy to capture a larger volume of gasoline sales even though sales per station declined. Station operators with Standard Indiana or Gulf franchises, for instance, frequently complained about the nearby location of another station selling their brand. According to the independents, the cumulative effect of the code rules jeopardized their continued existence. Particularly damaging were the increased labor costs resulting from maximum hour and minimum wage requirements and the refusal of major marketers to permit a significant differential between unbranded and branded products. Survival for a bit longer was won only by ignoring the rules. When the majors sought to reduce the margin by reducing prices, independents responded with an equivalent slash.[30]

Widespread noncompliance caused W. T. Holliday of Standard Ohio and Frank Phillips of Phillips Petroleum to fume at the chislers who gave rebates at retail outlets and stole their customers. Independents flouted the rules and attracted customers by giveaways, gaudy signs, hawkers on street corners, and other gimmicks. While the major firms spent millions on radio, newspaper, magazine, and billboard advertising, a Pittsburgh service station proprietor correctly observed, the code prohibited independents from giving premiums, stamps, or coupons with the sale of gasoline, the only methods of advertising available to them.[31]

The compliance record of the majors demonstrated virtuosity if not virtue. An independent refiner from El Dorado, Kansas, gathered evidence of illegal discounts offered by majors to dealers. Dan Danciger of Danciger Refineries, Tulsa, accumulated evidence that the majors sold high octane gasoline at regular octane prices, in effect an illegal discount. PCC, Danciger caustically noted, ignored such violations but jumped on poor and insignificant codebreakers. It was clear to Danciger: "The competition from the major companies through their selling a lower priced product and delivering a higher priced product . . . is affecting our sales a great deal more than the cut-price competition of the small plants."[32]

Independents and majors alike connived and dealt illicitly and, for the most part, went unpunished. Policing the marketing section of the code proved all but impossible. Price wars sprang up almost everywhere, and the price rules were unenforceable. After the collapse of efforts to win adherence to the marketing provisions of the National Petroleum Agency, PAB retained only the power of cajolery. In an effort to end the price wars, Ickes requested PCC to organize price stabilization committees in price-war locales. PCC complied, appointing a general stabilization committee, state chairs, and local committees normally composed of refiners rather than dealers. While some of these committees vigorously investigated charges of price cutting and the use of unfair trade practices, they possessed no authority and rarely accomplished much. Denver's committee, for instance, struggled unavailingly to prevent a large independent from cutting prices and to stop self-service gasoline stations from selling at one cent below the lowest retail price. Despite the best efforts of local committees, gas wars continued even after the reduction of hot oil production.[33]

After the Code

The top-heavy and incredibly complicated system of local, district, state, and national committees that administered the oil code unraveled when the U.S. Supreme Court pulled two critical threads. In *Panama Refining Co.* v. *Ryan* (January 1935), the Court invalidated Section 9(c) of NIRA; then, in the *Schechter Poultry Corp..* v. *United States* decision of May 1935, the Court struck down NIRA in its entirety. Even before the Panama decision, Ickes and a small minority within the oil industry pressed for the enlargement of federal power over oil production. Most within the industry campaigned for the extension of NIRA in its present form, an option eliminated by the Schechter case. Numerous smaller independents in Texas and Oklahoma wanted NIRA to expire, thereby denying the federal government any role in oil. A group of producing-state officials preferred a compact of producing states as the coordinating agency, with the federal role confined to the interdiction of hot-oil shipments. These same special interests had clashed over the formulation of NIRA and over the oil code. Now they were at it again, only this time the Court decisions against Section 9(c) and then against NIRA forced Congress to act with some alacrity.

The Cole committee, meeting in fall 1934 and early 1935, served as the primary theater for these debates and heard testimony on virtually all phases of the oil industry.[34] In early 1935, its principal concern was the formulation of legislation to replace the abrogated hot-oil clause of NIRA; but following the Schechter decision, its attention turned to devising a new federal policy for oil. The outlines for this debate were defined a year earlier with the introduction in both houses of the Thomas-Disney bill, largely the handiwork of Ickes and PCC. The bill authorized the federal government to allocate and enforce production quotas among the several states; it also called for a reorganized PAB, appointed by the secretary of Interior and housed within that department, and provided for mandatory import quotas. This legislation represented Ickes's response to the inability of PAB-PCC to stop the flow of hot oil from East Texas.[35]

Supporters of the Thomas-Disney bill resembled a political Noah's ark; a few individuals and an organization or two from each sector of the industry favored its passage. Although passed by the Senate, the bill died in the House, the victim of California and Texas oil interests and state officials from Texas who opposed any diminution of state sovereignty or any enlargement of Ickes's authority. Texas, as Governor-elect James V. Allred informed the Cole committee, refused to surrender state power over its natural resources and possessed sufficient power to police its own oil production, a position reiterated by E. O. Thompson of TRC. Blocked but unvanquished, PAB's Nathan Margold assured Ickes, "There is a general feeling of cheerfulness in the industry based on a belief that the oil administration will by some hook or crook be able to preserve conditions in spite of the defeat of the Thomas-Disney bill. There are the usual doubting Thomases, but they are in the minority."[36]

Congressional rejection of the Thomas-Disney bill contributed to the organization of the Federal Tender Board for Oklahoma City and East Texas which experienced some success in reducing the flow of hot oil during the last quarter of 1934.[37]

When on 7 January 1935, the Supreme Court invalidated Section 9(c) of NIRA, the tender board ceased functioning. Hot oil began to flow at once. Malcolm McCorquodale, chief FTB officer at Tyler, Texas, reported on 13 January that twenty-one refineries had reopened since 7 January, with ten using untendered oil. The state, McCorquodale asserted, "is in exactly the same position to stop hot oil it was two years ago," that is, untrustworthy.[38] In the face of this serious setback, Ickes called upon Congress for specific legislation to prevent the further demoralization of the industry. A number of bills were speedily introduced, several congealing into the Connally bill, which passed both houses on 22 February 1935. Known as the Hot Oil Act, the Connally law specifically prohibited interstate or foreign commerce in hot oil. The FTB was reestablished in East Texas.

Three months later in the Schechter decision the Supreme Court delivered the final blow. All code authorities ceased to exist. The PAB was reduced to a study group before finally expiring in March 1936, replaced as the administrator of the Hot Oil Act by the Petroleum Conservation Division of the Department of Interior. A flurry of legislative activity followed the Schechter announcement, as Congress sought a mechanism to allocate the demand for petroleum among the producing states. At this point it became clear that a majority of the oil industry and several of the producing states would obstruct any effort to devise a comprehensive system of federal controls. An editorial in *The Oil and Gas Journal* portrayed the industry as "harassed and bedeviled" by regulation and threatened by a new NRA with power to control prices and production for oil, gas, and coal. If you think the PAB was paternalistic, deluded, and inefficient, the editorialist warned his readers, you "Ain't Seen Nothin' Yet."[39]

The defeat of the Thomas-Disney bill in 1934 and the opposition the Connally bill engendered foretold the fate of any bills that enlarged federal authority beyond that already exercised in the Hot Oil Act. API's governing board, in a statement reminiscent of its position during the mid-1920s, assured the nation of the adequacy of oil supplies and rejected contentions that the industry required regulation. Others echoed those views, even though some, recently elected Gov. Ernest Marland of Oklahoma as an example, were less sanguine regarding the nation's reserves. Marland cautioned the industry against the danger of uninhibited production, counseling his colleagues to adopt state conservation measures with production limits or face more federal control. But the Schechter case afforded strong support for the antifederal control forces. E. O. Thompson of TRC expressed the prevailing sentiment in a telegram to Sen. Elbert D. Thomas, Democrat of Utah, "Any other effort of Federal Government to control the production of oil within the sovereign states will be held unconstitutional. . . . Respectfully urge that the state be left to handle the situation."[40]

Although Ickes kept PAB operating after Schechter, in anticipation of further oil legislation, the dismantling of NRA furnished the impulse and the opportunity to terminate the federal role in allocating production quotas to the states. In the Cole committee hearings, numerous witnesses paraded the old FOCB idea of an interstate oil compact before the congressmen. Officials from the Oil States Advisory Committee reiterated all the arguments in favor of a compact initially offered at the conference of oil-state governors called by Ickes back in March 1933. In 1933, the conference members supportive of the idea of a compact disagreed over the power to be vested in it and over the role of the federal government. Texas in 1933 and 1934 rejected a compact possessed of any authority over state production. Now, in 1935, Texas, led by Governor Allred and Commissioner Thompson, refused to consider a compact clothed with coercive powers to compel adherence to production quotas and vetoed the establishment of a permanent federal agency to cooperate with a compact authority to set production quotas. Finally, in early 1935, a compact was ratified by New Mexico, Kansas, Oklahoma, Texas, Colorado, and Illinois, the purpose of which was to conserve oil and gas by the prevention of physical waste through state conservation statutes. Article V of the Interstate Oil Compact (IOC) specifically stated that it was contrary to the purpose of the compact to limit production for the purpose of influencing price. The compact, then, conformed to the demands of Texas by providing no enforcement powers and no allocation of production among its members. Indeed, membership was possible for states such as Illinois without a prorationing law.[41]

Ickes and the Cole committee, seeking a compromise, produced a watered-down version of the 1934 Thomas-Disney bill. As refurbished, the bill contemplated congressional ratification of the compact, the regulation of imports, and a new and permanent PAB to administer the Hot Oil Act and recommend national production quotas to the compact authority. In effect, PAB would be purely advisory and encroach in no way on state sovereignty. The new Thomas-Disney bill hardly reflected Ickes's view of required legislation. On occasion, Ickes had articulated the opinion that the oil industry be

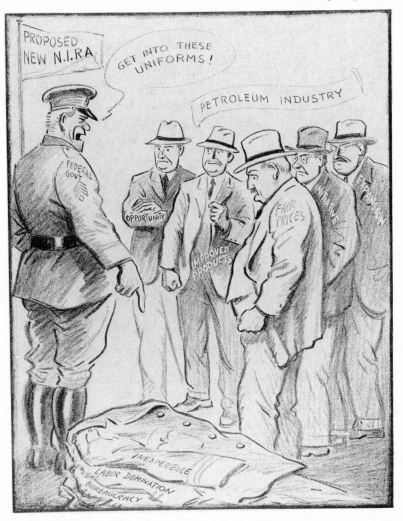

FIG. 5. *The trade journal spoke for many oilmen who opposed the hard-boiled regimentation of a second NIRA.*

Source: *The Oil and Gas Journal*, 33 (April 1935), 9.

defined as a public utility but wisely never pursued the idea in the legislative market place. He may have employed it as a threat, perhaps to compel the industry to accept federal regulation of production. Or it may be considered a vague wish, an "if I had my druthers" statement. He harbored no faith in the efficacy of voluntary agreement either within the industry or among the states. But he had to accept an eviscerated Thomas-Disney bill as the best he could get.

Ickes went down to defeat, undercut again by Roosevelt. Nash and Lear suggest that Roosevelt followed the political path of least resistance by adopting the compact approach coupled with the Hot Oil Act as the program that alienated the fewest interests. Following the Schechter decision, the president presented Congress an impressive set of reform demands—the social security bill, the Wagner labor bill, a banking bill, and a public utility holding company proposal. In addition, he was gearing up for an assault on the Supreme Court. Roosevelt pursued a soft path with oil so as not to jeopardize the passage of his reform package by antagonizing important Democratic National Committee members from Texas. Roosevelt did, however, offer some aid to Ickes by informing leading congressmen that he was opposed to the establishment of a PAB independent from Interior. Roosevelt obtained all his legislative demands. Interior retained its preeminence in oil. But Ickes could claim no victory. His ideas about conservation and national security and the obligations of the federal government were effectively diluted by the compromise measures.[42]

The irrelevance of the compact was amply demonstrated in 1937 and 1938 when new oil discoveries combined with recession and the deflationary effects of heavy inventories to provoke price wars and the flow of unprorated oil across state boundaries. The compact strategy failed to protect the industry from the consequences of flush production in Illinois or to a certain extent from California production. Neither of those states had prorationing laws, and California declined to join the IOC. In California, an ad hoc group of integrated firms cooperated, despite the opposition of independents and in defiance of the antitrust laws, to control production. But in Illinois, the sky was the limit for producers. Illinois production at 8 million barrels in 1937, tripled in 1938 and reached 97 million barrels in 1939. Although representing but 8 percent of national production in 1939, Illinois oil deranged Mid-Continent markets in 1938 and 1939 and accentuated the inherent weaknesses of IOC. In 1938 and 1939, Texas, Oklahoma, Kansas, New Mexico, and Arkansas ordered the shut-down of all wells for as long as a month at a time.[43]

Rather than expanding upon the production-control proposals of

FOCB, as Norman Nordhauser maintains, the New Deal accepted a less comprehensive compact than originally sponsored by the board.[44] By ratifying the compact, the federal government acquiesced to an agreement that permitted each state to act as it wished regarding oil production. State definitions of waste, defined by IOC specifically to exclude economic waste (production above market requirements), replaced federal conservation standards. IOC represented a substantial retreat from both the program sponsored by FOCB and the moderate position on oil controls reflected in NIRA and the oil code.

From Industrial Self-Government to Antitrust

The NIRA and NRA loosened the tongues of all the irascible elements in American society. Condemned by the left, pilloried by the right, criticized by the center, this New Deal experiment failed even to satisfy those responsible for its formulation and administration. That the intent was to save capitalism and destroy capitalism, to create a workers' democracy, a workers' tyranny, welfare capitalism, and corporate monopoly were all truths to those who showered invectives upon this effort to stimulate recovery and institute modest economic reform. Perhaps the blue eagles were buzzards, one cynic suggested, waiting to pick the remaining skin from our bones.

The oil code was the target for as much criticism as any of the other hundreds of codes, more perhaps, since this code utilized production quotas as a device to control prices as well as authorizing the president to fix the price of gasoline. It was attacked in general and in particular, by self-appointed spokespersons for the consuming public and by groups representing each sector of the oil industry. Just as no consensus emerged about NRA, so too did the oil industry disagree about the workability of the code; as with the NRA in general, the oil code suffered from the absence of a clear idea of what was intended. The Roosevelt administration, trying to reorganize American industry, did not project a picture of the shape of things to come. In the absence of a vision of a future structure, it is difficult to regard this experiment as a triumph for the planners. Perhaps it represented the ephemeral supremacy of planners in search of a plan.[45]

At best, the oil code reflected the momentary ascendancy of one or more oil industry interest groups. In each operational area of code authority—production, price, refining, marketing—equally strong interest groups contested the formulas adopted in 1933, and in key areas sabotaged the system. Few, if any, of the warring interests commanded followings that transcended their own numbers; that is, these interests were self-contained units functioning in a vacuum, unable to form alliances with a broader public.[46] The independents, led by Wirt Franklin, shaped the code and its administration in a manner favorable to their own interests, but represented only the IPAA.

The intractable and ultimately victorious opponents of the IPAA arrangements—independents from Texas, especially East Texas, Oklahoma, California-based majors, and others—may have exceeded the IPAA people in numbers, but they, too, labored without the support of a broad public. But this group of laissez-faire independents possessed one great advantage, a congruence of position with those in their states that proclaimed the inviolability of State rights. While PAB's Charles Fahy refused to believe that the industry desired a return to unregulated competition, that was precisely the goal of those who lobbied against the Connally bill and a new oil code.[47] In the end, this coalition, abetted by a conservative Supreme Court, undid the outwardly imposing but jerrybuilt edifice constructed so painstakingly by Ickes and assorted allies. After Schechter, this coalition, appealing to state sovereignty, successfully prevented the resurrection of a system containing a strong federal presence.

In the area of production controls, independent stripper well producers in Kansas and Oklahoma and Texas accepted controls from which they were immune and demanded fixed prices as well. They fought other independent producers in East Texas and Oklahoma City who opposed federal quotas, ignored state prorationing laws, and sold their oil regardless of price. The National Stripper Well Association supported, in 1935, a revitalized oil code while the other independents denounced the code and resisted its reimplementation. But both groups also fought the majors. The major producers disagreed, too.[48]

Refining and marketing exhibited similar division. In marketing, numerically the largest branch, the independent retailers were too numerous and too scattered to organize effectively for or against the code. These scores of thousands of small service station proprietors survived, individually, as best they could, abiding by or circumventing the code as circumstances demanded. In theory, these retailers, fighting for a life-sustaining margin between the price of their products and the price of the branded products of the majors, might have evoked some public support. Presumably, the motoring public preferred cheaper gasoline to more expensive gasoline. But no mechanisms existed to bring together the consumers and the retailers. In spite of the existence of a consumer counsel in NRA, the motoring public and consumers in general commanded scant attention from PAB-PCC or from the feuding camps in the industry.

A fusion of interests encompassing independents and a greater public seemed remotely possible if the issue of monopoly and the enforcement of the antitrust laws became the focal point. To construct such a union required the precise delineation of the conjunction between the general welfare and the antimajor attitudes of the independents. The current organizational structure of the industry produced socially undesirable results. Independent producers in Kansas and East Texas, independent refiners throughout the Mid-Continent and in California, and independent marketers in all parts of the nation generally agreed with the Independent Petroleum Association of California that the code provisions were destructive to small businessmen and beneficial to the majors. Each of the key code provisions provoked similar blanket condemnation from independents in all sectors of the industry.

A disturbing crescendo of assaults upon the New Deal by big business followed the collapse of NRA. With the recession of 1937, the antimajor, antimonopolistic refrain emanating from oil independents met a sympathetic response from New Dealers disenchanted with the concept of industry-government cooperation and impatient to lock horns with the malefactors of great wealth. After 1936, the New Deal marshaled its forces along the antitrust front: in petroleum already vaguely marked by the efforts of Ickes and others to define the oil industry as a public utility, and in electric power, established with concreteness by the Public Utilities Act of 1935.

Antitrusters composed an active faction among the critics of NRA. Senators Borah and Carter Glass, among others, disliked those provisions of NIRA that permitted practices violating the Sherman Act and accused NRA of fostering the domination of small firms by large, the actual elimination of small enterprise, and, thus, the strengthening of monopoly. The report of the National Recovery Review Board, the so-called Darrow board, appointed by Roosevelt in March 1934, denounced NRA on those very grounds and provided ammunition to the antitrusters. So, too, did the report of the lesser-known Petroleum Code Survey Committee on Small Enterprises, which investigated, among other matters, the impact of minimum wage and maximum hour provisions on small oil firms, the effects of code pricing on refining, and the consequences of code rules upon marketers; the report concluded that the code severely weakened nonintegrated firms.[49]

President Roosevelt's April 1938 call for a comprehensive study of monopoly power resulted in the establishment by Congress, in June, of the Temporary National Economic Committee (TNEC). TNEC published in 1941 the findings of its investigation of the oil industry. This study corroborated the belief of antimonopolists that since 1932 the major integrated oil companies markedly increased their prede-pression control of reserves and crude production and maintained a great supremacy in refining capacity, refining output, pipeline owner-ship, and marketing. TNEC's report concluded that NRA stabiliza-tion policies imposed a "form of monopolistic control," damaging to conservationist efforts and destructive to small firms. Explicit in this bill of particulars was the charge that the majors achieved this domi-nance through various forms of collusion and illicit cooperation. In a separate monograph published by TNEC, a writer for two oil firms denied all wrongdoing, explained the benefits of integration, and as-sured readers that consumer satisfaction was the primary objective of the industry.[50]

None of these disclosures produced any legislation or other concrete results. Demands for the breakup of the major integrated firms, pipeline divorcement, comprehensive regulation by an indepen-dent federal agency, compensatory taxation, and the abolition of the depletion allowance suffered the same fate as in prior years. In some states, the passage of antichain-store legislation aimed partly at the major companies. In 1936 and again in 1940, the Justice Depart-ment filed antitrust suits against two groups of integrated oil com-panies and other parties. But neither of these suits resulted in any convictions, and they had no apparent impact on concentration within the industry. Well before TNEC's findings were made public, the attention of Americans had shifted to the war in Europe and its implications for themselves; for all they may have abhorred or feared the violence that shook their world, they also began to enjoy the fruits of reinvigorated economic activity—jobs and a steady income.[51]

The antitrust campaign harvested little from the political field. Nash characterizes the antitrust approach as an aberration, a strategy far removed from the mainstream of New Deal oil policy as reflected in Ickes's preference for regulation. Nash further argues that the ob-session with monopoly bore little relation to the most pressing prob-lems of the industry: stabilization and conservation.

It is true that Ickes and his Interior colleagues disliked the antitrust bias of the Justice Department. After NRA, Interior encouraged mar-keting agreements among the majors and continued to support feder-ally mandated production controls. Ickes, in 1936, sought to deter the Justice Department from pursuing criminal prosecutions of the in-dicted oil companies. He advised the attorney general that prosecution could damage a still unstable oil industry, as well as the public interest.[52] Ickes remained wedded to the opinion that regulation rather than anti-trust action afforded the most efficacious method to protect the public interest. But there was no regulatory legislation, and there were antitrust laws that drew support from a long tradition of hostility toward monopoly.[53]

Antitrust was hardly an aberration, but reflected instead a strong but temporarily muted ideological component of the New Deal. New Dealers such as Thurman Arnold of Justice or Senator Borah viewed antitrust as a legitimate response to threats to the nation's free market system and to democratic government. If anything, the philosophy behind NRA was the sport. Moreover, thousands of oilmen insisted that monopoly was the central problem of the oil industry. To these independents, the obsession with stabilization and conservation totally ignored the awesome and ever-increasing power of the majors. To others, Ickes's regulatory approach masked threats every bit as dangerous as monopoly. All these positions contended for dominance within the New Deal coalition. One was no more an aberration than another.

The antitrust tradition contended that great size constituted prima facie evidence of monopolistic tendencies or practices that inhibited or even prevented the operation of a free and competitive market, that size or integration carried no inherent guarantee of efficiency, that integration permitted the shift of resources and costs or profits among operations to meet the competition of the nonintegrated firms, that the maneuverability of the large firms and their commonality of interests nurtured unfair competitive advantages, and that the aggregated power of the major integrated firms, controlling as they did the lion's share of the industry's resources, boded ill for democratic government.

During the New Deal, antitrusters such as Borah, a member of TNEC, repeatedly employed their arguments in efforts to separate the pipelines from the integrated firms. Pipeline control by the majors, now including product as well as crude lines, became even more complete during the 1930s; in 1938, fourteen companies owned 90 percent of the trunk lines and sixteen majors owned 96 percent of the gasoline pipelines. These pipeline companies did not act as common carriers. Dividends paid by the pipeline company to the owners, the only shippers, served as a form of rebate and as a competitive advantage over independents denied the use of the pipelines. Enormous powers and mutual interest conjoined to inhibit competition, or so the antimonopolists interpreted such developments.

These were not shocking revelations but merely an updating of information about a well-known tendency. In 1934, Senator Borah introduced bills for divorcement and to apply the commodities clause to pipelines. Similar bills followed in 1935, 1937, and 1939 but, as in the past, failed to muster sufficient support to overcome the concerted opposition of the major companies or of those congressmen who believed that the ICC possessed adequate authority to force pipelines to deal justly with all shippers. Even more damaging to the antitrusters, as A. Johnson observed, was their inability to demonstrate with hard data that the possession of pipelines by the majors unfairly buffered them against competition. Independent refiners, frequently the most articulate of divorcement adherents, never proved that divorcement would enable them to enter distant markets. Many producers, moreover, viewed divorcement skeptically and preferred to continue existing selling arrangements with the majors rather than risk the uncertainties of a new arrangement.[54]

Implicit in the assumptions of the antitrusters were prescriptions for structural change that would, as in the case of pipeline decentralization, strip from the majors their power to control transportation and thus market access. Unlike the adherents of regulation, like Ickes, or the sponsors of an industrial commonwealth (Hawley's term), the antitrusters shared a generalized notion of the future shape of American industry. That future could be (ought to be, according to TNEC) realized by preventing unfair trade practices through suits similar to those initiated in 1936 and 1940. Legislation could be passed that limited the size of the major firms by separating them into their constituent parts. Smaller and less powerful firms would then be left to contest for markets. Presumably, with the costs of monopoly eliminated, the public would benefit.

The scenario of the antitrusters lacked a certain specificity, to be sure. Could smaller firms offer quality products and new products at prices as cheap as the majors? How important was the competition of the independents in maintaining prices at a reasonable level? The efficiencies of bigness, the hallmark of American industry, still titillated Americans. Notwithstanding the depression and the gravely deflated reputation of big business know-how, Americans were unprepared to place the system in harm's way by adopting the nostrums of the antimonopolists. The objectives of the antitrusters were formulated with considerably more clarity than were the amorphous objectives of the NRA planners. The latter proved incapable of schematizing their version (vision) of a future corporate structure and its relationship with other institutions. Ickes, as an example, placed no greater trust in the willingness of the oil industry to act in the public interest than did the antitrusters. But he failed to convince the public that regulation would redound to the benefit of consumers or protect the public from the giants in the industry. Antitrusters, perhaps playing to a somewhat wider and more sympathetic audience, confronted public apathy and intense business opposition on Main Street and Wall Street.

Americans turned their back on both camps, to the great good fortune of the big oil companies and, as it turned out, to the great detriment of resource conservation and national security. Americans, it might be suggested, did not understand the stakes involved. By 1970, the twenty largest oil companies controlled 94 percent of proven reserves, up from 70 percent in 1937; 74 percent of crude production, compared with 53 percent in 1937 and 46 percent in 1926; 86 percent of refining capacity, compared with 76 percent in 1937 and 66 percent in 1926; and 79 percent of gasoline sales, up slightly, relatively, from 71 percent in 1926. This aggrandizement of economic power by the major firms, fostered by the federal government during World War II, fully corroborated the predictions of the antitrusters who labored futilely to reverse this trend during the 1930s and in earlier years.[55]

A Postscript

The demise of NRA symbolized, so Hawley tells us, the passing of the planners who had had their day. But in energy affairs, it might be suggested, a remnant of planners survived in both TNEC and the National Resources Committee (NRC).[56] Something more is said in Chapter 11 about the efforts of those groups to formulate a comprehensive energy policy. The studies of TNEC and NRC emphasized the interrelatedness of all energy sources and the inherent public interest in the energy industries, a public interest recognized by the Public Utilities Act of 1935 and the Natural Gas Act of 1938. The intentions of planners and antimonopolists meshed in this effort to define the energy industries as public utilities. Although bereft of statutory accomplishment in either coal or oil and overwhelmed by the emergency demands thrust on the nation by World War II, TNEC and NRC projected a concern for the future and for the general welfare that transcended narrowly conceived New Deal policies. While those policies recognized a national interest in a healthy oil industry, they denied the federal government adequate authority to regulate it in the public interest and were so complex as to be unadministrable (an even more dramatic failing of the coal code and its successors). From the perspective of the public interest, the oil compact-hot oil act formula did little more than treat a limited array of symptoms and restrict the federal government to the role of traffic officer.

Neither TNEC nor NRC succeeded in convincing Congress or the Roosevelt administration of the urgency of developing a comprehensive energy policy. In fact, separate administrations managed coal and oil during the war, a step backward it would seem from the precedent offered by the U.S. Fuel Administration. Planning for the future frightened some, presaging as it did an expansive federal role, and bored others less sensitive to evolving energy-reserve/energy-use equations. In defining the energy industries as public utilities, in grappling with prevalent manifestations of the public interest which emphasized abundant supply at cheap prices as almost a national birthright, in searching for ways to assure efficiency and economy in energy use, TNEC-NRC assumed a position along the leading edge in energy affairs. The concerns that challenged TNEC-NRC proved as crucial to the nation's postwar future as those that captured the attention of the more visible, more commanding, and more politicized factions in the New Deal coalition.

TEN

Federal Policies toward the Bituminous Industry during the New Deal

Coal's Internal Problems and Interfuel Competition

The depression that blighted the nation's hopes for the future struck a coal industry already reeling from a decade of hard times. In the years following World War I, as Chapters 5 and 6 explained, a series of devastating strikes in both the anthracite and bituminous industries caused severe fuel shortages throughout the land, prompting federal intervention and intense but inconclusive debate about the travail of coal and its relationship to the national economy. The efforts of coal mine owners to reduce costs by lowering wages precipitated the strikes. Cutthroat competition raged between mines, particularly the unionized mines north of the Ohio River and the nonunionized mines south of the river, as operators struggled to protect their normal markets or enter markets in key consuming areas (Map 3).

Among the ills sapping the strength of the industry, observers seldom failed to note productive overcapacity, the underemployment of miners and a shrinking work force, poor and drab mining communities located in degraded environments, and chaotic price conditions. John L. Lewis, president of the United Mine Workers of America (UMWA), and others characterized the industry as inefficient, backward, lacking in leadership, and congenitally incapable of reforming its own affairs.[1]

The internal disabilities of coal stemmed from the inability of the industry to compete with the other forms of energy that entered the

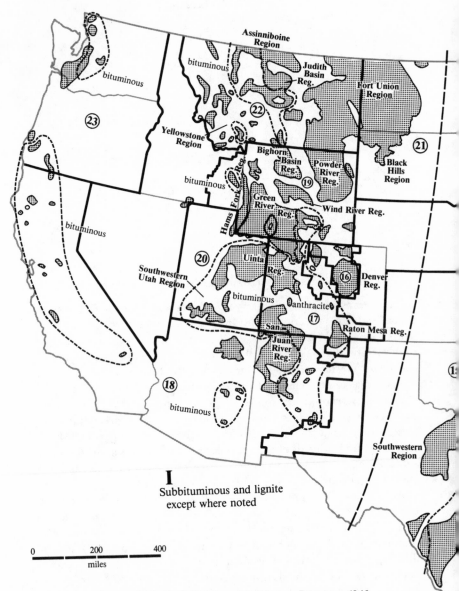

I
Subbituminous and lignite
except where noted

0   200   400
          miles

MAP 3 *U.S. Coal Fields and Producing Districts, 1940*

The critical producing districts were Districts 1, 2, 4, 6, and 11 in the North
and Districts 3, 7, and 8 in the South.

Source: Adapted from *Power*, 84 (December 1940), 72.

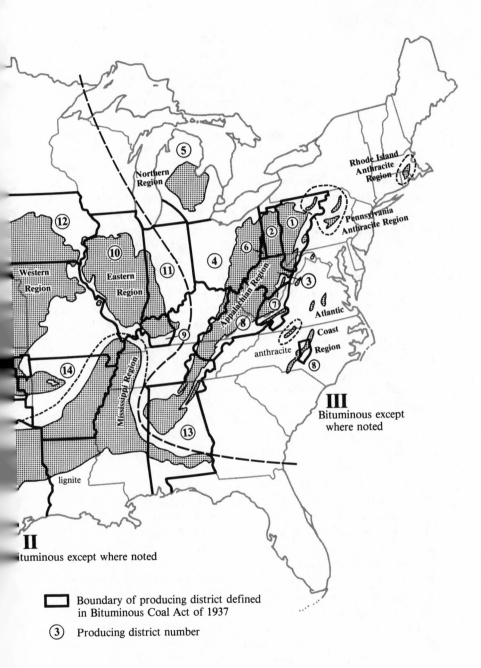

Northern Region

⑤

⑫

⑩

Western Region

Eastern Region

⑪

④

⑥

②

①

Rhode Island Anthracite Region

Pennsylvania Anthracite Region

③

Appalachian Region

⑦

⑧

Atlantic Coast Region

anthracite

⑧

III
Bituminous except
where noted

⑨

Mississippi Region

⑭

⑬

lignite

II
Bituminous except where noted

☐ Boundary of producing district defined
in Bituminous Coal Act of 1937

③ Producing district number

253

market during the initial third of the twentieth century. This situation is treated in this chapter as a prelude to studying the policy solutions evolved by the New Deal and represented by the National Recovery Administration (NRA) coal codes and the two National Bituminous Coal Commissions (NBCC) established by coal acts passed in 1935 and 1937. Only tangentially did these remedies cope with the consequences of interfuel competition; their fundamental objectives were increased wages, miner job security, and the establishment of industrywide collective bargaining. New Deal coal policy, then, treated symptoms rather than the illness and in applying its salves essentially ignored the shifting fuel mix that propelled the nation. As Grant Stauffer, official of several related coal mining companies in the Mid-Continent, and other operators understood only too well, any market or policy-induced influences that raised the price of coal relative to the cost of other forms of energy only aggravated the problem.[2]

Coal's competitive weakness relative to fuel oil, natural gas, and hydroelectric power, according to Charles O'Neil, official of a large District 1 mining company and the National Coal Association (NCA), cost the bituminous industry 122 million tons of production between 1919 and 1929. Stauffer corroborated this dismal assessment for the Mid-Continent by estimating that the output of the region's mines had fallen from above 17 million tons in 1912 to some 8 million tons in 1931 as a result of the invasion of markets by fuel oil and natural gas. While requirements for power and heat rose substantially in that region, new demand did not benefit the coal industry. Natural gas was a particularly strong competitor. According to Kenneth A. Spencer, president of the Southwest Interstate Coal Operator's Association, coal supplied 51 percent of regional industrial energy requirements in 1919, but only 22 percent in 1931; in the meantime, the contribution of natural gas increased from 18 percent in 1919 to 56 percent in 1931.

Similar gloomy calculations emanated from other regions of the nation, most emphasizing fuel oil competition and some reacting angrily to the impact of natural gas or hydroelectric. Citing as evidence the displacement of 700,000 tons of coal by fuel oil in Public Service Company of New Jersey electric generation, James D. Francis, associated with Appalachian Coals, Inc., a coal sales agency, warned an NCA audience that the low annual production figure of 310 million tons in 1932 was not the potential bottom; another 150 million tons could be lost to competing energy sources.[3]

These foreboding facts and portentous calculations echoed coal's problems of the 1920s; our summary in Chapter 6 (see pp. 142–46) was a grim preface to a more-of-the-same syndrome for the 1930s. In short, coal was continuing to lose out not only to other fuels but also to more efficient use of coal itself.

For example, such major coal consumers as the railroads and the public utilities increasingly turned to competing energy forms while simultaneously improving the efficiency of their coal-burning equipment. Between 1920 and 1929, kilowatt-hour (kwh) production by the electric utilities soared from 44 trillion kwh to 97 trillion and rose again to 142 trillion by 1940, an overall advance of over 200 percent. Coal consumption by the utilities rose by only 22 percent during the 1920s and 13 percent during the 1930s, in part because by 1940 generating equipment utilized less coal per kwh produced (1.3 pounds per kwh) than in 1920 (3 pounds per kwh) and in part because the utilities turned to other fuels. Natural gas consumption by the utilities increased almost ninefold during the two decades. Between 1936 and 1940, the use of other fuels by the utilities and the enhanced efficiency of generating equipment may have replaced above 20 million tons of coal annually. In New York, New England, and some states of the upper south, hydroelectric power also competed directly with both coal and fuel oil.

The use of coal by railroads followed a similar pattern. Between 1936 and 1940, railroad fuel oil consumption rose 32 percent while railroad coal consumption demonstrated no growth. For the entire two decades, railroad coal consumption dropped from 135 million tons in 1920 to 114 million in 1929 and 85 million in 1940.[4]

Concurrently, the competitors of coal continued to penetrate strategic coal-consuming regions, reducing the demand for coal among domestic and business consumers. Between 1929 and 1941, fuel oil sales rose by some 170 million barrels while coal production in 1941 was lower than the average production of the nonstrike years during the 1920s (see Table 11). Fuel consumption by household fuel oil burners increased more than sixfold between 1929 and 1941. Also, as in the 1920s, there were more and more apartment buildings, and more and more of these buildings employed fuel-oil furnaces. Fuel oil also found significant markets in commercial establishments such as hotels and office buildings. Furthermore, here again greater efficiency in coal use characterized new commercial and industrial coal-burning equipment. Finally, in the middle third of the nation, the brisk sale of gas home heating units and other gas equipment reduced coal usage and competed vigorously with fuel oil equipment. Coal operators in Indiana, Illinois, Kansas, and Colorado expressed dismay about the expanding natural gas pipeline network and sought to maintain coal's competitive position by opposing new pipelines (a tactic that attracted the support of the railroads) and by pressing for lower coal freight rates (a tactic that did not elicit railroad support).[5]

Coal's increasing vulnerability to the competition of other fuels combined with the devastating effects of the depression to jeopardize the future of the industry and the jobs of scores of thousands of coal miners. The productive overcapacity that precipitated price slashing, wage cutting, and strikes was not lessened by the depression. The coal industry in 1932 possessed a mining capacity of 653 million tons, while it actually produced 310 million and miners worked an average of only 146 days. The number of men employed fell sharply from an average of about 590,000 for the three years 1925–27, much reduced from the peak of 705,000 reached in 1923, to 406,000 in 1932. The number of mines in production also declined steadily after 1923, falling to 6,450 on the eve of the depression, down from a high of about 9,300 in 1922 and 1923, and slipping still further to about 5,400 in 1932. Thereafter and until 1941, the number of mines operating in a given year exceeded 6,000 excepting in the recession years of 1937–38, and the number of employed miners ranged between 421,000 in 1939 and 492,000 in 1937.

The halls of Congress resounded with the strident voices of operators who identified the UMWA as the chief cause of coal industry weakness, castigated the prejudicial action of the federal government, and complained about the unfair competitive tactics of oil and natural gas, about oil overproduction, about the harm caused by imports of cheap foreign oil, and about hydroelectric projects. This litany of grievances may have identified some symptoms of coal's problem but did not suggest or lead to effective countermeasures.

The remedial paths open to coal were two: either increase demand to match capacity, patently impossible during the depression and, if the 1920s are used as a standard, equally impossible during periods of prosperity; or reduce capacity to a level equal to demand by closing mines, consolidating mines into more efficient units, mechanizing all phases of the industry, and firing more miners, a politically unacceptable strategy during the New Deal.[6] The choice remaining—keeping as many mines open and as many miners employed as possible—was an expediential approach that ignored the competitive weakness of the industry but did serve short-run objectives of the UMWA and did attract some support from the coal operators.

During the 1920s, the coal operators sustained a fair degree of unity against federal intervention. When, in 1928, Secretary of Labor James J. Davis, appearing at a hearing on the coal industry, listed a series of coal industry weaknesses, all of which were well known and required some measure of federal involvement to remedy, NCA witnesses denied the existence of any internally generated difficulties save the unreasonable demands of the UMWA. This predictable response prompted John L. Lewis, UMWA president, to remark caustically that the "operators are apparently blind to developed facts. They do not seem to comprehend that the future holds nothing more than present profitless operations."[7] But the mine owners would soon have a plan to revitalize the industry through the organization of regional sales agencies which would, it was promised, reduce competition and stabilize prices.

Coal production plunged from 535 million tons in 1929 to 310 million in 1932 (see Table 11); and the average price per ton (FOB mine) fell steadily after 1922 from $3.02 to $1.78 in 1929, $1.31 in 1932, and then to a low of $1.03 in the early months of 1933, before recovering to reach an average annual price of $1.34. The profit' position of operators deteriorated despite wage cuts, mechanization, and the release of mine workers until between 1929 and 1932 the industry as a whole sold coal at prices below the cost of production.[8] Many mines closed, while those still operating shaved costs however they could and sought frantically to sell below competitors. Consumers, especially the large contract purchasers, such as utilities and railroads, exploited these conditions to force prices even below the average, a tendency condemned by John L. Lewis as well as the operators. To counter this market power, the operators of the seven Appalachian coal producing states gathered in 1931 at a conference called by the governor of Kentucky to discuss a countervailing strategy. The conference proposed that NCA devise an industrywide plan; NCA, in response, appointed a coal stabilization committee, which in turn recommended the formation of eighteen regional sales agencies.

A regional sales agency was to include all the operators within a designated territory. Each operator would contract with the agency to make it the exclusive sales agent for the firm's production. The agency would then deal directly with consumers: wholesalers, dock operators, utilities, railroads. Presumably, since the agency controlled the greater part of a region's production (70 percent was considered the minimum necessary to stabilize prices), higher prices would ensue and the baneful effects of intraregional competition be ameliorated. NCA viewed the sales agency scheme as a panacea and a defense against federal intervention and agreed to manage its legal defense in the courts, where it was certain to be tested under the antitrust laws. NCA, by

1933 cognizant of the inevitability of some sort of federal action, also orchestrated a lobbying campaign to assure that any legislation passed would permit the formation of sales agencies.

In December 1931, the operators of eight southern producing districts formed the first sales agency, Appalachian Coals, Inc. By 1932, the agency held contracts to dispose of 73 percent of the region's tonnage which normally competed with the production of northern fields in the Great Lakes market. Appalachian Coals quickly prepared its first coal shipment so as to get a test case in court. Two other coal agencies soon followed, Northern Coals, Inc., and Hocking Coals, Inc., while other producing districts laid plans for their establishment. Although Appalachian Coals successfully defended its legality before the Supreme Court in 1933, the advent of NRA terminated such experiments.

Eugene Rostow questions the ability of the agency plan to achieve coal industry stability since it merely upped the competitive stakes by substituting organized interregional competition for unorganized intraregional competition. As he points out, the Supreme Court upheld the validity of Appalachian Coals because the agency lacked the power to accomplish its major objective, the raising of prices. Its adherents, however, noted the leveling off of prices in key northern markets in late 1932 and early 1933 and a marked reduction in the shipment of consignment coal (coal without a known purchaser when shipped), a primary source of speculation and price cutting. But NIRA intruded. If the government had let us alone, lamented a Kentucky operator, "we would have gone along without any trouble."[9] Given the efforts of John L. Lewis and others to define the coal industry as a public utility, the Kentuckian's lament, however it reflected the preponderant opinion among coal operators, appears terribly naive.[10]

The Watson, Lewis, and Davis-Kelly Coal Bills

As thousands of underemployed and unemployed miners struggled in vain to provide basic necessities for their families and were ultimately compelled to accept whatever relief their counties and states provided, John L. Lewis in 1931 appealed to President Hoover to convene a conference between organized labor and the operators. But Hoover received this plea without enthusiasm and refused to take even this simple initiative. By 1930–31, those on relief in the mining counties of Ohio, Pennsylvania, West Virginia, and Kentucky, composed 20 to 25 percent of the entire population, and the bottom of the depression had still to be reached. But the operators controlling a majority of the tonnage opposed a conference, implying as it did a federal role, and Hoover, no friend of Lewis, yielded to their wishes. Nor did Hoover take an active part in the debates over several coal industry bills in Congress between 1928 and 1932, perhaps preferring, as James Johnson suggests, to allow the industry opportunity to employ the sales agency plan to achieve stabilization.[11]

The most important coal bills Congress attended to were the Watson bill of 1928, the Lewis bill of 1932, and the Kelly-Davis bill of 1932. These bills were quite similar, all grounded in part in the experience of the 1920s when strikes and transportation bottlenecks caused shortages in many parts of the nation and coal dealers boosted prices. Each bill recognized the intense competitiveness of the industry and were (the latter two bills in particular) sensitive to the deplorable conditions caused by the depression. Each bill gave the federal government, acting through an independent agency, the authority to coerce the industry, a power unwanted by Hoover who preferred industrial self-government. Each bill incurred the wrath of the NCA and most operators, although there were operators who admitted the necessity of federal regulation. None of the bills presented any surprises. None was as comprehensive as the Garfield proposals of 1919 or several of the bills introduced between 1919 and 1921 (see Chapter 5, pp. 110–12), which focused on production, price, and distribution. Under the Hoover administration, none stood an even chance of success.[12]

NCA and various regional operator associations damned the Watson bill of 1928 on every possible ground and denied its constitutionality. In the hearings on each later bill, the same coal industry witnesses restated the same objections. NCA's general counsel assured the Senate committee of coal's ability to resolve its own problems and characterized the bill, which included a collective bargaining section, as furthering the imperialistic effort of UMWA to monopolize all labor in the coal industry. An official of the National Retail Coal Merchants' Association accused the bill's sponsors of currying favor with the leadership of a discredited union that disregarded federal authority and the welfare of its own rank and file. John L. Lewis challenged the "truth of that vicious statement" which he found "gratuitously offensive," and Senator Wheeler pinned the witness to the wall by demanding substantiating evidence, which was not forthcoming.[13] Lewis offered his own analysis of the wellspring of coal obstructionism:

> Every agency which has investigated coal has been able to penetrate the mindless chaos and to disclose the existing evils in poignant detail. But few have ventured to suggest a remedy. A

bugaboo is met at the close of every analysis. Taboo, slogan, shibboleth smother reason under ancient metaphysical dogmas which pass current as economic laws among the half informed. There is an element in American business among whom the fear of governmental invasion of the sacred precincts of industrial management amounts to an obsession.[14]

Each of the bills created an independent bituminous coal commission and a mechanism to fix minimum prices by means of marketing pools or operator-controlled boards. The Lewis and the Kelly-Davis bills established production quotas, a tactic then employed by both Great Britain and Germany and resembling oil prorationing.[15] Senator Davis, Republican of Pennsylvania and former secretary of Labor, viewed the bill which he cosponsored as avoiding arbitrary government interference and guaranteeing industrial self-government. Davis urged the operators to agree upon a program of quota and minimum prices, subject to government review, and as a condition for exemption from the antitrust laws recognize the collective bargaining rights of the mine workers. The idea of production controls stimulated considerable controversy and was repeatedly rejected between 1933 and 1937. Labor was quite hostile to this device, believing that it would cause greater unemployment. The Watson bill, without explicit quotas, delegated to the commission authority to approve new railroad sidings and thus control the opening of new mines.

All three bills expressly exempted selling agencies from enforcement of the antitrust laws, placing their operations under the general supervision of the commission. But this provision offered insufficient inducement to attract operator support for bills otherwise totally objectionable. While Representative Kelly, somewhat ingenuously, portrayed his bill as simply carrying out the recommendations of the U.S. Coal Commission, the intent of the bills was best captured by Charles F. Hosfold, Jr., president of Butler Consolidated Coal Company and later chairman of NBCC.[16] In his view, these bills were based upon the propositions that coal is a natural resource that must be conserved, and that coal is a necessity that must be regulated in the public interest. NCA objected for precisely those reasons. In NCA's view, these bills subjected the coal industry, no different from any other industry, to regulations that did not apply to industry in general and placed the industry under a commission with undetermined but great power. Sen. Carl Hayden, Republican of Arizona, perceived the commission as a coal dictator. The entire system would, NCA asserted, do nothing but raise production costs and therefore prices, stimulate the increased use of competing fuels, and intensify all of coal's current problems. West Virginia operator Ashton File characterized the Davis-Kelly bill as a complete departure from anything "ever . . . proposed in this country among the industries."[17] Others labeled it socialistic.

Opponents of these bills, including the railroads, successfully prevented their passage. In the hearings on the Lewis and the Davis-Kelly bills, NCA recruited dozens of witnesses to testify, all of whom voiced the same objections. John L. Lewis seethed at these delaying tactics and angrily demanded a time limit on testimony, but to no avail. At the June 1933 annual meeting of NCA, Charles O'Neil congratulated the group for mounting such a splendid campaign; but, he warned, coal could not rest on its laurels, for a new administration had assumed power and new legislation affecting coal was making its way through the legislative maze.[18]

Coal under the NRA

As the Roosevelt administration set up shop in Washington in 1933, members of the coal industry understood that the days of nonregulation were about to end. For coal, the objective became not fighting legislation with the intent of defeating it, but influencing to the greatest extent possible the contents of legislation that would certainly be passed. Furthermore, by late April and early May 1933, coalmen were reasonably sure that separate legislation for coal, such as the Lewis or the Davis-Kelly bills, had been rejected by the new administration in favor of NIRA—the all-encompassing program.

Operators and their organizations did not accept the recovery experiment with favor or even with equanimity. They voiced serious objections to various parts of NIRA as it emerged from congressional committees. While they preferred NIRA to special coal legislation, from first to last organized coal objected to the labor provisions. NCA's president, C. E. Bockus, believed that NIRA was a "measure . . . radical enough to make even the boldest hesitate"; it would force industry under government control to a greater extent than ever tried "excepting possibly in Russia." NCA's membership adopted resolutions at its annual meeting in 1933 calling for amendments of NIRA that would, among other things, assure industry's participation in the act and, most critically, maintain the status quo in labor relations.[19]

The coal industry, much more than the oil industry, considered the labor provisions of NIRA as destructive of its best interests insofar as they could compel operators to bargain collectively with UMWA and increase wages while shortening the work day. However, the strenuous opposition of coal, especially its southern contingent, and other industries to eliminate or modify the labor provisions shattered against the intent of NIRA's architects to increase wages, employ as many miners as possible, and strengthen labor vis-a-vis industry. NCA deeply resented NRA's prolabor attitudes and verbally abused those in the coal industry who cooperated with organized labor. But these new thrusts became permanent fixtures in coal politics during the New Deal, and coal operators, pushed and shoved by strikes and New Dealers, accommodated to them quickly enough. Thus, the wage differentials existing between producing districts (or types of coal mining) rather than the absolute level of wages became a focal point of bitter contention during the period of code formulation and thereafter.[20]

Hammering out a producer's code proved no easy task and, as in the case of the oil code, required the intervention of NRA as a mediator between warring parties. Producers, wholesalers, retailers, and specialist handlers such as the coal dock operators all demanded and received their own code. NRA established a board to coordinate the implementation and operation of these separate codes, but it failed to resolve many of the issues that agitated these interests. Some producers sold directly to consumers. Was this producer or retail coal? Other producers sold to truckers who then sold to retailers or consumers. What kind of coal was that? Which code should fix the price of such coal?[21]

Within the producing branch of bituminous, which receives emphasis here, interregional differences grounded in the competitive structure of the industry engendered a struggle as intense as that simultaneously occurring in petroleum where independents and majors maneuvered to shape and control the code. Should there be a single code for the entire industry or separate codes for each producing district or groups of districts? How adjust interdistrict wage differentials? Since raising prices to a level adequate to pay minimum wages was a stated purpose of NRA, could reasonable prices be established that would not damage the competitive position of producing districts in their normal marketing areas? What of interfuel competition and the level of coal prices relative to the prices of other forms of energy? How would these divisive issues be mediated? These and other germane issues evaded satisfactory resolution under NRA and the Guffey acts which followed.

The writing of the coal code consumed several months, spawned numerous versions, and demanded a greater willingness to compromise on the part of Hugh Johnson and NRA than on the part of the operators. The operators in most districts, especially in the southern fields (Districts 3, 7, 8; see Map 3), the Ohio valley (Districts 9, 10, 11), and Iowa, Kansas, Missouri, and Oklahoma, expressed a strong preference for district codes and a persistent opposition to the national code advocated by Johnson at a meeting called by NCA in June 1933. Indiana, Iowa, and the Southwestern Coal Association submitted district codes. Prolific Illinois operators churned out eighteen codes. These codes frequently ignored the labor provisions of NIRA, recognized no outside regulatory authority (reflecting the belief of the operators that a code meant self-regulation and the relaxation of antitrust laws), and delegated the fixing of minimum prices to operator-controlled boards or sales agencies. As NCA explained it, the separate codes expressed the convictions of operators that the objectives of NIRA would be defeated if production costs were raised to a level that induced the replacement of coal by other fuels. NCA's *Bulletin 1200* advised its constituency to reject a code until NRA established a price relationship between coal and competing fuels.

At the June meeting, NCA did draft a model code of fair competition which incorporated the mandated labor provisions and even stipulated that prices be based upon the cost of production plus a fair margin of profit, a formula more precise than that adopted in the final code. But left to their own devices, most operator groups ignored both the model and NIRA. This struggle by a majority of the operators to impose a decentralized code structure on the industry confronted the demand of UMWA and operators in Districts 1, 2, and 6, supported by NRA, for a single code. The northern Appalachian coal operators viewed NRA and an industry code as weapons to equalize wages throughout the industry and negate the price advantage that southern nonunion operators exploited so successfully after 1924. A single code under a single code authority, and committed to industrywide collective bargaining, would more likely result in diminished wage differentials than a plethora of codes administered by autonomous producing districts. Groups of operators from Alabama, Georgia, Tennessee, and the Mid-Continent all advocated the maintenance of wage differentials and, even as late as September, insisted on district codes.

Even the northern operators, however, pressed for a system of district autonomy. By July, NCA reported that 70 percent of national tonnage supported a single code; but to attain this degree of unanimity NRA was compelled to accept an extraordinarily decentralized code. In September, after a final flurry of individual code submissions, Johnson bent before the prevailing winds. He achieved a single code but only at considerable cost. The end result can be considered a victory for a splintered industry and a defeat for New Dealers and others who believed that only centralized planning could bring permanent improvement to the embattled industry. Planners won few of their goals in the oil code and fewer still in the coal code.[22]

The code, as approved by Roosevelt on 18 September 1933, established code authorities in five geographical divisions. The president appointed one nonvoting member, and the remainder were selected by local coal associations. Division I, the largest, included every district east of the Mississippi, excepting Alabama, Georgia, and a few Tennessee counties (see Map 3). Each division could organize any number of subdivisional authorities, and at least seventeen of the latter were functioning in 1935, with seven in Division I. Presumably the division administered and enforced the code throughout its territory, but each subdivisional authority also possessed responsibility for code administration, enforcement, and price control. As a general advisory body, the code established the National Bituminous Coal Industry Board (NBCIB), consisting of representative operators from each division and additional presidential appointees. Theoretically, NBCIB would serve as the bonding agent of the system, providing guidance and recommending necessary code amendments to NRA and to the divisions.[23]

From the birth of the code to its demise in 1935, its decentralized structure militated against the coordination of activities among its numerous and atomistic parts. Unlike the Planning and Coordinating Committee of the oil code, NBCIB eschewed power, met rarely, and resisted any self-aggrandizement which would diminish the authority of the divisions. Moreover, the coal code lacked an administrative analogue to the Petroleum Administrative Board, which at least purported to speak for the public interest. At one of the infrequent meetings of NBCIB, convened at the insistence of NRA in January 1934, with coal prices still unformulated and noncompliance common, Donald Richberg, NRA's general counsel, reminded the operators that the code reflected their wishes. Its incompetent management must, therefore, rest on the shoulders of the industry. Richberg warned NBCIB that if it failed to eliminate the price wars then disturbing the industry, the Roosevelt administration would be compelled to develop separate and more stringent regulatory legislation.[24]

Richberg's criticisms and threats provoked no flurry of board activity. NBCIB could not be cowed into offering an amendment to the code to extend its authority over the divisions. Nor would the divisions exercise the authority delegated to them by the code, but instead deferred to their subdivisions in pricing and most other matters. In adopting such a low profile, the divisions acted in accordance with the wishes of operators who opposed the gathering of power in any body above the producing districts or subdivisions. When, in 1918, Harry Garfield realized that decentralization incurred unacceptable costs, he centralized power in USFA. Ickes attempted this during the life of the oil code but lacked adequate statutory authority. The coal code functioned without a head or center that could prevent the steady diffusion of power to the subdivisions. Thus the subdivisions evolved into the real locus of authority, buffered from NRA threats by the divisions and the code itself. Richberg's critique of code performance and operator culpability surprised few operators. The code had been designed to minimize outside interference and to protect operator or district autonomy.

The central task of the divisional and subdivisional code authorities was to establish sufficiently high minimum prices to permit the payment of minimum wages and furnish employment to as many miners as possible. Wages rather than the cost of production served as the standard, a fuzzy one indeed, for the determination of prices. Some members of the Division I authority doubted that stabilization could be achieved in the absence of production controls geared to national demand and allocated among the districts. District I conducted a brief experiment in production controls, but operator recalcitrance and UMWA opposition forced its abandonment. James W. Carter, president of Carter Coal Company, equated such controls with dictatorship, while UMWA feared that quotas would increase miner unemployment. NRA believed that price fixing would be sufficient to achieve the objectives of NIRA.[25]

Responsibility for establishing prices devolved upon the subdivisional authorities or the marketing associations recognized by them. Subdivisions did establish minimum prices in late 1933 and early 1934, but the methods employed varied widely from one subdivision to another.[26] Operators in Indiana and in Illinois acted independently of one another by establishing their own subdivisions. Indiana operators constructed a price schedule that offered it substantial advantages over competitors in Illinois and south of the Ohio. Division II lacked the authority to compel Indiana to negotiate a compromise with its competitors. The code lacked a precise and universally applicable formula for determining prices and lacked authority to compel the subdivision to coordinate their prices in common markets. Only haltingly in spring 1934 did the subdivisions of Division I establish an ad hoc group to undertake coordination and the complex task of classifying coal according to use-value.

Bitter conflicts over wage differentials, a hodgepodge of subdivisional judgments regarding the proper price of coal, blatant disregard for the code proscription against selling under a fair market price (Article IV, Section 1), and the widespread disregard of other injunctions against unfair trade practices (Article VI, Sections 6–18) produced a chaotic price structure in 1933 and most of 1934. Throughout the South, operators and code authorities, frequently allied with community organizations, damned Johnson for forcing wage increases on southern producers in Amendment 1 to the code (April 1934), thus weakening them relative to the North. Southerners correctly believed that the wage hikes reflected the control of NRA and the coal code by an alliance between UMWA and certain subdivisions of Division I. Western Kentucky operators contested the wage increases and criticized the coal prices fixed by Indiana, asserting that those factors combined with adverse freight rates to shut them out of markets north of the Ohio. Meanwhile, Alabama operators accused Kentuckians of dumping coal and cut their prices below the minimum to remain competitive. Shaft mine and strip mine operators in Missouri, Kansas, and Oklahoma, quarreling with one another over wage scales, coalesced temporarily to voice their fears about a threatened invasion of Indiana and Illinois coal. In the absence of an authority to compel the arbitration of these differences, each subdivision pursued its own self-interest in an effort to forestall other subdivisions from gaining some real or imagined advantage.

NRA held hearings on Amendment 1 in April 1934 and adjusted the wages of some subdivisions, but these concessions were not founded upon any firm data regarding either the value of a particular coal in a particular market area or on the cost of producing such coal. To devise such a price-setting formula, whether of the use-value type or cost-of-production type, was an enormous task—as both coal commissions learned between 1935 and 1940—and it was only partly accomplished during the life of the coal code. Hosford estimated that the code, prior to termination, recognized some 30,000 separate price classifications. Each price classification included several individual prices based upon the physical structure, chemical analysis, and use-value of a specific type of coal, thus generating a number of prices—at least 400,000—far beyond the ability of a decentralized code to administer. Division I's production control committee made precisely this point in advocating a quota system.[27]

Between 1933 and 1935, average national bituminous coal prices moved upward from a low of $1.31 per ton in 1932 to a stable price of about $1.75 in both 1934 and 1935. Reflecting posted or mine circular prices, these averages ignored the rampant price cutting of late 1933 and most of 1934 and were insensitive to the prices charged by wholesalers, retailers, and other middlemen such as truckers. The American Coal Wholesale Association expressed disgruntlement at the discounting and commission practices of illegitimate wholesalers. Retailers and operators inveighed against the truck mines that sold under the minimum price. On 27 December 1934, an NRA *Press Digest* reported newspaper stories of price wars that subverted the code's wage structure. By the end of 1934, NBCIB and NRA recognition of the inability of the current code organization to resolve interdivisional wage and price disputes induced NRA to centralize aspects of the price setting machinery.[28]

Amendment 6 originated with Division I, after some prompting by NRA, and sought to rectify the absence of a coordinating and arbitrating authority by the creation of a permanent National Coal Board of Arbitration (NCBA). In addition, the amendment revised the method of setting fair market prices. This proposal forced into the open the opposition of most subdivisions to surrendering any of their price-fixing authority to a superior body. Striking at rumors that NRA intended to vest pricing authority in the National Industrial Recovery Board, Divisions I, II, and III adopted resolutions in October 1934 identifying sources external to the coal industry—the oil code, natural gas pipelines, ICC, NRA—as the real troublemakers. The coal board sympathized with the position of the divisions, but strike threats from UMWA and hints from NRA that special coal legislation was in the offing prompted NBCIB grudgingly to adopt Amendment 6 and to select the members of the new arbitration board.[29]

NCBA was empowered to settle divisional and subdivisional disputes involving fair market prices and other trade practices and was limited only by NRA's right of final approval. In addition, Amendment 6 sought to regularize the pricing mechanisms by mandating that all code authorities abide by the classification standards imposed in Article VI and that all prices consider the needs of given market areas and of operators selling in their usual markets. As Glen Parker, James Johnson, and others have observed, NCBA arrived on the scene too late to achieve price coordination.[30]

The fragile structure of the coal code buckled under the weight of inordinate administrative complexity and the persistent assaults of critics within and without the industry. NRA's Consumers' Advisory

Board opposed all efforts of code authorities to expand their power over price while the railroads and other large consumers lobbied against wage increases that would inflate fuel costs. Assorted anti-trusters condemned the very concept of industrial self-government and attacked price fixing in coal and oil production controls with equal vigor. The National Recovery Review Board (Darrow board) in its report on the coal code concluded that the code was controlled by NCA, operated for the benefit of the large District I operators, and oppressed small operators.

Meanwhile, NCA, local coal associations, and code authorities, normally unable to cooperate with one another, targeted their weaponry on the threat of centralization that surfaced in late 1934 and was partly actualized by Amendment 6. So tenuous did the code structure appear in February 1935—the Panama case had invalidated a critical oil section of NIRA and a full-scale test of NIRA's constitutionality was only weeks away—that at least one subdivisional authority denied the legitimacy of NCBA. Given the incredibly complex price structure and the patent inability of code authorities to bring violaters to heel, it is unlikely that NCBA could have improved upon the code's operation.[31]

Assessments of the code emanating from federal sources generally insisted that the code saved the industry from collapse and that the experience demonstrated stabilization could be achieved only under government control. But the evaluations offered by the National Resources Committee and the National Resources Board and by others conveniently overlooked the criticisms of Henry Warrum, UMWA lawyer, and Rep. J. B. Snyder, Democrat of Pennsylvania, which were based upon the day-to-day operation of the code in the producing districts. The short-run and empirical perspective of Warrum and Snyder, that the code was collapsing internally, is more accurate than the overviews offered by the code's apologists. Warrum and Snyder displayed a greater realism than Donald Richberg or other NRA officials who frequently berated the industry for its failure to manage the code competently. J. D. A. Morrow, veteran of two decades of coal wars, explained to Richberg in January 1934 that the operators purposefully created a code with weak divisional authorities. The code, Morrow stated frankly, "is purely a competitive code. . . . We deliberately wrote it up to preserve competition."[32] Warrum and Snyder understood this more clearly than Richberg, just as they better understood the elemental importance of interfuel competition.[33]

The coal code was one of the few codes that mandated direct price fixing, and without doubt it posed the most complicated challenge. If a single price for coal was obviously impractical, how much less practical were thousands and thousands of coal prices. Surely reason called for a price system that recognized only a few average prices per producing district, after the fashion of the maximum prices established by the U.S. Fuel Administration. But this contravened custom, and the code, if it did nothing else, codified customary practice. Industrial self-government ran amuck under the coal code. But this, too, was a mere replication of historical patterns within the industry.

From the outset, with prices irrevocably tied to wages, the experiment took off on the wrong foot. It mattered little that the code ignored the cost of production and otherwise failed to specify a method for determining price. Both NBCCs included costs of production in their price formulas but experienced even less overall success than NRA. Price was merely symptomatic of coal's ills, and price setting could not work unless accompanied by and correlated with production controls. The urgent need, for the industry and for the public interest, was to assure that coal contributed efficiently to the nation's fuel requirements, an unapproachable goal under NRA or any other system that managed each fuel in isolation from all other fuels.

The Bituminous Coal Commissions

Hearings on the extension of NIRA and the coal code, underway prior to the Schechter decision of 27 May 1935, revealed widespread disagreement among the operators concerning the success of the code and the advisability of its renewal.[34] NCA's legislative committee unanimously opposed production controls but reached no common position on the question of code extension or the practicality of further price fixing. In the pre-Schechter months, individual operators and coal associations worked out their own alliances for or against code extension or special legislation. After Schechter, the industry split into pro- and anti-Guffey bill groups.[35]

Among the operators, both negative and positive evaluations can be found in profusion. Those directly involved as members of divisional or subdivisional authorities manifested a more favorable attitude than uninvolved operators. Operators from the eastern producing fields of District 1, interested in narrowing sectional wage differentials, accepted the code less reluctantly, responded less critically to such reforms as Amendment 6, and viewed NRA's extension more favorably than operators in the South and West. Kenneth Spencer of the Southwestern Coal Operators' Association denied any benefits from the code and blamed the code for inflating costs and weakening coal relative to competing fuels. This intraindustry division of opinion was sustained during the debates over both Guffey bills. In general, the high-labor-cost producers of northern Appalachia favored price fixing as a deterrent to the invasion of their markets by the low-labor-cost producers of the South who desired uninhibited price competition and the maintenance of interregional wage differentials. The southern producers, joined by many western operators, resisted all versions of the Guffy-Snyder bills.

Prior to Schechter, many industry members of the code authorities voiced their satisfaction with the code's operation, and some joined with other operators to form a Committee Against the Guffey Coal Bill. In this opposition they were sustained by the president and NRA officials who withheld support from the Guffey-Snyder bill. The Court's destruction of NIRA changed all this. Kenneth Spencer and James W. Carter, both members of the anti-Guffey committee, labored assiduously against new legislation and for an essentially unregulated coal industry. Simultaneously, other operators, among them Charles O'Neil and J. D. A. Morrow, formed a committee to support a revised version of the Guffey bill and on 20 May 1935 convened an operator conference representing 175 million tons of production. This National Conference of Bituminous Coal Producers agreed to draft a coal bill, using the Guffey bill as a basis for discussion, that would meet the Court's objections.[36]

Several versions of the Guffey-Snyder bill passed through the legislative grinder and formed the subject matter of congressional hearings, undergoing substantial transformations in the process. As originally introduced in the House as H.R.4461 and in the Senate as S.1417 in early 1935, the bill contained interesting features that were subsequently deleted. In order to reduce the capacity of the mining industry, the bill appropriated $300 million for the purchase of submarginal coal lands that would be placed in a federal coal reserve. Some of the funds were earmarked for the retraining of displaced miners.[37] Producer opposition and some labor apprehension about the immediate impact upon employment compelled the removal of this provision. The original bill also established a system of production controls, as had the Lewis and the Davis-Kelly bills, based upon quotas for each producing district. Proponents of the coal reserve and production quotas argued to no avail that these provisions dealt directly with the central problem of overcapacity and underemployment. But, as in the case of the coal reserves, producer opposition resulted in the deletion of production quotas from the final bill.

Despite an impressive preamble that declared the "production, distribution, and use of bituminous coal to be affected with a national public interest," the Bituminous Coal Conservation Act of 1935, approved by Roosevelt on 30 August 1935, was confined to minimum price fixing and the prohibition of unfair trade practices.[38] Neither of those objectives was sufficient to achieve industry stability even had the courts allowed the act to stand. As it passed, the Guffey Act was a replica of the coal code with those sections objected to in the Schechter decision removed. The bill pleased few either in committee or on the floor of each house where it passed with small majorities and only because of Roosevelt's strong support and, perhaps, a strike threat by UMWA. Its coal industry opponents denied the effectiveness of price fixing, argued that higher prices stimulated the substitution of other fuels for coal, damned it as an instrument of organized labor, and enjoyed the support of the National Association of Manufacturers, the railroads, and the owners of captive mines. According to a leading critic of the measure, H. R. Hawthorne, vice-president of Pocahontas Fuel Company, those opposed controlled 60 percent of national production, including about 18 percent contributed by captive mines. Supporters of the bill calculated that they represented 70 percent of commercial production. Thus, the antagonists each controlled a significant tonnage, attesting to the wide rift in the industry caused by the bill.[39]

The system spawned by the first Guffey Act had hardly organized when the Supreme Court struck it down in the Carter Coal decision (*Carter v. Carter Coal Co.*, 18 May 1936), the result of a suit filed the day after the act became operational in October 1935. After some delay, Congress passed a second Guffy Act, which, with certain administrative improvements and the deletion of constitutionally objectionable sections relating to organized labor and any mention of the public interest, replicated the first Guffey Act. The remainder of this chapter outlines the administrative systems established by the two coal laws and then focuses on the implementation of the second Guffey Act and the performance of the coal commission it established. This seems justifiable since the experience of the second commission strongly resembled that of the first in that it was similarly entombed in an essentially unworkable administrative mausoleum—and also failed to achieve its mandated objectives.

The laws of 1935 and 1937 established National Bituminous Coal commissions of five members and seven members, respectively, that were responsible for promulgating minimum prices and enforcing the code of unfair trade practices. To each commission, the president appointed two members representing the operators, two representing the miners, and the remainder representing the public.[40] Increasing the membership of NBCC(2) resulted in its factionalization, with the two operators, Hosford and Haymond, frequently joining forces with Maloney and Smith against Tetlow, Lewis, and Greenlee over patronage and over price fixing. Chairman Hosford denied the existence of the rift, but he did resign. The contention that embroiled NBCC(2) revolved around the procedures utilized to determine minimum prices; the proper role of the Consumers' Counsel (an office provided for by both acts) in determining prices; and the hostility of numerous groups of consumers to the prices set.[41] This is all returned to shortly.

Twenty-three district boards of varying size were established by both laws (see Map 3), and while the duties of the boards remained essentially unchanged, their actual power changed subtly. Under the first Guffey Act, the district boards established the minimum prices, subject to the approval of NBCC(1); while under the terms of the act of 1937, the boards "proposed" prices to NBCC(2), which then established them. This transfer of authority reflected a continuous trend to further centralize price fixing and, concomitantly, to reduce the autonomy and obstructiveness of the district boards. The act of 1935 was operational for about eight months, during which time minimum prices were announced for only a few states, none of significance as producers.

Each producing district fell into one of ten minimum price areas, the largest, Area I, encompassing Districts 1–4 and 6–8 (see Map 3). In December 1935, NBCC(1) issued Order No. 10, announcing public hearings preliminary to the establishment of minimum prices for Area I, and precipitated stiff operator resistance. Charles O'Neil denied the propriety of establishing prices before the courts settled the issue of the constitutionality of the law. Other operators asserted that price fixing would seriously disadvantage code members in their competition with noncode members.[42]

As of January 1936, only about 70 percent of national tonnage had assented to the code. The remaining 30 percent included some of the larger producers; one, the Carter Coal Company, instituted the suit that led to the demise of NBCC(1). In District 2, western Pennsylvania, and in the southern District 8, some 40 to 50 percent of the tonnage belonged to nonmembers. Code members in price Area I complained bitterly about price wars initiated by nonmembers and successfully thwarted the intention of NBCC(1) to announce a price schedule. The more powerful NBCC(2) did not enjoy greater success than its predecessor in setting minimum prices. Both labored under suffocating administration requirements and confronted hostile coalitions of nonmembers and consumers who took to the courts to emasculate the system.[43]

In theory, the establishment of prices occurred in the following way and is presented here to evoke, however faintly, the Byzantine nature of the system encumbering both commissions. The district boards gathered data on the cost per ton of producing coal at each mine—totalling 5,567 mines in price Area I—which formed the basis of determining the weighted average cost per district. Using this data, the commissions calculated the weighted average of total production costs for each minimum price area and resubmitted these figures to the district boards to be used as the basis for fixing minimum prices. The district boards established prices at each mine for the kinds, qualities, and sizes of coal produced in the district. Many districts recognized as many as fifty, sixty, or even seventy different sizes, a number the commissions persistently sought to reduce, while the operators just as persistently pressed for the recognition of even more sizes in order to improve their competitive position. And for any one size in any one district, there were innumerable qualities based upon chemical composition and other factors. In this step, the district boards were enjoined to give due regard to an adequate return to the operator, the relative market value of different kinds, sizes, and qualities of coal, the interests of the consuming public, and equity among the producers of the district.

Having accomplished all this and having received the approval of the coal commission—a phase never actually reached by NBCC(1) and only partially by NBCC(2)—meant the completion of about half the process, and that the simplest. The even more onerous task remained of coordinating district prices in common consuming market areas that the district boards were supposed to define but which the commission actually established when it became clear that the districts could not reach agreement. As of 1939, some 193 market areas had been defined. Presumably, the boards of districts shipping into common market areas initiated negotiations that would assure fair competition by taking into account the kinds, qualities, and sizes of coal used in the market area, equity between producers and districts, market values at points of delivery, and transportation charges. Regarding the last factor, one of extreme importance, the negotiators faced the problem of coordinating prices for coal moving by all-rail, all-river, and a combination of routes.

NBCC(1) was busily engaged in overseeing this task throughout the first quarter of 1936. Negotiations were in process among Districts 9, 10, and 11, Districts 16 and 17, and those districts belonging to minimum price Area I that competed in several dozen market areas. The issues separating these districts seemed insuperable. Districts 16 and 17 each accused the other of price cutting and other unfair trade practices. Districts 3 and 4 insisted, in December 1935, on the immediate establishment of minimum prices and the initiation of interdistrict coordination, while District 1 questioned the advisability of pursuing this course in the face of court suits brought by several large producers who were noncode members. The Voluntary Producers' Advisory Committee, set up by NBCC(1) to aid in the measurement of transportation-related costs, counseled the commission in December 1935 to postpone further price and coordination efforts until the constitutional issues were resolved. NBCC(1) rejected this advice, but the issues all became moot when the Supreme Court invalidated the first Guffey Act in May 1936.[44]

The legislative purposes of the first Guffey Act remained unrealized under NBCC(1), a result not entirely attributable to its hectic and brief life. Lacking the power to coerce the district boards into action and into consensus, the commission could only await the proposals of the individual boards regarding minimum prices and could do little more than apply moral suasion to facilitate coordination. Each mine owner functioned as a special interest, attuned to his own particular market problems and imbued with little faith in the willingness of his industry colleagues to treat him fairly. The act of 1935 attempted to guarantee equity and justice by erecting an administrative safety net, a worthy theoretical goal; but the net became a web, constraining rather than protecting, and so inflexible as to virtually assure failure. Thousands of mines were involved. The burden of manipulating tens of thousands of prices, each price an alchemy of measurable and subjective factors, proved a fatal obstacle to the effective operation of the law. Moreover, a sizable proportion of the tonnage ignored the law, refused to pay taxes, sought court injunctions against enforcement, and succeeded first in subverting the nascent price system and then in invalidating the law.

The history of the second commission supports the suggestion that brevity of life insufficiently explains the sorry performance of NBCC(1). In the second Guffey Act, Congress reproduced the first with the exception of the labor provisions. Arguments for and against the bill closely resembled those of 1935. A filibuster in the Senate, plus other obstacles, prevented until April 1937 passage of the Coal Conservation Act of 1937 (the Guffey-Vinson Act).

The wording of Section 2(a), which established NBCC(2), clearly vested in that body the power to determine and establish minimum prices, thus relegating the district boards to an advisory capacity, but NBCC(2)'s flexibility was severely constrained by the necessity of holding innumerable hearings at each step of the price-fixing process. The act of 1937 also required NBCC(2) to hold hearings to ascertain whether intrastate transactions in coal affected interstate commerce. If NBCC(2) decided this in the affirmative, which it did in several cases, then the law applied to that coal. As with the first Guffey Act, the new law permitted the establishment of cooperative sales agencies, a provision ignored by NBCC(1), included a list of unfair trade practices, and authorized NBCC(2) to intervene before ICC on coal rate issues. The Consumers' Counsel also survived in the act of 1937.[45]

The actual prices set and the arcane formulas employed to define them, involving as much bargaining as arithmetical calculation, may be the least important aspect of NBCC(2) and, perhaps, NBCC(1) as well. Of greater moment was the endless bickering over procedure and the ensuing procedural confusion that persisted until the duties of NBCC(2) were tranferred in 1939 to the Bituminous Coal Division of the Department of Interior. Too, the advocacy role of NBCC(2) and the Consumers' Counsel before ICC and other federal agencies elucidate the weakening position of coal in the nation's fuel mix, matters emphasized in the concluding pages of this chapter.

As NBCC(2) organized for action in mid-1937, the nation struggled to extract itself from a deepening recession which wiped out some of the economic progress made after 1933 in employment, higher wages, and productivity. Soft coal production dropped by 100 million tons from 1937 to 1938 (see Table 11). In October 1937, Roosevelt responded to the laying off of 130,000 miners by rebuking NBCC(2) for failing to announce minimum prices, a situation reflecting the commissions's inability to prod the districts, particularly Districts 1–8, to move swiftly in coordinating prices. At that moment, NBCC(2), the Consumers' Counsel, coal operators, and consumers were locked in a number of separate and debilitating fights over procedures and roles. Many coal operators called for the immediate announcement of fixed prices, but demonstrated little enthusiasm for the give-and-take necessary in market-area coordination. A number of operators, claiming to represent 65 percent of production (more like 25 percent, according to NBCC(2)), brandished their unremitting hostility for the act of 1937 by orchestrating noisy campaigns for the repeal of the law in 1937 and 1939. Despite operator resistance, NBCC(2) plunged ahead to a point in November and December 1937 when it did announce final minimum prices.[46]

NBCC(2) committed two mistakes that undid all its labors. First of all, in late October NBCC(2) adopted a rule that reduced rather than expanded the number of hearings convened during the gathering and manipulation of basic price data. Secondly, the commission decided that the public had no interest at this stage and barred the Consumers' Counsel from these proceedings. Partly as a result of these grievous errors, both the procedures and the prices were challenged by numerous parties who sought court injunctions, asserting that the prices had been arrived at arbitrarily and without due regard for the opinions of interested parties. During this stage, NBCC(2) mismanaged its relationship with the Consumers' Counsel, an office part of but not subordinate to NBCC(2), and headed by John Carson.

Two excellent accounts of Carson's efforts to carve out a meaningful role in the process of price establishment agree that his motivation sprang from no short-sighted inclination to push for the lowest possible prices.[47] As the records indicate, Carson believed that price stabilization was absolutely necessary but that the interests of producers, miners, and consumers had, somehow, to be balanced. Prices must not attain such a high level as to induce the substitution of other fuels or cause hardship to consumers or be set so low that operators could not make a profit or pay reasonable wages. Although NBCC(2) agreed with this in principle, the majority chose to deny Carson a substantial voice in price fixing by refusing to share coal production cost data with him and vetoing his demands that consumers be involved in the price-setting process. In a fit of paranoia, the commission set itself against the threat of dictation by the counsel. In one inexcusable exchange, Commissioner Maloney accused Carson of serving the interests of the railroads and the utilities.

In fact, Carson developed few contacts with small consumers, a shortcoming he admitted but worked with little success to rectify. Railroads and utilities and municipalities were organized and could articulate their position effectively; household consumers were unorganized, and Carson sought to protect them as well as the large consumers. While Carson advised NBCC(2) to extend the timetable for price fixing by permitting the appearance of consumers at hearings, the commission responded to pressure from Roosevelt, the UMWA, and many operators to establish the prices *now.* In doing his job, Carson could only be obstructive. NBCC(2) reacted with hostility and propelled Carson into an alliance with a mixed bag of consumer groups that opposed the prices set in late 1937.[48]

In October 1938, a plaintive letter from a Philadelphia coal dealer crossed the desk of the mayor of Atlanta asking why the city had filed suit against the Guffey Act and how the city could be so insensitive to the economic distress of small Georgia operators and their employees. Altanta's antagonism toward the policies of NBCC(2) typified that of many municipalities and other consumers who had obtained court injunctions in early 1938, preventing the commission from enforcing compliance with the prices announced in December 1937. Bethlehem Steel, the American Gas Association, Jackson County, Colorado, the city of Chicago, the governors of New England, the Associated Industries of New York State, Inc., among many others, resisted the implementation of the price schedule. The Consumers' Counsel filed a petition requesting suspension of the prices and new hearings. In February 1938, the U.S. Court of Appeals of Washington, D.C., granted a group of 200 railroads and the cities of Cleveland and Chicago a temporary injunction against the operation of the prices. NBCC(2) bowed to this consumer revolt, revoking all prices as of 25 February 1938. The entire process would be started all over again.[49]

Minimum prices actually became effective on 1 October 1940. Much had happened since February 1938. Operator opposition to the Guffey Act, while failing in 1939 to prevent renewal of the law, did convince Roosevelt to utilize the Reorganization Act of 1939 to abolish NBCC(2). The fiasco of February 1938 had cost the commission whatever political support it had once commanded. In 1939, just as NBCC(2) seemed ready to promulgate a new set of prices, following feverish efforts to develop coordinated prices in common consuming districts, Roosevelt centralized the administration of the Guffey Act by establishing the Bituminous Coal Division (BCD) in the Department of Interior.[50] The duties of the Consumers' Counsel devolved upon Interior's Office of the Solicitor. BCD, then, finally completed the price-fixing process initiated back in 1937, but by fall 1940 the nation's economy increasingly marched to the drum beat of war in Europe and Asia while the calamitous effects of the depression gradually faded away. By late 1940, average coal prices approached $2 per ton for the first time since 1926, and mine employment had risen by 100,000 since 1938. The attention of many in BCD shifted to the possibility of American involvement in the war and the potential of severe price inflation and inadequate coal production. The overcapacity in mining which so plagued the industry after World War I would appear to some as a godsend.[51]

Defending the Interests of Coal

In January 1934, a communication from C. E. Bockus, president of NCA, to Secretary of Labor Frances Perkins itemized the federal fuel policies considered damaging to the coal industry. Bockus complained of the unfair competition faced by coal as a result of federal policies toward petroleum, natural gas, and hydroelectricity. The inflation of coal prices by the coal code, coupled with the obvious inability of the government to reduce oil production and raise petroleum prices and the half-hearted efforts of the government to significantly reduce foreign crude imports, impinged unfavorably on coal's competitiveness. Natural gas remained unregulated, and NRA price policies were insensitive to the effects of dumping cheap fuel oil and natural gas in markets essential to coal's prosperity. In addition, Bockus wrote, the Reconstruction Finance Corporation and the Public Works Administration consistently promoted rail electrification and the exploitation of hydroelectric sites. The federal expenditure of $7.3 million to build a hydroelectric plant on the Loup River in Nebraska would displace, Bockus calculated, 200,000 tons of coal.

At a time like this, Bockus concluded, "no effort should be spared to preserve for the industry . . . all the market it now enjoys." In the following month, NCA focused its ire on the Roosevelt administration's hydroelectric programs, accusing Secretary Ickes of consciously working against the coal industry. Resolutions adopted in January 1934 by the National Bituminous Coal Industry Board condemned the appropriation of federal funds for hydro projects; this was a continuation of the NCA's antihydroelectric campaign during and after the debates on the legislation that established the Tennessee Valley Authority in May 1933.[52]

During the next several years, coal industry representatives beat a steady tattoo in the halls of Congress against policies deleterious to coal's interests. A large coal contingent opposed NIRA and the Guffey bills on the ground that raising coal prices without simultaneously controlling the price of other fuels could only diminish the demand for coal. Operators and marketers, occasionally joined by the UMWA, pressed for excise taxes or tariffs on imported oil, for the lowering of Canadian duties on American coal, and for other measures to buffer coal against competitive fuels. Under the code, the coal industry made little headway in shaping advantageous policies. But the industry gained a strategic ally with the formation of NBCC(1), which was endowed with the power to intervene before ICC on freight rates and was authorized (in Section 16 of the act of 1935) to concern itself with increasing the use of soft coal (a mandate repeated in Section 14 of the act of 1937). NBCC(1)'s brief career precluded much activity along these lines, but NBCC(2), including the Consumers'

Counsel, assumed an energetic role as the advocacy agency of the coal industry.[53]

NBCC(2) imbibed the prevailing views of the coal industry about the market vulnerability of coal. Not only did the commission intervene regularly before ICC with briefs against rate increases, but it demanded an equivalent status before the Federal Power Commission (FPC) and attempted to influence other federal agencies whose policies impinged on coal. Thus, in 1938, NBCC(2) filed a brief with the Department of State protesting the negotiation of a reciprocal trade agreement with Venezuela—part of the New Deal's "Good Neighbor Policy"—that would lower the oil import tax, a stance applauded by many oil independents. In its unsuccessful effort to defeat this trade agreement, strongly supported by Standard Indiana, which owned numerous wells in Venezuela, NBCC(2) argued that increased imports from Venezuela would displace 5 million tons of coal and destroy the jobs of 7,000 miners. On other fronts, NBCC(2) contested decisions of the Veterans Administration and the U.S. Housing Authority to burn fuels other than coal in their facilities.[54]

According to the act of 1937, ICC was required to inform both NBCC(2) and the Consumers' Counsel before deciding any cases involving coal transportation. From 1936 through 1939, the two commissions and the Consumers' Counsel frequently filed opinions protesting rate increases as inimical to coal's competitive position.[55] During those years, these agencies initiated a campaign to eliminate special rate surcharges authorized by ICC in 1931 and which the carriers wished to make permanent. In 1936, a five-cent-per-ton reduction in the surcharge on bituminous was won. In subsequent years, Carson and the commission prepared and submitted data substantiating coal's claims for further reductions and, as of 1939, had managed at least to forestall a marked increase in coal rates.

In this intervention, NBCC(2) engaged in a legitimate advocacy role. The coal industry, and parts of the oil industry as well, viewed ICC as the railroad's advocacy agency. According to NCA, ICC consistently protected the revenues of the railroads by maintaining high rates on coal which, in the mid-1930s, constituted 33 percent of the total carload freight tonnage and contributed 25 percent of freight revenue. Freight rates were critical in determining the market a producer could enter. NBCC(2) and the Consumers' Counsel functioned as a countervailing power to ICC and may have moderated somewhat ICC's usual permissive response to carrier demands for rate hikes.[56]

In other instances of NBCC(2)'s advocacy of coal's interests, the commission lost all sense of proportion as it flailed away at developments that, although damaging indeed to coal, represented the normal fruits of technological progress and promised benefits to millions of Americans. NBCC(2) and the coal industry waged a quixotic war with the natural gas industry and proponents of hydroelectric power. NBCC(2) did not engage in acts of industrial sabotage, but it did suffer from a case of bureaucratic dementia as it developed long and learned briefs against the introduction of natural gas service into new markets.

Throughout the 1930s, natural gas interests exploited improvements in pipeline technology to push their lines into new territories which, for the most part, welcomed the arrival of a new, clean, efficient fuel. Between 1928 and 1935, natural gas entered dozens of large cities in a score of states stretching from Florida to California to Illinois. Ambitious plans evolved to penetrate great northern markets such as Chicago and other cities along the Great Lakes; by 1932, a pipeline consortium, including the Insull interest, was constructing a line from Texas to Chicago. Before the establishment of NBCC, NCA and other coal organizations shouldered the responsibility for stemming the expansion of natural gas, appealing to the prolabor sentiments of New Dealers by warning that each new natural gas hookup threatened a coal miner's job. The organized coal industry supported New Deal efforts, successful only in 1938, to regulate interstate commerce in natural gas. Indeed, of all the advocates of the Natural Gas Act of 1938, coal insisted upon the most rigid regulatory formula.

With the passage of the gas law, NBCC(2) exerted every effort to gain a recognized standing before FPC, but the latter only permitted NBCC(2) to participate while refusing to recognize the commission as a party to the hearings. NBCC(2), along with UMWA and railroad interests, submitted numerous briefs challenging the applications of gas companies to serve particular markets. As gas companies appeared before FPC to obtain certificates of convenience and necessity that would permit the extension of natural gas service, NBCC(2) and its allies invented absurd claims about damage the public interest would suffer should certification be granted.

In 1938, the Kansas Pipeline and Gas Company sought to construct a line from the Hugoton field in Kansas to the Mesabi iron range in Minnesota. It would deprive coal of much business, and several UMWA locals, the American Retail Coal Association, the Southern Appalachian Coal Operators Association, and dozens of coal companies presented petitions to NBCC(2) and FPC arguing against the line. NBCC(2) prepared a long brief that stated, in effect: consumers should not be allowed to substitute natural gas for coal. Equally compelling arguments were advanced in 1939 when a gas line company proposed a line from Texas to the New York metropolitan area. In like manner, NBCC(2) tilted with the powerful Tennessee Valley Authority (TVA) whose dams controlled floods, contained soil erosion, and provided light and recreational facilities to hundreds of thousands of people. As an Alabama coal organization tellingly informed Roosevelt, TVA reduced the amount of coal consumed.[57]

A Litany of Failure

While NBCC(2) teetered on the brink of extermination in early 1939, Chairman Percy Tetlow defended the record of the two coal commissions by blaming the operators for unleashing the hounds of the federal courts on NBCC(1) and for obstructing in every possible way the price-fixing procedures of NBCC(2). Tetlow blasted the operators for trying to thwart UMWA's effort to gain a renewal of the wage agreement then in effect.[58] The operators, or at least those joined together in 1939 in a committee for the amendment of the coal act, regarded NBCC(2) as a creature of UMWA. But more to the point, the operators, including J. D. A. Morrow and James W. Carter, insisted that the act of 1937, as written, could not be made to function. Tetlow, too, admitted the complexity of the law. He also recognized that certain consumer interests sought to embarrass the commission at every turn. But Tetlow also believed that cooperation among reasonable men could make the law work. The practical criticism of the operators, saturated with self-interest though it was, struck closer to the heart of the matter than did Tetlow's vague faith in cooperation.[59]

A major bottleneck in the operation of the coal code was the sheer immensity of the technical task of setting tens of thousands of prices. But this difficulty, recognized by such contemporary students of coal policy as Parker, was regarded as less damaging than the decentralized structure foisted on the code by the operators. Other criticisms—failure to control overexpansion, absence of production controls, neglect of conservationist purposes—were also advanced by advocates of more complete regulation than the code or its successor statutes permitted. Just as compelling were the arguments of those, such as the National Resources Committee, who asserted the need for an integrated national fuel policy.[60] But the consequences flowing from the absence of production quotas and so forth can only be speculated about. The system would have worked differently with all those elements present.

If the absence of a centralized authority endowed with coercive powers to compel compliance doomed the code to certain failure, then the centralization of authority might have enhanced the chances of success. Both Guffey acts provided this centralized authority, the second more than the first. But success remained elusive. NBCC(2) actually survived long enough to implement the system, yet still missed its chance. According to the courts, it mismanaged the administrative procedures implicit in the law by denying various interests the right to present evidence at hearings prior to the establishment of prices. Although this was corrected, neither NBCC(2) nor BCD devised a satisfactory method of coordinating prices in common market areas. BCD conducted more hearings and gathered a mountain of evidence before announcing prices in October 1940, fifteen months after its formation. I am left to conclude that poorly constructed legislation and the complexity of the technical task, even though the mission was more adequately defined in the act of 1937 than in the coal code, constituted the key limiting factors. It almost seems that the system was designed to make failure likely. In modern parlance, we might call this a safe-fail system.

That miners achieved some basic gains is no testimony to the success of the code or of the two commissions but, rather, should be attributed to the endurance of the miners, to the single-mindedness of UMWA, and to New Dealers who believed that miners and other workers possessed rights that must be respected. For all that miners endangered their lives and risked their health every day, they never lived very high on the hog. Operators lost money, too. The Bureau of Foreign and Domestic Commerce estimated in March 1939 that coal mine owners had suffered a net loss of $125 million since 1937, or about twenty-five cents per ton, and with no end of losses in sight.[61]

Those deriving ideological sustenance from this account of federal ineptness must, of course, temper their satisfaction with the recognition that the coal industry deserved only the lowest of marks for its performance as producer, distributor, and employer. NCA and other coal associations and hundreds of operators adamantly contested all forms of federal control, denied a public interest in coal, sabotaged the operation of the code and the two Guffey acts by fair means and foul, and strove persistently (fortunately without success) to maintain a semifeudal labor system. UMWA repelled challenging unions, not all of which were owner-controlled, and viewed myopically, as did the operators and many public servants, the ills of the industry. Neither labor nor management could be accused of foresight or of developing progressive views. While the public interest in a stable and productive coal industry was ill served by New Deal coal policies and the coal industry, the public, too, must share the stigma of failure for naively defining good policy as that which seemed to provide a good at the cheapest price. The public—the cities of Atlanta, Chicago, or Cleveland, the chief executives of the New England states, as examples—did not understand its true interests in energy resources.

ELEVEN

A Prewar Policy Balance Sheet
for the Fuel Industries

COULD ANYONE have possibly offered a demurral to the thesis
posed by the National Resources Committee (NRC)?

> To protect the general welfare in our time—in an industrialized
> and urban economy—means above all else to build and maintain
> in good order a sound economic structure. In an industrial civili-
> zation the energy resources constitute the foundation stones of
> that structure.[1]

Of course, those with their eyes open might wonder, given the dreary
character of modern times, just when this sound economic structure
would emerge. Others, while agreeing that a sound economy promoted the general welfare, might well chart divergent paths to that future, depending upon their understanding of those worthy goals.
NRC's prescription anticipated an active federal role, not only in
energy but in the management of all resources, human and material.
However, as NRC penned its report, recovery from the depression remained elusive even after six or seven years of relatively intense federal intervention. The New Deal offered mixed signals regarding the
proper federal role in energy, extending it here and retracting it there,
offering significant economic buffers to some groups while ignoring
others; the New Deal's elliptical orbit around the central notion of a
planned economy brought it tantalizingly close at one moment while
carrying it frustratingly distant the next.

Had the New Deal been more unflinchingly ideological, it would
not have been American; had it been somewhat less flexible and less

the handmaiden of expediency, it might have been more successful. As it was, its energy policies, hovering somewhere between pragmatism and opportunism, were burdened from the start by the insistence of their authors that they satisfy the interests of all parties—producers, processors, distributors, transporters, employees, and consumers. Satisfying few while antagonizing many, New Deal fuel policies were buried in a stupefying administrative apparatus that only a Merlin could have penetrated. Only a New Deal agency such as NBCC(2) could announce unblinkingly that, among its tasks, it was engaged in the coordination of 400,000 separate coal prices and 1,000,000 individual freight rates.[2] Despite this bureaucratic impedimenta, historical trends in the nation's fuel-mix continued to evolve, but the touch of policy upon those changes differed from one energy source to another.

Uses of Energy

On the whole, NRC expressed a truth in writing, "Our problem . . . is not one of stretching a niggardly supply but rather that of wise use of a relatively favorable supply of presently available and potential energy resources."[3] While the proven reserves of each of the major energy resources—coal, oil, natural gas, and waterpower—seemed more or less large and adequate for many years, knowledgeable people in the fuel industries and government expressed some concern about such factors as rates of use, waste in production and use, and location of resources relative to use. The depression did not radically alter growth rates in national energy consumption, if compared with the 1920s: 21 trillion Btu in 1920, 24 trillion in 1930, 25 trillion in 1940 (there was a net decline 1930–35 but an advance between 1935 and 1940).[4] There was an increase in use of petroleum and natural gas, the fossil fuels with the most problematical proven reserves, while coal use fell. By 1940, coal supplied 50 percent of energy needs, compared with over 70 percent from 1900 through 1920 (see Table 11). In 1939, crude production stood at 1.2 billion barrels per year, with an estimated reserve of 15 billion barrels good for twelve years, compared with a reserve of fifteen years in 1930 and seventeen years in 1918 (see Table 12). Natural gas production declined in the early 1930s and then rose steadily after 1933, reaching 2.5 trillion cubic feet in 1939. Estimates of reserves ranged from 50 trillion to almost 100 trillion cubic feet, or a supply sufficient for twenty to forty years. Moreover, both oil and gas could be moved economically over great distances. Coal, the most plentiful fuel, was the most troubled economically. Reserves were not a problem—a century's worth remained in the ground—but some noted that the largest reserves were located furtherest from the greatest markets. If and when the nation had to turn again to coal, how would the reserves buried deep within the Rocky Mountains be moved to consuming areas east of the Mississippi?

Plentiful fuel reserves supplemented by the potential for additional hydroelectric generation, a favored technology of the New Deal and a focal point of bitter controversy, stimulated (as critics ever intoned) unconscionable waste and inefficient end-use.[5] American consumers expected cheapness, convenience, and abundance, demands not always concordant with such goals as conservation, end-use efficiency, or coal and oil industry stabilization. The wants of Americans, if not their interests, were well served by competition among the energy industries. In the marketplace, as in Washington, D.C. and many state capitols, the struggle for advantage, if not survival, exacerbated by the depression, pitted the energy industries one against the other. Coal experienced the least success in preserving its markets while the use of natural gas, oil, and electric power (cleaner and more convenient sources of heat and power) inexorably advanced in the home, office, and factory (see Chapter 6, pp. 142–46; Chapter 10, p. 255).

Each alternative energy use encroached directly upon coal use. The number of fuel oil burners in use rose from 674,000 in 1930 to 2.3 million in 1941, while the production of heating oil increased four times to 168 million barrels. The consumption of fuel oil by the railroads rose by almost 20 million barrels during the 1930s while coal burned by the railroads declined by 37 million tons during the 1920s and by another 13 million tons during the 1930s. The anthracite industry withered as oil and gas heat replaced anthracite in many eastern domestic markets and other householders accustomed themselves to the use of bituminous coal, obtainable at one-half the cost of anthracite. Industry in 1940 burned 100 million fewer tons of coal than in 1930. By 1939, electric motors produced 90 percent of industrial horsepower, compared with 82 percent in 1929 and 55 percent in 1919. Coal consumption by the electric utilities had risen during the decade but only by 10 million tons, and many electric and gas plants utilized fuel oil or, where available, natural gas.[6]

To a degree insusceptible to precise measurement, federal policies contributed to coal's malaise, a situation all too obvious to the organized coal industry and productive of much rancor. The coal industry orchestrated frequent campaigns against allegedly discriminatory federal policies—cheap foreign oil, the spread of natural gas service, hydroelectric projects, unfair rail freight rates—in which both NBCCs frequently served as coal's advocate.[7] Another federal initiative, the Electric Home and Farm Authority (EHFA), created in 1933 by NRA to finance sales of household electric and gas equipment for moderate-income families, also elicited intense opposition from coal and allied industries.[8]

EHFA contributed its mite to the steady growth of electric and gas equipment sales during the 1930s. The American Gas Association launched several nationwide sales campaigns during the 1920s and 1930s that were matched by promotions organized by the National Electric Light Association. Excepting the years 1932–34, Americans purchased over one million gas ranges annually during the 1930s; and the yearly sales of electric ranges surpassed 200,000 from 1936 through 1940. Americans purchased $254 million worth of electric appliances, not including radios, in 1930, not a prosperous year; by 1936, sales reached $341 million. In 1930, electricity reached 68 percent of all residential dwellings (but only 10 percent of farm homes) while in 1940, 79 percent of all homes were hooked up (including 33 percent of farm homes). By the late 1930s, natural gas was available to well over 7 million homes in thirty-five states. While EHFA played but a tiny role in this, it was, according to the coal industry, patently unfair; federal subsidies were not available to finance installations of new automatic coal stokers.[9]

But the technological tide that inundated the coal industry could not be stopped by political incantations or by delaying tactics. Officials of natural gas companies and of municipalities complained about the obstacles thrown in their paths by the coal industry, the railroads, and manufactured gas companies. For example, the railroads refused to grant rights of way for pipelines crossing railroad property and bringing natural gas to Detroit; the city finally got its gas but only after years of frustration and battles over this and other problems. Many other communities experienced similar debates and tangles.

Gradually but steadily natural gas became available to more towns and cities where it took its place not only as a significant energy source but also as a key factor in local and state politics. Simultaneously, New Deal hydroelectric programs coupled with financial aid for the refurbishment or installation of municipal power and light plants both revived interest in municipalization that had waned during the late 1920s and earned the everlasting enmity of the powerful investor-owned electric utilities. As high-voltage transmission wires were strung across the landscape, connecting homes in Los Angeles with the Boulder Dam generating plant or new TVA generating capacity with previously lightless homes, the average kwh-use per domestic consumer reached 952 in 1940, almost three times that of 1920 and almost two times that of 1930.

In local debates over energy, coal and oil associations assumed an active role. Chicago's oil burner association, in 1933, accused the Peoples Gas, Light, and Coke Company of employing unfair competitive tactics in its campaign to sell 60,000 heating units. A similar charge surfaced in Washington from the Western Burner Oil Distributors Association in 1934. According to the oil burner dealers in Oakland and Chicago, the gas companies offered free service, free parts, and rebates and sold equipment below cost, all forbidden to oil burner dealers by the oil code. For their part, the gas companies charged local coal and oil associations with spreading malicious propaganda about the danger of natural gas. The oil industry, of course, held its own as a result of a constantly growing demand for automotive fuel and lubricants. But coal did not. Speakers at the NCA convention of 1933 admitted to industry remissness in initiating practical research and product development programs. Research, however, could be a double-edged sword. Advances in the utilization of coal more often than not reduced the quantity required to produce the heat or power desired. By 1940, as the electric industry pushed ahead in the design of air-conditioning systems for domestic and commercial establishments, it was only a matter of time before coal disappeared from the household. It would not be missed.[10]

First Steps, and More First Steps

Responding to the gentlemen's agreement consummated among Kansas, Oklahoma, and Texas in 1931 to allocate oil production quotas according to predicted demand, Secretary of Commerce Robert P. Lamont congratulated the signers for taking a major first step toward a solution to the industry's problems. After the passage of several years, such agencies as the Petroleum Administrative Board and NRC, in assessing the oil code, the Connally Act, and the Interstate Oil Compact, referred to these developments as initial and tentative steps in the direction of industry stabilization and the conservation of oil and gas. While NRC and its predecessor units commended the coal code and the Guffey acts for improving the working conditions of the miners, they revealed their disappointment regarding the progress made in stabilizing the coal industry. In early 1938, a memorandum circulating among Department of Commerce employees called for a comprehensive study of fuel resources and electric energy as a preliminary to developing an integrated energy policy. The tenor of the memorandum bespoke scant regard for the accomplishments to date.[11]

The intrusion of the federal government—Congress, the executive branch, the independent agencies, the courts—into the affairs of the energy industries had been a constant since the early years of the twentieth century. Beginning in 1917, the Bureau of Mines operated a petroleum experiment station at Bartlesville, Oklahoma, which conducted research in oil and natural gas extraction and cooperated with dozens of operators, particularly independents, in resolving problems specific to day-to-day operations.[12] The USGS compiled statistics on all minerals and participated in the adminstration of the public domain. From time to time, other federal units established branches that focused on some aspect of energy. In 1913, the Department of Commerce and Labor created the Bureau of Foreign and Domestic Commerce which, in turn, established a coal and coke section and, later, electrical and fuels sections. In 1939, NCA requested Commerce to establish a separate coal unit that would provide the industry with current information regarding national and world markets. Industry regarded these units much more benignly than such newcomers as the Power Division of the Public Works Administration, created in 1934 to promote the construction of municipally owned gas and electric plants.[13]

While precedents for this type of activity stretched backward into the pre-World War I years, direct interference in the operations of the energy industries had been confined to federal court action taken under the antitrust laws or to strengthening and expanding the regulatory authority of ICC. World War I compelled the federal government to extend its purview beyond the antitrust theater of action into the realm of production, processing, distribution, and price. The Lever Act of 1917 and other laws authorized the government, acting through the U.S. Fuel Administration and other peer agencies, to design a fuel control program unsurpassed in comprehensiveness by any subsequent programs including those devised during World War II. World War I presented a unique challenge, evoking a moral intensity not easily replicated during peacetime, however threatening the problems.[14] Thus, the severe coal crises that occurred in 1919 and periodically thereafter engendered federal responses that only faintly resembled the programs of World War I.

When the depression shattered American complacency, the nation possessed a vast amount of information, raw and synthesized, about oil, coal, electric power, water power, and natural gas. Although the energy conundrums of the World War I era revolved around shortages, the details of production, processing, distribution, end-use, and pricing were well known for each of the energy industries. By spring 1918, administrators of the wartime fuel system were successfully meeting most fuel needs and moderating strong inflationary trends while remaining sensitive to weaknesses that would demand rectification should the war continue into 1919. With regard to oil, the Federal Oil Conservation Board's early efforts to define a complete conservation program, although prompted by fears of oil scarcity, emphasized the economic interrelatedness of all sources of energy.

While the initial versions of energy-related laws frequently included provisions reflecting advanced ideas, the New Deal's fuel measures became law only after skillful political surgeons neatly excised the innovative provisions. Petroleum legislation provided only weak price-fixing powers or denied it altogether while circumscribing federal authority to set and enforce quotas. A similar power vacuum characterized the Interstate Oil Compact, the adoption of which can be interpreted as a tactical move by producing states to forestall federal encroachment of state sovereignty.[15] PAB superficially resembled USFA's oil division but only because the organizational structure of both paralleled that of the industry. The responsibilities of the industry Planning and Coordination Committee in the area of refinery production more closely followed those of USFA, but the latter's oil division also carved out a central role in production, distribution, and pricing which PCC did not.[16]

Neither did the lessons learned under USFA or the Federal Fuel Distributor have any apparent influence on the coal code or the two NBCCs. USFA was staffed by a regiment of coal and oil industry officials, but they worked for a man from outside the industry who imposed his own organizational scheme on his agency and then changed it as circumstances dictated. The legislation establishing the two coal commissions allowed little flexibility. NBCC procedures hinged upon the worthy goal of treating all involved parties equitably and fairly. However, the commissioners lacked sufficient power to enforce their will on contumacious operators, many of whom chose not to participate, or to impose the fixed prices on willful consumers. Both commissions succumbed to a surfeit of fairness. In the final analysis, Congress was to blame for creating such an unworkable system.

The fuel policies of the New Deal, then, appear as ill-conceived measures that ignored past experience as well as the rationale behind such legislative proposals as the Watson, Lewis, or Davis-Kelly bills, all of which provided for production and price controls. Of almost as little moment to the lawmakers were the analyses of the fuel industries and accompanying policy recommendations drafted by existing agencies during the 1930s or by planning groups created by the Roosevelt administration. In the case of electric power and natural gas, however, some of these investigations and forays in planning did eventually bear fruit. But the call for a national energy policy remained unheeded as Pearl Harbor plunged the nation into the maelstrom of global war.

In 1923, the La Follette committee concluded that the oil industry "is clothed with a great public interest."[17] Somewhat earlier, the U.S. Coal Commission had similarly characterized the coal industry. FOCB's early reports implicitly supported such a definition, but couched it in nonpejorative language. The preamble of the first Guffey Act explicitly applied the idea of the public interest to the coal industry, a reference absent from the second Guffey Act. Harold L. Ickes persistently sought to so define the oil industry. The electric and gas utilities, too, became the target of regulators. As in coal and in oil, controversy swirled around the question of federal regulation of the interstate commerce of the electric and gas utilities. Threatening aspects of the holding company form of organization provided the Roosevelt administration with the opportunity to alter the structure of the utilities and to subject them to federal regulations. The efforts of planners contributed to these legislative achievements.

In 1933, Ickes created the National Planning Board as an arm of the Public Works Administration. Although focusing on land and water resources, the board did venture into minerals and energy in a report appearing in 1934. By that time, the original board had been replaced by the National Resources Board which published the report. In 1933, Roosevelt also appointed a Planning Committee for Mineral Policy, chaired by Secretary Ickes, which in 1934 became part of the National Resources Board and which prepared the minerals study appearing in the report of the National Resources Board.[18] While Congress refused to make these groups permanent, Roosevelt utilized executive authority to keep them in operation. In 1935, the National Resources Committee (NRC) succeeded the National Resources Board, and, in 1939, the former unit became the National Resources Planning Board. In 1943, Congress abolished the latter and expressly prohibited the transfer of its function to any other agency.

Throughout the life of the National Planning Board and its successors, a strange melange of antagonists coalesced to prevent the actual implementation of the planners' recommendations. Apprehension about the implications of national planning motivated some. Others were moved by the simple desire to thwart Roosevelt in all matters large or small. Large landowners in the South and West resisted changes in farm labor systems or in land use. Business and industrial organizations equated planning with socialism. Tunnel vision bound organized labor to a horizon limited by the needs of particular crafts or industries. Federal agencies such as TVA and FPC perceived the schemes of the planners as an invasion of jurisdictional turf. The jealous FPC became embroiled in controversy with the National Defense Power Policy Committee, a reconstituted amalgam of earlier hybrids.[19]

Each fuel or energy-related agency, each fuel or energy-related policy proposal, each policy that became law immediately spawned a host of antagonists united, often unnaturally, in their opposition to federal intervention. At every step those few advocates of total energy planning that the New Deal harbored were obstructed by powerful energy-industry and consumer and public coalitions. Only in the utility sector was a modicum of success achieved. Relative to the key fossil fuels and to the need for a national energy policy, the excellent report of the National Resources Committee remains the sole legacy.

Energy Planning

For many Americans, the terms "planning," "control," and "dictation" were interchangeable, threatening alike to individualism and to capitalism. In a free market economy, the role of government should be restricted to enforcing the customary rules of the game upon all players, a responsibility sufficiently flexible for all but the most rigid ideologues to permit such intrusions of federal power as ICC or FTC. As millions learned during the depression, when capitalism tottered, self-reliance offered little immunity against layoffs and foreclosures or against the psychic damage inflicted by soup lines and welfare queues. Still, American political culture refused to sanction European-style centralization or the capture of national government by demagogues. The task of the New Deal, as its numerous students have concluded, was to preserve capitalism, not oversee its demise.

While the enfeeblement of the national economy and its leading institutions provided almost unlimited opportunity for planning, and the New Deal enlisted many planners and scholars in its ranks, planners confronted the stern and unrelenting hostility of innumerable interest groups and their political representatives.[20] Interest groups within the energy industries fought in political arenas for or against legislation that promised advantages or disadvantages. The feuding segments of the oil industry displayed no unwavering allegiance to a governing political or economic principle but rather scrambled for the spoils of favorable legislation. During the NIRA experiment, politics effectively curbed the ambitions of planners. The politics of oil and coal transmuted a vague form of industry-government cooperation into de facto industry domination. Of all the energy industries, the investor-owned utilities and the electric industry associations mounted the most resolute and ideological attacks on federal intervention. Too, the exigencies of the moment—unemployment, failed businesses, pessimism and despair—demanded on-the-spot improvisation and desensitized Congress to the usefulness of a more leisurely exploration of future needs. The National Resources Board (NRB) and its successors, denied the breath of life by Congress, operated in the shadows, dependent upon presidential largess.

The congruence between energy planning and legislation was slight. But in formulating policy designs that went beyond the imperatives of the moment, NRB and its successors, particularly NRC, assumed a front-line position, just as they did in other matters that warranted national attention.[21] NRC defined the central issue as "not one of promoting or failing to promote the exploitation of energy resources" but rather "whether the nation shall permit this exploitation to continue without adequate regard for waste, for social objectives, and for future welfare—or shall endeavor to guide it into ways that are more effective for both economic and social objectives than it has followed in the past."[22] Customary methods of utilizing the nation's heritage of abundance were explicitly rejected as economically counterproductive and as damaging to the general welfare and specifically to national defense, a compelling concern during the final years of the 1930s. In a direct reference to the petroleum and coal industries, NRC wrote, "The free play of undirected capitalism cannot be relied upon to resolve unaided the maladjustments in these industries that have disturbed our national economy."[23]

Certain general notions and recommendations were stated in the study's "Findings and Recommendations," which served as a preface to staff studies of specific energy sources and other issues.[24] NRC, as had FOCB in its first phase, emphasized the interrelatedness of all fuels. Again and again, NRC returned to the fact of nonrenewability of conventional energy sources and the unlikelihood that solar, synthetic, or biomass substitutes would become economically viable in the near future. After domestic reservoirs have been depleted, what then? Consumption trends of the 1920s, only temporarily moderated by depression and certain of resumption once economic conditions improved, demanded that resources be conserved and waste eliminated.[25] Policies must be designed to foster the most efficient uses of scarce resources, a position first adopted by FOCB and then abandoned as a political liability. NRC, never directly engaged in the day-to-day politics of the energy industries as was FOCB, pressed for a distinction between superior and inferior uses of energy and suggested various means of discouraging inferior uses.

In devising a coordinated energy policy, NRC accommodated its recommendations to local, state, and regional developmental needs, particularly those impinging upon the uses of land and water.[26] In assigning the highest priority to policies serving the general welfare, NRC avoided the adoption of politically convenient but parochial views. To translate its general recommendations into concrete policy, NRC recommended the consolidation of responsibilities for energy in a single federal agency that would include representatives of the industries and other federal agencies. In its initial stages, this agency should have only advisory functions and concentrate on planning. In effect, the Energy Resources Committee of NRC, the author of this report, suggested that it be made permanent through legislation.[27]

Neither industry groups nor the states could provide the careful and coordinated management that the federal government could bring to petroleum, natural gas, coal, and electric power. Oil policies dependent upon state enforcement of state regulations precluded the adoption of a nationwide conservation program. Perceiving serious shortcomings in the Connally Act-Interstate Oil Compact system, NRC advocated legislation empowering the federal government to establish and enforce production quotas. This policy, pursued unsuccessfully by Secretary Ickes, represented an advance over the report of NRB, written during the NRA years, which avoided a stand on the issue of federal control. NRC viewed, erroneously as it happened, the second Guffey Act as a permanent advance but questioned the degree to which NBCC(2) was the procedural captive of the industry and suggested that the law best reflected the needs of the operators. NRC did not manifest a conspicuous interest in antitrust issues although it did report favorably on the Public Utility Holding Company Act of 1935, and it did address those antitrust issues relevant to oil and gas that affected key aspects of its recommendations.

NRC recommended policies of varying degrees of specificity for each of the fuels and for electricity. Reticence best describes NRC's approach to the electric industry, in marked contrast to the critical eye it cast on the oil and coal industries. Perhaps NRC believed that insufficient time had elapsed to warrant a critique of the new power policies and FPC's performance. NRC may have felt constrained by the large contribution that Secretary Ickes—through the National Power Policy Committee—made to the formulation of the new power policies. Whatever the cause, NRC's analysis of electric power is much weaker than its evaluations of the fossil fuels.

The elimination of physical and economic waste, broadly defined to encompass production, distribution, and land use, bound the separate proposals into a cohesive and self-supporting plan that was generally ignored in principle and flouted in practice. Few of the specific recommendations were new, most having appeared previously in some legislative proposal, in the reports of the U.S. Coal Commission, FOCB, or NRB, or from units within such agencies as PWA or NBCC. Virtually all the recommendations for an oil policy fit this pattern. The issues of unitization, prorationing, and the restriction of production to current market demand had been fought over since the early days of FOCB. NRC borrowed the idea of a federal oil reserve— and a federal coal reserve—from the 1920s. In 1934, the Planning Committee for Mineral Policy (see above, p. 291) supported a reduced tariff on foreign oil, arguing that national security demanded the preservation of American reserves. NRC accepted this argument. NRC displayed a certain caution about pipeline divorcement, unconvinced that divorcement would contribute to conservation, rational end-use, or national defense requirements. NRC's positions on tariffs and pipelines were consistent with its belief that national needs must take precedence over the demands of particular interests. Each separate policy component was linked to every other in a program designed to provide the nation with the necessary volume of fuel produced under optimal conditions and utilized in the most efficient manner.[28]

Proposals in which conservation and end-use considerations bulked large were offered for coal and natural gas. NRC, viewing the over-capacity of the coal industry as its most serious weakness, asserted that the viability of the industry demanded production as well as price controls. Pessimistic about the short-run prospects for coal, NRC believed the exhaustion of natural gas and oil fields would, at some future time, revitalize the industry.[29] In the meantime, coal must find its markets in competition with oil and gas. To ameliorate the economic disabilities of coal and to prolong the life of oil and gas fields, NRC suggested the use of both price regulation and taxation but clearly favored the latter.

As passed, the Natural Gas Act of 1938 granted FPC the power to regulate the wholesale rates of natural gas entering interstate commerce (similar to the authority exercised by FPC over the electric industry) and granted FPC authority over the expansion of interstate pipelines.[30] But the act and subsequent amendments proposed by FPC indicated that FPC harbored no ambition to engage in conservation. Indeed, the law and FPC policies sought the expanded use of gas at cheap rates for whatever purposes. The combined effect of the power and gas legislation divorced electric and gas companies and somewhat reduced concentration by breaking up the holding companies. All this, its proponents believed, would bring electricity and gas to more people at cheaper prices. This would stimulate growth and build a bigger and happier America.

A less sanguine approach was reflected in NRC's proposals that focused upon natural gas conservation and the discouragement of low-grade uses of the fuel. NRC's exposition of the case for selective taxation contradicted the intent of the Natural Gas Act of 1938. NRC, concerned with resource use and not with consumer convenience, deplored the burning of natural gas for electric production or other industrial purposes for which fuel oil or coal could serve just as efficiently. To reduce these wasteful uses, NRC advocated prorationing in the gas fields and a tax on gas sales below a certain price.

In 1934, NCA and elements within labor supported legislative proposals imposing an excise tax on natural gas used by main-line industrial consumers. Both NCA and NRC sought to raise the price of this "dumped" gas to a level at which coal could compete. NCA and NBCC(2), as Chapter 10 detailed, also opposed the extension of natural gas lines into new markets.[31] NRC considered the tax weapon more effective than pipeline regulation in bringing supply into equilibrium with demand at the points of most efficient use—the home, businesses, and certain industries requiring high-quality process heat. After World War II, FPC's policies toward natural gas yielded results antithetical to NRC's intentions.[32]

The reports of NRB and NRC assigned high priority to the multiple-use concept of water resource development, a thrust sustained by the National Resources Planning Board and bearing fruit in the Flood Control Act of 1944, which included provisions for power production.[33] NRC subscribed to NRB's opinion that private utilities were unlikely to press on with further development of hydroelectric sites. Both planning groups, of course, justified federal water-power projects because of their capacity to control flooding, supply drinking water, abate stream pollution, and provide other benefits in addition to cheap electricity. Regional power complexes stimulated economic growth and brought inestimable social benefits to masses of people, all of which nullified the opposition to federal hydro projects flowing from the private utilities and the coal industry. NRC, cognizant of the necessity of applying large-scale technology to regional waterways, also admitted the efficiency of smaller-scale technology in certain cases. PWA's power division, the National Power Policy Committee, and NRC all supported municipalization and the cooperation of adjacent communities in providing their own power. Not all hydro sites required such massive technology as the Tennessee or Colorado rivers. NRC advised the president to negotiate pooling agreements between federal power authorities and the private power industry. NRC also encouraged states to plan for future power needs and to offer support for municipal power projects.

In adopting this approach, NRC brought greater theoretical balance to the issue of power development than had the advocates of superpower who emphasized giant plants and large-scale technology while essentially ignoring the potential of small operations. NRC's attitudes closely resembled those expressed in a report of the National Association of Railroad and Utility Commissions published in 1928. NARUC seriously questioned the presumed benefits of superpower, arguing that small systems could apply modern engineering and management techniques just as economically and efficiently as giant systems. The report, anticipating the joint community action power programs of the 1970s, suggested that neighboring communities could form energy consortiums to generate and distribute electricity as cheaply or more cheaply than private systems.[34]

NRC's energy-policy recommendations sought flexibility but not at the expense of efficiency of end-use or of the imperatives of national defense. NRC's influence on policy during the remaining peacetime years was undetectable. NBCC(2) sank deeper into an administrative morass. Price wars and overproduction plagued both the oil and coal industries. The oil compact represented the triumph of state sovereignty over the public interest as defined by NRC. NBCC(2)'s attempted intervention before FPC in pipeline extension cases parodied NRC's analysis of the interrelatedness of fuels, distorted NRC's intent, and expressed the interest of only the coal industry. The motivation behind the Natural Gas Act conflicted with NRC's case for conservation and the use of high-grade gas. NRC's criticism of the diffusion of responsibilities for energy management among numerous and competing federal agencies ran afoul of the vested interests of established bureaucracies and of congressional indifference or hostility toward planning and coordination. A disinterested public and threatened interests within industry and government almost guaranteed that NRC's recommendations for a national energy policy would attract little attention. Pearl Harbor fully guaranteed such a result.

After the war, energy shortages disturbed the economy. Contracting markets and strikes fractured the tenuous peace that the war had forced upon the coal industry. In the 1950s, coal's prospects seemed little better than during the 1930s. In oil, hoary issues were resurrected. Independents and majors refought their version of the Battle of the Boyne. Depletion allowances became a sensitive issue. The question of oil import quotas, first surfacing during the 1920s, re-emerged in 1959 when President Dwight Eisenhower imposed mandatory oil import quotas. Independent distributors and retailers of gasoline accused the majors of oppressive and monopolistic practices. In 1952, the report of the President's Materials Policy Commission (the Paley commission) asked, "How can the nation minimize inferior uses of gas for which more abundant energy resources, notably coal, would serve as well?"[35] Efforts to deregulate natural gas fell before Truman and Eisenhower vetoes just as FPC, forced by the Supreme Court to expand its price-regulating jurisdiction in 1954, succumbed to pressures to keep prices artifically low.[36] Thus, NRC's thoughtful program for a national energy policy may have gone unheeded, but the problems it addressed did not disappear.

TWELVE

Before Pearl Harbor

W ORLD WAR II BEGAN when Germany unleashed its ground and air forces upon Poland in September 1939. There followed an interlude of relative calm—the so-called Phony War—which was broken in April 1940. With surprising swiftness and efficiency, the armed forces of Germany invaded and occupied Denmark and Norway, overran Belgium, the Netherlands, and Luxemburg, and destroyed French resistance, forcing France to sue for an armistice in June 1940. Only Britain stood firm, but imperiled by devastating air attacks and the threat of a massive cross-channel invasion. During these frightening months, the Roosevelt administration moved as quickly as political realities allowed to fashion machinery to oversee the strengthening of the nation's defenses and provide military goods and economic aid to the beleaguered enemies of Adolph Hitler. The shockingly easy Nazi conquest of France and the subsequent Battle of Britain tended to sharpen public awareness of the true character of the German threat.

In the months following the summer of 1941, the skeleton of a defense establishment emerged. Fuel resources clearly numbered among the most critical materials for waging war. While the experience of World War I seemed to demonstrate beyond contention the necessity for stringent fuel regulations (should the worst happen), it was, after all, still peacetime. Haltingly, steps were taken to assign responsibility for fuels and other energy forms to new agencies which jostled with such older agencies as the Federal Power Commission and the Bituminous Coal Division (BCD) for preference. Finally, two agencies were designated the principal fuel units: the Petroleum Coordinator for National Defense (established in May 1941) and the Solid Fuels Coordinator for National Defense (organized in November 1941).[1]

In 1940 and 1941, several federal agencies warned Roosevelt and the public to anticipate severe fuel shortages in the civilian sector as resources were diverted to defense preparations and to the remaining opponents of Nazism. These analyses emphasized that while productive capacity in both coal and oil seemed sufficient to meet rising demand in the immediate future, distribution and allocation facilities, unless coordinated, would quickly be overburdened and cause real scarcity in such key geographical areas as the Atlantic and Pacific coasts. Assessments of the energy situation drafted in the Department of Interior in 1940 and 1941 pointed to the almost total dependence of the West Coast upon petroleum and to the vulnerability of the East Coast oil supply to U-boat action against oil tanker traffic from Gulf ports.

East Coast markets received 42 percent of the 1.4 billion barrels of oil consumed in 1940, of which 92 percent arrived by oil tanker. The West Coast used 15 percent of national oil production, mostly from California fields, and was without access to a substitute fuel.[2] Coal was not to be counted upon as a substitute fuel in the eastern states because transportation facilities were incapable of handling a greater volume of coal traffic. The analysts emphasized that a marked increase in coal and oil use in key industrial sectors and by the military would shrink the supply available for civilian and nondefense users. In July 1941, officials of Socony Vacuum Company estimated a near-term gasoline deficiency of almost 50 percent if transportation services failed to improve.[3] These realistic projections of future supply needs were based upon continued American neutrality. Worse portended if the United States became a belligerent.[4]

The Emerging Control Apparatus

In June 1940, Assistant Secretary of War Louis Johnson reminded a meeting of fuel engineers of the heatless and lightless nights in 1917, of the paralysis of the railroad network in December 1917, and of the harsh Closing Order which followed. He assured his audience that the present administration had learned from that experience. "The confused efforts of 1917 will not be repeated," Johnson promised. "Our industrial mobilization is up-to-date . . . both practical and adequate."[5] That this assessment lacked frankness, Johnson would have been among the first to admit, privately. The structure that awkwardly and painfully emerged prior to Pearl Harbor consisted of a hodgepodge of separate agencies created under executive rather than legislative authority, each vested with limited mandates. Many Americans looked suspiciously, if not hostilely, upon even this jerry-built assemblage.

Roosevelt did receive at least two comprehensive proposals for the immediate application of formal controls to all phases of the energy industries. One, originating in the Energy Resources Committee (ERC) of the National Resources Planning Board, encompassed the fossil fuels and electric power. The second, drafted by H. A. Gray, director of the Bituminous Coal Division, dealt only with coal. Both explicitly called for highly centralized authority, and both ran afoul of the target industries as well as others who mistrusted any expansion of federal power or who refused to open their eyes to the marching of armed hordes in Europe and Asia.

The two schemes leaned heavily upon the fuel regulatory experience of World War I and rejected voluntarism as well as industry control as unworkable and essentially inimical to the public interest. ERC also pointed to the remarkable changes in production and transportation technologies and fuel-use patterns since 1917. Both Gray and ERC, thinking it highly likely America would be at war, believed this war would last considerably longer, span greater distances, and consume a vastly increased quantity of human and natural resources than World War I. While such considerations prevented ERC and Gray from merely dressing the policies of World War I in new clothes, their recommendations bore design resemblances to the measures administered by Harry A. Garfield and William G. McAdoo. Gray's proposal drew more directly upon the structure and procedures of the U.S. Fuel Administration than did ERC's.

Both proposals insisted on the vital need of immediate statutory authority to control production, transportation, storage, consumption, and prices. Current laws—the Connally Act, the Interstate Oil Compact, the second Guffey Act—were irrelevant to the crisis that deepened day by day. New laws were required to moderate the inescapable effects of submarine interdiction of coastal oil and coal traffic should war come. Similarly, increasing the capacity of railroads to carry both fuels to strategic market areas, particularly the East Coast, was of great urgency. Gray advocated the imposition of a revised form of the zone system for coal employed during the last war. ERC foresaw the need for legislation enabling the immediate construction of long-distance pipelines from producing districts to the refining areas of the Middle Atlantic states.

Control over coal production and the opening of new mines, the coordination of refining runs and the inevitable high demand for aviation gasoline and petroleum-based feed stocks for synthetic rubber, the building of new storage facilities—all demanded instant attention. Distribution must be both equitable and geared to the exigencies of defense or war. Fuel rationing, ERC and Gray both predicted, was highly probable. In Gray's scheme, the rationing mechanism and the assignment of priorities among coal users devolved upon a unified solid fuels organization. ERC and Gray also viewed price fixing as necessary. They were less clear where such authority should repose. While neither Gray nor ERC liked the notion of ubiquitous federal authority, they rejected the idea that informal government-industry cooperation could cope with the worsening crisis. ERC manifested greater reluctance than Gray to assign such sensitive duties to a single agency, preferring to diffuse authority among several existing and unborn agencies. President Roosevelt found the ERC formula more palatable than Gray's. He also chose not to seek statutory authority but instead, at least in the prewar days, to rely upon executive powers.[6]

The witches' brew of agencies Roosevelt concocted after 1939, each with a limited mandate that each sought to extend at the expense of some other office, fit perfectly with the mode of operation preferred by the president and caused great confusion. Roosevelt resurrected the Council of National Defense in 1940. The Vinson Act of June 1940 gave the executive greater power over the allocation of materials. Using that power, President Roosevelt organized one board within the council to deal with price stabilization and another board to handle materials priorities. After some permutation, and in response to the Lend Lease Act of May 1941 and to the transfer of fifty U.S.-flag oil tankers to British control in the same month, the price board evolved into the Office of Price Administration (OPA) and the priorities board first into the Office of Production Management (OPM) and finally into the War Production Board (WPB). OPA attempted to control prices even before the passage of the Emergency Price Control Act of January 1942. WPB, supposedly the focal point for industrial mobilization, suffered attenuation with the establishment of the Office of Economic Stabilization in 1942 and the Office of War Mobilization in 1943.

Other wartime agencies sprang into life, and the Council of National Defense lapsed into irrelevance. In December 1941, Roosevelt created the Office of Defense Transportation (ODT). The Foreign Economic Administration (FEA) of 1943 was the offspring of earlier boards. In 1942, the War Labor Board and the War Manpower Commission appeared. Still other agencies emerged during the war, entering the fray against the Axis and against other wartime offices and against older agencies such as FPC and ICC.[7] For instance, an interagency National Power Policy Committee and the Federal Power Commission regarded one another with distinct enmity. In the end, several agencies, including the solid fuels administration and WPB, uncomfortably shared certain powers over electricity and natural gas with a highly insulted FPC. And Leland Olds, FPC chair, and Harold Ickes, solid fuels and petroleum administrator and chair of the power committee, thoroughly distrusted one another.[8] Bureaucratic infighting centered around the fuel agencies and such supporting Interior branches as USGS and the Bureau of Mines. Engaged in recurrent jurisdictional battles with WPB, OPA, and other agencies, PAW and SFAW maneuvered to widen their field of operations by stripping other agencies of their authority over fossil fuels. In these campaigns, Ickes always attempted to win Roosevelt over to his side as well as muster congressional support.

Energy resources interested virtually all the above agencies. OPA wished to control fuel prices and fuel distribution at the retail level. ODT sought control over the transportation of fuel and demanded a sufficient supply for railroads, tankers, colliers, and trucks. WPB dictated the pace and type of plant expansion and defined production and end-use priorities. FEA asserted its authority over the export and import of fossil fuels. Such special-purpose agencies as the Defense Supplies Corporation and the Defense Plant Corporation influenced the fortunes of the energy industries and the evolving roles of PAW and SFAW. Negotiating—or precipitating—jurisdictional disputes with competing agencies consumed a large portion of the time of Ickes and his deputies. One senses that Ickes thoroughly enjoyed it. Through it all, Roosevelt resisted consolidation or the creation, for instance, of an energy or price czar.

The Fuel Agencies and Territorial Imperatives

While OPM and other agencies were established by executive order, PAW and SFAW derived their initial authority from letters written by Roosevelt to Ickes on 28 May 1941 and 5 November 1941, respectively. Why Roosevelt chose this mode is a mystery to me; that it was counterproductive seems clear. Neither office wielded substantive power. Ickes and his deputies were immediately compelled to negotiate with other agencies for authority sufficient to the task of coordinating the defense efforts of the fossil fuel industries. But the limited authority, delegated to the president by the Vinson Act, to requisition materials and to curb inflation severely delimited the purview of such key agencies as OPM and OPA. Agencies with little power were unlikely to admit PAW or SFAW to full partnership within their own narrow spheres of interest.

The president's letter of 28 May followed by one day his proclamation of an unlimited national emergency. In appointing Ickes petroleum coordinator (and later solid fuels coordinator), Roosevelt emphasized the urgency of coordinating the defense efforts of federal, state, and other government units, plus industry organizations and firms. The supply of both fuels must be accommodated, he insisted, to national defense needs. Each of the authorizing letters instructed the coordinator to gather pertinent information from all sources about all facets of the fuel industries. Both offices were expected to forward recommendations to all federal departments and agencies concerning the fuel situation for the purpose of "promoting the maintenance of a ready and adequate supply at reasonable price." In fact, at this time federal regulatory authority touched only tangentially upon either coal or oil production. The anomalous status of the fuel agencies notwithstanding, they were instructed to promote efficiency in all sectors of the fuel industries and to provide those industries with the necessary material and equipment to produce, transport, and distribute sufficient fuel for civilian use and defense programs.[9]

Convinced that war loomed on the horizon, Petroleum Coordinator Ickes moved quickly to establish relationships with OPM and OPA and to carve out a role for PAW in allocating the use of the depleted tanker fleet serving the East Coast.[10] But the U.S. Maritime Commission (superseded in 1942 by the War Shipping Administration) claimed preeminence over such matters. Admiral Emory Land, chair of the maritime commission, refused to concede anything to Ickes and, indeed, in 1942 advocated the transfer of control over petroleum from Interior to another agency. PAW also inaugurated a plan to speed oil to the coast by rail and launched a campaign to begin construction of a crude-oil pipeline from Texas to New York City. PAW, OPM, and OPA also grappled with the sensitive issue of maintaining a normal level of civilian supply. But no agency possessed the authority either to increase production or to reduce consumption. PAW could only issue "recommendations" to fuel and oil product users to curtail consumption voluntarily and to convert from oil to coal (see Chapter 13, pp. 319–20). Moral suasion proved useless. Ickes's powers were palsied by virtue of his original mandates. He lobbied vigorously for an executive order delegating to PAW virtually unlimited power over petroleum. A coalition of agencies objected strenuously and successfully to Ickes's demands.[11] The executive order of December 1942, which formally established PAW, did not resolve jurisdictional disputes.

While Ickes and his energetic deputy administrator, Ralph K. Davies, tried to convince the public of the realities of fuel availability, many people, even congressmen, believed the shortages to be a sham, perpetrated upon an unsuspecting public by the major oil companies and Washington bureaucrats. Sen. Francis T. Maloney, Democrat of Connecticut, spoke with acerbity of Ickes's oil shortage. At Senate hearings in August 1941, Ickes, Davies, and Admiral Land convincingly substantiated the magnitude of the crisis. Davies allayed the suspicion of some that the railroads hoarded cars.[12] Land nullified the charge that the British used American tankers for normal commerce. The testimony of Davies emphasized the absence of authority that inhibited PAW from dealing forcefully with the emergency. As Davies pointed out, PAW could only exhort, cajole, and recommend the adoption of conservation practices by the oil companies and consumers. This appeal for public cooperation, Davies complained, had failed miserably. Only the voluntary action of oil companies allowed the 10 percent curtailment of deliveries achieved in August. But this was insufficient. Ickes had already, in Recommendation No. 1, forewarned Americans that if voluntary conservation failed, rationing was certain to follow. While criticism abated somewhat, Congress chose not to further enlarge the war powers of the president. The vague status of PAW remained unclarified for a full year after Pearl Harbor.[13]

SFAW only appeared on the scene in the month prior to Pearl Harbor. In June 1941, the Advisory Committee of the Bituminous Coal Division—composed of management and labor—recommended that Ickes be appointed coordinator of the bituminous coal industry, a suggestion seconded and broadened by a group of anthracite producers. Both management and labor feared that the ineffectiveness of the coal division in coping with the deepening emergency would encourage the drift into a situation in which responsibilities for coal were diffused among several agencies headed by unfamiliar individuals. Ickes and Gray were known factors while both management and labor were familiar with the personnel of USGS and the Bureau of Mines. In spite of the powerlessness of the new agency, Ickes accepted responsibility. Given the source of the authorizing letter, he had little choice. With such overwhelming expertise at his disposal and armed with mountains of data as well as industry support, Ickes anticipated considerable latitude of action.[14]

The Structure of the Fuel Agencies

PAW and SFAW fashioned organizations modeled upon the operational structure of the relevant industries, just as had BCD, PAB, and USFA in prior years. Both created a system of vertically integrated divisions that reflected each step a particular fuel followed from mine or well to ultimate consumer. In addition, both fuel units were deeply interested in such potential problems as worker availability, labor relations, and the supply of equipment.[15] Both PAW and SFAW also appointed a full panoply of industry advisory committees, some of which dealt with industrywide operational concerns while other functioned within a particular district or region. The composition of PAW's chief industry advisory committee quickly became a source of internal discord, and the appointment of Ralph Davies exposed Ickes to a barrage of criticism.[16]

The essential divisions and duties of SFAW were well formed when the executive order of 19 April 1943 transformed the office into a full-fledged executive agency under its new title. Responsible for stimulating the production of as much coal as possible and assuring its best utilization, SFAW was logically organized into production, transportation, distribution and allocation, and conservation divisions and branches. These units sponsored a host of programs and responded to the demands of such agencies as PAW, ODT, and WPB. Determining the proper coal for a specific use, speeding up delivery, encouraging early storage and stockpiling, orchestrating conservation campaigns, and balancing rail and lake movements of coal were among the agency's primary duties. With the advent of coal shortages in 1942–43, SFAW also developed a distributor-controlled coal rationing system and defended it successfully against efforts of OPA to impose a coupon-rationing system. SFAW functioned as coal's claimant agency before various agencies. Obtaining mining equipment necessitated constant negotiation with WPB, which controlled the supply of materials. SFAW lavished particular attention on the maintenance of a stable mine labor force, appealing regularly to the War Manpower Commission and to Selective Service for miner deferments. As the European war ended, SFAW contested with the Department of State and the Foreign Economic Administration for control over the coal supply of liberated areas.

To manage these diverse tasks with limited personnel, SFAW depended heavily upon support from the industry. The agency established numerous advisory committees representative of the various branches of the industry and opened district and other local offices as well. At the apex of the industry committee network stood the Solid Fuels Advisory War Council, created in March 1942 and consisting of bituminous and anthracite producers, coke manufacturers, wholesalers and retailers, dock operators, and representatives from transportation industries and the United Mine Workers of America. Each of the industry interests also operated separately through standing committees, while each of the producing districts established under the Guffey acts also created machinery that dovetailed with the structure of the home office and the war council. Also, in 1943, belatedly according to critics within several peer agencies, Ickes and Gray formed an interagency Solid Fuels Requirements and Distribution Committee. Finally, in early 1944, SFAW, prodded by ODT, threatened by OPA, and confronted with severe shortages caused by the strikes of 1943, established area distribution committees and hundreds of local distribution committees to oversee the allocation of coal by dealers to domestic and small commercial consumers. Other committees appeared as necessary to manage discrete programs and special problems. Unanticipated emergencies, shifting war needs, the actions of other agencies, and numerous other imponderables must have ensured frequent usage of the wartime term "snafu."[17]

As with SFAW, PAW's primary responsibilities were quite clear when Roosevelt's executive order of 12 December 1942 gave final shape to the agency. As Chapter 13 reveals, its powers were the subject of much debate and politicking. Davies managed day-to-day affairs and exterted a strong, if not totally commanding, influence in policy decisions. In contrast with Davies, Gray's role at SFAW seems more muted and his relationship with Ickes more deferential. Ickes, while never relinquishing full command at PAW, relied upon Davies to push the industry in proper directions. At SFAW, Ickes did his own pushing of both labor and management and was shoved back in return, particularly by John L. Lewis of UMWA. Davies was also more likely than Gray to voice opposition to Ickes's decisions. Gray, for instance, favored the application of zoning to coal but accepted Ickes's veto without dissent. Davies, on the other hand, argued vigorously with Ickes about the role of the federal government in developing foreign oil fields.

Former industry officials, selected by Davies, filled most of the assistant deputy posts. J. Howard Marshall, also from Standard California, was appointed PAW's chief counsel, and other oil executives served as directors of the functional divisions and divisional subunits. The major oil companies furnished almost 40 percent of the personnel holding key PAW jobs. Other oil companies supplied about 35 per-

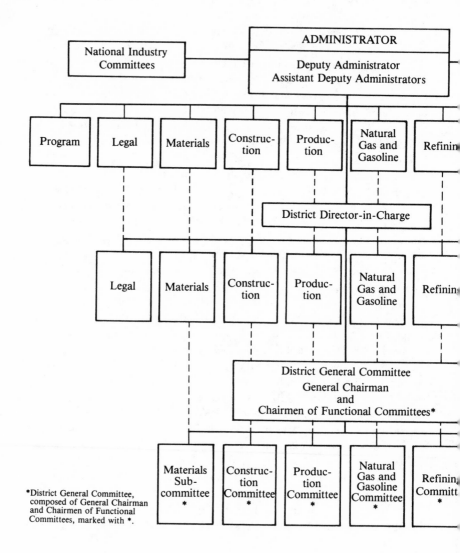

CHART 2. *Petroleum Administration for War*

Source: John W. Frey and H. Chandler Ide, *A History of the Petroleum Administration for War, 1941–1945* (Washington, D.C.: GPO, 1946), 27.

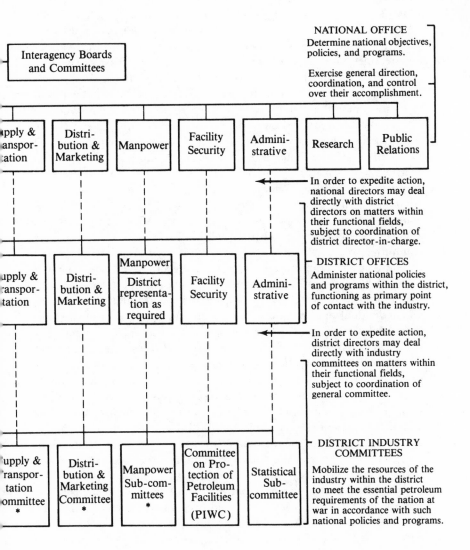

Interagency Boards
and Committees

NATIONAL OFFICE
Determine national objectives,
policies, and programs.

Exercise general direction,
coordination, and control
over their accomplishment.

| ▪pply &
▪anspor-
▪ation | Distri-
bution &
Marketing | Manpower | Facility
Security | Admini-
strative | Research | Public
Relations |

In order to expedite action,
national directors may deal
directly with district
directors on matters within
their functional fields,
subject to coordination of
district director-in-charge.

DISTRICT OFFICES

Administer national policies
and programs within the district,
functioning as primary point
of contact with the industry.

| ▪upply &
▪anspor-
▪tation | Distri-
bution &
Marketing | Manpower
District
representa-
tion as
required | Facility
Security | Admini-
strative |

In order to expedite action,
district directors may deal
directly with industry
committees on matters within
their functional fields,
subject to coordination of
general committee.

DISTRICT INDUSTRY
COMMITTEES

Mobilize the resources of the
industry within the district
to meet the essential petroleum
requirements of the nation at
war in accordance with such
national policies and programs.

| ▪upply &
▪ranspor-
tation
▪ommittee
* | Distri-
bution &
Marketing
Committee
* | Manpower
Sub-com-
mittees
* | Committee
on Pro-
tection of
Petroleum
Facilities
(PIWC) | Statistical
Sub-
committee |

cent, with the remainder coming from related industries or government agencies. As Ickes iterated and reiterated, the demand for public officials exceeded the supply of federal careerists. Still, opposition arose within antitrust and some independent circles to the appointment of Davies and his industry colleagues. During the war, various congressmen attacked PAW as a tool of the majors, citing as evidence the presence of Davies and other top oil company officials.[18]

Assistant deputy administrators supervised PAW's foreign and domestic operational units, which included divisions of production, refining, natural gas and natural gasoline, supply and transportation, and distribution and marketing. Industry advisory groups organized compatible sections and reported directly to the appropriate headquarters division. The Petroleum Industry War Council (PIWC), composed of influential industry leaders, has received most attention, but the five district committees possessed both advisory and substantive powers and may have exercised more influence than PIWC. Industry personnel filled virtually all staff positions on the district committees.[19]

The district committees implemented the orders of PAW and the War Production Board, serving as PAW's liaison and negotiator with the standing committees of PIWC, industry associations, companies, and individual operators. As the war ground on, PAW delegated additional duties to the districts, permitting them to make certain decisions without reference to the home office. In the critical matter of allocating limited supplies of drilling and storage equipment, as an example, the districts were authorized in 1943 to evaluate all applications for equipment and to forward those approved directly to WPB. In allocating crude to refineries, headquarters sketched out the general need—moving Texas crude to Mid-Continent refineries, for instance—and left it to the districts to work out the precise details. The district committees did not actively pursue greater authority. Indeed, in 1941 and 1942, they frequently resisted the enlargement of their jurisdiction, arguing that headquarters ought to retain responsibility. Davies countered by insisting that industry input must be paid for in the hard currency of shared responsibility. The elaborate district committee system reflected Davies's belief that controlled decentralization produced more rapid resolution of operational problems.[20]

An immediate uproar ensued over Ickes's initial appointments to PIWC. Independents accused Ickes of choosing a disproportionate number of representatives from the majors. PIWC reflected Ickes's intention to allow broad industry participation in PAW policy making while containing industry activity within a controllable body that reported directly to Davies and him. Everyone involved in the industry sensed that PIWC could exercise considerable influence on wartime mobilization and that once organized it would pay particular attention to policies that might affect the postwar world. Industry spokespersons, then and later, in stressing the importance of the council, generally exaggerated its actual contributions in shaping the policies adopted by PAW to achieve wartime goals. Without doubt, PIWC evolved into a key component of PAW, but it never dictated to the latter.[21]

Ickes ingenuously described PIWC as a body representative of the industry, a modern version of World War I's industry war council. That it was not representative—as everyone was perfectly aware—had little to do with favoritism or the political power of the API or the majors and much to do with the concentration of productive power within the industry. At an early conference between Ickes and the petroleum industry in June 1941, each of the many interests in attendance demanded representation on PIWC. Wildcatters from Kansas, gasoline wholesalers and retailers, wax manufacturers, and stove makers, among others, puffed themselves up as central to defense efforts. They exhorted Ickes and Davies to protect the "little guy" and when Ickes's appointments were announced, howled in anger at his neglect. For the most part, Ickes selected people from the larger production and refining companies that would provide the fuel to run the tanks and airplanes and that possessed the capacity to expand greatly their productivity or change the composition of their refinery runs. As a dozen or more independent organizations damned Ickes for passing over them, state associations of marketers, in April 1942, carried their grievances to Congress and the Department of Justice, accusing Ickes and Davies with furthering monopoly, a charge eliciting a sympathetic response from antitrusters.

Davies and other PAW officials attempted to assuage the bitterness of unrepresented interests by referring to the difficulty of selecting appropriate representatives from among the hundreds of thousands of retailers and by denying that PAW had lost sight of the smaller independents or that PAW policies would weaken the competitive position of small business. Although Ickes and Davies eventually offered a few places to the marketers, the larger companies and the most powerful trade associations retained their dominant position with PIWC. Ickes and Davies repeatedly expressed their commitment to fairness. They also recognized that some interests would play a larger role than others in the war effort. This, combined with Ickes's avowal to maintain existing historical competitive relationships within the industry, resulted in the bestowal of more benefits upon the larger firms than upon the smaller companies. Cities Service Corporation was deemed of greater significance than Derby Oil of Wichita, while the latter ranked above Economy Oil Company of Roanoke, Virginia, in the pecking order.[22]

The district committees and PIWC gradually evolved a reasonably smooth working relationship. The council's committee on petroleum economics submitted to PAW and the districts regular forecasts of district and national supply and demand, analyses of transportation problems, recommendations for refinery runs and yields, and studies of petroleum movement between districts. District committees worked closely with their twins in PIWC, and both exchanged information and advice with appropriate headquarters divisions. To mesh efficiently all these gears required time. The process of accommodation proceeded even while PAW and its subordinate units grappled with severe problems in 1941 and 1942 and while headquarters searched for favorable resolutions to jurisdictional conflicts with a plethora of competing agencies.

Much as Ickes disliked it, as fuels coordinator he worked for WPB. Until the creation in 1943 of the Office of War Mobilization (OWM), WPB reigned supreme. PAW and SFAW derived most of their amorphous authority from WPB, and the powers delegated by WPB legitimated the programs and policies of the fuel agencies. SFAW and PAW, acting as the priorities branch of WPB, prepared the coal and oil industry case for materials and equipment. These were presented to WPB, which until 1943 made the final decisions. WPB, in 1941 and 1942, vetoed PAW's requests for materials to construct large crude oil pipelines. The fuel offices also served as WPB's fuel procurement and fuel conservation agencies. WPB established needs and priorities; it was the job of the fuel offices to deliver the amounts required by the military and essential war industries. Unwilling to accept PAW or SFAW recommendations without review, WPB established its own energy-linked divisions. SFAW, PAW, and FPC considered those units as threatening to agency integrity. With the establishment of OWM, Ickes and his deputies habitually appealed to it when confronted with adverse WPB rulings.[23]

In their dealings with an office such as ODT, SFAW and PAW functioned as both claimant and supply agencies. The fuel administrations presented claims to ODT for rail and motor vehicle transportation while ODT claimed a portion of fuel supplies for the railroads. All three appeared before OPA's hundreds of local rationing boards as claimants for tires and gasoline.[24] Coordinator Ickes fumed about the subordination of his offices to WPB and circumvented it whenever possible. But his most stinging criticism was reserved for OPA.

Ickes and successive OPA administrators engaged in rancorous disputes over crude oil prices and over the system of rationing to be imposed upon coal and petroleum products. PAW inundated OPA with arguments for a hike in crude prices. OPA, ordered by the president in April 1941 to prevent price spiraling, refused to consider higher prices until the industry provided complete cost-of-production and operation figures. Once the Emergency Price Control Act legitimized OPA's authority, it proved invulnerable to the pressure exerted by Ickes and the industry. Simultaneously, Ickes criticized and opposed the method of rationing adopted by OPA and applied to petroleum products—and, if OPA had its way, to be applied to coal.[25]

In these contests, neither the fuel agencies nor OPA held transcendent power. Both appealed to WPB, to James Byrnes, chair of OWM, and to the president. Ickes also exploited congressional unhappiness with OPA in an effort to obtain legislation assigning the power to PAW to fix crude oil prices. Interagency competition for power and the consequences of the original presidential mandates assured the perpetual cloudiness of jurisdictional demarcations, tempting Ickes again and again to raid his neighbor's larder. As the war ended, desks at SFAW and FEA were awash with letters protesting one another's policies regarding the export of coal to Europe.

Ickes and Colbert

Ickes had not survived for so many years at Interior because of luck. He had demonstrated administrative competence, if not brilliance, and independence, described by detractors as narrow-minded obstinacy. After all this time, he had learned something about energy. Along with a handful of others in the federal service, and fewer still within the energy industries, Secretary Ickes clearly evinced an awareness of the national interest in and the interrelatedness of the primary sources of energy. NRC's energy report of 1939 had depended heavily upon Ickes's staff for data and for synthesis and ideas. He had experienced the negative effects of inadequate power in his role as head of the Petroleum Administrative Board and the Bituminous Coal Division. From his point of view, the authority delegated to him by Roosevelt to coordinate the defense efforts of the fuel industries was meager indeed. With no increments to power in the offing, Ickes necessarily danced to Jean Baptiste Colbert's tune. In a mercantilist world, additions to one's own wealth came only at the expense of someone else—in modern parlance, a zero-sum game. However much he delighted in this bloodless Hobbesianism, it was not self-gratification in a bureaucratic sense that impelled him.

Faith in the willingness of the general populace to make do with less was not one of Ickes's dogmas. War would require a massive production effort and all-encompassing regulation. Energy sufficiency would be the key to the entire war effort, a fact recognized by the Nazis in their campaigns against the Balkans, the Middle East, and the Soviet Union.[26] Inadequate authority widely diffused could only obstruct the fashioning of a mighty military engine. To appear as a supplicant before other agencies offended Ickes's sense of priorities and his perception of the efforts demanded to wage global war. Since Roosevelt would not enhance his authority, Ickes had no choice but to operate covertly, to play agencies against one another, to exploit whatever leverage he possessed to pry loose a piece of power from here or there, to call in his chits in Congress. An untoward result was that PAW responded most favorably to the importuning of the most powerful components of the oil industry. Independents resented this just as angrily as they had during the NRA-PAB years. But from Ickes's perspective, the cooperation of the largest integrated units was an undeniable imperative, to be won even at some cost to equity. That this fostered the further concentration of economic power was not of preeminent concern to PAW. While the alleged favoritism of PAW bared it to vocal assaults of antitrusters, the national emergency stymied the agency's enemies from advancing beyond rhetorical flourishes.

OPA's Leon Henderson sensed in Ickes a disdain for the consumer, for the little guy. OPA protected the general consuming public from the exploiters and price gougers, from landlords, from the major oil companies and their advocacy agency, PAW. OPA envisioned itself as the defender of fairness against powerful vested interests and normal human greed. Ickes, of course, could not agree that others championed equity or fairness more diligently than the fuel agencies. He did insist, however, that the perils confronting the nation demanded substantial concessions to efficiency. Everyone would have to do with less, and, perforce, the sacrifices of the less affluent would be disproportionately greater than the sacrifices of the more affluent. Donald Nelson of WPB, Henderson of OPA, and Ickes of PAW could all agree that the profligate energy consumption of Americans must be curtailed while the fruits of production increases must be channeled to the military and to essential industries. How to achieve this engendered many of the most vituperative disputes between the agencies collectively responsible for war production and distribution.[27] Overlapping and unclearly delimited duties abounded, providing a fertile field for agency aggrandizement, almost always at the expense of some other unit, and complicating the lives of those entering the system as petitioners.

THIRTEEN

Wartime Administration of Petroleum

"$\mathbf{F}$IRST I cover myself with gasoline and then gasoline is poured on top of the water in my portable tank after which both are ignited and I leap into the flaming tank." So daredevil Bee Kyle described to Petroleum Coordinator Harold L. Ickes in August 1942 the leap which thrilled countless spectators at Palisades Amusement Park. Kyle wished to know if this eighty-foot plunge "worked against defense" and should therefore cease for the duration.[1] If only everyone had been as obliging as Bee Kyle! Certainly many Americans, individually and collectively, cooperated with the government in pressing the war to a victorious conclusion. But to consider the war effort as the epitome of the American cooperative spirit exaggerates the actual good will with which Americans shouldered numerous burdens, some infinitely more onerous than others. Sanctions, too, were necessary; even those with good will required the cattle prod of law from time to time.

Commentators on the performance of the energy industries during the war tended to cast it in the mold of industry-government cooperation. A U.S. Chamber of Commerce booklet on the petroleum war organization, written in 1943, made it appear as if federal regulation was totally absent. During and after the war, Ralph K. Davies and Max W. Ball, an assistant to Davies, hailed the cooperative spirit and mutual confidence that permeated and defined the oil industry-government relationship. Later on, historians wrote glowingly of the federal-oil industry partnership and catalogued the sacrifices offered by industry on the altar of democracy.[2] In fact, even though Davies

316

and numerous other industry officials flocked to the capital to assume critical posts in government, the relationship between government and the energy industries resembled one between equals only in an Orwellian sense. By early 1942, federal authority was paramount. Industry recalcitrance became cooperation only under duress. At one time or another, most sectors of the fuel industries required coercion. In addition to the imposition of sanctions, the government offered inducements. Whenever possible, the carrot was preferred to the stick, but one or the other was normally necessary. None of this surprised Ickes, whose long experience with the oil industry counseled against a naive reliance upon voluntarism.

The Atlantic Seaboard Supply Crisis

Many federal and industry officials anticipated petroleum shortages of some magnitude along the East Coast should war come. As no one could predict when the worst would happen, attention in early 1941 focused upon the preparation of contingency plans. The crunch arrived more quickly than anyone expected, precipitated by the loan of fifty oil tankers (one-fifth of the tanker fleet) to Great Britain in May 1941 and impelling Roosevelt to create the petroleum coordinator's office (see Chapter 12, note 1). The new office, endowed with no authority, and other federal agencies cast about frantically for the means of supplying oil to the East Coast. The methods devised by PAW and other agencies to ameliorate this crisis patterned the course pursued after Pearl Harbor.

As early as March 1941, the Office of Production Management informed Congress that while crude production and refinery runs could be expanded by 25 to 30 percent, the tanker fleet would be hard pressed to move the additional volume even if not threatened by hostile naval forces. And tankers delivered almost 95 percent of the oil moving into the Atlantic states. Few believed that a sudden switch to rail delivery could eliminate the shortfall resulting from a reduction in tanker service. To fill the gap would require the railroads to increase their deliveries from 35,000 barrels per day (bd) to 1.4 million. Available rolling stock seemed inadequate to this task; nor could motive power dedicated to such other critical goods as food or coal be reassigned. Indeed, New England received about 65 percent of its bituminous requirements by colliers, which were as vulnerable as tankers.[3]

These disturbing facts determined that PAW plot a strategy to reduce fuel consumption in the East and substitute pipelines for both tankers and railroads. Since PAW possessed no authority to order shippers to move oil by rail rather than by water, industry and railroad cooperation was essential. It was immediately forthcoming; an ad hoc committee of major shippers acted with alacrity to uncover additional barges, tank cars, trucks, and pipeline space. These steps narrowed the delivery deficit to about 175,000 bd by September, leaving an estimated shortfall of some 12 percent if no further depletion of tanker capacity occurred and if consumption remained at normal levels.[4] But soon after the British returned most of the tankers, the Japanese attacked Pearl Harbor, and Germany declared war on the United States.

Prior to the tanker loan, the Allies had lost 406,000 dead weight tons (dwt) to enemy action and gained only 262,000 dwt by new construction. Tanker transfers from the United States replaced about 100,000 dwt of loss through October 1941. American belligerency permitted Germany to unleash its roving submarine packs against the defenseless colliers and tankers that plied the waters off the East Coast. I recall as a child strolling with my uncle along the beach at Point Pleasant, New Jersey, one evening early in the war. We were startled by a brilliant flash of light far out to sea that was quickly followed by a deep rumble. Sadly, my uncle told me that yet another oil tanker had fallen victim to Nazi subs. Many other unwitnessed explosions tore American ships apart, sending crews to death and darkness on the ocean floor. Between 7 December 1941 and mid-April 1942, the U.S. and its allies lost a hundred tankers while twenty-three new vessels were sent to sea. The net loss in tanker tonnage, under 100,000 in mid-February, soared to 250,000 by mid-March, and rose inexorably to a peak of 600,000 tons in mid-July 1942. In the spring and summer of 1942, losses were so heavy that the president confined all tankers to port.[5]

Thus, the partial resolution of the oil supply problem in September-November 1941 gave way to serious scarcity after Pearl Harbor. During those few prewar months, PAW and other agencies launched a multipronged campaign to satisfy defense industry and military demands and to reduce civilian consumption. But much confusion attended the halting steps taken by PAW and OPA, acting under authority delegated by OPM, to reduce gasoline use. While Ickes and his colleagues at OPM and OPA prepared to limit petroleum consumption in the eastern states, articulate Americans attacked the federal government for contriving the shortages to benefit the majors—or for some other nefarious purpose. For instance, in October 1941, an

editorial in *The Gasoline Retailer* expressed grave doubts about the need
to reduce gasoline use, implying that the scarcity was part of a plot to
drive the independents from business. After reading this, Ickes must
have suffered a déjà vu migraine. One oil company official criticized
Ickes and Davies for failing to convince the press and the public of
the reality of the fuel shortage.[6] In fact, PAW bombarded the press
with facts and figures demonstrating the impact of the tanker loan or
a war on fuel supply patterns along the eastern seaboard. The public,
however, absorbed information selectively, tuning out the somber
prognostications that flew from the typewriters of PAW information
officials. Bee Kyle's willingness to sacrifice was not emulated by all.

To identify the problem was simple enough. As winter approached,
receipts at eastern terminals fell 175,000 bd below normal, and storage tanks were rapidly drained. Gasoline consumption must be drastically curtailed and refiners induced to increase their runs of fuel oil.
The use of all fuels must be reduced in order to ease demand for
transportation. Unless these steps were taken, homes would be cold,
factories would close, and some utilities would run out of boiler fuel.
These facts held before as well as after Pearl Harbor, but prior to
7 December, the federal government possessed insufficient authority
to deal with them.

In July and August 1941, OPM instituted its civilian allocation
program, acting through PAW and OPA. Beginning in July, OPA and
PAW sought a 33 percent reduction in the consumption of motor fuels
in the Atlantic states (PAW Recommendation No. 1) by convincing
jobbers and wholesalers and retailers to limit sales to their customers.
This tactic achieved unsatisfactory savings for two basic reasons: Distributors and consumers generally ignored the recommendation; the
greater margin of profit in gasoline as compared with fuel oils encouraged refiners to continue producing sufficient gasoline to meet normal
demand. Consumers did not grasp the relationship between gasoline
and fuel oil supplies; nor did they wish to, as they sped along the
parkways to state parks and the seashore. Gasoline consumption rose
while fuel oil stocks fell to worrisome levels.

Voluntary conservation having failed, in August, Ickes and Davies,
his deputy administrator, recommended the reduction by some 15 percent of deliveries to distributors. OPM, in September 1941, did issue
Limitation Order (LO) L-8 to limit the distribution of motor fuel in
the eastern states. But so circumscribed were its powers to allocate
resources that L-8 depended upon voluntary compliance. In the meantime, PAW had issued recommendations to reduce the working hours

of service stations and to limit the hours of delivery to stations (Recommendations Nos. 4 and 3). Some stations complied and some did not.[7]

Order L-8 and accompanying PAW and OPA action alleviated the shortages developing along the East Coast. In late October, with the addition of forty tankers to the East Coast run, OPM suspended LO L-8. Ickes, Donald Nelson (OPM), and Leon Henderson (OPA) harbored little hope that better days lay ahead. While the three had evolved a working relationship during the short-lived crisis of fall 1941, certain disagreements had surfaced, and several serious problems had gone unresolved. Large petroleum shippers had cooperated in the substitution of railroad for tanker transportation, but the considerably higher freight charges for rail shipment jeopardized the continuance of their good will. Shipper demands were met by means of a compensatory adjustment program that subsidized oil companies for undertaking uneconomic war-related activities such as shipping by rail or moving crude to unusual destinations.[8] Ickes and Davies also devised command mechanisms to obtain proper refining yields from obdurate refiners. The most serious interagency controversies that emerged revolved around oil industry demands for price increases and the appropriate system to reduce fuel use along the Atlantic coast, or nationally if necessary.

All the problems of fall 1941 intensified in 1942 and thereafter as the federal government struggled to balance legitimate civilian energy needs against the essential demands of burgeoning war industries and a military machine that scattered 15 million men and women across the face of the globe. PAW and the other agencies early recognized that normal civilian requirements could not be met and that even if civilian use were reduced, existing transportation could not carry the fuel demanded by industry and the military.

PAW's evolving strategy included dealer-controlled fuel supply limitations for the East Coast and special controls for the West Coast, a massive emergency pipeline construction program to link Gulf oil fields with the refineries of the northeastern seaboard, crude price increases to stimulate discovery and production, and the conversion of fuel oil users to coal. Such strategies warrant separate treatment since their implementation depended upon the acquiescence of numerous agencies and trod upon a variety of interests. The conversion program, as an example, required the close cooperation of OPA, PAW, SFAW, and WPB and posed difficult questions about allocating steel to the manufacture of furnaces rather than tanks. Before dealing with these operational issues, the unflagging efforts of Ickes and Davies to win greater autonomy for PAW should be chronicled. The outcome of that campaign determined to a large degree the framework of the wartime regimen imposed upon petroleum and to some degree the position of strength from which the oil industry would step into the postwar world.

Defining the Limits of PAW's Authority

Throughout 1942, Ickes chafed under the restricted powers delegated by the War Production Board (OPM until January 1942) to PAW, the dispersal of authority over oil among several agencies, and the anomalous status conferred upon PAW by Roosevelt's letter of May 1941. Ickes repeatedly engaged in acrimonious jurisdictional disputes with WPB, OPA, and other federal units. In June 1941, Donald Nelson, WPB's head, suggested the creation of a national advisory committee for oil. Ickes interpreted this as a move to turn PAW into a branch office of WPB. Ickes's sensitivity to jurisdictional encroachment was sharpened in late 1941 when amendments to the Vinson Act of June 1940 and the passage of the First War Powers Act on 18 December 1941 endowed WPB with expanded powers and further subordinated PAW to WPB. WPB delimited PAW's field of action by delegating formal rationing powers to OPA in January 1942. The passage of the Emergency Price Control Act in the same month, a response to rising retail prices during 1941, granted OPA full authority over the price of most products, thereby obstructing, as Ickes viewed it, PAW's ability to stimulate new oil production. OPA hastened to establish fuel price and fuel rationing divisions, inevitably invading the domain staked out by PAW.

In April 1942, Nelson urged Ickes to speed up the production of toluene and butadiene, ingredients used in the manufacture of explosives, high-octane gasoline, and synthetic rubber. His dander up, Ickes lectured Nelson on the need for centralized direction to achieve maximum results and assigned to Davies the task of drafting a document that justified the centralization of control over oil in PAW. Completed in May, Davies's brief initiated PAW's campaign to gather to its bosom all authority over petroleum. Davies's argument emphasized the magnitude and complexity of mobilizing the giant oil industry for war, a fact soon forgotten by industry spokespersons. PAW, organized vertically to replicate the functional divisions of the industry, provided the integrated mechanism to efficiently control production, transportation, refinery runs and yields, distribution, and pricing. As Davies asserted, the ability of PAW to act quickly and effectively is "lost if the oil agency of government is made a mere subsidiary of another body such as WPB." The latter, as Davies described it, is organized "to deal only horizontally with numerous over-all industrial problems," lacking expertise to resolve specific oil industry problems.[9] Ickes and his staff rooted their proposal for oil administration reform in this administrative philosophy.

Ickes's plan, rumors of which stirred up apprehension within WPB in July, called for the creation of a War Petroleum Control Administration to serve as the focal point of contact between all government agencies and the oil industry. The purview of the new office would encompass everything coming out of the industry and everything going into the industry in the way of materials. Acknowledging that final decisions regarding the allocation of materials properly rested with WPB, Ickes suggested that WPB allocate the total amount of materials consigned to the industry—x tons of steel, y electric motors, etc.—to his office which would then determine intraindustry allocations. A similar approach was suggested for tankers, tank cars, trucks, tires, and so forth, thus freeing the oil administration from item-by-item negotiations with the War Shipping Board (WSB), the Office of Defense Transportation (ODT), and OPA. Ickes further proposed the lodging in his office of final authority over fuel rationing and the price of petroleum products purchased by units of the oil industry from other oil companies, thus permitting Ickes to establish crude oil prices. Prices to ultimate consumers would remain vested in OPA. In October, Ickes formally submitted a draft of an executive order to Roosevelt and to all relevant agencies and departments.[10]

Virtually every agency whose turf was threatened replied with scathing criticism. To WPB, the plan violated a basic principle: that control over production priorities and the allocation of all materials to industry remain concentrated in a single agency. Nelson castigated the coordinator's office for ignoring WPB determinations regarding refinery yields, implying that Ickes placed the profits of the oil industry before the war effort.[11] Under no circumstances, Nelson proclaimed, should WPB be stripped of sole authority for determining the total amount of oil required and the appropriate mix of essential refined products. WPB then proceeded to develop its own scheme to bring oil more fully under its control by relegating PAW to the role of a super stock clerk responsible for filling WPB's orders. For its part, OPA rejected the entire plan as inflationary and beneficial only to the oil industry. ODT, headed by ICC Commissioner Joseph B. Eastman, no fan of OPA, condemned Ickes's plan as unworkable. FPC expressed its unalterable opposition to the proposal because it would override all FPC functions under the Natural Gas Act.[12] The ICC, the Board of Economic Warfare, and other less fuel-oriented agencies demanded explicit assurances that nothing in Ickes's proposition would infringe upon their operations.[13]

By December 1942, when Ickes took his case to James F. Byrnes, head of the Office of Economic Stablization, the game was already lost. Indeed, in November, Nelson suggested that OPA control the delivery of fuel oil to war industries and deemphasized the oil-to-coal conversion program promoted by PAW. Only the determined opposition of Ickes to those changes restored the status quo. Nelson's foray may have convinced Ickes to accept a compromise executive order that created PAW as an executive agency but that essentially retained the jurisdictional status quo.[14]

Under the executive order of 2 December 1942, PAW remained a claimant agency for oil before WPB under the latter's controlled materials program and functioned as the instrument of WPB to achieve production goals decided upon by a newly created multiagency, Petroleum Requirements Board, chaired by Ickes. PAW could establish all necessary policies, plans, and programs for petroleum "provided that no directive issued hereunder shall conflict with any directive which may be issued by the chairman of the War Production Board."[15] His secessionist gambit checked, Ickes shifted his target to OPA, attempting through appeals to Byrnes and negotiations with WPB to strip OPA of its responsibilities over the distribution of oil products and through legislation to win the power to set crude oil prices. Subsequent sections take up these issues.

Ickes's quest for hegemony over petroleum won the support of spokespersons for various sectors of the oil industry who were confused and irritated by the number of agencies that meddled in oil affairs. IPAA, misunderstanding the jurisdictional compromise that created PAW, believed the executive order endowed PAW with greater power and flexibility than it actually possessed. Subsequent independent criticism of PAW can be traced, at least in part, back to IPAA's flawed perception. When PAW, frequently acting under the direction of WPB or OPA, failed to protect their interests vis-a-vis the majors, independents read it as the willful act of an agency run by and for the major firms. While independents occasionally erred in blaming PAW for policies favoring the majors, their general critique hit the mark.[16] The economic largess of the wartime cornucopia spilled in great abundance into the pantries of the majors.

From the birth of the oil coordinator's office to the end of the war, the oil industry distrusted the growing federal role in their business, fearing that it presaged permanent involvement. Both majors and independents recalled only too vividly Ickes's past advocacy of comprehensive federal controls over production. During the war, direct criticism by the majors remained muted, only surfacing fully in the hullabaloo over the Petroleum Reserves Corporation (PRC). However, in frequent statements the major-dominated PIWC expressed its unswerving dedication to an oil future free from federal regulation. Davies's testimony in November 1945 solidly supported this view. For their part, the independents also adhered to the idea of a fully competitive market; but whereas the majors insisted that such a condition already existed and required only protection, the independents viewed free competition as a goal to be achieved with the aid of the federal government.[17]

California independents in late 1941 and other independents in subsequent months demanded equal access to government contracts and condemned the magnitude of contracts let to the major companies.[18] Independents succeeded in enlisting the support of influential congressmen in their campaign to equalize benefits, but the urgency of wartime demand, the superior capabilities of the integrated firms, and the consumer-oriented price policies of OPA doomed them to failure. Sen. Harry S Truman might believe that the Standard Oil group "are still trying to choke the country to death," but what could he do as "one voice in the wilderness"?[19]

Subsequent investigations determined that the leading 100 corporations won 67 percent of the prime defense contracts. Eleven majors were among the 75 corporations receiving the largest federal construction subsidies. As a result of federal aid and economy of scale advantages, the largest companies (21 in some calculations and 26 in other counts) increased their share of crude production from 56 percent in 1941 (52 percent in 1939) to 64 percent in 1944 and their share of refining capacity from 76 percent in 1940 to 82 percent in 1945. Of the new refining facilities constructed during the war, 80 percent were operated by the 18 largest refiners. Many independents held PAW responsible for this acceleration of past trends. As best it could, PAW deflected such criticisms toward WPB and OPA, reminding the independents of its unceasing efforts to obtain higher crude oil prices and blaming OPA for all inequities.

As everyone knew, wartime mobilization inevitably lavished greater rewards upon the big integrated firms. Smaller marketers relied wholly on domestic and civilian consumption, the market hit hardest by rationing, while the larger companies shared this business and also supplied the government.[20] Repeated pledges by Ickes and Davies to protect existing competitive relationships prompted only mordant and cynical commentary from independents.

Wartime Production and Crude Prices

By mid-1943, petroleum producers and refiners were operating at over 90 percent of capacity and meeting projected goals. Crude oil production yielded 3.7 million barrels daily (mbd) in 1940, up 1.6 mbd from the depression trough of 1932, and reached a maximum of 4.6 mbd during 1945. Texas and California produced 55 percent of the crude in 1945, while Louisiana, Oklahoma, and Kansas pumped another 26 percent. From January through August 1945, refiners produced 487,000 bd of 100-octane gasoline, or six times the daily run of 1942. The daily production of fuel oil rose by 33 percent between 1940 and 1945, while motor fuel, tightly regulated, fell from 1.7 mbd in 1941 to 1.4 mbd in 1943 and then rose to 2 mbd in 1945.[21]

Oil states and their producers were a contentious lot, constantly bickering over quotas, complaining about shortages of materials for new oil wells and, especially in the early stages of the war, inadequate transportation, always angry about the level of crude prices, and, if small scale, ever suspicious of the big companies. Still, the tight controls worked rather effectively. The military never wanted for oil, factories produced remarkable quantities of war materials, and Walter Winchell's Mr. and Mrs. America were able to take an occasional Sunday drive.

The nation entered the war with a large reserve productive capacity.[22] In 1941, PAW recommended daily rates of production to state regulatory agencies who could use these estimates or ignore them in allocating quotas to each field.[23] After Pearl Harbor, PAW's directives carried the authority of law. To obtain sufficient oil for war use over an indefinite period of time, PAW calculated and imposed upon each field the maximum efficient rate at which oil could be withdrawn without excessive decline in reservoir energy. This standard was essentially maintained until mid-1944; thereafter, the hunger of the military machine required that production exceed the maximum efficient rate.

States such as Kansas and Colorado grumbled about low quotas but complied with PAW's directives. Texas and California, the largest producing states, normally ignored PAW quotas and produced well above the certified production rise. The Texas Railroad Commission found it extremely difficult to control production, resorting to field shutdowns from time to time. Patriotism, the constant admonitions of PAW, and periodic transportation shortages imposed some restraints.

While the productive life of fields in Texas and California might be shortened, sufficient oil was forthcoming.[24]

PAW and PIWC recognized that the satisfaction of wartime oil demand from already producing wells would quickly deplete reserves and cause serious supply problems in the future. PAW's policies, therefore, emphasized active exploration and discovery as well as the setting of maximum efficient rates of recovery for working fields and wells. The effort to add more to reserves than was withdrawn demanded the resolution of a host of complex problems, not all of which can be treated here. Davies and those majors with interests in foreign oil fields attempted to drum up support for the exploitation of overseas deposits, predictably drawing the fire of independent producers and refiners who disputed the need for oil imports or refineries located on foreign soil. Of greater immediate urgency for PAW were the polices adopted to regulate the flow of materials to producers and to fix crude price levels.[25]

As oil's claimant agency before WPB for well drilling and other production equipment, PAW's materials division pressed upon WPB the implications of the modest number of new wells completed, particularly by wildcatters. PAW arguments accentuated the fact that for every barrel of new oil discovered a greater volume was withdrawn— the ratio between 1941 and 1945 was 1:1.7. To moderate the consumption of strategic materials in the oil fields, WPB issued Order M-68 in December 1941. M-68 restricted the use of materials, especially steel, in production and legitimated well-spacing orders that PAW imposed in 1942 upon developing fields and even upon older fields when practicable. During the remainder of the war, first PAW and then the district committees processed requests for materials for the maintenance of old wells and the drilling of new wells, forwarding those approved to WPB. These restrictions reduced by 40 percent the number of drillings, all considered superfluous by PAW, and saved large amounts of metals.

While some producing states demanded that state regulatory agencies handle the allocation of materials, PAW, unable to win full administrative control over M-68, refused to relinquish any authority to the states. PAW utilized its limited control over materials allocation to pressure California and Texas producers into closer conformity with production quotas. PAW did attempt to increase the flow of materials to wildcatters, a key source of new oil discoveries. Ickes and the industry war council badgered WPB with proofs of the critical role played by wildcatters in the oil industry.[26] While they were at it, they importuned Donald Nelson for relief from the obstructive effects of low crude oil prices upon exploration and discovery, a condition laid directly at the door of OPA.

In October 1941, the petroleum coordinator forwarded to OPA a list of reasons supporting an immediate increase in crude oil prices: increased cost of materials and labor; higher taxes; rising transportation charges; to insure adequate supply; to prevent premature abandonment of stripper wells; to stimulate wildcatting; to develop new reserves. OPA permitted a small price increase and then slammed the price lid shut for the duration. In spite of the intense efforts of Ickes and Davies to pry the lid open, crude oil prices remained frozen at 1941 levels.[27]

Oil interests inveighed against the idiocy of OPA. Many producers fired burning letters across the desks of Ickes and Davies, unfairly blaming PAW for their alleged financial woes. PIWC, in October 1942, adopted a formal resolution demanding a crude price increase. PAW officials and industry witnesses sang the same refrain before numerous congressional committees, both during and after the war. IPAA celebrated Leon Henderson's resignation in December 1942, naively hoping for better days under the new OPA chief, former Sen. Prentiss M. Brown, the Senate sponsor of existing price legislation. But little changed under Brown or under his successor, Chester Bowles, a veteran New Dealer and, prior to his appointment, OPA's fuel administrator in Connecticut.

In 1944, the vitriolic Warren C. Platt, editor and publisher of *National Petroleum News*, characterized OPA as a "commie outfit," conspiring to destroy the oil industry, free enterprise, and democracy, in that order, for reasons known only to Platt. OPA was certainly the least popular wartime agency, its status challenged only by the local draft boards. Sellers griped about prices while buyers complained about rationing. Solid citizens dabbled in the active black market while calling for equity. OPA was an impossible agency to administer and was defended only by President Roosevelt and his two key political warriors, James F. Byrnes and Fred N. Vinson. Byrnes and Vinson brokered or arbitrated interagency disputes, balancing competing interests to win an acceptable middle position.[28] No matter what tactics were employed against OPA, Ickes and oil were stopped dead in their tracks by Byrnes and Vinson.

Ickes's tenacity over this issue owed much to his personal sense of probity, his self-righteous belief in the correctness of his position, and his perception of himself as a member of a small band dedicated to the protection of the public interest. Undeterred by their failure to budge OPA in 1942, PAW and its industry allies opened 1943 by escalating their offensive to force a price increase. OPA, ordered by the president to check inflation, disputed the legitimacy of a price rise. Producers foolishly refused to turn over all production cost data to OPA, strengthening the latter's position. OPA officials Sumner T. Pike and John K. Galbraith both denied the validity of PAW's claims, pointing to production increases under current prices and suggesting, much to the alarm of IPAA, that the U.S. should import cheaper foreign oil to fill immediate needs. Davies personally sympathized with this argument; he had advised Ickes in 1941 that "the petroleum resources of Mexico, Columbia, and Venezuela . . . must be considered to be reserves for the United States."[29] Nevertheless, he loyally pressed his chief's demands in numerous missives to his OPA counterparts. Unable to move OPA, Ickes, in October and November 1943, then presented his case to Byrnes at the Office of War Mobilization and Vinson at the Office of Economic Stabilization. They concurred with OPA's determination to hold the price line.[30]

By this time, Ickes had personalized OPA's opposition, viewing it as a vicious assault on his integrity as well as detrimental to the public interest. He rejected Vinson's offer of special subsidies for new production, for stripper wells, and for secondary recovery operations. Vinson argued that such incentive payments together with reimbursement for abnormal transportation charges would induce new production while protecting marginal producers. Ickes insisted that a general price increase was the easiest method of increasing production. As OPA organized meetings with the National Stripper Well Association, IPAA, and other producer groups to promote the subsidies, Ickes shifted his attention to Congress where he sought to turn producing-state influence and congressional antipathy toward OPA to the purposes of PAW. Considerable support for PAW's position developed in Wright Patman's Select Committee for Small Business and Clarence Lea's Special Subcommittee for Petroleum Investigation.

Bills surfaced in both houses that transferred OPA's authority over petroleum pricing and rationing to PAW. The House, in December 1943, passed a bill that advanced crude oil prices by thirty-five cents per barrel. Advocates of higher prices vitiated OPA's contention that the number of wells drilled had increased by pointing out that those gains were due entirely to the majors. OPA's defensive strategy, essentially labeling PAW as a stooge of the oil industry, contributed less to the defeat of these measures than did the lobbying of Byrnes and Vinson, armed as they were with the prestige of the president and the implicit threat of a presidential veto. Vinson's subsidization proposals deflected criticism by offering some benefits to smaller and marginal producers. Having been successfully bailed out, OPA bowed in the direction of the oil industry by appointing a crude oil advisory committee in 1945. Correctly viewed by IPAA as a mere ploy, the committee accomplished nothing.[31]

In his tawdry campaign to raise prices, Ickes, closely advised by Davies and his cadre of former petroleum officials, suffered from a skewed vision of the legitimacy of oil price increases. PAW, never insisting upon full disclosures, also lacked comprehensive cost-of-production figures. Davies undoubtedly knew more about such things than Ickes but could hardly be expected to argue against the official position of his industry. In the end, PAW's offensive shattered against Roosevelt's insistence that inflation be minimized.

During the price debates, cracks appeared in the facade of PAW-oil industry unity. An IPAA official stated flatly that PAW pursued policies contrary to the interests of independent producers. Others condemned PAW for filling most staff positions with employees of the major companies. Independent producers accused PAW's district committees of discriminating against them in reviewing applications for equipment. Independent refiners anticipated few benefits from the construction of new pipelines by the majors. In short, PAW may have emerged from its defeat in the price war with a tarnished image, its credibility as a spokesperson for a united industry somewhat dimmed.[32]

Controls over Refining and Transportation

PAW's program to increase the production of oil utilized practices developed during the 1920s and 1930s and familiar to those involved in the industry. In the refining, transport, and marketing sectors, however, the wartime emergency required an entirely new system, one that assured the proper crudes reached the appropriate refineries, for processing into the particular products called for by the military and essential war industries, and then transported expeditiously to distributors and end-users. Since supply fell below total demand, controls were imposed at each step, and the system was capped by gasoline and fuel oil rationing. The World War I experience offered few useful precedents. The industry in 1941 was much larger and its technologies much more complex. The demands generated by the new war called for a variety of specialized petroleum products and a volume of production of far greater magnitude.

America entered the period of defense preparation with substantial unused refining capacity, only a portion of which was reactivated by

Pearl Harbor. But a significant fraction of the surplus capacity was old, of small size, and unsuited for production of special products needed by the military, particularly the feed stocks for aviation gasoline, synthetic rubber, and explosives. PAW's refining division and the district committees assumed responsibility for negotiating contracts with industry for the production of stipulated quantities of particular products which were then sold to the Defense Supplies Corporation (DSC) under fixed-price or cost-plus contracts. The refining division determined the rate and type of refinery expansion as well as the location of new facilities, operating in the latter area through the Defense Plants Corporation (DPC), which provided all or part of the financing. Finally, the refining division allocated crude oil among and controlled runs within all refineries.

To coordinate these operations required a single-minded devotion to the detail of hundreds of separate contracts as well as the ability to shift resources from one refining program to another as the theater of operations of the armed forces shifted and expanded and as their product needs changed. All of this generated vituperative controversies over the allocation of crude to refineries, refinery runs, the awarding of government contracts, and the allocation of products to the civilian sector. PAW and OPA vied for dominance over distribution. The needs of the rubber program conflicted with the production of aviation gasoline. Independent refiners appealed to the refining division to stem the flow of domestic resources to the foreign refining industry. Independents accused PAW of favoring the majors in the awarding of contracts. From time to time, sketchy accounts of these disputes appeared in the newspapers, but for the most part a public airing was avoided as the contestants confined their wrangling to the ill-lit and uncomfortable offices of the agencies directly involved.[33]

The cooperation of the refining industry, especially the majors, was not immediately forthcoming when PAW and WPB attempted to shift refinery runs from gasoline to fuel oil in the months following the tanker loan. As PAW explained it, OPA's price schedules militated against the alteration of refinery yields in favor of fuel oil. This excuse triggered gnawing suspicions within WPB that PAW permitted profit considerations to guide refinery runs in spite of the alarming shortage of fuel oil in the East and the approach of winter. In the opinion of one WPB skeptic, PAW "apparently does not expect the industry to make changes . . . prior to assurance of . . . price changes to insure it against loss of revenue." a conclusion exposing Ickes to the charge of manipulating the shortages to force OPA to raise fuel and crude oil prices.[34] Once America entered the war, the new war powers delegated to WPB and then to PAW enabled the latter to compel a shift in yield ratios. But, concurrently, the coercive elements were softened by the favorable terms of the contracts awarded to the refiners. The negative attitude of the refiners during the six months prior to Pearl Harbor demonstrated the limitations of industry cooperation. Profitable contracts drew good will from the refining industry like a poultice.

The contracts financed by DSC and other subsidies compensated the larger refiners for extraordinary expenses accompanying the alteration of product yields. Small and nonintegrated firms that lacked the ability to produce specialized products enjoyed limited access to these bonuses. Even though crude supplies satisfied exploding demand, transportation shortages and the allocation of crude to the larger refineries threatened to close down many small and older plants in District 2. In 1943, PAW organized a crude oil pool in an effort to guarantee nonwar plants at least 80 percent of their prewar runs. In Districts 2 and 3, crude oil allocation committees determined allotments and forwarded district-wide claims for transportation to ODT. Independents greeted scornfully PAW's announced intention to treat low-priority refineries with some equity.[35]

The big bucks flowed to the big companies. Not only did the larger firms win the most lucrative federal contracts, but the larger oil companies employed federal funds to expand their refining capacity. Almost 90 percent of the $927 million expended on wartime refinery projects went to aviation gasoline production. Gov. Ellis G. Arnall of Georgia complained that his part of the country received less than its fair share of industrial development money. He was correct; of a total of $20 billion in federal funds spent on industrial expansion, the states of New York, Pennsylvania, Ohio, Indiana, Illinois, Michigan, Texas, and California received 75 percent. Louisiana, Texas, and California were notable beneficiaries of petroleum expansion, and within those states Standard Louisiana, Cities Service, Humble, the Texas Company, Shell, and Standard California enjoyed priority treatment in obtaining contracts from DPC. An additional $200 million was invested in refining facilities located in Mexico, Venezuela, the West Indies, and the Middle East. These installations were fully or partly owned and controlled by a handful of major firms.

Some funds flowed into other states and to nonmajors. Kansas and Oklahoma received about $52 million, of which $14 million went to Phillips and Continental Oil, $35 million in Champlin, and $3 million to National Oil, the latter two among the largest independents. Cities Service alone was awarded a $50 million contract to build its Lake

Charles, Louisiana, plant. While Davies might insist that a balance be struck in the letting of contracts to small and large firms, in fact imbalance prevailed. By the end of the war, the 18 largest majors owned or operated 80 percent of the new refining capacity. They received 85 percent of the $805 million channeled into aviation gasoline production while 30 of 234 independents divided the remainder. When Davies, in 1945, informed a Senate committee that nearly $1 billion worth of new refining facilities were built in dozens of large and small plants from coast to coast, he meant about three dozen and neglected to reveal the distribution of those funds by company.[36]

WPB strictly controlled contract awards. This assured government receipt of the product specified in the contract—a plant, a feed stock, a final product. Control by WPB did not mean the equal distribution of contracts among regions or among firms of various sizes. A contract award promised substantial benefits. A successful refiner could be certain of operating at close to capacity while selling to a captive market at a price independently negotiated through PAW-DSC. These cost-plus contracts permitted a price above that established by OPA for all other petroleum products. Other refiners received whatever crude was left and sold in a market strictly regulated by OPA's rationing and maximum price orders. Moreover, early in 1941, the petroleum industry demanded and won federal acceptance of the rule that the defense program would bear the cost of all new construction and additions. At the end of the war, refiners could either retain the facilities by repaying DPC the balance of the loan, already doubly amortized by sales realizations gained from the cost-plus contracts, or abandon the plants and be reimbursed by the government for all capital expenditures. Whatever the decision, the refiners had used these facilities at practically no cost.

PAW took pride in the 20 percent funneled to smaller firms, delighting in characterizing the entire operation as "one huge Nation-wide refinery."[37] Others looked askance at the consequences—increased control of production by the majors, independents refining 16 percent of the total run while eight Standard companies refined 39 percent, obsolete independent plants operating at two-thirds capacity, and the enhanced marketing position of the majors.[38]

However devoted congressional committees were to the protection of small businesses, the Patman and Lea committees in the House and the Truman committee in the Senate did not stay, let alone reverse, the momentum of concentration. The mind-set of those Americans directly engaged in mobilizing resources for a global war compelled them to imbibe as absolute truth the unproven assumption that Cities Service's Lake Charles plant with a 17,700 bd capacity operated more efficiently than National's Coffeyville, Kansas, plant with a capacity of 1,700 bd, sufficient for only seven B-29 missions over Japan. The 100-octane plants and the refineries producing feed stock for synthetic rubber received 100 percent of their crude requirements while most other refineries, invariably independents, received less than their normal demand.[39]

While speaking eloquently of equity and preservation of historical competitive relationships, Ickes and Davies contributed to decisions in 1941 that created the matrix for the war production system: one couched in the rhetoric of fairness yet only nominally devoted to it, one allowing some administrative innovation but impervious to any basic restructuring of the industrial system. Ickes, Davies, Nelson, and others, captives of the Cities Service syndrome, fostered greater concentration and giantism, thereby compounding the difficulties of those seeking compatibility between large-scale technology and democracy. But, after all, there was a war on! Humble's Baytown, Texas, refinery processed about 5 percent of all the crude used during the war and manufactured 10 percent of the aviation gasoline.[40] Such plants conformed more closely to the national image of proper scale than did the Coffeyville plant.

So it was too in matters of transportation where one big solution was sought to the problem of supplying the East Coast. In PAW's lexicon of production miracles, the construction of the "Big Inch" (crude) and the "Little Inch" (product) pipelines from Texas to the northeastern seaboard challenged the aviation gasoline program for first rank. In response to the abrupt decline in tanker deliveries in May 1941, PAW launched a campaign to build a 1,250-mile crude pipeline from Texas fields to Philadelphia and New York City. Even prior to the tanker loan, OPM and the National Resources Planning Board (NRPB) reported in favor of new pipeline construction only after all other modes of transportation had been fully employed, pointing out that a ton of steel used for pipelines was a ton not used for battleships. Ickes and Davies and most of the majors seized upon the pipeline solution and faithfully pursued it to a successful conclusion. In so doing, PAW necessarily deemphasized the overall contribution expected from trucks, barges, and tank cars, all far more suitable for short-distance service, as PAW would have it, and all inefficient consumers of energy.

As Ickes and Davies evolved their plan, highest priority was assigned the Texas–East Coast line, but other smaller lines were also supported. A victory was quickly won when Congress passed the Cole emergency pipeline bill in July 1941, in spite of hostile testimony from the U.S. Maritime Commission and other interests competing for steel. The Cole Act authorized the president to designate any pipeline as necessary to the national defense and confer upon its builders the right to eminent domain. PAW incorporated the Emergency Pipeline, Inc., soon changed to War Emergency Pipelines, Inc., as the agent to act with DPC in constructing lines at government expense; PAW also established a standing pipeline committee to evaluate pipeline proposals submitted by private parties.[41] PAW's pipeline committee responded negatively to several proposals and incurred the animosity of several southern states.[42] Map 4 displays some of the 13,600 miles of pipeline laid during the war.

Only the persistence of Ickes, the intercession of Roosevelt, and the deteriorating supply picture of the East Coast convinced WPB to relent in its opposition to the pipeline, a project requiring almost 400,000 tons of steel. In June 1942, after three earlier rejections, WPB authorized materials for the Texas-Illinois leg. WPB's initial vetoes derived from an erroneous belief that PAW attempted to maintain normal civilian consumption along the East Coast, a perception stemming from industry reluctance to alter refinery yields and the failure of voluntary rationing and its own limitation orders to reduce consumption. The imposition of mandatory rationing and various use-priorities in addition to vastly increased wartime demand convinced WPB of the pipeline's necessity. In October, WPB allocated steel for the extension of the Big Inch to New York and Philadelphia.

The Little Inch product line—requiring 300,000 tons of steel—from Beaumont, Texas, to Linden, New Jersey, also aroused opposition. NRPB and ODT condemned the line as impractical and unnecessary, arguing that the better utilization of barges, trucks, trains, and shorter pipelines would consume less material and less energy while moving products more efficiently and cheaply; PAW denied this. The correct position is impossible to determine. Mid-Continent refiners, fearing competition in their markets from Gulf refiners, also responded negatively to the proposal. District 2's refining committee, then chaired by the independent leader, Wirt Franklin, advocated the construction of the eastern leg first, hoping to stonewall the Texas-Indiana link. Ickes ignored the objections voiced by District 2, thereby strengthening the conviction of independents that he was indifferent to their interests, and gained WPB's approval for the entire system. Although suffering from numerous construction flaws, the Little Inch commenced pumping through to New Jersey in January 1944.[43]

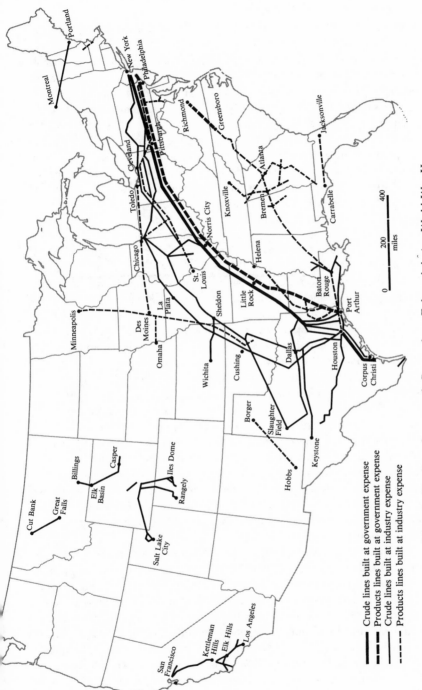

MAP 4. *Pipelines Constructed, Reversed, or Enlarged during World War II*

Source: John W. Frey and H. Chandler Ide, *A History of the Petroleum Adminis-tration for War, 1941–1945* (Washington, D.C.: GPO, 1946), facing page 102.

Crude lines built at government expense
Products lines built at government expense
Crude lines built at industry expense
Products lines built at industry expense

Pipelines composed a key segment of the transportation link between producing fields and the Atlantic Coast, but, as Table 14 shows, other forms of transportation supplied a greater proportion of the oil shipped to District 1 than the pipelines. Petroleum movements in other parts of the country depended even less upon trunk pipelines. Crude shipped from West Texas by tank cars supplemented California crude in the runs of California refineries. At times, flow through the Big Inch lagged because of inadequate crude inputs from Texas fields or because integrated firms in District 2 shipped crude from their Texas and Oklahoma fields through their own lines in order to guarantee supply. This practice contravened the intent of the crude oil pool arrangement and was unfair to small refiners who, lacking this option, frequently operated below capacity.

All these and myriad other puzzles were grappled with daily by PAW, ODT, and other agencies, sitting together in an Inter-Agency Committee on Petroleum and Liquids Transportation. ODT organized special committees on barges, trucks, and rail tank cars. And under various names, a tanker coordinating committee functioned. A permanent shortage of transportation, maintenance facilities, regular gasoline, tires, spare parts, and manpower compelled each scheme to undergo unanticipated permutations. As in other areas, military demands superseded even war industry requirements of the highest priority.[44] Adding to the carrying capacity of river and other inland water routes was bruited about as a viable alternative or supplement to pipeline and rail transport. But the dedication of scarce materials to tugboat and barge construction would, it was feared, diminish the fabrication of landing craft at Evansville, Indiana, and other places. Had time permitted, an objective evaluation of the best oil transportation package could have been conducted. As it was, a massive pipeline construction program afforded the simplest solution. No one knew whether the use of 700,000 tons of steel for the two lines moved more petroleum per ton of steel consumed than the employment of that steel in other forms of transport.

Shifting exigencies forestalled the evolution of a master transportation plan along the lines of World War I. As the European war ground to a halt in spring 1945, attention shifted to the Pacific theater and the dismaying prospect of a costly invasion of the Japanese home islands. PAW and ODT initiated discussions regarding a Texas-California pipeline, finally rejecting it as uneconomical. Both agencies assumed that tanker construction would escalate. However, in spring 1945, Vinson at the Office of War Mobilization and Reconversion decided to cut tanker construction by half, insisting over the objections

TABLE 14. *Movement of Oil into District 1, in Selected Periods, 1942–1945*
(thousand barrels per day)

	Total	By all pipelines	By Big and Little Inch	All-rail	All-ocean	Other water
1942 (Jan)	1,472	63	0	99	1,269	43
1942 (Dec)	1,074	158	0	740	112	64
1943 (Dec)	1,553	472	321	656	325	99
1944 (Dec)	1,746	740	531	523	376	108
1945[1]	1,815	733	520	505	451	127

[1] Average first six months.

Source: PAW, *A History of the PAW, 1941–1945* (Washington, D.C.: GPO, 1946), 433, 437, 449.

of PAW and ODT and the shipping interests that sufficient transportation was already available. PAW and ODT frantically sought to divert rail tank cars to the West, precipitating resistance from eastern interests who feared fuel shortages or some competitive disadvantage. As the agencies and regions stockpiled ammunition for another round in their war, the dropping of two atomic bombs forced the Japanese to surrender.[45]

Rationing and Fuel Conversion Programs

As fuel shortages spread along the Atlantic Coast in June and July 1941, PAW pleaded with consumers to limit their fuel use. PAW Recommendations Nos. 1, 4, and 6 and WPB Limitation Order L-8 (see above, p. 319) issued in August and September, did not succeed in restricting the distribution of motor fuel in the Atlantic Coast area. Gasoline consumption actually rose, and refiners chose not to increase their output of fuel oil. From the outset, Ickes warned Atlantic Coast residents of the inevitability of some form of rationing should voluntarism produce unsatisfactory savings. A feisty public refused to budge from its habits, ignoring exhortations to cut service station hours and drive less for pleasure. Orders to prevent the construction of new retail stations went unheeded.

Anticipating the failure of voluntarism, federal officials planned mandatory programs to effect the necessary conservation. Two agenda items dominated the numerous meetings during pre-Pearl Harbor days. One focused on the form rationing would take—that it would come was not disputed. The other centered upon a program to compel fuel oil users (and in some places natural gas users) to convert to coal and included a contingency plan to restrict electric consumption.[46] Both programs posed unprecedented administrative and logistical difficulties, requiring the careful coordination of activities by agencies that viewed one another as competitors rather than as home-front units engaged in a common cause.

Jurisdictional jealousies repeatedly intruded both before and after program implementation. OPA and PAW clashed over the rationing system, offering irreconcilable formulas for the achievement of equity in the distribution of fuels and vying for precedence in controlling the flow of petroleum to terminals (refiners in the critical areas were considered terminals) and distributors.[47] Similarly, several agencies professed a stake in the fuel substitution scheme because it implied the diversion of strategic materials from military hardware to coal-burning equipment and because it rested upon the assumption that sufficient coal could be produced and delivered to those who converted. Lastly, both programs required a degree of coercion that Americans were not used to. Since the demand for energy differed from one type of user to another and from one region to another, both programs imposed somewhat greater sacrifices upon some individuals, institutions, and regions than upon others, unleashing the predictable lamentations of the unfavored.[48]

Weak compliance mechanisms and uncertain authority explain the ineffectiveness of L-8, shortcomings corrected after Pearl Harbor by congressional delegation to the president of broad powers over materials. PAW and OPA, however, tendered conflicting schemes as to how best to apply the new power. To OPA, gasoline or tires or fuel oil were but commodities similar to many others and susceptible to user rationing. PAW, however, claimed pool-to-pump jurisdiction and would not relinquish control over distribution. Ickes developed a conservation package that protected his fiefdom and included rationing through distributor and retailer control over user supply, the substitution of coal for oil, and the easing of eastern scarcity by the construction of new pipelines. PAW's initial prognosis for conversion-induced savings anticipated the conversion of 300,000 of 1.2 million domestic oil burners in use in the northeast and the annual savings of 45 million barrels of oil by householders and industry. This was so extraordinarily optimistic that it might best be considered a tactic designed to weaken OPA's case for coupon rationing.[49]

By April 1942, WPB had decided to introduce the OPA gasoline rationing plan in July. Employing first a card system and then a coupon book system, the local rationing board assigned each user to a priority category based on need. Each coupon represented a gallonage value that could be raised or lowered as supply warranted. Once this basic decision was reached, the fuel conversion program became more or less disassociated from rationing. The decision, however, did not resolve the jurisdictional controversy between OPA and PAW. Remaining at issue was control of the flow from terminal operators through the many channels at the supplier level to the retail outlets.[50]

The dispute between OPA and PAW swirled around conflicting perceptions of how to achieve a fair distribution and resulted in the issuance of contradictory directives to suppliers. OPA's Gasoline Rationing Order No. 5 (and amendments), first issued on 11 May 1942, and Fuel Oil Rationing Order No. 11, effective in October and also employing the coupon system, mandated that each dealer receive a volume of fuel equal to coupon flow-back. In other words, the total gallonage represented by the coupons turned in by buyers determined the volume of new fuel supplied to a distributor or retailer. PAW's Directive No. 59, issued in September 1942, and frequently amended, established quotas for both the Atlantic states and the primary distributors within the region. It did not cover jobbers or retailers. They were covered by PAW Order No. 1, issued in December 1942. Initially, both regulations stipulated that the region and its dealers receive a fixed proportion of the gallonage sold during calendar year 1941. By adopting the historical base standard, PAW hoped to preserve existing competitive relationships which OPA's procedures would disturb. According to PAW, OPA's system favored the larger distributors and the retail outlets of the majors and large chains. OPA asserted that the purpose of rationing was to assure an equitable and orderly distribution to coupon holders and not to freeze competitive relationships, a consideration irrelevant to the war effort.

These two formulas were essentially imcompatible. Only gradually, imperfectly, and after resistance by PAW, were the two agencies able to synchronize their procedures. Their dichotomous approaches caused much confusion and in large measure explain the pestering anomalies that characterized fuel rationing and that inconvenienced and irritated innumerable consumers.

WPB accepted OPA's reasoning and, over Ickes's objections, suspended its distribution orders in favor of OPA's regulations. Unfortunately, WPB chose not to resolve fully the roiling jurisdictional conflict.[51] While PAW had lost out at the final point of sale, both agencies persisted in exercising total authority over dealer supply. PAW habitually ignored the coupon value of gasoline or fuel oil and provided a volume based upon its own calculations of a justifiable supply in a particular area. OPA, for its part, exerted but shaky control over regional and local price administrators who frequently permitted deliveries in excess of coupon value. In the absence of coordination, regional supplies frequently bore no relationship to the aggregate value of coupons in circulation. In places where the amount of gasoline available exceeded coupon value, consumers complained that rationing was unnecessary. In less favored places where coupon value exceeded supply, consumers called it a fraud.[52]

Initially, rationing was applied only to the East and Pacific Northwest, a minor victory for Ickes who insisted that PAW distribution restrictions adequately controlled consumption in other regions and that rationing in the heartland would not increase the fuel available along either coast. Whatever the accuracy of this position relative to total fuel supplies, it demonstrated the insensitivity of PAW to obvious political liabilities. Easterners howled about the magnitude of their sacrifices. Gasoline and transportation shortages as well as the need to conserve rubber led OPA in 1943 to extend the system throughout the nation. Ickes and midwesterners accused OPA of knuckling under to eastern politicians.[53]

In February 1943, Ickes floated a plan whereby WPB delegated all authority over rationing to PAW which then subdelegated it to OPA.[54] This focused authority in a single agency, dispersal being the target of much criticism, and assured PAW primacy in determining dealer supplies. Ickes interpreted the executive order establishing PAW as vesting it with responsibility for determining the timing, coverage, and amount of petroleum product rationing. The serious shortages of winter 1942–43 were compounded in their impact, Ickes claimed, by the incompetence of local rationing boards to establish priorities among competing industrial users of fuel oil. Moreover, local boards irresponsibly increased coupon values above the aggregate amount of gasoline available in their territory. Ickes belabored OPA for its intention to remove the ban on pleasure driving along the East Coast—instituted in January 1943 and revoked three months later—and its indifference to PAW steps to eliminate the use of credit cards for gasoline purchases and lower speed limits to 35 miles per hour. "Distribution programs and policies must be uniform," Ickes instructed Nelson, "and the agency responsible for supply must have unimpeded authority to prescribe such policies."[55]

Prentiss Brown, OPA chief, refuted Ickes on all points, claiming that coupon and flow-back rationing had reduced fuel consumption dramatically, achieving savings of 40 percent in heating oil use and 34 percent in gasoline use in District 1, whereas earlier limitation orders had produced paltry results. He categorically denied PAW imputations of irresponsibility in establishing coupon values, pointing to the shortcomings in PAW supply estimates and the intrusion of various factors in particular districts that warranted changes in coupon values. Brown strongly defended the local boards as more likely to make fair decisions than self-interested refiners and distributors. The civilian supply function, Brown averred, "is not likely to be effectively performed if split up among commodity czars."[56]

In the end, Nelson backed off from Ickes's plan, scrapping a policy statement drafted in March that conformed to Ickes's proposals. The opinion of Julius A. Krug, program vice-chairman at WPB, weighed heavily in Nelson's decision. Krug advocated the retention of the status quo and the establishment of an interagency Petroleum Rationing Policy Committee to arbitrate all disputes. ODT and the Bureau of the Budget also questioned the wisdom of enhancing the power of an agency that represented an industry. A WPB release of 2 July 1943, announcing the formation of the new committee, defined the new policy:

> Maintenance of petroleum supply and its distribution down to and including the retail outlet will continue to be the responsibility of the Petroleum Administrator for War. Quotas for the various rationed areas are to follow the pattern of rationed demand as shown by returned used coupons.[57]

What the first sentence bestowed, the second sentence swept away. Aside from a new committee, the prewar status quo prevailed.[58]

I have been unsuccessful in sorting out the relative merits of the claims advanced by OPA for flow-back rationing and by PAW for historical quotas. Within the industry, small and independent dealers complained of inadequate price margins and their inability to obtain delivery of their legal allotments. Some dealers attributed delivery problems to a concerted effort by the majors to monopolize transportation between refineries and terminals and retailers, thereby bypassing independent jobbers and guaranteeing supplies to the brand-name outlets. Tank truck fleets, such as those owned by the Texas Company or Standard Indiana, were more likely to receive some portion of their gasoline, tire, and spare part requirements than were the individual truckers who hauled fuel from jobbers to independent retailers. These disadvantages reduced sales at small outlets which then received a smaller flow-back volume, thus fostering inequity. Davies justified the historical quotas as a means of preserving small oil businesses. On the other hand, PAW's chief counsel, J. Howard Marshall, admitted in an in-house memo that historical quotas benefited primary suppliers but disregarded the needs of resellers and consumers. A formula that divides supplies on a historical basis, Marshall observed, "inevitably results in a failure of supply for some customers."[59] On the whole, interested parties outside the industry preferred coupon rationing and flow-back to oil industry rationing and historical quotas.

PAW and OPA ardently desired mastery over petroleum rationing. Fuel conversion, in contrast, while launched enthusiastically by PAW, SFAW, OPA, and WPB, soon became a millstone around their necks. Commitment to this program waxed and waned in each agency as they labored under their own moons. Throughout the last half of 1941, both PAW and WPB articulated the belief that oil-to-coal conversions would produce large savings and, operating in conjunction with limitation orders, obviate the need for stricter forms of rationing. In spite of the clamor against the scheme emanating from oil burner manufacturers and other sectors of the oil industry, WPB and PAW pushed ahead.[60] In March 1942, WPB issued LO L-56 which limited the installation of oil burning equipment and lowered fuel deliveries to East Coast and Pacific Northwest consumers with convertible equipment. During this period, SFAW, OPA, and military personnel were less sanguine concerning the program and warned of anticipated coal transportation bottlenecks, partly the result of the expanded use of railroads in crude oil transport, a shrinking supply of mine labor, and conflicting claims for strategic materials.[61]

By summer 1942, PAW's failure to prevent coupon and flow-back rationing for gasoline and the intent of WPB and OPA to impose fuel oil rationing in the fall noticeably weakened its crusading fervor for conversions. While PAW had estimated in 1941 that 25 percent of domestic oil heating units were convertible, Ickes in June 1942 lowered that figure to under 10 percent. Perhaps he was influenced by such state studies as Connecticut's which concluded that "comparatively few . . . heating units . . . could be converted to . . . bituminous."[62] But even as Ickes and Nelson questioned the viability of conversion, operating units persisted in the promotion of fuel substitution in the face of severe equipment deficiences and accumulating evidence of impending coal shortages. Mixed signals from Washington confused all involved at the local level, particularly coal dealers who were responsible for attesting to the convertibility of domestic equipment.[63]

Without warning, OPA issued an order in January 1943 that directed local rationing boards to compel the conversion of nonresidential building by withholding fuel oil rations. Oil users in the Middle Atlantic states shouted out against such coercion. PAW and SFAW scrambled to procure coal for the new consumers. PAW hastily issued interim Order No. 3, applying a rigorous definition of essential fuel oil use. OPA's unilateral action forced consideration of program practicality to the surface. The interested agencies quickly established a Conversion Policy Committee which, in April, undertook a comprehensive study of the availability of coal and equipment for conversion purposes in the heating season 1943–44. Its pessimistic findings prompted the suspension of the conversion program in September 1943.[64]

During the operational life of the conversion policy, its ramifications extended to electric power use and to natural gas use in the Mid-Continent and Appalachian regions. In September 1942, WPB promulgated LO L-94 which restricted the use of electricity in order to conserve fuel. Julius Krug, then head of WPB's power division, formulated and administered these restrictions, initially with the support of PAW and SFAW and then in the face of their growing hostility and the opposition of the utilities, electric users, and segments of the coal industry.[65] At first, PAW viewed L-94 as a way of reducing fuel oil consumption and of saving coal for use in the conversion program. But Krug's brand of bureaucratic imperialism soon alienated Ickes just as it had already antagonized FPC. PAW and SFAW soon perceived L-94, temporary brownout orders in 1942, and the national brownout mandate, Utilities Order U-9 of January 1945, as damaging to coal production and inconsequential as conservation measures.[66]

Efforts to rationalize fuel use by identifying user priorities collapsed in the Mid-Continent and Appalachian regions when unanticipated shortages of natural gas occurred in early 1942. Scarcity in Texas, Oklahoma, and Kansas forced WPB to issue LO L-31 in February 1942, curtailing natural gas consumption and forbidding new hookups. Orders to convert to coal proved impossible to enforce because sufficient coal was simply not available. Gas pipeline companies, with Krug's support, demanded materials for the construction of new pipelines from, as an example, the Hugoton field to Detroit. Eliciting a stream of protests from the coal industry, these proposals also collided with the steel requirements of the Big and Little Inch oil pipelines. PAW was already tearing up gas pipelines for reuse as oil pipelines. In January 1943, PAW Order No. 6 prohibited the drilling of new gas wells in the Hugoton and Panhandle fields.[67]

Senator Truman understood very well that people in Independence,

Missouri, stood to lose from forcible conversion. Senators Clyde M. Reed of Kansas and Kenneth S. Wherry of Nebraska feared the spread of hardship among some of their constituents. Pressure from such influential men compelled WPB and the fuel agencies to compromise their oil conservation program. As the *Kansas City Star* had predicted in September 1943, PAW speedily obtained WPB approval, authorized by amendments to L-31 and L-56, to permit conversion from coal- and gas-burning equipment to fuel oil.[68] Many agencies tinkered with fuel supply, but a grasp of the entire situation and authority to devise a program reflective of the actual availability of fuel eluded them all.

Putting PAW to Sleep

PAW's grand design to ensconce itself as the uncontested master of petroleum, regulating each stage through which oil flowed from wells to ultimate consumers, was consistently frustrated by Roosevelt's penchant for authority dispersed among competing agencies. Ickes and Davies jousted with a coalition of adversaries far more powerful than that confronting Harry A. Garfield during World War I. Compared with Garfield, Ickes managed a disarticulated fuel program: Petroleum was separated from coal, and at least three agencies planted their banners in the natural gas fields; a different agency administered maximum price policies; authority over distribution and end-use was diffused and subject to the penultimate decisions of WPB; and the requisite flexibility, possessed by Garfield and William G. McAdoo, to fashion a nationwide transportation system was missing.

Byrnes and Vinson as coordinate chiefs of staff for domestic mobilization hewed faithfully to the president's wishes concerning the delegation of authority among the numerous wartime agencies. WPB, initially regarded as the premier war mobilization office, while retaining its authority over materials allocation, gradually relinquished to the Office of War Mobilization its role as court of last resort in resolving disputes between various interests. But this diminution of WPB's status bestowed no advantages upon PAW. Too many other peer agencies blocked Ickes at every turn. A leading principle of bureaucratic politics posits as a primary objective the defense and maintenance, if not the enhancement, of original jurisdiction. Several agencies ganged up on the truculent Ickes in late 1942 to prevent the formation of a more powerful PAW. OPA displayed adeptness in defending its price and distribution powers against PAW incursions. Not even the exploitation of congressional antipathy toward OPA or the marshaling of the political power of the oil industry proved sufficient to compel the allied bureaucracies to grant concessions to PAW. Each office erected a high wall to contain its power and prevent its escape. New ideas seldom penetrated the barrier, and concessions to the opinions of others slipped (or sneaked) out even less frequently.

Ickes and his colleague-competitors sought efficiency in the production and use of materials critical to the war effort while simultaneously attempting to buffer the civilian sector against severe shortages of basic goods and runaway inflation. Most disagreements erupted over means rather than ends. Byrnes, Nelson, and Ickes promoted increased oil production. Ickes and the oil producers agreed upon crude price increases as the most efficient method of stimulating new finds and greater production. OWM, WPB, and OPA, concerned primarily with moderating inflationary pressure, offered indirect subsidies to producers. Some operational disputes, tanker space allocation as an example, simply went unresolved. Other areas of disagreement produced compromises, as in the case of the executive order of December 1942, that fell far short of PAW's initial demands. Still other points of contention, control over distribution comes to mind, called forth a species of jargon that must have left everyone befuddled. In such programs as pipeline construction or the creation of an aviation gasoline industry, PAW succeeded in establishing full control by convincing WPB of the short-term urgency of those ventures, this in the face of opposition from many who deplored their potential for further concentration within the industry.

These and other programs were quickly terminated following V-J Day. PAW's leaders had offered assurances to the oil industry and others that the agency harbored no ambition to perpetuate itself into the postwar period. In late August, PAW began lifting its controls and disbanding its many committees, a process virtually completed by late fall. Price controls on oil remained until 1946 as part of a general effort by President Truman to stem inflation, but PAW ceased making price recommendations to OPA as soon as the war ended. Ickes, and Davies after his chief resigned in February 1946, speedily wound up PAW's business, the agency being officially terminated in May 1946.[69] PAW did play a secondary role in the period between March and October 1945 when a series of strikes by refinery workers closed down 45 percent of the nation's refining capacity and threatened a severe oil shortage. But aside from recommending federal seizure, PAW launched no new operational initiatives.[70]

While closing one shop, Ickes laid plans to open another that would maintain a federal role in fuels; after Ickes's resignation, Davies pursued Ickes's plan to establish an oil and gas division within Interior. During the last days of PAW, Davies identified the PAW functions that could be passed on to the new unit. Truman, by executive order in June 1946, established such a division and appointed Davies's protege, Max Ball, as director. But the division was not endowed with the broad authority that Ickes had suggested.[71]

Much to his credit, the wartime course set by Ickes was motivated by long-term concerns as well as the needs of the moment. In letters of 1 and 8 December 1941, Ickes directed Roosevelt's attention to the question of domestic petroleum reserves. The secretary forcefully articulated the conviction that national security demanded the formulation of a national oil policy that encompassed foreign as well as domestic reserves.[72] In 1943, this became an even more critical issue as the oil surpluses accrued during the depression ran out and withdrawals surpassed the discovery of new reserves. PAW's application of the maximum efficient rate of recovery to each producing field could not be sustained even with the cooperation of state regulatory authorities. The fear of depleted reserves, not during the war but in some not too distant future, explains Ickes's relentless efforts to raise crude oil prices and provide equipment to drillers.

Doubts about America's future oil reserves underlay Ickes's active sponsorship of a leading role for the Department of Interior in the formulation of postwar resource and energy policies. Midway through the war, these nagging doubts stimulated his energetic advocacy of the Petroleum Reserves Corporation (PRC), an Arabian-American oil pipeline, and an Anglo-American oil treaty. Without sacrificing Ickes's trust, Davies strenuously opposed both PRC and the Arabian pipeline. The threat of a broadened federal role implicit in those proposals did, however, fracture the tenuous relationship forged between Ickes and powerful segments of the oil industry. PRC became anathema to the majors while independents and many majors nurtured an implacable hostility toward the Anglo-American treaty negotiated in 1944. The opposition of the major oil companies to the threat of federal intervention in the exploitation of foreign, particularly Middle Eastern, oil fields, the animosity of the independents toward any agreement that promised increased imports of foreign oil, and general Senate antipathy toward international trade agreements assured the failure of the treaty in 1947. But the issues so disturbing to the independents remained, surfacing again during the debates of the mid-1950s over the expedience of imposing oil import quotas.[73]

Nash claims that the wartime achievement in oil was possible "only because of a cooperative relationship of government and industry."[74]

In fact, the oil industry had no choice but to accede to the demands of the government, accommodate to a system imposed upon them, and, in general, temper their criticism of federal policy. True, small and independent oil firms frequently vented their anger at wartime practices they viewed as damaging to their competitive position. The more powerful elements within the industry, however, had little cause for complaint. The system of contracts, subsidies, and rebates fed them liberally while the various regulations did nothing to diminish their economic strength. But the self-imposed and prudent silence of leading elements of the oil industry ended with the establishment of PRC and subsequent decisions concerning foreign oil policies.

Ickes employed the rhetoric of cooperation but believed in the necessity of coercion just as he had during the depression. He was, however, forced by the steady state of emergency that accompanied his long tenure in office to concede more to the larger units of the oil industry than he, perhaps, wished. Independents viewed him as an adversary for almost fourteen years while the majors, overall, considered him acceptable. More often than not, the majors were able to accommodate to his views without sacrificing their corporate interests. Smaller firms possessed less flexibility. Ickes was inevitably drawn to the majors during the war, not by their patriotism but by their command over such a large proportion of the productive resources of the industry. He neither liked nor trusted the majors. But lacking the antitrust ideology that fortified a La Follette or a Borah, Ickes favored the majors because he needed them.

FOURTEEN

Wartime Administration of Solid Fuels

IN JULY 1940, the National Resources Planning Board recommended the implementation of an emergency system to forestall coal shortages and runaway coal prices. The report of NRPB recalled the experience of 1914–18 when transportation shortages of escalating severity finally compelled the issuance of the Closing Order of January 1918. To avoid a replication of the lightless and heatless days of the winter of 1917–18, NRPB advised the immediate increase in the coal carrying capacity of the railroads, especially those serving eastern terminals currently supplied by coastal shipping. NRPB emphasized the urgency of coordinating production and transportation, guaranteeing equity in distribution, and fixing maximum coal prices, powers lodged in the Bituminous Coal Division (BCD) by the Bituminous Coal Act of 1937.[1]

Others in 1940 and in 1941—Assistant Secretary of War Louis Johnson, Secretary of Interior Harold L. Ickes, the BCD director, Harold A. Gray, the industry Coal Advisory Committee of BCD— invoked similar memories in counseling the speedy establishment of an emergency coal administration. Predictably, these warnings went unheeded until after the first fuel supply crisis struck in the summer of 1941. One month before Pearl Harbor, Roosevelt designated Ickes as solid fuels coordinator. The authorizing letter of 5 November 1941 limited the new office to study and advisory responsibilities and subordinated it to the Office of Production Management.

These arrangements, entirely unsatisfactory to Ickes, lasted until April 1943, when a coal strike and the refusal of Congress to extend the second Guffey Act, thus terminating BCD, prompted the president

348

to issue an executive order endowing the Solid Fuels Administration for War (SFAW) with a modicum of permanence and authority. The executive order, however, sufficiently delimited the jurisdiction of SFAW to avoid jeopardizing the preeminence of the War Production Board or the peer status of other agencies. From April 1943 until the end of the war, SFAW's career mirrored that of PAW. Ickes and Harold Gray, deputy administrator of SFAW, contested with OPA over price policies and rationing. In both disputes the results were clear-cut. OPA's price-fixing authority superseded that of BCD's and was invulnerable to the challenges of SFAW while the latter fashioned and administered a rationing system impervious to the influence of OPA. Along the way, SFAW jousted with other agencies for the control of various programs.[2]

The Coal Supply Crisis of 1941–1942

By 1940, coal's share of aggregate energy consumption had shrunk from a peak of 77 percent in 1910 to about 50 percent; during the wartime years, it increased, by 1944, about six percentage points (SFAW figures) or remained relatively stable (as Schurr and Netschert suggest).[3] But shrinkage resumed during the first postwar decade. Coal's share of total Btu consumption dropped to 37 percent in 1950 and then to 29 percent in 1955. Petroleum and natural gas provided a stable share—about 41 percent—of the nation's energy needs during the war, but their portion rose to 53 percent in 1950 and reached 62 percent by 1955. Anthracite use declined more precipitously than bituminous. By 1950, anthracite production was only slightly more than half the tonnage mined in 1926 and a bit above two-thirds of wartime production. Bituminous production in 1950 stood at about five-sixths of the peak wartime production year and equaled the average annual production for the three years 1927–29 (see Table 11).

While anthracite production contracted rapidly, the proportion of anthracite burned by various consumers remained about the same, with 80 percent used in residential heating. After World War I, shipments of anthracite west of Pennsylvania diminished and, by 1940, 92 percent of total production warmed 6 million homes in Pennsylvania, New York, New Jersey, Delaware, Maryland, and Washington, D. C.; in those states anthracite fueled 54 percent of all domestic heating units. The primary consumers of bituminous changed gradually between 1929 (see Table 3) and 1944 and then drastically after the war (Table 15). In 1929, railroad and retail deliveries accounted for 253 million tons (mt), or 47 percent of total production (see Table 11); by

1953, those two consumer groups required only 89 mt, or 19 percent of production. Dieselization and electrification of railroads and the conversion of residential and commercial users to other fuels had severely reduced two of coal's principal markets. The greatly increased burning of coal to generate electricity—from 43 mt in 1929 to 112 mt in 1953—replaced only a fraction of the loss in railroad, residential, and commercial use.

TABLE 15. *Consumption of Bituminous Coal,*
by Consuming Groups, in Selected Years, 1929–1953
(percentage of total production)

	1929	1938	1943	1944	1953
Exports	1	<1	4	5	<1
Coke, beehive, and by-product	17	13	17	17	25
Electric utilities	8	10	12	13	25
Other industrial	23	31	24	23	27
Railroads	24	21	22	22	6
Delivered by retailers	23	20	21	20	13

Sources: Above Chapter 7, Table 13; Herbert E. Risser, *The Economics of the Coal Industry* (Lawrence: Bureau of Business Research, School of Business, University of Kansas, 1958), 54; Bituminous Coal Use, 1943–1944, Correspondence with Federal Agencies, WPB, January–March 1945, SFAW, RG 245.

Shifts also occurred in the regional consumption of soft coal as population rose or fell, as technological and other factors influenced rates of industrial growth, and as coal users switched to other fuels. Regional use patterns, displayed in Table 16, reflected more moderate changes than did use by consuming groups. Between 1917 (with production at 552 mt) and 1946 (with production at 534 mt), consumption in the Middle Atlantic states declined from 161 mt to 128 mt, and use in New England and the West North Central states fell from 89 mt to 68 mt. Meanwhile, coal use in the East North Central states rose from 188 mt to 230 mt. Changes in other regions were negligible. In all regions east of the Mississippi, the war fostered slight gains in coal use or protected against further contraction.[4]

TABLE 16. *Consumption of Bituminous Coal, by Regions, in Selected Years, 1917–1946[1]*
(percentage of total production)

	1917	1918	1929	1937	1943	1946
New England	5.9	5.4	4.7	4.5	5.4	4.9
Middle Atlantic	29.2	27.8	25.7	24.3	24.4	24.0
East North Central	34.1	36.0	41.2	41.5	41.8	43.0
West North Central	10.3	9.6	9.6	9.8	7.8	7.8
South Atlantic	8.0	8.3	7.9	9.6	10.1	10.6
East South Central	6.5	6.4	5.8	6.0	6.8	6.3
All other[2]	6.9	6.5	5.1	4.3	3.7	3.4

[1] Excludes railroad and steamship coal.

[2] Includes West South Central, Mountain, and Pacific states.

Sources: SFAW, "Report of War Activities, Revised to September, 1945," Mimeographed, Box 701, History of the Coal Agencies, SFAW, RG 245; Herbert E. Risser, *The Economics of the Coal Industry* (Lawrence: Bureau of Business Research, School of Business, University of Kansas, 1958), 146.

During World War I, coal served as the principal domestic, industrial, and transportation fuel. By World War II, while the quantity of coal burned had changed only marginally, the nation consumed two times more energy than in 1910. Although the relative importance of coal had diminished, it remained essential to electric utilities, steel, rolling mills, cement, railroads, and millions of households. Thus, NRPB and other agencies pressed for emergency coal planning in 1940 and 1941; and in spite of the inadequate powers over coal vested in OPM and BCD, the nation escaped the recurrence of a coal famine comparable to that of 1917. Coal shortages of greater severity occurred in 1942 and thereafter, but SFAW and WPB exercised sufficiently effective controls to avoid a crisis of the magnitude of 1917 even when coal strikes in 1943 closed down thousands of mines.

In April 1941, a coal strike precipitated the first coal emergency. Hardly had the mines reopened when the tanker loan forced the diversion of railroad rolling stock to the transportation of petroleum to eastern terminals. Between July and October 1941, delays in delivery depleted the coal stocks of steel and other plants in Pennsylvania and the lower Great Lakes states. BCD and Interior cooperated with OPM in recommending orders to ICC for the rerouting of coal to specific consumers. Shortages in New England and other tidewater markets and in the upper Great Lakes states never reached anticipated proportions: Coal production increased rapidly in May and June; large consumers heeded the admonitions of federal officials to order early and stock larger quantities; the railroads still possessed some unused carrying capacity in 1941; and unseasonably warm weather persisted into December. By November, when SFAW was organized, this particular emergency had evaporated. As deputy administrator Gray recognized, however, anticipated increases in demand for coal by defense industries and the exhaustion of surplus railroad carrying capacity would certainly aggravate distribution problems even if war could be avoided. Pearl Harbor assured that the weaknesses in coal transportation and distribution visible in mid-1941 would be quickly and greatly exacerbated.[5]

The brief mid-1941 coal crisis identified the weak links in the nation's coal supply network. SFAW inherited masses of data from BCD and the bituminous coal commissions. By 7 December, SFAW's staff, consisting largely of loaners from BCD, USGS, and the Bureau of Mines, had outlined a program to deal with actual and predicted exigencies. Acting as WPB's agent, SFAW implemented programs to moderate the impact of submarine interdiction of the collier fleet upon tidewater coal docks, to provision the upper Great Lakes, and to deal with supply shortages in the Pacific Northwest. Special programs were devised to channel fuel supplies to the critical regions by all available carriers and over routes not normally traversed.[6]

At the start of the war, New England produced no coal but consumed 22 mt annually while the West North Central states produced 11 mt but consumed 34 mt.[7] Pennsylvania accounted for most of the 140 mt mined in the Middle Atlantic states, which consumed 114 mt. The East North Central states burned 182 mt while producing 131 mt. The deficit for these northern regions totaled about 59 mt annually during the war. The South Atlantic states used 47 mt while producing 198 mt. The East South Central states consumed 32 mt and produced 110 mt. A surplus of 229 mt was available in the southern states east of the Mississippi. For all of the above regions, then, a surplus of 170 mt remained from which must be deducted virtually an equal amount consumed by railroads, steamships, and exports. Although coal use was of minimal importance in most parts of the western third of the country, special attention was given to utilizing the surplus production of the Mountain states to meet demands in the Pacific Northwest and some of the Plains states.

Leaving the western states out of the calculation for the moment, this accounting reflects an extremely tight supply-demand situation, one that verged upon crisis proportions as oil shortages along the East Coast prompted the initiation of the oil-to-coal conversion program and as war production engendered larger demands for coal. These supply-demand estimates also suggest the essence of the transportation dilemma. Coal from Kentucky and West Virginia, providing 36 percent of total production in 1944, had to be routed into Michigan, Wisconsin, Minnesota, and the Dakotas as well as toward tidewater docks for delivery to coastal states.

As had USFA during World War I, SFAW sought to balance the needs of New England and the upper Great Lakes and High Plains states. In establishing priorities, SFAW exposed itself to criticism from both regions, each of which felt discriminated against. As SFAW routed more southern coal into the North, northern operators immediately attacked the coal agency for fostering unfair competition, resurrecting an issue that had agitated the coal industry since 1919. Nothing in the extant documents lends credence to assertions that SFAW favored southern operators or that the agency exerted itself more forcefully to move coal to New England than to the upper midwestern states. Most war industry and the largest concentrations of urban population were located in the nation's northeastern quadrant.

New England burned about 26 mt of coal in 1944, up from the 19 mt consumed in both 1939 and 1940. In the latter year, tidewater arrivals accounted for 70 percent and all-rail for 30 percent. The German submarine menace greatly reduced receipts by colliers from Hampton Roads, compelling a substantial shift of deliveries from Hampton Roads to New York harbor where tugs and barges made the short trip to Boston and other New England ports and to all-rail which cost much more than delivery by collier.

Delivery figures for 1942 and 1943 attest to the success of SFAW and the transportation office in rearranging coal routing. Shipments from Hampton Roads were reduced by over 5 million tons; rail-water movement through New York increased by 3 million tons. All-rail deliveries to New England rose by 60 percent to 11 mt, or about 50 percent of receipts. In 1943, Hampton Roads deliveries fell by another 1.2 mt while the rail-water and all-rail routes rose by 2.2 mt. Altogether about 12 mt arrived in New England by rail and another 5.6 mt partly by rail. This shift required the use of 218,000 more coal cars than were employed in 1940.

Lake vessels carried 27 mt of coal in 1917 and 50 mt in 1941. By

1940, the share of lake cargo coal supplied by northern mines had fallen to 34 percent, compared with 63 percent during the early 1920s. War-engendered increases in demand were initially met by production increases in the southern Appalachian districts, which possessed the capability to supply the lake trade if unimpeded but could not provide sufficient high volatile coals to eastern industries at the same time. An expanded production of northern coal could satisfy a portion of lake demand but not all. By mid-1942, SFAW was inching toward a definition of priorities that diverted southern Appalachian coal eastward and reduced the lake shipment of coal for nonessential uses, largely residential and commercial. Lake cargo dock operators and southern Appalachian operators complied only fitfully with this plan until SFAW received authority in 1943 to institute a fully controlled distribution program. Until that time, OPA exploited SFAW's inability to obtain voluntary compliance by promoting a full-fledged coupon rationing system for coal. The lake supply problem was further complicated in mid-1942 by the assignment of many coal vessels to ore-carrying duties, a decision originating with WPB and ODT and futilely opposed by Gray.[8]

Well before the infusion of new authority into SFAW, that agency formulated distribution programs that achieved some success. Working through ODT, SFAW gave lake coal preferential treatment during the months prior to the official closing of lake navigation on 30 November. ODT guaranteed the availability of transport to move coal to New England after the lake shipping season ended. New Englanders fretted about this during each summer and fall because coal receipts invariably lagged behind peacetime norms for those months and because their region was a primary target in the oil conversion program. Lake dock operators in Detroit and elsewhere and consumers in Duluth and the Twin Cities feared that arrivals would be inadequate to carry them through the winter. Some suggested the greater use of railroads to meet Lake Superior requirements, but railroad unloading facilities were not available. SFAW promoted heavy early ordering by consumers dependent upon the lakes, a vast area from Michigan west to the Dakotas and south to eastern Nebraska and Kansas. Not everyone heeded this advice. Ickes admonished Gov. Payne H. Ratner of Kansas for the complacency of Kansans toward the war and fuel shortages. In turn, Ratner and Mayor John B. Gage of Kansas City, Missouri, questioned the accuracy of Ickes's estimates of coal supplies available to the Mid-Continent, emphasizing in particular the serious and intensifying scarcity of natural gas in the region.[9] Each region perceived its contributions to the war effort as of cardinal importance and therefore deserving of preferential treatment in the supply of fuels.

To improve lake supply, SFAW developed a program to commence shipments as early as weather permitted. Normally the shipping season opened on 15 April. Shipments prior to that date paid much higher insurance premiums. SFAW negotiated a compensatory plan with the War Shipping Administration, ODT, insurance underwriters, and shippers whereby preseason rates were reduced and the federal government repaid shippers the full cost of additional premiums. By 1944, a similar arrangement was in effect for postseason shipments. Under that scheme, the Maritime Commission provided reinsurance and a subsidy for vessels going forward without assured return cargoes. PAW also supported this program as a means of facilitating the movement of oil to eastern depots. Cold and monotonous duty faced the Coast Guard and other harbor crews responsible for breaking up the ice twenty-four hours a day.[10]

Government subsidies also stimulated coal shipments to New England. In a program modeled upon the compensatory adjustments applied to rail oil freight rates, the federal government paid rebates to northern dealers who brought in southern coals by all-rail or rail-water routes. Initially administered by OPA, these transportation subsidies, amounting to as much as $1.50 per ton, stirred up a clamorous hostility among District 1 producers who viewed it as patently unfair. Northern producers, however, could not guarantee sufficient production to fill New England's demands in addition to normal lake and Mid-Continent coal orders. Southern coal was essential, and federal programs, terminated in September 1946, spurred the movement of this coal into the coastal regions.[11]

A somewhat different mix of incentives was employed to secure an adequate supply of coal for the Pacific Northwest. During normal times, the region produced and consumed about 12 mt annually. However, regional coal production declined in 1941, 1942, and 1943, largely as a result of the drafting of miners and the flight of miners to safer and higher-wage jobs opening up in such cities as Portland and Seattle. By mid-1942, it was clear that regional coal production would fall short of local needs. Compounding the problem was the necessity to curtail fuel oil consumption, the region's primary fuel, as tankers were transferred to the Atlantic Ocean or commandeered for military use. To stimulate the export of the surplus coal production of the Mountain states to the Pacific Northwest, SFAW offered transportation subsidies and awarded delivery preferences to those placing early orders for Colorado and Wyoming coals. To free bituminous for western use, the relaxation of various regulations encouraged the consumption of sub-bituminous (lignite) along the eastern slope of the Rockies and in western Nebraska and Kansas.

In mid-1943, these incentives were combined with a joint Defense Supplies Corporation-SFAW program to purchase and stockpile bituminous for shipment to specific consumers and locales. In 1943, Defense Supplies Corporation (DSC) contracted with southern Colorado producers for over 500,000 tons of coal at a cost of $6.5 million.[12] Similar contracts were then offered to other western producers in 1944 and 1945. As expected, some eastern slope consumers, notably the Union Pacific Railroad, complained of the diminution of bituminous supplies in the western plains area. Eugene McAuliffe, former USFA official and president of the Washington Union Coal Company, a Union Pacific subsidiary, contested the need for regulations that shifted eastern slope coal to the west and impugned the ability of SFAW to comprehend the fuel situation in the Far West. Opposition also surfaced in Denver and Santa Fe, where politicians and coal dealers warned of impending coal shortages in the trans-Missouri expanse.[13]

These incentive programs worked reasonably well until early spring 1943. Intermittent coal strikes between April and November coupled with rising wartime energy demands both at home and in far-flung support and combat zones threw into disarray SFAW's efforts to fine tune coal supply and demand and necessitated the cancellation of PAW's oil conversion program. The utilization by SFAW of subsidies, rebates, government purchasing, and subcontracting reflected, on the one hand, the paucity of coercive powers it possessed and, on the other hand, the agency's dedication to retaining complete responsibility for coal.

SFAW concocted its patchwork program not because other mechanisms, perhaps more efficient and equitable, were unavailable, but because the strongest competing option was rationing controlled by OPA and thus threatening to SFAW's turf, while the second strongest option, some form of zoning, aroused the opposition of the coal industry. SFAW also functioned as the coal industry's advocacy agency and in opposing coupon-flow-back rationing echoed the inflexible rejection of rationing voiced by the Solid Fuels Advisory War Council and other industry groups. By 1943, many commodities were rationed. If applied to coal, rationing would have eliminated the need to lavish special favors upon the coal industry in order to win their cooperation. When, in late 1943, SFAW's authority was expanded, it was immediately put to use to counter OPA's ongoing campaign to ration coal. Thus, SFAW protected producers, distributors, and retailers at the expense of the public, and the jerrybuilt structure of 1942 grew like Simon Rodia's Watts Towers.

The Wartime Production of Coal

Following the economic slump of 1937, bituminous production increased steadily through 1944. Starting from a base of 349 mt in 1938, only 39 mt greater than the output in the worst depression year, 1932, annual tonnage rose by the following amounts: 49 mt in 1939, 66 mt in 1940, 53 mt in 1941, 69 mt in 1942, 7 mt in 1943 (a year of strikes), and 30 mt in 1944 when 620 mt were mined. Anthracite production, at 46 mt in 1938, attained a wartime peak of 61 mt in 1944 (see Table 11). Anthracite output proved less responsive to pressure for expansion because much of its capacity had been abandoned during the late 1920s and the 1930s, partly as a result of the conscious decision of a small number of producers to maintain high prices by limiting output.

Estimates of potential capacity in bituminous mining in 1940–41 ranged from 750 to 850 mt, but a plethora of limiting factors precluded the mining of such large quantities. In fact, SFAW estimates of total coal demand ranged from 550 mt in 1941 and 1942 to 610–630 mt for 1944 and 1945. Actual production closely approximated those estimates, and to that extent SFAW and the mining industry fulfilled their obligations. But serious difficulties arose at the production end which prevented the additional tonnage necessary to sustain the oil conversion program and which, in 1943, resulted in weighty deficits and a dangerous shrinkage of stocks. Factors impinging upon the supply side included: availability of new equipment and maintenance capabilities; official indecision as to the expediency of opening new mines or reopening abandoned mines; a diminishing supply of labor; the volatility of labor-management relations; prices.[14]

SFAW served as coal's claimant agency for spare parts, equipment, capital loans, and labor, operating through WPB and other agencies in much the same way as PAW. But, whereas PAW promoted the interests of an industry that produced goods used directly by the armed forces, the military machine consumed less than one percent of coal supply. Industry, not all war-related, used 74 percent of production, while residential use amounted to 12 percent, commercial and institutional 8 percent, and exports 4 percent. SFAW experienced greater difficulty in substantiating the essentiality of its claims upon finite resources than did PAW when it claimed steel for pipelines or construction materials for the building of aviation gasoline refineries.

Coal industry applications for new equipment or for permission to open new mines or to purchase mines already operating were subjected to close scrutiny, not only by SFAW but by agencies such as the Small War Plants Corporation (the mining branch of the Reconstruction Finance Corporation) and various units within the Departments of the Army and the Navy, as well as WPB. Approval by the latter units did not automatically follow a favorable verdict by SFAW. Industry requests to develop new capacity were investigated in detail. SFAW staff, recalling the experience of World War I when the rapid expansion of capacity contributed to the postwar malaise of the industry, reacted suspiciously to such applications and more often than not withheld approval.[15]

Applications for replacement equipment and parts for operating mines received swifter approval but then, of course, were subject to delays caused by the inability of coal equipment manufacturers to obtain the necessary materials for fabrication. Coal equipment manufacturers pressed for higher priorities and complained angrily about discrimination while assuring PAW that they possessed the capability to provide stokers and other equipment to consumers involved in the oil conversion program. Coal supply constraints finally forced the abandonment of mandatory conversion, a program viewed pessimistically by SFAW not because of potential supply problems but rather because of the lack of equipment. Requests were handled item by item and normally won approval if they promised to enhance production in a region of need and if the advantages of more coal outweighed the expenditure of other critical resources.[16]

Notwithstanding impressive mechanization after World War I, the labor intensiveness of the coal industry further complicated SFAW's task. In 1943, in deep shaft mines machines cut about 90 percent, loaded about 50 percent, and cleaned 25 percent of production. During the war, gains in productivity per man-shift were marginal. Strip mining, less labor intensive than underground operations, increased its proportion of total production from 12 percent in 1940 to 19 percent in 1944. But in the four states of Illinois, Kentucky, Pennsylvania, and West Virginia, accounting for 75 percent of national production, only Illinois matched the national average for surface mining with 21 percent stripped. West Virginia, the largest producer, stripped only 4 percent. Aggregate stripping in the four states contributed 10 percent to production. Surface mining, then, offered little potential for relieving demands upon labor and equipment.[17]

Tens of thousands of miners were vulnerable to the draft and receptive to the enticements of employers in less dangerous industries. Efforts to prohibit miners from changing jobs generally failed even when accompanied by threats of induction. In 1943, the Eastern Coal Company complained that the Kaiser shipyards had recruited twenty-eight families from one of its Kentucky mines. In the same year, Ickes informed Paul V. McNutt, chairman of the War Manpower Commission (WMC), that a government-financed rubber plant at Dunbar, West Virginia, had raided a nearby mine, reducing its work force by 111 men and jeopardizing the production of 50,000 tons annually. From 1941 through 1944, employment in all coal mines declined from 548,000 to 474,000, and the likelihood of an invasion of the Japanese mainland raised the specter of even more severe shrinkage in 1945 and 1946.

To compensate for a depleted labor force, SFAW endeavored in September 1942 to obtain the approval of the United Mine Workers of America and the operators to extend the work week of five days to six and from seven hours daily to eight. Unbelievably fractious negotiations spun on and on through March 1943. Miners covered by UMWA contracts demanded overtime pay for work above thirty-five hours and confronted the stiff resistance of operators. Northern operators and other operators of unionized mines feared widening cost differentials would weaken their competitive position. Both sides dilly-dallied, knowing the contract expired on 31 March 1943 and that a strike was likely. When Ickes tried to sweeten the package for the operators by agreeing to a general price increase, OPA refused to cooperate, arguing that a price adjustment in January 1943 more than covered any increases in cost attending a longer work week. James Byrnes, of the Office of War Mobilization, finally intervened and compelled OPA to raise prices. A forty-eight hour work week commenced when the miners returned to work following the strikes of November 1943.

To reduce the loss of miners to the draft, SFAW engaged in prolonged negotiations with WMC, both as a court of last resort and as an intermediary with General Louis B. Hershey, director of Selective Service, and scores of local draft boards. Agreements with WMC to offer individual and blanket deferments to miners met with loud objections from other unions and some opposition from UMWA. Moreover, local draft boards frequently ignored such agreements and drafted miners when their numbers came up. In 1943, over 30,000 miners entered the armed services. When the army agreed to release ex-miners over the age of thirty-eight, few identified themselves. Apparently, most ex-miners in that age category held rear echelon jobs and considered that duty safer than mining.

With the cooperation of Selective Service, a deferment program was implemented in 1944 which authorized SFAW to certify applications for deferment from miners between the ages of twenty-two and twenty-five with three years experience in a critical task. General Hershey ordered his state directors to comply with this agreement. Extended through February 1945, this program then encountered mounting pressure from the military for termination. SFAW warned WPB of production shortfalls of over 50 mt in 1945 if the labor force was further reduced. A final decision about mine labor had not been reached by V-E Day.[18]

Wildcat strikes, involving 17,000 anthracite miners from twenty-three locals, shut down about one-fourth of anthracite capacity in mid-January 1943. Precipitated by purely local grievances in this first instance, these walkouts reflected the intensifying labor-management hostility that ultimately led to an industry wide strike in April, sporadic wildcat strikes in subsequent months, and a UMWA-sanctioned strike in November. The strikes compelled SFAW to recalculate its vaguely optimistic supply-demand estimates for the coal year 1943–44, which posited a shaky equilibrium, to one anticipating serious deficits in the eastern producing and consuming districts. Expected shortages of anywhere between 20 and 50 mt, including a severe scarcity of metallurgical coals, forced SFAW and WPB to promulgate a series of emergency coal allocation orders to assure the supply of electric utilities, public institutions, and key war plants.[19] On 1 May, Roosevelt issued an executive order authorizing the Secretary of Interior to seize the mines. In July, Ickes established the Coal Mines Administration (CMA) to supervise the seized mines, numbering about 3,800, and maintain production.[20] The April strike somewhat quickened the pace of discussions within the Roosevelt administration concerning the strengthening of SFAW, and the second strike of 1 November served as the final catalyst. On 5 November, two days after a second executive order brought the mines once again under federal control, an executive order established SFAW as a bona fide executive agency, somewhat more autonomous than previously but still subordinate to WPB.[21]

Unlike the operators, the American Federation of Labor, the War Labor Board (WLB), and numerous politicians during these ten months of labor warfare, Ickes eschewed placing the entire blame on the miners or on John L. Lewis, president of UMWA. Ickes assumed the role of chief federal mediator between the disputants and damned both sides when they appeared intransigent. For all the bitter words that had passed between Ickes and Lewis over the years, they essentially trusted one another. The secretary sympathized with the miners' demands for higher wages and other benefits while displaying a healthy skepticism regarding the motives of the operators. Nevertheless, Ickes pilloried Lewis for permitting the strikes in the first place and thereby endangering national security and damaging the public interest.[22]

As the negotiations bogged down in October, a wave of wildcat strikes preceded a general strike on 1 November that terminated on 4 November when Ickes and Lewis approved a new wage settlement. At that time, both Ickes and Gray were convinced that the captive mines, particularly those owned by steel companies, were the most culpable in frustrating an agreement. Earlier, in June 1943, Ickes had reacted angrily when the WLB terminated the promising bargaining sessions he had initiated. Furious over WLB's obstructive intervention, Ickes offered Roosevelt his resignation as coal mines administrator, but retracted it at his chief's request and plunged anew into the fray. With the support of Byrnes, Ickes reopened negotiations in September. He was convinced that WLB conspired with the larger operators, including the steel companies, and the AFL-affiliated Progressive Mine Workers of America to destroy UMWA. In Ickes's view, the intractability of WLB, surpassing that of many independent operators in its obdurate rejection of most UMWA demands, and irresponsible demands for the induction of all strikers and the jailing of UMWA leaders, precipitated the strike of 1 November.

By December, producers of 400 mt of bituminous, or over 70 percent of production in 1942, had accepted the Ickes-Lewis agreement of 4 November. WLB persisted in withholding approval, some of its members still bitterly denouncing Lewis for blackmailing the country. Finally, pressure from Ickes and the president's men, Byrnes and Vinson, large consumers, and the eastern states forced WLB ratification in March 1944. By July, all mines were again in the possession of their owners. However, a new round of mine seizures followed the eruption of local work stoppages in August. During the remainder of the war, coal mines were alternately seized and restored as walkouts threatened or occurred. Most of the mines affected were captive. Virtually everyone involved in these events expected an industrywide strike when the current contract expired in April 1946.[23]

Strikes and new wage agreements compelled OPA to authorize periodic coal price increases, albeit reluctantly and only at the insistence of Byrnes and Vinson. In each instance, OPA rejected SFAW's price recommendations, manifesting distrust of the cost figures submitted. Committed to protecting the price ceiling established in April 1942 and ordered by Roosevelt to stem inflation, OPA naturally attempted to generate its own cost data.[24] As Ickes perceived it, OPA's establishment of industry price committees intruded upon SFAW's sphere of authority. Both sides then appealed their cases, first to WPB and then to either the Office of War Mobilization or the Office of Economic Stabilization. The two latter agencies supported OPA's right to establish such advisory bodies but also insisted that prices be raised. Ickes and successive price administrators held irreconcilable interpretations of the prerogatives employed by OPA under the price control act of 1942. With executive powers so diffused, neither party could impose its will on the other. OPA accused Ickes of pandering to the selfishness of the operators, a reiteration of charges leveled against PAW. In SFAW's eyes, OPA's rigidity, less reprehensible than WLB's because unmotivated by anti-UMWA prejudices, still reflected a shocking ignorance of the nation's energy needs. Never the twain shall meet; Ickes and OPA exchanged insults until the former resigned as Secretary of Interior in 1946.[25]

Federal responses to strikes, shortages of mine labor, and pricing policies attested to the limits imposed upon government power even during a war. Workers could not be shuffled around like so many robots to suit the needs of the war machine. SFAW and many other Americans viewed with distaste the use of coercive tactics, threatening induction for instance, to achieve a balance in labor supply. Roosevelt and Ickes championed labor's hard-won right to bargain collectively, regardless of its inefficiences; executive orders to seize the mines instructed the mine administrator to protect local grievance machinery. Notions of equity, devolving upon OPA from the two NBCCs and BCD, plunged the price administrator into the quagmire of setting coal prices almost lump by lump. Sad ironies also surfaced. SFAW indignantly vetoed a WMC suggestion to employ prisoners of war in the mines as verging on forced labor. SFAW pretended not to notice when operators and local unions conspired to turn away blacks who sought mine employment.

SFAW Wins Control over Distribution, 1943

Overall availability of coal in 1942 masked glaring deficiencies in the coal distribution system that only the strikes of 1943 thrust into the open. With supply apparently equaling demand, SFAW was content to manipulate shipments, channeling coal to the lake docks before ice closed the ports and then directing shipments to New England. SFAW relied entirely upon ODT and ICC orders to move the coal and monitored conditions by using ad hoc industry organizations and representatives of ODT and ICC at key terminals. SFAW not only lacked the power to act on its own (partially remedied by the executive order of 5 November) even after receiving WPB authority to act, but also functioned without internal sources of information. While some states, mostly in New England, had organized fuel administrations that consisted of representatives of the energy industries and consumers and that regularly reported to SFAW, most states utilized their public service commissions. The latter viewed energy needs from a narrow perspective, lacked experience in coal and petroleum, and were not in the habit of answering to federal agencies.

The fragility of this structure became apparent when the production losses caused by the strikes were calculated. The inadequacies of the producer-dominated organizations that SFAW inherited from BCD then blazed for all to see like a white way. Once demand exceeded supply, current and reliable information about stocks, storage capacity, and available transportation became imperative for intelligent decision making about the actual allotment of subnormal quantities of coal to myriads of consumers. But for reasons that escape me, SFAW chose not to resolve these weaknesses, proceeding instead to make allocation decisions before devising a reliable information network. SFAW persisted in its refusal to adopt a zoning system, a measure recommended by both ODT and NRPB but opposed by the industry, promising to study further the merits of zoning; but in reality opposed to it. In general, the coal industry resisted all administrative reforms that diluted its influence over distribution.

WPB Orders M-316 and M-318 laid the foundation for the distribution system fashioned by SFAW.[26] Between 4 May and 17 November 1943, SFAW issued a series of ten regulations that dealt with the distribution of bituminous (Regulation No. 1) and anthracite (Regulation No. 2), set priorities affecting lake supply and the supply of other regions (Regulation No. 3), defined the sources of lake coal (Regulation No. 4), limited stock on hand (Regulation No. 5), and fixed delivery quotas to industrial and other consumers (Regulation Nos. 6, 7, 10). In January 1944, SFAW Regulation No. 11 established the tidewater and the Great Lakes dock advisory committees. In February, Regulation No. 12 created a National Advisory Committee on Local Distribution and subordinate area and local committees to supervise the distribution of coal by retailers. These organizational reforms were enacted at the insistence of ODT and to counter another attempt by OPA to impose coupon rationing. Most subsequent regulations were refinements of or amendments to the first ten or were designed to resolve a particular problem in a specific area.[27]

Regulation No. 2 established an anthracite distribution system in the Middle Atlantic and New England states. Producers and wholesalers were ordered to maintain deliveries to retailers at a fixed percentage of sales recorded during the coal year 1 April 1941–31 March 1942, an application, as in petroleum, of the historical-base standard. This regulation did not proceed to the next step, that of limiting the amount of anthracite retailers could sell to ultimate consumers because OPA challenged the order even before its promulgation. In the ensuing debate, both OPA and SFAW also argued for the applicability of their conflicting distribution control systems to bituminous. OPA seized this opportunity to offer a general critique of the impending executive order that would regularize the authority of SFAW.

In the SFAW draft of a proposed executive order, prepared in February 1943, that agency retained exclusive control over coal rationing. Ickes and his counterpart at OPA, benefiting from their recently concluded bout over oil rationing, produced sophisticated rationales to substantiate their demands for administrative centralization over coal distribution. OPA reiterated its conviction that any course other than lodging complete responsibility with it would compromise the integrity of commodity rationing in the eyes of the public. SFAW disagreed, averring that the provision of sufficient coal depended upon its ability to regulate the flow from mine to final consumer. OPA, using essentially the same language aimed earlier at the executive order establishing PAW, lashed out at the draft because it created a coal czar. In that earlier encounter, WPB had thwarted Ickes's drive for autonomy in oil and had preserved OPA's authority over consumer rationing (see Chapter 13, pp. 326–31). In the coal dispute, SFAW emerged with primary responsibility for the distribution program while still functioning as an extension of WPB.[28]

The motivation for OPA's exertions against dealer limitation rationing derived not only from a bureaucratic impulse to protect and widen its administrative domain but from an unshakable belief in the equity of the coupon-flow-back method and apprehension concerning the discriminatory potential of dealer control. Residential consumers, the group least capable of protecting itself, burned 80 percent of anthracite production. A dozen large firms, mostly railroad companies, controlled 60 percent of production while twenty-nine corporations accounted for 80 percent. Many of these corporations either owned wholesaling firms or dominated them by means of exclusive contracts. These interlocking arrangements enabled the Pennsylvania producers to manipulate supply in order to maintain prices. While the degree of monopoly descriptive of anthracite did not compare with dozens of other industries in which one to four firms accounted for 75 percent of total production, the anthracite companies did wield great power over a key commodity.

In 1942 and 1943, congressional committees accumulated evidence attesting to the collusive efforts of New York City's largest coal dealers to determine the allocation of anthracite. According to the mayor of Freeport, Long Island, the larger dealers ruled the anthracite allocation committees established by Regulation No. 2 and exploited their position to assure their own supply while denying coal to smaller and independent coal yards.[29]

SFAW never responded in detail to these and similar allegations directed at retail bituminous dealers in different parts of the country. Instead, SFAW offered vague promises of fairness and expressions of faith in the basic integrity of retailers. SFAW then shifted the thrust of its case to the presumed impossibility of applying coupon rationing to hundreds of sizes and qualities of coal, insisting that the imposition of coupon rationing would cause operators to reduce production and severely limit the effectiveness of early ordering and stockpiling programs. Coal could not be stored at the mines. Each day mines produced as much as railroads or trucks could carry away. At least 20 percent of anthracite and 35 percent of bituminous moved directly from the mines to consumers, only a fraction of which, however, was destined for residential use. The volume of production could not, then, be geared to the time-consuming collection of coupons and their exchange for more coal. With some justification, SFAW considered coupons totally inappropriate in the industrial trade, much of which revolved around long-term contracts. Many of these points applied more tellingly to bituminous than anthracite, which had few special uses, and to industrial uses rather than residential, but SFAW shrewdly confused the two. SFAW successfully evaded the equity issue by diverting attention to technicalities and complexities that precluded the adoption of coupon rationing.

In June 1943, SFAW offered amendments to Regulation No. 2 that initiated dealer-controlled distribution of anthracite to consumers. Quotas were established, subject to change, and all consumers were promised access to coal. By that time, substantial quantities of anthracite had already been distributed—and not always fairly. As a result, thousands of homes in the Northeast were ill-heated, and long queues formed at retail yards. As fall ended and temperatures dropped, New York City, Manchester, New Hampshire, and other northeastern communities rushed desperate pleas for coal to SFAW. Water pipes froze and illness caused absenteeism. While the coal outlook for 1944 appeared even gloomier and coal yard lines in Passaic, New Jersey lengthened, SFAW repeatedly denied the need for coupon rationing, blaming present difficulties on transportation shortages, inadequate authority and diffused responsibility, and other factors external to the agency. Discouraged by the absence of support from WPB, OPA conceded in September 1943, without, however, relinquishing its right to press for coupon rationing at another time.

The actual weaknesses of the system justified OPA's persistent hostility. On 30 October, over the objections of the anthracite advisory committee, SFAW issued Regulation No. 6 in an attempt to correct abuses and to prepare for the strike promised for 1 November. Regulation No. 6 imposed tight SFAW supervision over the allocation practices of its distribution committees. In November, stung by proof that anthracite producers were shipping almost unburnable coal, SFAW set quality standards in Regulation No. 9. The refusal of producers to desist from sending anthracite on long hauls into western states, frequently for industrial steam-raising purposes, compelled SFAW to issue an order in December prohibiting western shipments.[30]

While OPA administrators may have been ignorant of the history of the industry-administered fuel distribution programs forged during World War I and employed again during the postwar coal crises, those experiences corroborated their suspicions concerning dealer control. USFA possessed substantially more power than SFAW and administered a nationwide network of state and local fuel administrations. Nevertheless, USFA moved quickly to centralize decision making and to force producer and dealer compliance with USFA price and distribution orders. In 1919 and 1922, the absence of vigorous enforcement measures permitted widespread profiteering and inequitable distribution. SFAW strengthened its leverage over coal distributors only gradually and imperfectly, perhaps influenced too strongly by the industry regarding the proper limits of regulation. OPA's distrust of industry-controlled distribution was well founded. SFAW's reluctance to develop effective and equitable controls reflected not an honest but naive reliance upon the good will of the industry but a selfish refusal to give up a poorly served responsibility. Domestic consumers would have been better served by OPA than they were by SFAW.

The distribution regulations issued by SFAW in 1943 to cope with the consequences of the coal strikes established the pattern of control adhered to through 1946. As the volume of available coal altered, new regulations superseded older orders and amendments to extant orders were designed to close loopholes, shunt coal to areas of scarcity, or achieve greater fairness. Almost without exception, the regulations of 1944 and 1945 limited the discretionary power vested in the distributors by the regulations of 1943. As an example, Regulation No. 2 did not prevent the hoarding of anthracite by residential consumers with storage space and the money to purchase coal early. This practice lessened the supply available to those who could not stockpile coal. Regulations No. 17 (April 1944) and No. 21 (March 1944) required consumers to file notarized declarations of annual use and stock on hand with retailers who then used these statements to allot coal and to reorder from their suppliers. SFAW, objecting to coupon rationing because of its administrative costs, imposed equally onerous burdens upon retailers. These reforms, moreover, did not eliminate the intrinsic inequities of the historical-based standard; homeowners with storage space and profligate users of coal were favored.[31]

Regulations governing the distribution of bituminous underwent similar permutations. As mentioned in the section just concluded, the purview of the orders encompassed: coal supplies for the lakes, New England, and other regions; the sources of supply for particular regions; stock limitations or preferential stockpiling for certain industries and for industry in general; delivery quotas to wholesalers and retailers; quotas for residential users of soft coal. In addition, SFAW strove for transportation efficiency and the conservation of coal. All this demanded close coordination and daily consultation with WPB, the agency responsible for defining the most efficient uses of all resources, and with ODT, ICC, and other agencies. As previously explained, in 1941 and 1942, SFAW initiated transportation and insurance subsidization programs to foster the movement of coal to the lakes and the Northeast.

The success of the distribution system hinged upon the efficient use of railroad, truck, and waterborne transport. From 1941 through 1943, the National Resources Planning Board vigorously advocated the application to coal transport of a zone system resembling that applied during World War I. As NRPB pointed out, coal constituted about 35 percent of total rail freight tonnage, therefore markedly affecting the overall use of rail facilities. Zoning would minimize the cross-hauling of coal of a similar type amd quality and the long-hauling of coal into areas that could be supplied by less distant mines. NRPB maintained that zoning would regularize the flow of coal to lake and tidewater docks and to key inland coal distribution terminals. More efficient and more numerous trips would add to the total stock of motive power and open-top cars, thereby relieving demands on rail transport and reducing congestion. By 1943, ODT and ICC had accepted the desirability of some form of zoning for the eastern third of the nation. Zoning appealed to ICC as a means of achieving a more rational division of railroad capacity, especially motive power, between the agricultural and coal industries, both of which made heavy demands upon railroads at about the same time. In September 1943, WPB also pressed the idea upon SFAW, but as of March 1944, SFAW had failed to respond. Having already rejected zoning several times, SFAW chose to ignore the latest version.[32]

NRPB anticipated that the coal industry would oppose the inescapable disruption of normal market relationships that accompanied zoning. In April 1942, the Solid Fuels War Advisory Council condemned zoning as totally unnecessary, arguing that the uninhibited operation of the market place resulted in the most efficient routing.[33] This position, adhered to tenaciously by northern operators, directly contradicted northern cries of unfairness and inefficiency leveled at southern operators who invaded northern markets after World War I. The strenuous efforts of both NBCCs to establish fair prices in common market areas foundered when confronted with the erratic shipping patterns of the coal industry. SFAW, however, adopted the industry stance, characterizing the World War I experience as a failure and denying the practicality of zoning in the present situation. While NRPB and ODT pointed to numerous examples of long- and cross-hauling, SFAW asserted that most of this had been eliminated before the war. Zoning would also, according to SFAW, obstruct the movement of critical metallurgical coals into areas where other grades of bituminous were available and would reduce the production of domestic grades.

As the quantity of resources consumed by the military burgeoned, SFAW multiplied its demands upon ODT and ICC for special regulations and car service orders which, in the aggregate, imposed a de facto zoning system upon large sections of the country. Anthracite shipments west of Pennsylvania were forbidden, as were bituminous shipments by lake and rail to the Pacific Northwest. Car shortages, rail congestion, and a persistent scarcity of coal forced SFAW to seek ODT-ICC authority to requisition cars and to impose coal embargoes in specific areas. Producers adjacent to the upper Ohio River received orders one week to ship east and the next week to ship north, compliance in each case depending upon the availability of transport.[34] Since many of these producers mined a similar quality of coal, the routing of coal trains could have been regularized by a systematic division of areal supply responsibilities. But SFAW, objecting to the alleged disruption of usual patterns implicit in zoning, proceeded to further confuse an already complex system with its numerous orders and counterorders. Each case of inadequate transportation was diagnosed as a discrete problem rather than as evidence of a generic flaw in a network requiring systemwide treatment. By 1944, rail congestion, bottlenecks at terminals, coal frozen in standing cars along obscure sidings, and car shortages were accepted as the norm. Thus, when SFAW ignored WPB's request for further study of zoning, WPB finally dropped the entire matter.

To equalize supply in the industrial sector and to prevent industrial hoarding, SFAW issued Regulations Nos. 4 and 5 in August and September, 1943, respectively. Failing to achieve these objectives, SFAW drafted Regulation No. 10 in November; it specifically curtailed further deliveries to industrial consumers with excessively large stocks. No apparent improvement in results followed because SFAW lacked subordinate units responsible for the enforcement of regulations at such key places as the lake docks or Ohio River terminals. Instead, SFAW relied upon the local offices of ODT, OPA, the Office of Civilian Supply, and in New England the state fuel administrations. Excepting the latter, these branches had neither the expertise nor the time to check out stocks held by utilities or other large industrial consumers. As a result, SFAW operated blindly in many instances. Inferior data rendered ineffective the most carefully constructed regulations. Straws in the wind formed the foundation for SFAW's national distribution program.[35]

In January 1944, Regulation No. 11 established tidewater and Great Lakes dock advisory committees, and in February, Regulation No. 12 created advisory committees on local distribution. The dock committees were organized to counter earlier NRPB criticisms of SFAW's transportation policies and to bury the issue of zoning. Similarly, the local distribution committees reflected SFAW's response to OPA criticisms of retail distribution procedures, echoed by ODT and WPB, and would, it was hoped, lay to rest OPA's efforts to impose coupon-flow-back rationing.

The two dock committees assumed responsibility for estimating the coal and transportation requirements of their respective regions and for determining allowable stockpiles for the large consumers in their regions. After filling all high-priority demands, at levels ranging from 90 to 110 percent of historical use, responsibility for the remaining coal passed into the hands of the local distribution committees.[36] The dock committees advised local committees as to projected quantities of coal available, and both sets of committees cooperated with ODT's local units in filling requests for transportation. An internally generated demand for accurate and current data did not serve as the catalyst for SFAW's tardy fabrication of a committee network; rather, criticism from peer agencies and their advocacy of programs threatening to SFAW's jurisdiction furnished the necessary impulse. Nevertheless, SFAW did develop the means to coordinate regional and local coal distribution.[37]

Short supplies of coal in 1944 and 1945 and the escalating demands of war industries necessitated the constant readjustment of the regulations issued in 1943. The local and regional network of committees, stretching from Hartford to Seattle, relayed quarterly assessments of demand to SFAW that in the aggregate predicted shortfalls for 1944–45 of 20 mt to 50 mt. Deficits were then parceled out among the less essential users of coal, and quotas were formalized in regulations. The key industrial regions east of the Mississippi received quotas of 100 percent, but categories of consumers within the region might receive less than a full share. Permissible deliveries to such nonessential consumers as the clay products industry and domestic consumers of both bituminous and anthracite varied between 85 percent and 95 percent of historical use. Weather conditions, transport availability, and other factors frequently required monthly changes in the quotas. Regulation No. 17, issued in March 1944, fixed quotas for anthracite delivery at 90 percent, but subsequent amendments reduced that to 87.5 percent and then to 75 percent. Regulation No. 18, issued in September 1944, then restored the original quota of 90 percent for areas of exclusive anthracite use and 87.5 percent for those areas that also used bituminous.[38]

Revisions of quarterly or annual delivery quotas affected other coal users, notably the utilities. While the utilities generally received 100 percent of historical use, the permissible size of stockpiles was frequently lowered or raised. In establishing stockpile limitations, SFAW rarely consulted with other agencies that shared jurisdiction over the utilities. In 1944 and 1945, SFAW and the Office of War Utilities of WPB haggled over the number of days' supply utilities could maintain in storage. SFAW set the allowable as it saw fit, adamantly refusing to acknowledge the right of prior consultation demanded by the utilities office. SFAW's posture in this petty issue reflected its pique at being ignored by WPB in formulating policies that mandated dimouts or blackouts.

In part, disagreement over the conservation of electricity stemmed from differing perceptions as to the purpose of reduced electric generation. In 1943, the coal strikes prompted SFAW to propose a national dimout and the elimination of all uses of electricity unrelated to the prosecution of the war or to essential civilian activity, especially outdoor advertising and use by the amusement and entertainment industries. But WPB would only agree to a voluntary conservation program drafted by the industry, which SFAW greeted with derision. By 1944, WPB's utilities office was evolving a more comprehensive plan for reduced electric use, based upon not only the supply of coal but also the supply of oil and natural gas. SFAW opposed this program because it would not save appreciable amounts of coal and, indeed, might cause a reduction in production in those areas in which the utilities relied exclusively upon coal. As Chapter 13 indicated, WPB did issue Utilities Order U-9. SFAW viewed this order as essentially a venture into the psychology of conservation rather than as a measure that would increase the supply of coal available to essential users. SFAW, it will be recalled, expressed similar doubts about the oil conversion program (see Chapter 13, pp. 342–43).[39]

As the winter of 1944 drew near, evidence from many parts of the nation pointed unmistakably to impending coal shortages of a disturbing magnitude, not only in the East but also in the Ohio and Mississippi valleys and west of the Missouri where natural gas supplies had fallen to alarming levels. This supply crunch was the product of many factors. In September and October, numerous local distribution committees in upstate New York voiced their concern over an apparent decline in coal receipts, echoing the apprehension of many communities in and between the New York and Philadelphia metropolitan areas and in New England as well. The committee in Camden, New Jersey, attributed the growing crisis to the production losses of 1943. Undoubtedly, the strikes were exacting their toll.

In Cleveland, Mayor Frank J. Lausche blamed the city's small coal supply, apparent in July, on discrimination and the erratic operation of the railroad routing system. Cleveland normally drew its coal from Districts 7 and 8, but SFAW Regulation No. 23 directed coal from those districts elsewhere. In Kansas City, Oklahoma City, and other Mid-Continent communities, the diminishing availability of natural gas, restrictions on oil use, inadequate coal production in Missouri and Kansas fields, and constraints on imports from producing fields to the east and west portended a measurable scarcity of winter fuels. Detroit and Mobile, in their appeals for larger allocations of coal, emphasized the unprecedented population growth accompanying the war. In both cities, the heating units in defense housing burned coal while many other residences had converted to coal. Coal allocations to these and other war-plant towns had not risen proportionately with population because the historical-use method of tabulating quotas was insensitive to dramatic increases in demand.[40] In hundreds of places, gasoline and tire rationing severely reduced imports by truck and strained coal delivery capabilities within the towns. In November 1944, an SFAW survey of 201 communities in 21 states revealed that the number of coal dealers had declined from 337 to 199 and that 32 percent of all coal consumers possessed no stored coal.[41]

In response to pleas for more coal, SFAW could only promise that each municipality or area would receive its fair share of a diminishing supply. Within each community, then, the burden of assuring equity of allocation rested directly upon the local distribution committee. In a memorandum of 6 June 1944, C. J. Potter, assistant deputy administrator of SFAW, emphasized the importance of the committees to the successful implementation of Regulation No. 21. The equitable distribution of coal to domestic consumers, Potter explained,

> cannot be secured unless those fuels move in conformity with . . . Regulation No. 21 during the spring and summer of this year. As you know, Regulation No. 21 does not provide for coupon rationing and the flowback of ration evidence; instead, the rationing scheme . . . is to see to it that all bins obtain a fair share of the available supply by limiting dealer deliveries. The . . . program cannot be carried out successfully unless an overwhelming majority of retail dealers of solid fuels cooperate.[42]

Potter then detailed the restrictions imposed by Regulation No. 21 and instructed the local committees on the proper procedures to be used to achieve its objectives.

Performance varied from committee to committee. Some communities were unable to organize committees and fell under the purview of area distribution managers. The greatest difficulty arose in places that had experienced a large influx of people seeking jobs in war industries. This created the problem of "coal orphans," people with no prior purchase record with area coal yards. In some places, the newcomers were left to shift for themselves. In other towns, in and around Syracuse, New York, as an example, local committees operated registration desks in public buildings where newcomers could file requests for coal. After determining need, the committees distributed the newcomers among local coal dealers. Each newcomer's share reduced the quantity of coal available to older residents. Communities that had experienced significant in-migration complained loudly about the lack of coal to meet the needs of prior residents, let alone thousands of new arrivals.

Some local committees, in Chemung and Tioga counties, New York, for instance, attempted to pool transportation so that two dealers did not use two trucks to haul partial loads to the same neighborhood. In Bridgeport, Connecticut, the committee promoted chimney cleaning and do-it-yourself conservation measures. In Montgomery, Alabama, on the other hand, the best efforts of SFAW area officials failed to arouse the enthusiasm of local dealers for any of these programs. Nor were letters absent from citizens in Atlantic City, New Jersey, Roanoke, Virginia, Peru, Illinois, or Reno, Nevada, attesting to the callously exploitive behavior of coal dealers. In Akron, Ohio, the refusal of coal dealers to cooperate so aggravated Ickes that he ordered his lawyers to explore the constitutionality of seizing the city's retail coal yards.[43]

After reading an enormous volume of fragmentary evidence from scores of places, I was left with the impression that most coal dealers struggled faithfully to comply with the regulations of 1944 and 1945. In general, dealer control worked, though somewhat less fairly and efficiently than the coupon-flow-back rationing applied to other commodities. The root of the difficulty lay in the historical-use method of calculating allocations of coal for residential use. Once locked into that criterion, dealers were obligated to conform whether or not it resulted in a fair division of coal among their customers. These inequities remained uncorrected during the harsh winter of 1944–45. They were perpetuated in Regulation Nos. 26 and 27, issued in April 1945, prior to V-E Day and when final victory in the Pacific still seemed to demand a bloody invasion of the Japanese home islands.

Winding Down SFAW

V-E Day and the subsequent improvement of coal supplies during the summer and fall of 1945 released the hitherto muted resentment over wartime restrictions. A cacophony of demands for the repeal of recently issued regulations bombarded the eardrums of SFAW. Given the new circumstances, distributors and consumers alike were convinced that limitation of deliveries to 80 percent of normal use and the stiffening of consumer declaration procedures were absolutely unnecessary. Moreover, the regulations did not apply to the entire nation but only to Minnesota, Iowa, the Dakotas, Louisiana, and the states east of the Mississippi. The legislatures of Minnesota and Wisconsin both drafted resolutions protesting the harshness of the quotas while the National Retail Coal Merchants Association condemned the consumer declarations as useless and unacceptably intrusive. SFAW refused to consider revocation until after V-J Day (and did revoke the regulations in September). But by that time, midway through the coal year, most dealers had accommodated to the requirements of the orders and were fearful that repeal would disrupt deliveries from their wartime sources of supply; in August and September, then, dealers expressed opposition to repeal.[44]

Weighty considerations explain the justifiable hesitancy of SFAW to lift the orders of spring 1945. Estimates made in March of coal production for the coal year 1945–46 warned of shortages approaching 40 mt. Wildcat strikes in April and May, resulting in the federal seizure of some 600 mines, forced an upward revision of the estimated deficits to 50 mt. The surrender of Japan in August relieved some of the pressure by permitting a shift in fuel supplies from war industries to peacetime uses. However, a new demand had arisen in Western Europe where wartime devastation and the dislocation accompanying the end of the war caused a dangerous shortage of coal, approaching 50 mt. To avoid widespread suffering in Western Europe, Ickes, President Truman, and officials of the Foreign Economic Administration (FEA) agreed that a large portion of the estimated European deficit must be supplied by the United States.

SFAW and FEA competed for control over the export program, with FEA tending to advocate immediate and massive shipments across the Atlantic while SFAW insisted that exports be balanced against American productive capacity and legitimate domestic requirements for the winter 1945–46. Beginning in April 1945, and extending through August, FEA proceeded to allocate millions of tons of coal to Europe, and also to Latin America, while SFAW issued Regulation No. 30, which required exporters to obtain licenses. SFAW then prohibited some shipments, particularly of high-quality and metallurgical coals, reduced the tonnage of others, and even determined the destination of some cargoes. In July, SFAW unilaterally imposed an embargo on all shipments of metallurgical coal to Portugal and Argentina and appeared ready to extend the embargo to all of Western Europe.

More was at issue than bureaucratic prerogatives. Truman endorsed the view of the State Department and WPB that satisfying the fuel requirements of Europe and Latin America was a prerequisite for the attainment of postwar foreign policy objectives. Ickes shared this opinion, only demurring when exports threatened domestic supply. In his view, the release of 2 million tons of scarce metallurgical coal to Portugal and Argentina, dictatorships cool to the Allied cause, would enrich a few producers who won contracts at higher-than-ceiling prices while harming industrial consumers who did not own mines and who sought metallurgical coal in the open market. FEA insisted that the export program, because of its greater urgency, should have priority over nonessential domestic uses. FEA's objections to SFAW's obstructive assault on FEA prerogatives wended their way to John W. Snyder, director of the Office of War Mobilization and Reconversion, who in August acknowledged most of the jurisdictional claims of FEA and instructed SFAW to allocate reasonable quantities of coal to FEA. With the conclusion of the war, SFAW turned its attention to liquidation and reluctantly dropped this issue.[45]

Between September and December 1945, SFAW lifted most controls over solid fuels and dismantled the local and area committee network.[46] For a moment, discussion within the agency and its Solid Fuels Advisory War Council shifted to the strategies necessary to obtain legislation that would reimpose minimum prices and prevent the reemergence of the destructive competitiveness of the pre-Guffey era. The war council also raised the issue of the alarming intrusion of natural gas and petroleum, particularly the dumping of cheap foreign crude, in "natural" coal markets. The council criticized the Roosevelt administration for its failure to implement legislation passed in April 1944 which authorized a five-year, $30 million program to build demonstration plants for the production of synthetic fuels. In March 1945, WPB vetoed a Bureau of Mines application to construct an oil shale development laboratory as unnecessary to the war effort. The National Coal Association, the coal-carrying railroads, and the coal war council united in demanding—unsuccessfully as it turned out—an amendment to the Cole Pipe Line Act that would prohibit pipelines built under the act from transporting natural gas.[47]

Before these and other prewar issues could capture the whole attention of the shrinking SFAW or of Interior, the latter contemplating various strategies to enlarge its dominion over energy policy, troublesome signals emanated from UMWA that virtually assured a strike on 1 April. In February 1946, Dan H. Wheeler, an assistant deputy administrator in SFAW, advised Acting Secretary of Interior Oscar L. Chapman to continue SFAW beyond February 1946, the expiration date targeted by the recently departed Ickes.[48]

On 1 April 1946, 330,000 miners went out on strike, closing most bituminous mines until 13 May. By executive order of 21 May, Truman ordered the secretary of Interior to seize the mines. Numerous wildcat strikes during the late spring and summer prolonged control by the Coal Mines Administration. In May, a railroad strike led to the seizure of the railroads and their operation by ODT. A seamen's strike in August and September resulted in an ICC embargo on all shipments to ports along the Great Lakes, Atlantic, Gulf, and Pacific coasts.

Coal production losses during the strike mounted to 37 mt. Panicky reports from around the country inundated SFAW. In late April, as deliveries to the lake docks declined by as much as 15 percent each week, the volume of coal stored shriveled to the lowest level in the memory of the dock operators. In anticipation of a severe coal famine, Connecticut resurrected its solid fuels administration and the legislature passed a bill authorizing local fuel administrators to purchase coal for distribution to those caught with empty bins. By fall, even though the mines were operating, coal was not moving freely. The seamen's strike had necessitated a shift to all-rail routes wherever possible, and this generated such great demands on the railroads that car shortages spread quickly. During six weeks ending 30 June, the Baltimore & Ohio alone delivered 35,000 fewer cars than shippers requested, causing rapid stock shrinkage at utilities in New York and New England. During three weeks in late June and early July, car shortages resulted in production losses of 1.5 mt. The Danville, Virginia, Chamber of Commerce informed President Truman that coal scarcity had forced the closing of textile and tobacco plants employing 16,000 people and that many families of returning veterans were without coal. The gloom of October deepened with the strike of 1 November 1946, lasting over a month and causing the loss of an additional 20 mt of coal.[49]

Coal losses between 1 April and 31 December 1946 amounted to 60 million tons. Coal available for delivery or held in stock by large consumers declined from 75 mt in late October to 55 mt by late November, 13 mt of which rested in utility yards. However, 141 utilities held less than fifteen days' supply, and another 68 stocked fuel for less than one month. The absence of mountainous piles of coal at Great Lakes and tidewater docks was all too obvious. Coal in household bins may have been as much as 10 mt below normal. To meet this emergency, less debilitating than the crisis of 1919 and 1922 because of the widespread use of natural gas and oil, SFAW issued Regulations Nos. 31 and 32, called upon the aid of ICC, and constructed a new priorities list for promulgation by the Office of War Mobilization and

Reconversion. A new round of federal mine seizures occurred in November. Whenever possible, SFAW reestablished local committees.[50]

Regulation No. 31 prohibited the export of coal suitable for residential and other high-priority uses. Regulation No. 32, with subsequent revisions, controlled the distribution of bituminous produced east of the Mississippi and required each producer to supply the same retail dealers as in 1944–45. In April and again in November, SFAW requested the issuance of service orders by ICC that froze the railroad transportation of coal, including that already in transit, until SFAW ordered it moved. SFAW then issued an order that listed such institutions as schools, hospitals, and federal, state, and local government buildings as the preferred recipients of the frozen coal. Other demands for coal were dealt with on a case-by-case basis. SFAW denied the applications of several steel companies for coal because they had not been identified as preferred. In early December, SFAW administrator Julius Krug warned movie house managers that they would be closed if the strike continued. Area distribution managers were authorized to release frozen coal within their jurisdictions; and, in keeping with the geographical limits of Regulation No. 32, controls over the movement of coal in most areas west of the Mississippi were lifted. ICC, in both April and November, dispersed available cars in conformity with SFAW instructions as to the points of greatest need. Many of the local committees reimposed dealer rationing. Utilities in twenty-one states were ordered to initiate brownouts. On 23 November, Krug strongly advised each governor to organize state and local fuel administrations, pointing out, as had the Federal Fuel Distributor in 1922–23, the limited authority available to the federal government to moderate the consequences of the shortages.[51]

Even as SFAW applied its stopgap remedies, it was the target of volleys of shrill criticism and, perhaps even worse, of much gratuitous advice. Capriciousness and irrelevance characterized much of the criticism. At best, opponents merely reiterated grievances prevalent during the war, especially the alleged discrimination in the distribution of coal among regions, states, and locales. Fuel officials in Connecticut asserted that coal earmarked for the state was siphoned off en route. Other states voiced similar and uncorroborated accusations. In general, nonproducing states may have received a fraction less than their proportionate shares as a result of interceptions of coal shipments by carriers and dealers in producing states. The freeze order sought to control forestalling. The degree of unfairness could not have been serious; residents in Stamford, Connecticut, suffered no greater deprivation than people in Cleveland or Danville.

Dealer-controlled distribution absorbed its measure of flack, both unjustly and justly. In July 1946, consumers blamed dealers for coal price increases ranging from $1.50 to $2.00 per ton, but dealers were only passing through a hike authorized by OPA as a result of the wage settlement. In truth, SFAW investigated dealer performance only cursorily, but those probes uncovered relatively few cases of profiteering, blackmarketing, or unequal treatment of consumers. The inability of low-income households to obtain fuel was viewed as a state or local responsibility. In both Connecticut and Vermont, state fuel officials effectively policed the dealers and contrived to furnish all households with some coal. In December 1946, the labor columnist Victor Riesel proposed that the federal government purchase, stockpile, and distribute coal to residential users. While sprinkling his idea with a liberal coating of social welfare rhetoric, Riesel aimed to break the power of UMWA. Given the magnitude of the emergency— the volume of coal lost, the coincidence of railroad and merchant marine strikes—SFAW and its peer agencies performed adequately in buffering the public against severe hardship.[52]

During the entire course of the emergency, hostile individuals demanded the immediate abolition of SFAW, and the agency consumed much valuable time in justifying its existence. Legally, SFAW would expire on 31 March 1947 along with the Second War Powers Act. Both Ickes in 1945 and Krug in 1946 had asserted that the controlling factor in determining the activities of SFAW would be the degree of stabilization achieved in labor-management relations. Neither wished to prolong the life of the agency beyond the time when coal production assured an adequate national supply. In January 1947, Secretary of the Interior Krug responded in that vein to Sen. Homer Ferguson, Republican of Michigan, who had accumulated several letters from constituents calling for the extinction of SFAW. One wonders where the senator had been hiding in November and December when coal piles dwindled away and workers were laid off. The coal supply of Detroit and other Michigan cities, particularly in the Upper Peninsula, depended entirely upon the efficient functioning of SFAW regulations. Coal industry organizations supported Krug's contention that SFAW should continue through the end of the 1946–47 coal year. No sooner had SFAW closed shop on 31 March than work stoppages during the first two weeks in April curtailed production by as much as 50 percent. In 1947 and 1948, coal shortages of varying intensity plagued the country. Then in 1949–50, the industry plunged into still another suicidal conflict, further weakening the competitiveness of coal by hastening the transition of consumers to other fuels.[53]

Conclusion

As of 1947, the federal role in coal had come full circle—perhaps the image of a spiral better captures the true historical progression from World War I through 1941. For a time, the demands of World War II revived the industry without markedly altering its structure. The industry remained divided between competing northern and southern sectors and between several thousand relatively small mines producing about 10 percent of total production and a few hundred firms supplying 60 percent of the coal. While the tonnage originating from the captive mines of steel and utilities companies climbed gradually, the independent firms retained their preponderant share of production into the 1960s.[54] Essentially, then, as a consequence of the persistent encroachment of other fuels in coal's normal markets, the competitive conditions of the 1920s and 1930s threatened to reemerge after the war with enhanced intensity.

In 1943, congressional refusal to extend the second Guffey Act resulted in the demise of the Bituminous Coal Division and its authority to fix minimum prices. Ickes lobbied vigorously for extension and considered the congressional negative unfortunate and extremely short-sighted. He attributed the defeat to a coalition of large producers, anchored by the captive mines, public utilities and other large industrial consumers, and a few municipalities, all with a record of opposition to the earlier coal acts and to the policies of both NBCCs and BCD. But John L. Lewis also fought renewal, apparently rejecting the location of administrative authority within the Department of Interior rather than in an independent agency. Most observers believed that the bill would protect the employees of the small producers who mined 40 percent of total tonnage. Those producers desired extension as a cushion against the anticipated postwar slump and as a defense against the competitive superiority of the large firms. Dan Wheeler and C. J. Potter, assistant deputy administrators of SFAW, and several congressmen belabored Congress and the administration for knuckling under to Lewis and his union. Interior, however, manifested no more willingness to compromise the issue of jurisdiction than UMWA. Interior preached the urgency of retaining authority to set minimum prices, and UMWA did not dispute this point. But to sacrifice control so that pricing authority survived proved beyond the moral capability of Interior.[55]

Within Interior, many people expected cutthroat competition to flare up again after the war. To reduce the deleterious consequences of impassioned labor-management strife and irrational intraindustry competition, Interior laid plans to recapture some of the authority of the two coal commissions and BCD. An in-house controversy surfaced between those who advocated a remedial strategy based upon minimum prices and others who proposed controls over production and capacity and the retraining of displaced miners, a program closely following the original version of the Guffey Act introduced in 1935. Secretary Krug, much to the disgust of John L. Lewis, did appoint a National Bituminous Coal Advisory Council in 1948. But congressional indifference and the persistent hostility of UMWA, large producers and consumers, and the coal-carrying railroads thwarted the designs of Interior.[56]

Postwar coal crises attended by a diminishing federal role suggest that neither government, the industry, nor consumers had absorbed any lessons of history. Labor and management alike permitted the pent-up antagonisms of half a century to cloud their vision of postwar America. By the mid-1950s, 160,000 fewer miners entered the shafts and pits than during the late 1940s. Sorely disadvantaged by such government policies as the oil depletion allowance, artificially low natural gas prices, and discriminatory rail rates and shortly to confront the foreboding challenges of nuclear generation and powerful environmental interests, the coal industry, aided and abetted by the federal government, labored to repeat the past.

FIFTEEN

Federal Fuel Policies, 1900–1946: An Evaluation

FEDERAL POLICIES toward the mineral fuels from 1900 to 1946 can be characterized as unsystematic, vague, and eminently minimal. Consider the nature of the four central problems that engaged the federal government during the first half of the twentieth century. Three problems (indeed, crises)—two wars and a depression, each exogenous to the evolution of an energy or fuel-use system—commanded the greatest attention. A fourth and endogenous problem of intrinsic importance, the competitive structure of the fossil fuel industries, became ensnared in the clutch of advocates of free enterprise and champions of trust busting. Even during the years of crisis, neither of those antagonists could transcend the traditional frameworks of their arguments; neither understood that the unique characteristics of energy resources raised issues that went beyond those of monopoly and a competitive market. Other endogenous aspects of the fuel industries—supply, demand, distribution, technology—were similarly crammed into the suffocating corsets of crisis management or free-market politics.

By the first third of the nineteenth century, a gradual energy transition was in progress in America, entailing the substitution of coal and new mechanical systems for wood and for human, animal, wind, and water power.[1] By the late nineteenth century, this shift was well under way and accelerating. The advent of petroleum fuels, the increasing use of coal, and the spread of electric and natural gas use propelled the transition at a more rapid pace during the initial decades of the twentieth century. America's increasingly energy-intensive economy featured the application of fossil fuels to more and more mechanical and process tasks and made ever-widening energy options accessible to a rising number of energy users. The rapidity of change and its ensuing bounty fostered a pervasive faith in the inherent economies of bigness achievable through the application of giant technology to industry. Only rarely does one encounter any questioning of the link between bigness and efficiency. Certainly the federal government acted during World War II as if superior efficiency flowed from large firms rather than small firms.

Did federal fuel policies influence the pace and direction of this ongoing energy transition during the first fifty years of the twentieth century? The answer must be a qualified "no," even if the scope of the question is broadened to include the considerable attention the federal government focused upon the electric and natural gas industries during the 1930s. Federal involvement in those industries can be categorized as either developmental or regulatory. The Tennessee Valley Authority and the Rural Electrification Administration represented the developmental thrust, while the Public Utilities Holding Company Act of 1935 and the Natural Gas Act of 1938 reflected a federal recognition of the need to regulate both the structure and the interstate marketing practices of natural gas and electric utilities. Therefore, one cannot simply assert that as of World War II the federal government remained without any energy policies. While many residents of rural areas were brought on line by the REA and while TVA and the Bonneville Power Administration contributed to the revival of lagging regional economies, the consequences of those regional initiatives for the fossil fuel industries were minimal and largely postponed, as were regulatory efforts, until after World War II. In the absence of any federal intervention in the utility industries and in the coal and petroleum industries, all would have arrived at about the same position at the conclusion of World War II.[2]

The federal government did evolve a political style for each of the energy industries. Fuel politics were an essential aspect of general national politics. But this is not to imply that the federal government contributed significantly to the energy transition. At points in time when federal action could have been effective and formative, as for example in dealing with coal industry weaknesses between 1916 and 1922, the government failed to act constructively. Lacking a working definition of the public interest in coal, federal policy makers operated without overarching goals and without the criteria necessary for selecting among policy alternatives. When federal officials did attempt to define the public interest in fuels, as during the first stage of the Federal Oil Conservation Board or during the hectic lives of the two

National Bituminous Coal commissions, the opposition of particular interests proved an insuperable obstacle. Thus, fuel policies from 1900 to 1946 broadly reflected the interests of the dominant segments of each fuel industry. [3]

Why were federal ventures into fuel policy making attended by such meager results? The National Coal Association and individual coal operators frequently appended the labels "stupid" and "ignorant" to congressmen and bureaucrats who dared to draft bills regulating coal. NCA's arrogance was matched only by its wrong-headedness. Neither stupid nor ignorant, the sponsors of such coal legislation as the Watson bill of 1928 or the Kelly-Davis bill of 1932 drew upon a massive coal industry data base compiled over the years by the Federal Trade Commission, the U.S. Coal Commission, the Bureau of Mines, and other federal units. The coal commission penned an admirable diagnosis of the ills plaguing the coal industry. With one exception, the information available about the structure and operation of the oil industry was equally reliable. That single exception—the accuracy of domestic reserve estimates—was, however, crucial to policy formulation.

Immediately following World War I, a roiling controversy erupted within oil circles about the sufficiency of domestic reserves. Two incompatible scenarios emerged. One emphasized the danger of rapidly depleting reserves as consumption surpassed discovery; the other insisted that adequate reserves existed or would be found to fulfill all future needs. Everyone recognized the guesswork involved in estimating reserves. To minimize the chances of error, the federal government needed access to the most up-to-date information possessed by the oil companies about their reserves. The oil companies insisted on the confidentiality of such data and refused to divulge it to federal agencies, all the while manipulating it for their own purposes. This lacuna diminished the likelihood of fashioning a rational oil program, or even defining critical problem areas.[4] Notwithstanding this inadequacy, ignorance is a weak explanation for the shortcomings of federal fuel policies.

In 1945, John M. Lovejoy, president of Seaboard Oil Company, told a Senate panel that private initiative and a free and competitive industry best served the public interest in oil. The senators also heard J. C. Hunter, president of the Mid-Continent Oil and Gas Association, liken federal intervention to waste, inefficiency, and demoralization.[5] Similar ideological incantations formed part of the warp and woof of oil rhetoric from the earliest days. If taken seriously, such weighty doctrinal utterances would highlight the paths chosen by the federal government in devising fuel policies. But neither big nor little oil remained fixed to their principles. Both exploited the formulas of laissez faire to achieve practical goals; both abandoned these truths whenever expediency instructed.

Satisfied with its position within the industry and anticipating even greater dominance, big oil logically denied the legitimacy of federal intervention—but not completely. Big oil also enshrined the oil depletion allowance as an inalienable right. Depression, combined with flush fields during the late 1920s and 1930s, spurred big oil to warmly embrace state and federal unitization, prorationing, and hot oil regulations. For its part, little oil believed that to reach the salvation implicit in a free market economy required a practical knowledge of sin. The independents demanded vigorous federal intervention to restore an open market. Oil import restrictions and pipeline divorcement and other antitrust measures, so the independents intoned, would safeguard their competitive position by exorcising the unnatural advantages enjoyed by the major integrated firms. Similar reasoning provoked the unstinting hostility of independents to production controls and to such sponsoring agencies as the Federal Oil Conservation Board and the Petroleum Administrative Board.

The coal industry appeared more consistently wedded to laissez faire. Both the bituminous and anthracite branches writhed with resentment when the federal government singled out coal for special attention, as in World War I, or when the coal operators sensed a sympathetic response to the demands of the United Mine Workers of America. But some manifested less resentment than others. All of coal demanded federal protection from the competition of other fuels, especially natural gas. Northern operators by the late 1920s were more amenable to federal action than southern operators. The conflicting competitive positions within coal determined attitudes toward the National Recovery Administration and the subsequent Guffey acts. A majority of productive capacity accepted these measures. Coal proved less resistant than oil to the controls imposed during World War II.

Ideology served as a convenient mask in the pursuit of special benefits. The fuel industries demonstrated a shrewd selectivity in marshaling the magic of laissez faire to protect or promote their interests. Within the federal establishment, political realities and the demands of the moment overwhelmed antitrusters and enthusiasts of comprehensive regulation. The search for the public interest in fuels launched by the La Follette committee and the U.S. Coal Commission and energetically pursued by Harold L. Ickes and the National Resources Committee came to naught, lost in the quagmire of contending special interests and unable to recruit a supportive public.[6]

The fragility of the federal commitment to the idea of the public interest in fuels was demonstrated between 1943 and 1946 when government initiatives to gain some control over the exploitation of foreign oil fields fell victim to the oil industry and anti-internationalist opinions in the Senate. Since World War I, individuals within and without government had insisted that national security considerations demanded the importation of cheap foreign oil. But during the 1920s and 1930s, the government played a diminutive role in overseas oil development. Private firms seized and retained the initiative, particularly in Mexico, South America, and the Middle East. Enormous wartime consumption of domestic supplies and anticipated postwar demand convinced Ickes and others that the diminishing curve of U.S. reserves required large-scale expansion of oil holdings in foreign areas. The major integrated firms with overseas interests insisted on their ability to accomplish this without federal interference. Ickes determined that national security required active federal participation. As a first step, he convinced President Roosevelt to create the Petroleum Reserves Corporation in June 1943. PRC possessed the authority to buy or otherwise acquire reserves of oil outside the United States.[7] PRC then negotiated an agreement with the American Arabian Oil Company whereby PRC would finance the construction of a pipeline from fields in Saudi Arabia and Kuwait to the Mediterranean Sea.[8]

Intense oil industry opposition immediately confronted Ickes and PRC. The Petroleum Industry War Council condemned government participation in oil ownership or other operations. Ralph K. Davies, Ickes's deputy administrator, dissented vigorously as did a host of independent oil organizations. The overseas majors desired this oil for themselves; the independents lashed out at the prospect of enlarged oil imports. Oil industry spokespersons, especially members of the Petroleum Industry War Council, the American Petroleum Institute, and the Independent Petroleum Association of America, conjured up an image of themselves as frightened patriots engaged in a last-ditch defense of private enterprise against the evil of nationalization and socialism. Faced with the intransigence of the oil industry and swayed by the temperate but more convincing counsel of the trusted Davies that an Anglo-American oil agreement was of infinitely greater importance to future national security, Ickes backed down. PRC gradually faded into obscurity.[9]

Once attuned to the threat of an expanded federal role in oil, industry closely monitored the negotiations between England and the United States that produced the Anglo-American oil agreement of 1944 (revised and accepted by England in 1945) which presumably prepared the way for an international petroleum agreement and an international petroleum council. Ickes and Davies labored diligently to negate the contention of large sectors of the industry that this agreement would lead inevitably to the imposition of peacetime controls over oil. API, in 1946, announced its support of the agreement with England, reflecting the political power of those major firms with overseas interests. But Ickes and Davies were unsuccessful in their courtship of majors such as Sun Oil or the independents of IPAA, both of which feared the competition of foreign oil. These opponents aimed an ideological barrage at the Senate, condemning the agreement that "violated their notion of the right order of things in a capitalist world."[10]

Independents had fought cheap foreign oil since at least 1918. The Anglo-American agreement opened a new front in an old war. In the end, practical considerations doomed the chances of Senate ratification in 1947. Coal entered the trenches in opposition to the treaty, as did the major coal-carrying railroads. But of greater moment, as Craufurd D. Goodwin suggests, was the escalation of international tensions that occurred in the postwar years. The Cold War and the political instability of the Middle East argued against greater dependence upon overseas oil supplies. Cultivating our own garden, as the independents had insisted for years, made sense to many in those early days of the Truman Doctrine when Turkey, Greece, Italy, and France seemed to hover on the edge of a communist takeover.[11]

This limited excursion into the field of foreign oil policies yields the conclusion that ideological flexibility and pragmatic assessments of benefits and losses motivated opinion makers in the oil industry and in the government as well. Oil leaders evaluated policy by calculating short-term economic impacts. Federal officials tended to subordinate larger goals to immediate political imperatives. Both world wars and the depression chronicle this process.

Wartime is an unpropitious moment in which to initiate reform. While emotions run high, they are confined to narrow channels. Survival and victory supersede all other goals. Not surprisingly, then, neither world war produced much planned improvement in American society. Change, yes, but reform, no.[12] During the depression, opportunities for necessary reform proliferated. Significant steps were taken in banking and the stock exchange, in labor relations, and in old age security. In the area of energy, programed change restructured the electric and natural gas utilities. Innovative programs encouraged the extension of electric service to rural and other consumers and constructed large-scale, multiple-purpose river valley projects. Coal and oil, however, essentially escaped the reformist impulse.

During both wars, controls of varying degrees of rigor were imposed on the fossil fuel industries. The experiences of World War I taught the necessity of centralized control, a lesson imperfectly assimilated by World War II managers. Diffused and conflicting mandates far more accurately characterize the World War II design than the World War I system. The controlling agencies of the second war grew like an ameoba, slithering about to engulf whatever seemed necessary at the time. This amoeboid structure constantly generated new likenesses of itself. Agency proliferation, a trait of the New Deal, defined the World War II experience. Each new unit sought self-aggrandizement at the expense of existing agencies. While a shooting war raged in Africa, Asia, and Europe and on the seas in between, a bureaucratic war dominated fuel politics in Washington, D.C. Harold L. Ickes presided at the center of this third front.

Jurisdictional disputes weakened the effectiveness of World War II fuel regulations that were, in fact, inferior in scope and authority to those employed during the Great War. Harry A. Garfield's regime possessed a coercive authority superior to that at the disposal of Ickes. Americans not only tolerated such stringent measures as the Closing Order of January 1918, but demanded the consistent application of federal power to control prices and assure the equitable allocation of scarce resources. During the second conflict, the war managers denied the relevance of the earlier experience to the current emergency, founding their claim on the vast differences in magnitude involved. This spurious argument overlooked the essential ingredients of World War I policy: coercion, a national system, and the concentration of authority over fuels in a single agency. Ickes mistakenly rejected advice to create a zone system for coal similar to that applied in 1918. Ickes did crusade for the autonomy of both the coal and oil administrations. Agency independence, however, did not conform to the administrative style preferred by President Roosevelt.

Roosevelt and Ickes in 1940 ignored the importuning of the National Resources Planning Board to impose emergency controls over coal. The ad hoc structure that evolved, centering on the Solid Fuels Administration for War, demonstrated more success in repelling assaults on its jurisdiction than in bringing order to the production and distribution of coal. Chaos reigned as usual. Wildcat strikes, snarled transportation, ill-considered fuel substitution schemes (more the fault of PAW), inequitable distribution by coal dealers, hoarding by large users—all skewed distribution in favor of the largest producers and consumers. The defeat of coupon rationing was a victory won by SFAW at the price of equity.

After the war, the federal government abandoned coal to its own destiny. Nothing done by the government during the depression or World War II infused the industry with new strength. The operators and their sorely abused workers quickly retreated into the self-destructive Battle of the Boyne attitudes of prior decades, leaving the industry ill-prepared to defend its markets against postwar incursions by natural gas, fuel oil, and, ultimately, the nuclear electric industry.

World War I proved that in the absence of preventive measures, the large oil firms would thrive while the small firms grew thin. This disproportionate sharing of benefits and burdens reoccurred during World War II. As a result, both wars endowed the elemental tension between the major integrated oil companies and the independents with renewed intensity. Federal policies, particularly those governing the letting of war contracts, enhanced the dominance of the giant firms. Small refiners scrambled for the crumbs. While the federal government governed the industry, Davies and scores of other lend-lease officials from the big firms administered the system and dwelt cozily within the federal mansion.

Antitrusters and such congressional bodies as the Truman committee were unable to mitigate the consequences of such favoritism. Wartime exigencies convinced Ickes and Donald Nelson, as Garfield and his contemporaries were earlier convinced, that biggest meant best. Thus, the largest oil companies garnered the lion's share of federal largess. No wonder that less criticism of the system, often touted as a cooperative attitude, originated from the major firms than from the independents.

Applying the analogue of war to the New deal makes sense in certain cases but not in the fossil fuel industries, that is, unless bayonet-wielding troops forcing the shutdown of Oklahoma City and East Texas oil fields constitute an equivalent. New Deal fuel policies submerged critical fuel (or energy) considerations in the nonenergy related purposes of the National Recovery Administration. In doing so, the legitimate concerns voiced by USCC and FOCB fell between the cracks. The Kelly-Davis bill of 1932 addressed coal as a natural resource and a necessity that should be regulated in the public interest. NRA and the two Guffey acts defined the coal industry in terms of labor-management relations, the objective being to raise coal prices so as to employ more miners. This policy achieved the New Deal's short-run political objectives. The coal industry, as a supplier of a valuable form of energy, was damaged in the intermediate term. The more humane policy offered by the Kelly-Davis bill proposed to remove redundant miners from the shafts and train them for other productive work. As for oil, the New Deal expended little mental energy in guiding the industry into a conservationist mode or into a less top-heavy structure. Increasing oil profits was the principal objective of New Deal policies.

During the years bracketed by the two world wars, the deliberations and proposals of the early FOCB and NRC afford welcome relief from the stream of unimaginative and irrelevant fuel policies that passed into law. FOCB contributed the concept of conservation by means of end-use control. That its endeavors failed to provoke a change in mentality about energy should not detract from this achievement. FOCB also brought to an early focus the steadily growing concern over oil supplies and national security. But the board was victimized by the politics of oil as well as by the magnificent oil discoveries of the late 1920s and the depression that swiftly followed.

The National Resources Committee, exiled to an orbit distant from the center of power in the New Deal, suffered less from political hostility than from general indifference, its inability to influence events clearly exposed in natural gas policy making. NRC approached natural gas as a scarce resource that ought to be burned only for superior uses. It advocated various mechanisms to discourage promiscuous use and to encourage conservation. But the Natural Gas Act of 1938 and subsequent interpretations of the law by the Supreme Court and the Federal Power Commission emphasized low rates and expanded use for whatever purposes.

NRC, although very much a creature of its time, did at least preach the interrelatedness of all fuels and the nonrenewability of conventional sources of energy. It transcended the habitual fuel-by-fuel approach by offering a holistic view of energy. The committee's proposals were rooted in a responsible notion of the public interest and the imperatives of national security. As a rational means of guaranteeing that the rights of private property did not trample upon the public interest, NRC adopted a regulatory approach to the fuels and to electric power. But its formulas were without political appeal. Ignored, and finally terminated during World War II, NRC composed the best public statement on energy that appeared before the war and, perhaps, after the war as well.[13]

Only with difficulty and charity can one identify successes in the checkered history of federal fuel policies. The fuel-by-fuel focus of yesteryear has yet to metamorphose into an "energy" concept. Supply-side solutions dominate analyses of the energy conundrum. Not even the shock of the Arab embargo in 1973 and the energy crunch of following years forced the birth of energy policies that dealt comprehensively with end-use. In an age of economic decline at home and with only the tattered remnants of power surviving overseas, we would serve ourselves well by scrutinizing the energy diseconomies implicit in boiling lima beans on an electric stove. An unhappy sense of dèjá vu distresses the student of fuel policy formation in the twentieth century.

At times in spite of and at times as a result of federal policies, the giants that ruled petroleum became almost impervious to political oversight; and during the decades following World War II, extended their reach into coal, uranium, and other sources of energy. So strong and resilient are they that they prospered while everyone else suffered from the Organization of Arab Petroleum Exporting Countries embargo and the events that flowed from the Iranian revolution. Warnings that this would come to pass, first voiced at the turn of the century and never again absent from oil politics, went unheeded. Only a Pangloss might suggest the future will be different.

That much abused term, "the public interest," figured prominently in the rhetoric of fuel policy formation after World War I, and still does. More often than not, its use shrouded the machinations of special interests, not all of which were corporate. Predictably, the fuel industries employed the term selfishly. Sadly enough, the failure to discover the public interest in fuels stemmed from the self-delusion of the general public, narcotized by the wildly optimistic pronouncements of federal and private-sector information mongers that we were secure in our supply of cheap energy. Succumbing to such sky-is-the-limit prompts, the public foolishly equated its best interests with cheap energy and absolute freedom of use. Given the heritage of abundance that spurred America's growth over more than three centuries, it was too much to expect the emergence of a new mentality, no matter how dire and prescient the warnings.

NOTES

Manuscript Collections
as Abbreviated in the Notes

BCD, RG 222   Bituminous Coal Division Records. Record Group 222. National Archives.

BFDC, RG 151   Bureau of Foreign and Domestic Commerce Records. Record Group 151. National Archives.

CF Papers   Charles Fahy Papers. Franklin Delano Roosevelt Library, Hyde Park, New York.

CIC, RG 158   Capital Issues Committee Records. Record Group 158. National Archives.

CWCR, RG 50   Connecticut War Council Records. Record Group 50. Connecticut State Library, Hartford, Connecticut.

DC, RG 40   Department of Commerce Records. Record Group 40. National Archives.

DI, RG 48   Department of the Interior Records. Record Group 48. National Archives.

FFD, RG 89   Federal Fuel Distributor Records. Record Group 89. National Archives.

FMcN Papers   Frank McNaughton Papers. Harry S Truman Library, Independence, Missouri.

391

FOCB PAB, RG 232	Federal Oil Conservation Board. Petroleum Administrative Board Records. Record Group 232. National Archives.
FTC, RG 122	Federal Trade Commission Records. Record Group 122. National Archives. This group includes the Bureau of Corporation Records.
HAG Papers	Harry A. Garfield Papers. Library of Congress.
HST Papers	Harry S Truman Papers. Harry S Truman Library, Independence, Missouri.
JC Papers	James Couzens Papers. Library of Congress.
KCMoPL	Clippings File in the Kansas City, Missouri, Public Library.
LO Papers	Leland Olds Papers. Franklin Delano Roosevelt Library, Hyde Park, New York.
NBCC, RG 150	National Bituminous Coal Commission Records. Record Group 150. National Archives.
NRA, RG 9	National Recovery Administration Records. Record Group 9. National Archives.
PAUS, RG 49	Printed Archives of the United States. Record Group 49. National Archives.
PAW, RG 253	Petroleum Administration for War Records. Record Group 253. National Archives.
RBSO	Records of the Bureau of State Organizations.
RFC, RG 234	Reconstruction Finance Corporation Records. Record Group 234. National Archives.
RKD Papers	Ralph K. Davies Papers. Harry S Truman Library, Independence, Missouri.
RLW Papers	Ray Lyman Wilbur Papers. Herbert Hoover Presidential Library, West Branch, Iowa.
SFAW, RG 245	Solid Fuels Administration for War Records. Record Group 245. National Archives.
STP Papers	Sumner T. Pike Papers. Harry S Truman Library, Independence, Missouri.
TC Papers	Thomas T. Connally Papers. Library of Congress.
TJW Papers	Thomas J. Walsh Papers and Walsh-Erickson Papers. Library of Congress.

USCC, RG 68   United States Coal Commission Records. Record Group 68. National Archives.

USFA, RG 67   United States Fuel Administration Records. Record Group 67. National Archives.

USGS, RG 57   United States Geological Survey Records. Record Group 57. National Archives.

VM Papers   Victor Murdock Papers. Library of Congress.

WEB Papers   William E. Borah Papers. Library of Congress.

WGMcA Papers   William G. McAdoo Papers. Library of Congress.

WIB, RG 61   War Industries Board Records. Record Group 61. National Archives.

WPB, RG 179   War Production Board Records. Record Group 179. National Archives.

WW Papers   Woodrow Wilson Papers. Microfilm. Library of Congress.

Introduction

1. Mark Bennitt, ed., *History of the Louisiana Purchase Exposition . . . St. Louis World's Fair of 1904* (St. Louis: Universal Exposition Publishing Co., 1905; reprinted by Arno Press, 1976), 612–23.

2. Bureau of the Census, *Historical Statistics of the United States, Colonial Times to 1957* (Washington, D.C.: GPO, 1960), 402, 410; Sam H. Schurr, Bruce Netschert, et al., *Energy in the American Economy, 1850–1975: An Economic Study of Its History and Prospects* (Baltimore: Johns Hopkins University Press for Resources for the Future, Inc., 1960), 35–36.

3. Schurr, Netschert, et al., *Energy in the American Economy*, 35.

4. *Historical Statistics*, 506.

5. As a general rule, the term *Mid-Continent* refers to Kansas, Oklahoma, and Texas, and occasionally Arkansas and northern Louisiana. It is also used with reference to coal (Colorado is frequently included with the producing states mentioned above) as well as oil and natural gas.

Chapter One

1. For the above three paragraphs: Hale, "The Marketing of Bituminous Coal," Box 1, Entry 4, USCC, RG 68; FTC report of a conference in Kansas City, Mo., July 1916, Coal Investigation, D.S. 40-1-2-5, FTC, RG 122; FTC, *Report on Anthracite and Bituminous Coal*

Situation and the Relation of Rail and Water Transportation to the Present Fuel Problems, June 20, 1917, 65th Cong., 1st sess., 1917, H. Doc. 193, vol. 35, 17, 20; *Bradstreet's A Journal of Trade, Finance, and Public Economy* 29 (12 August 1901): 515, 29 (23 January 1901): 23; W. C. Trapnell and Ralph Ilsley, *The Bituminous Coal Industry with a Survey of Competing Fuels* (Washington, D.C.: Federal Emergency Relief Administration, 1935), 32.

2. Correspondence with the U.S. Fuel Administration, August–September 1917, Coal Investigation, COR5 UNI58 Part 1, FTC, RG 122; Trapnell and Ilsley, *Bituminous Coal Industry,* 68.

3. Between 1896 and 1916, the steam tonnage of the merchant marine rose from 50 to 75 percent. In other words, wind tonnage still claimed 25 percent of total tonnage as late as 1916. USFA, *Report of the Engineer's Committee, 1918–1919* (Washington, D.C.: GPO, 1919) 173–74.

4. FTC, *Report on Anthracite and Bituminous,* 17–20 passim; Hale, "Marketing of Bituminous"; USHR Committee on Interstate and Foreign Commerce, *Report on Discrimination and Monopolies in Coal and Oil,* 59th Cong., 2d sess., 1907, H. Doc. 561, 1–3, 49–63 (This report, submitted by the ICC, focused on the eastern coal-carrying railroads).

5. For the above six paragraphs: Hale, "Marketing of Bituminous"; Jackson Walker Coal & Mining Co., Kansas City, Mo., to L. A. Snead, USFA, 7 December 1917, BCon, Box 1064, USFA, RG 67; USFA and Southwest Coal Bureau Report . . . for 1917, Kansas City, Mo., May 1918, RBSO, Missouri, File S., ibid.; New England Coal Supply in 1908, Box 364, Coal, 21A-A4, Technical or Commodity File, WIB, RG 61; FTC, *Report on Anthracite and Bituminous,* 3; *The Retail Coalman,* 28 (January 1916): 87–90.

6. *Historical Statistics,* 350, 411, 462; Joseph E. Pogue, *The Economics of Petroleum* (New York: John Wiley & Sons, 1921), 48; Bureau of the Census, *Thirteenth Census of the United States, 1910: Manufactures, 1909,* vol. 10 (Washington, D.C.; GPO, 1913), 657; Sam H. Schurr, Bruce Netschert, et al., *Energy in the American Economy, 1850–1975: An Economic Study of Its History and Prospects* (Baltimore: Johns Hopkins University Press for Resources for the Future, Inc., 1960), 35–36.

7. These themes are explicit and implicit in numerous books, among the most useful of which, in order of dates of publication, are: Ida M. Tarbell, *The History of the Standard Oil Company* (New York: Macmillan, 1904); Pogue, *Economics of Petroleum;* George Ward Stocking, *The Oil Industry and the Competitive System: A Study of Waste* (Boston: Houghton Mifflin, 1925); Arthur M. Johnson, *The Development of American Petroleum Pipelines: A Study in Private Enterprise and Public Policy, 1862–1906* (Ithaca: Cornell University Press, 1956); Henrietta M. Larson and Kenneth W. Porter, *History of Humble Oil and Refining Company: A Study in Industrial Growth* (New York: Harper & Brothers, 1959); Harold F. Williamson et al., *The American Petroleum Industry: The Age of*

Energy 1899–1959, vol. 2 (Evanston: Northwestern University Press, 1963); Alfred T. Chandler, Jr., *Strategy and Structure: Chapters in the History of the Industrial Enterprise* (Cambridge, Mass.: M.I.T. Press, 1962); Arthur M. Johnson, *Petroleum Pipelines and Public Policy, 1906–1959* (Cambridge, Mass.: Harvard University Press, 1967); August W. Giebelhaus, *Business and Government in the Oil Industry: A Case Study of Sun Oil, 1876–1945* (Greenwich, Conn.: JAI Press, 1980).

8. *Thirteenth Census: Manufactures, 1909*, 10:657, 662 and *Mines and Quarries, 1909*, 11:269; Williamson et al., *American Petroleum Industry*, 2:61–63, 78; Johnson, *Pipelines, 1862–1906*, 27–31, 51–69 passim; FTC, *Report on Petroleum Industry: Prices, Profits, Competition* (Washington, D.C.: GPO, 1928), 46; Stocking, *The Oil Industry*, 50–52; *Oildom*, 7 (September 1917): 448, 8 (April 1918): 251.

9. Williamson et al., *American Petroleum Industry*, 2:165–66; Giebelhaus, *Sun Oil*, 287–90.

10. Prior to the dissolution of Standard, such non-Standard firms as Union, Gulf, and the Texas Company, although becoming very large, were referred to as the independents. By World War I, Standard, Gulf, Sinclair, and a dozen such others were known as the majors and all others, some integrated and some not, as independents. "Independent" as it appears in this text refers to these latter-day independents who generated the furor and controversy in oil politics.

11. Max West, "The Mid-Continent Oil Field", 6A, BC, 4198 part 1, FTC, RG 122, Oil Investigation, Kansas; Prairie Oil & Gas Co., BC, 2826 part 26, ibid.; FTC, *Report on Pipeline Transportation of Petroleum* (Washington, D.C.: GPO, 1916), 91, 406–10; Williamson et al., *American Petroleum Industry*, 2:88, 93; Schurr, Netschert, et al., *Energy in the American Economy*, 101–2; *Petroleum Industrial Review for 1915*, compiled . . . by the Oil, Paint and Drug Reporter (New York: 10 July 1916), 43.

12. *Petroleum Industrial Review for 1915*, 71–76; FTC, "The Gasoline Investigation, Conference with Representative Jobbers, Refiners, and Others Interested in the Petroleum Industry" (Washington, D.C.: 12–13 June 1916, typescript), Gasoline Investigation, 8508-570-2-1–3, FTC, RG 122.

13. Williamson et al., *American Petroleum Industry*, 2:113–49 passim, 169, presents a uniformly excellent review of the technological advance of the industry; Stocking, *The Oil Industry*, 242.

14. Williamson et al., *American Petroleum Industry*, 2:168, 242–60. For an illuminating and exciting account by geologists of oil exploration in South America, see Ralph Arnold et al., *The First Big Oil Hunt: Venezuela, 1911–1916* (New York: Vantage Press, 1960).

15. John Burrows, Oklahoma City, to BCorp. 10 April 1905, BCorp, 2824, FTC, RG 122; Oil Investigation, Standard Oil Co.–Subsidiary Companies etc., 1906–7, BCorp, 3495 part 1, ibid.; *Report of the Commissioner of Corporations on the Petroleum Industry (Part 1: Position of the*

Standard Oil Company in the Petroleum Industry) (Washington, D.C.: GPO, 1907), 298–99; Petroleum Industrial Review for 1915, 74; Oildom, 7 (September 1917): 450; Williamson et al., American Petroleum Industry, 166, 210–12, 217–27.

16. Kanotex statement to BCorp, 1907, Oklahoma Oil Investigation, 1424-5, FTC, RG 122; Kansas Oil Refining Co. statement to BCorp, 1913, Oklahoma Oil Investigation, 1424-2, ibid.; Chanute Refining Co. statement to BCorp, 1913, Oklahoma Oil Investigation, 1424-1, ibid.; FTC, "Gasoline Investigation, Conference," ibid.

17. Response to FTC inquiry by J. C. McDonald president, Standard Oil Co. of Kansas, 1916, Oklahoma Oil Investigation, 7100-73, ibid.

18. For the above paragraphs on gas: "Artificial Gas in the United States, 1901–1920," Box 652, Gas, 21A-A4, Technical or Commodity File, WIB, RG 61; Herbert B. Dorau, ed., Material for the Study of Public Utility Economics (New York: Macmillan, 1930), 3–5, 8, 11; Delos F. Wilcox, Municipal Franchises: A Description of the Terms and Conditions Upon Which Private Corporations Enjoy Special Privileges in the Streets of American Cities, 2 vols. (New York: McGraw-Hill, 1911) 1:139–41, 466; Harold C. Passer, The Electrical Manufactures, 1875–1900: A Study in Competition, Entrepreneurship, Technical Change, and Economic Growth (Cambridge, Mass.: Harvard University Press, 1953), 149–50; Arthur A. Bright, Jr., The Electric-Lamp Industry: Technological Change and Economic Development from 1800 to 1947 (New York: Macmillan, 1949), 152; Louis Stotz and Alexander Jamison, History of the Gas Industry (New York: Press of Stettiner Brothers, 1938), 250–51; USHR Committee on Interstate and Foreign Commerce, To Make Gas Pipe Lines Common Carriers, Hearings on S. 3345, March 18, 1914, 63d Cong., 2d sess., 1914, 4–5, 11–16.

19. After World War II, the railroad market for coal virtually disappeared.

20. "Electric power" and "power" are used synonymously throughout this study.

21. For the above four paragraphs: Bituminous Coal Trade Association, A Report to the Bituminous Coal Trade Association on the Present and Future of the Bituminous Coal Trade, 1908 (New York: H. S. Fleming, 1908), 3–4; Oil Investigation, Kansas-Crude Oil-Fuel Oil, BC, 3241 part 1, and H. H. Tucker, Jr., Uncle Sam Oil Co., Kansas City, Kansas, to Commissioner of Corporations, 16 November 1906, Oil Investigation, Missouri-Inspection-Competitive Methods–Standard Oil Co., 4202, BC, FTC, RG 122; McCollam Papers, Southern Historical Collection, University of North Carolina Manuscripts Division, Chapel Hill, Box 5, Folder 79. McCollam operated a sugar plantation; Schurr, Netschert, et al., Energy in the American Economy, 76–79, 105, 113; Pogue, Economics of Petroleum, 158; Williamson et al., American Petroleum Industry, 2:179–80; Stocking, The Oil Industry, 122–23; The Retail Coalman, 38

(April 1916): 45; Jacob Martin Gould, *Output and Productivity in the Electric and Gas Utilities* (New York: National Bureau of Economic Research, 1946), 52.

22. For the above three paragraphs: Allen R. Foote, *Economic Value of Electric Light and Power*, 2d ed. (Cincinnati: Robert Clarke & Co., 1899), 46–48, 54–56; Passer, *Electrical Manufacturers*, 196–203; John G. Clark, *Towns and Minerals in Southeastern Kansas: A Study in Regional Industrialization, 1890–1930* (Lawrence: State Geological Survey of Kansas, 1970).

23. *The Retail Coalman*, 40 (May 1922): 65.

24. Ibid.: 65–66.

Chapter Two

1. Sam Bass Warner, Jr., *The Urban Wilderness: A History of the American City* (New York: Harper & Row, 1972); William Frederick Cottrell, *Energy and Security: The Relation Between Energy, Social Change, and Economic Development* (New York: McGraw-Hill, 1955), 111–13; Allan R. Pred, *The Spatial Dynamics of U.S. Urban-Industrial Growth, 1800–1914: Interpretive and Theoretical Essays* (Cambridge, Mass.: M.I.T. Press, 1966), chap. 4; Robert H. Wiebe, *The Search for Order, 1877–1920* (New York: Hill and Wang, 1967) skillfully evokes the varied responses of Americans to the new technological and economic thrusts of the period.

2. Graham R. Taylor, *Satellite Cities: A Study of Industrial Suburbs* (New York: D. Appleton, 1915), 91–105, 127–49, 165–77; Sam Bass Warner, Jr., *Streetcar Suburbs: The Process of Growth in Boston, 1870–1900* (Cambridge, Mass.: Harvard University Press, 1962); Mark H. Rose and John G. Clark, "Light, Heat, and Power: Energy Choices in Kansas City, Wichita, and Denver, 1900–1935," *Journal of Urban History*, 5 (May 1979): 345; Donald J. Bogue, *The Structure of the Metropolitan Community: A Study of Dominance and Sub-dominance* (Ann Arbor: Horace H. Rackham School of Graduate Studies, University of Michigan, 1949), 7–8; David Ward, *Cities and Immigrants: A Geography of Change in Nineteenth Century America* (New York: Oxford University Press, 1971), 128–30, 134–39.

3. Rose and Clark, "Light, Heat, and Power," 348–49.

4. For the above two paragraphs: Eric E. Lampard, "The Evolving System of Cities in the United States: Urbanization and Economic Development," in H. S. Perloff and L. Wingo, Jr., eds., *Issues in Urban Economics* (Baltimore: Johns Hopkins University Press, 1968), 102–3; Christopher Tunnard and Henry H. Reed, Jr., *American Skyline: The Growth and Form of Our Cities and Towns* (Boston: Houghton Mifflin, 1955), 206. Other essential works include: John Marston Fitch, *American Building: The Forces That Shape It* (Boston: Houghton Mifflin, 1948) and *American Building 2: The Environmental Forces that Shape It*, 2d ed.,

rev. (Boston: Houghton Mifflin, 1972); Carl W. Condit, *Chicago, 1910–1929: Building, Planning, and Urban Technology* (Chicago: University of Chicago Press, 1973). For smoke pollution, I am indebted to Joel A. Tarr's paper, "Transport Fuels and Environmental Quality of Twentieth-Century Cities," delivered at the Conference on Power, Transport, and Public Policy in Modern America, Michigan Technological University, 25–27 September 1981.

5. "America's Electrical Week on the Pacific Coast," *Journal of Electricity, Power and Gas*, 37 (16 December 1916): 459–65; Rose and Clark, "Light, Heat, and Power," 344–48; P. F. Walker, "Industrial Development in Kansas, Section 2, Industrial Development Map," *Bulletin of the University of Kansas*, 23 (15 June 1922): 14–15.

6. Between 1900 and 1920, innumerable books and articles appeared, which offered to guide homeowners, and especially women, in making choices of household equipment. The extent to which promises of liberation were realized has been questioned. See Ruth Schwartz Cowan, "The 'Industrial Revolution' in the Home: Household Technology and Social Change in the 20th Century," *Technology and Culture*, 17 (January 1976): 1–23; and Corlann G. Bush, "The Barn Is His, the House Is Mine: Agricultural Technology and Sex Roles," in George H. Daniels and Mark H. Rose, eds., *Energy and Transport: Historical Perspectives on Policy Issues* (Beverly Hills: Sage Publications, 1982) 235–59.

7. "Energy industries" encompasses coal, oil, natural gas, and power, both fuel-generated and hydroelectric. "Fuel industries," the focus of this work, includes all the above, particularly coal and oil, but not power.

8. For an intelligent exposition of the fuel-by-fuel politics that dominated energy policy making in the 1960s and 1970s, see David Howard Davis, *Energy Politics* (New York: St. Martin's Press, 1974), 18–42 passim.

9. Thomas K. McCraw, "Regulation in America: A Review Article," *Business History Review*, 49 (Summer 1975): 160. Others who assert the uselessness of the term include: Robert A. Dahl and Charles E. Lindblom, *Politics, Economics, and Welfare* (New York: Harper Torchbook, 1963) and Frank Sorauf, "The Public Interest Reconsidered," *The Journal of Politics*, 19 (November 1957): 616–39.

10. Richard E. Flathmam, *The Public Interest: An Essay Concerning the Normative Discourse of Politics* (New York: John Wiley & Sons, 1966), 13. A strong defense of the term and an attempt at definition form the substance of Virginia Held, *The Public Interest and Individual Interests* (New York: Basic Books, 1970), which contains an excellent bibliography. I am indebted to Robert Simon, professor of philosophy at Hamilton College, for introducing me to these studies.

11. John Rawls, *A Theory of Justice* (Cambridge, Mass: The Belknap Press of Harvard University Press, 1971). My concept of the public

interest recognizes the probability that its precise meaning may shift with time and under changing circumstances. One can argue that American belligerency in 1917 was not in the public interest. Once the fighting had been joined, however, it was in the public interest that the war be won.

12. *First Annual Report of the Public Utilities Commission, Kansas City, Missouri, April 17, 1911* (Kansas City: n.p., 1911); Delos F. Wilcox, *Municipal Franchises: A Description of the Terms and Conditions Upon Which Private Corporations Enjoy Special Privileges in the Streets of American Cities,* 2 vols. (New York: McGraw-Hill, 1911), 2:750.

13. Alfred M. Leeston et al., *The Dynamic Natural Gas Industry: The Description of an American Industry from the Historical, Technical, Legal, Financial, and Economic Standpoints* (Norman: University of Oklahoma Press, 1963), 263; USHR Committee on Interstate and Foreign Commerce, *To Make Gas Pipe Lines Common Carriers, Hearings on S. 3345, March 18, 1914.* 63d Cong., 2d sess., 1914, 11–16. Events in Kansas City can be followed in Clippings File, Gas Companies, KCMoPL.

14. The capture thesis and its adherents, notably Gabriel Kolko, *The Triumph of Conservatism* (Glencoe: Free Press, 1963) and *Railroads and Regulation 1877–1916* (Princeton: Princeton University Press, 1965), are discussed in numerous works. For two different contexts, see James P. Johnson, *The Politics of Soft Coal: The Bituminous Industry from World War I through the New Deal* (Urbana: University of Illinois Press, 1979), 3–5; and McCraw, "Regulation in America," 162–73. McCraw disposes of "public interest" as a justificatory theory for regulation, but he does not inform the reader as to his own notion of the meaning of the term.

15. Proponents of supply-side theories who rely on "free" market forces to allocate economic resources would do well to follow the history of natural gas in Kansas between 1900 and 1920. Rates fluctuated wildly even when supplies were adequate. When supplies diminished, KNG arbitrarily cut off the gas supply of entire towns and discriminated in favor of industrial consumers and against domestic consumers. For an introduction to this tangled story, see John G. Clark, *Towns and Minerals in Southeastern Kansas: A Study in Regional Industrialization, 1890–1930* (Lawrence: State Geological Survey of Kansas, 1970).

16. J. Leonard Bates, *The Origins of Teapot Dome: Progressives, Parties, and Petroleum, 1909–1921* (Urbana: University of Illinois Press, 1963), 21–55, 97–199 passim. See also Keith W. Olson, *Biography of a Progressive: Franklin K. Lane, 1864–1921* (Westport, Conn.: Greenwood Press, 1979), 108–19; and Burl Noggle, *Teapot Dome: Oil and Politics in the 1920's* (New York: W. W. Norton, 1965).

17. Among the federal bodies that functioned during those years were: The United States Industrial Commission (1899); the Department of Commerce and Labor with its Bureau of Corporations (BCorp) (1903), which was transformed into the independent FTC in

1914; and the Bureau of Mines (1907). The United States Geological Survey in the Department of the Interior also touched upon the energy industries.

18. Bruce Bringhurst, *Antitrust and the Oil Monopoly: The Standard Oil Cases* (Westport, Conn.; Greenwood Press, 1979), 68.

19. Harold F. Williamson et al., *The American Petroleum Industry: The Age of Energy 1899-1959*, vol. 2 (Evanston: Northwestern University Press, 1963), 7–9, essentially ignores intraindustry opposition to Standard; Arthur M. Johnson, *The Development of American Petroleum Pipelines: A Study in Private Enterprise and Public Policy, 1862–1906* (Ithaca: Cornell University Press, 1956), 186–97.

20. James R. Garfield to the President, 2 May 1906, BCorp, Doc. 4196, FTC, RG 122; *Report of the Commissioner of Corporations on the Transportation of Petroleum, May 2, 1906* (Washington, D.C.: GPO, 1906); and *Report of the Commissioner of Corporations on the Petroleum Industry (Part 1, Position of the Standard Oil Company in the Petroleum Industry)* (Washington, D.C.: GPO, 1907). Bureau investigation of the oil industry persisted through the establishment of the FTC. The major effort, the Oklahoma Oil Investigation of 1909/13/15, focused on the pipeline companies in the Mid-Continent field. These documents comprise a separate manuscript file, Oklahoma Oil Investigation, BCorp, FTC, RG 122. See also USHR Committee on Interstate and Foreign Commerce, *Report on Discrimination and Monopolies in Coal and Oil*, 59th Cong., 2d sess., 1907, Doc. 561. A Senate resolution in 1913 extended the sphere of the investigation to include all phases of the petroleum industry, an extension reiterated in a resolution of 1914, by which time the FTC had succeeded the Bureau, FTC, *Annual Report, 1916*, 22.

21. August W. Giebelhaus, *Business and Government in the Oil Industry: A Case Study of Sun Oil, 1876–1945* (Greenwich, Conn.: JAI Press, 1980), 31–34, emphasizes the centrality of Standard's competition in the expansion of Sun. Sun's managers always kept one eye on what Standard was doing.

22. For the above five paragraphs: Johnson, *Pipelines, 1862–1906*, 201–16, 219–34, notes that President Roosevelt used the data gathered in Kansas to lobby in favor of the Hepburn Act; see also his *Petroleum Pipelines and Public Policy, 1906–1959* (Cambridge, Mass.: Harvard University Press, 1967), 55–56, 72–81; FTC, *Report on Pipelines Transportation of Petroleum* (Washington, D.C.: GPO, 1916), 24–25, 413; Walter T. Munn to T. A. Carroll, special agent, Department of Commerce, 12 November 1913, Oklahoma Oil Investigation, BCorp, Doc. 1424-5, FTC, RG 122; Charles Moreau Harger, "Kansas' Contest with Standard Oil," *Moody's Magazine*, March 1906, 425–29, in BCorp, Doc. 2874, FTC, RG 122; E. L. Gross interview, BCorp, Doc. 3209, part 3, FTC, RG 122; Oil Investigation, Kansas-Refining Oil, BCorp, Doc. 3303, part 3, FTC, RG 122; Bringhurst, *Antitrust and the Oil Monopoly*, 67–68, 86–88; Henrietta M. Larson and Kenneth W. Porter, *History of*

Humble Oil and Refining Company: A Study in Industrial Growth (New York: Harper & Brothers, 1959), 19–21, 42–46, 52–53.

23. Alfred D. Chandler, Jr., *The Visible Hand: The Managerial Revolution in American Business* (Cambridge, Mass.: The Belknap Press of Harvard University Press, 1977), 376.

24. USHR Committee on Mines and Mining, *Hearings on Petroleum and Gasoline* (Washington, D.C.: GPO, 1916), 62–68, 108; FTC, "The Gasoline Investigation. Conference with Representative Jobbers, Refiners and Others Interested in the Petroleum Industry, Washington, D.C., June 12–13, 1916," 3 vols. typescript, 1:6–13, 141–42,. Gasoline Investigation, Doc. 8508-570-2-1-3, FTC, RG 122; USHR Committee on Interstate and Foreign Commerce, *Hearings on H.R. 13916, Laying an Embargo Upon Crude Petroleum, etc., April 15, 1916*, 64th Cong., 1st sess., 1916, 6–17; USHR Committee on Interstate and Foreign Commerce, *Hearings on H.R. 16581, A Bill to Regulate the Transportation of Oil by Means of Pipelines, May 15–16, 1914, Parts 1 and 2*, 63d Cong., 2d sess. 1914, 5–6, 35; FTC, *Annual Report of the Federal Trade Commission for the Fiscal Year Ended June 30, 1917* (Washington, D.C.: GPO. 1917); ibid., 1922; and ibid., 1925; Johnson, *Pipelines, 1906–1959*, 176–77.

25. Crude-oil prices at the well remained fairly stable from 1907 through 1915, then increased rapidly from 1916 through 1920 as wartime demand, in Europe and at home, accelerated and as older fields played out. Thereafter, prices gradually declined through 1929, but never to the lower levels obtaining between 1907 and 1914. W. C. Trapnell and Ralph Isley, *The Bituminous Coal Industry with a Survey of Competing Fuels* (Washington, D.C.: Federal Emergency Relief Administration 1935), A-8.

26. It is interesting to note that in Giebelhaus, *Sun Oil*, chaps. 2 and 3, not a single connection is made between Sun's growth and federal or state policies.

27. USHR Committee on Interstate and Foreign Commerce, *Report on the Alleged Coal Combination*, 52d Cong., 2d sess., 1893, H. Rept. 2278.

28. Arthur E. Suffern, "Coal for the People," *Atlantic Monthly*, 136 (December 1925): 844; National Resources Committee, *Energy Resources and National Policy* (Washington, D.C.: GPO, 1939), 16.

29. For the above five paragraphs: USHR, *Discrimination and Monopolies in Coal and Oil, 1907*, 1–3, 8–15, 30–31, 63–64; USHR Committee on Interstate and Foreign Commerce, *Freight Rates on Coal, Hearings on H. Res. 217 . . . August 22, 1913*, 63d Cong., 1st sess., 1913, 3–6, 11–12, 20–23; USHR Committee on Interstate and Foreign Commerce, *Hearings on Mining and Transportation of Coal, H. Res. 13354, Prohibiting Common Carriers from Owning or Leasing Coal Lands, February 5 and May 8, 1914*, 5–6, 21–22, 40–42; FTC, *Report on Anthracite and Bituminous Coal Situation and the Relation of Rail and Water Transportation to the Present Fuel Problem*, 65th Cong., 1st sess., 1917, H. Doc. 193, vol. 35

passim; Exhibit submitted to FTC and Coal Industry Hearings, Denver, 26 July 1916, concerning the unfair competition by Railroad Companies and Subsidiaries, Bituminous Coal Investigation, Doc. 8508-574-2-2, FTC, RG 122; Johnson, *Pipelines, 1862–1905,* 251; Joseph T. Lambie, *From Mine to Market: The History of Coal Transportation on the Norfolk and Western Railway* (New York: New York University Press, 1954), 255–57.

30. Johnson, *Politics of Soft Coal,* 30–31; F. G. Tryon, "The Irregular Operation of the Bituminous Coal Industry," reproduced from the *American Economic Review Supplement,* vol. 11, no. 1, 21 March 1921, published by the American Economic Association, Bituminous Coal Investigation, Doc. 1/COR5 INT3, FTC, RG 122, 1–3.

31. Johnson, *Politics of Soft Coal,* 30–31.

32. F. W. Vaughan, Victor-American Fuel Co., Denver, Colo., to ICC, 8 August 1916, Coal Investigation, COR5 VIC5, FTC, RG 122; "USFA and Southwest Coal Bureau Report on Zone 17 and the Indiana and Illinois coal that moved into those states for 1917, Kansas City, Mo., May 1918," typescript, Records of the Bureau of State Organizations, Missouri, File S, USFA, RG 67; F. G. Tryon and W. F. McKenney, USGS, "Economic Phases of Coal Storage," prepared for the Federated American Engineering Societies, 1923, Coal Investigation, 1/COR5 INT3, FTC, RG 122; Johnson, *Politics of Soft Coal,* 29–30.

33. Gerald D. Nash, *United States Oil Policy, 1890–1964: Business and Government in Twentieth Century America* (Pittsburgh: University of Pittsburgh Press, 1968), 11.

34. Giebelhaus, *Sun Oil,* 10.

35. Obscure Bureau of Mines publications do reflect some concern with fuel end-use problems, and these can be considered as designed to serve a general public. See, as examples, Samuel B. Flagg, *City Smoke Ordinances and Smoke Abatement,* Bureau of Mines Bulletin 49 (Washington, D.C.: GPO, 1912); or R. S. Blatchley, *Waste of Oil and Gas in the Mid-Continent Fields,* Bureau of Mines Technical Paper 45 (Washington, D.C.: GPO, 1913); or L. P. Breckenridge and S. B. Flagg, *Saving Fuel in Heating a House,* Bureau of Mines Technical Paper 97 (Washington, D.C.: GPO, 1917).

Chapter Three

1. David M. Kennedy, *Over Here: The First World War and American Society* (New York: Oxford University Press, 1980). Chapter 2 recounts this story with great skill and insight.

2. Garfield, son of President James A. Garfield and brother of Commissioner of Corporations and Secretary of the Interior James R. Garfield, came to his job, after a brief stint as an assistant in Herbert Hoover's Council of National Defense Food Committee, from the pres-

idency of Williams College. Garfield and President Wilson were close friends, Garfield having taught politics at Princeton from 1903 to 1908 when Wilson was president of the university.

3. In 1915, FTC initiated a study of the Indiana and Illinois coalfields, which in midyear was extended to include the Mid-Continent fields. Price and supply problems in 1916 prompted the House to pass Resolution 352, the Rainey resolution, directing the FTC to inquire into all aspects of coal. In 1917, the FTC published its findings as *Report on Anthracite and Bituminous Coal Situation and the Relation of Rail and Water Transportation to the Present Fuel Problem*, 65th Cong., 1st sess., 1917, H. Doc. 193, vol. 35.

4. FTC, "Transcript of Proceedings with Railroad Purchasing Agents and Municipal Public Utilities, Washington, April 26, 1917," Coal Investigation, Docket Section 40-1-2-13, FTC, RG 122; Statement re bituminous coal by L&N Railroad, 25 April 1917, Coal Investigation, 8508-589-21, FTC, RG 122.

5. For the above three paragraphs: *The Retail Coalman*, 28 (January 1916): 39, 28 (February 1916): 39, 28 (April 1916): 37; 29 (December 1916): 40; 30 (January 1917): 65; *Washington, D.C., Times*, 1 November 1916, and *Philadelphia Public Ledger*, 10 November 1916, Clippings in *Coal Investigation* CLi5 Part 1, FTC, RG 122; FTC, *Anthracite and Bituminous Coal Situation*, 4–5, 11, 14; Coal prices, Kansas City, Coal Investigation, TAB5 KAN5, FTC, RG 122; Philadelphia coal prices, Coal Investigation, SCH5 HOT5, FTC, RG 122; Oklahoma City and other coal prices, PRi5 #9, FTC, RG 122; FTC, "The Gasoline Investigation, Conference with Representative Jobbers, Refiners and Others Interested in the Petroleum Industry, Washington, D.C., June 12–13, 1916," 3 vols. typescript, 1:6–13, 35–43, 109–16, Gasoline Investigation, Doc. 8508-570-2-1-3, FTC, RG 122; USHR Committee on Mines and Mining, *Hearings on Petroleum and Gasoline* (Washington, D.C.: GPO, 1916), 127.

6. Some critics of the concept of the public interest question the validity of declaring one industry as affecting the public interest more than another industry. Surely a supply of coal was more essential to the public interest than a supply of oilcloth or percolators.

7. Provision for CND was written into the Army Appropriation Act of 1916. It consisted of the secretaries of War, Navy, Interior, Agriculture, Commerce, and Labor plus an advisory council of seven specialists in the fields of transportation, labor, general industry, finance, mining, merchandise, and medical sciences. Secretary of War Newton I. Baker served as chairman. Dr. Franklin H. Martin, *Digest of the Proceedings of the Council of National Defense During the World War* (Washington, D.C.: GPO, 1934), 37; CND, "A Report from the Director of the Council of National Defense and of Its Advisory Commission to the Chairman," Mimeographed (Washington, D.C., 28 May

1917), 3–4. For a superb discussion of the origin, organization, and philosophical essence of the CND and the War Industries Board, see Robert D. Cuff, *The War Industries Board: Business-Government Relations during World War I* (Baltimore: Johns Hopkins University Press, 1973). Cuff emphasizes CND's search for a cooperative, noncoercive, voluntaristic mode of managing the war and offers essential qualifications to the view that the Wilson administration created a centralized and comprehensive war directorate.

8. Ibid., 5, 8–9, 41–42; CND, *Community Council Circular No. 1* (Washington, D.C., December 1917), 1–4, and *Circular No. 2* (May 1918), 2.

9. Cuff, *War Industries Board*, 73–85; CND, *First Annual Report . . . for the Fiscal Year Ended June 30, 1917* (Washington, D.C., 1917), 57–59, and *Second Annual Report, 1918* (1918), 217–19; CND, *Report from the Director*, 26–27; Frank Haigh Dixon, *Railroads and Government, Their Relations in the United States, 1910–1921* (New York: Charles Scribner's Sons, 1923), 111–13.

10. Representative of coal industry personnel on the committee were J. F. Welborn, president of Colorado Fuel and Iron Company, Denver, the largest firm in the Rocky Mountain field, which owned or operated steel works, twenty-seven coal mines, and innumerable coke ovens; and Harry N. Taylor, vice-president of Central Coal and Coke Company, Kansas City, Missouri. Central Coal owned twenty-six mines in the Mid-Continent, and Taylor had past service as an officer in various operator associations. The public representatives included John Mitchell, former president of the UMWA and chairman of the New York Industrial Commission; Van H. Manning, director of USBM; and George Otis Smith, director of USGS. *Coal Age*, 11 (12 May 1917): 1–3; Peabody Committee, Coal Investigation, 1/COR5 SEN5 part 2, FTC, RG 122. CND also appointed other energy-related committees: Gas and Electric Service, Oil (chaired by A. C. Bedford, president of Standard Oil of New Jersey), and Electric Rail Transportation.

11. John P. White to CND, 23 May 1917, Office of the Secretary, 1–53 (part 1), DI, RG 48. Peabody's committee, ignoring UMWA opposition, intervened in numerous wildcat strikes, implicitly defining all strikes as inimical to the public interest.

12. For the above two paragraphs: CND, *First Annual Report, 1917*, 32–33; CND Committee on Coal Production to the Coal Operators of the U.S., 14 May 1917, Office of the Secretary, 1–53 (part 1), DI, RG 48; F. S. Peabody, chairman, Committee on Coal Production, to W. S. Gifford, director, CND, weekly reports of 12 May, 5, 11, and 30 June 1917, ibid.; Committee of Lake Shippers to Francis S. Peabody, 15 May 1917, ibid.; Daniel Willard to Franklin Lane, Secretary of the Interior, 8 May 1917, Office of the Secretary, 1-53 Railroads, DI, RG

48; Arthur Arctander, Bronx County Property Owners' and Business Men's Association, N.Y., to William L. Calder, USS, 15 May 1917, Coal Investigation, COR5 BRO62, FTC, RG 122; J. G. Holden, secretary, Bronx Citizens' Association, N.Y., to Henry Bruckner, USHR, 28 May 1917, ibid.; Miss M. E. Cavanaugh, Kansas City, to FTC, 8 May 1917, Coal Investigation, COR5 CAV5, FTC, RG 122; Sam M. West, secretary, Cassidy Southwestern Commission Co., Kansas City, to FTC, 8 May 1917, Coal Investigation, COR5 CAS5, FTC, RG 122.

13. FTC, *Anthracite and Bituminous Coal Situation*, 25; David L. Wing, assistant chief economist, FTC, memorandum for Commissioner Murdock, Box 106, VM Papers; M. C. Wooster, "Memorandum on a plan for the regulation of the coal industry by the [FTC], August 13, 1917," Coal Investigation, MEM5 WIN5, FTC, RG 122; Letters and pamphlets pertaining to railroads, April–August 1917, Office of the Secretary, 1-53 Railroads, DI, RG 48; J. G. Puterbaugh, "Supply of Coal Will Be Largely Question of Cars," in *Oklahoma City, Oklahoma*, 8 July 1917, Box 366, Clippings, 21A-A4, Technical or Commodity File, WIB, RG 61; USS Committee on Interstate Commerce, *Hearings on S. 2354 . . . Price Regulation of Coal and Other Commodities, June 22 and 26, 1917, Part 1*, 65th Cong., 1st sess., 1917, 272–74 (and Lewis testimony, 72–75; Colver testimony, 216–19, 225); for the Lever Act and the appointment of Garfield, see *General Orders, Regulations and Rulings of the United States Fuel Administration*, compiled by the Legal Division of the Administration (Washington, D.C.; GPO, 1920), 9–19, 26–27; Kennedy, *Over Here*, 123.

14. Cuff, *War Industries Board*, 94–98; Kennedy, *Over Here*, 143.

15. Garfield memorandum handed to the president, 17 July 1917, Box 130, HAG Papers; J. Wilson Howe to Uncle Woodrow, c. August 1917, Box 91, ibid.; J. F. Gallbreath, secretary, American Mining Congress, to the Honorable Woodrow Wilson, 16 August 1917, Coal Investigation, COR5, AME4, FTC, RG 122; letters in August to Wilson, including one from Senator Frank B. Kellogg, Minnesota, Series 4, Case File 664, WW Papers.

16. NRCMA claimed a membership of 25,000 by 1918, handling 80 percent of retail tonnage. By early 1918, NCA claimed a membership that produced two-thirds of total tonnage. For the first organizational efforts, see *The Retail Coalman*, 31 (November 1917): 41; *Proceedings of the First Annual Convention of the National Coal Association, May 28–29, 1918* (Philadelphia, 1918), 4–8 passim; NRCMA, *First Annual Meeting, May 20–21, 1918, Atlantic City, N.J.* (Washington, D.C., 1918), 1, 3, 4; [NRCMA], *The Coal Merchant*, 1 (25 March 1919): np. Oil organizations are noted in Chapter 4.

17. Robert Cuff, "Harry Garfield, the Fuel Administration, and the Search for a Cooperative Order During World War I," *American Quarterly*, 30 (Spring 1978): 48, 53; Kennedy, *Over Here*, 43, 95–98, 118–23;

Garfield testimony before USS Subcommittee of the Committee on Manufactures, *Hearings on Shortages of Sugar and Coal, Part 3,* 65th Cong., 2d sess., 1918, 627.

18. N. S. Schroeder, director, "Final Report of the Bureau of State Organizations, 1917–1919," 1919 Typescript, RBSO, Box 745, USFA, RG 67. Among USFA's most important units were the Bureau of Production, Distribution Division, Oil Division, Bureau of State Organizations, Bureau of Conservation, Bureau of Prices, and the Engineers Committee on Production Costs.

19. For the above two paragraphs: Cuff, *War Industries Board,* 8–9; NRCMA, *First Annual Meeting,* 1; USFA, *Final Report of the United States Fuel Administration, 1917–1919, Report of the Administrative Division, 1917–1919, Part 2, Reports of Bureaus with Headquarters in Washington, D.C., Report of the Oil Division* (Washington, D.C.: GPO, 1921), 232–44, 261–68; J. D. A. Morrow to William Hard, 13 September 1918, Box 130, HAG Papers; *Saward's Journal,* 5 (June 1922): 98.

20. USFA dealt most notably with the Capital Issues Committee (CIC), which originated through the efforts of the Treasury Department, the Federal Reserve Board, and major investment banking houses. Designed to discourage investment in nonessential activities, CIC was legitimated in the legislation that created the War Finance Corporation (WFC). CIC, however, lacked all compulsory authority and depended wholly upon the employment of extralegal pressure and the cooperation of private financial institutions. Both CIC and WFC are discussed later, particularly in Chapter 4, which deals with petroleum and electric power. See Woodbury Willoughby, *The Capital Issues Committee and War Finance Corporation,* The Johns Hopkins University Studies in Historical and Political Science, Series 52, No. 2 (Baltimore: Johns Hopkins University Press, 1934). WGMcA Papers Boxes 188–95 contain material on CIC, and, or course, the chief source is CIC, RG 158.

21. WIB was created by CND in July 1917, superseding the General Munitions Board. On 4 March 1918, Wilson redefined the board's functions, giving it, among other duties, the authority to establish priorities. The priorities division of WIB included representatives of the Food Administration, the War Trade Board, the Shipping Board, USRA, and USFA.

22. For the last two paragraphs: Cuff, *War Industries Board,* 102, 153–54, 158; USS Subcommittee of the Committee on Interstate Commerce, *Car Service Shortage, Hearings on S. 636 . . . May 3, 1917,* 65th Cong., 1st sess., 1917, 9, 18–28; Car shortages, Office of the Secretary, 1-53 Railroads, DI, RG 48; J. G. Puterbaugh, president, The McAlester Fuel Company, to FTC, 22 June 1917, Coal Investigation, COR5 McC2, FTC, RG 122; Dixon, *Railroads and Government,* 111–13.

23. For an account that emphasizes the centrality of price fixing, blaming on the prices established all the failures and problems of

USFA, and asserting, erroneously, that coalmen were without influence in USFA, see James P. Johnson, "The Wilsonians as War Managers: Coal and the 1917–1918 Winter Crisis," *Prologue: The Journal of the National Archives*, 9 (Winter 1977).

24. Cuff, *War Industries Board*, 94–98; Harry Taylor in USS, *Price Regulation of Coal*, 91–92; items from the Coal Investigation, FTC, RG 122 include: the Kansas Buff Brick and Manufacturing Company to FTC, 4 June 1917, COR5 KAN6; Frank McAllester, attorney general of Missouri, "Abstract of Evidence...on...Coal," 1917, COR5 MIS5; Fuel Engineering Company of N.Y. to FTC, May–September 1917, COR5 FUE5; William F. Notz, memo concerning *Denver Post* fight against Colorado coal operators, 3 October 1917, MEM5 NOT5. William T. Galligan, fuel administrator for Colorado to Garfield, 15 March 1918, Colorado. Folder 2, RBSO, USFA, RG 67; newspaper references from Boxes 365–66, Clippings, 21A-A4, Technical or Commodity File, WIB, RG 61; William A. Cullop to Wilson, 5 July 1917, Series 4, Case File 664, WW Papers.

25. Johnson, *Politics of Soft Coal*, 12, 43–48; Cuff, *War Industries Board*, 105–9; Keith W. Olson, *Biography of a Progressive: Franklin K. Lane, 1864–1921* (Westport, Conn.: Greenwood Press, 1979), 142–45; Josephus Daniels, *The Wilson Era: Years of War and After, 1917–1923* (Chapel Hill: University of North Carolina Press, 1946), 244–45; Peabody testimony before USS Subcommittee of the Committee on Manufactures, *Hearings on Coal, Part 3*, 1524–35.

26. For the above three paragraphs: For opposition, see *The American Coal Journal*, August 1917, and Chamber of Commerce of the United States of America, "Reduce the Coal Requirements," *War Bulletin No. 16*, 27 August 1917, np; *General Orders, USFA*, 52–160, for various coal district price orders; USFA, *Final Report, 1917–1919*, 240–41; Memorandum for Secretary Brachen, FTC, 18 November 1917, Coal Investigation, REP5 TOB5 Part 1, FTC, RG 122; *Denver Post*, 19 January 1918, Box 367, Clippings, 21A-A4, Technical or Commodity File, WIB, RG 61.

27. Arthur Capper to Garfield, 12 October 1917, Kansas, Alphabetical file, RBSO, USFA, RG 67; Emerson Carey to USFA, Kansas, Folder 2, RBSO, USFA, RG 67; *General Orders, USFA*, 199–202, for retail price orders.

28. Dealer margins for 1917–18 were arrived at by calculating the average gross margin each dealer received in 1915 for each size and grade of coal—a figure often determined by sheer guesswork—plus 30 percent of that gross margin as compensation for inflation, a formula prescribed in the 1 October order.

29. For the above three paragraphs: *The Retail Coalman*, 31 (October 1917): 78; USFA to Wallace Crossley, fuel administrator for Missouri, 5 April 1918, and Crossley to USFA, 12 April 1918, Missouri, Folder 3, RBSO, USFA, RG 67; William G. McAdoo to Woodrow Wilson, Box

523, WGMcA Papers; W. K. Prudden, fuel administrator for Michigan to Joseph J. Crawley, president, Detroit Board of Commerce, 29 May 1918, and assistant secretary, Federal Fuel Administration, Michigan, to Wayne County Fuel Committee, 28 June 1918, Box 6, JC Papers; William J. Galligan to USFA, 17 November 1917, 15 March 1918, 29 July 1918, and USFA to Galligan, 23 July 1918, Colorado, Folders 2 and 3, RBSO, USFA, RG 67; Retail prices of anthracite coal, Box 369, 21A-A4, Technical or Commodity File, WIB, RG 61.

30. Clippings regarding hoarding, in Coal Investigation, CLi5 Part 1, FTC RG 122; for rules governing coal deliveries to domestic consumers and for orders and regulations governing jobbers and distributors, *General Orders, USFA*, 444–78; USFA, *Final Report, 1917–1919*, 222–27; for opposition to Denver's public coal yards, NRCMA, *First Annual Meeting*, 11–14, Resolutions Two, Eleven, and Twelve.

31. For the above three paragraphs: USS, *Hearings on Coal, Part 3*, testimony of USFA officials, 559, 763; NCA, *First Annual Convention, 1918*, 124–27; Days worked by miners and other data, Box 16 Entry 36, USCC, RG 68; Anthracite Bureau of Information, 1918, Coal Investigation, REP6 ANT5, FTC, RG 122; F. G. Tryon, "The Irregular Operation of the Bituminous Coal Industry," Coal Investigation, 1/ COR5 INT3, FTC, RG 122; W. C. Trapnell and Ralph Ilsley, *The Bituminous Coal Industry with a Survey of Competing Fuels* (Washington, D.C.: Federal Emergency Relief Administration, 1935), 32.

32. The Bear Canyon Coal Company, Colorado, to W. J Galligan, Colorado fuel administrator, 28 March 1918, for a priority rating for equipment requests, Colorado, Folder 2, RBSO, USFA, RG 67; USFA new mine policies, Box 161, TJW Papers; Letters and memorandum of Garfield regarding new mines, Boxes 126–27, HAG Papers; Tryon, "Bituminous Coal Industry," 2–4.

33. Kennedy, *Over Here*, 101, 103–13; Cuff, *War Industries Board*, 86, 104, 238. See also Grosvenor B. Clarkson, *Industrial America in the World War: The Strategy Behind the Line, 1917–1918* (Boston: Houghton Mifflin, 1923).

34. For a superior exposition of the opinion that federal regulation seriously weakened the nation's railroad system, see Albro Martin, *Enterprise Denied: Origins of the Decline of American Railroads, 1897–1917* (New York: Columbia University Press, 1971).

35. *Proceedings of a Conference of Owners of Railroad Securities, Baltimore, May 23, 1917* (np: Organization of the National Association of Owners of Railroad Securities, 1917), Box 557, WGMcA Papers; ICC to Fairfax Harrison, chairman, Executive Committee Special Committee on National Defense, ARA, 7 November 1917, Box 191, ibid.; and [William G. McAdoo], "Efficiency of Railroad Management," Box 559, ibid.; FTC, *Anthracite and Bituminous Coal Situation*, 11, 23–24; USS, *Car Service Shortage*, 10–11, 45–48; Martin, *Proceedings of CND*, 188; Robert Y. Thomas, Jr., congressman, Kentucky, to Wilson, 12 April 1918, Series

4, Case File 664, WW Papers; USS, *Hearings on Coal, Part 3*, 761.

36. For the above three paragraphs: CND *Second Annual Report, 1918,* 217–19 for the official view of railroad war committee performance. See also Marlen Pew article in *Railroad Man's Magazine*, 34 (November 1917), 353–65; J. G. Puterbaugh to FTC, 22 June 1917, Coal Investigation, COR5 McC2; and Charles J. Tobias, report on Oklahoma coal situation, 21 November 1917, Coal Investigation, REP5 TOB5 Part 15, FTC, RG 122; Emerson Carey to USFA, 22 October 1917, RBSO, Kansas, Folder 2, USFA, RG 67.

37. [William G. McAdoo], "Efficiency of Railroad Management," Box 559, WGMcA Papers; Newton D. Baker to McAdoo, 28 October 1917, Box 190, ibid.; Byron R. Newton, collector of the Port of New York, to McAdoo, 5 November 1917, Box 191, ibid.; Clipping, *New York Tribune*, 23 January 1918, Box 195, ibid.; Committee of Lake Shippers to Francis Peabody, CND, 15 May 1917, attacked the plan to govern the pooling of lake cargo coal at Lake Erie ports, Office of the Secretary, 1-53 (part 1), DI, RG 48; Garfield to Wilson, 6 September 1917, Box 91, HAG Papers; USS, *Price Regulation of Coal*, 90; USS, *Hearings on Coal, Part 3*, 1219.

38. [William G. McAdoo], "Efficiency of Railroad Management," Box 559, WGMcA Papers; and Irving T. Bush, chief executive officer of the War Board of the Port of New York, to McAdoo, 27 November 1917, Box 523, ibid.; USS, *Hearings on Coal, Part 3*, 773–83; Letters from Emerson Carey, Kansas fuel administrator, to USFA, 9–20 December 1917, RBSO, Kansas, Folder 2, USFA, RG 67; Coal Operators of Kansas, Colorado, Oklahoma, New Mexico, Wyoming, and Utah to Priorities Committee, 5 November 1917, Box 371, 21A-A4, Technical or Commodity File, WIB, RG 61.

39. McAdoo to Wilson, 6, 14, 15, and 24 December 1917, and Fairfax Harrison, chairman, Special Committee on National Defense, ARA, to Francis Newlands, chairman, USS Committee on Interstate Commerce, 10 December 1917, Box 523, WGMcA Papers; Samuel Untermeyer, office of the Commissioner of Internal Revenue, to McAdoo, 14 December 1917, Box 193, ibid.; and [William G. McAdoo], "Efficiency of Railroad Management," Box 559, ibid.; McAdoo to T. W. Sims, chairman, USHR Committee on Interstate and Foreign Commerce, 11 December 1918, OS, 1-53 (Railroads), DI, RG 48; Garfield to Wilson, 26 November 1917, Box 92, HAG Papers; Vardaman remarks in USS, *Hearings on Coal, Part 3*, 627, 734–35. In March, Congress passed *An Act to Provide for the Operation of Transportation Systems While Under Federal Control, for the Just Compensation of Their Owners, and for Other Purposes*. McAdoo's authority under this act was extended by presidential proclamation of 29 March 1918.

40. McAdoo to Josephus Daniels, Secretary of the Navy, 31 December 1917, Box 194, WGMcA Papers; Correspondence relating to trenches in Central Park, March 1918, Box 524, ibid.; Garfield to New-

ton D. Baker, 24 March 1922, recalled the conference of 16 January, Box 85, HAG Papers; Garfield's Closing Order, BC, Box 1080, USFA, RG 67; Defense of the Fuel Administration and New York Merchant Association to Wilson, 17 January 1918, BC, Box 1093, ibid.; Policies on Shipping Coal, and Lodge Attacks on USFA, BC, Box 1099, Speeches, ibid.; Franklin K. Lane to Gavin McNab, 23 January 1918, Office of the Secretary, 1-53 (part 1), DI, RG 48; Kennedy, *Over Here,* 123–25.

41. According to Francis Peabody in USS, *Hearings on Coal, Part 3,* 1158–61, he had suggested a zoning plan to Garfield in September, which the railroads opposed but ICC approved. Perhaps the ICC possessed sufficient authority to enforce compliance, but the ICC refrained from even applying its car service powers. Without federal control of the railroads, zoning could not be effectively implemented. One week before Wilson established USRA, the ARA national defense committee submitted to Garfield a zoning proposal similar to that adopted; Fairfax Harrison, ARA, to Garfield, 19 December 1917, Office of the Secretary, 1-53 (part 1), DI, RG 48; for the zoning order, *General Orders, USFA,* 213–362. Thereafter, no essential changes were made. USFA, *Final Report, 1917–1919,* 255. Zoning markedly affected the Mid-Continent oil industry; this is attended to in Chapter 4.

42. USFA, *Report of the Distribution Division, 1918–1919, Part 1, Distribution of Coal and Coke,* by C. E. Lesher (Washington, D.C.: GPO, 1919), 40.

43. Crossley to Garfield, Telegram, 13 March 1918, RBSO, Missouri, Folder 3, USFA, RG 67; and Resolutions and Suggestions of the Fuel Administrators of Arkansas, Oklahoma, Texas, Missouri, Kansas, Colorado, Iowa, and Nebraska addressed to Garfield, Kansas City, Missouri, Conference, 6 May 1918, RBSO, Colorado, Folder 3, ibid.

44. For the above three paragraphs: NCA, *First Annual Convention, 1918,* 124–27; Petition of New England Manufacturers to the President, 19 February 1918, Series 4, Case File 664, WW Papers; Richard Ramsay Mead, *An Analysis of the Decline of the Anthracite Industry Since 1921* (Philadelphia: n.p., 1935), 37–41; W. K. Prudden, fuel administrator, Michigan, to James Couzens, Wayne County Fuel Committee, 18 June 1918, Box 6, JC Papers; McAdoo to Wilson, 27 February 1918, Box 524, WGMcA Papers; Cuff, *War Industries Board,* 90–93, 116–19, 133–34, 191–97, for the tortuous evolution of a priorities system; P. B. Noyes, "Non-Essential Industry? There is None," *The Nation's Business,* February 1918, 24–25, BC, Box 1080, Defense of the Fuel Administration, USFA, RG 67.

45. For the above four paragraphs: Preference Lists 1 and 2, Bernard M. Baruch, chairman, *American Industry in the War. A Report of the War Industries Board* (Washington, D.C.: GPO, 1921), 325–54, Appen-

dix 11; USFA, *Report of the Distribution Division, Part 1*, 8–9, 28–30.
USFA, *Final Report, 1917–1919*, 247; Garfield on protecting all indus-
tries, Box 126, HAG Papers; USFA to State Fuel Administrators and
District Representatives, "The Distribution Program," Washington,
D.C., 25 May 1918, Executive Office, Box 2104, USFA, RG 67; USFA
Press Release No. 393, 21 February 1918, Coal Investigation, PUB5
UNI5 Part 1, FTC, RG 122; F. A. Hope, USFA, to Wallace Crossley,
6 February 1918, Missouri, Folder 2 and Emerson Carey to Garfield,
Telegrams, 6 and 7 February 1918, Kansas, Folder 3, and Carey to
E. Q. Trowbridge, USFA, 1 October 1918, Kansas, Folder 6, and
Resolutions and Suggestions of the Fuel Administrators, 6 May 1918,
Colorado, Folder 3—all in RBSO, USFA, RG 67. USFA defined slack
as coal that passed through a screen with bars not less than three-
quarters of an inch apart. Slack, then, was fine coal; prepared sizes
were larger pieces. Taylor argued the suitability of slack for domestic
purposes. Most home furnaces, however, could not burn it efficiently
without modifications, which users would have to pay for.

46. Cuff, *War Industries Board*, 133–34; Baruch, *American Industry in
the War*, 365–67, 381–82; CND, "Curtailment of Non-war Construction," *Bulletin No. 113*, 11 September 1918, Office of the Secretary, 1-53
(part 5), DI, RG 48. WIB, *Circular No. 21*, 3 September 1918, formalized the evaluation procedures for construction permits; FTC to
National Association of Window Glass Manufacturers, 24 June 1918,
Coal Investigation, COR5 NAT17, FTC, RG 122; for general information on building restrictions, BC, Box 1090, Misc., USFA, RG 67. For
specific curtailment orders, see: "Order Establishing a Regulation to
Restrict Fuel Consumption by the Manufacturers of Common Building
Brick, April 13, 1918," and orders relating to florists and common
window-glass manufacturers, Coal Investigation, PUB5 UNI5 Part 1,
FTC, RG 122; USFA, "Order Establishing a Regulation to Restrict
Fuel Consumption by Manufacturers of Cement, August 8, 1918,"
Executive Office, Box 2736, USFA, RG 67; for automobiles, *Oildom*, 8
(July 1918): 387.

47. For a sample of industry responses, see BC, Boxes 1070–71,
1075, and 1085–86, USFA, RG 67.

48. Correspondence between Galligan and USFA, May–December
1918, RBSO, Colorado, Folders 3 and 4, USFA, RG 67. All restrictions were lifted by USFA order of 30 November 1918. Breweries received special attention that was unwanted and politically motivated.
The Lever Act prohibited the use of food and feeds in the production
of distilled liquors. WIB refused to achieve full prohibition by destroying the brewing industry through administrative decree. Following the
lead of the food administration, which ordered a reduction in the al-
cohol content of beer, ale, and porter, thus reducing grain consumption by one-half, WIB opted to reduce by 50 percent the coal supplied

to the industry. USFA issued an order to that effect in July 1918. Prohibition groups applied great pressure on local and federal USFA officials to close saloons completely.

49. Resolutions and Suggestions of the Fuel Administrators, 6 May 1918, RBSO, Colorado, Folder 3, USFA, RG 67; on Idaho's inability to obtain Kansas cement, G. B. Graff, secretary, Boise Commercial Club, Boise, Idaho, to William E. Borah, 22 February 1918, Box 61, Railway Matters, 1917–1918, WEB Papers.

50. James Ingles, WIB, to William Ritter, WIB, 25 July 1918. Box 365, Coal, 21A-A4, Technical or Commodity File, WIB, RG 61.

51. For the above three paragraphs: H. R. Hatfield. WIB to Edwin Gay, U.S. Shipping Board, 23 September 1918, Box 364, Coal, 21A-A4, Technical or Commodity File, WIB, RG 61; Federal Fuel Committee for Kansas City, Order No. 11, 8 July 1918, Missouri, Folder 8, and W. J. Galligan to USFA, 14 February 1918, Colorado, Folder 2, and "Coal Price Hike Unjust to Poor, Alderman Says," *Kansas City Post*, 28 September 1918, Clippings, Missouri, Alphabetical File—all in RBSO, USFA, RG 67; Philadelphia rationing, Executive Office, Box 48, USFA, RG 67; J. F. McGee, fuel administrator for Minnesota, to P. Noyes, USFA, 17 July 1918, BC, Box 1086—House Heating, USFA, RG 67.

52. USFA to State Fuel Administrators and District Representatives, "Distribution Program," 25 May 1918, Box 2104, USFA, and "Tentative Suggestions for Opinion and Order Concerning Coal Jobbers," 29 July 1918, Box 156, USFA, and "Order Establishing Various Regulations for the Better Control of the Retail Distribution of Coal and Coke," 8 March 1918, Box 1572—all in Executive Office, USFA, RG 67; USFA, *Final Report, 1917–1919*, 222; John H. Rees, 30 Post Avenue, New York, to USFA in New York, 26 September 1918, BC, Box 1086—House Heating, USFA, RG 67.

Chapter Four

1. USFA, *Report of the Distribution Division, 1918–1919, Part 1, Distribution of Coal and Coke*, by C. E. Lesher (Washington, D.C.: GPO, 1919), 11–17.

2. For the above three paragraphs: USRA, *Fuel Conservation Circulars 1–21*, 16 June 1918–15 November 1919, mimeo compilations; USFA, *Final Report of the United States Fuel Administrator, 1917–1919, Report of the Administrative Division, 1917–1919, Part 2, Reports of Bureaus with Headquarters at Washington, D.C., Report of the Oil Division, 1917–1919* (Washington, D.C.: GPO, 1921), 244–51; "The Economical Use of Coal in Railway Locomotives," *University of Illinois Bulletin 16*, (Urbana, September 1918); USRA and USFA, *The Production and Conservation of Fuel, Addresses Delivered at the Tenth Annual Convention of the International Railway Fuel Association, Chicago, May 23–24, 1918* (Washington, D.C.: GPO,

1918); USHR Committee on Interstate and Foreign Commerce, *Emergency Power Bill, Hearings on H.R. 12776, Part 1, August 23 to 27, 1918,* 65th Cong., 2d sess., 1918, 129–31; Letters regarding interconnections at Richmond, March–April 1918, Office of Director, 110.116, USGS, RG 57; Final Reports, Building Materials Division, WIB, December 1918, 1-D1, Chairman's Office, WIB, RG 61; Schedule for Manufacturers of Furnaces, October 1918, Furnaces, Box 647; Mark L. Requa, Oil Division, USFA, to F. Darlington, chief, Power Division, WIB, 11 September 1918, Petroleum Production, Texas and Oklahoma, and Estimate of Coal Saving for 1918, USFA BCon, Coal Consumption, Box 370, 21A-A4, Technical or Commodity File, WIB, RG 61; Conference on isolated plants in New York, Box 1090; Miscellaneous pamphlets on fuel efficiency 1918, Box 1092, and electric systems in Tulsa, Box 1144, Tulsa, Oklahoma, BC, USFA, RG 67.

3. BCon, USFA conference on illumination, 1918, BC, Box 1095, Reports H–K; S. W. Stratton, director, Bureau of Standards, to G. N. Allen, BCon, USFA, 30 October 1918, BC, Box 1087, Lamps, USFA, RG 67.

4. *General Orders, Regulations and Rulings of the United States Fuel Administration,* compiled by the Legal Division of the Administration (Washington, D.C.: GPO, 1920), 532–43; Associated Engineers Company to Garfield, 8 January 1918, BC, Box 1062, Electric Lighting, A–E, USFA, RG 67; Garfield to Secretary of Commerce, 30 August 1918, General Records, 75024-134, DC, RG 40; Crossley to P. B. Noyes, USFA, 9 July 1918, RBSO, Missouri, Folder 4; Galligan to Noyes, 20 August 1918, RBSO, Colorado, Folder 3; Arkansas Valley Railway Light and Power Co., Pueblo, Colorado, to W. J. Galligan, 28 August 1918, BC, Box 1075, Cement A–K, USFA, RG 67; USHR, *Emergency Power Bill,* 42–46, on curtailment of power sales to Pennsylvania cement plants.

5. For the above four paragraphs on domestic and commercial conservation, all the following are from USFA, RG 67: Philadelphia rationing, 1918, and Fuel Committee, Greenwich, Conn., "Your Winter Coal," 1918, Executive Office, 48; Wallace Crossley, "Emergency Orders for Committeemen," 16 January 1918, and "Order Relative to Conservation of Coal, Light, and Heat," 17 January 1918, RBSO, Missouri, Folder 8; Carey to County Chairman and County Committeemen, 30 January and 2 February 1918, RBSO, Kansas, Folder 3; Edward Bok to Garfield, 19 November 1917, BC, Box 1094; Publicity-Magazines and Bok to P. B. Noyes, 24 June 1918, and Noyes to Bok, 26 June 1918, BC, Box 1094–Publicity, A–L. Material on early closing is scattered about in RBSO and BC, Boxes 1061 and 1090. USFA absorbed bitter criticism from prohibitionists for allowing saloons and breweries to remain open. In reply, USFA insisted that it could only be concerned with fuel and not with the merits of the liquor question. That being the case, saloons were treated as mercantile establish-

ments. As for breweries, fuel and grain curtailment forced many out of business. See BC, Box 1061, Early Closing, Box 1067, Breweries, and Box 1098, Saloons.

6. For skip-stop, all of the following are from USFA, RG 67: Charles E. Stuart, power and light section, conservation bureau, Memo, 8 July 1918, BC, Box 1091, Office memos; Emerson Carey to Stuart, 8 October 1918, BC, Box 1173, Skip-stop, Kansas; for Kansas City, BC, Box 1142, Skip-stop, Missouri. See also "D. E. Druen, Assistant Superintendent of Power, Kansas City Railways, Effects 35 Percent Reduction in Generating Costs," *Power*, 57 (27 March 1923): 170.

7. For references to Tag Day: RBSO, Kansas, Folder 3; Colorado, Folder 6, USFA, RG 67; USFA, *Final Report, 1917–1919*, 34, 256, 271.

8. Sam H. Schurr, Bruce Netschert, et al., *Energy in the American Economy, 1850–1975: An Economic Study of Its History and Prospects* (Baltimore: Johns Hopkins University Press for Resources for the Future, Inc., 1960), 36; Bureau of the Census, *Thirteenth Census of the United States, 1910, Vol. 11, Mines and Quarries, 1909, General Report and Analysis* (Washington, D.C.: GPO, 1913), 288; and *Fourteenth Census of the United States, 1920, Vol. 11, Mines and Quarries, 1919, General Report and Analytical Tables and Reports for States and Selected Industries* (Washington, D.C.: GPO, 1922), 310.

9. Quoted in Joseph E. Pogue, *The Economics of Petroleum*, (New York: John Wiley & Sons, 1921), 196.

10. USFA, *Final Report, 1917–1919*, 268; Hearings before CIC re War Financing of Public Utilities, 8 February 1918, CON5 WAR7, CIC, RG 158; P. A. Norris, fuel administrator for Oklahoma, to Steam Plants Using Natural Gas, 24 September 1918, RBSO, Oklahoma, Folder 7, and Robert Treat memo to W. A. Williams, Oil Division, USFA, 26 June 1918, BC, Box 1144, Tulsa, Oklahoma, USFA, RG 67; *First Annual Report of the Public Utilities Commission, Kansas City, Missouri, April 17, 1911* (Kansas City: np, 1911), 17; *Kansas City Times*, 25 July 1913, 4 January 1917, Clippings, KCMoPL.

11. For the above three paragraphs, all the following are from USFA, RG 67: USFA to Oklahoma Natural Gas Company of Tulsa, 2 September 1918, OD, Box 2756, F42; Wilcox memorandum to Treat, 1918, BC, Box 1144, Tulsa, Oklahoma; District Engineer, USFA, to Mr. Haley, Oklahoma City Oil Division, September 1918, OD, Box 2759, Office memos; USFA to Oklahoma Fuel Supply Co., 6 August 1918, OD, Box 2755, E209; Kansas Natural Gas Co. to USFA, 7 August 1918, OD, Box 2755, E148; Oklahoma Natural Gas Co. to Natural Gas Bureau, USFA, 19 July 1918, OD, Box 2550, #2188.

12. All the following are from USFA, RG 67: USFA to secretary, Chamber of Commerce, Kansas City, Missouri, [1917], OD, Box 2457, E502; W. G. Williams, district engineer, USFA, to W. C. Robinson, director of Oil Conservation, 12 August 1918, OD, Box 2759, Investi-

gation No. 1; "Kansas City Gas Situation, Report of Investigation . . . [of] the Condition of the Gas Mains . . . August 1917," OD,
Box 2515, #1494; Kansas City, Kansas, Chamber of Commerce to Oil
Division, USFA, 26 July 1918, OD, Box 2515, #1492; W. A. Wads-
worth, Kansas Gas and Electric Co., to W. G. Williams, district engineer, USFA, 23 August 1918, and *Wichita Beacon*, 3 September 1918,
and *Wichita Eagle*, 12 September 1918, OD, Box 2758, J7; *Kansas City
Times*, 26 September 1918, Clippings, OD, Box 2759, Investigation No.
8; Kansas Natural Gas Co. production figures, 1917–1918, OD, Box
2515, #1498; Crossley to Mark Requa, director of Oil Division, 26
September 1918, Telegram, RBSO, Missouri, Folder 5; Kansas City
Gas Co., Kansas City, Missouri, to USFA, 18 and 21 September 1918,
OD, Box 2756, E354.

13. Items from USFA, RG 67 included: USFA, *Proclamation by the
President of the United States, September 25, 1918 and Rules and Regulations
Governing Licensees Engaged in the Business of Importing, Manufacturing, Distributing, and Transporting Crude Oil, Fuel Oil, Gas Oil, Kerosene, Gasoline,
and Natural Gas* (Washington, D.C.: GPO, September 1918), BC, Box
1091, Oil; Louisville rationing, 1918, Executive Office, 3518–3519. Also
used were: M. L. Requa memorandum for H. A. Garfield regarding
licensing, 29 August 1918, Box 127, HAG Papers; USFA Press Release
No. 1002, 21 January 1919, Coal Investigation, PUB5 UNI5 Part 1,
FTC, RG 122.

14. See Table 4; Harold F. Williamson et al., *The American Petroleum
Industry: The Age of Energy, 1899–1959*, vol. 2 (Evanston: Northwestern
University Press, 1963), 261–67.

15. Statement of H. G. James, Western Petroleum Refiners Association, in FTC, "Conference with Representative Jobbers, Refiners, and
Others Interested in the Petroleum Industry," 13 January 1916, 245–
48, Gasoline Investigation, Docket Section 40-1-5-3, FTC, RG 122;
USFA, *Final Report, 1917–1919*, 277, 296; FTC, *Advance in the Price of
Petroleum Products (1920) House Document 801*, 66th Cong., 2d sess., 1920
vol. 97, 5; George Ward Stocking, *The Oil Industry and the Competitive
System: A Study in Waste* (Boston: Houghton Mifflin, 1925), 105–7; *Oildom*, 7 (November 1917): 527.

16. As the United States and Great Britain attempted to coordinate
the use of shipping in 1917, the United States sought to exploit its
maritime power by compelling the British to withdraw a large tonnage from the Persian Gulf and Indian Ocean routes for use in the
North Atlantic. According to David Kennedy, *Over Here: The First
World War and American Society* (New York: Oxford University Press,
1980), 326–27, the United States was "more reluctant than the British
to sacrifice their peacetime commerce to the cause of winning the
war." For recent analyses of U.S. world oil policies, see Edward W.
Chester, *United States Oil Policy and Diplomacy: A Twentieth Century Over-*

view (Westport, Conn.: Greenwood Press, 1983), and William Stivers, *Supremacy and Oil: Iraq, Turkey, and the Anglo-American World Order, 1918–1930* (Ithaca: Cornell University Press, 1982).

17. *Oildom,* 7 (January 1917): 7, and (May 1917): 214, worried about federal control of the oil industry; Williamson et al., *American Petroleum Industry,* 2:168–69; Robert D. Cuff, *The War Industries Board: Business-Government Relations during World War I* (Baltimore: Johns Hopkins University Press, 1973), 272–73; Gerald D. Nash, *United States Oil Policy 1890–1964: Business and Government in Twentieth Century America* (Pittsburgh: University of Pittsburgh Press, 1968), 24–29, treats oil as a monolithic interest group, misunderstands the authority over oil conferred on USFA by the Lever Act, and uncritically accepts the rhetoric of cooperation employed by the oil committee in explaining how the system operated; Burt Lyon to Bernard Baruch, CND, 31 July 1917, Box 1039, 21A-A4, Technical or Commodity File, WIB, RG 61.

18. David Howard Davis, *Energy Politics* (New York: St. Martin's Press, 1974), 46–47, completely misconstrues the issues leading to the formation of USFA, stating that the agency was established to cope with the oil problem and take control away from the oil industry. While it is valuable to place current energy difficulties in a historical context, that context must be described accurately.

19. Wilson to Garfield, 17 December 1917, Box 92, HAG Papers.

20. Mark L. Requa to Garfield, 11 December 1917, ibid.

21. USFA, *Final Report, 1917–1919,* 261–68; *Oildom,* 8 (February 1918): 7; USFA Bureau of State Organizations, "Petroleum and Its Products, Instructions by the Oil Division of the USFA," 27 August 1918, Executive Office, 2774, USFA, RG 67.

22. Williamson et al., *American Petroleum Industry,* 2:268–70; *Oildom,* 8 (April 1918): 208; Committee on Conciliation and Cooperation, 1918, OD, Box 2469, Entry 686, USFA, RG 67. Darby also served as vice-chairman of PWSC's Advisory Committee on Production, Mid-Continent field.

23. Williamson et al., *American Petroleum Industry,* 2:285–87; *Oildom,* 7 (January 1917): 3 and 8 (January 1918): 5, Manning testimony in USS Committee on Public Lands, *Leasing of Oil Lands, Hearings on S.45, A Bill to Encourage and Promote the Mining of Coal, Phosphate, Oil, Gas, Potassium, and Sodium on the Public Domain, Part 1, June 13, 1917,* 65th Cong., 1st sess., 1917, 23; Van H. Manning, in response to a Senate Resolution of 11 September 1918, *Production of Crude Oil,* 65th Cong., 2d sess., 1918, S. Doc. 280; Mark Requa to Garfield, 27 March 1918, POL5 OIL5, CIC, RG 158; USFA, *Final Report, 1917–1919,* 277.

24. For the above three paragraphs: Testimony regarding the naval reserves in USS, *Leasing of Oil Lands,* 98–107, 111–19, 176–79; Franklin H. Martin, *Digest of Proceedings of the Council of National Defense during the World War* (Washington, D.C.: GPO, 1934), 212–15; Josephus Daniels, *The Wilson Era: Years of War and After, 1917–1923* (Chapel Hill:

University of North Carolina Press, 1946), 246–48; *Oildom*, 7 (December 1917): 608; Manning to Requa, 15 October 1918, Office of Director, 110.116, USGS, RG 57. Documents from CIC, RG 158 included: C. L. Davidson, Wichita, auxillary committeeman to CIC, to Asa E. Ramsey, chairman, Subcommittee on Capital Issues, Kansas City, Missouri, 16 May 1918, POL5 OIL5; CIC policy respecting application by oil development companies, 1918, POL5 OIL5; CIC Bulletin #5, 24 August 1918, POL5 OIL5; CIC minutes, CAP5 MIN5 Part 5, File designation APP5, contains scores of applications and information on their disposition.

25. Liberty Oil and Refining Corp. to J. C. Miller, governor, Kansas City Federal Reserve Bank, 18 June 1918, APP5 LIB54; and Apex Refining and Drilling Co. to CIC, 9 September 1918, APP5 APE5; and Cities Service–CIC correspondence, APP5 CIT1, all in CIC, RG 158.

26. Oil well supplies, 1917, and E. B. Parker to Requa, 3 October 1918, Oil Well Supplies, 21A-A4, WIB, RG 61; from OD, USFA, RG 67: Kansas City Bolt and Nut Co. to USFA, 16 May 1918, and USFA to Priorities Committee, WIB, 19 September 1918, Box 2687, #391, Kansas City Bolt and Nut Co.; Kaw Boiler Works to USFA, 9 February 1918, Box 2516, #150, Kaw Boiler Works Co.; and Kaw Boiler Works Co. to PWSC, 20 September 1918, Box 2687, #391, Kaw Boiler Works Co; Requa to CIC, 7 October 1918, POL5 OIL5, CIC, RG 158.

27. *Oildom*, 7 (October 1917): 483–88.

28. Pogue, *Economics of Petroleum*, 238–41, 246; Williamson et al., *American Petroleum Industry*, 2:39, 292–93; USFA, *Final Report, 1917– 1919*, 285–87, 296–98; Kansas City Refining Co. reports to FTC, 1917–18, Oklahoma Oil Investigation, 7336-150-1, FTC, RG 122. Oil companies were required to submit various reports (used by USFA) to the Bureau of Mines and the FTC that described their weekly and monthly operations. Oil refiners complained loudly about these time-consuming obligations and as soon as the war terminated asserted the principle of confidentiality to obstruct the continued gathering of these data by FTC. Typical reports are filed in OD, Boxes 2653–54, USFA, RG 67.

29. Henrietta Larson and Kenneth W. Porter, *History of Humble Oil and Refining Company: A Study in Industrial Growth* (New York: Harper & Brothers, 1959), 65; *Oildom*, 7 (May 1917): 217–18; North American Refining Co. to USFA, Telegram, 6 June 1918, Box 2653, File N, OD, USFA, RG 67; see Box 7336, Oklahoma Oil Investigation, FTC, RG 122, for letters and reports from Kansas City Refining Co., Atwood Refining Co. (Oklahoma City), Occidental Oil and Refining Co. (Wichita), Railroad Men's Refining Co. (El Dorado, Kansas), and Wright Producing and Refining Co. (Tulsa).

30. Garfield to Wilson, 23 April 1918, Box 92, HAG Papers; regarding FTC charges of profiteering, Bedford to Victor Murdock, FTC, 11

February 1918, Box 105, and Lewis H. Haney, assistant chief economist, FTC, to Murdock, 19 June 1918, Box 106, VM Papers; Williamson et al., *American Petroleum Industry*, 2:287–93; Garfield price announcement, Clipping, 10 September 1918, OD, Box 2469, Entry 678, USFA, RG 67; USFA, *Price Fixing Bulletin 11*, November 1918, Fuel Oil Prices, 21A-A4, Technical or Commodity File, WIB, RG 61; *Oildom*, 8 (June 1918): 329.

31. USFA, *Final Report, 1917–1919*, 34, 256, 271; *Oildom*, 8 (December 1918): 973; *Daily Oil News Report*, 10 September 1918, on Senate response to gasless Sundays, in OD, Box 2469, Entry 678; and USFA news release for Oil Division, 21 October 1918, Oil Division; and Advisory Committee on Distribution (Atlantic Division), PWSC, to Requa, 30 September 1918, Box 2491, #1012, Gasoline Conservation, USFA, RG 67.

32. USFA, *Proclamation by the President, September 25, 1918*; Requa memorandum for Garfield, 29 August 1918, Box 127, HAG Papers; *Oildom*, 8 (February 1918): 21; Garfield to Wilson, 28 January 1918, Box 92, HAG Papers, on the first phase of oil industry licensing; USFA, "Revised Rules and Regulations Governing Licensees Engaged in the Business of Distributing Fuel Oil," 18 March 1918, Coal Investigation, PWB5 UNI5 Part 1, FTC, RG 122; Highway Transport Committee, CND to Priorities Committee, WIB, 14 October 1918, Box 655, 21A-A4, Technical or Commodity File, WIB, RG 61.

33. For USFA's response to the refiners' plight, Requa memorandum to Garfield, 21 August 1918, and Garfield memorandum for internal use, 11 September 1918, Box 127, HAG Papers; H. G. James statement at FTC Conference with Oil Jobbers, 1916, Gasoline Investigation, Docket Section 40-1-5-3, FTC, RG 122; Oklahoma-Kansas Refining Co. to USFA, 22 August 1918, and USFA reply, 23 August 1918, OD, Box 2549, #2186, Oklahoma-Kansas Refining Co., USFA, RG 67.

34. *Oildom*, 7 (January 1917): 11, 7 (March 1917): 110, 7 (September 1917): 450, 7 (November 1917): 538–39, 8 (January 1918): 14, and 8 (March 1918): 143; USRA Division of Transportation, Car Service Section, *Bulletin No. 4*, 14 March 1918, Box 557, WGMcA Papers; items on shortage of oil cars, December–March 1918, Box 2478, Entry 850; Report of Manager, Inland Traffic, OD, USFA, 1918, Box 2462, #588; O. M. Conley, W. E. MacEven, Advisory Committee on Tank Cars, PWSC, to Refiners of the Mid-Continent Field, Kansas City, Missouri, 30 August 1918, Circular Letter No. T-90, Box 2462, #588, Conley, O. M. (all from Oil Division, USFA, RG 67); Stocking, *The Oil Industry*, 98–99; American Petroleum Institute, *Bulletin 2 No. 104* (25 August 1920): n.p.

35. Crossley to USFA, 13 November 1918, RBSO, Missouri, Folder 6, and WIB Priorities Division, Circular No. 59, 21 November 1918, BC, Box 1097, Restrictions, Industrial, and Suspension of zoning and

price orders, 1 February 1919, Executive Office, 345 (all in USFA, RG 67); CIC correspondence, November 1918, POL5, POS5, CIC, RG 158; Cuff, *War Industries Board*, 261; *The Coal Merchant*, 1, no. 2 (5 March 1919), n.p., no. 3 (5 April 1919), n.p., no. 6 (20 May 1919), n.p.; M. H. Gerry to Walsh, Telegram, 30 November 1918, Box 161, TJW Papers; NRCMA, *Meeting of the Executive Committee, Washington, D.C., November 11, 1918* (1918), 4–7, and *Meeting of the Executive Committee, Cincinnati, January 27–28, 1919* (1919), 9–11; [USRA], *Annual Report of Walker D. Hines, Director-General of Railroads, 1919, Division of Operations* (Washington, D.C.: GPO, 1920), 7.

36. Cuff, *War Industries Board*, 9–10, 147, 265 passim; Kennedy, *Over Here*, 137, 140, 142 passim. WIB chairman Bernard Baruch contrived a picture of rather complete federal control in *American Industry in the War, A Report of the War Industries Board* (Washington, D.C.: GPO, 1921).

37. Report of the Section on Housing to the Chairman of the Committee on Welfare Work, Conference Held in Washington, 21 September 1917, Section on Housing, Committee on Labor. Advisory Committee of CND, Office of the Secretary, 1–53 (Part 3), DI, RG 48; John D. Kelby to Crossley, 31 July 1918, RBSO, Missouri, Folder 4, USFA, RG 67; Cost of Living Studies by the Railroad Wage Commission, Washington, March 1918, Office of the Secretary, 1–197, DI, RG 48.

38. Nash, *United States Oil Policy*, 38; Williamson et al., *American Petroleum Industry*, 2:292; National Resources Committee, *Energy Resources and National Policy, Report of the Energy Resources Committee of the U.S. National Resources Committee* (Washington, D.C.: GPO, 1939), 210–11.

Chapter Five

1. Conference among Harry A. Garfield, National Coal Association, and United Mine Workers of America, 11–14 February 1919, Box 127, HAG Papers.

2. American Coal Wholesaler *Bulletin*, 100 (4 September 1919): 1–3.

3. Testimony of Walker D. Hines, USS Subcommittee of the Committee on Interstate Commerce, *Hearings on the Increased Prices of Coal, Part 1*, 66th Cong., 1st sess., 1919, 240.

4. For the above four paragraphs: Committee on Public Administration Cases, *The Consumers' Counsel and the National Bituminous Coal Commission, 1937–1938* (Washington, D.C.: Committee on Public Administration Cases, 1949, rev. ed., 1950), 102: USFA, *Final Report of the United States Fuel Administrator, 1917–1919, Report of the Administrative Division, 1917–1919, Part 2, Reports of Bureaus with Headquarters at Washington, D.C., Report of the Oil Division, 1917–1919* (Washington, D.C.: GPO, 1921), 27; F. G. Tryon, "The Irregular Operation of the

Bituminous Coal Industry," Coal Investigation, 1/COR5 INT3, FTC, RG 122; USCC, Report on irregular production, by months, 1913–22, Box 16, Entry 36, USCC, RG 68; Stocks of Coal in the Hands of Consumers, 1 October 1916–1 June 1920, Box 364, 21A–A4, Technical or Commodity File, WIB, RG 61; USS, *Hearings on the Increased Price of Coal*, 44–50, 90–99, 228–29; NCA, *The Weekly Digest* (became *Coal Review* in March 1920), 4 (23 July 1919): 1–3, 18, 4 (10 September 1919): 7, 4(1 October 1919): 13; *The Coal Merchant*, 1 (5 May 1919), np. See also Ellis Hawley, "Secretary Hoover and the Bituminous Coal Problem, 1921–1928," *Business History Review*, 42 (Autumn 1968): 252–53, for Hoover's solution to the coal dilemma.

5. For the above three paragraphs: For the most important hearings and other studies, see USS Committee on Interstate Commerce, *Railroad-Car Shortage, Hearings on S. 4733, A Bill to Amend Sections 207 and 210 of the Transportation Act, 1920*, 66th Cong., 2d sess., 1920; USS Select Committee on Reconstruction and Production, *Hearings . . . pursuant to S. Res. 350 . . . Coal and Transportation*, 66th Cong., 3d sess. 1920–21; USS Committee on Manufactures, *Hearings on S. 4828 on the Publication of Production and Profits in Coal, 3 vols., 1921*, 66th Cong., 3d sess., 1921; USS Subcommittee on Interstate Commerce, *Hearings on the Coal Problem*, 67th Cong., 1st sess., 1921; United States Coal Commission, *Report of the United States Coal Commission in Five Parts, Part 1, Principal Findings and Recommendations, 1923* (Washington, D.C.: GPO 1925); Edward T. Devine, *Coal, Economic Problems of the Mining, Marketing, and Consumption of Anthracite and Soft Coal in the United States* (Bloomington, Ind.: American Review Service Press, 1925); Walton H. Hamilton and Helen R. Wright, *The Case of Bituminous Coal* (New York: Macmillan, 1925); Helen Wright, *Coal's Worst Year* (Boston: Richard G. Badger, 1924).

6. For the above three paragraphs, see: USHR Committee on Rules, *Hearings on the Creation of a Committee for Investigation of Coal Situation*, 66th Cong., 1st sess., 1919, 19; USS, *Hearings on Coal Problem*, 21; USS, *Coal and Transportation*, 567–72; NCA, *The Weekly Digest*, 4 (16 July 1919): 15, and 4 (30 July 1919): 1–6, on the Huddleston bill; *The Retail Coalman*, 40 (January 1922): 44, and Glen L. Parker, *The Coal Industry: A Study in Social Control* (Washington, D.C.: American Council on Public Affairs, 1940), 89, on the Frelinghuysen bill; James P. Johnson, *The Politics of Soft Coal: The Bituminous Industry from World War I through the New Deal* (Urbana: University of Illinois Press, 1979), 111–12, for the Kenyon bill; John A. Ryan to William E. Borah, 2 April 1921, and Borah–George W. Perkins letters, February 1922, Box 109, Coal Bill A, WEB Papers; NCA to Walker D. Hines, 11 January 1919, Series 4, Case File 664, WW Papers; Statement of Harry N. Taylor in USS, *Increased Price of Coal*, 67; *The Coal Merchant*, 2 (January 1920): 11; National Retail Coal Merchants Association to Federal Fuel Distributor, 3 April 1923, Box 43, Entry 33, FFD, RG 89; *Oildom*, 13

(July 1922): 12; American Engineering Council, *Industrial Coal: Purchase, Delivery, and Storage* (New York, Ronald Press, 1924), iii, 7–9, 25–30 passim.

7. For an excellent economic analysis of the immediate postwar years, see National Resources Planning Board, *After the War—1918–1920: Military and Economic Demobilization of the United States, Its Effect upon Employment and Income* (Washington, D.C.: NRPB, 1943).

8. USFA, *Final Report, 1917–1919*, 15; NELA, *Bulletin*, 6 (July 1919): 387; USS, *Increased Price of Coal*, Hines statement, 228–29, 240, and statement of John Callahan, traffic manager, NCA, 90–99, and statement of J. D. A. Morrow, vice-president, NCA, 49–50; *The Coal Merchant* 1 (15 August 1919): 2; American Coal Wholesaler *Bulletin*, 102 (18 September 1919): 3–4.

9. Walker D. Hines to the president of the Senate, "Distribution of Coal and Coke," 66th Cong., 2d ses., 1920, S. Doc. 235, 4 (This was Hines's response to the Pomerene resolution); USCC, "Report on irregular production," 20 September 1923, Box 16, Entry 36, USCC, RG 68; Bituminous coal loaded at mines in cars, 1 November–13 December 1919, in NCA, *The Weekly Digest*, 5 (28 January 1920): 1; for the labor-management negotiations, see Johnson, *Politics of Soft Coal*, 102–7.

10. Hines, "Distribution of Coal and Coke," 1–2; American Coal Wholesaler *Bulletin*, 108 (1 November 1919): 1–4, 108 (8 November 1919): 1–3; USRA press release 31 October 1919, Box 79, Railroads (2), WEB Papers; Garfield to Hines, 30 October 1919, Box 129, HAG Papers.

11. USFA, *Final Report, 1917–1919*, 17–19; NCA, *The Weekly Digest*, 4 (3 December 1919): 1, 4–5, 10–11, (17 December 1919): 1–6; *The Coal Merchant*, 1 (20 December 1919): 1, severly critized Wilson's rejection of Garfield's award as motivated by an attempt to strengthen the UMWA; Harry A. Garfield to President Wilson, 11 December 1919, Box 128, HAG Papers; American Coal Wholesaler *Bulletin*, 120 (10 January 1920): 4.

12. Devine, *Coal*, 197; *The Coal Merchant*, 2 (April 1920): 8, 3 (February 1921): 5; USS, *Coal and Transportation*, 17; American Coal Wholesaler *Bulletin*. 107 (25 October 1919): 7–8; ICC, *34th Annual Report December 1, 1920* (Washington, D.C.: GPO, 1920), 6–7.

13. Hines telegram to all CCC regional directors, 29 October 1919, and USRA press notice, 31 October 1919, Box 79, Railroads (2), WEB Papers.

14. Map of coal distribution and consumption, 1917, Box 377, 21A-A4, Technical or Commodity File, WIB, RG 61; Distribution of shipments of bituminous coal from 3 August 1918 to 1 February 1919, by producing fields and classes of consignees, Box 1, Entry 4I, USCC, RG 68. The absence of coordination continued into the period of ICC control.

15. USFA/USRA reimposed certain restrictions on street lighting and advertising signs and the evening operation of businesses, but compliance was negligible. Hines, "Distribution of Coal and Coke," 2, 5, 10; Henry B. Spencer, chairman, "Report of the Central Coal Committee," in *Annual Report of Walker D. Hines, Director-General of Railroads, 1919* (Washington, D.C.: GPO, 1920), 8–11; American Coal Wholesaler *Bulletin*, 108 (1 November 1919): 4; *The Coal Merchant*, 2 (March 1920): 1–3; NCA, *The Weekly Digest*, 4 (10 December 1919): 21; Walker D. Hines instructions to regional directors, 31 October 1919, Box 79, Railroads (2), WEB Papers; Thomas J. Walsh correspondence, December 1919, Box 266, TJW Papers; F. G. Tryon and W. F. McKenney, "Economic Phases of Coal Storage," 1923, Coal Investigation, 1/COR5-INT3, FTC, RG 122. Railroad influence on price aroused the ire of UMWA president Frank J. Hays in January 1919. According to Hays, the railroads beat down coal prices by offering 100 percent car supply to those selling at the lowest price. Hays was repeating an accusation that surfaced in 1916. Hays statement, 11 January 1919, Series 4: Case File 664, WW Papers.

16. For the Transportation Act of 1920, which Secretary McAdoo attacked as a Republican giveaway to the railroads, see Box 560, WGMcA Papers. For unfavorable assessments of the act, see Merle Fainsod and Lincoln Gordon, *Government and the American Economy* (New York: W. W. Norton, 1941, rev. ed., 1948), 261–74, and David M. Kennedy, *Over Here: The First World War and American Society* (New York: Oxford University Press, 1980), 253–58; Production of bituminous coal, by months, 1913–22, Box 16, Entry 36, USCC, RG 68.

17. USS, *Coal and Transportation*, testimony of Clyde B. Atchison, ICC, 157–58, and testimony of James J. Storrow, 2, 20; Memorandum, CND, 18 May 1920, regarding the congestion of the nation's railways, Office of the Secretary, 1–53 (Part 8), DI, RG 48; ICC, *34th Annual Report*, 13–14; *The Coal Merchant*, 2 (September 1920): 1, 6.

18. Johnson, *Politics of Soft Coal*, 107–8; Spencer, "Report of Central Coal Committee," 8; USRA, *Annual Report of Walker D. Hines, Director-General of Railroads, 1919, Central Western Region* (Washington, D.C.: GPO, 1919), 6–7; George O. Smith, USGS, to Herbert Shenton, executive secretary, U.S. Bituminous Coal Commission, 19 May 1920, Office of the Secretary, 1–53 (Part 8), DI, RG 48; USS, *Coal and Transportation* 80–81.

19. *Proceedings of the Fourth Annual Convention of the National Coal Association, New York City, May 1921* (New York: np, 1921), 21–22; USS, *Coal and Transportation*, 161; ICC, *34th Annual Report*, 15–17.

20. USS, *Coal and Transportation*, testimony of Clyde B. Atchison, ICC, 159–60, 163–65, testimony of Daniel B. Wentz, president, NCA, 285–87, testimony of James J. Storrow, 11–14, testimony of John W. Lieb, vice-president, New York Edison, 69–73, testimony of Walter H. Johnson, vice-president, Philadelphia Electric Co., 214, 219; *The Coal*

Merchant, 2 (July 1920): 2, 13, (August 1920): 7, (October 1920): 1; ICC, *34th Annual Report*, 14–15, 20–22.

21. For the above two paragraphs: USS, *Coal and Transportation*, testimony of John McGee, Minnesota fuel administrator, 26, 29, 33, witnesses from central New York, 61–64, testimony of Clyde Atchison, 162–70, testimony of Daniel Wentz, 725, testimony of August G. Gutheim, testimony of J. D. A. Morrow, vice-president, NCA, 533, 578, ARA Car Service Division, 678–81, 725; ICC, *34th AR*, 18–20.

22. For the above two paragraphs: USS, *Coal and Transportation*, testimony of Wentz and Morrow on the Indiana fuel administration, 574, 735. The Indiana Act permitted the fixing of mine-mouth prices and the licensing of dealers. It required coal producers to ship coal at the fixed price to any dealers that the administration prescribed. "An Act Creating a Special Coal and Food Commission in Indiana, July 31, 1920," Box 117, Entry 153, USCC, RG 68; Governors of Wisconsin, North Dakota, and South Dakota to Wilson telegram, July 1920, and William L. Frierson, acting Attorney General, to Wilson, 10 July 1920, Series 4: Case File 664, WW Papers.

23. The United States was a very minor participant in a world coal trade still dominated by Great Britain and centered around Western Europe. In that region, and notably in Great Britain, the coal industry suffered from the same disabilities that so weakened the American industry. During the 1920s, the British government adopted several of the policies that Americans only discussed, particularly measures designed to reduce overcapacity, moderate competition, and stabilize labor costs. None of these steps retarded the ever-downward slide of the industry in the face of oil, gas, and hydroelectric competition and increased coal production in those countries that served as Britain's main foreign markets. See International Labour Office, *The World Coal Mining Industry*, Studies and Reports, Series B, No. 31 (Geneva: ILO, 1938), and Neil K. Buxton, *The Economic Development of the British Coal Industry from Industrial Revolution to the Present Day* (London: Batsford Academic, 1978).

24. New England governors telegram to Wilson, 10 July 1920, Robert Wooley, ICC, to Joseph Tumulty, 15 June 1920, U.S. Shipping Board to Wilson, 14 June 1920, and American Coal Wholesale Association to Wilson, 12 June 1920, Series 4: Case File 664, WW Papers; USS, *Coal and Transportation*, testimony of Storrow, 5–7, testimony of David A. Ellis, Commissioner of Public Utilities, Boston, 225, testimony of Alfred M. Barrett, NYC public service commissioner, 65–68; Hines, "Distribution of Coal and Coke," 5, 10; W. S. Benson, chairman, U.S. Shipping Board, to J. W. Alexander, Secretary of Commerce, 14 June 1920, Alexander to Benson, 25 June 1920, NCA press release, 16 June 1920, and J. D. A. Morrow, vice-president, NCA, to J. W. Alexander, 18 June 1920, all from 75341-32 (1918–1922), DC. RG 40.

25. Harry N. Taylor, "The Future of the Bituminous Industry," in NRCMA, *Addresses Delivered at the Third Annual Meeting, Detroit, Michigan, June 10–12, 1920* (Philadelphia: NRCMA, [1920]), 18.

26. For the above two paragraphs: Production of bituminous coal by months, 1913–1922, Box 16, Entry 36, USCC, RG 68; *Coal Review,* 4 (11 January 1922): 8, and ibid. (8 February 1922): 5; USS, *Coal and Transportation,* testimony of J. W. Lieb, 309, and Chairman Calder exchange with Wentz, 306–8; Wright, *Coal's Worst Year,* 195–97; *The Coal Merchant,* 3 (February 1921): 1, 4; ibid. (March 1921): 2; ibid. (April 1921): 2; *Proceedings of the Fourth Annual Convention, NCA,* 14–17.

27. J. D. A. Morrow, vice-president, NCA, "The Coal Strike Set for April," *American Industries,* 22 (April 1922): 13–14; *The Black Diamond,* 20 (20 May 1922): 477–78; *Electrical World,* 79 (21 January 1922): 117, warned its readers of a possible coal strike; ibid., 79 (4 February 1922): 245, (18 February 1922): 345; Johnson, *Politics of Soft Coal,* 114–16.

28. *Coal Review,* 4 (11 January 1922): 8; ibid. (8 February 1922): 5; American Engineering Council, *Industrial Coal,* 367–68.

29. USGS, "The Coal Supply in the Event of a General Strike April 1," 8 March 1922, Box 2, Entry 6; Production of Bituminous Coal by Months, 1913–1922, Box 16, Entry 35, USCC, RG 68.

30. *Saward's Journal* 5 (29 April 1922): 1; ibid. (29 July 1922): 242, 248; ibid. (5 August 1922): 262, 264; Edward A. Tyman, "What the Coal Strike Involves," *American Industries,* 23 (August 1922): 13; USGS, News Release, 3 June 1922, 80769 part 1, General Correspondence, DC, RG 40; Fuel administrator for Massachusetts to wholesale and retail coal dealers and consumers of bituminous coal, 29 August 1922, Box 9, Entry 20, USCC, RG 68.

31. For the above two paragraphs: Wright, *Coal's Worst Year,* 20, 40–41; *Coal Review,* 4 (15 March 1922): 1; ibid. (24 May 1922): 9–10; ibid. (7 June 1922): 1; ibid. (14 June 1922): 3; ibid. (14 July 1922): 1; ibid. (14 July 1922): 11; *The Coal Merchant,* 4 (June 1922): 2, 16; USCC, "Coal Situation as of June 3, 1922," Box 9, Entry 20, USCC, RG 68; "Hoover Obtains Price Agreement," *American Industries,* 22 (July 1922): 20; Hawley, "Hoover and the Coal Problem," 257–59; Production of Bituminous Coal by Months, 1913–1922, Box 16, Entry 36, USCC, RG 68; *Saward's Journal,* 5 (29 July 1922): 248; *Final Report of the Federal Fuel Distributor* 2–3; Heber Blankenhorn, Bureau of Industrial Research, New York, to Senator Borah, 15 August 1922, Box 109, Coal Bill, August–November 1922, WEB Papers; ICC, *36th Annual Report, December 1, 1922* (Washington, D.C.: GPO, 1922), 9–10; "Federal Government Action during the Coal Crisis," prepared by C. E. Spens, federal fuel distributor, 6 October, 1922, General Correspondence, 80769 part 1, DC, RG 40; B. J. Dunn, Wichita, to Hoover, 6 September 1922, Box 18, Kansas, FFD, RG 89.

32. ICC, *36th Annual Report*, 13; Spencer Press Releases, 2 August–9 September, Box 11, FFD, RG 89; for PFDC orders directing coal to the Great Lakes, Box 6, Kentucky, and for efforts to cope with railroad recalcitrance, Box 7, Missouri, and Box 15, Colorado, and for tonnage moved, Box 11, FFD, RG 89; "Federal Government Action During the Coal Crisis," by Spens, General Correspondence, 80769 part 1, DC, RG 40.

33. ICC, *36th Annual Report*, 10–13; Spencer to governors' fuel committees, 30 August 1922, Box 11, Authorizations Issued, FFD, RG 89; Hoover to Borah, 18 August 1922, General Correspondence, 80769 part 1, DC, RG 40; *The Black Diamond*, 13 (23 September 1922): n.p. *Cushing's Survey*, 1 (14 September 1922): n.p.; ibid. (21 September 1922): n.p.; ibid. (28 September 1922), n.p.; Borah–George W. Perkins letters, February 1922, Box 109, Coal Bill A, WEB Papers; Walsh correspondence, August 1922, Box 255, TJW Papers. By the second week in September, car shortages—cars called for by mines but unavailable—had reached 26,000, a number sufficient to move over one million tons. At the peak of the crisis, in October and November, car shortages averaged 43,000 weekly and remained above 20,000 until the final week of April 1923, American Engineering Council, *Industrial Coal*, 93.

34. *Coal Review*, 4 (19 April 1922): 3–5; ibid. (24 May 1922): 26; *The Retail Coalman*, 40 (July 1922): 36–44; See Borah correspondence in Box 109, Coal Bill B, and Coal Bill, August–November 1922, and Box 130, Coal Commission; Wright, *Coal's Worst Year*, 111–20. All USCC preliminary and final reports were signed by: John Hays Hammond, chairman, Edward T. Devine, Clark Howell, Thomas R. Marshall, Charles P. Neil, and George Otis Smith. F. G. Tryon, a leading authority on the coal industry, was borrowed from the Bureau of Mines to serve as statistical advisor.

35. For the above four paragraphs: from FFD, RG 89, Consolidated Coal and Coke Co., Denver, correspondence with FFD and the Union Pacific Railroad Co., October 1922, and Colorado and New Mexico Coal Operators Association, Denver, to FFD, 6 October 1922, and Denver and Rio Grande Western RR to FFD, 10 October 1922, Telegram, FFD to J. C. Roth, ICC, 6 October 1922, and Roth to FFD, 7 October 1922, indicating that ICC turned the car problem over to ARA, Box 15, and Minnesota, Wisconsin, North and South Dakota fuel administrators to FFD, 17 December 1922, Box 38, Entry 28, and George H. Webb, fuel administrator, Rhode Island, to FFD, 2 November 1922, Box 28, Rhode Island; *Cushing's Survey*, 1 (5 October 1922): n.p.; ibid. (12 October 1922): n.p.; Wright, *Coal's Worst Year*, 180.

36. From Box 38, Entry 28, FFD, RG 89: O. J. Larson, member of Congress, Duluth, to C. E. Spens, FFD, 1 November 1922; FFD to Delaware, Lackawanna and Western Railroad Co., 3 November 1922;

Fuel administrators of Minnesota, Wisconsin, North and South Dakota to FFD, 17 December 1922; Spens, FFD, to director of distribution, Pennsylvania Fuel Commission, 22 December 1922, and reply, 27 December 1922.

37. ICC, *37th Annual Report, December 1, 1923* (Washington, D.C.: GPO, 1923), 52–53.

38. In 1922, twenty-eight states organized fuel commissions by executive or by legislative action. Not all, however, possessed the extensive authority of the commissions in New York, Massachusetts, Michigan, Ohio, and Indiana that could set prices and dealer margins, license coal dealers, certify the quality of coal, and control fuel distributors. Coal Investigation, REP 3 HO5 Part 1, FTC, RG 122.

39. For the above two paragraphs: FFD Press Releases, August–October 1922, Box 11, and FFD to Kruger Lumber Co., Abilene, Kansas, 2 October 1922, Box 18, Kansas, FFD, RG 89; *Final Report of the Federal Fuel Distributor,* 8–9; The Anthracite Emergency of 1922–23 and How It Was Handled, Submitted to the USCC on Behalf of the General Policies Committee of Anthracite Operators, 21 April 1923, Box 3, Entry 8; and NCA *Bulletin No. 246,* 7 February 1923, Box 18, Entry 43, USCC, RG 68; *The Retail Coalman,* 41 (October 1922): 49; ICC No. 14624. Transportation and Distribution of Anthracite Coal, 27 February 1923, Box 48, ICC, FFD, RG 89; Wright, *Coal's Worst Year,* 177–79. See also Harold K. Kanarek, "The Pennsylvania Anthracite Strike of 1922," *Pennsylvania Magazine of History and Biography,* 99 (April 1975): 207–25.

40. *Electrical World,* 79 (25 March 1922): 567; ibid. (1 April 1922): 617–18; John W. Lieb, "Electricity and the Coal Supply," *American Industries,* 23 (May 1923): 36–40.

41. Hawley, "Hoover and the Coal Problem," 262–63; Johnson, *Politics of Soft Coal,* 117–18.

42. A preliminary report on bituminous was submitted on 15 January 1923. In July and August 1923, fourteen of fifteen topical studies of anthracite were forwarded to Congress. Topical reports on bituminous were completed during the following month. Box 17, USCC, RG 68.

43. For the above two paragraphs: *Report of the U.S. Coal Commission, 1, 1923* (1925), x–xi, 259–78; James A. Emery, general counsel, National Association of Manufacturers, "Need for a National Coal Policy," *American Industries,* 23 (November 1922): 27; Hawley, "Hoover and the Coal Problems," 264–65; Devine, *Coal,* 2–3, 321–76 passim; Walter Barnum, president, NCA, "What the Bituminous Coal Industry Has Done for Itself and for the Nation," presented at the International Conference on Bituminous Coal, Pittsburgh, 16 November 1926, Box 161, TJW Papers; Report of the president, E. C. Mahan, in *Eleventh Annual Meeting, National Coal Association, November 14–16, 1928* (Cleveland: n.p., n.d.), 8–10.

44. Floyd W. Parsons, "Coal Remedies," *The Saturday Evening Post*, 14 October 1922, 29, 137–38, 141–42, and his articles in the issues of 16 September 1922 and 30 September 1922; Editorials from various newspapers on the USCC reports in Box 8, Clippings Notebook, USCC, RG 68; Reprints of editorials from New York papers, 1925–26, in Julia Emily Johnsen, comp., *Government Regulation of the Coal Industry* (New York: H. W. Wilson, 1926), 54–66.

45. For excellent treatment of these strikes, see Harold K. Kanarek, "Disaster for Hard Coal: The Anthracite Strike of 1925–26," *Labor History*, 15 (Winter 1974): 44–62; Robert H. Zieger, "Pinchot and Coolidge: The Politics of the 1923 Anthracite Crisis," *Mississippi Valley Historical Review*, 52 (December 1965): 566–81, and "Pennsylvania Coal and Politics: The Anthracite Strike of 1925–26," *Pennsylvania Magazine of History and Biography*, 93 (April 1969): 244–62. See also Hawley, "Hoover and the Coal Problems," 266–67; Parker, *The Coal Industry*, 68–84; Johnson, *Politics of Soft Coal*, 118–22.

46. *The Coal Merchant*, 6 (January 1924): 3–4; Parker, *The Coal Industry*, 70–73; USHR Committee on Interstate and Foreign Commerce, *Hearings on Coal Legislation, [March 30–May 14, 1926], Parts 1–3*, 69th Cong., 1st sess., 1926, 4–7, remarks of Representative Allen T. Treadway, Republican, Massachusetts, 8–10, testimony of Representative Meyer Jacobstein, Democrat. Rochester, New York, 32–61, testimony of Representative Mayhew Wainwright, Republican, New York, 104–5, exchange between Representative Hamilton Fish, Jr., Republican, New York, and Representative John G. Cooper, Republican, Ohio 164–71, testimony of Harry L. Gandy, executive secretary, NCA, 247–56, 283, testimony of Eugene McAuliffe, Union Pacific Coal Co., and Washington Union Coal Co., 339.

47. Johnsen, *Government Regulation of Coal*, 103–4; H. Blankenhorn, *New York Leader, Labor's Daily Newspaper*, to Borah, 30 October 1923, and Borah to Herbert Croly, *The New Republic*, 23 October 1923, Box 130, Coal Commission, and Gifford Pinchot, governor, Pennsylvania, to Borah, 18 January 1924, Box 151, Coal Legislation, WEB Papers; Hawley, "Hoover and the Coal Problems," 267–68.

48. *Cushing's Survey*, 1 (5 July 1923): n.p.

Chapter Six

1. Chester A. Gauss, "Selling Labor-Saving Appliances, Selling the Man of the House," *The Central Station*, 21 (July 1921): 16–20.

2. Technologically induced changes in metropolitan growth patterns receive some attention in R. D. McKenzie, *The Metropolitan Community* (New York: McGraw-Hill, 1933); Donald J. Bogue, *The Structure of the Metropolitan Community: A Study of Dominance and Subdominance* (Ann Arbor: University of Michigan, Horace H. Rackham School of Graduate Studies, 1949); John R. Borchert, "American Metropolitan

Evolution," *Geographical Review,* 57 (July 1967): 301–32.

3. Sam H. Schurr, Bruce Netschert, et al., *Energy in the American Economy, 1850–1975: An Economic Study of Its History and Prospects* (Baltimore: Johns Hopkins University Press for Resources for the Future, 1960), 35–36.

4. For the above two paragraphs: Memorandum for Dr. G. O. Smith, on quantity of coal required to heat a house, 26 June 1923, Box 22, USGS, RG 57; A. L. Freehoffer, commissioner, Idaho Public Utilities Commission, to W. E. Borah, 7 January 1919, regarding hearings before the commission on electric house heat versus coal; *The Retail Coalman,* 40 (March 1922): 59; *The Coal Merchant,* 1 (15 November 1919): 6–7; ibid., 4 (July, August, September 1922): 9; ibid., 6 (March 1924): 6; Richard R. Mead, *An Analysis of the Decline of the Anthracite Industry Since 1921* (Philadelphia; n.p., 1935), 57; National Industrial Conference Board, *The Competitive Position of Coal in the United States* (New York: NICB, 1931), 31, 94–95; Shurr, Netschert, et al., *Energy in the American Economy,* 126–27.

5. Foreign crude, at first Mexican and then Venezuelan and Columbian, supplied a significant portion of the fuel oil burned along the Atlantic coast. Mid-Continent producers and refiners believed that the imports narrowed the market for domestic oil, and they demanded tariffs or import quotas. See Chapter 8, pp. 197–201; Williamson et al., *The American Petroleum Industry: The Age of Energy, 1899–1959,* vol. 2 (Evanston: Northwestern University Press, 1963), 444–48, 450; Mead, *Decline of Anthracite,* 82; W. C. Trapnell and Ralph Ilsley, *The Bituminous Coal Industry with a Survey of Competing Fuels* (Washington, D.C.: Federal Emergency Relief Adminstration, 1935), 109, 154; Shurr, Netschert, et al., *Energy in the American Economy,* 77–78, 106; U.S. Bureau of the Census, *Historical Statistics of the U.S., Colonial Times to 1957* (Washington, D.C.: GPO, 1960), 162; Charles H. Huntley, General Electric Company, "Getting Power and Saving Coal," *American Industries,* 22 (January 1922): 7–10, 47; *Electrical World,* 74 (12 July 1919): 88; Report of the Massachusetts Fuel Commission, 1923, Box 117.153, USCC, RG 68.

6. John W. Lieb, vice-president, New York Edison Company, "Electricity and the Coal Supply," *American Industries,* 23 (May 1923): 40; Walton H. Hamilton and Helen R. Wright, *The Case of Bituminous Coal* (New York: Macmillan, 1925), 10, 179–80; Edward T. Devine, *Coal: Economic Problems of the Mining, Marketing and Consumption of Anthracite and Soft Coal in the United States* (Bloomington, Ill.: American Review Service Press, 1925), 22–23.

7. Remarks by Welch in FTC, Informal Conference with API, 24 January 1927, Petroleum Investigation, Docket section 40-1-5-17, FTC, RG 122.

8. Summary of Statistics of Petroleum, 1914–29, Box 3, FOCB, PAB, RG 232; USBM, *Petroleum Refinery Statistics, 1926, Bulletin 289*

(Washington, D.C.: GPO, 1927), 11, and ibid., *1927, Bulletin 339* (1929), 36; FTC, *Advance in the Price of Petroleum Products*, 66th Cong., 2d sess. 1920, H. Doc. 801 vol. 97, 19.

9. *Oildom*, 7 (January 1917): 3, 13; USGS, Memo [from Director George O. Smith] for the Secretary of the Interior, 23 June 1917, and Manning to CND, 1919, Office of the Secretary, 1-242 (Part 1), DI, RG 48; Lewis, "Our Future Supplies of Petroleum Products," address before Independent Oil Men's Association Convention, Denver, 1920, Box 1036, 21A-A4, Petroleum, Technical or Commodity File, WIB, RG 61; Joseph E. Pogue, *The Economics of Petroleum* (New York: John Wiley & Sons, 1921), 19, 249, 289–90; O'Neal in *Oil and Gas Journal*, 21 (28 December 1922): 70; Ruth W. Ayres, "The Petroleum Industry," in George B. Galloway, ed., *Industrial Planning Under Codes* (New York: Harper & Brothers, 1935), 186. See Earl Cook, *Man, Energy, Society* (San Francisco: W. H. Freeman, 1976), 98–99.

10. As a result of the migratory nature of underground oil, the owner of one tract of land could pump oil that migrated from adjoining tracts, thus diminishing the amount of oil recoverable from those contiguous tracts. The law recognized the producer's title to the oil or gas pumped, and this became known as the rule of capture. Offset drilling became the standard procedure in the fields. Wells were drilled close to property lines with the specific purpose of counteracting the wells drilled on adjoining properties. For an excellent discussion of these practices, see Erich W. Zimmermann, *Conservation in the Production of Petroleum: A Study of Industrial Control* (New Haven: Yale University Press, 1956), 96–100.

11. For the above two paragraphs: O'Donnell in *Oildom*, 13 (January 1922): 6; API, *American Petroleum: Supply and Demand, A Report to the Board of Directors of the American Petroleum Institute by a Committee of Eleven Members of the Board* (New York: McGraw-Hill, 1925), 3–5; Response of state geologists, 1924 and 1925, Office of Director, 143.5, USGS, RG 57; *Denver Post*, 28 October 1925; Pogue, *Economics of Petroleum*, 262–84, 292–99; FTC, *Report on Petroleum Industry: Prices, Profits, and Competition* (Washington, D.C.: GPO, 1928), 2; Zimmermann, *Conservation*, 125–26; Williamson et al., *American Petroleum Industry*, 2: 300–304, views the fear of oil depletion as unwarranted and emanating from sources hostile to the industry; James John Hayden, *Federal Regulation of the Production of Oil* (Washington, D.C.: Callaghan, 1929), 4–5.

12. M. L. Requa, *The Petroleum Problem: Some Fundamentals of the Petroleum Problem* (n.p., reprinted from *The Saturday Evening Post*, 1920); Requa (USFA), Manning (BM), and Smith (USGS) to Harry A. Garfield, 28 February 1919, Office of the Secretary, 1-242 (Part 1), DI, RG 48, called for immediate federal leadership in strengthening the American presence overseas; Pogue, *Economics of Petroleum*, 294; FTC, *Report . . . on Foreign Ownership in the Petroleum Industry* (Washington,

D.C.: GPO, 1923), 38. For extensive treatments of these issues, see John A. Brown, late president, Socony Vacuum Oil Co., "The Role of Private Enterprise in the Development of Oil Resources," 1–9, and Eugene Holman, president, Standard Oil Co. (New Jersey), "American Oil Companies in Foreign Petroleum Operations," 18, in Leonard M. Fanning, ed., *Our Oil Resources* (New York: McGraw-Hill, 1945); Gerald D. Nash, *United States Oil Policy 1890–1964: Business and Government in Twentieth Century America* (Pittsburgh: University of Pittsburgh Press, 1968), 53–60; John A. De Novo, "The Movement for an Aggressive American Oil Policy Abroad, 1918–1920," *American Historical Review,* 41 (July 1955): 854–76; Williamson et al., *American Petroleum Industry,* 2: 516–32; R. W. Ferrier, *The History of the British Petroleum Company,* vol. 1, *The Developing Years, 1901–1932* (Cambridge: Cambridge University Press, 1982), 376–77, 463; William Stivers, *Supremacy and Oil: Iraq, Turkey, and the Anglo-American World Order, 1918–1930* (Ithaca: Cornell University Press, 1982), 23–49, 87–91, 119–24; Edward W. Chester, *United States Oil Policy and Diplomacy: A Twentieth Century Overview* (Westport, Conn.: Greenwood Press, 1983), 214–28.

13. Zimmerman, *Conservation,* 114, and for reservoir theory, 121–24; Pogue, *Economics of Petroleum,* 204–5; R. H. Fernald, "Fuel Wastes: Causes, Effects, Remedies," in Clyde L. King, ed., *The Price of Coal,* 223–24; David Moffat Meyers, "Fuel Conservation: The Need for a Definite Policy and Its Requirement," paper presented at the fuel session of American Society of Mechanical Engineers Annual Meeting, New York, 7 December 1920, Box 10, Alph. D, FOCB, PAB, RG 232; George Ward Stocking, *The Oil Industry and the Competitive System: A Study in Waste* (Boston: Houghton Mifflin, 1925), 134–35, 177–79.

14. The 1940 movie *Boom Town,* featuring Spencer Tracy, Claudette Colbert, Hedy Lamarr, and Clark Gable, graphically depicted the waste attending the coming in of a flush field and the individualistic and competitive attitudes of the wildcatters engaged in such risky ventures.

15. For the above three paragraphs: Stocking, *The Oil Industry,* 117–19; Nash, *U.S. Oil Policy,* 15; Zimmermann, *Conservation,* 135–46, 252–26; Ayres, "The Petroleum Industry," 187. Important to my understanding of the regulatory process in Texas was Edward W. Constant's "State Management of Petroleum Resources, Texas, 1910–1940," in George H. Daniels and Mark H. Rose, eds., *Energy and Transport: Historical Perspectives on Policy Issues* (Beverly Hills: Sage Publications, 1982), 157–75.

16. For Teagle's remarks, API, *Bulletin,* 125 (18 November 1920): n.p., and Welch's comment in ibid., 144 (24 February 1921): 4; for the Randall resolution, USHR Committee on Mines and Mining, *Hearings on Petroleum and Gasoline,* no Cong., no sess., 1916, 3–6.

17. Stocking, *The Oil Industry,* 115–16. During World War II, Stocking, as head of the fuel price division of the Office of Price Administra-

tion, battled against the monopolies to keep oil prices stable; Arthur M. Johnson, *Petroleum Pipelines and Public Policy, 1906–1959* (Cambridge, Mass.: Harvard University Press, 1967), 173, 187. For Teapot Dome, see J. Leonard Bates, *The Origins of Teapot Dome: Progressives, Parties, and Petroleum, 1909–1921* (Urbana: University of Illinois Press, 1963), and Burl Noggle, *Teapot Dome: Oil and Politics in the 1920s* (New York: W. W. Norton, 1965).

18. FTC, *Advance in the Price of Petroleum Products* (1920), *Foreign Ownership in Petroleum Industry* (1923), and *Petroleum Industry* (1928). The latter originated in a Senate resolution of 1926 ordering a study of gasoline prices and expanded to include all phases of the industry. For Congressional hearings, see USS Committee on Manufactures, *Investigation into Prices and Conditions in the Oil Industry*, 67th Cong., 2d sess., 1922, S. Rept. 877, and USS Subcommittee of the Committee on Manufactures, *Hearings on the High Cost of Gasoline and Other Petroleum Products*, 67th Cong., 2d and 4th sess., 1923, 2 vols., called the La Follette committee and considered by the oil industry the most hostile investigation.

19. The discussion of the depletion allowance in David Howard Davis, *Energy Politics* (New York: St. Martin's Press, 1974), 49–50, is error-ridden and misleading. For the industry view of its origins and its significance, see Petroleum Industry War Council, *Report of the Committee on Cost and Price Adjustment to the PIWC* (Washington, D.C.: PIWC, 1943), 5. Jon R. Bond, "Oiling the Tax Committees in Congress, 1900–1974: Subgovernment Theory, the Overrepresentation Hypothesis, and the Oil Depletion Allowance," *American Journal of Political Science*, 23 (November 1979): 661, finds no evidence of oil state overrepresentation on the tax committee; Nash, *U.S. Oil Policy*, 85–86; Zimmermann, *Conservation*, 198–99.

20. Williamson et al., *American Petroleum Industry*, 2: 58–59; Zimmermann, *Conservation*, 186–87; Nash, *U.S. Oil Policy*, 73–81, offers a sympathetic account of Secretary of the Interior Albert B. Fall and views Teapot Dome as retarding the development of federal oil policy regarding defense requirements; Van H. Manning to Newton T. Baker, chairman, CND, 1921, on the nation's oil situation, Office of the Secretary, 1-242 (Part 1), DI, RG 48; USBM, *Production and Consumption of Crude Petroleum and Other Mineral Oils, September 18, 1918*, 64th Cong., 2d sess., 1918, S. Doc. 280, cover; USS, *Hearings on High Cost of Gasoline*, 1: 591.

21. Johnson, *Petroleum Pipeline Policy, 1906–1959*, 142–43, 195–99, 206; S.J. Res. 107 (Hoch-Smith resolution), 30 January 1925, and Before the ICC, ICC Docket No. 18458; ICC Docket No. 17000 (Part 4); Rates on Petroleum and Petroleum Products, *Brief for the Eastern Truck Line Carriers* (1925), Box 10, Alph. E, FOCB, PAB, RG 232; USS, *Hearings on High Cost of Gasoline*, vol. 1, see conclusions for committee recommendation of divorcement, 48–49, testimony of W. H. Gray,

president of the National Association of Independent Oil Producers, 585–89; *Annual Report of the FTC for the Fiscal Year Ended June 30, 1924,* 92, and FTC, *Petroleum Industry* (1928), xviii; Trapnell and Ilsley, *Bituminous Coal Industry,* 34; Fayette B. Dow, "The Role of Petroleum Pipelines in the War," *Annals of the American Academy of Political and Social Science,* 230 (November 1943): 93–94.

22. August W. Giebelhaus, *Business and Government in the Oil Industry: A Case Study of Sun Oil Company, 1876–1945* (Greenwich, Conn.: JAI Press, 1980), 114, 117–18; For the completely negative attitude of API speakers at the third annual convention, *Oil and Gas Journal,* 21 (14 December 1922): 10; W. C. Teagle to Hubert Work, chairman, FOCB, 15 July 1925, 143.5, and George Otis Smith to Secretary of Commerce, 16 October 1924, for a good summary of Doherty's views and Smith's reaction, 143.4, both in Office of the Director, USGS, RG 57; FOCB, *Complete Record of Public Hearings, February 10 and 11, 1926* (Washington, D.C.: GPO, 1926), 23 for Teagle statement; 131 for Requa statement. For a more positive analysis of cooperative initiatives, see Nash, *U.S. Oil Policy,* 6–15.

23. National Resources Committee, *Energy Resources and National Policy* (Washington, D.C.: GPO, 1939), 210, accepted the judgment of the U.S. Temporary National Economic Committee, *Control of the Petroleum Industry by Major Oil Companies* (Investigation of Concentration of Economic Power, *Monograph No. 39,* by Roy C. Cook) (Washington, D.C.: GPO, 1941) that FOCB was formed because of the rise of oil stocks and a weakening of the price structure. Invariably, New Dealers viewed FOCB as the tool of the majors. Davis, *Energy Politics,* 49, attributes the board's formation to Coolidge's efforts to avoid another Teapot Dome. For more informed views as to the president's motivation, see Zimmermann, *Conservation,* 125; Johnson, *Petroleum Pipeline Policy, 1906–1959,* 210; Nash, *U.S. Oil Policy,* 82–85, considers Doherty and Secretary of the Interior Hubert Work as instrumental in the creation of FOCB. In a letter to Coolidge of 11 August 1924, Doherty suggested the appointment of a committee of lawyers to develop uniform oil conservation legislation for each state and a permanent commission to study all aspects of the oil question, Box 12, Board File, FOCB, PAB, RG 232; Norman S. Nordhauser, "Origins of Federal Oil Regulation in the 1920s" *Business History Review,* 47 (Spring 1973), 64–65, provides a balanced explanation.

24. None of the secondary sources cited in note 23 above offers a discussion of FOCB's attention to end use. Virtually all sources begin their treatment of the board by discussing the notions of unitization and prorationing and the influence of Doherty in advocating these techniques to stabilize the industry.

25. API, *American Petroleum,* 1; Giebelhaus, *Sun Oil,* 127–28; Nordhauser, "Oil Regulation in the 1920s" 66–67; Henrietta Larson and Kenneth W. Porter, *History of Humble Oil and Refining Company: A Study*

in *Industrial Growth* (New York: Harper & Brothers 1959), 251–57; Newspaper Clippings 1924–1925, Box 34, vol. 1, FOCB, PAB, RG 232.

26. Rochester memorandum for Secretary Work, 15 August 1927, Box 9, FOCB, PAB, RG 232.

27. API, *American Petroleum*, 3–5.

28. FOCB, *Hearings*, 134, and a similar cautionary statement against the techological quick-fix by Doherty, 26–27.

29. For the discussion of FOCB's end-use thrust, See National Industrial Conference Board, *Oil Conservation and Fuel Oil Supply* (New York: NICB, 1930), v–vi, 57–58, 159; USBM, *Petroleum Refinery Statistics, 1926, Bulletin 289*, 28, and ibid., *1927, Bulletin 339*, 38, and *Crude Petroleum* (1918), 5–6; Williamson et al., *American Petroleum Industry*, vol. 2, chapter 11; Pogue, *Economics of Petroleum*, 155, 163; *Report of the Federal Oil Conservation Board to the President of the United States, September 1926, Part 1* (Washington, D.C.: GPO, 1926), 5–6, 9–12, and *Report 2 . . . January 1928* (Washington, D.C.: GPO, 1928), 3, 5–9; drafts of Report 2 of FOCB, 1928, Box 1, FOCB, PAB, RG 232. During the 1920s, the Anglo-Persian Oil Co. opened several shale oil refineries in Scotland. They operated only spasmodically during the late 1920s owing to low crude oil prices. See John H. Nelson, *Petroleum Refineries in Foreign Countries*, U.S. Department of Commerce Bureau of Foreign and Domestic Commerce, Trade Information Bulletin No. 494 (Washington, D.C.: GPO, 1927), 19–20.

30. Stocking, *The Oil Industry*, 250; B. Stanley Nelson, "Fuel Oil and Its Utilization," 794–879, and Samuel S. Wyer, "Natural Gas," 902–13, in Raymond F. Bacon and William A. Hamor, eds., *American Fuels*, 2 vols. (New York: McGraw-Hill, 1922), vol. 2; API, *Bulletin*, 144 (24 February 1921): 7–9; Larson and Porter, *Humble Oil*, 260; J. A. Doyle, vice-president, W. S. Rockwell Co., New York, to FOCB, 10 February 1925, Box 10, Alph. D.; and Leon D. Becker, executive secretary, American Oil Burner Association, to Secretary of the Interior, 26 February 1926, Box 9, FOCB, PAB, RG 232; FOCB, *Hearings*, Beaty statement, 11, Teagle statement, 19, Becker statement, 27, Nicholas statement, 148.

31. For the above two paragraphs: FOCB, *Hearings*, Doherty statement, 29; "Those Who Would Regulate Coal Industry May Drag in Oil Also," *National Petroleum News*, 7 December 1927, in Box 35, vol. 5, FOCB, PAB, RG 232; Giebelhaus, *Sun Oil*, 129–33; Zimmermann, *Conservation*, 127–28; for the ten questionnaires and digests of responses to each, Box 26, Questionnaires, FOCB, PAB, RG 232.

32. E. W. Clark speech as reported in *The Manufacturer and Industrial News Bureau*, 39 (June 1927): 12–13.

33. Nordhauser, "Oil Regulation in the 1920s," 58–59; Williamson et al., *American Petroleum Industry*, 2: 316–21, 347; Zimmermann, *Conservation*, 160; Nash, *U.S. Oil Policy*, 95–96; George Otis Smith, chairman

of the FOCB Advisory Committee, "FOCB Conservation Policy One of Cooperation," Typed, [1928], Office of Director, 143.5, USGS, RG 57.

34. Address delivered by Borah at the International Advertising Association, Denver, 28 June 1927, Box 10, Alph. B. FOCB, PAB, RG 232.

Chapter Seven

1. August W. Giebelhaus, *Business and Government in the Oil Industry: A Case Study of Sun Oil Company, 1876–1945* (Greenwich, Conn.: JAI Press, 1980), 136–37.

2. Cushing to Borah, 7, 13, 21, 25 April 1925, Box 176, Coal Legislation, WEB Papers; Barnum, president, NCA, "What the Bituminous Coal Industry Has Done for Itself and for the Nation," presented at the International Conference on Bituminous Coal, Pittsburgh, 16 November 1926, Box 161, TJW Papers.

3. Southeastern Millers Association to Hoover, 12 May 1924, and *The New England Coal Dealer*, May 1924, Box 80769. National Associations, General Correspondence, DC, RG 40; C. R. Goldmann, Retail Coal Dealers Association of Texas, Dallas, to Hoover, 22 April 1925, 243.1, General Coal and Coke, BFDC, RG 151.

4. *New York World*, 30 January 1925, Clipping in Box 34, vol. 1, FOCB, PAB, RG 232.

5. National Industrial Conference Board, Inc., *The Competitive Position of Coal in the United States* (New York: NICB, 1931), 151.

6. Chapters 8 and 9 treat the evolution of oil policies during the Hoover and Roosevelt administrations, while Chapter 10 studies the New Deal's NRA coal codes and the National Bituminous Coal Commission.

7. The proportion of anthracite to total coal production, 17 percent for the three production years 1911–13, fell to 14 percent in 1923 and 12 percent in 1929. For anthracite markets, see Edward T. Devine, *Coal, Economic Problems of the Mining, Marketing and Consumption of Anthracite and Soft Coal in the United States* (Bloomington, Ill.: American Review Service Press, 1925), 84–85; Richard R. Mead, *An Analysis of the Decline of the Anthracite Industry Since 1921* (Philadelphia: n.p., 1935), 67, 99–100.

8. Committee on Public Administration Cases, *The Consumers' Counsel and the National Bituminous Coal Commission, 1937–1938* (Washington, D.C.: Committee on Public Administration Cases, 1949, rev. ed., 1950), 102; W. C. Trapnell and Ralph Ilsley, *The Bituminous Coal Industry with a Survey of Competing Fuels* (Washington, D.C.: Federal Emergency Relief Administration, 1935), 16–32, 67; Adam Thomas Shurick, *The Coal Industry* (Boston: Little, Brown, 1924), 361; Glen L.

Parker, *The Coal Industry: A Study in Social Control* (Washington, D.C.: American Council on Public Affairs, 1940), 50–53.

9. Harold F. Williamson et al., *The American Petroleum Industry: The Age of Energy, 1899–1959*, vol. 2 (Evanston: Northwestern University Press, 1963), 302–3.

10. Production in Kansas, stable during the 1920s, declined as a proportion of the national total from a peak of 13 percent in 1918 to under 5 percent in 1927–29. Production in Oklahoma increased steadily from 1919 through 1927. However, its share of national production declined from a peak of 35 percent in 1915 to around 23 percent in 1923–26, rising then to 30 percent in 1927 when the Oklahoma City field came in, and then falling steadily through 1944 when it leveled out at 8 percent. Texas production skyrocketed in the 1920s, and its share of domestic production advanced from under 20 percent in 1922 to 45 percent in 1932. California, a separate oil province, experienced a dramatic increase in production in 1923 and remained relatively stable during the remainder of the decade. California's share of the total fell from 35 percent to 25 percent. Erich W. Zimmermann, *Conservation in the Production of Petroleum: A Study of Industrial Control* (New Haven: Yale University Press, 1957), 143, 151, 160, 162, 171.

11. See Albert L. Danielsen, *The Evolution of OPEC* (New York: Harcourt Brace Jovanovich, 1982), 81–89, for an interpretation of the Interstate Oil Compact and market demand prorationing that blends smoothly into his account of the events leading to the formation of OPEC.

12. As Williamson et al., *American Petroleum Industry*, 2: 438, explains it, many of the shut-down refineries, averaging 164 yearly for the five years 1922–27, consisted of small Mid-Continent operations, producing a limited range of products by means of obsolete techniques, which found it difficult to compete with larger, more efficient, and more advantageously located refineries.

13. Ibid., 341; George W. Stocking, *The Oil Industry and the Competitive System: A Study in Waste* (Boston: Houghton Mifflin, 1925), 261–63; Joseph E. Pogue, *The Economics of Petroleum* (New York: John Wiley & Sons, 1921), 92; see also sources used for Table 13.

14. Eugene V. Rostow, *A National Policy for the Oil Industry* (New Haven: Yale University Press, 1947), 58–62; Williamson et al., *American Petroleum Industry*, 2: 307, 360–62; James J. Hayden, *Federal Regulation of the Production of Oil* (Washington, D.C.: Callaghan, 1929), 104–6; Arthur M. Johnson, *Petroleum Pipelines and Public Policy, 1906–1959* (Cambridge, Mass., Harvard University Press, 1967), 179–87, 195–99, 206; *Annual Report of the Federal Trade Commission for the Fiscal Year Ended June 30, 1924* (Washington, D.C.: GPO, 1924), 92; FTC, *Report on Petroleum Industry: Prices, Profits, and Competition* (Washington, D.C.: GPO, 1928); USS Subcommittee of the Committee on Manufactures, *Hear-*

ings on the High Cost of Gasoline and Other Petroleum Products, 67th Cong., 2d and 4th sess., 1923, 2 vols., 1: 48–49, 585–86. For an earlier consideration of divorcement, see USHR Committee on Interstate and Foreign Commerce, *Hearings on H.R. 16581, A Bill to Regulate the Transportation of Oil by Means of Pipelines, May 15 and 16, 1914, Parts 1 and 2*, 63d Cong., 2d sess., 1914.

15. U.S. Coal Commission, *Report of the United States Coal Commission in Five Parts (Part 1, Principal Findings and Recommendations, 1923)* (Washington, D.C.: GPO, 1925), 6; Trapnell and Ilsley, *Bituminous Coal Industry*, 2; Parker, *The Coal Industry*, 43–44, 50–53; Operator's Committee on Reorganization of the Bituminous Coal Industry, Chicago, 5 December 1922, Box 1, Entry 5, E-5, USCC, RG 68.

16. For the above three paragraphs: NICB, *Competitive Position of Coal*, 151; *The Retail Coalman*, 42 (March 1923): 55; ICC, *34th Annual Report, December 1, 1920* (Washington, D.C.: GPO, 1920), 6–7: *American Petroleum Institute Bulletin* 2 (25 August 1920), n.p.; Memorandum re Northwest Dock Operators, 24 April 1923, by J. A. Adams, and ICC hearings of November 1922 re dock companies and rail rates, and Indiana Coal Trade Bureau statement, February 1923, in Box 117.153, USCC, RG 68; Parker, *The Coal Industry*, 43–48; Eugene Rostow, "Bituminous Coal and the Public Interest," *The Yale Law Journal*, 50 (February 1941): 553–55.

17. Walton H. Hamilton and Helen R. Wright, *The Case of Bituminous Coal* (New York: Macmillan, 1925), 149–52; Jacob H. Hollander, special investigator, Notes on Freight Rates on Anthracite Coal, 18 June 1923, Box 1, Entry 4, and Statement to the USCC on Coal Transportation, submitted by the Bituminous Operators' Special Committee, 4 September 1923, Box 4, Entry 8, both in USCC, RG 68; testimony of J. D. A. Morrow, vice-president, NCA, USS Select Committee on Reconstruction and Production, *Hearings . . . pursuant to S.R. 350 . . . Coal and Transportation*, 66th Cong., 3d sess., 1920–21, 578; ICC rejection of USCC mine-rating plan, 1924, Box 48, ICC, FFD, RG 89; Devine, *Coal*, 293.

18. Rostow, *National Policy for Oil*, 58–60; Joseph T. Lambie, *From Mine to Market: The History of Coal Transportation on the Norfolk & Western Railway* (New York: New York University Press, 1954), 333–34; Williamson et al., *American Petroleum Industry*, 2: 104–9, 344–45, 354, 438; Johnson, *Pipelines, 1906–1959*, 187, 206.

19. Railroad operating revenues, at $6.3 billion in both 1920 and 1929, fluctuated between a low of $5.6 billion in 1921 and 1922 (corresponding with the coal strike) and a high of $6.5 billion in 1926. Freight revenues averaged $4.3 billion annually for the five years 1920–24 and $4.8 billion for the succeeding five years. These figures attest to a no-growth decade for the railroads. During this decade, the tonnage of lake coal traffic increased—steadily—by 47 percent, U.S. Bureau of the Census, *Historical Statistics of the United States, Co-*

lonial Times to 1957 (Washington, D.C.: GPO, 1960) 434, 454; *API Bulletin*, 176 (11 August 1921): n.p.; Trapnell and Ilsley, *Bituminous Coal Industry*, 34, 100; Merle Fainsod and Lincoln Gordon, *Government and the American Economy* (New York: W. W. Norton, 1941, rev. ed. 1948), 263–65.

20. Potter remarks in Lambie, *From Mine to Market*, 331; USCC, *Report* 1: x–xi, 259–78; *Electrical World*, 79 (15 March 1922): 567; John W. Lieb, "Electricity and the Coal Supply," *American Industries*, 23 (May 1923): 36–40; Coolidge to the Secretaries of War, Navy, Interior, and Commerce, 19 December 1924, Box 223, FOCB, PAB, RG 232.

21. By order of production in 1926 the sixteen largest firms were: Standard Oil (California) (12.6 percent), Gulf Oil Corporation (10.6 percent), Standard Oil (New York) (8.5 percent), Standard Oil (New Jersey) (7.9 percent), Tide Water Oil Co. (6 percent), The Texas Co. (5 percent), Ohio Oil Co., a former Standard subsidiary (4.9 percent), Standard Oil (Indiana) (4.6 percent), Marland Oil Co. (4.5 percent), Phillips Petroleum Co. (4.3 percent), Union Oil Co. of California (3.7 percent), Prairie Oil and Gas Co., a former Standard subsidiary (3.7 percent), California Petroleum Corp. (3.6 percent), Sinclair Consolidated Oil Corp. (3.1 percent), Cities Service Co. (3 percent), Pure Oil Co. (2.9 percent).

22. FTC, *Petroleum Industry* (1928), xvii, 25, 29; *Independent Petroleum Association of America Monthly*, March 1931, Box 12, Board File, FOCB, PAB, RG 232; Williamson et al., *American Petroleum Industry*, 2: 63, 165–66, 329–30, 440–41; Fainsod, *Government and American Economy*, 622.

23. In 1929, Cities Service supplied 18 percent of all the gas and above 2 percent of the oil produced; Standard of New Jersey supplied 9 percent of gas and 8 percent of domestic oil. Cities Service was also a major electric power holding company. Trapnell and Ilsley, *Bituminous Coal Industry*, 34–35.

24. See Chapter 1, notes 5 and 6; Report on Railroad Coal Companies, 1923, and Report on Coal Owned by Anthracite Companies, 1923, in Box 1, Entry 4, USCC, RG 68; *Report of the U.S. Coal Commission, 1923*, 1: 48, 66.

25. Hamilton and Wright, *Bituminous Coal*, 42; USHR Committee on Interstate and Foreign Commerce, *Hearings on Coal Legislation, March 30, 31, and April 1, 2, 6, 7, and 8, 1926. Part 1*, 69th Cong., 1st sess., 1926, 247–50.

26. *Report of the U.S. Coal Commission, 1923*, 1: 3–5; Devine, *Coal*, 84–85; Harold M. Watkins, *Coal and Men: An Economic and Social Study of the British and American Coalfields* (London: George Allen & Unwin, 1934), 32; Mead, *Decline of Anthracite*, 11–16, 41–43; Harold K. Kanarek, "Disaster for Hard Coal: The Anthracite Strike of 1925–1926," *Labor History*, 15 (Winter 1974): 45; Jacob H. Hollander, special investigator, Notes on Investment Returns of the Railroad Coal Companies, 18 June 1923, Typed, Box 1, Entry 4, USCC, RG 68.

27. Lambie, *From Mine to Market*, 251–59; Paul L. Murphy, *The Constitution in Crisis Times, 1918–1969* (New York: Harper & Row, 1972), 33–35; Arthur Cecil Bining and Thomas C. Cochran, *The Rise of American Economic Life* (New York: Charles Scribner's Sons, 1964), 536–38; FTC, *Annual Report. 1921*, 30, ibid., *1922*, 24, ibid., *1923*, 43–44, on a court reversal of an FTC order against gasoline station franchises; Parker, *The Coal Industry*, 89.

28. *Report of the U.S. Coal Commission, 1923*, 1: 1–2, 52.

29. McAuliffe testimony in USHR, *Hearings on Coal Legislation*, 339. McAuliffe was president of two coal companies owned by the Union Pacific line.

30. For the above four paragraphs: Robert H. Zieger, "Anthracite Crisis," *Mississippi Valley Historical Review*, 52 (December 1965): 577–80, and "Pennsylvania Coal and Politics: The Anthracite Strike of 1925–1926," *Pennsylvania Magazine of History and Biography*, 93 (April 1969): 254–61; Devine, *Coal*, 52–58; Watkins, *Coal and Men*, 121; Frank L. Burns Coal Co., New York, to Senator Borah, 28 November 1925, and Curley to Borah, 20 November 1925, Box 176, Coal Legislation, WEB Papers; *The Coal Merchant*, 6 (January 1924): 3–4; USHR, *Hearings on Coal Legislation*, 4–7, 128, 144, 269, 339.

31. USS, *Hearings on High Cost of Gasoline*, 3, 13.

32. Williamson et al., *American Petroleum Industry*. 2: 329.

33. Ibid., 375–95, for an excellent discussion of the complicated issue of cracking patents. Cracking became increasingly important in gasoline refining during the 1920s, yielding by 1929 one-third of the gasoline produced. Cracking increased the yield of gasoline per barrel of crude and produced a superior product. The licensing practices of the patent owners, according to the independents, denied them access to this technology and weakened their competitive condition. A federal suit initiated in 1924 against the patent holders was finally dismissed in 1931.

34. USS Committee on Manufactures, *Investigation into the Prices and Conditions in the Oil Industry*, 67th Cong., 2d sess., 1922, S. Rep. 877 6–7; FTC, *Advance in the Price of Petroleum Products*, 66th Cong., 2d sess., 1920, H. Doc. 801, vol. 97, 2, and *AR 1924*, 92, and *Petroleum Industry* (1928), xvii, xix.

35. Clippings from *New York Post*, 26 February 1925, *New York World*, 1 March 1925, Box 34, vol. 1, and *Washington Herald*, 24 May 1927, *The Nation*, 25 May 1927, Box 34, vol. 4, FOCB, PAB, RG 232.

36. Gerald D. Nash, *United States Oil Policy 1890–1964: Business and Government in Twentieth-Century America* (Pittsburgh: University of Pittsburgh Press, 1968), 97, writes: "The Coolidge years saw the development of a slowly emerging consensus on national oil policies, both among leaders in the industry and in various branches of state and federal government." My interpretation emphasizes contention, divisiveness, and the search by the majors and the independents for a

political solution that would serve their particular interests. See also
Ruth W. Ayres, "The Petroleum Industry," in George B. Galloway,
ed., *Industrial Planning Under Codes* (New York: Harper & Brothers,
1935), 190–92, 197–98; Ronald B. Shuman, *The Petroleum Industry:
An Economic Survey* (Norman: University of Oklahoma Press, 1940),
127, 161.

37. Harry L. Gandy, executive secretary, NCA, to Alexander Forward, managing director, AGA, 6 December 1927, Power and Gas
Investigation, 4437/HEA5, FTC, RG 122.

Chapter Eight

1. Preliminary Draft of Report on Petroleum by Committee on
Tariff Bargaining Concerning Petroleum Exports, Planning Commit-
tee for Mineral Policy, 11 October 1934, Office of the Secretary, 1-287,
DI, RG 48; National Resources Committee, *Energy Resources and Na-
tional Policy, Report of the Energy Resources Committee to the U.S. National
Resources Committee* (Washington, D.C.: GPO, 1939), 134.

2. USHR Subcommittee of the Committee on Interstate and Foreign
Commerce, *Hearings on H.R. 441, Petroleum Investigation, Parts 1–5*, 73d
Cong., recess, 1934, Wolverton, Part 1, 252–53, Farrish, Part 1, 744,
Phillips, Part 3, 1662. This body was known as the Cole committee
after its chairman, William P. Cole, Jr., Democrat, Maryland.

3. For the above four paragraphs: Erich W. Zimmermann, *Conservation in the Production of Petroleum: A Study of Industrial Control* (New
Haven: Yale University Press, 1957), 125–26, 144–45; August W.
Giebelhaus, *Business and Government in the Oil Industry: A Case Study of
Sun Oil Company, 1876–1945* (Greenwich, Conn.: JAI Press, 1980),
133–35; Northcutt Ely, *Oil Conservation Through Interstate Agreement*
(Washington, D.C.: FOCB, 1933), 92; Henrietta M. Larson and Kenneth W. Porter, *History of Humble Oil and Refining Co.: A Study of Industrial Growth* (New York: Harper & Brothers, 1959), 320; W. H. Gray,
president, National Association of Independent Oil Producers, Tulsa,
to Hubert Work, Secretary of the Interior, 14 December 1926, FOCB,
Box 10, G, PAB, RG 232; Ray Lyman Wilbur, Secretary of the
Interior, to editor, *Houston Oil Weekly*, 21 May 1930, Office of the Secretary, 1-242 (Part 3), DI, RG 48; Requa–Doherty–Borah correspondence, 1927, Box 234, Oil, WEB Papers.

4. Harold F. Williamson et al., *The American Petroleum Industry: The
Age of Energy, 1899–1959*, vol. 2 (Evanston: Northwestern University
Press, 1963), 729; Eugene Holman, "American Oil Companies in
Foreign Petroleum Operations," in Leonard M. Fanning, ed., *Our Oil
Resources* (New York: McGraw-Hill, 1945), 22–29; Gerald D. Nash,
*United States Oil Policy 1890–1964: Business and Government in Twentieth
Century America* (Pittsburgh: University of Pittsburgh Press, 1968), 53–
55; USS Committee on Commerce, *Hearings on S.J. Res. 238 and*

S. 5818, Regulating Importation of Petroleum and Related Products, Part 2, January 30, 31, February 2 and 3, 1931, 71st Cong., 3d sess., 1931; USHR Committee on Ways and Means, *Hearings on HR. 16585, Regulating Importation of Petroleum and Related Products, February 13, 14, 16, and 17, 1931,* 71st Cong., 3d sess., 1931.

5. For the above two paragraphs: USS, *Importation of Petroleum, Part 2,* 90–91, Capper, 110–11, Pan American, 133–35, New England, 136, 179, Savannah, 141–47, Tydings, 148; USS Committee on Finance, *Hearings on HR. 10236, Revenue Act of 1932, An Act to Provide Revenue, Equalize Taxation, and for Other Purposes,* 72d Cong., 1st sess., 1932, Wirt Franklin, 434–35, NCA, 564–70; Letters from Texas Republicans and Democrats to Sen. Tom Connally in December 1930–February 1931 supporting a stiff tariff, Box 144 Oil Tariff, TC Papers.

6. USS, *Importation of Petroleum, Part 2,* Requa, 208–33; Zimmermann, *Conservation,* 129; Doherty to FOCB, 11 November 1931, FOCB, Box 11, 1931, and E. S. Rochester, secretary, FOCB, Memorandum re the Proposal for Tariff on Oil, 5 February 1930, FOCB, Box 10, 1930, and FOCB Press Release, 2 April 1931, FOCB, Box 32, Press Releases, 1929–32, PAB, RG 232; Joe I. Cromwell, president of the Cromwell-Franklin Oil Co., Oklahoma, and a director of IPAA, commented sardonically that these and other concessions "were done for the benefit of importers of foreign oil." He asserted that FOCB "is not interested in supplying 'markets' for American oil producers—and is even willing to see our markets taken away from us." Joe I. Cromwell, "Oil Proration and the Federal Oil Conservation Board," IPAA *Bulletin No. 29* (c. 1929), in Box 20, Oil, FOCB, RLW Papers.

7. W. S. Fitzpatrick, Prairie Oil and Gas Co., Independence, Kansas, to E. B. Reeser, president, API, 2 January 1931, FOCB, Box 18, Kansas–Oklahoma field, PAB, RG 232; Wesley E. Disney, member of Congress, 1st Oklahoma District, to President Hoover, 1 June 1931, Telegram, General Correspondence, 82231-17, Part 1, DC, RG 40; Larson and Porter, *Humble Oil,* 322–23, 537–38.

8. USS, *Revenue Act of 1932,* 438–41, 447, 479–521, 564–70 passim.; Revenue bill of 1932, Box 7, TJW Papers; Williamson et al., *American Petroleum Industry,* 2: 548, 552; Larson and Porter, *Humble Oil,* 537, 548; Zimmermann, *Conservation,* 196.

9. USS, *Importation of Petroleum, Part 2,* 208–33.

10. Merger negotiations between Prairie and Sinclair commenced in 1927, and in 1932 a much-weakened Prairie merged with the strong and diversified Sinclair. Williamson et al., *The American Petroleum Industry,* 2: 339–40, 347–49; Arthur M. Johnson, *Petroleum Pipelines and Public Policy, 1906–1959* (Cambridge, Mass.: Harvard University Press, 1967), 139–43, 153–60.

11. Zimmermann, *Conservation,* 172–73, 204; Ely, *Oil Conservation,* 295–98; Correspondence between Ray Lyman Wilbur and API, December 1930, FOCB, Box 18, Kansas–Oklahoma field, PAB, RG 232.

12. See Chapter 2, pp. 40–42; Chapter 6, pp. 155–56; and Chapter 7, pp. 176–77 for earlier Mid-Continent demands for divorcement which were endorsed by FTC in reports of 1917, 1922, and 1925 (see Chapter 2, note 24) and which stemmed in part from ICC refusal to enforce the common carrier clause.

13. USHR Committee on Interstate and Foreign Commerce, *Pipelines, Hearings on HR. 16695, February 17–18, 1931,* 71st Cong., 3d sess., 1931, Hoch, 1–2, 9–10, 55, Bowles, 15–19, Ritchie, 38–39, 46, Landon, 60; C. O. Ross, Coffeyville, Kansas, to Sen. Borah, 26 December 1930, Box 321, Oil (1), WEB Papers; Petition to President Hoover from Coffeyville, Kansas, 20 December 1930, Telegram to Secretary of Interior Wilbur from Chanute, Paola, Sedan, Garnett, Moran, Iola, Carey, [Southeastern] Kansas, 20–23 December 1930; Tulsa oil producers meeting with USGS official in attendance, 27 December 1930, Northeastern Oklahoma oil producers' committee meeting in Tulsa re Prairie, 8 January 1931, and telegrams and letters protesting the Prairie decision forwarded by Sen. George McGill, Democrat, Kansas, and President Hoover, January 1931, FOCB, Box 18, Kansas–Oklahoma field, PAB, RG 232.

14. The report of Walter M. W. Splawn, University of Texas economist, was commissioned by the House Committee on Interstate and Foreign Commerce, which, in a House resolution passed on 19 January 1932, was assigned the task of investigating all common carriers other than railroads, Johnson, *Pipelines, 1906–1959,* 219–21.

15. *Oildom,* 13 (May 1922): 17; *Kansas City Times,* 29 March, 2, 12, 15 April 1921, 15 June 1925; FTC, *Report on Petroleum Industry: Prices, Profits, and Competition* (Washington, D.C.: GPO, 1928), 9, 51, 226–27; Williamson et al., *American Petroleum Industry,* 2: 468–76, 482–88.

16. The Ethyl Corporation, formed in 1923 by General Motors and Jersey Standard, controlled the manufacturing, licensing, and marketing of leaded, high-octane, antiknock gasoline—the premium grade—during the 1920s and 1930s. Other petroleum companies sought diligently to develop their own premium grades in competition with Ethyl's licensees, while others were purchasing Ethyl. See Williamson et al., *American Petroleum Industry,* 2: 501–2; Giebelhaus, *Sun Oil,* 72–75.

17. For the above five paragraphs: Williamson et al., *American Petroleum Industry,* 2: 499, 503–5, 680; FTC, *Annual Report, 1921,* 30, ibid., *1922,* 24, ibid., *1923,* 43–44; Ronald B. Shuman, *The Petroleum Industry: An Economic Survey* (Norman: University of Oklahoma Press, 1940), 128–34, 138–41; George W. Stocking, *The Oil Industry and the Competitive System: A Study in Waste* (Boston: Houghton Mifflin, 1925), 270–73; René de Visme Williamson, *The Politics of Planning in the Oil Industry Under the Code* (New York: Harper & Brothers, 1936), 45; Larson and Porter, *Humble Oil,* 539–42; *Kansas City Star,* 7 June 1931; Westland Oil Company, Minot, North Dakota, to Sen. Walsh, 11 February 1931, Box 7, TJW Papers; Memorandum from FTC re Lease and Agency,

Lease and License Methods of Marketing Petroleum Products, 28 October 1933, Box 86, FTC; and Ralph Horween, National Association of Gasoline Retailers, to Charles Fahy, Department of the Interior, 26 February 1934, Box 99, NAGR, PAB, RG 232.

18. *Report 4 of the Federal Oil Conservation Board to the President of the United States, May 28, 1930* (Washington, D.C.: GPO, 1930), 8; *Bulletin of the Independent Oil Men of America,* 23 April 1929, in Box 198, TJW Papers; National Resource Committee, *Energy Resources and National Policy,* 387; for a hostile contemporary analysis of FOCB, see Myron W. Watkins, *Oil: Stabilization or Conservation, A Case Study in the Organization of Industrial Control* (New York: Harper & Brothers, 1937), 45–47, 251–52; For a somewhat later positive analysis of FOCB, see Zimmermann, *Conservation,* 301–2, 307; George Otis Smith, chairman, Advisory Committee of the Oil Conservation Board, "Federal Oil Conservation Board's Conservation Policy One of Cooperation," Typed, n.d., Office of Director, 143.5, USGS, RG 57.

19. For the above three paragraphs: Zimmermann, *Conservation,* 121, 131–32, 147–48; Shuman, *Petroleum Industry,* 256–60; Stanley Gill, *A Report on the Petroleum Industry of the United States, Prepared for Presentation to the Sub-Committee on Petroleum Investigation of the Committee on Interstate and Foreign Commerce, House of Representatives, 73rd Congress* (n.p., 1934), ix, 9, 87–93, 187–90 passim, in a highly technical study accepted the idea of an optimum rate of flow for each well but condemned unitization and prorationing, as proposed by FOCB, as financially beneficial only to the large oil companies; National Resources Committee, *Energy Resources,* 220; Ely, *Oil Conservation,* 3–14; FOCB, *Report 4,* 17–24.

20. James G. Stanley to Work, 15 February 1926, FOCB, Box 12, Board File, PAB, RG 232.

21. Hoover to Wilbur, 9 December 1930, Box 20, Oil, General, 1929–1931, RLW Papers.

22. Shuman, *Petroleum Industry,* 261–63; Zimmermann, *Conservation,* 130, 145; James J. Hayden, *Federal Regulation of the Production of Oil* (Washington, D.C.: Callaghan, 1929), 10–11; Nash, *U.S. Oil Policy,* 102–3; Ely, *Oil Conservation,* v–vi; on the Committee of Nine, Box 198, TJW Papers; from FOCB, PAB, RG 232: Resolution of the Board of Directors, API, 5 December 1927, Box 11, 1930; Secretary Work, FOCB, address to the Committee of Nine, 10 December 1927, and Summary of recommendations to FOCB by American Bar Association Committee of Nine, 28 January 1928, Box 9; *Washington Herald,* 6 December 1927, on Doherty attack, Box 35, vol. 6; and *National Petroleum News,* 23 November 1927, 17 April 1929, Box 34, vol. 4; FOCB to the President, 5 April 1929, re API resolutions adopted at Houston meeting, 1929, calling for production controls, Box 20, Oil, FOCB; Department of Interior Memorandum for the President, 12 April 1929, re FOCB response to API resolutions, Box 21, Oil, Oil Conservation Policy, April–May 1929.

23. Williamson et al., *American Petroleum Industry*, 2: 322–25; Zimmermann, *Conservation*, 160; from FOCB, PAB, RG 232: Clippings from *Inland Oil Index*, 28 January 1927, *Tulsa World*, 10 February 1927, *Christian Science Monitor*, 14 May 1927, *Salt Lake City Tribune*, 26 May 1927, *Oildom*, 27 June 1927, *National Petroleum News*, 27 July 1927, in Box 35, vol. 4; Okmulgee District Oil and Gas Association to FOCB, 17 May 1927, and minutes of the meeting of Mid-Continent oil producers, particularly those operating in the Seminole field, held in W. C. Teagle's office, New York City, 25 May 1927, Box 9; and the Paden Oil Co., Oklahoma City, to FOCB, 10 January 1928, Box 8.

24. Williamson et al., *American Petroleum Industry*, 2: 542–45; Oil compact conference, FOCB, Box 15, File 8, PAB, RG 232; *Oil and Gas Journal*, 6 June 1929.

25. For public land withdrawal: Zimmermann, *Conservation*, 186–87; Williamson et al., *American Petroleum Industry*, 2: 545–46; Nash, *U.S. Oil Policy*, 101; Remarks of Secretary of Interior Work in FOCB, *Complete Record of Public Hearings, February 10 and 11, 1926* (Washington, D.C.: GPO, 1926), 4–5; For earlier Hoover endorsement of changes in the leasing act of 1920, Hoover to Work, 2 January 1926, general correspondence, 82231-17 part 1, DC, RG 40; Department of Interior Press Release, 16 March 1929, implementing withdrawal and other items, in Box 199, TJW Papers; From RLW Papers: E. C. Finney, solicitor, memorandum for Secretary Wilbur, 4 March 1930, Box 20, Oil, FOCB, 1929–1936; Hoover's remarks to the press, 15 March 1929, and Julian I. Sears, acting director, USGS, to Secretary Wilbur, 15 March 1929, and Sears's memorandum for Mr. Burlew, 16 March 1929, Box 20, Oil, Oil Conservation Policy, February–March 1929.

26. For other conference-related material in FOCB, PAB, RG 232: *National Petroleum News*, 19 June 1929, Box 35, vol. 7, letters from Oklahoma independents to FOCB, May–June 1929, and Independent Oil Men of America to Secretary Wilbur, 8 June 1929, Box 15, File 8.

27. Both Giebelhaus, *Sun Oil*, 138–40, and Nash, *U.S. Oil Policy*, 99–105, view the Colorado Springs meeting as a failure. If compared with Harding and Coolidge, Nash judges Hoover's oil policy to be inept. Coolidge did create FOCB, but beyond that he did nothing and Harding did even less. Both of Hoover's predecessors were essentially disengaged from oil issues. Hoover's inability to influence events in oil looks worse because times were so bad that drift seems inexcusable. Harding and Collidge had the good fortune to be drifters on placid waters.

28. Demand forecasting began in March 1930. The Voluntary Committee first predicted the future consumption of refined products with separate estimates for gasoline, fuel oil, and so on—then the necessary production to meet that demand, and finally the allowable production for each producing district. These forecasts continued under the NRA oil code and were then taken over by the Bureau of Mines. Even the

bitterest opponents of quotas recognized the accuracy of the forecasts. Report of the Voluntary Committee on Petroleum Economics made for FOCB, 25 March 1930, FOCB, Box 6, PAB, RG 232; Demand for Motor Fuel, 11 November 1932, from the Voluntary Committee on Petroleum Economics, Office of the Secretary, 1-242 (Part 2), DI, RG. 48; Zimmermann, *Conservation*, 130; Ely to Wilbur, 30 April 1931, Box 30, Oil, FOCB, 1929–1936, RLW Papers.

29. Oil States Advisory Committee to Secretary Wilbur, 9 April 1931, Box 4, and FOCB release, 10 April 1931, Box 32, Press Releases, 1929–32, and Clippings, *Rocky Mountain News*, 16 July 1931, *United States Daily*, 23 September 1931, Box 36, vol. 11, all in FOCB, PAB, RG 232; Nash, *U.S. Oil Policy*, 125–27; Ely, *Oil Conservation*, 20–21, notes 10 and 11; from Box 20, RLW Papers: Ely to Wilbur, 30 April 1931, Oil, FOCB, 1929–1936; To Secretary Wilbur: Suggestions with Reference to an Interstate Oil Conservation Compact, 17 March 1931, Box 20, Oil, Oil Conservation Compact, 1931.

30. FOCB Release, 7 August 1931, FOCB, Box 32, Press Releases, 1929–1932, PAB, RG 232.

31. Ibid.; Larson and Porter, *Humble Oil*, 452–55; Johnson, *Pipelines, 1906–1959*, 211; Zimmermann, *Conservation*, 151–53; Petroleum Administration Board, *Report on the Cost of Producing Crude Petroleum; December, 1935* (Washington, D.C.: GPO, 1936), 10–12; A. V. Boswell Co., Oklahoma City, to Sen. Borah, 15, 22, 24 December 1930, Box 321, Oil (1), WEB Papers; Unitization in Oklahoma City, 1929, Box 15, File 9, and H. H. Champlin to Secretary Wilbur, 18 October 1930, Box 18, Kansas–Oklahoma Fields, and *Denver Post*, 5 June 1931, Box 36, vol. 11, in FOCB, PAB, RG 232.

32. For the above five paragraphs: Larson and Porter, *Humble Oil*, 70–71; PAB, *Report on Cost*, 11–13; James A. Veasey, general counsel, Carter Oil Company, Tulsa, Oklahoma, to E. S. Rochester, secretary, FOCB, 14 March 1932, and A. L. Derby, president, Derby Oil and Refining Corporation, Wichita, Kansas, to Rochester, 24 February 1932, Box 14, Letters from Oil Industry, and Clippings, March–August, 1931, Box 36, vols. 10–11, FOCB, PAB, RG 232.

33. Ames quoted in Ely, *Oil Conservation*, 162.

34. Larson and Porter, *Humble Oil*, 454; B. M. Parmenter, Oklahoma City, to Sen. Borah, 28 April 1931, and J. Edward Jones, New York City, to Harry H. Woodring, governor of Kansas, 19 August 1931, Box 321, Oil (3), WEB Papers; Independent Petroleum Association of America, *Bulletin* (January 1933): 7.

35. Memorandum for chairman, Technical and Advisory Committee, from Wilbur, 20 April 1932, FOCB, Box 12, File 13, PAB, RG 232; Linda J. Lear, "Harold L. Ickes and the Oil Crisis of the First Hundred Days," *Mid-America*, 63 (January 1981): 3–5.

Chapter Nine

1. Ellis W. Hawley, *The New Deal and the Problem of Monopoly: A Study in Economic Ambivalence* (Princeton: Princeton University Press, 1966), 3–15.

2. Ickes statement in USHR Committee on Interstate and Foreign Commerce, *Crude Petroleum, Hearings on HR 5010 to Aid the States in the Conservation of Crude Petroleum . . . April 18–19, 1933,* 73d Cong., 1st sess., 1933, 16–17.

3. Linda J. Lear, "Harold L. Ickes and the Oil Crisis of the First Hundred Days," *Mid-America,* 63 (January 1981): 5–8; Gerald D. Nash, *United States Oil Policy, 1890–1964: Business and Government in Twentieth Century America* (Pittsburgh: University of Pittsburgh Press, 1968), 131–32; Conference of Governors of the Oil Producing States, March 27–29, 1933, Office of the Secretary, 1-242 (general), DI, RG 48.

4. USHR, *Hearings on Crude Petroleum,* 1–17 passim, 22–25, 27; Lear, "Ickes," 10–13; Nash, *U.S. Oil Policy,* 132–33; René de Visme Williamson, *The Politics of Planning in the Oil Industry Under the Code* (New York: Harper & Brothers, 1936), 49–57; opposition to and defenses of IPAA in Box 395, Oil (1), WEB Papers.

5. Arthur M. Johnson, *Petroleum Pipelines and Public Policy, 1906–1959* (Cambridge, Mass.: Harvard University Press, 1967), 223–24; Merle Fainsod and Lincoln Gordon, *Government and the American Economy* (New York: W. W. Norton, 1941, rev. ed., 1948), 575, 630; USHR, *Hearings on Crude Petroleum,* 2, 25, and Committee on Ways and Means, *Hearings on Conservation of Petroleum, Pursuant to HR. 5720 . . . June 1 and 2, 1933,* 73d Cong., 1st sess., 1933, 16; The Petroleum Administration, 1935, Typed, Box 172, PAB #8, PAB, RG 232.

6. Ben Wilkins, Montana Motor Oil Co., Great Falls, to J. E. Erickson, 4 April 1934, Box 49, WEB Papers.

7. For the above three paragraphs: Williamson, *Planning in Oil Under the Code,* passim; Accounts of code writing are available in Nash, *U.S. Oil Policy,* 135–39, and August W. Giebelhaus, *Business and Government in the Oil Industry: A Case Study of Sun Oil Company, 1876–1945* (Greenwich, Conn.: JAI Press, 1980), 206–11; Fainsod and Gordon, *Government and the American Economy,* 582; Charles Fahy, "Independence Within Sound Public Policy," 7 December 1934, I32.2:Ad2, PAUS, RG 49; For independent attacks on the code, Box 391, NRA (Oil) and NRA, Small Business (1), WEB Papers; From PAB, RG 232, T. B. Brown, secretary, [Emergency National Committee of 54 for Petroleum Industry], to Hugh S. Johnson, 15 August 1933, Box 40, B; Frank S. Craven, Tulsa, to NRA, 17 June 1933, and NRA to Craven, 21 June 1933, Box 40, C; Marvin Lee, vice-president, IPAA, to Senator George W. McGill and Congressman W. A. Ayers, 3 August 1933, Box 41, I; Independent Oil Distributors Association, Minneapolis, to NRA, 22 July 1933, Box 41, G.

8. Nash, *U.S. Oil Policy,* 139–40.

9. Executive Order, 11 July 1933, prohibited the interstate transportation of hot oil and assigned administrative responsibility to Ickes, General Records, 82272-1, DC, RG 40; Executive Order, 14 July 1933, authorized the Secretary of Interior to appoint an administrative body to carry out the provisions of the oil code, The Petroleum Administration, Box 172, PAB #8, PAB, RG 232.

10. Ickes also appointed a Petroleum Labor Policy Board to administer the labor provisions of NIRA and, in October 1934, a Federal Tender Board to stop the hot oil pouring out of East Texas. Presumably, the Tender Board would cooperate with the Division of Investigation of Interior to enforce compliance with NIRA Section 9(c), The Petroleum Administration, Box 172, PAB #8, PAB, RG 232.

11. Ibid.; Williamson, *Planning in Oil Under the Code,* 58–60.

12. Article 2 of the code established maximum hours and minimum wages in the production, refining, transportation, and marketing branches, with wages reflecting differentials between regions and, for service stations, the size of the community. As in other industries, the prescribed minimum wages caused definite hardship to small family firms and small partnerships, provoking much opposition to and evasion of the code. Many critics of the code, even those sympathetic with the idea of minimum wages and collective bargaining, viewed this feature as beneficial to larger firms and potentially destructive to small businesses. For the code, "A Code of Fair Competition for the Petroleum Industry," 19 August 1933, Box 50, PAB, RG 232; For correspondence from small businesses allegedly harmed by the code, Box 391, NRA, Small Businesses (1), WEB Papers. See also Report of Petroleum Code Survey Committee on Small Enterprise [c. 1934], Box 15, Reports, CF Papers; United States Department of Interior, *Decisions of the Petroleum Labor Policy Board, February 6, 1934 to March 13, 1935* (Washington, D.C.: GPO, 1935).

13. This power assumed importance when the debate over price fixing revealed the unyielding hostility of the majors and many independents, yet the refining of hot oil and widespread gasoline price wars threatened to sabotage the production controls and undermine the entire code.

14. "A Code of Fair Competition for the Petroleum Industry," 19 August 1933, Box 50, PAB, RG 232.

15. These marketing agreements are returned to in a subsequent section on marketing.

16. Giebelhaus, *Sun Oil,* 214.

17. This is compatible with the conclusions of Lear, "Ickes," 8–9, but less so with Norman E. Nordhauser, *The Quest for Stability: Domestic Oil Regulation, 1917–1935* (New York: Garland, 1979), 107–8, or Nash, *U.S. Oil Policy,* 140–42, both of whom overemphasize Ickes's attachment to price fixing. Ickes did acknowledge the urgent necessity of

raising crude oil prices, but he repeatedly asserted that this could best be achieved through production controls.

18. Williamson, *Planning in Oil Under the Code*, 61–62.

19. For the above four paragraphs: Ibid., 38, 58–60; Myron W. Watkins, *Oil: Stabilization or Conservation? A Case Study in the Organization of Industrial Control* (New York: Harper & Brothers, 1937), 177–87; Ruth W. Ayres, "The Petroleum Industry," in George B. Galloway, ed., *Industrial Planning Under Codes* (New York: Harper & Brothers, 1935), 200; PAB, *Report on the Cost of Producing Crude Petroleum* (Washington, D.C.: GPO, 1936), 1; Ickes's testimony in USHR Subcommittee of the Committee on Interstate and Foreign Commerce, *Hearings on HR. 441, Petroleum Investigation, Parts 1–5*, 73d Cong., recess, 1934, Part 1, 192. From PAB, RG 232: Letters from the oil industry for and against the price schedule, Boxes 267–68; Memorandum re price control by Nathan Margold, chairman, PAB, 5 October 1933, Box 171, PAB #1; Secretary of the Interior and Administrator of the Petroleum Industry Harold L. Ickes to Donald R. Richberg, National Emergency Council, 15 August 1934, Box 100, National Emergency Council. Summary of major problems confronting the Petroleum Administration and the Industry, 30 August 1934 [a draft for Ickes's consideration], Office of the Secretary, 1–290 (Part 1), DI, RG 48.

20. Lear, "Ickes," 9–10; Erich W. Zimmermann, *Conservation in the Production of Petroleum: A Study of Industrial Control* (New Haven: Yale University Press, 1957), 136, 194; Allocation by state of daily average crude production, September 1933–16 December 1933, Box 490, PAB, Washington office, PAB, RG 232. For the Oklahoma City field: PAB, summary report of the work of PAB for the week ending 26 January 1934, Office of the Secretary, 1-266 (Part 1), DI, RG 48; E. B. Swanson, PAB, memorandum for Mr. Margold, 26 June 1934, Box 223, Oklahoma Corporation Commission, and [several] special agents of Department of Interior, Oklahoma City, to Rhodes McPhail, assistant director, Division of Investigation, Department of the Interior, 4 August 1934, Box 653, Oklahoma, General, PAB, RG 232; USHR, *Petroleum Investigation, Part 3*, testimony of Hugh C. Ivey, special agent in charge at Oklahoma City, 1529–30, 1535, and testimony of C. C. Brown, Oklahoma Corporation Commission, 1544–45.

21. In 1932, a state court in Texas and the U.S. Supreme Court in *Champlin Refining Co.* v. *Oklahoma Corporation Commission* upheld laws limiting oil production to market demand.

22. For the above four paragraphs: Harold E. Williamson et al., *The American Petroleum Industry: The Age of Energy, 1899–1959*, vol. 2 (Evanston: Northwestern University Press, 1963), 543–45, 691–92; Williamson, *Planning in Oil Under the Code*, 67–68; Zimmermann, *Conservation*, 155–57; Henrietta M. Larson and Kenneth W. Porter, *History of Humble Oil and Refining Company: A Study in Industrial Growth* (New York: Harper & Brothers, 1959), 484–85; Ickes testimony in USHR,

Petroleum Investigation, Part 1, 180, and *Part 3,* testimony of Ernest O. Thompson, TRC, 1767, 1782, 1815–18, which blamed the Department of Interior and PAB for failing to enforce section 9(c) of NIRA until much damage had been done, and testimony of Norman L. Meyers, executive secretary, PAB, 1975, which disputed Thompson's statements. Box 15, CF Papers, contains much correspondence for late 1934 that documents petty controversies over jurisdiction between FTB and the investigatory division of Interior and between FTB and TRC. From PAB, RG 232: Secretary of Interior and Administrator of the Petroleum Industry Harold L. Ickes to Donald R. Richberg, National Emergency Council, 15 August 1934, Box 100, National Emergency Council; Wilburn Cartwright to Ickes, 24 October 1934, and Margold to Cartwright, 30 October 1934, Box 98, Mid-Continent Oil and Gas Association; Correspondence of Homer Hoch and Ickes, September–October 1934, Box 223, Kansas Corporation Commission.

23. Larger oil companies purchased tank-car gasoline from the smaller refiners; hence this buying arrangement was called the Tank Car Stabilization program. Even in normal times, integrated refiners commonly purchased some of their gasoline from independents and then sold it under their own brand name.

24. *Citizens of Washington, You Are Being Robbed* [c. 1934], Box 91, Independent Service Stations of America, PAB, RG 232, a tract supporting Initiative Bill 83, which would permit the state to store and sell gasoline to wholesalers and retailers at prices lower than those charged by the majors.

25. For the discussion of refining regulations: Williamson, *Planning in Oil Under the Code,* 38–40; Watkins, *Oil: Stabilization or Conservation,* 65–67, 86–87, 155–61; Eugene V. Rostow, *A National Policy for the Oil Industry* (New Haven: Yale University Press, 1947); USHR, *Petroleum Investigation, Part 1,* 359–60; Fahy, "Independence Within Sound Public Policy," PAUS, RG 49; Report of the Petroleum Code Survey Committee on Small Enterprises [c. 1934], Box 15, Reports, CF Papers. From PAB, RG 232: Agreement of 7 December 1933 establishing the National Petroleum Agency, and National Petroleum Agency, an agreement, 5 February 1934, and memorandum to the secretary, a brief résumé of two agreements submitted by the Petroleum Industry, 14 June 1934, Box 56; For independent refiner opposition to the agency, [25 Mid-Continent refiners] to Ickes and Wirt Franklin, 26 February 1934, Box 58; Danciger Refineries, Inc., to Ickes, 13 December 1933, Box 54, C; Consumers' Advisory Board objections, December 1933, Box 56; Nathan Margold to Borah, 22 January 1934, Box 395, Oil (1), WEB Papers.

26. Beatty in USHR, *Petroleum Investigation, Part 1,* 200.

27. New Deal controversies focusing upon pipelines, freight rates, import tariffs, or quotas reiterated the arguments of earlier years. Little purpose would be served to repeat them here. Without implying

anything regarding the legitimacy of demands for divorcement or import restrictions, let it suffice to say that import restrictions were continued under the code but did not satisfy all nonimporters and that Roosevelt chose not to employ his power to institute divorcement proceedings and was criticized by independents and others. PAB did intervene before ICC to stay a reduction of pipeline rates that would further the marketing advantage of the pipeline owners. For imports, see Chapter 8, p. 200 and USHR, *Petroleum Investigation, Part 3*, 711–13, 1396–98, 1403–11. For transportation, see Chapter 8, pp. 202–3, and Arthur M. Johnson, *Petroleum Pipelines, 1906–1959* (Cambridge, Mass.: Harvard University Press, 1967), 222–23, 226–28, 238–53; USHR, *Petroleum Investigation, Part 3*, 719–35, for a report on pipelines prepared by petroleum economist Joseph E. Pogue in 1932; and Box 196, Pipe Lines, PAB, RG 232.

28. USHR, *Petroleum Investigation, Part 1*, for Ickes, 195, and comments by others, 556–57, ibid., *Part 3*, 1620–21; Williamson et al., *American Petroleum Industry*, 2: 679–86; Williamson, *Planning in Oil Under the Code*, 44–46; FTC conducted investigations of the lease and agency device during the 1920s. Even as NIRA came up for debate, FTC probed those contracts. The study continued as the oil industry wrote the oil code, and the study continued after Roosevelt accepted the code. Some within PAB believed that FTC avoided a decision. Memorandum for the Commission [FTC] re Lease and Agency, Lease and License Methods of Marketing Petroleum Products, by Robert E. Healy, chief counsel, 28 October 1933, Box 86, FTC, and Charles Fahy, PAB, to John W. Frey, PAB, 7 May 1935, Box 486, Lease and Agency, PAB, RG 232.

29. Summary of major problems confronting the Petroleum Administration, 30 August 1934, Office of the Secretary, 1-290 (Part 1), DI, RG 48.

30. USHR, *Petroleum Investigation, Part 1*, testimony of John W. Frey, PAB, 553; A. Hiplop, Vine Service Station, Glendale, California, to Senator Borah, 30 July 1934, Box 391, NRA, Oil, WEB Papers; E. C. Shanks, executive secretary, National Association of Petroleum Retailers, Milwaukee, to Charles Fahy, PAB, 1 December 1934, Box 130, #1 Stabilization Program, PAB, RG 232.

31. USHR, *Petroleum Investigation, Part 1*, Holliday testimony, 241, ibid., *Part 3*, Phillips testimony, 1614–15; Boyer Motor Co., Pittsburgh, to Senator Borah, 6 February 1934, Box 395, Oil (2), NRA, Oil, WEB Papers. The owner of a Los Angeles firm that supplied green glassware and various trinkets to filling stations observed, "The larger companies can use billboards, but the individual dealer cannot give out even a calendar that serves as his billboard." Joe L. Frankel, Advertising Novelty House, Los Angeles, to Borah, 14 July 1934.

32. Danciger to Howard Bennette, Western Petroleum Refiners Association [and PCC members], Tulsa, 30 November 1933, Box 83,

Danciger Refineries, Inc., and C. W. Rice, El Dorado Refining Co., to A. V. Borque, Western Petroleum Refiners Association, 6 September 1934, Box 486, Margin Statistics, PAB, RG 232.

33. For price wars, PAB, summary report to the secretary of the work of the PAB for the week ending 2 June 1934, Office of the Secretary, 1-266 (Part 2), DI, RG 48; and for Denver, 1934–1935, Box 81, Colorado Enforcement, PAB, RG 232; and for Kansas City, *Kansas City Star*, December 1938, for the stabilization program, Box 130, PAB, RG 232.

34. The Cole committee was the Special Subcommittee on Petroleum Investigation of the House Committee on Interstate and Foreign Commerce, chaired by William P. Cole, Democrat, Maryland. See USHR, *Petroleum Investigation, Parts 1–5*, cited frequently above.

35. For hearings on S. 3495, the Thomas-Disney Bill, see USS Subcommittee of the Committee on Mines and Mining, *Federal Petroleum Act, Hearings on S. 3495, a Bill to Regulate Commerce in Petroleum and For Other Purposes*, 73d Cong., 2d sess., 1934, and the Cole committee hearings cited in note 34 above. For preliminary drafts of the bill, see Amos L. Beatty, chairman, Planning and Coordination Committee, to Charles Fahy, PAB, 20 March 1934, and Beatty, Federal Legislation on Petroleum, Statements and Arguments Addressed to the Subcommittee of the House Committee on Interstate and Foreign Commerce, n.d., both in Box 14, CF Papers.

36. Nathan Margold, Summary report of activities of PAB through 28 July 1934, Office of the Secretary, 1-266 (Part 1), DI, RG 48.

37. For the Thomas-Disney bill's advocates, Department of the Interior, Memorandum for the Press, 30 April 1934, Box 51, and material in Box 172, PAB #8, PAB, RG 232; E. C. Shanks, executive secretary, National Association of Petroleum Retailers, Milwaukee, to Ickes, [April, 1934], Box 14, CF Papers; Testimony of H. B. Fell, National Stripper Well Association in USHR, *Petroleum Investigation, Part 1*, 1506–7; For opposition, from California in Box 395, Oil, Thomas Bill, WEB Papers and USHR, *Petroleum Investigation, Part 3*, Allred testimony, 1727, and Thompson testimony, 1771.

38. McCorquodale to Fahy, Box 14, CF Papers.

39. *The Oil and Gas Journal*, 25 April 1935, n.p.; for the establishment of the Petroleum Conservation Division, 14 March 1936, Office of the Secretary, 1-322 (Part 1), Oil and Gas Division, DI, RG 48.

40. For the views of API and Marland, *Tulsa World*, 6 November 1934, *New York Times*, 13 November 1935, and *Tulsa Tribune*, 13 November 1935, in Boxes 494–95, API, PAB, RG 232; Thompson to Thomas, 29 May 1935, Box 14, CF Papers.

41. Memorandum to the secretary, 30 October 1935, from the PAB, Office of the Secretary, 1-290 (Part 6), DI, RG 48; John W. Frey, "The Interstate Oil Compact," in National Resources Committee, *Energy Resources and National Policy, Report of the Energy Resources Committee to the*

U.S. National Resources Committee (Washington, D.C: GPO, 1939), 397–401.

42. HR. 9053, Petroleum Administrative Board [Thomas bill], 74th Cong., 1st sess., 1935, H. Rept. 1801; J. W. Adams, memorandum on Interstate Oil Compact of 11 February 1935, Power and Gas Investigation, REP6 ADA5 INT5, FTC, RG 122; G. W. Holland, director, Petroleum Conservation Division, memorandum to the secretary, 24 September 1936, on IOC, Office of the Secretary, 1-290 (part 7), DI, RG 48; *Dallas News*, 13 August 1935, on IOC and Ickes, scrapbook, 1935, TC Papers; Nash, *U.S. Oil Policy*, 151–52; [Jane D. Ickes, ed.], *The Secret Diary of Harold L. Ickes: The First Thousand Days, 1933–1936* (New York: Simon & Schuster, 1954), 413–18; William E. Leuchtenburg, *Franklin D. Roosevelt and the New Deal, 1932–1940* (New York: Harper & Row, 1963), 150–51; Linda J. Lear to John G. Clark, 30 June 1982.

43. Williamson et al., *American Petroleum Industry*, 2: 540, 558–60; Zimmermann, *Conservation*, for Illinois, 167, 201–3, 212–15, 232–33; National Resources Committee, *Energy Resources*, 33; Rostow, *National Policy for the Oil Industry*, 28; Ronald B. Shuman, *The Petroleum Industry: An Economic Survey* (Norman: University of Oklahoma Press, 1940), 267–69; Larson and Porter, *Humble Oil*, 529–34; Metals and Minerals Division, Bureau of Foreign and Domestic Commerce, reports of December 1937–November 1938, Box 1339, Reports, BFDC, RG 151.

44. Norman E. Nordhauser, "Origins of Federal Oil Regulation in the 1920s," *Business History Review*, 47 (Spring 1973): 70–71.

45. Hawley, *New Deal and Monopoly*, 15, portrays the NRA period as dominated by economic planners and industrial rationalizers.

46. The labor-intensive coal industry touched a broader base represented by organized labor and its supporters as well as by those opposed to the labor provisions of NIRA and the codes. Coal politics also involved shifting coalitions of consumer interests such as the utilities, while those promoting the interests of coal intervened in the affairs of natural gas, oil, and, of course, the railroads.

47. Fahy, "Independence Within Sound Public Policy," PAUS, RG 49.

48. The Cole committee criticized the Mid-Continent Oil and Gas Association for its inability to make concrete recommendations regarding federal oil policy. Clarel B. Mapes, general secretary, defended the organization by pointing to the diversity of its membership. Representative Charles A. Wolverton, Republican, New Jersey, thought the association rather useless, in USHR, *Petroleum Investigation, Part 3*, 1599.

49. For the above three paragraphs: Hawley, *New Deal and Monopoly*, 36–50, for the conflicting goals that made their way into NRA and the codes, ibid., 95–97, for the Darrow report; Watkins, *Oil: Stabilization or Conservation?*, concludes that the oil stabilization program caused increasing concentration.

50. Hawley, *New Deal and Monopoly,* 412–14 and passim, for an intelligent discussion of the origins of TNEC; U.S. Temporary National Economic Committee, *Control of the Petroleum Industry by Major Oil Companies (Investigation of Concentration of Economic Power, Monograph No. 39),* by Roy C. Cook (Washington, D.C.: GPO, 1941), 4–7, 13–14, and passim, and *Review and Criticism on Behalf of Standard Oil Co. (New Jersey) and Sun Oil Co. of Monograph No. 39 with Rejoinder by Monograph Author (Investigation of Concentration of Economic Power, Monograph No. 39A)* (Washington, D.C.: GPO, 1941), 13, 39–41, 46–61; National Recovery Review Board, "Second Report to the President of the United States. Report on Petroleum, Typed, Office of Secretary, 1-286, DI, RG 48; Independent Petroleum Association of California to Borah, 24 July 1934, Box 391, NRA, Oil, WEB Papers; E. C. Shanks, executive secretary, National Association of Petroleum Retailers, to Charles Fahy, 1 December 1934, Box 130, #1 Stabilization Program, PAB, RG 232; Memorandum for the administrator re Report of Petroleum Code Survey Committee on Small Enterprises, 22 March 1935, by Charles Fahy, Box 14, CF Papers.

51. Shuman, *Petroleum Industry,* 141–42; Larson and Porter, *Humble Oil,* 551–52; Johnson, *Pipelines, 1906–1959,* 268–73. For a good summary of opinions about IOC and the Hot Oil Act, see USHR Subcommittee of the Committee on Interstate and Foreign Commerce, *Petroleum Investigation, Hearings on HR. 290 and H. 7372 . . . Five Parts,* 76th Cong., 3d sess., 1940.

52. Ickes to Attorney General, 24 December 1936, Office of the Secretary, 1-290 (Part 8), DI, RG 48.

53. Nash, *U.S. Oil Policy,* 152–55; Rostow, *National Policy for Oil,* 78.

54. TNEC, *Control of the Petroleum Industry,* 19–20, 23–24, 39; Shuman, *Petroleum Industry,* 106–7; Rostow, *National Policy for Oil,* 11; Johnson, *Pipelines, 1906–1959,* 228, 232, 235, 268–83 passim. For divorcement, see USHR Committee on Interstate and Foreign Commerce, *Hearings on . . . Oil and Oil Pipe Lines, June 1–7, 1934,* 73d Cong., 2d sess., 1934, and USS Subcommittee of the Committee on the Judiciary, *Hearings on Petroleum Marketing Divorcement . . . March 31, April 2, 20–21, 1938,* 75th Cong., 3d sess., 1938.

55. The oil crisis of 1973 precipitated still another assault on the largest integrated firms. Senator James G. Abourezk, Democrat, South Dakota, offered an amendment in 1975, supported by forty-five senators, to break up the large oil companies and limit their ownership in other energy areas. Andrew S. McFarland, *Public Interest Lobbies: Decision Making on Energy* (Washington, D.C.: American Enterprise Institute for Public Policy Research, 1976), 73; Robert Engles, *The Brotherhood of Oil: Energy Policy and the Public Interest* (Chicago: University of Chicago Press, 1977), 14, 20; for earlier statistics, Williamson et al., *American Petroleum Industry,* 2: 564–65; TNEC, *Control of the Petroleum Industry,* 4, 9–10, 34; USHR Committee on Interstate and

Foreign Commerce, *Pipe Lines, Hearings on HR. 16695 . . . February 17–18, 1931*, 71st Cong., 3d sess., 1931, 15.

56. Hawley, *New Deal and Monopoly*, 15; for the origins of NRC, see Marion Clawson, *New Deal Planning: The National Resources Planning Board* (Baltimore: Johns Hopkins University Press for Resources for the Future, 1981).

Chapter Ten

1. Lewis in USS Committee on Interstate Commerce, *Hearings on S. 4490, A Bill to Regulate Interstate and Foreign Commerce in Bituminous Coal . . . and to Create a Bituminous Coal Commission, Part 1, December 14 and 17, 1928*, 70th Cong., 2d sess., 1929, 24–33; NRC, *Energy Resources and National Policy, Report of the Energy Resources Committee to the U.S. National Resources Committee* (Washington, D.C.: GPO, 1939), 1; Glen L. Parker, *The Coal Industry: A Study in Social Control* (Washington, D.C.: American Council on Public Affairs, 1940), 8–12.

2. Stauffer in USS Subcommittee of the Committee on Mines and Mining, *Hearings . . . to Create a Bituminous Coal Commission, Part 1, March 14, 17, 22, April 18–22, 1932*, 72d Cong., 1st sess., 1932, 408–23. Stauffer was president of three firms with six mines in four states that produced 800,000 tons annually.

3. W. C. Trapnell and Ralph Ilsley, *The Bituminous Coal Industry with a Survey of Competing Fuels* (Washington, D.C.: Federal Emergency Relief Administration, 1935), 111–12; USS, *Hearings to Create a Bituminous Coal Commission* (1932), O'Neil, 352, and Stauffer, 422; USS Subcommittee of the Committee on Interstate Commerce, *Hearings on S. 1417, Stabilization of the Bituminous Coal Mining Industry*, 74th Cong., 1st sess., 1935, 444–45, for Spencer's remarks; National Coal Association, *Fourteenth Annual Meeting, June 15–7, 1933* (n.p., n.d.), 29–31, for the Francis remarks.

4. Efficiency factors damaged coal as well. Railroads moved 12,452 gross ton miles of freight per ton of coal in 1923, while in 1939 one ton of coal moved 17,774 gross ton miles of freight. A similar trend occurred in steel where the quantity of coking coal consumed per ton of pig iron fell by 19 percent between 1918 and 1938. For railroads, Waldo E. Fisher and Charles M. James, *Minimum Price Fixing in the Bituminous Coal Industry* (Princeton: Princeton University Press, 1955), 418, and for steel, NRC, *Energy Resources*, 108; see also Table 3. For this paragraph: U.S. Bureau of the Census, *Historical Statistics of the U.S., Colonial Times to 1957* (Washington, D.C.: GPO, 1960), 358, 507–8; Harold F. Williamson et al., *The American Petroleum Industry: The Age of Energy, 1899–1959*, vol. 2 (Evanston: Northwestern University Press, 1963), 666; NICB, *The Competitive Position of Coal in the United States* (New York: NICB, 1931), 32; Ralph Hillis Baker, *The National Bituminous Coal Commission: Administration of the Bituminous Coal Act, 1937–1941*,

Johns Hopkins University Studies in Historical and Political Science, Series 59, no. 3 (Baltimore: Johns Hopkins University Press, 1941), 25–26; FPC, *Consumption of Fuel for Production of Electric Energy, 1941* (Washington, D.C.: FPC, 1942) in Power Resources Division, Box 38, USGS, RG 57.

5. NRC, *Energy Resources*, 176; Williamson et al., *American Petroleum Industry*, 2: 662–63; Richard Ramsay Mead, *An Analysis of the Decline of the Anthracite Industry Since 1921* (Philadelphia: n.p., 1935), 79; Louis Stotz and Alexander Jamison, *History of the Gas Industry* (New York: Press of Stettiner Brothers, 1938), 170, 211–17; Parker, *Coal Industry*, 8–9; NCA, *14th Annual Meeting*, 110; Carrie E. Demeritt, "Report on Natural Gas Industry, 1931," Power and Gas Investigation, REP6, DEM5, NAT8, FTC, RG 122.

6. In 1928, Secretary of Labor James J. Davis argued forcefully for consolidation and advocated the amendment of antitrust laws to foster mergers and cooperative endeavors. His position stimulated rebuttals from Sen. Burton K. Wheeler, Democrat, Montana, and others who opposed any exemptions to the antitrust acts. For this reason, Senators Wheeler, Borah, and O'Mahoney, among others, distrusted the NIRA and the code system. USS, *Bituminous Coal Commission Hearings* (1928), 13–14, 17–19.

7. For the above four paragraphs: Department of the Interior, Bureau of Mines, Coal Economics Division, "Bituminous Coal Tables, 1913, 1923, 1931–1934," Box 187, Tables, NBCC, RG 150; Committee on Public Administration Cases, *The Consumers' Counsel and the National Bituminous Coal Commission, 1937–1938* (Washington, D.C.: Committee on Public Administration Cases, 1949, rev. ed., 1950), 102; USS, *Bituminous Coal Commission Hearings* (1928), for Davis, 4–7, for Charles O'Neil, NCA, 346–48.

8. Committee on Public Administration Cases, *Consumers' Counsel*, 102; Fisher and James, *Price Fixing*, 435; Parker, *Coal Industry*, 10, 62.

9. NCA, *14th Annual Meeting*, 41–45.

10. For the above four paragraphs: Eugene Rostow, "Bituminous Coal and the Public Interest," *The Yale Law Review*, 50 (February 1941): 557–61, and *A National Policy for the Oil Industry* (New Haven: Yale University Press, 1947), 81–82; Parker, *Coal Industry*, 163–66; Sidney A. Hale, "The Bituminous Coal Mining Industry," in George B. Galloway, *Industrial Planning Under Codes* (New York: Harper & Brothers, 1935), 167–68; NCA, *14th Annual Meeting*, 9, 14, 24, 32, 34–45; Lewis statement in USS, *Bituminous Coal Commission Hearings* (1928), 37–38; USS, *Hearings to Create a Bituminous Coal Commission* (1932), 14–15, 130–31.

11. James P. Johnson, *The Politics of Soft Coal: The Bituminous Industry from World War I Through the New Deal* (Urbana: University of Illinois Press, 1979), 131–33; Trapnell and Ilsley, *Bituminous Coal Industry*, 6–7; Baker, *National Bituminous Coal Commission*, 36.

12. For the Watson bill (S. 4490 in 1928 and S. 2888 in 1930), USS, *Bituminous Coal Commission Hearings* (1928); for the Lewis bill (HR. 9924 and revisions in 1933) and the Kelly-Davis bill (S. 2935), USS, *Hearings to Create a Bituminous Coal Commission* (1932). Rep. David J. Lewis, Democrat, Maryland, was an ex-miner and the son and grandson of coal miners. His bill devoted considerable attention to guaranteeing decent living and working conditions.

13. Roderick Stephens, chairman, Governmental Relations Committee, NRCMA, in USS, *Bituminous Coal Commission Hearings* (1928), 63, and Lewis and Wheeler responses, 64.

14. Ibid., 35.

15. A production allotment plan was discussed at the 1931 Kentucky conference, Parker, *Coal Industry*, 101. From time to time coal experts called the attention of Congress to the organization of the coal industry in Great Britain and Germany. Following World War I, the depressed position of British coal called forth various government efforts to promote mergers, establish sales agencies, and otherwise regularize production and stabilize prices and wages. See H. Townshend-Rose, *The British Coal Industry* (London: Allen and Unwin, 1951), 15–33. The coal cartel system in Germany is explained in Archibald H. Stockder, *Regulating an Industry: The Rhenish-Westphalian Coal Syndicate, 1893–1929* (New York: Columbia University Press, 1932).

16. Parker, *Coal Industry*, credits Hosford with suggesting the first minimum price proposal while serving on a coal stabilization committee in Pennsylvania.

17. USS, *Hearings to Create a Bituminous Coal Commission*, (1932), 701.

18. NRC, *Energy Resources*, 405–6; Parker, *Coal Industry*, 98–104. For the statements of various witnesses: USS, *Bituminous Coal Hearings*, *Part 2* (1929), NRCMA testimony, 56–60, Ohio Coal Operators Association, 81–82, Association of Railway Executives, 115–18, NCA, 181f., for National Association of Manufacturers and American Wholesale Coal Association, 223–30; USS, *Hearings to Create a Bituminous Coal Commission* (1932), Sen. James J. Davis, 3, 6, Sen. Carl Hayden, 27, 49, Charles F. Hosford, Jr., 112–27, Rep. David J. Lewis, 211–14, Charles O'Neil, 361–64, John L. Lewis, 415, M. C. Kelly, 539, Association of Railway Executives, 617–18; NCA, *14th Annual Meeting*, 160–61.

19. NCA, *14th Annual Meeting*, Bockus remarks, 8, and resolutions including granting the president authority to embargo imports and aimed at cheap foreign oil, and proposing a national excise tax to pay for the administration of the act, 164.

20. See Johnson, *Politics of Soft Coal*, chapter 6, for an excellent discussion of the revival of UMWA and the impact of NIRA, the code, and the labor boards under the code on miners' wages and employment. Johnson views NRA as beneficial to the union cause

and productive of short-run economic and social gains for miners but as generally detrimental to economic recovery and to the coal industry. Also, see Hale, "Bituminous Industry," 168–70; NCA, *Bulletin No. 1202*, 8 July 1933, Box 931, No. 25, NCA, 1933 (Folder 2), NRA, RG 9.

21. The historical accounts of the coal code utilized in this chapter and already cited in above notes—Hale, Johnson, Parker, Rostow, and Trapnell and Ilsely—devote little if any attention to the nonproducer codes. In August 1934, NRA considered abandoning the wholesale code, only approved in March, and placing wholesalers under the bituminous code. Wholesalers strenuously objected and managed to hang on until the code period ended. American Wholesale Coal Association, *Proceedings, Fourteenth Convention . . . April 26–27, 1935* (n.p., n.d.), 5–7; Coordination Board, Box 861, No. 24.1, Folder 2, and NCA, *Bulletin No. 1210*, 19 August 1933, Box 931, No. 25, NCA, 1933 (Folder 2), and Meeting of the Coordinating Board with Retail Solid Fuel Authority, Pittsburgh, 22 June 1934, Box 863, No. 24.2 (Amendment #5) (Folder 2), NRA, RG 9.

22. Parker, *Coal Industry*, 106–10; Hale, "Bituminous Industry," 175–76; NCA, *14th Annual Meeting*, 166–81, 198; Southwestern Coal Association Code, Box 50, PAB, RG 232. From NRA, RG 9: Illinois codes, August 1933, Box 930, No. 24, Trade Practices, Enterprises; NCA, *Bulletin*, 1197 (10 June 1933) through 1209 (12 August 1933), Box 931, No. 25, NCA, 1933 (Folder 2); On October 2, 1933, Hugh Johnson signed a blanket approval sanctioning most divisional and subdivisional codes, although he was essentially ignorant of the contents; Box 873, No. 24.5, Code Authority, Organization (Folder 2).

23. Code of Fair Competition for the Bituminous Coal Industry, 18 September 1933, Box 875, No. 24.8, Documents (A–Z), NRA, RG 9. Article 3 provided for maximum hours of labor, Article 4, minimum rates of pay, Article 5, conditions of employment including the right to bargain collectively and the abolition of child labor. Article 6 defined unfair trade practices and mandated the establishment of fair market prices. Article 7 identified the administrative bodies, including a National Coal Labor Board with divisional units. Article 8 enjoined the industry to maintain safe working conditions. Schedules were attached with the basic minimum wages for the various producing districts. Also from NRA, RG 9: List of subdivisional authorities, Box 865, No. 24.5, Code Authority (A–Z).

24. Richberg's remarks, NRA, *News Release No. 2818*, 19 January 1934, Box 867, No. 24.5, Code Authority, NBCIB, NRA, RG 9.

25. Parker, *Coal Industry*, 124–25; Hale, "Bituminous Industry," 176–77. From NRA, RG 9: Committee on Production Control and Proration of Output, Divisional Code Authority No. 1, proposed amendment, 7 February 1934, to grant NBCIB authority to set industrywide production quotas, Box 863, No. 24.2, Amendment 2; John J.

Atwater, vice-president, William C. Atwater Coal Co., "Proration in the Coal Industry," *Coal and Coal Trade Journal*, 8 February 1934, 91–92, and James W. Carter opposition to quotas in *Saward's Journal*, 19 May 1934, Box 930, No. 24, Trade Practices, Production Control.

26. Article 6, Section 1 of the code permitted the consideration of competition with other fuels in fixing fair market prices. Section 2(a–d) indicated that prices take account of grades and sizes used in various consuming markets. Code of Fair Competition for the Bituminous Coal Industry, 18 September 1933, Box 875, No. 24.8, Documents (A–Z), NRA, RG 9.

27. For the above three paragraphs, from NRA, RG 9: Heath S. Clark, president of Rochester and Pittsburgh Coal Co., memorandum on Production and Price Control, 3 January 1934, Box 930, No. 24, Trade Practices, Production Control; Western Kentucky complaints, Box 861, No. 24.2 (A–Z); Alabama, Box 861, No. 24.2 (Folder 1); Hearings on Amendment 1, April 9–11, 1934, Box 862, No. 24.2 (Folder 4); On the modification of Amendment 1, 22 April 1934, which became Amendment 2, Box 863, No. 24.2 (Amendment 1); Amendment 3, 4 June 1934, ordered specific wage adjustments in Missouri, Kansas, Arkansas, and Oklahoma for shaft and strip mining, Box 863, No. 24.2 (Amendment 3). Hosford, in Box 32, Transcripts, NBCC, RG 150; USS Committee on Interstate and Foreign Commerce, *Hearings on S. 4668, A Bill to Regulate Interstate Commerce in Bituminous Coal . . . June 3, 12–13, 1936*, 74th Cong., 2d sess., 1936, remarks of J. N. Snider, vice-president of Consolidated Coal Co.

28. Committee on Public Administration Cases, *Consumers' Counsel, 1937–1938*, 102; Parker, *Coal Industry*, 49; American Coal Wholesale Association, *Proceedings 14th Convention*, 12, 23; Remarks of J. D. A. Morrow, NBCIB member, on truck mines, minutes of the meeting of NBCIB, 16 January 1934, Box 868, No. 24.5, Code Authority, NBCIB (Folder 3), and NRA *Press Digest*, 27 December 1934, Box 864, No. 24.2 (Amendment 6) (Folder 1), NRA, RG 9.

29. Johnson, *Politics of Soft Coal*, 210; Divisions 1–3 to NRA, 8 October 1934, Box 863, No. 24 (Amendment 5) (Folder 2), and memorandum on the price provisions of the coal code from the Consumers' Advisory Board, January 1935, Box 864, No. 24.2 (Amendment 6) (Folder 3), NRA, RG 9.

30. Parker, *Coal Industry*, 119–20; Johnson, *Politics of Soft Coal*, 210; minutes of meeting of Division 1 Divisional Market Committee and letter of committee to NRA, 27 February 1935, Box 866, No. 24.5, Code Authority, Committees, and NBCIB to NRA, 1 February 1935, Box 867, No. 24.5, Code Authority (NCBA), NRA, RG 9.

31. Johnson, *Politics of Soft Coal*, 204–7; Consumers' Advisory Board, Box 864, No. 24.2 (Amendment 6) (Folder 2), and Association of Railway Executives with Regard to Proposed Amendments to the Bituminous Coal Code, 9 April 1934, Box 863, No. 24.2 (Amendment

3), NRA, RG 9; For the Darrow report, Box 391, NRA, Darrow Report, WEB Papers.

32. Remarks of Morrow in minutes of the meeting of NBCIB, 16 January 1934, Box 868, No. 24.5, Code Authority, NBCIB (Folder 3), NRA, RG 9.

33. NRC, *Energy Resources*, 407–8; National Resources Board, *A Report on National Planning and Public Works in Relation to Natural Resources and Including Land Use and Water Resources with Findings and Recommendations* (Washington, D.C.: GPO, 1934), 402; Parker, *Coal Industry*, 114, 131; Hale, "Bituminous Industry," 162, 179–83; Baker, *National Bituminous Coal Commission*, 46–47; USHR, *Hearings on H.R. 8479*, Snyder comments, 20–22, Warrum testimony, 25.

34. In early May, the Senate Finance Committee reported favorably on a joint resolution to extend NRA, NCA, *Bulletin No. 1351*, 4 May 1935, Box 932, No. 25, NCA, 1935 (Folder 3), NRA, RG 9. Other pre-Schechter hearings on special coal legislation known as the Guffey-Snyder bills to replace the coal code include: USS Subcommittee of the Committee on Interstate Commerce, *Hearings on S. 1417, Stabilization of the Bituminous Coal Mining Industry*, 74th Cong., 1st sess., 1935, and USS Committee on Interstate Commerce, *Report No. 470 to Accompany S. 2481, To Stabilize the Bituminous-Coal-Mining Industry . . . and For Other Purposes*, 74th Cong., 1st sess., 1935. The key post-Schechter hearing was USHR Subcommittee of the Committee on Ways and Means, *Hearings on H.R. 8479, Stabilization of Bituminous Coal Mining Industry*, 74th Cong., 1st sess., 1935.

35. Legislative Committee, NCA, 16 January 1935, Box 864, No. 24.2 (Amendment 6) (Folder 1), and minutes of meeting of the NBCIB, 16 January 1934, Box 868, No. 24.5, Code Authority, NBCIB (Folder 3), and NCA, *Bulletin No. 1358*, 1 June 1935 for pro- and anti-Guffey forces.

36. For the above two paragraphs: Spencer remarks in USS, *Hearings on S. 1417*, 446. From NRA, RG 9: for reflections of operator sentiment, Box 874, No. 24.5, Code Authority, Organization (Folder 5); NCA, *Bulletin No. 1352*, 11 May 1935, *Bulletin No. 1355*, 21 May 1935, *Bulletin No. 1358*, 1 June 1935, *Bulletin No. 1360*, 11 June 1935, Box 932, No. 25, NCA, 1935 (Folder 3); Baker, *National Bituminous Coal Commission*, 294–95.

37. The contents of the original bill owed much to Henry Warrum, chief counsel of UMWA, operators in Division I, and the National Resources Board, *Report on Planning and Natural Resources* (1934), 391–403, which, in promoting a national resources policy, argued for the regulation of coal production, capacity, stocks, and price, and specifically suggested a coal reserve. See also Johnson, *Politics of Soft Coal*, 217–19.

38. "An Act To stabilize the coal mining industry," Box 2, Subject

Matter, 1935–1936, NBCC, RG 150. The Bituminous Coal Conservation Act of 1935 is also referred to variously as the Coal Conservation Act of 1935, the first Guffey Act, the Guffey coal bill, the Guffey-Snyder bill, the Guffey-Synder Act of 1935, the Guffey Act of 1935.

39. For the above two paragraphs: Baker, *National Bituminous Coal Commission*, 47–52, 81–84; Parker, *Coal Industry*, 135, 140; USS, *Hearings on S. 4668 to Regulate Bituminous Coal* (1936), James A. Emery (NAM), 106, J. Noble Snider, Consolidated Coal Co. (the second largest company), argued against the bill, 125; USS, *Report No. 470 to Stabilize the Bituminous Industry* (1935), 2–4, for a positive assessment of the initial version of the Guffey bill; USHR, *Hearings on H.R. 8479*, the UMWA-operator coalition favoring the Guffey bill, 26–27, remarks of H. R. Hawthorne, 228–32, testimony of Thomas Moses, president, H. C. Frick Coal Co. (a mine owned by U.S. Steel), 300–311.

40. Four men served on both commissions (hereafter referred to as NBCC(1) and NBCC(2): Charles F. Hosford, Jr., mine operator and chairman of both commissions; Percy Tetlow, UMWA official who succeeded Hosford as chairman of NBCC(2) in 1938; W. H. Maloney, lawyer; C. E. Smith, newspaperman. George E. Acret, lawyer, served on NBCC(1). T. S. Haymond, operator, J. C. Lewis, UMWA official, and Percy E. Greenlee, newspaperman, served on NBCC(2).

41. See Baker, *National Bituminous Coal Commission*, 68, 108–13, 117, 325–28; Committee on Public Administration Cases, *Consumers' Counsel, 1937–1938*, 39–43. For the Consumers' Counsel, see p. 276 below.

42. The act of 1935 established an excise tax of 15 percent of the mine price of all bituminous sold or disposed of. Each operator who accepted the code received a rebate of 90 percent of the excise tax. The act of 1937 imposed an excise tax of 1 percent on all coal and an additional tax of 19.5 percent on the coal disposed of by noncode members.

43. For the above two paragraphs: USS, *Hearings on S. 4668 to Regulate Bituminous Coal*, 20. From NBCC, RG 150: Order No. 10 in List of General Orders Promulgated by NBCC, Box 15, Chronological Record; NBCC, "Release No. 41," 19 December 1935, and "Release No. 53," 7 February 1936, Box 166, Releases; Tonnage Represented, 25 January 1936, by districts, Box 11, Statistics (General); NBCC, Transcript . . . of Report of Conference Held Pursuant to Special Order No. 10, Washington, D.C., 27–28 December 1935, Box 32, Transcripts.

44. Fisher and James, *Price Fixing in Bituminous* provides virtually a price-by-price discussion and is almost as complicated as the system itself. For the above three paragraphs, all from NBCC, RG 150: On sizing and coal classification, to NBCC from Hugh B. Lee, chairman, District 11, 1935, Box 11, Prices; Transcript . . . of Report of Conference Held Pursuant to Special Order No. 1, Washington, D.C., 21–22

November 1935, the reduction of sizes, Box 32, Transcripts; NBCC, "Releases," Nos. 25, 28, 51, 62, 21 November 1935–21 March 1936; Transcript . . . of Preliminary Conference in re Districts 9, 10, and 11, 10–11 February 1936, Box 32, Transcripts; Minutes of Meeting, Voluntary Committee of Producers, 12 November 1935, Box 1, Voluntary Committee of Producers; Voluntary Producers' Advisory Committee to NBCC, 13 December 1935, Box 11, Prices (General); Before the NBCC In Re: Coordination of Prices between Districts 16 and 17, [1936], Box 11, Prices (General).

45. USS Subcommittee of the Committee on Interstate Commerce, *Hearings on S. 1 to Regulate Interstate Commerce in Bituminous Coal, and For Other Purposes, March 1, 2, 8, and 15, 1937*, 75th Cong., 1st sess., 1937, 12; for the House, USHR Committee on Ways and Means, *Report No. 294 to Accompany HR. 4985 to Regulate Interstate Commerce in Bituminous Coal, and For Other Purposes*, 75th Cong., 1st sess., 1937; Parker, *Coal Industry*, 143; NRC, *Energy Resources*, 409–13; Baker, *National Bituminous Coal Commission*, 63–71; Johnson, *Politics of Soft Coal*, 231–33; The Bituminous Coal Act of 1937, Box 3071, General Files, A–AD, BCD, RG 222. This record group contains the records of NBCC(2).

46. Parker, *Coal Industry*, 144–47; Baker, *National Bituminous Coal Commission*, Baker, 80, 156–57; Committee on Public Administration Cases, *Consumers' Counsel, 1937–1938*, 65–67; Rostow, "Bituminous Coal," 573. From BCD, RG 222: Charles W. Shinnamon, executive secretary, District 3, to NBCC, 11 November 1937, Box 3074, All Commissioners; NBCC to Georgia and Florida Railroad, 31 August 1937, Box 3088, LE–MA. The activities of the Operators Committee for Amendment of the Coal Act of 1937 are well documented in DC, RG 40, 80769 part 5(1), (2), (3) and in Box 3074, All Commissioners, 1939, BCD, RG 222.

47. Committee on Public Administration Cases, *Consumers' Counsel, 1937–1938*, 1–2, 25–37, 43–45, 70–72, passim; Baker, *National Bituminous Coal Commission*, 225–26, 233–37.

48. In addition to the sources cited in note 47, see: Consumers' Counsel, NBCC, to the Congress of the United States, 27 December 1938, by John Carson, Consumers' Counsel, Box 3075, All Commissioners, August–December 1938, and correspondence to NBCC(2) for and against the price-fixing procedures and the prices, December 1937, Box 3074, All Commissioners, December 1937, and Procedure and Steps Necessary for Establishment of Prices Under the Bituminous Coal Act of 1937, Box 3088, LE–MA, BCD, RG 222.

49. Baker, *National Bituminous Coal Commission*, 159–62; Committee on Public Administration Cases, *Consumers' Counsel, 1937–1938*, 80–81. From BCD, RG 222: A. E. Nichols, president, Sitnik Fuel Co., Philadelphia, to Mayor W. B. Hartsfield, Atlanta, 21 October 1938, Box 3075, All Commissioners, August–December 1938; AGA to Charles F. Hosford, Jr., 1937, and Bethlehem Steel Co. to NBCC, 17

November 1937, and governors of Vermont, Maine, Connecticut, Massachusetts, New Hampshire, and Rhode Island to NBCC, 4 November 1937; and John Carson, memorandum to NBCC, Subject: Requests for Information from NBCC, 2 December 1937, Box 3074, All Commissioners; Atlanta's opposition in Box 3077, Court Cases; Railroads and Cleveland in court and NBCC revocation of prices, 24 February 1938, Box 3074, All Commissioners, January–March 1938; Jackson County, Colorado, commissioners to NBCC, 6 January 1938, Governments, Jackson County, Colorado, and Chicago before the U.S. Court of Appeals, January term, 1938, Governments, Chicago, SFAW, RG 245.

50. In 1943, Congress allowed the Bituminous Coal Act of 1937 to expire, and BCD was liquidated. By that time the Solid Fuels Administration for War was fully operational.

51. Parker, *Coal Industry,* 145–47; Baker, *National Bituminous Coal Commission,* 9–10, 120–28, 133–34, 242–45; Committee on Public Administration Cases, *Consumers' Counsel, 1937–1938,* 102, 112–18; regarding the abolition of NBCC(2), Box 3075, All Commissioners, January 1939, BCD, RG 222.

52. From NRA, RG 9: Bockus to Perkins, 16 January 1934, and Clipping, *New York Herald Tribune,* 20 February 1934, Box 932, No. 25, NCA, 1934, (Folder 6); NBCIB Resolution, 17 January 1934, Box 867, No. 24.5, Code Authority, NBCIB. NCA antihydro resolution, 29 October 1934, REP95 FED6 Part 1, and NCA, *The Facts About the Billion Dollar Water Power Development of the Federal Government, The Menace to the Coal Industry of the TVA and Similar Projects* (NCA, 1934), Power and Gas Investigation, COR5 NAT5, FTC, RG 122.

53. USS, *Hearings to Create a Bituminous Coal Commission* (1932), 350, for statement of Charles O'Neil, and USS, *Hearings on Bituminous Industry* (1935), 455, for testimony of J. G. Puterbaugh, spokesman for Oklahoma's operators; J. D. Battle, executive secretary, NCA, to Thomas Walker Page, chairman, Committee for Reciprocity Information, U.S. Tariff Commission, 5 March 1935, Box 12, Imports and Exports, NBCC, RG 150; Appalachian Joint Conference of Bituminous Producers and Miners to U.S. Senate, 24 March 1934, re an excise tax on imported oil, TC Papers, Box 144, S.1302.

54. Baker, *National Bituminous Coal Commission,* 56, 189, 212–15. From BCD, RG 222: Before the Department of State . . . Committee for Reciprocity Information, Proposed negotiation of a Trade Agreement between the United States and Venezuela involving Crude Petroleum and Fuel Oil, Brief in Behalf of NBCC, 6 August 1938, Box 3077, Competition, Foreign; Correspondence of NBCC with Veterans Administration and U.S. Housing Authority, March 1939, Box 3076, Competition of Other Fuels-Domestic.

55. Rostow, "Bituminous Coal," 581–84, argues that the minimum prices established by BCD for operators shipping partly by river (ex-

river) were set high enough to negate any advantage ex-river operators might derive from utilizing this cheaper form of transportation, thus buffering all-rail shippers from this competition and denying consumers cheaper coal prices. It seems to me that John Carson made a similar charge against NBCC(2), but I cannot find the source. However, NBCC(2)'s briefs to ICC sought rate reductions for southern as well as northern shippers, Percy Tetlow, chairman, NBCC, to John D. Battle, executive secretary, NCA, 27 October 1938, Box 3073, Chairman, Percy Tetlow, BCD, RG 222.

56. For the above two paragraphs: Baker, *National Bituminous Coal Commission*, 195–212; NRC, *Energy Resources*, 78; NCA, *14th Annual Meeting* (1933), 161–63; NBCC(1), "Releases," Nos. 58, 59, 2–65, 3–66, 67, 28 February 1936–15 June 1936. From BCD, RG 222: Traffic Division, NBCC, Freight Rates, August 1937, Box 3073, Coal Industry Reports Freight Rates; ICC, *Fifteen Percent Case, 1937–1938, Ex Parte No. 123, In the Matter of Increases in Rates, Fares, and Charges, Decided March 8, 1938*, Box 3086, IN-LE; Samuel P. Huntington, "The Marasmus of the ICC: the Commission, the Railroads, and the Public Interest," *Yale Law Journal*, 61 (April 1952): 483, describes railroad rates between 1929 and 1945 as being well above general price levels and attributes the differential to ICC reliance upon the railroads for political support.

57. For the above three paragraphs: Stotz and Jamison, *Gas Industry*, 299–302; NRC, *Energy Resources*, 179; USHR Subcommittee of the Committee on Interstate and Foreign Commerce, *Natural Gas, Hearings on HR. 11662 to Regulate the Transportation and Sale of Natural Gas in Interstate Commerce and For Other Purposes, April 2, 3, 7, 14, 15, 1936*, 74th Cong., 2d sess., 1936, 71, 77–79, for testimony of John D. Battle, executive secretary, NCA; Carrie E. Demeritt, Report on the Insull Interests, 1932, Power and Gas Investigation, REP6 DEM5 INS5, FTC, RG 122; for resolutions and petitions against Kansas Pipeline and Gas Co. application, Box 3075, All Commissioners, August–December 1938, and for Alabama Coal Trade Extension Organization, Birmingham, to the president, 11 February 1939, Box 3075, All Commissioners, January 1939, BCD, RG 222.

58. UMWA went on strike 1 April and reduced bituminous production to about 20 percent of demand. By May, when the strike ended in most fields, stocks were dangerously low—particularly in the northeast.

59. From Box 1340, Secretary, BFDC, RG 151: Memorandum of a conference [with BFDC and Richard C. Patterson, Jr., Assistant Secretary of Commerce] held in the office of the chairman of NBCC, 20 February 1939, and conferences between Richard C. Patterson, Jr., and a committee for the amendment of the coal act, 10 February and 17 March 1939, and W. W. A Janssen, chief, Metals and Minerals Division, BFDC, to Richard C. Patterson, Jr., 10 February 1939.

60. Parker, *Coal Industry,* 132–33, 177–78; Rostow "Bituminous Coal," 543, 588; NRC, *Energy Resources,* 416.

61. Metals and Minerals Division, BFDC, to Assistant Secretary Patterson, 17 March 1939, Box 1340, Secretary, BFDC, RG 151.

Chapter Eleven

1. NRC, *Energy Resources and National Policy, Report of the Energy Resources Committee to the U.S. National Resources Committee* (Washington, D.C.: GPO, 1939), 36.

2. *Second Annual Report of the National Bituminous Coal Commission, Fiscal Year Ended June 30, 1938 with Additional Activities to November 15, 1938* (Washington, D.C.: GPO, 1939), 14.

3. NRC, *Energy Resources,* 31.

4. Sam H. Schurr, Bruce C. Netschert, et al., *Energy in the American Economy, 1850–1975: An Economic Study of Its History and Prospects* (Baltimore: Johns Hopkins University Press for Resources for the Future, Inc., 1960), 35–36; NRC, *Energy Resources,* 290–91, 294–95.

5. In 1933, hydroelectric power contributed 36 percent of a total electric production reaching 103 billion kwh. By 1940, hydroelectric production had increased from 37 billion kwh in 1933 to 52 billion kwh, contributing some 29 percent of the 180 billion kwh generated in that year. FPC estimated feasible undeveloped waterpower generation at 273 billion kwh, U.S. Bureau of the Census, *Historical Statistics of the U.S., Colonial Times to 1957* (Washington, D.C.: GPO, 1960), 506; NRC, *Energy Resources,* 298–99.

6. Harold F. Williamson et al., *The American Petroleum Industry: The Age of Energy, 1899–1959,* vol. 2 (Evanston: Northwestern University Press, 1963), 662–66; Schurr, Netschert et al., *Energy in the American Economy,* 76, 113, 186; Richard R. Mead, *An Analysis of the Decline of the Anthracite Industry Since 1921* (Philadelphia: n.p., 1935), 98–115.

7. National Bituminous Coal Industry Board Resolution, January 1934, against the appropriation of Public Works Administration funds for hydroelectric projects, Box 868, No. 24.5, Code Authority, NBCIB (Folder 2), NRA, RG 9; NCA, *The Facts About the Billion Dollar Water Power Development of the Federal Government* (Washington, D.C.: NCA, August 1934), Power and Gas Investigation, COR5 NAT5, FTC, RG 122; FPC Release No. 1718, September 1941, denying that the proposed St. Lawrence River power project competed with coal, FPC General Files, Box 80, Coal: Electric Power Generation, LO Papers.

8. EHFA was transferred to TVA in 1934 and then in 1935 incorporated in Washington, D.C., and attached to the Reconstruction Finance Corporation, where it remained until liquidated in 1942. Reconstruction Finance Corporation press releases, 1937–39, and other items relating to EHFA in EHFA, General Files, 020, 020.1, and 020.2, RFC, RG 234.

9. U.S. Bureau of the Census, *Historical Statistics of the U.S., Colonial Times to 1970, Part 2* (Washington, D.C.: GPO, 1975), 700–701; Louis Stotz and Alexander Jamison, *History of the Gas Industry* (New York: Press of Stettiner Brothers, 1938), 170, 279–282; NRC, *Energy Resources,* 106; USHR Subcommittee of the Committee on Interstate and Foreign Commerce, *Natural Gas, Hearings on HR 11662 to Regulate the Transportation and Sale of Natural Gas in Interstate Commerce and For Other Purposes, April 2, 3, 7, 14, 15, 1936,* 74th Cong., 2d sess., 1936, 11–12, 149–50.

10. For the above three paragraphs: John Bauer and Nathaniel Gold, *The Electric Power Industry: Development, Organization, and Public Policies* (New York: Harper & Brothers, 1936), 32–34, 50, 95–96, 108, 114; for Detroit, Frank P. Fisher, consulting engineer, "The Gas Rate Problem in Detroit," 15 April 1935, *Detroit News,* 4 September 1935, and other documents, Power and Gas Investigation, REP6 ODE5 FIS5, FTC, RG 122; NCA, *Fourteenth Annual Meeting, June 15–17, 1933* (np, nd), 45–79 passim; NRC, *Energy Resources,* 102; NCA, *Bulletin No. 1212,* 2 September 1933 re Chicago, Box 931, No. 25, NCA, 1933 (Folder 2), NRA, RG 9; Western Burner Oil Distributors Association to PAB, 24 September 1934, Box 145, WBODA, Oakland, Calif., PAB, RG 232.

11. Robert P. Lamont, "The Petroleum Industry," address before the API, 11 November 1931, General Correspondence, 82272-1, and Draft Message of Information on Energy Resources, February 1938, General Correspondence, 87570, both in DC, RG 40; Suggestions Regarding Natural Resource Industries in the Proposed Extension of the Recovery Act, by C. K. Leith, Planning Committee for Mineral Policy, National Resources Board, 23 January 1935, Box 100, National Resources Board, and "The Petroleum Administration," Box 172, PAB #8, both in PAB, RG 232; Summary Report to the Secretary of the Work of the PAB for the week ending 5 January 1934 and 28 July 1934, Office of the Secretary, 1-266 (Part 1), DI, RG 48; NRB, *A Report on National Planning and Public Works in Relation to Natural Resources and Including Land Use and Water Resources with Findings and Recommendations* (Washington, D.C.: GPO, 1934), 403; NRC, *Energy Resources,* 3, 19, 22–23.

12. In mid-1982, budget cuts by President Reagan threatened to eliminate the Bartlesville facility, one of five Energy Technology Centers and the only one that concentrated on oil research. Independent operators questioned the wisdom of closing the only federal center that had consistently benefited them. Independents relied heavily on Bartlesville for current information on petroleum technology—in particular techniques for enhanced oil recovery, a critical concern of operators working old fields, Tammi Harbert, "Dismantling DOE," *The American Oil and Gas Reporter,* 25 (May 1982): 11, 157. Independents drilled nine of every ten oil and gas wells in 1979, discovered one-half

of the nation's oil, and produced 38 percent of it, Howard Peacock, "Oildom's most independent people," *Exxon USA*, 19 (1980): 16.

13. On the Bartlesville experiment station, USHR Subcommittee of the Committee on Interstate and Foreign Commerce, *Hearings on HR 441, Petroleum Investigation, Part 3*, 73d Cong., recess, 1924, 1637–40, 1945–72; H. V. Moffat, "What the Mineral Leasing Law Has Contributed to the Development of the Oil Industry," USGS Conservation Branch, "Papers Presented at a Conference of Oil and Gas Supervisors and Mining Supervisors at Washington, D.C., March 7–12, 1932," Mimeographed, Office of Director, 701, USGS, RG 57; on the units composing BFDC, Box 66 Metals and Minerals, Box 931, Box 1337, Metals and Minerals, and NCA to BFDC, 15 August 1939, Box 931, Coal Division, BFDC, RG 151; PWA Press Section, Release No. 1522, Office of the Secretary, 1-264 (Part 1), DI, RG 48.

14. See William E. Leuchtenburg, "The New Deal and the Analogue of War," in John Braeman et al., eds., *Change and Continuity in Twentieth Century America* (New York: Harper & Row, 1964), 81–143. Presidents Johnson and Carter both learned how flimsy the "moral equivalent to war" appeal actually was in marshaling support for antipoverty and energy policies.

15. Erich W. Zimmermann, *Conservation in the Production of Petroleum: A Study of Industrial Control* (New Haven: Yale University Press, 1957), 209–10.

16. Gerald D. Nash, *United States Oil Policy 1890–1964: Business and Government in Twentieth Century America* (Pittsburgh: University of Pittsburgh Press, 1968), 140, detects a functional and structural kinship between PAB and USFA; for PCC, see Chapter 9, pp. 226, 229.

17. See Chapter 7, p. 188.

18. NRB, *Report on National Planning, Part 4, Report of the Planning Committee for Mineral Policy*, 389–449.

19. For the official documents relevant to the planning boards, see Marion Clawson, *New Deal Planning: The National Resources Planning Board* (Baltimore: Johns Hopkins University Press for Resources for the Future, 1981), 290–321; Otis L. Graham, Jr., *Toward a Planned Society: From Roosevelt to Nixon* (New York: Oxford University Press, 1976) 52–57.

20. For the actors involved in New Deal planning, see Clawson, *New Deal Planning*, chapter 5.

21. Arlene Inouye and Charles Susskind, " 'Technological Trends and National Policy,' 1937: The First Modern Technology Assessment," *Technology and Culture*, 18 (October 1977): 593–621, have described NRC, *Technological Trends and National Policy* (1937), as the pioneering venture in technology assessment, an effort in forecasting that, while constrained by the imperatives of the Depression, accurately described contemporary technological trends and confronted the question of the impact of technology in the future. Similarly,

NRB's studies of state and regional planning, land and water use, and other subjects merit commendation as pioneering efforts. See Clawson, *New Deal Planning*, 327–46, for a list of reports and studies flowing from these national planning units.

22. NRC, *Energy Resources*, 8.

23. Ibid., 30.

24. Ibid. treated four general themes: the economics of the energy industries; the size and location of energy reserves, including potential hydroelectric sites and an analysis of possible substitutes such as synthetic fuels; technology and conservation, including end use; and the implications of the above for public policy. In this concluding section, pieces were written on the Connally Act, the Interstate Oil Compact, the Guffey Acts, and power policy.

25. Dolores Greenberg, "Perspectives on Conservation," paper presented to the Hunter College/Exxon Energy Project, June 1977, typed, 4–8, for the long-term planning implicit in President Theodore Roosevelt's approach to conservation and the rejection of such goals by those advocating preservation or unrestrained use.

26. See NRB, *Report on National Planning*, v–vi, and subsequent sections on water resources.

27. One-half of the ten-member Energy Resources Committee were from various branches of the Department of the Interior, the dominant federal force in energy matters. Interior expansionism seemed threatening to both FPC and the Corps of Engineers, neither of which manifested much enthusiasm for NRC's report. FPC was particularly hostile to any schemes that hinted of an Ickes connection; NRC, *Energy Resources*, v, 1–8, 30–36.

28. For the above two paragraphs: Ibid., 19, 22–23, 33, 69, 88, 90, 92, 210, 226–35; NRB, *Report on National Planning*, 33–36; Preliminary Draft of Report on Petroleum by Committee on Tariff Bargaining Concerning Petroleum Exports, 11 October 1934, Office of the Secretary, 1-287, DI, RG 48.

29. As oil prices soared after 1973, and particularly following the Iranian revolution of 1979, coal production increased dramatically from 650 million tons in 1975 to over 800 million tons in 1981. A large export market developed, and observers heralded the rebirth of the coal industry. By 1982, however, inflation, recession, and declining rates of growth in electric consumption had turned strong demand into a coal glut. In terms reminiscent of the 1920s and 1930s, Carle Bagge, president of NCA, complained of production increases approaching 10 percent while demand rose by under 4 percent. He worried about a production overcapacity approaching 150 million tons and the depressed prices that surpluses and a slackening export market would bring. Bagge viewed federal policies toward the environment, the railroads, and other industries as damaging to coal's

interests, "Coal—The Other Glut," *New York Times*, 16 May 1982, Section 3.

30. The Supreme Court upheld the law's constitutionality in 1942. In a very significant case, the Supreme Court in *Phillips Petroleum Co. v. Wisconsin* (1954) decreed that FPC must regulate wellhead prices. Prior to that decision, FPC had denied its authority to regulate gas at points of production, even when the gas was sold in interstate commerce. This decision brought most independent producers under FPC jurisdiction.

31. While the market for natural gas was much less extensive than for electricity, improved pipeline delivery technologies during the 1930s permitted the extension of natural gas to 2 or 3 million new customers in several new states. Still, a phenomenally large untapped market remained. Of the thirteen states served by natural gas, metered customers as a percentage of total population reached 24 percent only in Texas, 17 percent in Ohio, and 10 percent or less in the remaining eleven states. G. P. Watkins, "Report on Production, Distribution, and Interstate Movement of Gas by Holding Company Group in 1930," Power and Gas Investigation, REP5 WAT5 GAS5 Part 2, FTC, RG 122.

32. NRB, *Report on National Planning*, 33, 35, 391, 400; NRC, *Energy Resources*, 3, 44, 90–91, 94, 117–22, 179. NRC's conclusions relative to waste in producing coal were very similar to R. W. Shumway, NBCC, "Conservation in the Production of Bituminous Coal," 4 January 1937, Typed, Box 3073, Coal Industry Reports, Conservation, BCD, RG 222; NCA, *Bulletin No. 1253*, 24 February 1934, Box 932, No. 25, NCA, 1934 (Folder 6), NRA, RG 9.

33. The planning board released six studies on water problems during 1939–40. Clawson, *New Deal Planning*, 333–35; Craufurd D. Goodwin, ed., *Energy Policy in Perspective: Today's Problems, Yesterday's Solutions* (Washington, D.C.: Brookings Institution, 1981), 172.

34. NRC, *Energy Resources*, 3–4, 242, 266–69; NRC, "State Planning: A Review of Activities and Progress, Electric Power Problems," 1935, Office of the Secretary, 1-293 (Part 1), DI, RG 48; *Report of the Special Committee on the Generation and Distribution of Electricity of the National Association of Railroad and Utilities Commissioners* (New Orleans: np, 1928). By 1977, over ninety joint-action power-supply projects were in operation or being organized. In most cases, state legislation or even an amendment to the state constitution was required to authorize cooperating municipalities to jointly finance the construction of new generating facilities or to own facilities jointly with private companies and cooperatives. Communities were then required to seek voter approval of revenue bond issues. In Kansas, Missouri, Virginia, and other states such legislation confronted strong resistance from the investor-owned utilities, *Public Power*, September–October 1977, 20–28.

35. Quoted in Zimmerman, *Conservation*, 242, n. 8.

36. Goodwin, ed., *Energy Policy*, 132–34; David Howard Davis, *Energy Politics* (New York: St. Martin's Press, 1974), 98–100; John G. Clark, "The Energy Crisis of 1919–1924 and 1973–1975: A Comparative Analysis of Federal Energy Policies," *Energy Systems and Policy*, 4 (1980): 245; USS Select Committee on Small Business, *Hearings . . . on the Fuel Situation in Chicago, December 14, 1950*, 81st Cong., 2d sess., 1950, 1–13; USS Committee on the Judiciary, Subcommittee on Antitrust and Monopoly, *Hearings Pursuant to SR 334 on Marketing Practices in the Gasoline Industry, Part 1, July 14–16, 1970*, 91st Cong., 2d sess., 1970, 2–7.

Chapter Twelve

1. Petroleum Coordinator for National Defense became the Petroleum Coordinator for War (PCW) following Pearl Harbor and the Petroleum Administration for War (hereafter PAW) in December 1942. In a similar transformation, Solid Fuel Coordinator for National Defense became the Solid Fuels Administration for War (hereafter SFAW) in April 1943.

2. Office of the Secretary, 1-188 Coal Administration, DI, RG 48; Consumption of Fuels for Residential Use, 1940, Correspondence with Federal Agencies, WPB, SFAW, RG 245.

3. Conference on Petroleum Conservation called by the Office of Petroleum Coordinator for National Defense, July 3, 1941, Office of Secretary, 1-188 Petroleum Administration (Part 1), DI, RG 48. This dismal projection stemmed from the consequences of the transfer in May 1941 of fifty oil tankers from East Coast service to the British.

4. For the above two paragraphs; E. B. Swanson, Petroleum Conservation Division, confidential memorandum to Secretary Ickes, May 23, 1940, 1-188 Petroleum Administration (Part 1) and H. A. Gray, director, Bituminous Coal Division, memorandum for the Secretary, 15 November 1941, 1-188 Coal Administration (Part 1), both in Office of the Secretary, DI, RG 48; Glenn E. McLaughlin memorandum to Mr. Watkins, National Resources Planning Board, on the Relation of Oil and Coal to National Defense, 15 July 1940, Box 45, Energy Resources Committee, LO Papers; PAW, *A History of the PAW, 1941–1945*, prepared under the direction and editorship of John W. Frey and H. Chandler Ide (Washington, D.C.: GPO, 1946), pp. 444, 449.

5. National Coal Association, *Bulletin No. 1841*, 29 June 1940, 1, 3.

6. The Energy Resources Committee consisted of representatives from NRPB, including Ralph J. Watkins, who served as chairman, the Bureau of Mines, USGS, Petroleum Conservation Division, Bituminous Coal Division, the Securities and Exchange Commission, FPC, and the War and Navy departments. For the above four paragraphs: For the rationing of petroleum products, see Chapter 13, 337–42; coal rationing, see Chapter 14, pp. 362–67, 371–73; H. A. Gray,

director, Bituminous Coal Division, Memorandum to Ickes, 13 June 1941, Ickes, Secretary of the Interior, 1941–42, SFAW, RG 245. From Box 45, Energy Resources Committee, LO Papers: Memorandum to Dr. Watkins on the emergency program of the coal industry, 15 July 1940; John Frey, "The Applicability of World War Type of Control to the Current Petroleum Industry," July 1940; Minutes of the ERC, 16 August 1940; ERC, A Program of Planning for the ERC, c. 1940.

7. This material is in part summarized from Historical Records Office, OPA, "Chronological Outline of Events and Situations in OPA History to July 1943" (January 1944), Mimeograph, Box 748, Historical Records Project, and Foreign Economic Administration, *A Brief Historical Statement* (1944), Box 769, PAW, RG 253. See also such agency histories as PAW, *A History of PAW,* personal-official histories such as Donald M. Nelson, *Arsenal of Democracy: The Story of American War Production* (New York: Harcourt, Brace, 1946), and such secondary works as David Novick et al., *Wartime Production Controls* (New York: Columbia University Press, 1949).

8. For Ickes versus Olds, from LO Papers: numerous documents from NDPPC in Boxes 41–43; for Olds's interpretations of the machinations of private power and the intentions of Ickes, see Olds, memorandum of a talk with John Scott, 2 November 1938, and memorandum of a conference with Assistant Secretary of War Louis Johnson, 3 November 1938, Box 41, Folder 3, and Preliminary Notes of Fortas's Draft for Power Policy Report on FPC Plan, 12 August 1941. According to Olds, Ickes and his stooges were up to no good, Box 43, FPC.

9. For the above two paragraphs: Roosevelt to Ickes, 28 May 1941, Office of the Secretary, 1-188 Petroleum Administration (Part 1) and letter of 5 November 1941, Office of the Secretary, 1-188 Coal Administration (Part 1), both in DI, RG 48.

10. Chapter 13 attends in detail to PAW responsibilities and programs. Chapter 14 does the same for SFAW. While focusing upon agency performance in functional areas, both chapters analyze interagency friction over administrative territory and responses to fuel crises that erupted from time to time. The supply crisis of 1941 is treated more fully in those chapters and serves in this chapter only as the setting for the emerging role of PAW and, in less detail, for SFAW.

11. Conference on Petroleum Conservation called by the Office of Petroleum Coordinator for National Defense, 3 July 1941, Office of the Secretary, 1-188 Petroleum Administration (Part 1), DI, RG 48; Ickes to Admiral Land, USMC, 16 July 1941, and Ralph K. Davies to Land, 25 August 1941, Box 16, General Correspondence, RKD Papers. From PAW RG 253: Re Tanker Control Board, 1941–1942, Box 748; Statement relating to Tanker Policy, 26 August 1941, Box 644, Statements relating to policy; correspondence between PAW and USMC, July–August 1941, Box 645, Maritime Commission. E. S. Land, ad-

ministrator, War Shipping Administration, Memorandum 21 February 1942, WPB, RG 179.

12. Producers proved more reluctant to alter their normal shipping practices than railroads did in supplying abnormal transportation services. Freight rates for oil by railroad were higher than tanker rates. In July and August, a number of the larger shippers absorbed those costs. Chapter 13 describes the freight compensation system that finally emerged, as well as the successful efforts to increase railroad deliveries.

13. PCND Recommendations, 1-188 Petroleum Recommendations (Part 1) and clipping of the Pegler column, 1-188 General, both in Office of the Secretary, DI, RG 48; Frank McNaughton's reports on the oil shortage, August 1941, Notes on the Maloney Hearings, 22, 29 August 1941, FMcN Papers.

14. SFAW account of war activities, Box 701, History of the Coal Agencies, SFAW, RG 245; for the authorizing letter of 5 November 1941, see note 9 above.

15. Prior to V-J Day, both agencies played an active role in the seizure and operation of mines and refineries that were shut down by strikes.

16. Davies left his position as vice-president of Standard Oil of California to join PAW. No effort is made to discuss each division, branch, or committee that emerged during the war; an overview only, and that set in a static framework, is presented here.

17. For the above two paragraphs, from SFAW, RG 245: SFAW Committee system, 18 November 1946, Inter Bureau Correspondence, Division of Power, Department of Interior; Solid Fuels Advisory War Council, Minutes of first meeting, 10 March 1942, Ickes, Secretary of Interior, 1943–1944; Report of SFAW, 1945, Government Advisory Committees, A–Z. From Office of the Secretary, DI, RG 48: SFAW Order delegating authority to regional bituminous coal managers, 1 May 1943, 1-188 Coal Mine Operations (Part 1); Abe Fortas, acting director, SFAW, to Ickes and Secretary of the Navy Knox, February 1944, 1-188 Coal Committee (Part 1).

18. PAW, *A History of PAW*, 352–53. California independents protested the Davies appointment, and a bill was introduced into Congress to prevent the appointment of oil-industry officials to the coordinator's office. Independent Petroleum and Consumers Association, Los Angeles, to members of the California Legislature, 12 September 1941, Box 15, Folder 1, and clipping from *Los Angeles Times*, 1941, Box 16, General Correspondence, RKD Papers.

19. District 1 (New York City) encompassed the entire Atlantic seaboard; District 2 (Chicago) included the Great Lakes states, the Plains states of the midcontinent, and Kentucky and Tennessee; District 3 (Houston) included the Gulf states; District 4 (Denver) administered affairs in the Rocky Mountain states; and District 5 (Los

Angeles) handled the Pacific coast. These districts were created by Recommendation No. 1, August 1941. Ickes also established a National Conference of Petroleum Regulatory Agencies to advise on matters of production controls, but this group faded into obscurity.

20. From PAW, RG 253: Petroleum Coordinator for National Defense, Functions of District Directors, 30 January 1942, Box 671, R. K. Davies File; Reports of various subcommittees of Districts 1–3, February–May 1942, Box 6001, Office of Directors-in-Charge, 1942, District 2, Transportation; PCND, Conference with Petroleum Industry Committee chairmen, 11–12 August 1941, set II, Box 9.002.2.

21. The policy pronouncements of PIWC's Petroleum Economics and National Oil Policy committees minimized the role of government in mobilizing the industry for war, strongly denied the need for government regulation, and expressed the unswerving conviction that national security could only be achieved through the uninhibited operation of the free marketplace. See, for example, George A. Hill, Jr., *Trends in the Oil Industry in 1944 (Including United States Foreign Oil Policy) As Presented to Petroleum Industry War Council, January 12, 1944* (Washington, D.C.: PIWC, 1944).

22. For the above three paragraphs, from PAW, RG 253: Ickes establishment of PIWC, Box 644, Statements relating to policy, 28 November 1941; A Conference between the Department of the Interior and Representatives of the Petroleum Industry, Washington, D.C., 19 June 1941, Box 9.002.2; E. Holland, president, National Association of Petroleum Retailers, Milwaukee, to Ickes, 12 June 1941, and John W. Frey, special assistant, PCND, to Ray McBride, president, Petroleum Marketers Association of Oklahoma, Tulsa, 5 August 1942, Box 18.050; Indiana Independent Petroleum Association to W. R. Boyd, Jr., chairman, Petroleum Industry Council for National Defense [and API president], 16 January 1942, and Walter Hochuli, director of marketing, PAW, memo for Davies, 6 November 1943, and Eastern States Gasoline Dealers Conference protest to PAW, 7 December 1941, and PIWC resignations through 1943, Box 20.067, PIWC, 1941–1943; J. Elmer Thomas, weekly report ending 4 April 1942, Box 92.181.84; Davies to Paul H. Wade, Economy Oil Company, Roanoke, Virginia, 19 December 1941, Box 671, Davies file.

23. For PAW-WPB relationship, see Box 654, WPB, PAW, RG 253; for natural gas, internal correspondence of WPB featuring Julius A. Krug, head of OPM's power branch, Donald Nelson, chief of OPM-WPB, and for correspondence with FPC in 1941 and 1942, 623.07, WPB, RG 179.

24. See, for examples, Correspondence with Federal Agencies, ODT, SFAW, RG 245.

25. Reports of price fixing, August 1941, Reports, January–August 1941, FMcN Papers; Ickes to Roosevelt, 6 August 1941, and Ickes to Henderson, 14 August 1941, and OPA Civilian Allocation Program for

Motor Fuel in the Atlantic Coast Area, 15 August 1941, Office of the Secretary, 1-188 Petroleum Administration (Part 2), DI, RG 48. From PAW, RG 253: OPA price freeze, June 1941, and Henderson to Davies, 23 August 1941, Box 27.073.2, June 1941–June 1942, and Notes on a meeting of California Assembly Interim Oil Investigation Committee, Los Angeles, 25 October 1941, Box 9.002.2, and Industry arguments for increased crude prices, Box 664, Statements relating to policy, 17, 27 October 1941.

26. Ickes to Roosevelt, 1 December 1941, Office of the Secretary, 1-188 Petroleum Administration (Part 4), DI, RG 48.

27. Estimates of fuel needs for waging war prepared by the fuel agencies corresponded much more closely with actual consumption than did the estimates of the military, particulary for aviation gasoline. OPA, however, defended its fuel rationing program against PAW's charges of inefficiency by questioning the accuracy of PAW's forecasts of regional and local demand and supply.

Chapter Thirteen

1. Bee Kyle, Palisades Park, New Jersey, to Harold Ickes, 18 August 1942, Telegram, Box 15, folder 1, RKD Papers.

2. U.S. Chamber of Commerce, *Petroleum War Organization* (Washington, D.C.: np, 1943), 1–5; Max W. Ball, "Fueling a Global War, An Adventure in Statecraft," *Ohio Journal of Science*, 45 (January 1945): 29–43. In 1946, Ball became director of the Division of Oil and Gas, Department of the Interior; Davies testimony in USS Special Committee Investigating Petroleum Resources, *Hearings on Wartime Petroleum Policy Under the Petroleum Administration for War*, 79th Cong., 1st sess., 1946, pp. 40–41; John A. Brown, ex-president, Socony Vacuum Oil Company, "The Role of Private Enterprise in the Development of Oil Resources," in Leonard M. Fanning, ed., *Our Oil Resources* (New York: McGraw-Hill, 1945), 2–3; Henrietta M. Larson and Kenneth W. Porter, *History of Humble Oil and Refining Company: A Study of Industrial Growth* (New York: Harper & Brothers, 1959), 570–72; Harold F. Williamson et al., *The American Petroleum Industry, 1899–1959*, vol. 2 (Evanston: Northwestern University Press, 1963), 753.

3. Tankers to Great Britain, Box 748, PAW, RG 253 and Office of the Secretary, 1-188 Petroleum Administration (Part 1), DI, RG 48; statement of Robert Wilson, OPM, to USHR Subcommittee of the Committee on Interstate and Foreign Commerce, Petroleum Investigation, 27 March 1941, Box 1231, Petroleum Conservation Division, PAB, RG 232; Petroleum movement into District 1, 1940–1943, Box 622.5, WPB, RG 179.

4. Officials of Gulf Oil, Standard of New Jersey, The Texas Company, Atlantic Refining Co., Socony-Vacuum Oil Co., Tidewater Associated Oil Co., Cities Service, Consolidated Oil, Sun Oil, American

Oil, and Shell Oil Co., to Davies, 4 September 1941, Box 15, RKD Papers.

5. C. S. Snodgrass memorandum to Davies re tanker losses, 21 October 1941, Box 15, Confidential Memorandum, and Ickes to Roosevelt, 21 March, 15 April 1942, Box 15, Correspondence with Roosevelt, RKD Papers; Tanker losses and construction, Box 769, PAW, RG 253; Ad hoc oil industry committee on tankers to Ickes, 16 April 1942, and Ickes to Roosevelt, 20 April 1942, Office of the Secretary, 1-188 Petroleum Administration (Part 7), DI, RG 48.

6. Clipping from *The Gasoline Retailer*, October 1941, Office of the Secretary, 1-188 Petroleum Administration (Part 4), DI, RG 48; Frederick W. Williamson, Louisiana oil official, to Davies, 29 October 1941, Box 770, October 1941, PAW, RG 253.

7. For the above two paragraphs, all from PAW, RG 253: PCND Recommendations re East coast fuel supply, Recommendations 1, 3, 4, 6, Box 748; Ickes to Leon Henderson, 14 August 1941 and Ickes to Nelson, 23 October 1941, Box 644, By Other Agencies; PAW telegrams to principal suppliers on Atlantic coast, Box 768, June–July 1941; Limitation Order L-8, Box 671, R. K. Davies File.

8. Oil companies calculated in April 1942 that they absorbed additional transportation costs of about $100 million in shipping by rail. A portion of this was recovered when OPA allowed small increases in gasoline and fuel oil prices in fifteen eastern states in January and March 1942. Beginning in August 1942, relief came in the form of reimbursements from the Defense Supplies Corporation, a subsidiary of the Reconstruction Finance Corporation, to shippers for unusual transportation costs. This program continued during the war and was utilized to move crude from the Gulf to the West coast and to Mid-Continent refiners. Through September 1945, almost $900 million in rebates was returned to shippers. I did not find an accounting of these expenditures that identified the recipients. PCND memorandum on the petroleum supply of the Atlantic coast states, 2 April 1942, Box 622.01, WPB, RG 179; from PAW, RG 253, PAW-OPA-RFC discussions relating to transportation subsidies, May–August 1942, Box 92.181.84, and Connally-Steagull bill, Box 20.050.3. PAW, *History of PAW*, 362–65. See also Box 144, War Petroleum Corporation Correspondence, TC Papers.

9. For the above two paragraphs: Nelson to Ickes, 4 April 1942 and Ickes to Nelson, 17 April 1942, Box 532.114, WPB, RG 179; OPA, "Chronological Outline of Events and Situations in OPA History to July 1, 1943," January 1944, Mimeographed, Box 748, Historical Records Project, PAW, RG 253; Davies, "Necessity for Separate Functional Regulation of the Oil Industry," May 1942, Typed, ibid.

10. Independently of PAW, Sen. Tom Connally submitted a bill creating a War Petroleum Corporation authorized to make loans to producers. Connally withdrew his bill when independent opposition

surfaced and because PAW's proposal was more palatable to the oil industry. Furthermore, Roosevelt, Ickes, and Nelson preferred to operate through existing agencies; see Box 144, War Petroleum Corporation Correspondence, TC Papers; Milton Katz memorandum to Donald M. Nelson re War Petroleum Control Administration, 10 July 1942, Box 622.007, WPB, RG 179; Ickes to Roosevelt, 4 August 1942, Box 747, Executive Orders, PAW, RG 253.

11. A report prepared by the National Resources Planning Board (NRPB) for WPB and released on 8 August 1942 stated the need for a drastic alteration of refinery yields to obtain 59 percent fuel oils and lubricants compared with a normal yield of 47 percent and the expedition of toluene, aviation gasoline, and butadiene production. But the report indicated that all this was under way and that the goals could be met through fuel conversions, the continued restriction of nonessential gasoline use, and the speeding up of the construction of special-purpose refineries. Nelson did not draw upon these findings in formulating his response to Ickes's suggestions, NRPB, "Energy Supply and Requirements for the War Program, Interim Report," prepared for WPB by the Industrial Section, NRPB, 27 August 1942, Box 46, LO Papers.

12. By this time, FPC's authority over electric power had been undercut by OPM orders regarding power pooling and interconnections, while its control over natural gas had gradually migrated to OPM and the petroleum coordinator—a process that can be traced from documents in Box 623.07, WPB, RG 179.

13. "The WPB and Petroleum Industry Control," 31 August 1942, Box 622.007, WPB, RG 179. From Box 747, Executive Order, PAW, RG 253: Davies memorandum to Ickes re responses to proposed executive order, 11 September 1942, and Joseph A. Fanelli memorandum for Davies re WPB and FPC responses to proposed executive order, 12 September 1942, and Draft of executive order to establish PAW, 21 October 1942.

14. Ickes to Byrnes, 23 December 1942, Box 622.01, and Nelson to Ickes, 11 November 1942 and Nelson to Ickes, 25 November 1942, Box 622.007, WPB, RG 179; Ickes to Harold D. Smith, director, Bureau of the Budget, 17 November 1942, Box 747, Executive Order, PAW, RG 253.

15. Executive Order No. 9276, Establishing the Petroleum Administration for War and Defining Its Functions and Duties, 2 December 1942, Box 644, PAW, RG 253. Some WPB officials viewed the executive orders establishing PAW, SFAW, and ODT as sapping the authority of WPB. One administrator complained that those agencies adopted the position that they could review all the directives or priorities to determine their necessity and means of implementation. The orders establishing PAW and SFAW did not permit such action. If Ickes or Eastman exceeded his authority, the fault lay with WPB

for not bringing him to heel. See W. Y. Elliott, director, Stockpiling and Transportation Division, WPB, to Nelson, 28 May 1943, Box 622.007, WPB, RG 179.

16. From PAW, RG 253: IPAA, *Report No. 338* (29 September 1942) and *Report No. 343* (3 December 1942), Box 20.0503, and North Carolina Oil Jobbers Association, *Bulletin No. 84* (28 September 1942), Box 18.050, and Natural Gas and Natural Gasoline Division, PAW, Weekly Report for 20 February 1943, on the Kansas City hearings of February 1943.

17. PRC, treated briefly in Chapter 15, was created in June 1943 and attracted immediate opposition from all sectors of the oil industry. Davies's remarks in USS, *Wartime Petroleum Policy*, 226. Ickes's coolness toward antitrust strategies had earned him the enmity of independents during the Depression. During the war, Ickes evinced positive hostility toward antitrust suits and such other antimajor strategies as divorcement and import quotas. See Ickes to Senator Chandler, 16 July 1941, Box 768, July 1941, on the inappropriateness of such action during the emergency, and IPAA, *Report No. 317* (19 February 1942), on the need to control imports, Box 20.050.3, PAW, RG 253.

18. Under Secretary of the Interior Wirtz memorandum to Ickes, 15 May 1941, Office of the Secretary, 1-188 Petroleum Administration (Part 1), DI, RG 48. A full exposition of the independents' case appears in USS Special Committee Investigating Petroleum Resources, *Hearings . . . The Independent Petroleum Company, March 19–22, 27–28, 1946*, 79th Cong., 2d sess., 1946.

19. Truman to Frank B. Grumbine, Jamesport, Missouri, 27 June 1942, Senatorial and Vice-Presidential File, HST Papers; Testimony of Ben A. Moyle, manager, Owl Refining Company, Long Beach, California, in Notes on a Meeting of the California Assembly Interim Oil Investigating Committee, 25 October 1941, Box 9.002.2, PAW, RG 253. Among the allies of the independents were: Wright Patman, Democrat, Texas, and chairman of the House Committee on Small Business; Clarence Lea, Democrat, California, and chairman of the House Special Subcommittee on Petroleum Investigation of the Committee on Interstate and Foreign Commerce; Sam Rayburn, Speaker of the House; Jennings Randolph, Democrat, West Virginia; Senator Truman, Democrat, Missouri, and chairman of the Special Committee to Investigate the National Defense Program; and Senator Joseph C. O'Mahoney, chairman of the Committee on Public Lands and Surveys.

20. USHR Committee on Small Business, *United States Versus Economic Concentration and Monopoly: An Investigation of the Effectiveness of the Government's Efforts to Combat Economic Concentration* (Washington, D.C.: GPO, 1947), 71, 97: USHR Select Committee to Conduct a Study and Investigation of the National Defense Program in Its Relation to Small Business. . . , *Hearings on H. Res. 64 . . . Part Three. Policy*

and Procedures of the Office of Price Administration Relative to Crude Oil Price, June 12–13, 1945, 79th Cong., 1st sess., 1945, 1426; Eugene V. Rostow, *A National Policy for the Oil Industry* (New Haven: Yale University Press, 1947), 10–11; Civilian Production Administration, *War Industry Facilities Authorized July 1940–August 1945, Listed Alphabetically by Company and Plant Location* (Washington, D.C.: 30 July 1946), Office of the Secretary, 1946, SFAW, RG 245; Davies to John A. Brown, General District Committee for District 1, in care of Socony-Vacuum Oil Co., New York, 26 January 1942, Box 671, R. K. Davies File, PAW, RG 253; Ickes to Freda Kirchwey, *The Nation*, 12 January 1944, an eight page response to an article charging that the majors controlled PAW, Office of the Secretary, 1-188 Petroleum Administration (Part 22), DI, RG 48.

21. Davies to Byrnes, Office of War Mobilization, 3 August 1943, Box 677, R. K. Davies File, PAW, RG 253, PAW, *History of PAW*, Appendix 12; Williamson et al., *The American Oil Industry*, 2: 750; Erich W. Zimmermann, *Conservation in the Production of Petroleum: A Study of Industrial Control* (New Haven: Yale University Press, 1957), 140.

22. Depression-shrunk markets, state production controls, and the Connally Act contributed to this reserve capacity. In spite of the opposition of many independents, the Connally Act was extended indefinitely in 1942; see Box 144, S.1302 and Box 145, Connally Hot Oil, TC Papers.

23. Prorationing did not extend to the entire production of a state. California had no regulatory agency at all; neither did Illinois. Both ignored the Interstate Oil Compact Commission. Only 42 percent of Oklahoma's production in 1940 and 4 percent of its producing wells were subject to prorationing; Prorationing in Oklahoma, Box 6001, Office of the Director in Charge, District 2, Production Committee, PAW, RG 253.

24. Zimmermann, *Conservation*, 190; USS, *Wartime Petroleum Policy*, 80–81; Clipping, *Denver Post*, 23 January 1942, Office of the Secretary, 1-188 Petroleum Quotas (Part 1), DI, RG 48; Hamman Exploration Company, Houston, Newsletter, 4 May 1942, Box 144, War Petroleum Correspondence, TC Papers. From PAW, RG 253: Ickes to Kansas Corporation Commission, 25 May 1942, Box 672, R. K. Davies File; Davies to TRC, 20 March 1942, ibid.; Davies to TRC, 21 February 1944, Box 681, R. K. Davies File; Davies memorandum re California production and unitization, 7 May 1945, Box 683, R. K. Davies File.

25. Some of the issues relating to an expanded American role in foreign oil fields are glanced at in Chapter 15. IPAA, *Report No. 353* (29 April 1943), on restricting oil imports, Box 20.050.3, PAW, RG 253; For early discussions of the ownership of offshore deposits, see Ickes to Truman, 19 April 1943, in which Ickes recommended against litigation at the present time since all production was subject to PAW conservation directives, Senatorial and Vice-Presidential Files, HST

Papers; Ronald B. Shuman, *The Petroleum Industry: An Economic Survey* (Norman: University of Oklahoma Press, 1940), 275.

26. PAW, *History of PAW,* 443–44; Petroleum Industry War Council, *Report of the Committee on Cost and Price Adjustment* (Washington, D.C.: PIWC, 1943), 33; Ickes to Nelson, 1 May 1943, Office of the Secretary, 1-188 Petroleum Administration (Part 16), DI, RG 48; from PAW, RG 253: PAW, *PAW Redistribution Program No. 2, Program and Instructions* (Washington, D.C.: GPO, 1943), for procedures to redistribute used equipment and equipment from abandoned wells and for remarks on well spacing and the implications of M-68, Box 6001, Office of the Director in Charge, 1942–1943, District 2, Production Committee; Davies's thoughts on M-68 addressed to industry officials, Congressmen, and WPB, Box 672, R. K. Davies File; and statement of case for allocations of new drilling equipment to oil fields, October 1943, Box 20.067, PIWC, September 1942–December 1943.

27. Arguments for a price increase, October 17 and 27, 1941, Box 644, Statements Relating to Policy, and Davies to Galbraith, 28 January 1942, on OPA Ceiling Order No. 88, Box 671, R. K. Davies File, and OPA Ceiling Order No. 88, 2 February 1942, Box 27.037.2, July–December 1942, all in PAW, RG 253. Within OPA, John K. Galbraith, deputy administrator of the price division, adopted the most rigid position relative to price. Sumner T. Pike, veteran New Dealer, SEC commissioner, and then head of the fuel price division, tried to convince Galbriath that specific price adjustments might be warranted. Pike, for example, argued in favor of a price advance for Pennsylvania-grade crude, used largely as a lubricant, as an incentive to reverse declining production. Pike agreed with Galbraith that prices should remain frozen for Mid-Continent and Gulf crudes; Pike to Galbraith and Henderson, July–September 1941, Box 4, File OPA, STP Papers.

28. Warren C. Platt to Chester Bowles, OPA, 13 June 1944, Box 5997, Miscellaneous, District 2, PAW, RG 253; Richard Polenberg, *War and Society: The United States, 1941–1945* (Philadelphia: J. B. Lippincott, 1972), 36.

29. Davies memorandum to Ickes, 15 October 1943, Box 15, Correspondence with Roosevelt, RKD Papers.

30. From PAW, RG 253: OPA-PAW correspondence regarding price and costs of production, Box 27.073.2, June 1941–June 1942; Kentucky Oil and Gas Association to Henderson and to Ickes, 20 October 1941, Box 6001, Office of the Director in Charge, 1942, District 2, K, Miscellaneous; PIWC resolution, October 1942 and Minutes of Meeting of PIWC, 1 and 2 September 1943, and PIWC, *Report of Committee on Cost and Price Adjustment* (1943), Box 20.067, PIWC, September 1942–December 1943; Davies testimony before USHR Committee on Interstate and Foreign Commerce, 23 November 1942, Box 753; IPAA, *Report No. 345* (28 December 1942), Box 20.050.3; Davies to

Vinson, 4, 19 October 1943, and Price Increase Materials presented to Vinson, October 1943, Box 1048, A-H. From the Office of the Secretary, DI, RG 48: Ickes to Clyde T. Ellis, USHR, 18 November 1941, 1-188 Petroleum Administration (Part 4) and Prentiss Brown to Ickes, 7 August 1943, 1-188 Petroleum Administration (Part 19). Pike to Henderson, 24 November 1942, Box 4, File OPA, STP Papers.

31. For the above two paragraphs, from Office of the Secretary, DI, RG 48: Ickes to Vinson, 4 November 1943, and Ickes to Byrnes, 25 November 1943, 1-188 Petroleum Administration (Part 21); and *New York Herald Tribune* 14 December 1943, 1-188 Petroleum News Summary; and *Investor's Reader* (Merrill, Lynch, Fenner & Beane), 1 (15 December 1943), 1-188 Petroleum Administration, General; Ickes to Vinson, 25 May 1944, 1-188 Petroleum Administration (Part 23). Gulf Coast Refiners Association, notes to members, 4 October 1944, and J. D. Sandifer, Jr., president, National Stripper Well Association, to Pike, 4 October 1944, Box 4, File OPA, STP Papers. From PAW, RG 253: Adolph H. Levy report on House committee hearings, 31 August 1943, Box 9.002.2; on transfer of powers to PAW: re S. 1266, September 1943, Box 678, R. K. Davies File; for reports of congressional proceedings, IPAA, *Report No. 355* (31 May 1943), *No. 356* (14 June 1943), *No. 359* (8 July 1943), *No. 360* (20 July 1943), and so on through January 1944, Box 20.050.3. For a convenient summary of independent criticisms of OPA, see USHR, *Hearings on OPA*, 1291–93, 1299–1309 passim.

32. Oil successfully defended depletion allowances against the forays of OPA and other enemies such as Secretary of Treasury Henry M. Morganthau and Senator Robert La Follette. The independents refused to scuttle those tax advantages in return for a general price increase. IPAA, *Report No. 314* (10 January 1942), *No. 319* (20 March 1942), *No. 339* (12 October 1942), *No. 348* (19 February 1943), Box 20.050.3, PAW, RG 253; for independent grievances, A. H. Levy memorandum for Davies, re Patman House Select Committee on Small Business, 15 April 1943, Office of the Secretary, 1-188 Petroleum Administration (Part 16), DI, RG 48.

33. For the duties of the refinery division, PAW, "Budget Justification, Fiscal Year Ending June 30, 1946 (1945)," Box 748, and E. J. Bullock, Director-in-Charge, "Narrative of Wartime Activities of PAW, District 2, 1945," Box 5995, Office of the Director in Charge, 1944–1945, District 2, PAW, RG 253; PAW, *History of PAW,* 191–213; George A. Hill, Jr., *Trends in the Oil Industry in 1944 (Including United States Foreign Policy) as Presented to the Petroleum Industry War Council, January 12, 1944* (Washington, D.C.: PIWC, 1944); Larson and Porter, *Humble Oil,* 566-67, 589–95. These accounts glide facilely around all commotion and attribute the impressive production results to industry-government cooperation. Williamson et. al., *American Petroleum Industry,* 2: 766–71, discusses domestic consumption and ration-

ing but scarcely glances at manifestations of industry-government or interagency antagonisms.

34. Clinton Scilipote, Executive Office of the Chairman, WPB. Memorandum, 16 October 1942, Box 622.007, WPB, RG 179.

35. For the above two paragraphs, from PAW, RG 253: Davies to Henderson, OPA, 11 November 1942, and E. B. Swanson to Davies, 15 October 1943, Box 673, R. K. Davies File; Ray B. McBride, Penoco Oil Company, Tulsa, to PCND, 10 August 1942, Box 6.002; D. Oty Grace, Grace Independent Oil Co., St. Charles, Missouri, to Ickes, 28 February 1942, Box 9.002.2; for the crude oil pool, W. W. Vandeveer, District 2, Chicago, to PAW, 30 December 1943, Box 5997, Supply and Transportation, District 2. The districts are geographically defined in Chapter 12, note 19 above.

36. Alfred J. Wright, "Recent Changes in the Concentration of Manufacturing," *Annals of the Association of American Geographers*, 35 (December 1945): 147–48, 159, 161, USHR, *United States Versus Economic Concentration*, 108–10; USS, *Wartime Petroleum Policy*, 11, 148–50. From Office of the Secretary, DI, RG 48: remarks by Governor Arnall printed in *Congressional Record*, 78th Cong., 1st sess., 24 September 1943, 1-188 Petroleum Administration (Part 22), and Construction Progress, Major 100-Octane Plants, 1944, 1-188 Petroleum Administration (Part 21). From PAW, RG 253: Davies to Jesse Jones, RFC, 7 April 1942, and Davies memorandum on aviation gasoline plants, 15 April 1942, and Priorities for 100-Octane Program, 6 June 1942, R. K. Davies File; WPB Directive for War Time Construction, Box 26.073.1, 1942.

37. USS, *Wartime Petroleum Policy*, 137.

38. USS, *The Independent Petroleum Company*, 51–64, 338–39.

39. PAW found itself between a rock and a hard place in the bitter dispute between the synthetic rubber program and the demands of the military for aviation gasoline, both programs dependent upon some of the same feed stocks. Vitriol flowed liberally between William M. Jeffers, director of the Rubber Reserve Corporation, an RFC subsidiary, and a coalition consisting of Ickes, Nelson, and the Departments of the Army and Navy. The latter group resented Jeffers's success in grabbing high-priority materials for rubber plants. For the many ramifications of this dispute, see William M. Tuttle, Jr., "The Birth of an Industry: The Synthetic Rubber 'Mess' in World War II," *Technology and Culture*, 22 (January 1981): 35–67.

40. Larson and Porter, *Humble Oil*, 589. See Langdon Winner, *Autonomous Technology: Technics-out-of-control As a Theme in Political Thought* (Cambridge, Mass.: MIT Press, 1979) for a somewhat deterministic characterization of giant technology as self-perpetuating and autonomous.

41. The Cole Act was necessary because some states, Georgia for one, refused to permit pipelines to cross railroads. Ickes, the presi-

dent, and the secretaries of War and the Navy all wrote the Georgia legislature, but to no avail. Secretary of the Navy Knox conversation with Ickes, 3 July 1941, Office of the Secretary, 1-188 Petroleum Administration (Part 1), DI, RG 48. War Emergency Pipelines, Inc., was a nonprofit organization organized by eleven oil companies and responsible for the design, engineering, and construction of both major pipelines. DPC reimbursed the consortium for all out-of-pocket costs. Davies to A. J. May, chairman, USHR Committee on Military Affairs, 2 December 1942, Box 672, R. K. Davies File, PAW, RG 253.

42. The promoters of one line—Trans America Pipeline from West Texas to Savannah or Charleston—enlisted congressmen from Texas, Mississippi, Florida, Georgia, South Carolina, and Maryland and flooded PAW, WPB, and other offices with promotional material and criticisms of other pipelines. In spite of intense pressure from Congressmen L. Mendel Rivers, Democrat, South Carolina, and chairman of the Petroleum subcommittee of the Committee on Naval Affairs, and John E. Rankin, Democrat, Mississippi, Ickes refused to recommend its designation as National Defense Pipeline; WPB seconded this decision. Data on Trans America from Box 748, PAW, RG 253. A classic white elephant emerged in the Canol pipeline from Alaska to a refinery in underdeveloped oil fields in Canada. The Army promoted this to supply its Alaska forces in spite of the opposition of virtually everyone knowledgeable about oil. After spending $100 million of a budgeted $135 million, Congress began asking whether it should be continued.

43. For the above two paragraphs, the Big Inch, from PAW, RG 253: Pipeline Conference Summary, 26 June 1941, Box 6.002; Davies to Nelson, 3 December 1941, Box 671, R. K. Davies File; Temporary Joint Pipeline Subcommittee, Districts 1, 2, and 3, Report of the Tulsa Pipeline Conference, 23–26 March 1942, and PAW release of transcript of radio program by Davies on the Big Inch and other oil problems, Box 671, unfiled, 1942. WPB, Supply of Petroleum Products Summary, April 1942, and W. G. Fritz, NRPB, Memorandum on pipelines, Box 622.01, WPB, RG 179. From Office of the Secretary, DI, RG 48: Ickes to Nelson, 20 February 1942, 1-188 Petroleum Administration (Part 4), Ickes to Vinson, 20 April 1942 and Ickes to Roosevelt, 21 April 1942, 1-188 Petroleum Administration (Part 7). For the Little Inch, from Office of the Secretary, DI, RG 48: Ickes to Nelson, 3 March 1943, and Ickes to Senator Joseph F. Guffey, 9 March 1943, 1-188 Petroleum Administration (part 15). From PAW, RG 253: IPAA, *Report No. 350* (11 March 1943), Box 20.050.3; Davies to Nelson, 3 April 1943, Davies to DSC, 26 January 1944, and Davies to Chairman Charles F. Roeser, District 3, 18 February 1944, Box 680, R. K. Davies File. WPB, Report on the Movement of Petroleum, 6 February 1943, Box 622.5001, WPB, RG 179.

44. See Polenberg, *War and Society*, 226–34, for the efforts of Nelson

to commence reconversion to civilian production as early as mid-1943, his gradual eclipse and ultimate replacement, and the emergence of OWM as the superior mobilization agency.

45. For the above three paragraphs, from PAW, RG 253: J. R. Parten, director of transportation, PAW, Memorandum on pipeline operation, 2 September 1943, Box 1048, A–H; Davies to Wright Patman, 21 March 1945, on the California pipeline, Box 683, R. K. Davies File; Report of the Joint Committee on Barges, Inland, and Intra-Coastal Waterways for Districts 1, 2, and 3, May 1942, Box 6001, District 2, Transportation; PAW memos on tanker shortages, December 1944, Box 1049, I–Z; Davies to Vinson and Vinson to Davies, Ickes, and J. Munroe Johnson, director, ODT, April–June 1945, Box 1049, I–Z. For minutes of Interagency Committee on Petroleum and other Transportation, 1944–1945, Box 622.5007, WPB, RG 179. By the end of the war, the American tanker fleet consisted of 750 vessels of 11.4 million deadweight tons, an increase of over 500 ships and 9 million dwt over the 1942 totals.

46. For the conversion programs imposed during World War I, see Chapter 3, pp. 77–78 and Chapter 4, pp. 83, 90–92. These programs were not referred to by World War II's managers and, indeed, were irrelevant to the problems of 1941.

47. Chapter 14 describes Ickes's opposition to the application of coupon rationing to coal. Coal conversion is treated here because it was a PAW program. In effect, PAW appeared before SFAW as a claimant for fuel to supply those who converted to coal.

48. For the above three paragraphs, from Office of the Secretary, DI, RG 48: Ickes to East Coast Governors, 8 August 1941, and Ickes to Senator Charles W. Tobey, 12 August 1941, and E. B. Swanson, director of research, PCND, to Davies, 13 August 1941, 1-188 Petroleum Administration (Part 2). From PAW, RG 253: John W. Frey, director of marketing, PCND, note relative to meeting on rationing, 5 August 1941, Box 6.002; Ickes to Nelson, 26 September 1941, Box 768, By Other Agencies. PAW, *History of PAW,* 402–3, 407.

49. Residence use of fuels in 1940, Correspondence with Federal Agencies, WPB, SFAW, RG 245; Conference on Petroleum Conservation, 3 July 1941, Office of the Secretary, 1-188 Petroleum Administration (Part 1), DI, RG 48.

50. Meeting of Motor Vehicle Commissioners from the states of District 1, Washington, D.C., 10 April 1942, CWCR; Henderson to Ickes, 7 May 1942, Office of the Secretary, 1-188 Petroleum Administration (Part 7), DI, RG 48; WPB, Minutes of Meeting, 28 April 1942, Box 622.01, WPB, RG 179.

51. WPB, "Comments Regarding Responsibility for Controlling Petroleum Movements at the Supplier Level, 1942," Box 622.007, and WPB, Minutes of Meeting, 28 April 1942, Box 622.409, WPB, RG 179; OPA, "History to July 1, 1943," 24, 36, Box 748, Historical Re-

cords Project, PAW, RG 253; Ickes to Knox, 11 July 1942, on retention of limitation orders even with coupon rationing, Office of the Secretary, 1-188 Petroleum Administration (Part 9), DI, RG 48.

52. PCND, Conference of Dealers on Fuel Oil, 28 September 1942, Box 9.002.2, PAW, RG 253; Davies memorandum on gasoline rationing allotment for District 1, 29 June 1942, Box 15, Confidential Memoranda, RKD Papers; Memo to John Schoonmaker, Connecticut representative of PAW, Hartford, Connecticut, 10 February 1943, Box 75, PAW, CWCR.

53. For expressions of interregional animosity and Ickes's responses, from Office of the Secretary, DI, RG 48: La Guardia to Ickes, 15 September 1942, and Ickes to Frederic A. Delano, NRPB, 5 August 1942, 1-188 Petroleum Administration (Part 10); Ickes to Senator Truman, 27 November 1942, 1-188 Petroleum Administration (Part 12). From PAW, RG 253: Report on Eastern insistence that rationing be extended nationally, Box 9.002.2; Frank Phillips, chairman, Petroleum Industry Committee for District 2, "Solve the East's Petroleum Problem Without Rationing the Midwest!" 1942, Box 16.010.12; PIWC, *Report on Cost and Price*, 18, for factors determining the civilian supply of gasoline.

54. According to WPB files, this plan actually originated within the WPB general counsel's office, which drafted a letter for Ickes to submit to Nelson in February, Box 622.40171, WPB, RG 179. In a letter to Nelson of 15 February 1943, Ickes sketched out the changes desired and acknowledged the assistance of WPB staff, ibid. While the subdelegation device may have been suggested by WPB, Ickes's quest for full authority over rationing antedated this correspondence. See Ickes to Byrnes, 23 December 1942, Box 622.01, WPB, RG 179.

55. Ickes to Nelson, 15 March 1943, Box 622.007, WPB, RG 179: William J. Gottlieb, president, Automobile Club of New York, to Senator Robert F. Wagner, 2 June 1943, Box 676, R. K. Davies File, PAW, RG 253. For the ban on pleasure driving, all from Office of the Secretary, DI, RG 48: Clippings from the *New York Times*, 2 June and 16 July 1943 and *Washington Post*, 8 January 1943, 1-188 Petroleum News Summary (Part 1) and Ickes to Robert Moses, New York State Council of Parks, 18 March 1943, 1-188 Petroleum Administration (Part 15). On credit cards, Box 5995, Petroleum Directive No. 62, 29 December 1942, PAW, RG 253.

56. Brown to Nelson, 30 March 1943, Box 622.007, WPB, RG 179.

57. WPB release, 2 July 1943, ibid.

58. Krug to Nelson, 18 June 1943, and Wayne Coy, acting director, Bureau of the Budget, to Nelson, 15 June 1943, ibid. In January 1943, Krug had shown much irritation at PAW's "casual response" to shortages of industrial fuel oil in New England and New York. Krug did not trust PAW. He alluded to reports proving distributor discrimination during the first months of rationing. Krug correspondence, January

1943, Box 622.4017, WPB, RG 179. For such a report, "Summary of Rationing Compliance, June 1942," Office of the Secretary, 1-188 Petroleum Administration (Part 9), DI, RG 48.

59. Marshall memorandum, 19 April 1944, Box 681, R. K. Davies File, PAW, RG 253. See also correspondence between D. Oty Grace, Grace Independent Oil Co., St. Charles, Missouri, and PAW, February–April 1942, Box 9.002.2, PAW, and Davies to Bowles, 27 August 1943, Box 678, R. K. Davies File, PAW, RG 253.

60. OPM took a small but symbolic step in October 1941 by banning oil burner installation in defense housing constructed along the Atlantic coast, a prohibition extended across the country in 1942 and still in effect in November 1944. Defense Housing Order No. 1192, OPM, reported in *New York Times*, 15 October 1941, Box 18.050, PAW, RG 253; W. C. Leland, Jr., OPM, to J. Douglas Brown, OPM, 25 October 1941, on oil burner industry response, Box 422.205, WPB, RG 179; Survey Report, Grand Island, Nebraska, 7 November 1941, Box 2019, Denver Office, November 1944, SFAW, RG 245.

61. WPB, Limitation Order L-56, 14 March 1942, By Other Agencies, PAW, RG 253; H. E. Eastwood, colonel, U.S.A., member of End Products Committee, WPB, dissenting statement on conversion, July 1942, Box 442.01, 1941–1942, WPB, RG 179.

62. Report on Use of No. 2 Fuel Oil in Connecticut, 1942, Box 74, Conversion, CWCR; Ickes to Nelson, 30 June 1942, Box 422.01, 1941–1942, WPB, RG 179.

63. In October and November 1942, an exchange between PAW's division of marketing and WPB's plumbing and heating branch indicated that lack of coal-burning equipment severely retarded conversion. Everyone involved was loath to upgrade steel priorities for the manufacture of grates and coal stokers at the expense of military hardware. Paul A. Best, assistant director of marketing, PCND, to Henry S. Norris, chief, Plumbing and Heating Branch, Box 26.073.1, July–December 1942, and for other items, Box 442.01, 1941–1942, WPB, RG 179; New England Coal and Coke Co., to Wesley L. Sturgis, State Fuel Administrator, Hartford, 13 January 1943, Box 74, Coal, CWCR.

64. WPB itemization of program problems, and WPB, End Products Committee, report on conservation, 24 July 1942, and A. Hill, Jr., WPB, to Nelson, 3 August 1942, on PAW irresponsibility, in Box 442.01, 1941–1942, and Henderson's order, Box 440.1, 1943, all from WPB, RG 179; PAW Order No. 3, Box 674, R. K. Davies File, PAW, RG 253; formation of a conversion committee with representatives from eight federal units, Correspondence with Federal Agencies, ODT, June to December 1943, SFAW, RG 245; Davies to Nelson, 21 September 1943, on suspension of the program, Box 440.01, 1943, WPB, RG 179.

65. Krug came to WPB as deputy director general of distribution

from a post as manager of power for TVA. Krug and Ickes had clashed earlier when the former stopped construction on public power projects. Ickes charged Krug with favoring private power. After a brief Navy stint, Krug succeeded Nelson in 1944 as head of WPB. He followed Ickes as Secretary of Interior in 1946.

66. U-9 prohibited certain commercial uses of lighting and restricted white-way lighting and other ornamental uses, prompting a barrage of criticism from the advertising and utilities industries. U-9 actually lowered coal production in areas where the utilities burned slack coal, a consequence similar to that experienced during World War I; see Chapter 3, pp. 77–78, and Chapter 4, pp. 84–85. Utility responses to 1943 brownout orders; Correspondence with federal agencies, Smaller War Plants Corporation, 1943, SFAW, RG 245. For other SFAW items: R. B. Griffith, Denver, Weekly Report for week ending 3 February 1945, Box 2019, Denver Office, February 1945; WPB, Utilities Order U-9, 15 January 1945 and Edward Falck, director of war utilities, to Julius A. Krug, chairman, WPB, 16 March 1945, Correspondence with Federal Agencies, WPB, January–March 1945.

67. From PAW, RG 253: the Cities Service position and various pipeline proposals, Box 181.96, Natural Gas, Natural Gas and Natural Gasoline Division, Weekly Reports, 1942–1943; on L-31 and conversion, PAW and WPB discussions, Box 26.0731, January–June 1942.

68. PAW estimated oil savings through conversion at 80 million barrels for 1942–1943. In eastern Kansas and western Missouri alone, gas shortages of 10 billion cubic feet required the substitution of at least one million barrels of oil. Nine factories in and around Charleston, West Virginia, sought oil or coal to replace 5 billion cubic feet of natural gas. The PAW estimate, then, must be reduced, but by how much cannot be calculated. Clippings, *Kansas City Star*, 14, 15 September 1943, and *Kansas City Times*, 15 September 1943, and F. J. Halstead, area district manager, Kansas City SFAW, to H. A. Gray, SFAW, 15 September 1943, Central File, Kansas City Office, September–October 1943, SFAW, RG 245. For Appalachia: PAW, Natural Gas and Natural Gasoline Division, Weekly Reports, January 1942–June 1944, Box 181.96, Natural Gas, PAW, RG 253; WPB amendments to L-31 and effect in West Virginia, Correspondence with Federal Agencies, WPB, SFAW, RG 245.

69. From R. K. Davies File, PAW, RG 253: Davies to Grady Tripplett, editor, *Petroleum News*, 30 August 1944, Box 682; Davies to Michael W. Straus, Assistant Secretary of Interior, 12 April 1945, Box 683; other items concerning liquidation in Box 684, September 1945–May 1946.

70. Strikes began in March 1945 at the huge Lake Charles, Louisiana, plant of Cities Service. Strikes in Kansas City followed shortly thereafter. PAW, under presidential authority, took over the operations of these plants and others that struck in succeeding

months. In September 1946, the Oil Workers International Union, CIO, authorized a nationwide strike. President Truman, acting on the recommendation of PAW and the armed forces, then issued an executive order under which the Department of the Navy seized and operated the refineries. This confrontation can be followed in Boxes 683–684, R. K. Davies File, PAW, RG 253.

71. See Box 15, Oil and Gas Division, RKD Papers. Also consult Craufurd D. Goodwin, ed., *Energy Policy in Perspective: Today's Problems, Yesterday's Solutions* (Washington, D. C.: Brookings Institution, 1981), 14–20, 32–46, 75–76.

72. Ickes to Roosevelt, 1, 8 December 1941, Box 15, Correspondence with Roosevelt, and Davies memorandum re oil in Mexico, 24 June 1944, Box 15, Confidential Memoranda, RKD Papers.

73. Among the many excellent studies of the penetration of the Middle East by American oil companies are: Anthony Sampson, *The Seven Sisters: The Great Oil Companies and the World They Made* (London: Hodder & Stoughton, 1975) and Michael B. Stoff, *Oil, War, and American Security: The Search for a National Policy on Foreign Oil, 1941–1947* (New Haven: Yale University Press, 1980).

74. Gerald D. Nash, *United States Oil Policy, 1890–1964: Business and Government in Twentieth Century America* (Pittsburgh: University of Pittsburgh Press, 1968), 158.

Chapter Fourteen

1. Wilbert G. Fritz to Dr. Watkins, NRPB, on the emergency coal program, 10 July 1940, Box 45, Energy Resources Committee, LO Papers.

2. From Office of the Secretary, DI, RG 48: Roosevelt to Ickes, 5 November 1941, 1-188 Coal Administration (Part 1); Ickes to Henry L. Stimson, Secretary of War, 16 May 1942, 1-188 Coal Administration (Part 2); Executive Order, 19 April 1943, 1-188 Coal Administration. SFAW, "Report of War Activities, Revised to September 30, 1945," Mimeographed, Box 701, History of the Coal Agencies, SFAW, RG 245; Ralph Hillis Baker, *The National Bituminous Coal Commission, Administration of the Bituminous Coal Act, 1937–1941* (The Johns Hopkins University Studies in Historical and Political Science, Series 59, No. 3) (Baltimore: Johns Hopkins Press, 1941), 618–26.

3. Supply of heat and power, Btu equivalent, 1940–44, Correspondence with Federal Agencies, WPB, January–March 1945, SFAW, RG 245; Sam H. Schurr and Bruce Netschert et al., *Energy in the American Economy, 1850–1975: An Economic Study of Its History and Prospects* (Baltimore: Johns Hopkins University Press for Resources for the Future, 1960), 36.

4. Anthracite production and use, Office of the Secretary, 1-188 Coal Administration, DI, RG 48; see sources for Tables 15 and 16.

5. From Office of the Secretary, DI, RG 48: Harold A. Gray memorandum for Secretary Ickes, 15 November 1943, 1-188 Coal Administration (Part 1), and Conference on Petroleum Conservation, 3 July 1941, 1-188 Petroleum Administration (Part 1).

6. In addition, OPA promulgated a temporary price freeze in April 1941 and one year later issued Maximum Price Regulation No. 120 for coal. Price ceilings are returned to in a subsequent section. For this paragraph, Baker, *The National Bituminous Coal Commission*, 308; FPC, New York Regional Office "Memorandum Report on New England Fuel Situation, Résumé of Results of Field Investigation, March 30 to April 2, 1942," Inter Bureau Correspondence, FPC, SFAW, RG 245.

7. These figures are derived from the sources cited in Table 15 and do not include railroad or bunker coals or exports.

8. For the above three paragraphs, from SFAW, RG 245: SFAW, "Report of War Activities to 1945," Box 701, History of Coal Agencies; Meeting of the Solid Fuels Advisory Committee, 10 March 1942, Government Advisory Committees, S–Z. From Office of the Secretary, 1-188 Coal Administration (Part 2), DI, RG 48: Loss of Coal Vessels, January–April 1942; Ickes to Nelson, 20 April 1942, on colliers and railroad rolling stock; H. A. Gray Memorandum for the Secretary, 13 May 1942; Priorities for Lake Vessels, May 1942.

9. Gray memoranda to Ickes, 5 and 12 March 1942, Ickes, Secretary of Interior, 1941–42, and ODT to SFAW, 21 September 1943, Correspondence with Federal Agencies, ODT, June–December 1943, and Gage to Ickes, 26 September and 14 October 1942, Correspondence with Cities, Kansas City, Missouri, SFAW, RG 245; Ickes-Ratner correspondence, 1 July 24, 30 September 1942, and Ickes to Gage, 21 September 1942, Office of the Secretary, 1-188 Coal Administration (Part 2), DI, RG 48.

10. Meeting of the Solid Fuels Advisory War Council, 10 March 1942, Government Advisory Committees, S–Z, SFAW, RG 245; Dan H. Wheeler memorandum for the Secretary, 1-188 Coal Administration (Part 17), and W. W. Vandeveer, chairman, Tanker Transportation Subcommittee, District No. 2, to Major J. R. Parten, Division of Transportation, PCW, 18 July 1942, Office of the Secretary, 1-188 Petroleum Administration (Part 10), DI, RG 48.

11. From SFAW, RG 245: Solid Fuels Advisory War Council Minutes, 6 May 1942, Government Advisory Committees, S–Z; Charles O'Neil, chairman, Bituminous Coal Production Board, District No. 1, to Leon Henderson, OPA, 7 May 1942, Bituminous Coal Producers Advisory Boards No. 1–2, 1941–47; Gray memoranda to Ickes, 31 March and 8 May 1942, Ickes, Secretary of Interior, 1941–42; OPA to SFAW, 19 September 1946, Correspondence with Federal Agencies, OPA, 1946. Federal subsidies for coal transportation, 1946,

Office of the Secretary, 1-188 Coal Administration (Part 16), DI, RG 48.

12. By 1944, in response to the coal strikes of 1943, SFAW had obtained the approval of WPB to negotiate DSC guarantees of payment for the shipment and delivery of bituminous to anthracite dealers, the latter having no credit relationships with bituminous producers or wholesalers. In a typical arrangement, DSC, on instructions from SFAW, contracted with the Delaware, Lackawanna and Western Coal Company to receive and ship 22,000 tons of bituminous to designated recipients. In addition to full reimbursement for all costs, D,L & W received fifteen cents per ton as a service fee. SFAW, "A Preliminary Memorandum with Respect to a Proposed Program for Alleviating the Domestic Coal Shortage in the Northeast, January 1944" and DSC to SFAW, 29 January 1944, Correspondence with Federal Agencies, Defense Supplies Corporation, 1943–44 and DSC to D,L & W, 28 June 1945, re Bituminous Coal Contract No. 167-M-4, Correspondence with Federal Agencies, DSC, 1945–1946, SFAW, RG 245.

13. For the above two paragraphs, from SFAW, RG 245: NRPB Report on Fuel Supplies of the Pacific Northwest, 2 March 1942, Correspondence with Federal Agencies, NRPB; Sheridan-Wyoming Coal Co. to SFCND, 14 May 1942, Field Office, Denver, Correspondence District 19, RU-SH; Reports from the Denver Office of SFAW, 1942, Central File, Denver Office, January–December 1942; SFAW to DSC, 10 February 1944, Correspondence with Federal Agencies, DSC, 1943–1944; Copy of a letter from Eugene McAuliffe to the president of the Union Pacific Railway Company, 17 August 1943, Correspondence with Federal Agencies, ODT, June–December 1943. McAuliffe to Ickes, 2 March 1942, Office of the Secretary, 1-188 Coal Administration (Part 1), DI, RG 48; Alfred J. Wright, "Recent Changes in the Concentration of Manufacturing," *Annals of the Association of American Geographers*, 35 (December 1945): 163–65.

14. From Correspondence with Federal Agencies, WPB, SFAW, RG 245: Office of Civilian Supply, "Anthracite Coal Supply and Requirements," 26 January 1943; SFAW reports on bituminous coal requirements, 1943, 1944, and 1945. These reports are also filed in Government Advisory Committees, S–Z.

15. ICC also shared responsibility in this matter because of its authority to approve or disapprove the construction of spur lines to the mines. ICC normally referred such applications to SFAW for a recommendation but did not always adhere to SFAW's conclusions. See ICC-SFAW correspondence, 30 March, 7, 13 April 1944, regarding an application of the Baltimore and Ohio railroad for new track to an undeveloped coal deposit, Correspondence with Federal Agencies, ICC, SFAW, RG 245.

16. For the above two paragraphs, from Correspondence with Fed-

eral Agencies, SFAW, RG 245: RFC to SFAW, 20 May 1942, RFC; Applications to Small War Plants Corporation, RFC; Certification Supervisory Unit correspondence with SFAW, Navy Department, 1942–43; Defense Plant Corporation to WPB, 3 July 1944, Defense Plant Corporation. J. D. A. Morrow, president, Joy Manufacturing Co., to Ickes, 7 September 1943, Office of the Secretary, 1-188 Coal Administration (Part 6), DI, RG 48.

17. SFAW, "Report of War Activities to 1945," Box 701, History of Coal Agencies, SFAW, RG 245; Hubert E. Risser, *The Economics of the Coal Industry* (Lawrence: University of Kansas School of Business, Bureau of Business Research, 1958), 70–71.

18. For the above four paragraphs, from Correspondence with Federal Agencies, SFAW, RG 245: WMC, "Labor Market Problems of the Bituminous Coal Industry, Western States," 10 February 1943, and correspondence between SFAW and WMC relative to raids on mine labor, and Ickes to McNutt, 29 February 1944, WMC; regarding the extended work week, see SFAW-OPA letters, August–October 1943, OPA, July–September 1943, and Byrnes to Chester Bowles, OPA, 3 September 1943, War Mobilization and Conversion. For data on the work week dispute not found in SFAW files, see Office of the Secretary, 1-188 Coal Administration (Part 3), DI, RG 48.

19. WPB Order M-316 (bituminous), 30 April 1943, and M-318 (anthracite), 1 May 1943, prohibited delivery to and accepting delivery by any consumer with more than ten days' supply. These orders delegated administrative authority to SFAW and empowered SFAW to issue necessary supplemental directives and orders, Correspondence with Federal Agencies, WPB, March–April 1944, SFAW, RG 245. A subsequent section will deal with distribution and allocation programs.

20. Executive Order 9340, 1 May 1943, Office of the Secretary, 1-188 Coal Mine Operations (Part 2) DI, RG 48. Although lodged in Interior and distinct from SFAW, CMA necessarily was an extension of the latter. CMA was terminated in 1945, prior to the end of the war. Ickes negotiated a contract with DSC for funds to operate 2,800 bituminous and 250 anthracite mines, Correspondence with Federal Agencies, RFC, SFAW, RG 245.

21. Clipping, *New York Times*, 18 January 1943, regarding anthracite strike, Office of the Secretary, 1-188 Petroleum News Summary (Part 1), DI, RG 48; News Release, 11 January 1943, of Truman attack on John L. Lewis and Truman to Lewis telegram, Senatorial and Vice-Presidential Files, HST Papers.

22. For exciting and revealing exchanges between Ickes and Lewis, see National Joint Wage Conference of Mine Operators and UMWA, Washington, 30 November 1943, 1-188 Coal Mine Operations (Part 7) and SFAW conference with operators and UMWA, April 1944, 1-188 Coal Conference, both in Office of the Secretary DI, RG 48.

23. From Office of the Secretary, DI, RG 48: Ickes to Roosevelt, 2 June 1943, Coal Mine Operations (Part 2); Ickes to William H. Davis, chairman, WLB, 29 December 1943, and Department of the Interior, "Analysis of the NWLB Actions in the Coal Controversy to January 1944," 1-188 Coal Mine Operations (Part 8). From Ickes, Secretary of the Interior, 1943–44, SFAW, RG 245: Gray memorandum to Ickes, 2 November 1943 and C. J. Potter memorandum for Ickes, 22 June 1944. Dan H. Wheeler memorandum for Ickes concerning coal mine takeovers, 15 October 1945, Ickes, Secretary of the Interior, 1945, SFAW, RG 245.

24. OPA issued its first coal price freeze on 3 April 1941, two days after the miners struck, and revoked it in May. BCD, responding to rising coal prices in July and August, held hearings—still in progress in December—on whether to invoke its powers to establish maximum prices. The Emergency Price Control Act of 30 January 1942 enlarged federal authority over prices, and the Roosevelt administration decided to vest responsibility for coal prices with OPA rather than BCD. In April, OPA issued Maximum Price Regulation No. 120 for coal on the basis of grade-size-market formulas constructed by BCD.

25. From Correspondence with Federal Agencies, SFAW, RG 245: OPA, "Statement of Considerations Involved in the Issuance of Maximum Price Regulation No. 120," 30 January 1943, and SFAW-Office of Economic Stabilization correspondence, December 1942–March 1946, OES; Ickes to Prentiss Brown, 21 June 1943, and to Chester Bowles, 14 October 1943, and other SFAW-OPA correspondence, OPA, October–December 1943, October–November 1945. Minutes of the Meeting of Solid Fuels Advisory War Council, 14 February 1945, Government Advisory Committees, S–Z, SFAW, RG 245.

26. See above, note 19.

27. For the regulations, Office of the Secretary, 1-188 Coal Regulations (Part 1), DI, RG 48.

28. For key documents that explain the position of both OPA and SFAW, see the following from Correspondence with Federal Agencies, SFAW, RG 245: Prentiss Brown, OPA, to F. J. Bailey, Bureau of the Budget, 2 April 1943, and Joel Dean, OPA, to A. C. C. Hill, WPB, 14 June 1943, OPA, January–June 1943; Ickes to Brown, 31 July 1943, and Nelson, WPB, to Gray, SFAW, 25 August 1943, and Gray to Nelson, 28 August 1943, WPB, August 1943. Also, Minutes of the Meeting of the Solid Fuels Advisory War Council, 15 September 1943, Government Advisory Committees, S–Z, SFAW, RG 245. See, SFAW, "Considerations Dealing with the Rationing of Anthracite and Bituminous Coal," 20 July 1943, Office of the Secretary, 1-188 Coal Administration (Part 5), DI, RG 48.

29. From SFAW, RG 245: Thurman Arnold, Assistant Attorney General, Memorandum to the Attorney General, 17 July 1942, re anti-trust violations in New York City, Correspondence with Federal Agen-

cies, Justice Department; Correspondence between SFAW and USS Special Committee Investigating the National Defense Program, March 1943, Government Advisory Committees, S–Z; Clinton M. Flint, mayor, Village of Freeport, Long Island, to Roosevelt, 27 October 1943, Executive Office of the President, 1941–44; Wright Patman, chairman, House Select Committee on Small Business, to Ickes, 4 November 1943, Correspondence with Federal Agencies, Select Committee on Small Business; SFAW, "Report on War Activities to 1945," Box 701, History of the Coal Agencies, denied the self-serving nature of the industry advisory committees.

30. For the above three paragraphs, from SFAW, RG 245: SFAW, "Report on War Activities to 1945," Box 701, History of the Coal Agencies; Report of the Solid Fuels Administration for War, 1944, Government Advisory Committees, S–Z; Gray Memorandum for Ickes, 12 August 1943, and C. J. Potter Memorandum for Ickes, 31 December 1943, Ickes, Department of Interior, 1943–44; Gordon C. Cooke, Chairman, National Anthracite Distribution Committee and President of the Delaware, Lackawana and Western Coal Co., to Ickes, 12 November 1943, on the breakdown in enforcement owing to inadequate personnel, Government Advisory Committees, C–N. For regulations and amendments, see note 27 above.

31. For regulations and amendments, see note 27 above; for Ickes's understanding of Regulation No. 17, Ickes to Senator Owen Brewster, 5 May, 1944, Office of the Secretary, 1-188 Coal Administration (Part 9), DI, RG 48.

32. From Correspondence with Federal Agencies, SFAW, RG 245: NRPB, "Summary of Recommendations, Energy Supply and Requirements for the War Program, Interim Report," August 1942, and Ralph J. Watkins, Assistant Director, NRPB, to Ickes, 17 November 1942, and SFAW Memorandum on Zoning, 9 September 1942, NRPB, and Zoning report of the Subcommittee on Haulage Conservation of the Traffic Requirements and Priorities Committee, WPB, September 1943, WPB. Ralph J. Watkins to Joseph L. Weiner, Office of Civilian Supply, 2 October 1942, Box 46, Energy Supply and War Programs, LO Papers.

33. Minutes of the Solid Fuels War Council Meeting, 8 April 1942, Government Advisory Committee, S–Z, SFAW, RG 245.

34. When transportation problems arose, SFAW normally applied to ODT for relief. If car service was involved, ODT then recommended an order to ICC. SFAW also applied for exemptions to car service orders that ICC issued to achieve some general purpose but that affected coal movement. A call for a rail embargo, as in January 1945 when severe weather tied up rail lines in the Northeast, generally originated with ODT. SFAW was consulted prior to the application of the embargo, and relevant exemptions were issued for coal transport.

See numerous documents in Correspondence with Federal Agencies, ODT, SFAW, RG 245.

35. Subsequent amendments—revised Regulation No. 10 (April 1944)—and new regulations—Regulation No. 23 (July 1944), amended four times—altered stockpiling limitations to reflect available supply in particular districts. See note 27 above.

36. A quota above 100 percent encouraged early ordering and stockpiling.

37. For the above two paragraphs, from Correspondence with Federal Agencies, SFAW, RG 245: SFAW-ODT correspondence, November–December 1943, regarding SFAW use of ODT units and branches of the Massachusetts Solid Fuels Administration, ODT; SFAW–Office of Civilian Defense correspondence, June–July 1942, Office of Civilian Defense, 1943–47. Also from SFAW, RG 245: SFAW, "Report on War Activities to 1945," Box 701, History of the Coal Agencies; Functions of Area Advisory Committees and Community Committees on Emergency Distribution, 1944, Bituminous Coal Producers Advisory Boards No. 1–2, 1941–47; Tidewater Dock Coal Advisory Committee, Boston, April 1944, Government Advisory Committees, S–Z.

38. From Office of the Secretary, DI, RG 48: Economics and Statistics Division, SFAW, "Bituminous Coal Requirements, 1943–1944," September 1943, 1-188 Coal Administration (Part 6); Ickes to Senator Owen Brewster, 5 May 1944, 1-188 Coal Administration (Part 9), on Regulation No. 17. From Ickes, Secretary of the Interior, 1943–44, SFAW RG 245: C. J. Potter Memoranda for Ickes, re Regulations No. 17 and 18, 22, 30 March, 17 May 1944; Robert F. Duemler, chief, Anthracite Distribution Division, SFAW, memorandum for Undersecretary of the Interior Abe Fortas, 21 October 1944.

39. From Office of the Secretary, DI, RG 48: Ickes to Nelson, 1 May 1943, 1-188 Coal Mine Operations (Part 2); WPB-SFAW exchanges regarding coal savings and the coastal dimout, February–April 1943, 1-188 Coal Administration (Part 3). From SFAW RG 245: Office of War Utilities, WPB, *Report on Voluntary Conservation Program for Electric Utilities* (War Production Board, July 1943), and Edward Falck, Office of War Utilities, WPB, to Ralph K. Davies, Deputy Administrator, PAW, 17 January 1945, on Utilities Order U-9, Correspondence with Federal Agencies, WPB; Reports from the Denver, Colorado, Office of SFAW on electric blackouts and area coal production, November 1944–March 1945, Central File, Denver Office, October 1944–March 1945.

40. From SFAW, RG 245: for upstate New York, W. H. Kresan, chairman, SFAW Area Committees for District 5, to Potter, SFAW, 3 October 1944, Bituminous Coal Production Advisory Boards No. 1–2, 1941-47, and J. S. Miner, public welfare officer and chairman,

Emergency Coal Committee, Port Chester, Rye, Harrison Area, to Potter, 2 February 1945, Government Advisory Committees, C–N; for New York City, Brice P. Disque, chairman, New York City Area Advisory Committee on Local Distribution, Minutes of the 12th Meeting, 1 February 1945, and for Philadelphia, SFAW Office at Philadelphia to SFAW, 31 January 1945, Government Advisory Committees, A–C; for Cleveland, Lausche to Ickes, 21 July 1944 and Lausche to H. A. Smith, Area Distribution Manager, SFAW, Cleveland, 24 July 1944, and Potter to Lausche, 4 August 1944, Correspondence with Cities, Cleveland; for Kansas City and Oklahoma City, E. N. Ahlfeldt, Area Distribution Manager, Kansas City, to Potter, 5 January 1945, and W. P. Kelly, SFAW, to Ahlfeldt, 5 January 1945, Kansas City Office, January–April 1945; for Detroit, J. L. Newbold, chairman, National War Council of the Retail Solid Fuel Industry, to Potter, 29 July 1943, Government Advisory Committees, C–N; for Mobile, R. M. Weinecker, chairman, Solid Fuel District Advisory Committee, ODT, Mobile, to Ickes, 20 October 1943, Government Advisory Committees, A–C.

41. SFAW survey, November 1944, Correspondence with Federal Agencies, WPB, September–December 1944, SFAW, RG 245.

42. Potter memorandum for Ernest N. Ahlfeldt, Area Distribution Manager, Kansas City Office, 6 June 1944, Area Advisory Committees on Local Distribution, Area II, SFAW, RG 245.

43. From SFAW, RG 245: W. H. Kresan, chairman, SFAW Area Committee for Area 5, to Potter, 3 October 1944, Bituminous Coal Production Advisory Boards No. 1–2, 1941–47; SFAW to Office of Civilian Defense, Montgomery, Alabama, 24 April and 5 September 1944 and 12 January 1945, Correspondence with Federal Agencies, OCD, 1943–47; Clipping, *Cortland Standard*, New York, 26 September 1944, Correspondence with Cities; citizen complaints in Executive Office of the President, 1945; Potter Memorandum for Ickes, re Akron, 29 January 1945, Ickes, Secretary of the Interior, 1945. Bridgeport, Conn. Fuel Committee's furnace cleaning week, Box 74, Fuel Correspondence, CWCR.

44. From SFAW, RG 245: Wisconsin and Minnesota resolutions, 1945, and Audrey C. Lucking, Cincinnati, to Truman, 15 September 1945, Executive Office of the President, 1945; Potter memoranda to Ickes, 12 September and 21 November 1945; Retail Coal Merchants Association, Pittsburgh, to Michael W. Straus, Assistant Secretary of the Interior, 20 June 1945, Office of the Secretary, Straus; National Anthracite Distribution Committee Minutes of Meeting, 22 August 1945, Government Advisory Committees, C–N.

45. From Office of the Secretary, DI, RG 48: Ickes to Henry L. Stimson, Secretary of War, 31 May 1945, 1-188 Coal Administration (Part 10); see 1-188 Coal Administration (Part 11) and (Part 12) for files on European coal shortages. From SFAW, RG 245: for SFAW-FEA

correspondence, April–August 1945, for instance, SFAW to FEA, 4 July 1945 and FEA response, 6 August 1945, on SFAW export embargoes, FEA; Potter memoranda to Ickes, 27 March and 4 July 1945, on the impact of exports on domestic supply, Ickes, Secretary of the Interior, 1945; Truman to Ickes, 21 May 1945, Executive Office of the President, 1945; John W. Snyder, OWMR, to Ickes, 14 August 1945, Correspondence with Federal Agencies, OWMR.

46. The subsidization and reinsurance of coal shipments on the Great Lakes remained in effect partly because of striking lake tugboat crews. These programs were abandoned in March 1946, SFAW to OWMR, 7 November 1945, Correspondence with Federal Agencies, OWMR, SFAW, RG 245.

47. From SFAW, RG 245: SFAW, "Report on War Activities to 1945," Box 701, History of the Coal Agencies; Solid Fuels Advisory War Council Minutes of Meeting, 14 November 1945, Government Advisory Committees, S–Z; R. B. Griffith, Denver Office, to SFAW, 22 July 1946, Central File, Denver Office, January–September 1946. On pipeline disposal, Ralph K. Davies, PAW, to Burton K. Wheeler, chairman, Senate Committee on Interstate Commerce, 13 March 1945, Box 683, R. K. Davies Files, and Davies to W. Stuart Symington, administrator, Surplus Property Administration, 3 October 1945, Box 684, R. K. Davies Files, PAW, RG 253; and Memorandum on disposal of Big and Little Inch pipelines, 10 December 1945, Box 90, Petroleum, LO Papers. On synthetics, Davies testimony before House and Senate committees, 1943, on the bill authorizing demonstration plants, Box 748, and Davies to Krug, chairman, WPB, 3, 16, March 1945, Box 683, R. K. Davies Files, PAW, RG 253.

48. Wheeler to Chapman, 25 February 1946, Office of the Secretary, 1-188 Coal Administration (Part 13), DI, RG 48.

49. For the above two paragraphs, from Office of the Secretary, DI, RG 48: ICC embargo, 5 September 1946, and Wheeler memorandum to Krug, 8 August 1946, and B. Morcell, Coal Mines Administrator, to Krug, 31 August 1946, 1-188 Coal Administration (Part 16), and Summary of Strikes, 1 May–31 May and 1 November–30 November 1946, 1-188 Coal Reports (Part 1). From SFAW, RG 245: "Arrangements for the Coordination of Transportation During the Railroad Strike Emergency–May 17–26, 1946," and SFAW to ODT, 24 July 1946, on car shortages, Correspondence with Federal Agencies, ODT; W. A. Reiss, Lake Dock Advisory Committee, St. Paul, to Krug, 24 April, 4 May, 2, 29 August 1946, Government Advisory Committees, C–N; Dan H. Wheeler weekly reports to the Secretary, 29 July–6 September 1946, Krug, Secretary of the Interior, August–September 1946; Danville, Virginia, Chamber of Commerce to Truman, 13 October 1945, Telegram, Executive Office of the President, 1945. House of Representatives, State of Connecticut, House Bill No. 1237, Box 74, Legislation, and correspondence of the New Haven

Chamber of Commerce, July–August 1946, Box 74, Fuel Correspondence, CWCR.

50. Wheeler Memorandum for Krug, 28 March 1946, Krug, Secretary of the Interior, 1946, SFAW, RG 245. From Office of the Secretary, DI, RG 48: Number of Electric Power Utility Plants and Net Tons of Bituminous Coal in Stock on 1 October 1946, classified by days, supply, 1-188 Coal Administration (Part 16), and Revised Estimates of Total Coal Available (as of 7 December 1946), 1-188 Coal Administration (Part 17).

51. From SFAW, RG 245: Wheeler memoranda for Krug, 18, 22, 26 April, 2 May 1946, and SFAW car seizures, November 1946, Krug, Secretary of the Interior, 1946. From Office of the Secretary, DI, RG 48: Coal freeze order of 16 November 1946, and SFAW Priority List, November 1946, and Krug to Donald M. Nelson, president, Society of Independent Motion Picture Producers, Hollywood, California, 7 December 1946, 1-188 Coal Administration (Part 16), and Krug to all governors, 23 November 1946, 1-188 Coal Administration (Part 17). For Kansas City's experience with dimouts, dealer rationing, area coal production, industrial stocks, and other strike-related items, Clippings, Coal, Kansas City, KCMoPL.

52. For the above two paragraphs: State Solid Fuel Committee Meeting, 16 October 1946, at Hartford, Box 74, Fuel Committee, other items in Box 74 and folders in Box 75, CWCR; *Kansas City Times*, 15 July 1947, on prices, Clippings, Coal, Kansas City, KCMoPL; Clipping of Victor Riesel column, *New York Post*, ? December 1946, Office of the Secretary, 1-188 Coal Administration (Part 17), DI, RG 48.

53. From Office of the Secretary, DI, RG 48: Wheeler, "Necessity for Continuance of Regulation, May 29, 1946," 1-188 Coal Administration (Part 15); Krug to Ferguson, 23 January 1947, 1-188 (Part 17). From SFAW, RG 245: Krug to John W. Snyder, OWMR, 3 June 1946, Correspondence with Federal Agencies, OWMR; Wheeler weekly report, 23 July 1946, Krug, Secretary of the Interior, 1946. See reports on the effects of the steel and coal strikes on industrial production, November 1949–January 1950, 243.1, U.S. Coal and Coke (1927– 1950), BFDC, RG 151.

54. By the mid-1970s, forty noncoal corporations, led by petroleum and gas companies, produced 63 percent of the nation's coal; see Richard H. K. Vietor, *Environmental Politics and the Coal Coalition* (College Station: Texas A & M University Press, 1980), 19–20.

55. From Guffey Act Extension File, SFAW, RG 245: Ickes to Burton K. Wheeler, chairman, USS Committee on Interstate Commerce, 2 September 1943; F. La Guardia, mayor, city of New York, to Senator Joseph F. Guffey, 12 March 1941; attitudes of various members of USHR Committee on Ways and Means, May–August 1943; Letters endorsing extension from Wisconsin dock operators, Northwestern

Pennsylvania Coal Operators Association, Alabama and Utah coal operators, Michigan Retail Coal Merchants Association, and others, along with many unfavorable letters, 1943.

56. From Office of the Secretary, DI, RG 48: regarding the creation of a solid fuels division in Interior, January 1947, 1-188 Coal Committee (Part 2), and G. A. Lamb, Pittsburgh Consolidation Coal Co., to Krug, 25 June 1947, on the need for an industry advisory committee, 1-188 Coal Administration (Part 11); Department of the Interior, "Plans for Reconversion from War to Peace-Time Basis," Mimeograph, c. 1945, Plans for Reconversion, SFAW, RG 245; Craufurd D. Goodwin, ed., *Energy Policy in Perspective: Today's Problems, Yesterday's Solutions* (Washington, D.C.: Brookings Institution, 1981), 138–43.

Chapter Fifteen

1. Dolores Greenberg, "Reassessing the Power Patterns of the Industrial Revolution: An Anglo-American Comparison," *The American Historical Review*, 87 (December 1982): 1237–61, cautions against exaggerating the speed and scale of the shift from animate to inanimate sources of power during the nineteenth century. See also Louis Hunter, *A History of Industrial Power in the United States, 1780–1930*, vol. 1, *Waterpower in the Century of the Steam Engine* (Charlottesville: University of Virginia Press, 1979).

2. The immediate impact of the Natural Gas Act of 1938 was postponed as a result of World War II. The act was designed to encourage natural gas use. The Federal Power Commission, prodded by court interpretations, did so after the war. Federal policies also promoted the spread of electric power. Hydroelectric installations reduced coal and petroleum use by some fraction hardly felt by petroleum and only slightly exacerbating the weak competitive position of coal.

3. For the post–World War II years, scores of studies of the energy scene make a similar point. As Richard H. K. Vietor, "Market Disequilibrium and Business-Government Relations in Oil Policy, 1947–1980," *Materials and Society*, 7 (1983): 389, writes: "With few exceptions government decision making sacrificed considerations of necessary long-term adjustment to short-term pressures of distribution conflict. If the polity benefited from any of these policies, it was more than likely coincidental."

4. For a contemporary analysis of this problem, see Aaron Wildavsky, *The Politics of Mistrust: Estimating American Oil and Gas Resources* (Beverly Hills: Sage Publications, 1981).

5. USS Special Committee Investigating Petroleum Resources, *Hearings . . . Petroleum Requirements—Postwar, October 3–4, 1945.* 79th Congress., 1st sess., Lovejoy, 60, Hunter, 105.

6. The idea of the public interest was applied to both the interstate electric power and natural gas industries. However, both of these cases

represent more an application of antitrust ideas than any recognition of the position of those industries in the nation's energy mix.

7. PRC was a subsidiary of the Reconstruction Finance Corporation.

8. USS Special Committee Investigating Petroleum Resources, *Hearings . . . American Petroleum Interests in Foreign Countries, June 27–28, 1945.* 79th Cong., 1st sess., 1945, 20; Blaire Bolles, "Oil: An Economic Key to Peace," *Foreign Policy Reports,* 20 (1 July 1944): 86–90.

9. For oil industry opposition, see George A. Hill, Jr., *Trends in the Oil Industry in 1944 (Including United States Foreign Oil Policy). As Presented to the Petroleum Industry War Council, January 12, 1944* (Washington, D.C.: 1944), 12–13. Hill was an IPAA official; John A. Brown, late president of Socony-Vacuum Oil Company, "The Role of Private Enterprise in the Development of Oil Resources," in Leonard M. Fanning, ed., *Our Oil Resources* (New York: McGraw-Hill, 1945), 4–6; Craufurd D. Goodwin, "Truman Administration Policies toward Particular Energy Resources," in Craufurd D. Goodwin, ed., *Energy Policy in Perspective: Today's Problems, Yesterday's Solutions* (Washington, D.C.: Brookings Institution, 1981), 71–73; Notes of various meetings between Ickes and Davies and Abe Fortas, Michael Straus, and a subcommittee of PIWC, 1–2 February 1944, Confidential Correspondence, 1940–1948, Box 15, RKD Papers.

10. Eugene V. Rostow, *A National Oil Policy for the Oil Industry* (New Haven: Yale University Press, 1947), 114.

11. For the above two paragraphs: Box 13, folders 1, 2, 4, RKD Papers provides a blow-by-blow account of the progress of the Anglo-American treaty through 1947; Craufurd D. Goodwin, "Truman Administration Policies," in Goodwin, *Energy Policy in Perspective,* 82–86; Rostow, *National Policy for Oil,* 110–14.

12. See David M. Kennedy, *Over Here: The First World War and American Society* (New York: Oxford University Press, 1980); John M. Blum, *V Was For Victory: Politics and American Culture During World War II* (New York: Harcourt Brace Jovanovich, 1976); Richard Polenberg, *War and Society: The United States, 1941–1945* (Philadelphia: J. B. Lippincott, 1972).

13. The President's Material Policy Commission (Paley Commission), formed in 1951, embraced material resources in general. Its conclusions regarding energy, described by Goodwin as "by and large upbeat," advanced little, if at all, beyond those of NRC. It may have taken a step backward in downplaying the significance of end-use conservation in favor of supply-side remedies. Craufurd D. Goodwin, "The Truman Administration: Toward a National Energy Policy," in Goodwin, *Energy Policy in Perspective,* 52–61.

Index